Lecture Notes in Computer Science   4402

Commenced Publication in 1973
Founding and Former Series Editors:
Gerhard Goos, Juris Hartmanis, and Jan van Leeuwen

Editorial Board

David Hutchison
  Lancaster University, UK
Takeo Kanade
  Carnegie Mellon University, Pittsburgh, PA, USA
Josef Kittler
  University of Surrey, Guildford, UK
Jon M. Kleinberg
  Cornell University, Ithaca, NY, USA
Friedemann Mattern
  ETH Zurich, Switzerland
John C. Mitchell
  Stanford University, CA, USA
Moni Naor
  Weizmann Institute of Science, Rehovot, Israel
Oscar Nierstrasz
  University of Bern, Switzerland
C. Pandu Rangan
  Indian Institute of Technology, Madras, India
Bernhard Steffen
  University of Dortmund, Germany
Madhu Sudan
  Massachusetts Institute of Technology, MA, USA
Demetri Terzopoulos
  University of California, Los Angeles, CA, USA
Doug Tygar
  University of California, Berkeley, CA, USA
Moshe Y. Vardi
  Rice University, Houston, TX, USA
Gerhard Weikum
  Max-Planck Institute of Computer Science, Saarbruecken, Germany

T0182052

Weiming Shen   Junzhou Luo
Zongkai Lin   Jean-Paul A. Barthès
Qi Hao (Eds.)

Computer Supported Cooperative Work in Design III

10th International Conference, CSCWD 2006
Nanjing, China, May 3-5, 2006
Revised Selected Papers

 Springer

Volume Editors

Weiming Shen
National Research Council Canada - IMTI, Canada
E-mail: weiming.shen@nrc.gc.ca

Junzhou Luo
Southeast University, Nanjing 210096, China
E-mail: jluo@seu.edu.cn

Zongkai Lin
Chinese Academy of Sciences, Beijing, 100080, China
E-mail: lzk@ict.ac.cn

Jean-Paul A. Barthès
Université de Technologie de Compiègne
BP 529, 60205 Compiègne, France
E-mail: barthes@utc.fr

Qi Hao
National Research Council Canada, Canada
E-mail: qi.hao@nrc-cnrc.gc.ca

Library of Congress Control Number: 2007927711

CR Subject Classification (1998): H.5.3, H.5.2, H.5, H.4, C.2.4, D.2.12, J.6, D.4, H.2.8

LNCS Sublibrary: SL 3 – Information Systems and Application, incl. Internet/Web and HCI

ISSN   0302-9743
ISBN-10   3-540-72862-7 Springer Berlin Heidelberg New York
ISBN-13   978-3-540-72862-7 Springer Berlin Heidelberg New York

This work is subject to copyright. All rights are reserved, whether the whole or part of the material is concerned, specifically the rights of translation, reprinting, re-use of illustrations, recitation, broadcasting, reproduction on microfilms or in any other way, and storage in data banks. Duplication of this publication or parts thereof is permitted only under the provisions of the German Copyright Law of September 9, 1965, in its current version, and permission for use must always be obtained from Springer. Violations are liable to prosecution under the German Copyright Law.

Springer is a part of Springer Science+Business Media

springer.com

© Springer-Verlag Berlin Heidelberg 2007
Printed in Germany

Typesetting: Camera-ready by author, data conversion by Scientific Publishing Services, Chennai, India
Printed on acid-free paper   SPIN: 12070909   06/3142   5 4 3 2 1 0

Preface

The design of complex artifacts and systems requires the cooperation of multidisciplinary design teams using multiple commercial and proprietary engineering software tools (e.g., CAD, modeling, simulation, visualization, and optimization), engineering databases, and knowledge-based systems. Individuals or individual groups of multidisciplinary design teams usually work in parallel and separately with various engineering software tools which are located at different sites. In addition, individual members may be working on different versions of a design or viewing the design from different perspectives, at different levels of detail.

In order to accomplish the work, it is necessary to have effective and efficient collaborative design environments. Such environments should not only automate individual tasks, in the manner of traditional computer-aided engineering tools, but also enable individual members to share information, collaborate, and coordinate their activities within the context of a design project. CSCW (computer-supported cooperative work) in design is concerned with the development of such environments.

A series of international workshops and conferences on CSCW in design started in 1996. The primary goal of the workshops/conferences is to provide a forum for the latest ideas and results on the theories and applications of CSCW in design, research on multi-agent systems, Grid-/Internet-/Web-based applications, electronic commerce, and other related topics. It also aims at promoting international scientific information exchange among scholars, experts, researchers, and developers in the field. The major topics of CSCWD workshops /conferences include:

- Techniques, methods, and tools for CSCW in design
- Social organization of the computer-supported cooperative process
- Knowledge-intensive cooperative design
- Intelligent agents and multi-agent systems for cooperative design
- Workflows for cooperative design
- VR technologies for cooperative design
- Internet/Web and CSCW in design
- Grids, Web services and Semantic Web for CSCW in design
- CSCW in design and manufacturing
- Cooperation in virtual enterprises and e-businesses
- Distance learning/training related to design
- Applications and testbeds

The 1st International Workshop on CSCW in design (CSCWD 1996) was held during May 8-11, 1996 in Beijing, China and the second one (CSCWD 1997) was held during November 26-28, 1997 in Bangkok, Thailand. After the two successful workshops, an international working group on CSCW in Design was created and an International Steering Committee (ISC) was formed in 1998. The ISC then coordinated two workshops (CSCWD 1998, July 15-18, 1998 in Tokyo, Japan and CSCWD 1999, September 29 - October 1, 1999 in Compiègne, France). During the annual ISC meeting held at CSCWD 1999, the ISC decided to change the name from the "International Workshop on CSCW in Design" to the "International Conference on CSCW in Design". The Fifth International Conference on CSCW in Design (CSCWD 2000) was then held from November 29 to December 1, 2000 in Hong Kong, China, followed by CSCWD 2001 during July 12-14, 2001 in London, ON, Canada; CSCWD 2002 during September 25-27, 2002 in Rio de Janeiro, Brazil; CSCWD 2004 during May 26-28, 2004 in Xiamen, China; and CSCWD 2005 during May 24-26, 2005 in Coventry, UK.

The 10th International Conference on CSCW in Design (CSCWD 2006) was held during May 3-5, 2006 in Nanjing, China. It was a milestone for the CSCWD Working Group. Two volumes of conference proceedings were published with 260 papers selected from about 600 submissions. This book includes 76 articles that are the expanded versions of the papers presented at CSCWD 2006. The book is organized in topical sections on CSCW techniques and methods, collaborative design, collaborative manufacturing and enterprise collaboration, design methods and tools, agents and multi-agent systems, Web services, Semantic web, and Grid computing, knowledge management, security and privacy in CSCW systems, workflow management, and e-learning.

With the rapid development of Internet- and Web-based technologies, the application of CSCW technologies to design is becoming more and more promising. In the area of application of collaboration technologies to engineering design, the depth and width of such applications go far beyond the traditional definition of concurrent engineering. In fact, a new field called collaborative engineering has emerged. Collaborative engineering has been applied not only to design, but also to manufacturing (or construction in civil engineering), enterprise collaboration, and supply chain management. Collaborative design is carried out not only among multidisciplinary (product development) teams, but also across the enterprise boundaries (including customers and suppliers).

However, when CSCW technologies are used to implement applications in industry, security and privacy issues become critical. The number of papers on this topic submitted to CSCWD conferences has increased significantly during the past years. This will continue, particularly with more practical techniques and applications.

We have seen a great potential of applying Web services, Semantic Web and Grid computing technologies to collaborative design, although traditional CSCW techniques including context awareness and synchronized communication are still required.

Agent technology is still one of the most important technologies for implementing collaborative design systems. However, it is important to combine with other technologies adopted by industry, particularly Web Services. With the combined efforts of IEEE and FIPA (Foundation for Intelligent Physical Agents) and the availability of IEEE standards on software agents, agent-based collaborative design systems will be widely developed and deployed in industry. Agent-based cooperative workflow is becoming an active research topic, with applications for the coordination of highly distributed collaborative design systems, as well as collaboration and coordination among various departments or among collaborating enterprises.

CSCWD conferences will continue to be a focused international forum for researchers over the world working on the foundations and applications on CSCW in design, manufacturing, and other related areas.

March 2007

Weiming Shen
Junzhou Luo
Zongkai Lin
Jean-Paul Barthès
Qi Hao

Table of Contents

CSCW Techniques and Methods

Collaborative Design

Collaborative Manufacturing and Enterprise Collaboration

Design Methods and Tools

Agents and Multi-Agent Systems

Web Services, Semantic Web, and Grid Computing

Knowledge Management

Security and Privacy in CSCW Systems

Workflow Management

E-Learning

Cognitive Dust: A Framework That Builds from CSCW Concepts to Provide Situated Support for Small Group Work

Terence Blackburn[1], Paul Swatman[1], and Rudi Vernik[1,2]

[1] University of South Australia, School of Computer and Information Science,
City West Campus, South Australia 5000
{terence.blackburn, paul.swatman, rudi.vernik}@unisa.edu.au
[2] Defence, Science and Technology Organisation,
PO Box 1500 Edinburgh South Australia 5111
rudi.vernik@dsto.defence.gov.au

Abstract. The aim of this paper is to describe a framework that extends and combines two CSCW theories, Situated Action (SA) and Distributed Cognition (DC), to provide situated support for human activities in small workgroups. SA characterises teamwork as unpredictable, ill structured or emergent (often all of these) and people need creative processes to find solutions to their problems. In order to provide support, we draw on DC. We extend this concept into a framework called Cognitive Dust, which is composed of cognitive processes and anything observable in a focus domain. Cognitive Dust, which is collected through a multi modal infrastructure, allows us to measure complexity in various aspects of workspace activities and we use complexity as a marker for creativity. This allows us to identify when creativity is occurring and suggests opportunities for providing dynamic, contextually relevant, situated support for the group. This paper describes Cognitive Dust, which is the first step in a research project that will ultimately enable a computer infrastructure to provide group support without human assistance.

1 Introduction

In practice, a substantial amount of teamwork is heuristic at best and, as a result, only predictable in the short term and in a broad sense. At worst, teamwork is unpredictable. This is either an unavoidable consequence of a characteristic of the task (planning, design) or too little or too much information flowing to a team (e.g. command and control teams, requirements engineers). At times it may be both. If teamwork, then, is hard to predict, this presents a challenge for researchers who want to provide support for cooperative work. It would seem evident that prescriptive approaches would encounter difficulties in providing contextually useful support in an unpredictable activity at any arbitrary point in time. If we consider the concepts in Situated Action [1], which describe the unpredictability of group work processes, it may be useful to consider teamwork support from a situated perspective. This means that support approaches should consider the nature of an activity at any point in time, its

W. Shen et al. (Eds.): CSCWD 2006, LNCS 4402, pp. 1–12, 2007.
© Springer-Verlag Berlin Heidelberg 2007

context, environment and any resources required or available. Our research, then, looks at providing situated computer support for small work groups. The support is non prescriptive and will eventually consist of an infrastructure that can observe a group and make contextually relevant decisions without the intervention of humans.

The purpose of this article is to outline our approach for observing small groups at work but it stops short of describing how we translate our observations into data models. In particular we describe a conceptual framework called Cognitive Dust. This framework builds on the established CSCW concepts of Situated Action and Distributed Cognition. It is not a separate theory but rather an extension and combination of these existing ideas and with a different focus. The design goal for the framework is to identify (as far as possible) all evidence of human communication in small work groups, traces of cognitive processing in its various manifestations, specific machine observable data and the creative processes that are required to deal with the unpredictable or ill structured nature of teamwork.

We define Cognitive Dust as "anything observable in our focus domain" (our current research is constrained to the synchronous work activities of small groups in colocated environments). In addition to observations that humans make, we also include observations that can be made by a computer infrastructure.

Humans can make observations that include the presence of other group members, the location of technological artefacts in the workspace, communicative actions (verbal and non verbal) and evidence of cognitive processing. Cognitive Dust builds on the concept of Distributed Cognition [2] but rather than just identifying and investigating an existing cognitive system, we also include systems that may be unconnected or have existed previously. For example, for the length of time it took for a set of designers and tradesmen to build a workspace, they formed a distributed cognitive system. This group communicated and made decisions that included the size and layout of the room, which technologies would be installed and the location of public screens. The decision about screens, for example, is important to current workspace users when making decisions about what information should be displayed on them during the current task. Users observe the location of the screen which represents cognitive processes in a previous system. A substantial amount of Cognitive Dust is representative of some type of cognition but humans have limits that generally constrain their observations to their primary senses such as sight and hearing. The case is reversed for computers, which have complementary faculties.

Computer sensors are not very developed in the areas of sight and sound (through video and audio devices) although they can see and hear more that any person when using arrays of cameras and microphones. Their shortcomings become evident when they try and make sense of what they see and hear [3]. However, they have abilities in areas where humans have poorly developed senses and biometrics is one such area. Changes to human pulse rates, levels of skin conductivity and heart rates, for example, can be monitored efficiently (albeit with intrusive devices). These physiological conditions can be indicative of changes in human emotional states that may not be evident to other group members but which may have an influence on team processes.

We have developed a concept of a *third party observer* (a computer infrastructure). This *observer* currently represents a set of multi media devices that includes cameras and microphones, as well as technologies that capture keyboard and mouse events in group work. This enables us to record a substantial amount of cognitive dust although it represents a subset of what is generated and what is potentially available in a work-space. We have begun modeling the dust into abstract, syntactic models that in the future will link to semantic models of group behaviour described in the theoretical literature.

In the next section we describe some of the key underlying ideas that characterise work in small groups. In Section 3 we expand Distributed Cognition into our concept of Cognitive Dust and this is followed by a description of how humans process *dust* naturally. In the same section we juxtapose the method that computers use to process the *dust*. We then discuss some of the issues and challenges associated with this research and finally we conclude and articulate some of the future directions that we have identified for this work.

2 Key Concepts

Researchers have examined many dimensions of small group work including tasks, roles, communication, processes, conflict and many others. In this section we focus on the ill structured and emergent nature of work processes and this is followed by a discussion that links the creative processes required to manage this ill structuredness with complexity. We do not look at higher level creative processes, creative actors or methods for building more creative artefacts. We take the view that some level of creative or cognitive input – commonly called thinking - is required to manage the surprises, interruptions, opportunistic shortcuts and mistakes that exist in group work. We finish the section with a description of where we focus our support interventions.

2.1 Structured and Ill Structured Work

Structured process modeling, which includes workflow, is often driven by static models and usually focuses on conceptual or "ideal" workflows rather than "real world" work activities, which need to accommodate interruptions and errors but can also benefit from opportunistic short cuts and redundant tasks. Flexible workflow models [4-5] are useful in activities that are specified at higher levels of abstraction but have been considered as inadequate for the types of project room activities described in this research [6].

We posit that work processes that are not (formally) structured are either semi structured or ill structured. ("Structure" refers to predefined processes.) The ill structured processes are what we term "creative" due to the cognitive effort required to execute them or find solutions. There is no premeditated focus on creativity per se, but instead a recognition that arbitrary work tasks may be performed in a different way each time they are executed [1] and the path that people choose to navigate through their tasks is *emergent*.

2.2 Situated and Emergent Work

People seldom follow predefined work processes although they may use them as a guide to undertake their tasks. Instead, they are propelled by influences such as their environment, social elements (such as people), instinctive factors, values and context [7]. Work processes, then, become self defining and emergent and this is a central tenet of Situated Action [1]. The environment is used as a resource to support planning processes and overcome restrictions. SA claims that plans, such as agendas for meetings, are descriptions of activities or resources that can be referred to for guidance and may just be used to define a starting point in an activity. Therefore, there is a difference between representations of work paths encapsulated in plans and process models and the path that real work follows. This path is usually directed by one or more members of the group.

Situated Action modeling describes problems and solutions each as being unique. They can be instances of the same task abstraction but with slightly different inputs, influences or outputs. The structuring of activity does not precede the "solution finding" activity but instead grows immediately from the opportunistic and flexible interactions between people in a setting using their available resources. An example can be found in military planning [8]. This is a highly prescriptive, well documented, structured activity [9] and popular belief would expect the planning process to mirror the description. However, when planners start their planning activity, their doctrine becomes merely a guide to remind the participants of the required outcomes and expected end state of the plan. At the level of human interaction, the planning process becomes emergent and the course navigated through the process is creative in nature and different each time the exercise is repeated. The resulting goal is always similar in nature but different in detail. We label these emergent activities as creative and Situated Action, then, motivates us in our characterisation of group work processes.

2.3 Creativity and Complexity

In order to support creative activities of the type described in this article, we seek evidence of the existence of creativity and some metric to indicate variance. We are currently using *complexity* (as measured by the number of concepts) as a marker for creativity. By recording the requirements engineering (RE) process and analysing both the dynamic complexity of requirements models and the engineer's decision making record [10], we have identified unexpected patterns of complexity during the design process (see Figure 1A). (Many common tools are available to calculate the number of concepts but the concepts themselves are derived from data that represents a class of Cognitive Dust.)

The cyclic structure in this diagram, which appears characteristic of the complexity within developing requirements models is comprised of interleaved periods of incremental learning or evolution (E), "creative opportunism" or insight (I) and restructuring of the problem space or revolution (R). This id called the Catastrophe Cycle Model (CCM) of the requirements modeling process.

A single slightly modified CCM cycle is depicted in Figure 1B. The first part of the evolutionary stage (label A) might comprise semi structured activities, such as information gathering, and creative processes may become apparent when people start to mentally process this information. At this point, the number of concepts that require processing is increasing along with the associated complexity. During the incubation period (label B), complexity, while level, may still be high and indicate the presence of creativity. This might be characteristic of an activity such as categorizing ideas. Creativity would be evident, during the ill structured insight phase (label C) if complexity increases markedly and this is due to the increased cognitive effort required to manage the extra processing. This might be the evaluation phase of a brainstorming session and it spills over into D, in the figure, when it becomes apparent which of the final ideas is likely to be the most useful in the solution space. This revolutionary phase, which is semi structured, is likely to require less mental processing as complexity is decreasing, and less cognitive effort is required to reconceptualise the final candidates in the model. The variable levels of complexity indicate that the RE process is less formal or structured than previously conceived but rather semi structured or ill structured with levels of creativity appearing during different parts of the cycle. Complexity, calculated from Cognitive Dust, might provide opportunities for providing support interventions.

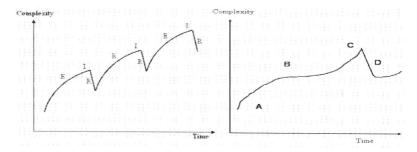

Fig. 1A. The Catastrophe Cycle model   **Fig. 1B.** A single cycle of the model

2.4 Situated Support

Our focus is on intervening in group activities by providing timely and contextually relevant support actions. Examples of intervention include: automatically reconfiguring a workspace, as determined by current activities; recognising when and how to reform sub groups into a main group to discuss an important issue; or prefetching information and displaying it on public screens. A support service needs to be partly autonomic and partly interactive. For example, the service may prefetch and load data automatically, but a user should also have the flexibility to request ad hoc data sets. This could allow a service to coordinate goal oriented activities accordingly to a pre-selected sequence of events but offer the flexibility of changing the order as determined by human input.

Having described examples of support, we need to identify the level at which we intervene. Our work model consists of a taxonomy of *processes, activities* and *actions. Processes*, which are at the top of the taxonomy, are repeatable and coarse grained. An example would be the description of a common class of meetings where participants: accept apologies, read the minutes of the previous meeting, discuss current agenda items, call for further items of general business and close the meeting. *Activities* would feature within any of the items in the *process* and include discussing ideas, brainstorming and making choices. *Actions* are the communication primitives within the activities and include speaking, listening, pointing and gazing. We have positioned our support at the level of *activities*. This is because *processes* are too abstract and contain little variance, and *actions* are too fine grained, unpremeditated and, consequently, hard to predict. *Activities* combine a blend of repetition (processes) and unpredictability (actions). Support strategies are comprised of short sequences of actions (predictable and based on action histories) that are be found in activities. Using a previous example, if a group is discussing a specific topic, a support mechanism could proactively load contextually useful data onto the nearest public display and let group members scroll through candidate data sets and select any as they see fit. *Loading the data* is a repeatable set of actions that make up a small activity but the unpredictable content to be loaded is based on the conversation. This is an example of dynamically processing Cognitive Dust (see Section 4). In this case, the dust represents all of the words in the conversation as well as the locations of the people and screens. Keywords that identify the relevant /candidate data sets can be selected by a text mining tool and an inferencing strategy can determine when the data should be loaded on the nearest public screen.

3   Distributed Cognition and Cognitive Dust

We seek to gain an understanding of people's behaviour, what activities they engage in and what artefacts they use, and, given a series of actions in an activity, to predict a succeeding action. We start with the external, symbolic representations of human cognition in a workspace, referred to as External Cognition [11]. In this approach, the representations are used for "computational offloading". It describes how people use their environment to reduce the cognitive effort required in work activities. For example, writing notes on a white board acts substitutes as a mental persistence mechanism for the information and using a calculator substitutes for mental processing. An alternative view [12] models the representations as "information resources" in a similar fashion to SA. These resources (which include plans, goals, histories and states), are associated with an interaction strategy, which, along with the information resources, links the devices, representations and activities in a workspace.

Distributed Cognition (DC) also takes a holistic view of a system or a view where all of the relevant artefacts are linked. It is comprised of a set of cognitive representations and models the creation, representation, mediation and propagation of these cognitive artefacts in the environment [13]. DC tries to identify how internal human processes can transcend the boundaries of the mind and exist in the environment. People are regarded as nodes for creating and mediating cognition at the same level as keyboards or displays. Once the cognitive representations exist external to the actor, devices can independently propagate the representation, mediate it to other devices (or humans) or capture and store it in a data model.

We are not satisfied that the theories we have examined adequately support the interpretation of the *complete* set of entities, artefacts and representations that exists in a small group workspace. We seek to build on these existing theories of External and Distributed Cognition and find a more encompassing yet focused approach that can adequately define observable human actions (with a high level of confidence), workspace artefacts and computer observable phenomena.

Cognitive Dust allows us a more encompassing model of a workspace. In addition to cognitive representations and technological/human interactions, we also include other artefacts and entities. Non verbal behaviour (NVB), for example is an important communication channel for establishing power, dominance and leadership in a group.

This channel needs to be processed to indicate an order of importance for deciding which people to support in times of confusion or contention for attention. To extend the example we have been using, if a sidebar conversation is occurring in a subgroup that is located near a public display, contextually relevant data can be automatically added to the screen to support the conversation based on the keywords generated by the *dominant* person (or people). In addition, unique identifiers are required for each device in the workspace as well as state information to query whether the device is available. Interpersonal interactions are also important. For example, if two of the people are conversing, using the same keywords, the rate and volume of speech has increased and progress in the sidebar group has halted (along with other indicators), then a level of conflict might exist, which could require an intervention.

All of these examples contain many different classes of Cognitive Dust. The NVB is a form of communication and creates a power hierarchy, the shared focus of the subgroup communicates shared intent and the conflict also communicates important information to the group. These communications are all cognitive in origin, are included in the cloud of dust and need to be processed by both people and a technological infrastructure.

4 Human and Computer Processing of Cognitive Dust

Humans observe and interpret Cognitive Dust naturally in almost any environment. They usually interpret it correctly because they have been practicing since they were very young. They are able to focus on any arbitrary set of *dust motes* but they also have the ability to identify and filter the important representations in a system, intuit meaning from them and, in the case of a small work group, provide contextually useful support. It's a very different matter for a computer infrastructure.

4.1 Human Processing

To explain how humans interpret Cognitive Dust, we describe a team of sixteen engineers (plus their leader), who design deep sea expeditions and space missions [14]. Their room has large public displays; the engineers each have a computer on a long shared desk and they use various technologies for visualising information and sharing data. Work is hectic, very focused and lasts about three hours per session. This is a sensorially rich environment. Each engineer constantly must visually and aurally monitor a variety of communication channels in the room and process large amounts of dust. To do this they: listen to others in their immediate conversation; monitor information on public screens; listen for keywords in other conversations that might effect them (or that they can contribute to); look for errors in their part of the project; interact with technologies, including publishing information when requested; subscribing for information when required; register the locations of other members in the room and who they are talking to; and be aware of the team leader's directions. Over time they gain experience at simultaneously processing all of these channels and they build a private mental network of where each person fits into the project along with a map of dependencies that dictates the order of tasks. Each person must monitor their own parts of the project but the team leader must monitor all of the activities in the room. The engineers are successful at processing all of the Cognitive Dust. However, it takes some months of practice to operate efficiently at such a high level and it would be only reasonable to allow a computer infrastructure some length of training period to become effective.

4.2 Computer Processing

To enable a computer infrastructure to provide support in a manner similar to humans, we must equip it with the ability to select and process the key classes of dust that will ultimately produce useful meaning. This may be achieved by providing the infrastructure with "eyes and ears" to observe the dust in the system.

The "eyes and ears" in our research are embedded within a research and development environment called LiveSpaces [15]. This platform extends current research into ubiquitous workspaces (where computer hardware becomes less visible and workspace interfaces become more natural). It supports collaborative, colocated activities such as design meetings, complex presentations and evaluation sessions. The LiveSpaces architecture comprises a transparent set of workspace applications, services and devices, which are integrated and coordinated by way of the Event Heap [16]. This core data abstraction is a messaging system that allows applications to post or request events. The associated Data Heap facilitates information movement or temporary persistence by allowing any application to request or place data into a public store. Device services manage light controllers or large public screens, and any user with a single mouse and keyboard can control any public display. These capabilities are possible due to the service and device saturation in the workspace. A plethora of sensors is used to monitor temperature, light intensity, artefact location and digital traffic. There are also arrays of cameras, microphones and radio frequency identification (RFID) tags, which form the eyes and ears of our multi modal observation facility. Using this infrastructure, the dust is collected, filtered, abstracted, modeled and (ultimately) analysed to create a level of *understanding* that will enable the infrastructure to provide situated support for creative human activities.

The origins of different classes of dust are modeled in Figure 2. We start at the top of the figure by classifying workspace participants as either present (label A) or absent (label B). Our current focus in this work is on colocated, face to face groups. An individual's cognitive properties are classified as internal (label D) and external representations (label C), of which the latter are either transient (label E) or persistent (label F). At this point, absent individuals can still contribute to the persistent cognitive representations with artefacts such as: notes, emails, diagrams previously drawn on a whiteboard or making personal files available (dotted link from label B to label F).

Transient cognitive artefacts have a substantial influence in this research and produce the most dust. They represent many of the observable human communicative actions and include: speech (label G), which can be processed with technologies such as transcription services (label K); gestures and other non verbal communications, such as body language (label I) and gaze (label M), which are observed with video; and non visible actions (label H) such as the use of keyboards and mice (label L).

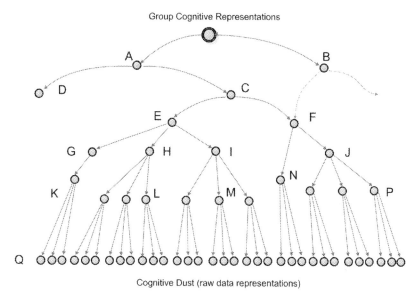

Fig. 2. Different classes of Cognitive Dust and their origins

Each of these communication channels can be observed and raw data recorded (label Q) by our multi modal infrastructure. (Computer observable data, such as the biometric examples mentioned earlier, are also observed at the level of Q.) These raw data "dust collectors" can collect the cognitive dust in machine formats such as wav files for sound or mpeg files for video. (Spoken) utterances in a wav file, for example, can be parsed for further analysis such as concept mapping [17] or transcription [18].

The persistent cognitive representations (label F) are stored in a variety of media and include: computer files of different types (label N); paper artefacts containing maps or bullet points; white board or e-Beam pictures (label P); and written standard operating procedures (SOPs). To the extent possible, these are assimilated, analysed and aggregated with the transient artefact representations to form a rich representation of workspace activities. Once the data is captured within a technological infrastructure, it can be syntactically abstracted and analysed at different levels.

5 Discussion

It would be reasonable to ask why should we go to the effort of developing theory when there is already a well developed research domain for observing meetings and analysing (with limited success) their audio and video records [19]. The reason is that these projects are accumulating huge repositories of data from which little *meaning* can be extracted and the task of aggregating the important channels is problematic. One of our goals is to distill human comprehension from our observations and identify the important workspace activities that will inform our support efforts. For example, if two people are both talking and pointing in an activity, we will know which person has control of the floor and where we should direct support. Cognitive Dust is important for identifying this order of importance and for helping us to articulate this human understanding.

Humans have been learning to observe and understand Cognitive Dust for all of their lives. They bring with them to the observational activities many years of experience in interpreting human behaviour and communication, with its accompanying confirmatory feedback. This is in contrast to current computer infrastructures that may have an elementary level of vocabulary, a paucity of contextual knowledge and a poor understanding of social rules. These contrasting positions set us a number of challenges such as knowing which sets of dust should be observed and analysed, and which sets can be safely ignored. As humans we set up internal maps of what is important to us in a group setting such as which people are most likely to influence our work as well as the dependencies in the group. These need to be uncovered so that they can be analysed and recorded. Another issue might be to differentiate between structured activities that (also create dust and) already have manually invoked support mechanisms and the less structured, creative activities that exhibit rising levels of complexity.

It is the ill structured activities that we seek to support. We use SA to motivate our characterisation of how people carry out their tasks in group work. Because these tasks are unpredictable and emergent, people need to supply cognitive input or creative processing to find useful solutions. How do we support these unpredictable activities? We have observed rising and falling levels of complexity associated with similar tasks [20]. If we use complexity as a marker for creativity, we may be able identify these creative periods. How do we identify complexity? This is where we draw on DC. We have extended DC to include anything observable in a workspace including machine observable characteristics, static objects and residues of previous cognitive systems. We have labeled this frame work as Cognitive Dust and within the dust we can identify changes in artefacts, which include conversations and digital outputs. To date we have counted the number of concepts in an artefact to measure complexity and this may provide the link to creativity although other issues remain unresolved (such as when complexity is not a marker for creativity).

A final example of issues that will need to be addressed is one that humans also manage poorly. In any group of people, each person will hold and maintain a different perspective of the world, (which will also be different from that created by a computer infrastructure; our *third person observer*). This is because we do not articulate our complete local view during communication. Many times we make assumptions based on context or past experience and these assumptions may turn out to be different from what we expected. It is not always reasonable to claim that the leader or most dominant person in the group has the most important view so we must go through a process of reconciling multiple views of the world to arrive at a shared frame of reference. The third person may also have to do this although views can become irrelevant or redundant and this is a complication that will need to be addressed.

6   Conclusions and Future Work

The main contribution of this paper is the description of Cognitive Dust, which is a framework that is composed of cognitive systems, interactions, artefacts and different communication channels. It is a concept that builds on CSCW theories and suggests an alternative way of supporting work in small groups. This is achieved through observing the activities in a workspace and using a multimodal infrastructure to filter, abstract and analyse the *dust* to provide useful, dynamic situated support for creative processes. We are extending this work by articulating, at a fine grained level, semantic descriptions of activities in these workspaces, in addition to syntactically abstracting the dust from video footage and technology use during meetings. Our goal is that when the top down (semantic) approach meets the bottom up (syntactic) approach, we will divine meaning that can be formalised for inferencing and providing support.

We defined Cognitive Dust as "anything observable in our focus domain" however our domain so far has been constrained to synchronous, colocated groups. However, there is nothing intrinsic to either "synchronous", "same place", "formal place" or "anyplace", which makes the problem we are addressing (or the approach we are taking) special. Most creative teamwork occurs in networks of synchronous collaboration multi-linked to asynchronous collaborations, which may take place in the office, in the coffee shop or anywhere. It is simply easier to collect cognitive dust in synchronous/formal situations. In associated work, we extend our study of creative teamwork to investigate support approaches for work between meetings and between groups.

References

1. Suchman, L.: Plans and Situated Actions. Cambridge University Press (1987)
2. Hollan, J., Hutchins, E. and Kirsh, D.: Distributed cognition: toward a new foundation for human-computer interaction research. ACM Transactions on Computer-Human Interaction 7 (2000) 174-96
3. Oliver, N., Garg, A. and Horvitz, E.: Layered representations for learning and inferring office activity from multiple sensory channels. Computer Vision and Image Understanding 96 (2004) 163-180
4. Sadiq, S., Sadiq, W. and Orlowska, M.: Pockets of Flexibility in Workflow Specification. Lecture Notes in Computer Science 2224 (2001) 513
5. Mangan, P. and Sadiq, S.: On Building Workflow Models for Flexible Processes. Proc. Thirteenth Australasian Database Conference (ADC2002). Melbourne, Australia (2002)
6. Carroll, J., Neale, D., Isenhour, P., Rosson, M. and McCrickard, D.: Notification and awareness: synchronizing task-oriented collaborative activity. International Journal of Human-Computer Studies 58 (2003) 605-632
7. Lave, J.: Cognition in Practice. Cambridge: Cambridge University Press (1988)
8. Blackburn, T., Vernik, R. and Bright, D.: Identifying Cognitive Activities and Processes in a Military Planning Training Exercise. Proc. OZCHI 2004. Wollongong, NSW (2004)
9. Zhang, L., Falzon, L., Davies, M. and Fuss, I.: On Relationships between Key Concepts of Operational Level Planning. Proc. 5th International Command and Control Research and Technology Symposium. Canberra (2000)
10. Nguyen L. and Swatman, P.A.: Complementary use of ad hoc and post hoc design rationale for creating and organising process knowledge. Proc. 33rd Annual Hawaii International Conference on System Sciences (2000)
11. Scaife, M. and Rogers, Y.: External Cognition: how do graphical representations work? International Journal of Human-Computer Studies 45 (1996) 185-213

12. Wright, P., Fields, R. and Harrison, M.: Analyzing Human-Computer Interaction as Distributed Cognition: The Resources Model. Human Computer Interaction 15 (2000) 1-41
13. Hutchins, E.: Cognition in the wild. Cambridge, Mass: MIT Press (1995)
14. Mark, G.: Extreme Collaboration. Communications of the ACM 45 (2001) 89-93
15. Vernik, R., Blackburn, T. and Bright, D.: Extending Interactive Intelligent Workspace Architectures with Enterprise Services. Proc Evolve2003, Enterprise Information Integration. Sydney, Australia (2003)
16. Johanson, B., Fox, A. and Winograd, T.: The Interactive Workspaces Project: Experiences with Ubiquitous Computing Rooms. IEEE Pervasive Computing 1 (2002)
17. Smith, A.: Automatic Extraction of Semantic Networks from Text using Leximancer. Proc. HLT-NAACL. Edmonton (2003)
18. Sladek, J., Zschorn, A. and Hashemi-Sakhtsari, A.: Speech-to-Text Transcription in Support of Pervasive Computing. Proc. Inaugural Asia Pacific Forum on Pervasive Computing. Adelaide, SA (2003)
19. Nijholt, A., Akker, R. and Heylen, D.: Meetings and Meeting Modeling in Smart Surroundings. Proc. Social Intelligence Design: Third CTIT Workshop. Enshede, The Netherlands (2004)
20. Raisey, D., Tan, K., Swatman, P., Blackburn, T. and Nguyen, V.: An Empirical Study of the Evolving Dynamics of Creative Teams in Action. Proc. CIDMDS. London, UK (2006)

Evaluation of Contextual Information Influence on Group Interaction

Márcio G.P. Rosa[1], Marcos R.S. Borges[2], and Flávia M. Santoro[3]

[1]Faculdade Ruy Barbosa
Rua Theodomiro Batista, 422 - Rio Vermelho – Salvador
Cep: 41940-320, BA, Brasil
marciorosa@frb.br
[2]Departamento de Ciências da Computação and NCE/UFRJ
Caixa Postal 2324, Rio de Janeiro, 20001-970, RJ, Brasil
mborges@nce.ufrj.br
[3]Departamento de Informática Aplicada , UNIRIO
Av. Pasteur, 458. Rio de Janeiro, 22290-040, RJ, Brasil
flavia.santoro@uniriotec.br

Abstract. In groupware development, one of the most important work-group support issues is providing information about the context under which a group interacts. Research has been done in order to clarify the relationship between context and group work. The goal of this paper is to describe an experiment aimed at evaluating Interaction Context relevance on the collaboration level in group interactions supported by groupware and to establish a way to specify context aspects in groupware design. A case study was set up and carried out with this purpose.

1 Introduction

One of the most important work group aspects in supporting collaboration is providing information about the context under which an interaction occurs. This kind of information helps group members to know each other and be aware of their goals and of the issues that influence them. With this information at hand, the group should be able to increase their level of awareness and collaboration. Context is not only the initial predefined state of a collaborative environment: it is part of the interaction [8].

Although this information would be very important to support and foster collaboration, it is, generally, not effectively available to group members in groupware applications [1][17]. One of the most significant obstacles is identifying the types of contextual information relevant to each situation.

The goal of this paper is to describe an experiment aimed at evaluating Interaction Context relevance on the collaboration level in group interactions supported by groupware and to establish a way to specify context in groupware design.

This paper is divided into three parts. In the first part, the concept of awareness and context is presented for CSCW domain. We then describe an experiment plan to evaluate and identify contextual information need in a specific collaborative system; and, finally, the experiment results are discussed.

W. Shen et al. (Eds.): CSCWD 2006, LNCS 4402, pp. 13–22, 2007.
© Springer-Verlag Berlin Heidelberg 2007

2 Contextual Information Relevance in Group Work

In CSCW literature, we find various references to the term "context" associated with the set of information that group members need in order to become aware of the environment in which they are performing collective tasks. Terms such as "awareness information" and "awareness mechanisms" are generally used to refer to features that supply this kind of information. According to Greenberg [13], context has to be considered as a dynamic construction in five dimensions: (1) period of time, (2) usage episodes, (3) social interactions, (4) internal goals, and (5) local influences. Although contextual elements in some situations are steady and predictable, this is not always true: situations that apparently present similar contexts can differ greatly.

Context is the representation of knowledge that involves a situation, while awareness can be appraised as the act of becoming contextualized or, in other words, perceiving the context where the group is acting. Each member can distinguish the same context information in different ways; therefore, the act of perceiving is associated with individual cognition. Context and awareness must be considered together in the groupware domain.

Brézillon [7] summarized the comprisal of context information by attempting to answer the questions: "Who?", "What?", "When?", "How?", "Where?" and "What for?". By analyzing the questions proposed by Brézillon, we can observe a strong relation between context and awareness. Researchers have proposed conceptual frameworks for analysis and classification of awareness information [12][16]. In these frameworks, we observe aspects related to perception through the answers to five of the above questions: "Who?", "What?", "When?", "How?", and "Where?".

We proposed a conceptual framework as the first step in the direction towards evaluating the importance of context in interactions supported by groupware as well as what types of contextual information should be considered [17]. The conceptual framework suggests that contextual information is clustered in five main categories: (1) information about people and groups, (2) information about scheduled tasks, (3) information about the relationship between people and tasks, (4) information about the environment where the interaction takes place and (5) information about tasks and activities already completed. This paper focus on third main category. This category is further divided into two context types; Interaction and Planning.

3 Case Study: Evaluating the Collaboration Level

We conducted an experiment in order to validate the dimensions described in the framework and to discuss whether making this information available actually stimulated collaboration in the scenario studied. A group would perform a collaborative design task supported by groupware: at first without Interaction Context element help, and then, secondly, having access to that information. We aimed at observing the impact of this type of contextual information in collaboration among the group members. The experiment was planned as follows:

- **Hypothesis:** The availability of mechanisms for creating and accessing Interaction Context information helps group members to keep aware of the context where they are acting, encouraging collaboration within the group.

Interaction Context consists of information that details the actions or sequence of steps performed by the group, while working together. For example, Group member 1 placed Object 1; Group member 2 connected Object 1 to Object 2, Group member 1 commented this relationship through an annotation. CO2DE implements basically two interaction context mechanisms: versioning and annotation. Versioning allow participants to build particular versions of the diagram presenting them through masks (Figure 1). Annotations are used to communicate opinions about the elements of the diagram. To evaluate our hypothesis group members drew up a diagram with and without version evolution control and annotation inclusion.

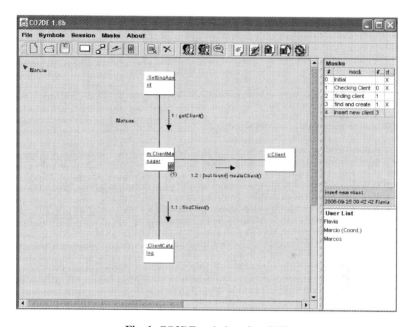

Fig. 1. CO2DE main interface [15]

- **Task Domain: Software Design.** The experiment was a simulation of a software design phase, specifically modeling Collaboration Diagrams using UML(Unified Modeling Language). The Collaboration Diagram shows the objects, their relationships, and the sequence of messages exchanged among the objects.
- **Groupware: CO2DE (Collaborate to Design).** CO2DE is a tool that supports the construction of the UML Collaboration Diagram by a team [15]. One of its main features is a shared workspace, with a WYSIWID interface, and generation of diagram versions, implemented using the mask metaphor [4]. The main interface of CO2DE is depicted in Figure 1.
- **Participants' description:** The group was made up of four computer science students, experienced in groupware use. The participants formed a system design team.
- **Interaction characterization:** A design problem was presented to the group: software requirement scenarios, represented by UML Use Cases, a brief description of the system and a Class Diagram. The participants were supposed to interact and

discuss among themselves in order to build a solution on how those requirements should be implemented by the programmers. The solution would be provided in the Collaboration Diagram format. The participants drew up the diagram. During the experiment, each participant in his workstation was to add objects (rectangles), links (lines connecting the objects) and messages (arrows). Synchronous and asynchronous communication resources were available to the participants.

- **Evaluation goal: Collaboration Level.** The objective was to investigate the influence of contextual information in the collaboration level, observed during diagram construction and in the final result. The evaluation was made in terms of version evolution, member contributions, message exchange and annotation inclusion. Chats (synchronous communication) have also been considered in analysis.

3.1 Experiment Description

The experiment was held in two phases: for each one, a scenario was considered to be modeled. Both scenarios expressed system operations with a similar degree of complexity. The difference between the two phases was the possibility of using some Interaction Context awareness resources supplied by CO2DE.

Phase 1: Use of CO2DE without the versioning resources and annotations
Participants drew up an Interaction Diagram throughout a 30-minute interval session. Aiming at simulating the absence of a participant during part of the session, one of the participants was called out after 8 minutes, returning in the 15 final minutes. In this phase, it was not possible to use versioning and annotation resources, since this was the control group. By the end of the modeling session, the result was expressed in the final version of the diagram, with no intermediate versions.

Phase 2: Use of CO2DE with the versioning and annotation resources
In this phase, the experimental group developed the diagram using version generation and annotation resources. It also lasted 30 minutes, and the same procedure of taking out one of the participants for a period of time was used.

Before the beginning of the first phase, the group was introduced to both scenarios to be modeled; the specific Class Diagram was presented for each scenario. The participants were instructed to construct the solution in a collaborative way, exchanging messages and manipulating the objects in a shared workspace.

The hypothesis was evaluated through the measurement of items presented on Table 1. We analyzed issues related to group work evolution:

The number of contributions was of good quality, bearing session duration in mind. It helped to point out that the information about the interaction context stimulated participation and collaboration. We called contribution any kind of manipulation of the shared objects, for example, the insertion of a symbol, a message, or an annotation. When a participant includes one of these elements he is making a contribution to the diagram building process, and collaborating with his group.

The messages exchanged and annotation numbers have been high, also depicting the high degree of participation and collaboration. The absent members obtained information that made it easier for them to start to participate and collaborate.

Diagram evolution occurred in a set of well-defined versions, demonstrating that the group members were aware of the context in which they were performing.

Table 1. Metrics

Criteria	Metric Unit	Type of Metrics	Collecting Instrument
Communication (degree of interaction and participation in discussions)	Number of messages exchanged	Quantitative/ objective	Number of messages recorded in log
	Quality of messages exchanged	Qualitative/ subjective	Analysis and classification of messages recorded in log
Collective construction (degree of contribution)	Number of contributions in the diagram	Quantitative/ objective	Number of symbols, messages, and annotation per element in the diagram and log
	Quality of contributions in the diagram	Qualitative/ subjective	Analysis of the diagram produced and the questionnaire
Coordination (degree of organization)	Commitment with the work process definition	Qualitative/ subjective	Questionnaire and observation
Awareness (degree of understanding of the process)	Understanding of tasks and relationships	Qualitative/ subjective	Questionnaire and observation

The participants were also requested to answer a questionnaire about the work done after the two-phase interaction. The answers provided helped us to consolidate and interpret the results, as they are summarized in Table 5.

3.2 Phases Organization

Before each stage, a Use Case, describing the situation to be modeled, was presented. The Use Cases were studied by the groups, so that an agreement about the problem could be reached, in order to avoid context mismatch [5]. Afterwards, a modeling session was initiated, in which each participant used the workstation tool in a laboratory.

4   Analysis of Results

The accomplishment of the experiment in two phases aimed at evaluating the influence of context information availability in the collaboration level by comparing the result in each situation. However, this type of evaluation is not trivial. Group performance depends on a number of factors, amongst which members´ behavior, personality and social and economic motivation, as well as political views. All these aspects interfere in the way people use groupware, making identification and control of all variables difficult or even impossible [3].

The evaluation criteria in Table 1 could not be analyzed separately, as collaboration cannot be measured by each of these alone. Even distinct criteria combination does not lead to conclusive results, but only suggests that context information influences collaboration.

4.1 Comments Related to Communication

Participant 1 was chosen to be absent in part of the modeling sessions. Regarding the volume of messages exchanged in each phase, the latter did not oscillate significantly, as can be observed from Table 2. However, in the first stage, Participant 1 took 6 minutes approximately to interact again with the group after his arrival. Yet, in the second stage, this time decreased to 2 minutes, which indicates a faster contextualization process. This information, combined with the answer to Question 8 (summarized in Table 5), also shows a positive influence of the versioning resource and chat.

Regarding message quality, we classified the messages through Freitas' proposal [11]: (1) socialization; (2) relevant content; (3) no content. Table 3 illustrates the total number of messages and relative percentages.

By analyzing Table 3, we notice a replacement from socialization messages (in the first session) to no-content messages (in the second session). As regards content messages (messages related directly with diagram construction), the percentage was practically the same. Thus, it was not possible to reach to a conclusion, only through information quality evaluation. However, by examining these messages in detail, we have understood that, in the first stage, when the group worked only in the single mask, conflicts appeared quickly and were fully solved through chat. In the second stage, despite the fact that they also existed, (in a less significant number), the group dealt with these faster, either by talking through chat, or by creating simultaneous versions. The versions allowed, at the same time, that a participant present a solution proposal and observe the other members' proposals.

Table 2. Number of messages exchanged

Phase	Part. 1	Part. 2	Part. 3	Part. 4	Total
1st	3	33	18	28	82
2nd	5	25	19	26	75

Table 3. Message classification

Phase	Socialization	Relevant content	No content
1st	7 – 8,5%	71 – 86,6%	4 – 4,9%
2nd	2 – 2,7%	64 – 85,3%	9 – 12%

4.2 Comments Related to Collective Construction

The volume of contributions during diagram construction displayed a reduction of approximately 15% from the first phase to the second, as can be observed on Table 4. This fact, combined with the reduction in number of conflicts occurred in the second

Table 4. Number of contributions

Phase	Part. 1	Part. 2	Part. 3	Part. 4	Total
1st	58	54	54	31	197
2nd	51	57	34	25	167

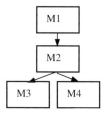

Fig. 2. Version tree generated during the 2nd phase experiment interface

Table 5. Conclusions extracted from the answers to the questionnaire

Question	Average Result	Observations
1. Usage of annotation feature allowed for decision and rationale registration of group actions.	2.25	The annotation feature was not very used because of the type of interaction (synchronous) chosen for the experiment. Nevertheless, we believe that if the group had been concerned about the absent participant, it would have been worth and effective.
2. Reading information posted on annotations helped understand way group work was carried out.	2.25	
3. This information allowed the group to be aware of decisions made, fostering collaboration among its members.	2.75	
4. Usage of more than one diagram version, during a session, establishing parallel sub-sessions facilitated the group work follow-up.	3.25	The average results in Questions 4, 5, 6 and 7 show that participants considered the featured versioning worthwhile. The group affirmed that versions facilitated work follow-up, demonstrating that participants could understand the context.
5. Usage of more than one diagram version, during a session, establishing parallel sub-sessions, stimulated participation and collaboration in work.	3.25	
6. While a participant selects one version through context-based chat and annotations, he can be aware of contributions from other group members.	3.25	
7. In case 6 is positive, this fact helps the collaboration among group members, allowing for the inclusion of new contributions.	3.25	
8. For a participant entering a modeling session already begun, the versioning feature helps understand the work performed by other group members.	3.00	Participants demonstrate that information through diagram versions, annotations and chat help participants absent from the session for a time period.
9. At the moment a participant creates a new version, additional information about its goal would make it easier to understand the evolution of the diagram.	3.75	The average obtained shows that, in spite of versioning being an efficient feature for contextualizing the group, relevant information about the versions is still out.

phase, points to a possible reduction of the degree of uncertainty and equivocality. Thus, the convergence of opinions among group members was easily reached; therefore, a reduced volume of contributions was necessary.

Contribution quality was evaluated through the analysis of the result of modeling sessions. In both phases, it was evidenced that the diagrams were correct and well-constructed. We could notice that the annotation resource was not used, with chat being the mechanism chosen for communication. Some hypotheses can be raised to justify this fact: the interaction was synchronous; thus, it was very natural to discuss through this channel.

The questionnaire answers to Questions 6, 7 and 8 pointed that, in the case of a longer experiment, the group would probably recognize the importance of providing context resources for the absent members. In this case, annotations could be used in association with the diagram. Despite the short session duration, the versioning feature was used, and the evolution of the diagram based on versions, as a hierarchy of masks, is presented in Figure 2. This hierarchy of masks represents the stage of the diagram since it was first created in the beginning mask (M1) up to the end of session, with two possible final masks (M3 and M4). However, it was not possible to distinguish whether the use of masks fostered collaboration among group members or helped the absent member to get contextualized in a faster, efficient manner.

4.3   Comments Related to Awareness

Analysis of coordination and awareness was carried out through the application of a questionnaire. The majority of questions were presented in an affirmative manner, and participants answered by indicating one, among four alternatives: (1) strongly disagree, (2) disagree (3) agree (4) strongly agree. The numbers suggested a scale of values, in which the average results for each question had been calculated. Table 5 presents the questions, average results, and comments taken from each one of them.

5   Conclusions and Future Work

This paper describes an experiment aimed at evaluating the Interaction Context relevance on the collaboration level and establishing a way to characterize context in groupware design. The experiment is considered one step towards offering assistance to groupware designers wanting to include contextual elements in their tools.

The analysis of the experiment carried out indicates that the availability of mechanisms to access Interaction Context information, like versioning and annotation, helps group members keep aware of circumstances in which they are acting, thereby fostering collaboration.

In other domains, context has become the focus of research [2][6][9-10][13-14], demonstrating its relevance. It could also be evidenced, through the use of annotations and answers in the questionnaires, that different types of interactions - synchronous and asynchronous - need different mechanisms for contextualization.

Finally, after the evaluation of collected data, we noticed that the results would be more conclusive if more frequent, complex and longer modeling sessions were performed.

As future work, we plan to implement a new version of CO2DE in order to make available additional Interaction Context, as well as modify the existing awareness mechanism in order to display this new information. After this implementation, we intend to perform a new experiment aimed at evaluating issues related to context mismatch and loss of context [5].

Acknowledgement. The work of Professor Marcos R. S. Borges was partially supported by a grant from CNPq (Brazil) No. 305900/2005-6.

References

1. Alarcon, R.A., Guerrero, L.A., Ochoa, S.F., Pino, J.A.: Context in Collaborative Mobile Scenarios. Fifth International and Interdisciplinary Conference on Modeling and Using Context. Workshop on Context and Groupware. CEUR Proceedings, Vol. 133. Paris, France (2005)
2. Agostini, A., de Michelis, G., Grasso, M.A., Prinz, W., Syri, A.: Contexts, Work Processes, and Workspaces. Journal of Collaborative Computing 5(2-3) (1996) 223-250
3. Araujo, R.M., Santoro, F.M., Borges, M.R.S.: A Conceptual Framework for Designing and Conducting Groupware Evaluations. International Journal of Computer Applications in Technology 19(3/4) (2004) 139-150
4. Borges, M.R.S., Meire, A.P., Pino, J.A.: An interface for supporting versioning in a cooperative editor. Proceedings of the 10th International Conference on Human-Computer Interaction, Vol. 2. Crete, Greece (2003) 849-853
5. Borges, M.R.S., Brézillon, P., Pino, J. A., Pomerol, J.-Ch.: Dealing with the effects of context mismatch in group work. Decision Support Systems (accepted for publication)
6. Brézillon, P.: Context in problem solving: A survey. The Knowledge Engineering Review 14(1)(1999) 1-34
7. Brézillon, P., Borges, M.R.S., Pino, J.A., Pomerol, J.-Ch.: Context-awareness in group work: Three case studies. Proceedings of the 2004 IFIP International Conference on Decision Support Systems. Prato, Italy (2004) 115-124
8. Coutaz, J., Crowley, J.L., Dobson, S., Garlan, D.: Context is Key. Communications of The ACM 48(3)(2005) 49-53
9. Dey, A.K., Salber, D., Abowd, G.D.: A Conceptual Framework and a Toolkit for Supporting the Rapid Prototyping of Context-Aware Applications. Human-Computer Interaction 16(2-4) (2001) 97-166
10. Dourish, P.: Seeking a Foundation for context-aware computing. Human-Computer Interaction 16(2,3-4) (2001) 229-241
11. Freitas, R.M.: A Reengenharia Participativa apoiada por uma ferramenta de groupware: CEPE, um editor cooperativo para elicitação de processos. Master Dissertation. Instituto de Matemática e Núcleo de Computação e Eletrônica, UFRJ, Brazil (2003)
12. Gutwin, C., Stark, G., Greenberg, S.: Support for Workspace Awareness in Educational Groupware. ACM Conference on Computer Supported Collaborative Learning (1995) 147-156

13. Greenberg, S.: Context as a Dynamic Construct. Human-Computer Interaction 16(2-4) (2001) 257-268
14. Leake, D., Bogaerts, S., Evans, M., McMullen, D.F.: Contextual Support for Remote Co-operative Troubleshooting: Lesson From a Naturalistic Study. Fifth International and Interdisciplinary Conference on Modeling and Using Context. Workshop on Context and Groupware. CEUR Proceedings, Vol. 133. Paris, France (2005)
15. Meire, A.P., Borges, M.R.S., Araujo, R.M.: Supporting Collaborative Drawing with the Mask Versioning Mechanism. In: Favela, J., Decouchant, D. (eds.): Proceedings of 9th International Workshop on Groupware. Autrans, France. LNCS 2806 (2003) 208-223
16. Pinheiro, M.K., Lima, J.V., Borges, M.R.S.: A Framework for Awareness Support in Groupware Systems. Proceeding of CSCWD 2002, Vol. 1. Rio de Janeiro (2002) 13-18
17. Rosa, M.G.P., Borges, M.R.S., Santoro, F. M.: A Conceptual Framework for Analyzing the Use of Context in Groupware. In: Favela, J., Decouchant, D. (eds.): Proceedings of 9th International Workshop on Groupware. Autrans, France. LNCS 2806 (2003) 300-313

Modeling Contexts in Collaborative Environment: A New Approach

Guiling Wang, Jinlei Jiang, and Meilin Shi

Dept. of Computer Science and Technology, Tsinghua University,
Beijing, 100084, P.R. China
{wgling, jjlei, shi}@csnet4.cs.tsinghua.edu.cn

Abstract. Context awareness, context sharing and context processing are key requirements for the future CSCW, HCI and Ubiquitous computing systems. However, research issues of collaborative context have not been completely addressed till now. While arguing that a generic context model is very important for building context-aware collaborative applications, this paper proposes a new semantic rich context modeling approach, Ontology for Contextual Collaborative Applications (OCCA), for collaborative environments. Based on OCCA, mechanisms for context query, context matching and collaboration awareness control are devised using semantic query and reasoning technology to support the three perspectives of a context model, i.e., information space, interaction space and collaboration control. We present an evaluation study on the features and performance of OCCA and context query services.

1 Introduction

Context and context awareness have been hot topics in recent years, especially in three communities: CSCW, HCI and Ubiquitous Computing. As a result, several context models have been proposed and several context-aware applications have been applied into ubiquitous computing environment, collaborative environment and human-computer interaction environment [1-9]. The new trend of context and context awareness research is to develop context services middleware as an infrastructure for distributed, heterogeneous and autonomous environments.

To build such an infrastructure, in our opinion, two levels are involved: at the conceptual level, a conceptual context model should be given to categorize the concepts and the relationship between them and to define the functions of application, and at the architectural level, a common and consistent architectural model should be given to define the hierarchy, the modules and their interactions. Services provided for context-aware applications include Provider & Consumer Services, Directory Services, Context Query/Event Services, Aggregation/Composition Services, Information Memory Services, Reasoning Services and Control Services. In this view, some of the most important projects on context-aware applications in distribution environment are summarized in Table 1.

Context awareness in CSCW is different from that in ubiquitous computing. Specific context factors are often taken into account by ubiquitous computing like location,

W. Shen et al. (Eds.): CSCWD 2006, LNCS 4402, pp. 23–32, 2007.
© Springer-Verlag Berlin Heidelberg 2007

time and people while the collaborative context like group, role and process, which is very important to CSCW applications, is not considered in ubiquitous computing environment. In collaborative environment, there is lack of a generic mechanism to model the context functions and concepts and to implement common services and architecture. Among the emerging models (Table 1), ENI (Event and Notification Infrastructure) [10] is the only CSCW-specific model which is different from other ubiquitous computing-specific models, but it is an incomplete work because most of the common services are not implemented. In our view, the characteristics of collaborative context should be taken into account from an integrated view. It is our aim to develop a CSCW-specific, complete and generic context model. We propose a generic model of context that focuses on modeling and designing context within collaborative environment.

This paper initially analyzes the functions of a context model in a collaborative environment. Next, a conceptual context model is proposed. And then the implementation of context services is explained. In the last section the paper is summarized and the future work is outlined.

Table 1. A comparison of context modeling

	Conceptual model	Architecture						
		Sensor/ Consumer	Directory Service	Context Query/ Event Service	Aggregation /Composition Service	Information Memory Service	Reasoning Service	Control Service
Context Toolkit [1]	Key-Value Model	Context widgets/ Actuator services	Discovers	No	Aggregators	No	Interpreters	No
Context Fabric [8]	Markup Scheme Model	Sensor/ application, context spec language	Sensor management service	Context event & query service	Automatic Path Creation service	No	No	Privacy
Gaia [9]	Ontology based Model	Context provider/ Consumer	context provider lookup service	Implemented by context consumer	context synthesizer	Context History	Ontology server	No
CoBrA [2]	Ontology based model	Context Acquisition Component/ Agent	Broker directory service	Implemented by Broker Behavior	Broker Behavior	Knowledge Base	Inference Engine	Privacy Policy
ENI [10]	Markup scheme model	Sensor/ Indicator	No	ENI	Situation module	Context module	No	No

2   The Functions of Context Model

In our view, context can be defined as any information that can be used to characterize the situation of entities in the collaborative space. On the one hand, the traditional groupware systems didn't model context explicitly. Context information is embedded in function modules during system development. In this way, the context services are fixed and hard to be changed. The system lacks a special context module, which results in difficulty with context services reuse. On the other hand, an integrated collaborative space can promote linking, navigation and querying of resources before, after, and while a collaborative action occurs. So it is very important to model the context for a collaborative environment.

First of all, every entity has its context in a collaborative space. For example, a person at work wants to know who are his (or her) collaborators as well as their profiles and present statuses. This information promotes cooperating among people. These contexts form the information space dimension of the context model for a collaborative environment, with which users can query any information, including historical and real-time information. Secondly, in an interaction space, various collaborative tools co-exist, users need different interaction patterns in different contexts. Based on the context model, system can help users switch to the proper groupware, fetching the collaborative documents on demand. Lastly, the collaboration control mechanism based on this context model can be more flexible and intelligent. For example, a policy of access control based on the context of a person is much richer in semantics than that based on role.

3   The Conceptual Model and OCCA Ontology

The Denver Model for Groupware Design [12] is a useful model describing the generic elements of any groupware application. Based on the Denver model, Rosa et al proposed a conceptual model for context-aware groupware [4]. However the Denver model doesn't take into account the element of collaboration tool. Various tools play different roles in a collaborative environment. The Denver model lacks the capability of modeling the tool element because its aim is for independent groupware rather than an integrated collaborative environment.

In order to make up for this lack of tool element of the Denver model, we propose a conceptual model that classifies contextual information into 8 categories: Person Context; Task Context; Process Context; Artifact Context; Tool Context; Environment Context; Collaboration Control Policy Context; and Historical Context. We define an Ontology for Contextual Collaborative Applications (OCCA) to present this conceptual model.

$$OCCA = \{Per, Tsk, Process, Art, Tool, Env, Pol, His\}$$

OCCA is used for description of human, task, process, artifact, tools, environment, policies, and the history of these entities. OCCA is written in OWL [13] and maintained by Protégé 3.0[14]. *Per, Tsk, Process, Art, Tool, Env,* and *Pol* are the names in XML namespace, and *His* is the record composed of other context information's history. Figure 1 shows OCCA in upper layer. The classes in upper layer model the generic concepts in collaborative environment such as *Person, Group, Role, Task, Process, Artifact, WorkSpace, Policy* and so on. Most of the classes in lower layer are sub-classes of the classes in Figure 1. They model the domain relevant concepts for applications in diverse fields. For instance, concepts like *Professor, Lecturer*, etc., in cooperative learning and *Driver, Passenger*, etc., in cooperative design are described. Due to space limit, the classes and properties in lower layer are not presented in this figure and are not discussed in this paper.

For modeling person context, OCCA defines such personal information as name, email, homepage, interests, identification in some chat tools, the related project, belonging group and so on. Elements like per: membership, per: Project, per: hasRole, per: Role and per: Group are the basic concepts or properties in collaborative applications. Persons in a common group share their contexts in the workspace.

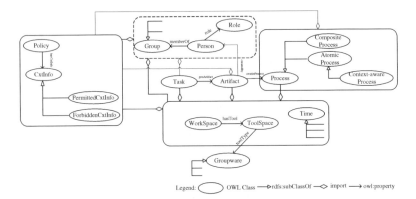

Fig. 1. OCCA in upper layer

Task is one of the core concepts in OCCA. OCCA defines vocabulary for describing task properties, restrictions, and plan. This description is used for task contextual information querying and reasoning. The basic properties of a task in OCCA include the name of the task (tsk: name), the description of the task (tsk: desp), the deadline of the task (tsk: deadline), the group which is in charge of the task (tsk: groupInCharge), the artifacts generated by the task (tsk: genArtifact), the attendee of the task (tsk: attendee), and the workspace where users do the task (tsk: inWorkspace). Such information is useful for users to query task information during their collaboration.

Process is another core concept in OCCA. Process:AtomicProcess is subclass of process:Process, which represents an action taking place during task run. Process: CompositeProcess is a subclass of process:Process, which represents a composite process composed of several activities. Process: ContextawareProcess is also a subclass of process: Process, and it has some special properties to generate the query request for context information in runtime. The details will be discussed in another paper.

The class OCCA: Artifact represents a set of artifacts. Artifacts are those objects produced or consumed during an interaction. Individuals of this class can have a set of properties like art: name, art: fileSize, art: fileType, art: createdBy, art: createdOn and art: modifiedOn to characterize its identification, size, type, creator, create time and modified time. It also has properties like art: createdIn and art: lastmodifiedBy with their values in the process: Process and per: Person respectively.

When building a contextual collaborative environment, it is very useful to describe kinds of collaboration tools, their characteristics, and their status. The class tool: Groupware is used to describe all the meta-information about collaboration tools in the environment. It has properties like tool: workTimeType, tool: workLocationType, tool:groupSize and tool:participant. Their domain is tool: Groupware and their range is tool: TimeOrLocationType, which is an enumerated class composed of value "common", "predictable" and "unpredictable". For example, the tool: workTimeType property and tool: workLocationType property of a teleconference system are both "common" because such a system only supports users who work at the same time (synchronous) and at the same place. Tool:groupSize has a data type of integer. The range of tool:participant is per:Person, which describes the constraints on person using this tool. Thus the properties are used to select a proper collaboration tool and transfer the document into the tool automatically.

OCCA ontology defines a vocabulary for representing policy of collaboration awareness. In a collaborative environment, the policy of collaboration awareness is defined by users and is used to allow or forbid the awareness information access or presentation to other users. Classes of pol: Policy and pol: CxtInfo are defined to represent the policy and the information. Properties like pol: fromGroup/pol: toGroup, pol: fromPerson/pol:toPerson, pol: fromRole/pol: toRole, pol: fromWorkSpace/to: toWorkSpace, pol: fromToolSpace/pol: toToolSpace, pol: fromProcess/pol: toProcess, pol: Artifact and pol: fromTime/pol: toTime are defined to represent the condition of who, where, and when the publishers or receivers are.

Environment contexts include information which can influence the users' actions like the location, workspace, time and so on. This information can be described based on OCCA. The agent can reason about the environment context to trigger some services.

When a task or activity is completed, personal profiles are changed or an artifact is modified, Information about them is stored for reference and tracking purpose. This is called historical context which is very important for a collaborative environment. Sometimes it is called the collaborative memory of a system.

4 Context Services

Previously we have built up an infrastructure for distributed, cross-organization and collaborative environment, called LAGrid [11]. Although we have also developed several groupware like the whiteboard, video-conference system and workflow management system, they haven't been integrated flexibly in a grid infrastructure. To support such a flexible integrated collaborative environment, we added context-aware support to current infrastructure by exploiting Contextual Collaborative Space (CCS). CCS is a new extension of LAGrid service-oriented middleware implemented for OCCA.

In the current version of CCS, the collaborative applications at the same time are context sensors/providers. The applications generate the ontology instances and store them in the knowledge base in real time. The ontology introduced above is also stored in the knowledge base. On top of the knowledge base, we use a reasoner which can derive new knowledge from the knowledge base. The reasoner supports OWL-DL inference and $\mathcal{AL}$-log inference which is a hybrid integration of ontology reasoning and rule based reasoning. In order to implement information space, interaction space and collaboration control mechanisms for the contextual collaborative space (CCS), we design new services like Context Query & Memory Service, Inference Service and Control Service based on the knowledge base and the reasoner.

4.1 Context Query and Memory

Information space is divided into 3 parts: group information space, private information space and historical information space. During the collaborative work, individuals of every class in OCCA are declared in collaborative information space by context sensor services. Context is visualized as a graph so that users can navigate all the elements in the environment together with their associate attributes and the relationships between them.

Every entity in collaborative environment has its context. The context is dynamic with some properties having different values at each collaborative situation. For storing, retrieving and aggregating dynamic context information, RDF dataset and named graph model defined in [15] is used.

Context Memories can be seen as RDF datasets composed of Person Context Memory, Task Context Memory, Artifact Memory, etc. Each context memory (CM_i) is a RDF dataset as follows:

$CM_i = \{Cxt, (<u_1>, Cxt_1), (<u_2>, Cxt_2), \ldots (<u_n>, Cxt_n) \}$, where Cxt is the aggregate graph, and each $<u_i>$ is a distinct URI. $(<u_i>, Cxt_i)$ is a named graph. Cxt_i, which is described in Cxt, is a set of facts and the situation within which those facts are believed to be true. When a new collaborative entity is created or changed, a graph Cxt is created and stored into CM together with the situation.

Track of document or task can be implemented easily based on this model. An example of a track is as the following: "query the word documents modified during Oct.2005 by Alice, return the documents' name, creator and the task name within which the document was modified". Table 2 shows the query expression in SPARQL that supports RDF dataset. For context query and context memory, Jena [16], which supports SPARQL language, is used for RDF document parsing and query.

Table 2. A context query expression

```
SELECT  ?name ?creatorname ?taskname
WHERE{
        ?g  inTask  ?task .
        ?task hasname ?taskname .
        GRAPH ?g
        {?doc  rdf:type art: WordDocument;
               art:modifiedOn ?date;
               art:modifiedBy ?mPerson;
             art:name ?name;
             art:creatBy ?creator .
          ?creator per:name ?creatorname .
          ?mPerson per:name "Alice".
          FILTER
          (?date > "2005-09-30"^^xsd:date
            && ?date < "2005-11-01"^^xsd:date)
        }
      }
```

4.2 Context Service Matching

In a contextual collaborative space, the metadata of the context services are published in a central server for further discovery. We advertise the service descriptions by sending the message to a so-called "information service". The information service assigns it a unique ID, stores it in the repository and sends it to the inference service to be added to the subsumption hierarchy. When a collaborative action is planned, a request is submitted to the information service. The inference service computes the match degree between the request and each advertisement in the repository. The most matchable one is returned with its unique ID. Then the requester can query more detailed characteristics of the tool in the information service using this unique ID.

For example, in the interaction space, the characteristics of the collaboration tools like whiteboard, video-conferencing, threaded discussions and so on are encapsulated as web services. We want to publish a whiteboard to the information service with some restrictions on the participants' size and location like this: i). Group's size must be less than 5. ii) Participants must be from some city. So the advertisement can be written as presented in Table 3 in description logic (DL) notation. It is submitted to information service and WBAdvert is matched and returned with the subsumption relationship of *Query* $\sqsubseteq$ *WBAdvert*. The implementation is based on Pellet used in conjunction with Jena [17].

Table 3. An advertisement and query of the whiteboard

WBAdvert =	Query =
ServiceProfile ⊓	ServiceProfile ⊓
∀item (∀ type.WB ⊓	∀item(∀type.WB ⊓
∀workTimeType.common ⊓	∀workTimeType.common ⊓
∀workLocationType.common ⊓	∀workLocationType.common ⊓
< 5 groupSize ⊓	= 3 groupSize ⊓
∀partici-	∀partici-
pant.(Person⊓∀location.City)))	pant.(Person⊓∀location.Beijing))

4.3 Collaboration Awareness Control Policies

Policies are increasingly used for behavior control of complex systems, allowing administrators to modify system behavior without changing source code. Semantic-rich policy representations based on a common ontology can facilitate interoperation, and the policy representation based on description logic can simplify policy analysis and conflict detection.

Based on OCCA, the publisher and receiver of the shared collaboration awareness information can define control policy in a declarative way. With whom the awareness information is shared is determined both by the profile, location, task, related artifact and time period of the publisher and by those of the receiver.

The cascading characteristic of context is indicated as "the collaboration spaces associated with broader contexts are also visible within an inner context" [18]. Contexts are nested following the structure of task, activities, role, workspace and organization. For example, G1 represents an organization and G1.1 represents a department of this organization in Figure 3. Thus the collaborative awareness information generated from G1.1 can be seen as generated from G1 and the information which will be sent to G1 will also be sent to G1.1. The group information view is the aggregation of the nested context and others. It can save the storage cost and processing cost by inheriting the outer context.

Describing the cascading characteristics of the collaborative awareness information goes beyond the expressive capabilities of OWL DL. So we take advantage of the expressive power of rules to depict it. In this paper, we use $\mathcal{AL}$-log [19], a hybrid approach combining ontology language and rule language. The example above can be described in $\mathcal{AL}$-log as follows:

```
toGroup(C, G11)  :- toGroup(C, G1) , partOf(G11, G1) &
                    C:CxtInfo , G1:Group , G11:Group
fromGroup(C, G1):- fromGroup(C, G11) , partOf(G11, G1) &
                    C:CxtInfo , G1:Group , G11:Group
```

More powerful cascading characteristics can be described based on the relation between different properties:

```
toPerson(C, P):- toGroup(C, G) , memberOf(P, G)&
                 C:CxtInfo , P:Person , G:Group
```

In the following rule, pol represents a control policy on collaborative awareness information sharing. It is specified by John saying that the context information could be shared with a group at meeting room if and only if the publisher is doing some action on some word documents of CSCW topic.

```
permits(pol,cxt):-
policyOf(pol,p) , name(p,John) , toGroup(cxt,mg) , fromPerson(cxt,sender)
& pol:Policy , p:Person , cxt:CxtInfo , mg:MeetingRoomGroup , sender:Person
⊓ ∃AttendIn.CSCWRelatedTask
```

The concepts in this rule which have not been introduced in Section 3 are defined as the following:

```
CSCWRelatedTask = Task ⊓ ∃GenArtifacts.CSCWWordArtifact;

CSCWWordArtifact = WordArtifact ⊓ ∃Topic.{CSCW}; WordArtifact ⊑ Artifact
```

5   Evaluation

Compared with other most important context-aware models in Table 1, OCCA is a context model especially for collaboration applications. OCCA is designed towards a distributed, heterogeneous context-aware collaboration environment. It is ontology based and adopts the standard OWL as its description language. The architecture model based on OCCA has been introduced in section 4. CCS adopts the service-oriented architecture and has developed some key services. Also Table 4 presents another feature of OCCA in our collaborative environment. Which context information is used in implementing the three kinds of functions is showed in this table. Observed that the most frequently used context information are description of human, task, artifact and tool, we can say that OCCA has the feature of focusing more on internal context instead of outer context.

We evaluated the context query performance against the artificial RDF named graph dataset which is generated according to the real world collaboration scenario. The test ontology defines 48 classes and 35 properties for description of a collaborative learning group, the task and the artifact. We created 8 datasets with different sizes of class instances and properties. The size of the datasets is from 600KB to 9MB. The test was done on a windows 2003 server with the configuration of AMD Athlon(tm) XP 1600+ at 1.40GHz and 768MB RAM. The java environment is J2SE 1.5.0_04 and the max java heap size is 512MB. The test module is based on Jena 2.4 ontology toolkit with an Oracle 9i database as the back-end. The Oracle9i database server runs on a VMware workstation with windows 2003 server OS, AMD Sempton™ Processor 2800+ at 1.61GHz and 740MB RAM. All of the ontology data is loaded in database in advance so that they needn't be re-loaded while performing query. We performed a SPARQL query on Named Graphs both with RDFS reasoner and OWL reasoner 5 times on each dataset. We measured the average query time as shown in Figure 2. The results show that the query time is within 25 seconds for the knowledge base of about 1000 class instances (about 9MB) in our prototype when only RDFS inference is needed. But for the complex query that need OWL inference, the query time can be 8 minutes long. The observation suggests us cache the query results for non-real-time tasks. Also we can split the instances and classes or load the data in common use in the main memory in order to reduce the query response time.

Table 4. Ontology used in different scenario

	Per	Tsk	Proc	Art	Tool	Env	Pol	His
Context Query	√	√	√	√	√	√	√	√
Collaborative Tools Switching	√	√	×	×	√	×	×	×
Collaboration Awareness Control	√	×	×	√	×	×	×	×

√used; ×not used.

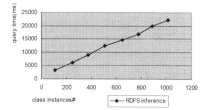 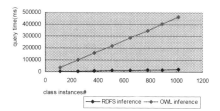

Fig. 2. Context query time

6 Conclusions and Future Work

The context model described in this paper is the first attempt to give a generic semantic rich model for integrated context-aware collaborative environments. This model focuses on context information sharing and collaborative work rather than an individual's context awareness and reasoning.

OCCA is used for description of 8 kinds of generic entities for collaborative applications and the domain relevant concepts for collaborative applications in diverse fields. Its query and inference mechanism is based on OWL and $\mathcal{AL}$-log. This paper presents the context services devised for the architecture. Also we evaluate the features of OCCA and the performance of the context services. There are still several issues to be resolved. The $\mathcal{AL}$-log reasoner that can work with Jena is still in progress and needs further development and performance evaluation for collaboration control.

Acknowledgments. This work is supported by the National Natural Science Foundation of China under Grant No. 90412009.

References

1. Dey, A.K. and Abowd, G.D.: A Conceptual Framework and a Toolkit for Supporting the Rapid Prototyping of Context-Aware Applications. HCI 16(2001) 97-166
2. Chen, H.: An Intelligent Broker Architecture for Context-Aware Systems. PhD.Dissertation proposal. University of Maryland (2003)
3. Brezillon, P., Borges, M., Pino, J. and Pomerol, J.-C.: Context-Awareness in Group Work: Three Case Studies. IFIP International Conference on Decision Support Systems (2004)
4. Rosa, M.G.P., Borges, M.R.S. and Santoro, F.M.: A Conceptual Framework for Analyzing the Use of Context in Groupware. The 9th International Workshop on Groupware: Design, Implementation, and Use. LNCS 2806 (2003) 300-313
5. Steinfield, C., Jang, C.-Y., .Pfaff, B.: Supporting Virtual Team in Collaboration: The TeamSCOPE System. Proceedings of the International ACM SIGGROUP Conference on Supporting Group Work (1999) 81-90
6. Bradley, N.A., Dunlop, M.D.: Towards a User-centric and Multidisciplinary Framework for Designing Context-aware Applications. First International Workshop on Advanced Context Modeling, Reasoning And Management (2004)
7. Hong, J.I.: Context Fabric: Infrastructure Support for Context-Aware Systems. Qualifying Exam Proposal (2001). URL: http://www.cs.berkeley.edu/~jasonh/quals/quals-proposal-context-fabric.pdf
8. Ranganathan, A. and Campbell, R.H.: A Middleware for Context-Aware Agents in Ubiquitous Computing Environments. ACM/IFIP/USENIX International Middleware Conference (2003)
9. Gu, T., Pung, H.K., Zhang D.Q.: A Service-Oriented Middleware for Building Context-Aware Services. Journal of Network and Computer Applications 28(1) (2005) 1-18
10. Gross, T., Prinz, W.: Modelling Shared Contexts in Cooperative Environments: Concept, Implementation, and Evaluation. Computer Supported Cooperative Work: The Journal of Collaborative Computing 13(3-4) (2004) 13-34
11. Wang, G., Li, Y., Yang, S., Miao, C., Xu Jun, Shi, M.: Service-oriented grid architecture and middleware technologies for collaborative e-learning. IEEE International Conference on Service Computing (SCC2005) 67-74
12. Salvador, T., Scholtz, J., Larson, J.: The Denver model for groupware design. ACM SIGCHI Bulletin archive 28(1)(1996)
13. McGuinness D.L., van Harmelen, F.: OWL web ontology language overview (2004). URL: http://www.w3.org/TR/2004/REC-owl-features-20040210/
14. The Protege Ontology Editor and Knowledge Acquisition System (2006). URL: http://protege.stanford.edu/
15. SPARQL Query Language for RDF (2006). URL: http://www.w3.org/TR/rdf-sparql-query/
16. Jena – a semantic web framework for Java (2006). URL: http://jena.sourceforge.net/
17. Pellet OWL Reasoner (2006). URL: http://www.mindswap.org/2003/pellet/
18. Lei, H., Chakraborty, D., Chang, H., Dikun, M.J., Heath, T., Li, J.S., et al.: Contextual Collaboration: Platform and Applications. IEEE International Conference on Services Computing (SCC 2004). Shanghai, China (2004)
19. Donini, F.M., Lenzerini, M. et al.: AL-log: Integrating Datalog and Description Logics. Journal of Intelligent Information Systems 10(3) (1998) 227-252

A Hierarchical Cooperation Model for Application Self-reconfiguration of Sensor Networks

Liang Liu, Huadong Ma, Dan Tao, and Dongmei Zhang

School of Computer Science and Technologies,
Beijing University of Posts and Telecommunications,
Beijing 100876, China
laurelliu@sina.com.cn, mhd@bupt.edu.cn

Abstract. Application self-reconfiguration is essential in order to complement the flexibility and adaptability for sensor networks in the environment monitoring domain. In this paper, we mainly focus on the issue of application self-reconfiguration from the point of cooperation. Based on our previous works, we conclude the features of cooperation in sensor networks, and propose a hierarchical cooperation model to describe the cooperative manners. Finally, we utilize the layered cooperation model to realize application self-recon-figuration in sensor networks.

1 Introduction

Sensor networks are composed of a large number of sensing devices with computation, communication and sensing capabilities [3-4]. Advances in sensors and wireless technologies enable sensor networks to be deployed for a wide range of monitoring applications. Physical environment monitoring is the main application domain of sensor networks [5-7].

Because the objects in environment are dynamic and unpredictable, there are two key issues of environment monitoring in sensor networks: (1) Flexibility. The main method of improving flexibility is reconfiguring applications. Because sensor nodes can't store all possible codes of applications in their constrained memories, application reconfiguration needs to provide a powerful mechanism to adapt component-based distributed applications to dynamic environment. (2) Adaptability. The sensing data coming from dynamic environment can be influenced by various factors, and users' requirements to the applications are diverse, so it is difficult to predict all possible applications in the initial deployment of sensor networks. Even if we know all the possible states of environment, we wouldn't predict its exact state at a given time. For example, in a building environment monitoring system, most nodes only collect temperature data under normal situation. But under certain situation, such as abnormal high temperature, some sensor nodes need to collect smoke data adaptively. In order to perform the sensing application efficiently, sensor networks should be aware of the variations of environment conditions dynamically at runtime and reconfigure the applications adaptively.

In our previous work [1-2], we employed an Environment Adaptive Application Reconfiguration (EAAR) mechanism to describe the process of application

W. Shen et al. (Eds.): CSCWD 2006, LNCS 4402, pp. 33–42, 2007.
© Springer-Verlag Berlin Heidelberg 2007

self-reconfiguration for sensor networks. However, we can find that the process of self-reconfiguration is a cooperative one, and EAAR mechanism doesn't consider the cooperative relation and cooperative manner during the whole process of self-reconfiguration.

Taking advantage of the benefits provided by CSCW [10-14], we have presented the novel conception of Sensor Networks Supported Cooperative Work (SNSCW) [8]. SNSCW is a distributed calculation environment which is based on sensor networks technology, distributed calculation technology, multimedia technology and artificial intelligence technology. The role of sensor nodes in sensor networks is much as the role that a person plays in the society. So, the cooperation among nodes has the basic features of cooperation among people, which can be seen as a simplified human cooperation. Cooperators supported by sensor networks are mainly divided into users (human) and sensor nodes. And cooperation supported by sensor networks is mainly divided into two levels: one is cooperation between user and intelligent nodes, it represents the cooperation between human and environment; the other is the cooperation among sensor nodes.

In this paper, we mainly focus on the issue of application self-reconfiguration for sensor networks from the point of cooperation, and employ a hierarchical cooperation model of sensor networks to realize EAAR mechanism. First, we describe the EAAR mechanism briefly, which partitions the application self-reconfiguration of sensor networks into three modules. Moreover, we summarize the cooperative relationship among multiple cooperators in sensor networks. In particular, we propose a hierarchical cooperation model for sensor networks. Based on the cooperation model, we design a typical application self-reconfiguration system to realize EAAR mechanism.

The rest of the paper is organized as follows. Section 2 describes the EAAR mechanism briefly. In Section 3, we conclude the feature of cooperation in sensor networks. Section 4 details a hierarchical cooperation model for sensor networks. In Section 5, we implement EAAR mechanism using the hierarchical cooperation model. Finally, Section 6 concludes the paper.

2   Environment Adaptive Application Reconfiguration Mechanism

In our previous work [1-2] , we have proposed an Environment Adaptive Application Reconfiguration (EAAR) mechanism. This mechanism can effectively provide a solid theoretical foundation for application self-reconfiguration in sensor network. In this section, we will introduce this application self-reconfiguration mechanism.

EAAR mechanism executes application self-reconfiguration according to a sensing-analyzing-performing process. In this way, sensor nodes are aware of the variation of environment, and analyze how to reconfigure application, and then perform application reconfiguration referring to the results of analysis. In order to sense the changes dynamically, we denote environmental information as rule-based knowledge, and utilize the knowledge to analyze environment data, and determine which applications should be supported in the current environment. Figure 1 illustrates the model of this mechanism composed of three modules: Decision Making, Script Providing and Scripts Executing.

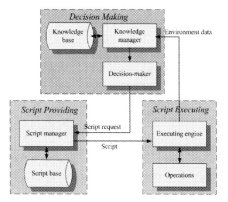

Fig. 1. Environment aware self-reconfiguration model

- **Decision Making** is responsible for detecting changes and determining whether they can cause reconfiguration. This module includes three components: knowledge base, knowledge manager, and decision maker. Knowledge base stores knowledge defined by users. The relationship between environment states and corresponding applications can be described using rule-based knowledge. The knowledge can be denoted as the following formula: P->Q (or IF P THEN Q), where P is a prediction, Q is an action when P is satisfied. By utilizing knowledge manager, users can define domain knowledge and submit them to knowledge base, and decision maker can call knowledge. Decision maker combines the knowledge and the collected data from sensors with the task's running state of current node to determine where, when and how to reconfigure, and then send request to script manager.
- **Script Providing** generates, stores, manages and sends scripts to appointed nodes. This module includes two components: script manager and script base. Script base stores scripts defined by users or generated by script manager. Scripts can migrate between nodes via multi-hop communication. A lightweight script language is needed in our model to meet the constraints of sensor nodes. Script manager is responsible for generating and managing scripts. Utilizing it, scripts can be extracted from script base according to requirements. Moreover, if needed, script manager can generate scripts according to the requirements.
- **Script Executing** is responsible for executing application scripts transmitted from Script Providing. This module consists of two components: executing engine and operations. Executing engine executes scripts deployed on nodes. It works as a lightweight script interpreter and map scripts to lower-layer operations. Operations are the units of execution functionality, which can be configured and assembled using different ways to perform different applications.

In general, a sensor network system starts at Decision Making module, and executes Script Providing module if a script request message is sent which indicates some nodes need to be reconfigured. The sensor network executes Script Executing module if scripts delivery is successful, then it returns to execute Decision Making module once new scripts have been performed and new environment data have been collected.

3   Cooperation in Sensor Networks

The cooperation in the sensor networks contains two aspects. On one hand, sensor network mainly pays attention to the interaction between human and environment, it introduces quantized environmental data into human activities, and informs about the changes of environment to human. On the other hand, every node in the sensor networks is an independent individual with basic ability of cooperation. With the continuously complex calculation, the future calculation environment of sensor networks will be an open, distributed, and coordinative one. So, the support for the cooperation among sensor nodes will be a main feature in future calculation environment of sensor networks. Thus, we conclude that: (1) Cooperators supported by sensor networks are mainly divided into users (human) and sensor nodes. (2) Cooperation supported by sensor networks is mainly divided into two levels: one is cooperation between user and intelligent nodes, it represents the cooperation between human and environment; the other is the cooperation among sensor nodes.

As to the cooperation between human and sensor nodes, they are more often a user-executor relationship that always reflected as: user customizes work to sensor nodes (executor), the executed results of the nodes can be used by users' application. User here initiates the cooperation. Meanwhile, because of the intelligence of node, it can also initiate cooperation. After analyzing the changes of environment or the previous works, the nodes actively query whether the user needs some work.

As to the cooperation among the nodes, their relationships are uncertainty according to different applications, but there are two fundamental ones: (1) Peer relation. The cooperators have the same roles and functions in cooperation; have the common way of communication; share information and tools with each other. (2) Master-slave relation. In the process of cooperation, the master node mainly coordinates the works of slave nodes, and maintains some sharing information relative to the cooperation. The slave is the executor of the specific operations.

4   A Hierarchical Cooperation Model for Sensor Networks

After analyzing the relationships and interactions among the cooperators, we know that the cooperation between user and nodes is simple, and structural. But the cooperation among intelligent nodes is more complicated. Thus, we propose a hierarchical cooperation model, which contains two independent cooperation models as to the two-layer cooperation, and make a formal description of the cooperation model among intelligent nodes.

4.1   Cooperative Model Between Human and Sensor Nodes

As to the cooperation between people and nodes, because their relationship is user-executor, and these nodes can be seen as a logical entity, the interaction between human and nodes can be abstracted as individual-individual. On the basis of these conclusions, we can build series of system primitives based on the speech-acts theory [9] to describe and control the cooperative process between human and nodes.

Based on the speech-acts theory, we introduce two action rings, shown as Figure 2, to describe the cooperation model between human and nodes.

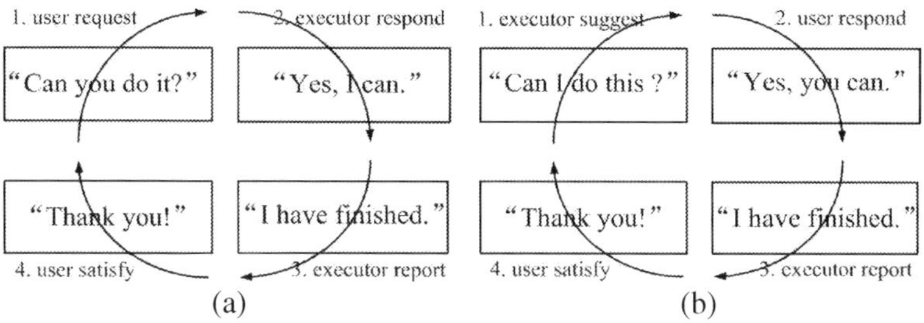

1. user request	2. executor respond	1. executor suggest	2. user respond
"Can you do it?"	"Yes, I can."	"Can I do this ?"	"Yes, you can."

"Thank you!"	"I have finished."	"Thank you!"	"I have finished."
4. user satisfy	3. executor report	4. user satisfy	3. executor report

(a)   (b)

Fig. 2. Action rings of the cooperation model between human and sensor nodes. (a) Human initiates cooperation (b) Node initiates cooperation.

Figure 2(a) describes a typical controlling ring that is proposed by Medina-Mora. The cooperation is initiated by human. The user firstly tells the sensor nodes what to do, and then sensor nodes judge if they could follow the user's orders according to their own abilities and present state, if yes, they execute the user's commands, and then return the results or suggestions to the user who will deal with the result or make some operation based on the suggestions.

Figure 2(b) is the extension of Figure 2(a) due to the intelligence of nodes, the cooperation is initiated by nodes, sensor node can analyze the changes of the environment or the previous works, and give the user suggestions, or warning on changes of environment, then the user can take proper actions.

4.2 Cooperative Model Among the Sensor Nodes

Due to the complicated relationships and the diversity interaction among sensor nodes, it is necessary for us to build a layered cooperation model, which can integrate the features of multiple cooperation modes, the reasons are: (1) Sensor nodes always both have the peer relationship and the master-slave relationship, which require that the cooperation should be hierarchical. (2) Nodes on different levels always have different cooperative activities, which require the cooperation model integrate the features of multiple fundamental cooperation models.

So, we introduce layered abstract model (activity-task-cooperation) to sensor network. Although the interaction and cooperation among nodes are classified into synchronous ones and asynchronous ones, and the interactive media includes various types, such as temperature, audio and video sensed by sensors, commands and code scripts, they are all based on the fact that activity is made up of nodes and interactive media; task is a set of relative activities; cooperation is a set of independent tasks with common aims and complete semantics.

Let $N = \{N_1, N_2, ..., N_n\}$, where N_i denotes the ith node; let $S = \{S_1, S_2, ..., S_m\}$, where S_i denotes the ith type of the medium; receiving ($\leftarrow$), transmitting ($\rightarrow$),processing ($\downarrow$)and sensing ($\uparrow$) are basic operations of a certain medium, and let $O = \{\leftarrow, \uparrow, \rightarrow, \downarrow\}$. $\sigma(O)$ is a set contains all the subset of O.

Let $M_{i,j} (\forall i \in [1,n], \forall j \in [1,m])$ denotes the medium, which type is S_j. It is sensed by N_i, or N_i transforms the existing medium $M_{i',j'}$ into $M_{i,j}$, that is: $M_{i,j} = N_i \uparrow S_j$ or

$M_{i,j} = N_i \downarrow M_{i',j'}$. $M = \{M_{i,j} \mid \forall i \in [1,n], \forall j \in [1,m]\}$ denotes the set of all media in this system.

The expression of operation $\uparrow$ can be depicted as $M = N \uparrow S$; the expression of operation $\downarrow$ can be depicted as $M = N \downarrow M$; the expression of operation $\rightarrow$ and $\leftarrow$ can be depicted as $N \rightarrow M$ or $M \leftarrow N$.

Definition 1. Let $D_k(M_{i,j})(\forall i, k \in [1,n], \forall j \in [1,m])$ denotes the authority of N_k for accessing medium $M_{i,j}$, thus, $D_k\left(M_{i,j}\right) \in \sigma(O)$. If $D_k\left(M_{i,j}\right) \neq \phi$, then N_k can access $M_{i,j}$, which can be described as $N_k \in M_{i,j}$, that is $N_k \in M_{i,j} \equiv D_k\left(M_{i,j}\right) \in \sigma(O) \wedge D_k\left(M_{i,j}\right) \neq \phi$.

When every node at least accesses one medium, and every medium at least has been accessed by two different nodes (at least one sends, one receives), or the medium is transformed into another one by a node. Once at least one of the above conditions is satisfied, we can consider they comprise an activity. The definition of activity is formalized as follow.

Definition 2 (Activity). Let $D_k = \bigcup D_k\left(M_{i,j}\right)$ denotes N_k 's access authority to all the different media, $\{\leftarrow, \rightarrow\} \subseteq D_k\left(M_{i,j}\right) \bigcup D_k\left(M_{i,j}\right)$ $\forall i, k \in [1,n], \forall j \in [1,m]$, and $D_K \neq \phi$, $\exists k, k' \in [1,n], k \neq k', N_k \in M_{i,j}, N_{k'} \in M_{i,j}$, when $\{\leftarrow, \rightarrow\} \subseteq D_k\left(M_{i,j}\right) \bigcup D_k\left(M_{i,j}\right)$ or $\exists k, j' \in [1,n]$, $M_{k,j'} = N_k \downarrow M_{i,j}$, the set of sensor nodes N and media M comprise the activity A.

In the process of cooperation, existential relation can describe some restricted relationship between node and media, activity and activity.

Definition 3. Let $E = N \bigcup M$ denotes all the entities in an activity, and the signal "a" denotes *Existential relation*. Assume the boolean variable ε_{E_i} represents whether E_i exists. If the existence of E_i relies on E_j, then it is described as ε_{E_i} a ε_{E_j} .

The semantic interpretation of Existential relation relies on the type of entities. For instance, $\varepsilon_{M_{ij}}$ a ε_{N_k} represents that the existence of medium $M_{i,j}$ relies on node N_k (typically, when $i = k$, $M_{i,j}$ is sensed by N_k); ε_A a ε_{N_k} represents activity A can't begin without N_i's parting in; and $\varepsilon_{M_{ij}}$ a $\varepsilon_{M_{i,j}}$ represents having to access $M_{i',j'}$ before accessing $M_{i,j}$.

Generally speaking, one task consists of many activities, and these activities are relative. For example, in heterogeneous sensor networks, before high-end node executes A_i, lower-end node has to execute awakening activity A_j, that is A_i a A_j. We call a series of relative activities as a task.

Definition 4 (Task). Assume $A_1, A_2, ..., A_n$ are several relative activities, iff $\forall i \in [2,n]$, $\exists j \in [1,n]$ and $i \neq j$, if exists A_i a A_j, then these activities make up task T, which can be described as $T = \{A_1, A_2, ..., A_n\}$.

Here we suppose that A_1 is the initial activity of the task, which is independent of any other activities. So, a task is a set of activities, it will terminate only when all the interactions terminate.

Cooperation is a set of tasks. These tasks have the common objective, and they are always the peer relation, executed by different group in the sensor networks. They are independent with each other.

Definition 5 (Cooperation). Cooperation C is a set of tasks $T_1, T_2, ..., T_n$, that is, $C = \{T_1, T_2, ..., T_n\}$.

Three abstract levels of the cooperation model consist of activity, task, and cooperation. The model is illustrated by Figure 3.

In this model, the relationship between cooperation level and task level represents the division of works and cooperation among groups during the cooperative work, while the relationship between task level and activity level represents interaction between the sensor nodes and coordinative activities. This model can describe cooperative work among sensor nodes entirely.

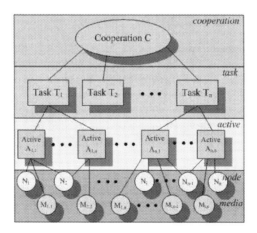

Fig. 3. Three-level cooperation model

5 Implementation of Application Self-reconfiguration in Sensor Networks

In order to correspond to the cooperation model, we propose a cluster-based architecture for sensor network. There are three types of nodes deployed in sensor networks: sensor nodes (N_i), cluster heads (H_j) and Sink node (S), the set of nodes

$N = \{N_1, N_2,...,N_i,...,H_1,H_2,...H_j,...,S\}$. Sensor nodes are simple and inexpensive, while cluster heads are much powerful and richer in resource. A cluster head organizes sensor nodes around it into a cluster. An overall sensor network can be divided into several clusters. And there is one sink node in a sensor network, which is responsible for controlling and maintaining the topology of sensor network. The types of media contain environment data (S_d), analysis results (S_r), scripts (S_s), that is $S = \{ S_d , S_r , S_s \}$. The structure of system is shown as Figure 4.

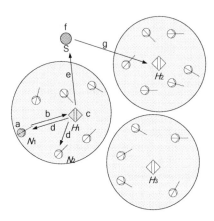

Fig. 4. Procedure of application self-reconfiguration in cluster-based sensor network

As far as the hierarchical cooperation model is concerned, the process of application self-reconfiguration for the whole sensor network can be considered as *cooperation*, and the self-reconfiguration process for each cluster can be considered as *task*. We regard all kinds of operations and interactions among sensor nodes and cluster head during the self-reconfiguration process as *activity*. Therefore, sink node organizes and manages multiple tasks; cluster head divides a self-reconfiguration task into multiple activities and cooperates the corresponding sensor nodes to perform these activities efficiently.

During the self-reconfiguration process, Decision Making module can run onto two different types of nodes. Decision Making module on sink node will determine when and how adjust the set of tasks (e.g. add a new task, delete a task) according to analysis results coming from cluster heads. Decision Making module on cluster head will decide the cooperation and interaction among multiple sensor nodes according to the sensing data. Script Providing module runs on the cluster head, and generates scripts for multiple sensor nodes by the result from Decision Making module. Script Executing module runs on the sensor node, interprets and executes scripts.

The process is detailed as follows:

a. Sensor node N_1 executes the current operation, and gathers the corresponding data ($M_{d,1}$), that is $M_{d,1} = N_1 \uparrow T_d$;

b. N_1 transmits $M_{d,1}$ to cluster head H_1, that is $N_1 \rightarrow M_{d,1}, H_1 \leftarrow M_{d,1}$;

c. H_1 analyzes these data, generates the corresponding analysis result $(M_{r,1})$, thus generates the corresponding scripts $(M_{s,1})$ according to the above analysis result, that is $M_{r,1} = H_1 \downarrow M_{d,1}, M_{s,1} = H_2 \downarrow M_{r,1}$;

d. H_1 transmits $M_{s,1}$ to the corresponding sensor nodes (e.g. N_1 and N_2), and determines cooperates N_1 and N_2 to monitor together, that is $H_1 \rightarrow M_{s,1}, N_1 \leftarrow M_{s,1}, N_2 \leftarrow M_{s,1}$;

e. H_1 transmits the reconfiguration information $(M_{r,1})$ to sink node (S), that is $H_1 \rightarrow M_{r,1}, S_1 \leftarrow M_{r,1}$

f. S generates analysis results $M_{r,s}$ by $M_{r,1}$, and decides whether other clusters need join in or retreat from this reconfiguration process, that is $M_{r,s} = S \downarrow M_{r,1}$

g. S transmits $M_{r,s}$ to the corresponding cluster head (H_2), and we assume that S want cluster 2 to join into this reconfiguration process here, that is $S \rightarrow M_{r,s}, H_2 \leftarrow M_{r,s}$.

6 Conclusion

Based on our previous works, this paper first utilizes a hierarchical cooperation model to implement the process of application self-reconfiguration in sensor networks. Compare to the general description of application self-reconfiguration, our description from the point of cooperation further analyzes the cooperative relation and cooperative manners among multiple entities in sensor networks. Therefore, the hierarchical cooperation model is useful for designing and implementing the self-reconfiguration system of sensor networks. Moreover, our cooperation model can be not only used to describe the application self-reconfiguration, but also to describe and model many other cooperative issues in sensor networks.

Acknowledgments. This work is supported by the National Natural Science Foundation of China (Grant No. 90612013), the National High Technology Research and Development Program of China (Grant No. 2006AA01Z304), Beijing Natural Science Found (Grant No. 4062024) and the NCET of MOE, China.

References

1. Zhang, D., Ma, H., Liu, L. and Tao, D.: EAAR: An Approach to Environment Adaptive Application Reconfiguration in Sensor Networks. Proceedings of the International Conference on Mobile Ad-hoc and Sensor Networks (MSN'05). Wuhan, China (2005)
2. Liu, L., Ma, H., Tao, D., Zhang, D.: A Push-based Paradigm for Environment-adaptive Application Reconfiguration in Clustered Sensor Networks. Proc. of the 3rd International Conference on Mobile Ad-Hoc and Sensor Systems (MASS'06). Vancouver (2006)
3. Akyildiz, I.F., Su, W., Sankarasubramaniam, Y. and Cayirci, E.: Wireless sensor networks: a survey. Computer Networks 38(4) (2002) 393-422
4. Culler, D., Estrin, D., Srivastava, M.: Overview of sensor networks. IEEE Computer 37(8) (2004) 41-49

5. Lin, C., Federspiel, C.C. and Auslander, D.M.: Multi-sensor single-actuator control of HVAC systems. URL: http://www.cbe.berkeley.edu/research/briefs-wirelessxyz.htm
6. Holman, R., Stanley, J., Ozkan-Haller, T.: Applying Video Sensor Networks to Nearshore Environment Monitoring. IEEE Trans. on Pervasive Computing 2(4) (2003) 14-21
7. Herzog, R.K. and Konstantas, D.: Continuous monitoring of vital constants for mobile users: the MobiHealth approach. Proceedings of IEEE-EMBS. Cancun, Mexico (2003)
8. Liu, L., Ma, H., Tao D. and Zhang, D.: A Hierarchical Cooperation Model for Sensor Networks Supported Cooperative Work. Proceedings of the 10th International Conference on Computer Support Cooperative Work in Design. Nanjing, China (2006)
9. Searle, J.: Speech Acts. Cambridge: Cambridge University Press (1969)
10. Gelernter, D. and Carriero, N.: Coordination Languages and their Significance. Communications ACM 35(2) (1992) 97-107
11. Palmer, T.D., Fields N.A.: Computer Supported Cooperative Work. Computer 27(5) (1994) 15-17
12. Grudin, J.: Computer-supported Cooperative Work: History and Focus. Computer 27(5) (1994) 19-26
13. Zheng, Q. and Li, R.: A Modeling and Implementing Method of CSCW. Chinese Journal Computers 21(S1) (1998) 270-271
14. Wu, W., Peng D., Lin Z., Liu, P. and Deng, W.: Research of Coordination Mechanism of Distributed Multi-tasks in CSCW. Computer Engineering 23(5) (1997) 3-7

Developing Ubiquitous Collaborating Multi-Agent Systems Based on QoS Requirements

Rahat Iqbal[1], Nazaraf Shah[2], Anne James[1], Babak Akhgar[2], Muhammad Younas[3], and Kuo-Ming Chao[1]

[1] Distributed Systems and Modelling Research Group,
Faculty of Engineering and Computing,
Coventry University, United Kingdom
{r.iqbal, a.james, k.chao}@coventry.ac.uk
[2] Informatics Research Group,
Faculty of Arts, Computing, Engineering and Sciences
Sheffield Hallam University,
United Kingdom
{n.shah, b.akhgar}@shu.ac.uk
[3] Department of Computing,
Oxford Brookes University, Wheatley Campus,
Oxford, United Kingdom
m.younas@brookes.ac.uk

Abstract. Addressing the issues of Quality of Service (QoS) from user perspective is gaining increasing importance in ubiquitous collaborating systems. However, it is difficult to perform an effective and rigorous analysis of QoS user requirements using traditional methods of investigation. To acknowledge this fact, researchers need to move literally as well as metaphorically from the laboratory to the field. In this respect, applying ethnographic methods of investigation can unfold the social aspects of work practices in the "real world". In this paper, we address the issues of QoS in terms of user requirements. We also present an approach based on ethnography and multi-agent systems to address these issues in an effective way by mapping a user mental model onto intelligent agents. We apply an ethnographic approach in order to understand and elucidate the semantics, functionality and detail QoS requirements for a collaborative system in an academic domain. Secondly, we employ agent technology for modelling a collaborative system based on user profiles and preferences.

1 Introduction

An important aspect of designing for ubiquitous collaborating systems is addressing the issues concerning QoS from user perspective. To date, most of the research on QoS is system oriented that focuses on traffic analysis, scheduling, and routing [1]. We believe that little attention has been paid to a user perspective of these issues in the past, while the rapid proliferation of ubiquitous computing in recent years has encouraged researchers to move beyond the system oriented QoS issues and address such issues from user perspective.

W. Shen et al. (Eds.): CSCWD 2006, LNCS 4402, pp. 43–52, 2007.
© Springer-Verlag Berlin Heidelberg 2007

Addressing user level QoS issues in ubiquitous computing is gaining increasing acceptance due to the fact that the user interface has moved to the real world. One of the major applications of ubiquitous collaborating systems is to support human-human communication and collaboration in an unobtrusive way, by constantly monitoring humans, their activities and their intentions [2-3].

To acknowledge and address the issues of QoS from user perspective, researchers need to move literally as well as metaphorically from the laboratory to the field. In this respect, applying ethnographic methods of investigation can provide detailed QoS requirements by unfolding the social aspects of work practices in the "real world". Ethnography has successfully been applied to various complex, large scale and domestic workplaces [4-6]. The aim is to effectively analyse working practices in order to aid the system development process. Computer systems that are developed without any systematic help from the social sciences (sociology, psychology, linguistics, anthropology, etc.) may not thoroughly address the needs of the users [8]. Ethnographic research intends to obtain a deep understanding of the people, the organisations, and the broader context of the work, which they undertake.

We should take into account the experience of previous research that has shown that users may not accept a relatively high-speed service unless it is also predictable, visually appealing and reliable [1][7].

Importantly the growing realization is that most systems fail not for technical reasons but because they do not resonate with the work as it is actually done as a "real-world" and "real-time" phenomenon [8]. And eventually, they do not address the quality metrics from user perspectives. Bouch and Sasse argued that many QoS factors could be obtained by interacting with users' judgments of quality [7].

In order to ensure that QoS requirements are met in the development of ubiquitous collaborating systems, we need a computation paradigm that provides an effective coordination model and reasoning capability. Intelligent agents provide an effective computational model that allows realising the social aspects of collaborative systems. One of the key characteristics of this model is to simulate the reasoning and action processes of humans. They also model approximation of human problem solving behaviour. Therefore, this model allows us to map user requirements related to QoS onto intelligent agents' mental attitudes. Such attributes of agents enable us to understand and explain system behaviour in terms of mental attitudes such as belief, desire and intention (BDI) [6]. Given this perception, multi-agent systems can be used to conceptualise QoS criteria and thus ensure maintenance of QoS during a task performance. The belief component represents the information the agent has about its environment and its capabilities, desire represents the state of affairs the agent wants to achieve and intention corresponds to the desires the agent is committed to achieve. BDI architecture has also been called deliberative architecture [9-11].

The rest of the paper is organised as follows. Section 2 discusses the proposed approach. This section also describes the components of the proposed approach. Section 3 presents the analysis of Document Management System (DMS). Section 4 discusses communication and collaboration patterns between agents in the context of DMS. Besides the discussion, this section also takes into account implementation considerations. Section 5 concludes this paper and provides a direction for future research.

2 Proposed Approach: Ethno-Agent

We propose an approach based on ethnography and the intelligent agent paradigm. Both ethnography and multi-agent systems take into account the social aspects of the working environment. Therefore, they can be integrated to provide a unified framework that could be used for user requirements as well as for system implementation. More precisely, ethnography provides a "rich", "textual" and "concrete" exposition of the analysis of working practices while multi-agent systems provide an efficient computation model.

The outcome of the ethnographic analysis results in detailed description of the findings. Such findings are mapped to the internal components of intelligent agents such as belief, desire, and intention. Our proposed approach allows us to include ethnographic findings of the problem domain in multi-agent systems by using higher level of abstraction. Thus, it ensures that user requirements concerning QoS are included in the design and implementation of the system.

We use an effective and rigorous ethnographic framework that helps to organise ethnographic research findings. We use three viewpoints for each of ethnography and Multi-Agent Systems (MAS). In ethnography, these viewpoints are referred to as:distributed coordination; awareness of work; and plans and procedures [12]. In MAS these viewpoints consist of : plans and actions; belief; and coordination protocols [11].

In the subsequent sections, we discuss different viewpoints of the ethnographic model and the BDI model of intelligent agents. We also map the concepts of the ethnographic model onto the BDI model of MAS as shown in Table 1.

In the subsequent subsections, we briefly discuss the components of the proposed approach.

Table 1. Mapping description

Ethnography	Artificial Intelligent Agents	Level of analysis
Distributed coordination	Coordination protocols	Social Behavioural analysis
Plans and procedures	Plans and actions (desire and intension)	Functional analysis
Awareness of work	Belief	Structural analysis

2.1 Distributed Coordination

Distributed coordination refers to the fact that the tasks are carried out as: part of patterns of activity; operations with the context of a division of labour; "steps" in protracted operations; and contributions of continuing "process" of activity [12]. The activities are dependent upon each other. Distributed coordination involves coordinating the interdependencies between the activities and describes how the tasks are performed [12].

In the development of MAS, distributed coordination highlights the importance of actions and tasks within the system and describes the manners and means by which work is coordinated. It also emphasises the implications to support coordination mechanisms. Similar to human society, effective coordination is also essential in MAS in order to achieve commons goals among autonomous agents. The role of coordination is to maintain various forms of interdependencies that occur in a system of interdependent agents [13]. Systems that are capable of solving problems cooperatively must employ standards, or mutually agreed upon ad-hoc coordination mechanisms in order to manage dependencies among their interrelated activities.

A variety of coordination mechanisms have been developed to address the problem of coordination in MAS. These mechanisms range from social laws [14] that constrain the acceptable behaviours of agents, to explicit coordination models [13][15] and interaction protocols [13] used to guide a society's behaviour.

2.2 Plans and Procedures

Plans and procedures provide a prominent means by which distributed coordination is achieved. A wide range of artefacts such as plans, schedules, manuals of instruction, procedures, job descriptions, formal organisational charts, and workflow diagrams are all examples of plans and procedures which allow people to coordinate their activities [12]. It is important to understand how "plans and procedure" are used to organise activities. Hughes and his colleagues further clarify their role and suggest that a consideration of plans within cooperative work should identify the different actors and their potential relationship to plans and procedures [12].

In MAS, each agent has its own plan library. An agent's plan is an implementation of well-defined business functionality or a part of it. A plan is a recipe or a set of actions that an agent uses to achieve its goal. Plans are arranged in a plan library. Such arrangement provides a flexibility to extend an agent's functionality in a modular way. A BDI agent plan consists of three parts; the plan's context, the plan's relevance and a recipe of actions that is executed to achieve a desired goal. A plan is invoked to achieve a goal and always executed in a given context.

2.3 Awareness of Work

The third component of the ethnographic model refers to the way in which the work activities are made available to others [12]. The physical layouts of workplaces can affect the ability of people to make reciprocal sense of the others' activities. In the workplace, the visibility or intelligibility takes place through talking aloud as someone works or maybe through the representation of the work to be done (forms, memos, worksheets etc.) which make obvious the current stage of the work.

In an agent contextual information can be stored in its belief in order to provide context awareness during execution of its plan. A plan that is valid in one context may not be valid in another context for achieving the same goal.

In BDI agents framework such as JACK [16] the context aware functionality is implemented by a context method of a plan. A plan's context method is executed in order to determine the applicability of the plan to achieve a given goal in current context. Context methods always operate on agents' beliefs to confirm or refute the presence of a given fact.

3 Analysis of a Document Management System

The Document Management System (DMS) is an asynchronous collaborative application. Its purpose is to support the development and maintenance of modules of different disciplines in the University. A module is a taught unit at the university. In this section, we mainly describe the activities involved in DMS. For more detail, readers are referred to [17].

The coordination work in the university can be viewed as sub-activities performed by actors according to a division of labour. In DMS there are routine workflows between the administrator, the lecturer, the subject group leader, the subject quality group (SQG) and the Module Approval and Review Panel (MARP). Common resources such as a module document support the interdependencies between such activities. A common resource, such as a module document, constrains each activity. The interdependence between the activities in the university is known in advance. For instance in the DMS a "Revise/Compose activity" will enable the "Review activity". Eventually, the "Review activity" will initiate the "Approve/Disapprove" activity carried out by the MARP. Mostly, this activity occurs only when new modules are introduced or substantial changes are made on the existing modules. The "Approve/Disapprove" activity involves the external moderator and the same people who are involved in the SQG where requirements for new modules are discussed The MARPs are constituted as required to assess the quality of new or revised modules within a subject area. This process leads to approval or disapproval of that module. The revision process is reviewed and finalised by the SQG. A glossary of terms describing actors and their roles is shown in Table 2.

Table 2. A glossary of terms of the DMS

Name	Type	Description
Lecturer (M. Leader)	Actor	Person who views and edits the module
Administrator	Actor	Person who views, adds, deletes, and archives module and views logbook
Subject Leader	Actor	Person who interacts with the module leader and the administrator and assists the module leader to revise the module
SQG	Actor	Person who views logbook and module, and accepts or rejects module
MARP	Actor	Person who views logbook and module, and approves/disapproves module
Module	Object	The document on which different operations are carried out by different actors
Logbook	Object	Book on which different operations are carried out by different actors to keep record
Maintain MID	Activity	Activity performed by the administrator to keep updated record of modules
Revise	Activity	Activity performed by lecturer to revise the module
Review	Activity	This activity performed by SQG in order to make a decision on the acceptance or rejection of modules for quality purposes
Approval	Activity	This activity performed by MARP in order to approve or disapprove modules. This activity involves subject leader, SGQ and external moderator

4   Design and Implementation Considerations

The structure of the university is such that different actors have different roles to play in order to coordinate with each other to perform their daily tasks. The actors are aware of their roles and know their responsibility in the academic environment. The administrator assigns different roles to different actors.

The role-activity model is developed to illustrate different roles related to DMS. This is diagrammatically shown in Figure 1. Only those actors mainly concerned with DMS are included. This model identifies the activity units for each role. The role-activity model describes the identification of activity unit, and the association of these activity units with functional roles. We identify only those activities which represent functionality and provide some results for a functional entity represented by a functional role.

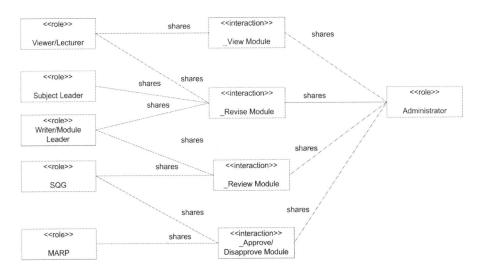

Fig. 1. Role-Activity Model of DMS

We identify and design agents and their functionalities based on the functional roles and activities of the actors involved in the DMS. The agents in the DMS work together in order to construct the artefact, alter the state of the artefact, or inspect the artefact. These agents achieve their goals through communication and collaboration. Figure 2 graphically depicts the patterns of communication that may occur during communication and collaboration amongst actors.

The agents collaborate with each other through message passing. A brief description of such communication patterns is given in Table 3. The administrator agent is responsible for resolving any conflicts that may arise among the associated agents. The notification plays an important role in this scenario. For example, the lecturer agent automatically generates a notification and sends it to the SQG agent when the module is ready for inspection. Similarly, the SQG agent notifies the lecturer and the administrator that the module has been reviewed.

There exists one to one mapping between each actor and agent due to the distinct functionality of each actor. We have designed the following agents corresponding to each actor in the system.

1. LecturerAgent
2. AdministratorAgent
3. SubjctLeaderAgent
4. SQGAgent
5. MARPAgent

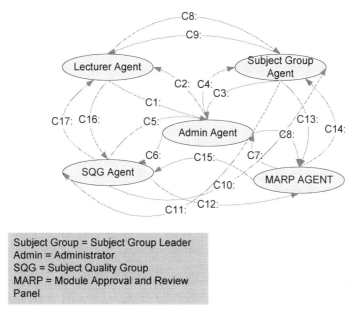

Fig. 2. Communication patterns in DMS

4.1 Communication Language and Protocols

The agents communicate using standard FIPA ACL (Agent Communication Language) and KQML (Knowledge Query and Manipulation Language).

We use FIPA ACL for agents' communication in the system. The FIPA ACL is built upon speech act theory [18]. The agent's standard communication languages facilitate the interaction between independently developed agents.

The interaction protocols are defined as a standard sequence of messages that agents follow during interactions. The messages that pass between the agents contain information about interaction protocols and type of the message.

1. Communication Patterns. We provide a brief description of communication patterns that may occur between an Administrator agent and other agents in the system. Similar patterns of communication and collaboration exist for the other agents in the systems as shown in Figure 2.

- C1: AdministratorAgent receives a request for module description from Lecturer Agent
- C2: AdministratorAgent replies to LecturerAgent by sending module description if it has received a valid module ID in request or reply with NotUnderstood message if module ID is not valid.
- C3: AdministratorAgent receives a request from SubjectLeaderAgent for module description.
- C4: AdministratorAgent sends a reply in response to C3. If the request message contains a valid module ID then module description is sent otherwise NotUnderstood message will be sent to the SubjectLeaderAgent.
- C5: AdministratorAgent receives an inform message from SQGAgent; the message contains an agenda.
- C6: AdministratorAgent sends an inform message to SQGAgent in response to C5.
- C7: AdministratorAgent receives an inform message from MARPAgent; the message contains an agenda.
- C8: AdministratorAgent sends an inform message to MARPAgent in response to C7.

2. Coordination. Coordination is a process by which an agent reasons about its local actions and the (anticipated) actions of others to try to ensure that community acts in a coherent manner. Coordination is a key problem in distributed artificial intelligence [13]. The intelligent agent paradigm provides an effective way of managing flexible coordination at service level by using higher level protocols and coordination models.

For successful coordination, agents maintain the model of each other's future interactions. They use these models in order to guide their future actions. If the agent beliefs about other agents' future commitments are wrong, it will result in chaotic behaviour. Without coordination, the benefit of a decentralised system cannot be achieved.

Following the design considerations discussed above, we have implemented a prototype [19] of the MAS using components of the JADE [20] agent development environment and the JACK framework [16]. The JACK agent framework is based on the BDI model, whereas components of JADE are used for communication based on ACL.

Table 3. Communication pattern of the administrator agent in DMS

Task	Collaboration	Comm. Name	Message Type	Content
Receive module	Lecturer	C1	Request	Module ID
Send module (vie, edit)	Lecturer	C2	Inform	Module description
Receive module	Subject leader	C3	Request	Module ID
Send module (view, edit)	Subject leader	C4	Inform	Module description
Receive dates	SQG	C5	Inform	Agenda
Send module (for acceptance)	SQG	C6	Inform	Module description
Receive dates	MARP	C7	Inform	Agenda
Send module (for approval)	MARP	C8	Inform	Module description

5   Conclusions and Future Work

In this paper, we have addressed the issues of QoS from user perspectives. This has been achieved by mapping ethnographic analysis onto a computational model of intelligent agents. We argue that we should not only focus on system level QoS metrics but should also acknowledge and address the QoS issues from the user perspective. We believe that little attention has been paid to these issues in the past. In this paper, we also present an approach based on ethnography and multi-agent systems to address these issues in an effective way. We apply the ethnographic approach in order to understand and explain the semantics, functionality and detailed user requirements of ubiquitous collaborating systems. Secondly, we employ artificial intelligent agents for communication and collaboration purposes based on user profiles and preferences. We have demonstrated the usefulness of this approach by presenting a real life case study of DMS. Our future work will include detail description of QoS issues from the user perspective and drawing a map from the user mental model to artificial agents.

References

1. Bouch, A., Kuchinsky, A., Bhatti, N.: Quality is in the eye of the beholder: Meeting users' requirements for internet quality of service. Proceedings of CHI-2000 (2000) 297 -304
2. Sturm, J., Iqbal, R., Kulyk, O., Wang, C., Terken, J.: Peripheral Feedback on Participation Level to Support Meetings and Lectures. Proceeding of Designing Pleasurable Products Interfaces (DPPI 2005). Eindhoven, The Netherlands (2005) 451-466
3. Iqbal, R., Sturm, J., Terken, J., Kulyk, O., Wang, C.: User-Centred Design and Evaluation of Ubiquitous Services. Proceedings of the 23rd International Conference on Design of Communication: Documenting and Designing for Pervasive Information. Coventry, UK (2005) 138-145
4. Crabtree, A., Hemmings, T., Rodden, T., Mariani, J.: Informing the Development of Calendar System for Domestic Use. Proceedings of the 8th European Conference on Computer Supported Cooperative Work (ECSCW 2003). Finland (2003) 119-138
5. Clarke, K., Hughes, J., Dave, M., Rouncefield, M., Sommerville, I., Gur, C., et al.: Dependable Red Hot Action. Proceedings of the 8th European Conference on Computer Supported Cooperative Work (ECSCW 2003). Finland (2003) 61-80
6. O'Brien, J., Rodden, T., Rouncefield, M., Hughes, J.: At Home with the Technology. ACM Transaction on Computer-Human Interaction 6 (1999) 282 -308
7. Bouch, A. and Sasse, M.A.: It ain't what you charge it's the way that you do it: A user perspective of network QoS and pricing. Proceedings of IM'99. Boston, MA (1999)
8. Goguen, J. and Linde, C.: Techniques for requirements elicitation. Proceedings of the IEEE International Symposium on Requirements Engineering (1993)
9. Rao, A.S., Georgeff, M.P.: Modelling Rational Agent within a BDI Architecture. Proceedings of Knowledge Representation and Reasoning. Cambridge, Massachusetts, USA (1991) 473-483
10. Rao, A.S., Georgeff, M.P.: BDI Agents: From Theory to Practice. Proceedings of the First International Conference on Multiagent Systems. San Francisco (1995)
11. Shoham, Y.: Agent-Oriented Programming. Artificial Intelligence 60 (1) (1993) 51-92
12. Hughes, J., O'Brien, J., Rodden, T., Rouncefield, M. and Blythin, S.: Designing with Ethnography: A Presentation Framework for Design. Proceedings of DIS'97. Amsterdam, Netherlands (1997) 147-58

13. Jennings, N.R.: Commitments and Conventions: The Foundation of Coordination in Multi-Agent Systems. The Knowledge Engineering Review 8 (3) (1993) 223-250
14. Shoham, Y. and Tennenholtz, M.: On the Synthesis of Useful Social Laws for Artificial Agent Societies. Proceedings of the National Conference on Artificial Intelligence. San Jose (1992) 276-281
15. Wooldridge, M., Jennings, N.R.: Intelligent Agents: Theory and Practice. Knowledge Engineering Review 10 (2) (1995) 115-152
16. JACK™ Intelligent Agents, Agent Oriented Software. URL: http://www.agent-software.com/shared/home
17. Iqbal, R., James, A.: Towards the Development of CSCW: An Ethnographic Approach. Proceedings of Human Computer Interaction (2004) 19-34
18. Searle, J.R.: Speech Acts. Cambridge University Press, Cambridge, UK (1969)
19. Iqbal, R., Shah, N.H., James, A., Younas, M., Chao, K.M.: A User Perspective of QoS for Ubiquitous Collaborating Systems. Proceedings of Computer Supported Cooperative Work in Design Conference (2006) 1-5
20. Java Agent Development Framework. URL: http://sharon.cselt.it/projects/jade/

Olympus: Personal Knowledge Recommendation Using Agents, Ontologies and Web Mining

Juliana Lucas de Rezende[1], Vinícios Batista Pereira[1], Geraldo Xexéo[1,2],
and Jano Moreira de Souza[1,2]

[1] COPPE/UFRJ – Graduate School of Computer Science
[2] DCC/IM - Institute of Mathematics
Federal University of Rio de Janeiro, PO Box 68.513, ZIP Code 21.945-970, Cidade
niversitária - Ilha do Fundão, Rio de Janeiro, RJ, Brazil
{juliana, vinicios, xexeo, jano}@cos.ufrj.br

Abstract. There are many initiatives in the scientific community to produce
knowledge management and CSCW systems. However, it is difficult to promote the easy information share among learners. In this paper we present
Olympus, a multi-agent system to help learners share not only what the information content is, where the information is, and who have the information
needed by the learner, but also how to use the available knowledge. Olympus
uses agent technologies, ontologies and data mining to create knowledge chains
in a semi-automatic way, which is a job that usually would take a lot of effort.
The agent monitors the learner's web navigation activities. From there, another
agent classifies its content using an ontology, creates and recommends a knowledge chain to the learner. As a sub-product of this work we establish a knowledge base with classified web pages contents.

1 Introduction

The Internet became an important way to make information available to people who
needs to acquire new knowledge faster and in a much greater volume than in the past.
There are communities of practice which act as a method to complement teaching in
the traditional classroom, to acquire knowledge in evolution [1], and to improve the
learner's performance [2]. They are called learning communities. One of the principles of Wenger for cultivating communities of practice is the knowledge sharing to
improve personal knowledge. Another issue related to making a successful community should be to assist the members in building up their personal knowledge [3].

To complement the learning process, we considered a process to promote knowledge building, dissemination, and exchange in learning communities. The need of a
number of individuals to work together raises problems in the CSCW domain [4].

Knowledge design [5] is defined as a science of selecting, organizing and presenting the knowledge in a huge knowledge space and in a proper way, so it can be
sensed, digested and utilized by human beings efficiently and effectively. It aims to
offer the right knowledge to the right person in the right manner at the right point of
time. According to Xexeo [6], the design activity has been described as belonging to a

W. Shen et al. (Eds.): CSCWD 2006, LNCS 4402, pp. 53–62, 2007.
© Springer-Verlag Berlin Heidelberg 2007

class of problems that have no optimal solution, only satisfactory ones. They are complex, usually interdisciplinary in nature and require a group of people to solve it. Designing knowledge is similar in principle to designing computer software. It takes time, careful thought and creativity to do it well. The biggest difference is that you cannot just load the knowledge into someone's brain like you can do with software in a computer; you need an implementation procedure to build the knowledge in the learner's mind [5].

1.1 Motivation

To complement the learning process, a system has been developed to promote knowledge building, dissemination, and exchange in learning communities. This system is called the Knowledge Chains Editor (KCE), and is based on a process for building personal knowledge through the exchange of knowledge chains (KCs) [1]. It is implemented over COPPEER[1]. The process differential is the addition of "how to use" the available knowledge to "authors" (who), "localization" (where), and "content" (what), which are commonly used.

The KC is a structure created to organize knowledge structure and organization. A KC is made up of a header (which contains basic information related to the chain) and a knowledge unit (KU) list. Figure 1.a presents an example where Class is a prerequisite of Inheritance, and Overriding is a successor of Inheritance. The other way to organize knowledge is by composition. When a KU is formed by composition of other KUs, it can be represented like Figure 1.b. In this example, Class is composed by Attribute and Method.

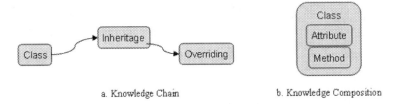

a. Knowledge Chain   b. Knowledge Composition

Fig. 1. Knowledge organization

Conceptually, knowledge can be decomposed into smaller units of knowledge (recursive decomposition). For the sake of simplification, it was considered that there is a basic unit which can be represented as a KU (structure formed by a set of attributes).

To build his KC, the learner can use the KCE (shown in Figure 2). In the case of questioning, he must create a KU whose state is "question". At this moment, the system starts the search. It sends messages to other peers and waits for an answer. Each peer performs an internal search. This search consists of verifying if there are any KUs similar to the one in the search. All KUs found are returned to the requesting part.

---

[1] COPPEER [6] is a framework for creating very flexible collaborative peer-to-peer (P2P) applications. It provides non-specific collaboration tools as plug-ins.

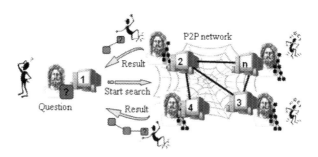

Fig. 2. KCE architecture

The creation of a KU of type "question" is obviously motivated by the learner's need to obtain that knowledge. So far, we have considered the existence of two motivating factors for the creation of available KCs. The first would be a matter of recognition by the communities, since each KU created has a registered author. The second would be the case where the professor makes them available "as a job", with the intention of guiding his students' studies.

However, we were aware that the learner needs more motivation to create new KCs. In the attempt to solve this problem, in this work we present a proposal to improve the creation of new KCs, which is a system called Olympus. The Olympus's main goal is to recommend potential KCs that can be accepted, modified or even discarded by the learner. These KCs will be created from the data collected by monitoring (carried out by a software agent[2]) learner navigation. Olympus had been developed based on the proposal presented in [8].

The remainder of this paper is organized as follows. The main concepts of web mining and ontologies are presented in the next two sections. Section 4 presents the proposed idea and the prototype developed. Conclusions are given in section 5.

2   Collaborative Learning Ontologies

Ontology is a formal specification of concepts and their relationships. By defining a common vocabulary, ontologies reduce concept definition mistakes, allowing shared understanding, improved communications, and a more detailed description of resources [9].

According to Guarino [10] the ontologies can be categorized in 4 types: top-level, domain, task and application. *Top-level ontologies* describe very general concepts like space, time, object, etc., which are independent of a particular problem or domain. *Domain ontologies* and *task ontologies* describe, respectively, the vocabulary related to a generic domain (like medicine or automobiles) or a generic task or activity (like diagnosing or selling), by specializing the terms introduced in the top-level ontology. *Application ontologies* describe concepts depending both on a particular domain and task, which are often specializations of the related ontologies.

---

[2] A Software Agent [7] can be defined as a complex object with attitude.

A more generic ontology can become easily, more specific in accordance with the necessity. However, to transform a specific ontology into a more generic one can be a difficult task. In this work we first created a domain ontology and, from this one, we created a more specific ontology which was more appropriate to our needs.

The prototype developed has been instantiated to the Java learning community, and the first ontology created was a domain ontology which describes the object oriented (OO) language concepts. After this, specific properties were added to the created ontology to incorporate thesaurus functionalities. In this way the software agent can search in the ontology for words found in the text and correlate web pages with ontology concepts, transforming the domain ontology.

All classes that symbolize concepts from an OO language inherit of a superclass called "Concept". In our case, this superclass contains a property named keyword, which is used on the page classification, and if we need to add new properties related to the classification it is enough to make it in the Concept class. To transform the new ontology in a domain ontology it is enough to remove the Concept class.

The OO language ontology was instantiated to Java to be used as a specific base of knowledge by the application. With the concepts and relations instantiated, it is possible to compare the keywords found in the page mining process with the ontology keywords. The attribution of weights to the page keywords makes possible the probabilistic classification of the page according to the ontology concept.

The relationship between the ontology concepts can be used to support decisions about the concept represented by a page. When the page has the occurrence of keywords that are concepts related to the same concept, the page can be classified as a representation of the common concept.

For example, in Figure 3, we have an ontology that has the concept Package related to the concept Class, and Package java.util related to Class, Vector and HashTable. If the page has keywords, with the same weight, referring to the java classes Vector and HashTable, the system can consider that both are related to Package java.util and can classify the page as a reference to Package.

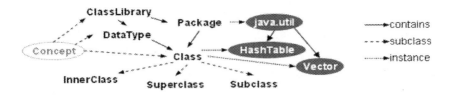

Fig. 3. Example of an ontology

The collaborative learning ontology [11] is the system of concepts for modeling the collaborative learning process, such as "learning goal", "learning group type", and "learning scenario". When the ontologies are in use, they are usually arranged in three layers. The top layer is the negotiation level that corresponds to negotiation ontology. The intermediate layer corresponds to the collaborative learning ontology. Here, only important abstracts for negotiation from agent level remain as the necessary scope of information at an abstract level. The negotiation level is the level that represents the important information for negotiation at an abstract level. The bottom layer is the agent level that corresponds to the individual learning ontology.

This work contemplates only the two lower layers of a collaborative learning ontology, as it captures the learner's personal learning process, which supports the lowest layer; and allows the exchange of learning processes, creating the necessary information for the highest layer.

3   Web and Text Mining

In a simplified way, we can say that web mining can be used to specify the path taken by the user while he is navigating on the web (Web Usage Mining) and to classify the navigated pages (Web Content Mining) [12-13]. However, there is a problem that cannot be solved only using web mining, and this is the difficulty in calculating the information hierarchy. This problem can be solved with the use of ontologies.

In addition to the availability of little (if any) structure in the text, there are other reasons why text mining is so difficult. The concepts found in a text are usually rather abstract and can hardly be modeled by using conventional knowledge representation structures. Furthermore, the occurrence of synonyms (different words with the same meaning) and homonyms (words with the same spelling but with distinct meanings) makes it difficult to detect valid relationships between different parts of the text [14].

3.1   User Web Navigation

We make use of web usage mining when the data is related to the user navigation, this means, when we store and analyze the order of the navigation pages, the visit length for each page, and the exit page. This information will be important for verifying, respectively, what the order of the navigated concepts is, after page classification; and which pages are relevant when the user does not follow the structure of a site and goes to a new site on the same subject, or stops studying the subject [12].

3.2   Page Content Analysis and Classification

Once the relevant pages are selected using web usage mining, the web content mining can be used to analyze and to classify the page content [12]. In this kind of mining the input data is the HTML code of the page and the output data is one or more possibilities of classification of the page in accordance with the considered ontology.

In order to simplify the page classification we used an automatic summarization technique (AST) that extracts the most relevant sentences from the page [14]. First, the AST applies several preprocessing methods to the input page, namely case folding, stemming and removal of stop words. The next step is to separate the sentences. The end of a sentence can be defined as a "." (full stop), an "!" (exclamation mark), a "?" (question mark), etc. In HTML texts, we can also consider tags of the language.

Once all the sentences of the page were identified, it is necessary to give a "weight" to each remaining word based on its HTML tag (see Table 1) and to compute the value of a *TF-ISF* (term frequency – inverse sentence frequency) measure for each word. For each sentence s, the average *TF-ISF* weight of the sentence, denoted *Avg-TF-ISF(s)* is computed by calculating the arithmetic average of the *TF-ISF(w,s)* weight over all the words *w* in the sentence. Sentences with high values of *TF-ISF* are considered relevant.

Once the value of the *Avg-TF-ISF(s)* measure is computed for each sentence *s*, the final step is to select the most relevant sentences, i.e. the ones with the largest values of the *Avg-TF-ISF(s)* measure. In the current version of our system this is done as follows. The system finds the sentence with the largest *Avg-TF-ISF(s)* value, called the *Max-Avg-TF-ISF* value. The user specifies a threshold on the percentage of this value, denoted *percentage-threshold*.

Sentences with high values of TF-ISF are selected to produce a summary of the source text. According to Larocca [14] this technique has been evaluated on real-world documents, and the results are satisfactory.

4 Personal Knowledge Chains Semi-automatic Building

The main goal of this work is to automatically build knowledge chains to be recommended to the learners. As has been previously stated, the learner can accept, modify or even discard these KCs. For this to be possible, the proposal is to extend the Knowledge Chains Editor (KCE) [1], to automatically build personal KCs.

In order for this to occur, we need an ontology of the considered domain. The goal is to determine the sub-groups of navigated concepts (concepts found in the navigated pages), and relate them to the pages.

The architecture of Olympus is given in Figure 4.

The software agent called Argus observes the learner's navigation through web pages. It sends the web pages to the agent Hera, which stores the page content and the time spent on each page.

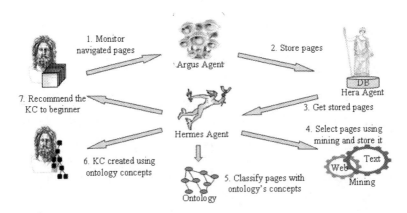

Fig. 4. Olympus architecture

After this, the agent called Hermes has the responsibility for mining the navigation and the page content to determine the sub-group of ontology navigated concepts related to the navigated pages and to create a graph from this. With all this information, Hermes can build a potential KC that will be recommended to the learner.

It is necessary to point out that the new KC will be recommended to the same learner that is navigating on the web. He/She will decide if he/she wants to add (or not) the recommended KC to his/her personal knowledge. From this point onwards, if the learner accepts the KC, it can be exchanged between the community members using the KCE.

4.1 Olympus - Knowledge Chains Recommendation System

The Argus agent is responsible for observing the learner's navigation and sending the navigated page content, the visited length and the times that it has been accessed by the Hera agent, which store all information. In this first stage, the agents only create a database of web pages and access information (Web Usage Mining). At a later stage, with a frequency determined by the user, the Hermes agent will select, from the stored pages, the pages that are related to the subject discussed by the community (The subject must be known because it is necessary to have an ontology on it in the community). This will be made by comparing the content of the web page with a set of keywords (ontology concepts) related to the subject in question. In this way, the stored pages are filtered, with only the ones that are in fact of interest to the community remaining. This also solves any problems related to user privacy, since those pages that are not related to a community subject are discarded.

With this set of stored pages, the system has a guided graph, because the navigation order has been stored. As the system goal is to make a KC with the concepts studied by the learner, it is necessary to use text mining techniques to classify the pages in accordance with the described concepts of the ontology. This classification is based on the proposals of Desmontils [15] and Jacquin [16]. However, instead of using a thesaurus with an ontology, we have improved our ontology by adding, in all concepts, a vector of attributes with the keywords related to the concept. Thus, we can do the mining and the classification only using the ontology.

At this time, the system needs to remove all the stop words from the text on a page. Then it is necessary to give a "weight" to each remaining word, based on its HTML tag. The weights are given in accordance with the values given in Table 1.

Table 1. Higher coefficients associated with HTML markers [15-16]

HTML marker description	HTML marker	Weight
Document Title	<title></title>	10
Keyword	<meta name="keywords"... content=...>	9
Hyper-link	<a href=...></a>	8
Heading level 1	<h1></h1>	3
Bold font	<b></b>	2
...	...	...

Once the frequency and the weight of the keywords on a page are compared with the ontology concepts, the page receives degrees of relevance. With this relationship between pages and ontology concepts, the graph of pages can be transformed into a knowledge chain. This KC will be recommended to the learner, and he/she can decide what to do with it.

As there are many software agents "working" for the learners, a lot of KCs will be created. Therefore, it is possible to identify absent concepts in the navigation of one learner that have already been studied by another, and recommend KUs, concepts, pages and even the users who know the concepts the learner does not know.

4.2 Example

The following example shows how a KC is created from the learner's navigation through web pages. Figure 5 shows the web pages navigated by the learner and Figure 6 shows the community ontology (arrows represent a non hierarchical relationship).

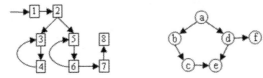

Fig. 5. Web page navigation   **Fig. 6.** Community Ontology

In the first stage, web mining will be performed, and according to the keywords found on the web page, it may match partially with one concept from ontology and partially with another. In this case there is a relevance degree for each concept relating to the page. Therefore, for each page the result is:

```
Page 1: a 60%; b 10%; c 30%; ...
Page 2: a 0%; b 0%; c 100%; ...
...
```

After relating the web pages to the most relevant ontology concepts, the software agent will create a learning path in the ontology, which is a learning ontology a → c → d → e → ... and the creation of the KU is initiated, mapping the web pages on the learning ontology.

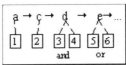

At this time the KUs are created using the learning ontology and all the information on the learner's navigation through web pages. In this example, it is necessary to study "attribute", then study "class", to study "object".

As has been said before, a KU is a structure formed by an attribute set. These attributes are grouped into categories: General (name, description, keywords, author, creation date, last use date), Life Cycle (history, current state, contributors), Rights

(intellectual property rights, conditions of use), Relation (the relationship between knowledge resources), Classification (the KU in relation to a classification system) and Annotation (comments and evaluations of the KUs and their creators). Many of these attributes can be automatically filled, which facilitates the creation of new KCs.

5   Conclusions and Future Work

The growing number of learning communities which communicate online makes possible to exchange, and use chains of explicit knowledge as a strategy for creating personal knowledge. Today, we have the WWW (who, what, where) triad, where "who" is the people who have the knowledge, "what" is the knowledge itself, and "where" is its location - in our case, the peer in which it is located. Using knowledge chains, we hope to add "how to use" the available knowledge to the existing triad.

Apart from KCE, there are other tools that stimulate knowledge sharing in communities. These include WebWatcher [16], which is a search tool where the learner specifies his/her interests and receives the related pages navigated by the other community members. OntoShare [17] uses software agents which allow the user to share relevant pages. MILK [18] allows the communities to manage knowledge produced from metadata. The main difference between these tools and the KCE is that they are focused on sharing "where" and/or "with whom" the knowledge can be found. KCE adds the sharing of "what" and "how to use" this knowledge.

As has been previously stated, to motivate the learner in the creation of new KCs, we propose a personal knowledge recommendation system that uses software agents technology to monitor learner navigation; uses web mining to plot the path taken by the user while he is navigating on the web and to classify the navigated pages; and uses learning ontologies in addition to all the information collected for the creation of new KCs.

The experimental use of the extended KCE shows evidence that, when used by a learner to build a personal KC, the hypothesis that he/she creates more new KCs, that he/she will achieve a reduction in the time dedicated to studying a specific subject as well as gaining a more comprehensive knowledge of the subject studied has been confirmed. In order to evaluate whether the KCE's goal has been reached, experiments aimed at obtaining qualitative and quantitative data that would make the verification of the hypothesis under consideration possible must be carried out.

It is necessary to emphasize that it is not the goal of this work to ensure that the learner has assimilated everything in his/her KCs. Our goal is to stimulate the creation of new KCs, so that the knowledge network can expand, and better assist the community members. This is a relevant point, because it is very difficult to motivate users to share knowledge.

Due to the fact that this work is still in progress, many future projects are expected to take place. The most important are: improving the algorithm used to map the web page on the ontology nodes, and extending the monitored domain, considering any media manipulated by the learner, instead of only the navigated web pages.

Acknowledgments. This work was partially supported by CAPES and CNPq.

References

1. Rezende, J.L., da Silva, R.L.S, de Souza, J.M., Ramirez, M.: Building Personal Knowledge through Exchanging Knowledge Chains. Proc. of IADIS Int. Conf. on WBC. Algarve, Portugal (2005) 87-94
2. Pawlowski, S., Robey, D., Raven A.: Supporting shared information systems: boundary objects, communities, and brokering. Proc. 21th Int. Conf. on Information Systems. Brisbane, Australia (2000) 329-338
3. Tornaghi, A., Vivacqua, A., Souza, J.M.: Creating Educator Communities. Int. Journal Web Based Communities (2005) 1-15
4. Rezende, J.L., de Souza, J.F., de Souza, J.M.: Peer-to-Peer Collaborative Integration of Dynamic Ontologies. Proc. 9th Int. Conf. on CSCWD. Coventry, UK (2005)
5. Leitch, M.: Human Knowledge Design. Undergraduate Project. February (1986)
6. Xexeo, G., Vivacqua, A.S., de Souza, J.M., Braga, B., D'Almeida Jr., J.N., Almenero, B.K., et al.: COE: A Collaborative Ontology Editor Based on a Peer-to-Peer Framework. International Journal of Advanced Engineering Informatics 19(2)(2005) 113-121
7. Bradshaw, J.M.: An Introduction to Software Agents. In: Bradshaw, J.M. (eds.): Software Agents. MIT Press (1997)
8. Rezende, J.L., Pereira, V.B., Xexeo, G., de Souza, J.M.: Building a Personal Knowledge Recommendation System using Agents, Learning Ontologies and Web Mining. Proc. 10th Int. Conf. on CSCWD. Nanjing, China (2006)
9. Gruber, T.R.: Toward Principles for the Design of Ontologies Used for Knowledge Sharing. Int. Journal of Human-Computer Studies 43 (1995): 907-928
10. Guarino, N.: Formal Ontology in Information Systems. Proc. of FOIS'98. Trento (1998)
11. Supnithi, T., Inaba, A., Ikeda, M., Toyoda, J., Mizoguchi, R.: Learning Goal Ontology Supported by Learning Theories for Opportunistic Group Formation. In: Lajoie, S.P. and Vivet, M. (eds.): Artificial Intelligence in Education. IOS Press (1999)
12. Zaïane, O.R.: Web Mining: Concepts, Practices and Research. Conference Tutorial Notes. XIV Brazilian Symposium on Databases (SBBD 2000). João Pessoa, Paraíba, Brazil (2000)
13. Cooley, R., Mobasher, B., Srivastava, J.: Web Mining: Information and Pattern Discovery on the World Wide Web. Proc. 9th IEEE Int. Conf. on Tools with Artificial Intelligence. Newport Beach, CA, USA (1997)
14. Neto, J.L., Santos, A.D., Kaestner, C.A.A., Freitas, A.A.: Document clustering and text summarization. Proc. of the 4th Int. Conf. Practical Applications of Knowledge Discovery and Data Mining (PADD-2000). London: The Practical Application Company (2000) 41-55
15. Desmontils, E., Jacquin, C.: Indexing a web site with a terminology oriented ontology. In: Cruz, I.F., Decker, S., Euzenat, J. and McGuinness, D.L. (eds.): The Emerging Semantic Web. IOS Press (2002) 181-197
16. Joachims, T., Freitag, D., Mitchell, T.: Webwatcher: A tour guide for the world wide web. Proc. of the 15th IJCAI. Nagoya, Japan (1997) 770-775
17. Davies, J., Duke, A., Sure, Y.: OntoShare – A Knowledge Management Environment for Virtual Communities of Practice. Proc. of the Int. Conf. on Knowledge Capture (K-CAP03). Sanibel Island, Florida, USA (2003)
18. Agostini, A., Albolino, S., De Michelis, G., De Paoli, F., Dondi, R.: Stimulating Knowledge Discovery and Sharing. Int. ACM Conf. on Supporting Group Work. Sanibel, Florida. ACM Press (2003) 248-257

Constraint Information Visualization Methodology for Cooperative Design

Xiaoping Liu, Hui Shi, Zhengqiang Mao, and Qiang Lu

VCC Division, School of Computer & Information, Hefei University of Technology,
Hefei 230009, P.R. China
lxp@hfut.edu.cn

Abstract. It is difficult to manage constraint information in cooperative design due to its variety and changeability. The concept of Constraint Information Visualization (CIV) in cooperative design and CIV framework comprising the CIV methodology are put forward to control cooperative design flow efficiently, detect constraint conflicts early and negotiate the contradiction under the support of visualization. On the basis of classification and representation of constraint information, this paper discusses the importance of CIV and its formalized description for cooperative design. The procedure of visual mapping and harmony evaluation is given in details. The main step of visual mapping is divided into classification mapping, structure and harmony mapping and detailed property mapping. Visual Mapping implements mapping from constraint information to visual representation with corresponding mapping modes. The concepts of local harmony and global harmony are also proposed for cooperation. An application of CIV verifies CIV methodology, which will direct a new way to implement complicated constraints management in cooperative design.

1 Introduction

Cooperative design is a process full of continuous repetitions, experiments, selections and cooperation, which involves a large number of important constraint information to be organized. Firstly, with the increase of the system complexity, the quantity of constraints exponentially accelerates. Secondly, the dynamic characteristics of network also increase the difficulties in representing and managing constraint information. Thus, at present, research on constraint in cooperative design is intensive and extensive to make full use of constraint information. Paper [1] applies search heuristics that consider the simultaneous effect of design to improve the productivity and predictability. Paper [2] presents an approach based on constraints network to support concurrent and cooperative design. Lottaz et al. [3] gives a constraint satisfaction tool-box providing an intuitive interface to specify numeric constraint satisfaction problems on continuous variables.

How to control the "confusion network" structure of constraint relation in cooperative design is a key problem. Explicit and vivid representation methods for solving the problem are in urgent need. So constraint visualization methodology is created to control design flow efficiently, detect constraint conflicts early and decrease contradiction

W. Shen et al. (Eds.): CSCWD 2006, LNCS 4402, pp. 63–72, 2007.
© Springer-Verlag Berlin Heidelberg 2007

extension speed. The concept of CIV, as a subset of information visualization, has been proposed by the group of authors. The relative research has also been initialized by us in different application areas such as engineering design [4] and cooperative design [5]. There are also several relative papers that focus on similar points. In paper [6], authors build a prototype tool for browsing constraint systems for the layout of graphical objects. Two approaches have been described to visualize constraint systems in the visualization rules of TRIP systems. Paper [7] presents a hierarchically structured constraint-based data model for solid modeling in the virtual reality environment. Cruzt et al. [8] presents a constraint-based data visualization system supporting a visual query language with its efficient constraint solver. The main difference between these researches and ours is that focus of us is visualization itself of constraint information for effective design.

Based on wide research on constraints in cooperative design, the group of authors has firstly applied the concept of CIV to cooperative design. Multi-orientation, multi-angle and multi-space characteristics of visualization help to visualize the invisible, abstract, complicated and dynamic relations in visual forms, which are useful to better comprehension for constraint information, and to assure efficiency of cooperative design. Our previous research on cooperative design included cooperative template design environment [9] and its mechanism [10]. Based on the constraint information, task information and network information obtained from the cooperative design environment, this paper focuses on CIV methodology including visual mapping module and harmony evaluation module, which is implemented under the support of cooperative design environment [9-10] and enriches the research methods of constraint information in cooperative design.

2 Constraint Information in Cooperative Design

2.1 Constraint Information Characteristics and Classification

Cooperative design is an unceasingly repeated process full of selection, communication and experiments. Much constraint information has to be dealt with during it. Based on the necessity of constraint in engineering design, three main characteristics are concluded in cooperative design environment that are complexity, variety and changeability. Based on constraint characteristics, constraint information can be classified as follows:

1) Classification according to representation
   - Value constraint: A value constraint gives a certain value to the right object restrained.
   - Expression constraint: An expression constraint comprising other parameters and symbols defines the limits to be restricted through rule-based solving.
   - Semantic constraint: Semantic constraints are composed of specific keywords based on a corresponding normative set of rules.
2) Classification according to domains
   - Geometric constraint: Topological constraints, structural constraints and dimensional constraints are obviously included.

- Physical constraint: Physical constraints define the restraints on mechanics, optics and so on.
- Temporal and Spatial constraint: Constraints on design priority, interval and storage capacity all belong to this type.

3) Classification according to coupling degree

- Loose constraint: The variable constrained has indefinite value.
- Strict constraint: The variable constrained has definite value.

4) Constraints can also be classified as dynamic constraint, static constraint, direct constraint, indirect constraint, inner constraint, outer constraint and other types produced if necessary according to characteristics.

2.2   Constraint Information Presentations

During the design process, the representations of constraint information are various according to different conditions. One constraint may be represented in several forms by mutual transformation.Extended Backus-Naur Form (EBNF) has been adopted to descript the presentations of constraint information following the grammar of TDML [9], the main part is given as follows:

Constraint ::= '<Constraint>'*General? Rules? Relations?* '</ Constraint >'
General ::= '< General >' (*domain table | if | default | express | string | graph | semantic*)+ '</ General >'
Rules ::= '<Rules>' (*table | if | default | express | string | graph*)+ '</Rules>'
Relations ::= '<Relations>' (*UpComponent | LeftComponent | Parallel | Tangency*)+ '</Relations>'
UpComponen ::= '<UpComponent>' *Component1 Component2 xDistance yDistance zDistance* '</UpComponent>'
domain ::= '< domain >' *Geometric Physical Chemistry Temporal Spatial* '</domain>'
table ::= '<table>' *Varname TableName DatabaseName QueryItem Condition* '</table>'
if ::= '<if>' *Varname Condition ifValue ElseValue* '</if>'
express ::= '<express>' *range Varname Value* '</express>'
semantic ::= '<semantic >' *constraintWord Varname*+ '</semantic>'
range ::= '<range >' '>' | '>=' | '<' | '<=' '</ range >'
Varname ::= '<Varname>' *Name* "." *Name* '</Varname>'
Name ::= '<name>' *Name* '</name>'
Value ::= '<Value>' *numberValue | expressValue | stringValue* '</Value>'
constraintWord ::= '*precedence*' | '*importance*' |'*exchange*'
numberValue ::= ('+' | '-')? ([0-9])+ ('.' [0-9]+)?
expressValue ::= *expressValue* ('+' | '-' | '*' | '/') *expressValue* | '(' *expressValue* ')' | *numberValue* | *Name* "." *Name*
stringValue ::= Char*

3   CIV Concept and Framework

3.1   Concept of CIV in Cooperative Design

Information represented in visual forms assists users to get insight into the data for simplifying and speeding up the analysis process. As a subset of information visualization, CIV in cooperative design is a process comprising controlling changeable constraints, mapping constraints to visual patterns and evaluating the balance state of system. The transformation of constraints can be observed in multiform visual forms. The balance state is visualized as well for conflict detection and negotiation.

Based on the integrated summary of rich visual techniques and various visual mapping modes, the visualization model can be concluded as: CIV= < C, OP, M, G, F, HE, TA >. Among this, constraint set C= $\{c_i|1{\leq}i{\leq}n\}$ means a set of constraint expressions. OP= $\{o_i|1{\leq}i{\leq}n\}$ integrates the constraint operation and simplification functions. M= $\{m_i|1{\leq}i{\leq}n\}$ is a set of mapping modes. The set of graph elements G= $\{g_i|1{\leq}i{\leq}n\}$ contains selectable graph elements to be visualized as representation units. The set of mapping methods F= $\{f_i|1{\leq}i{\leq}n\}$ mainly contains a great many visible methods, carrying on the combination and organization of graph elements for mapping modes. Symbol n is the number of constraints to describe. HE means harmony evaluation model which is to be specified in the following section. TA records detailed information of design tasks and designers. The roles in cooperative design can be divided into two categories: the controller and the designer. The controller stores all of the constraint information and corresponding design task information. The designer is mainly responsible for completing the design task and communicating with relative designers. During the cooperative design process, control task of CIV belongs to the controller with assisted cooperation of the designers.

3.2 CIV Framework

Based on the introduction of the concept of CIV, the CIV system framework is constructed. As Figure 1 shows, it consists of four main modules: Constraint Modeler, Visual Mapping Manager, Harmony Evaluation Module and Task Manager. Constraint Modeler is mainly responsible for the constraint extraction and representation. Simplified constraint data structure is abstracted from this module. Visual Mapping Manager contains multiple mapping rules and modes with analyzing and filtering function as an interface between constraint information and graphic elements. It is mainly responsible for the mapping between constraint information and visual forms. The Visualization

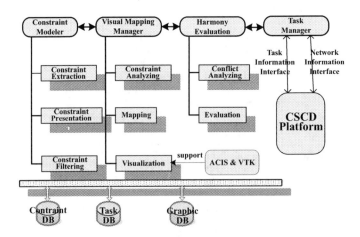

Fig. 1. CIV framework

module is supported by the 3D Geometric Modeler - ACIS, and the Visualization Toolkit (VTK), which is an open source software system for 3D computer graphics, image processing, and visualization. As the key module in this framework, harmony Evaluation Module provides constraint conflict analysis and conflict negotiation functions for detecting the balance state of the whole system and seeking the optimal design state to improve the design efficiency. Task Manager offers a network platform with task information for other modules. As a communication interface with cooperative design platform, it integrates cooperative design flow with CIV framework. The information transmission among four modules forms the whole workflow.

4 Visual Mapping

Visualization techniques are helpful to find rules and represent complicated, dynamic constraint information in visual and direct forms. However information may not match the actual physical objects automatically under most circumstances. If the constraints change, the corresponding visual forms will change immediately. The solution to the key problem is to find out new patterns to represent useful information full of rules to meet complex need.

   Just as mentioned above, visual mapping among constraint information, mapping modes and graph elements, as a complex procedure, plays a great role in CIV framework. It refers to three sets including M-mapping mode, G-graph element, F-mapping method which are integrated in CIV model. Mapping mode includes three levels: The first level is classification mapping, which partitions constraint information into various categories according to their background and meanings, and maps them into different structures. The second level is structure mapping and harmony mapping, which undertakes the task to build a direct bridge between constraint information and graph elements. Structure characteristic is the essential commonness between information and visual forms, such as tree, graph structure. As for harmony mapping, compatible visual techniques are key to visualize and solve constraint conflicts. The last level is detailed property mapping, which maps the properties of information to ones of visual forms in details based on structure, such as color, size, and quantity. Graph element is a graph set, integrating basic elements for selection, like lines, shapes, bodies, structures. Mapping method is a combination and organization of graph elements to meet the needs of mapping modes. Figure 2 presents the whole procedure of visual mapping.

   As follows, the formalized description of mapping is given: M= {M1, M2, M3} = {Classification Mapping, Structure Mapping and Harmony Mapping, Detailed Property Mapping}; M1 (C) = C'; M2 (C') = C''; M3 (C'') = C''';VF = CF (C''', G, F) = CF (M3 (M2 (M1(C))), G, F). Among this, M1 () is the function to realize Classification Mapping, M2 () is the function to implement Structure Mapping and Harmony Mapping, M3 () is the function to complete Detailed Property Mapping. CF () is the function to execute the mapping between constraint information and graph elements with mapping modes. VF is a meaningful visual structure.

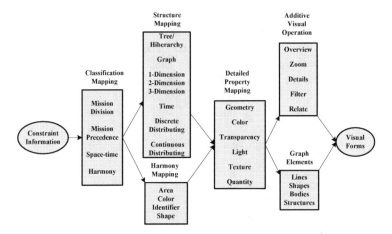

Fig. 2. Procedure of visual mapping

5 Harmony Evaluation

CIV is used to watch balance and development of the whole system state, including coordinating the distributed design tasks with optimal and visualized methods, detecting constraint conflicts early, decreasing contradiction extension speed and controlling design flow efficiently. Constraint harmony, as a key module of CIV framework, is an evaluating system for keeping balance efficiently.

5.1 The Creation of Harmony Evaluation

Engineering design is at root a constraints satisfaction problem (CSP) [11] [12]. As for cooperative design in network, conflicts are easier to occur for collaboration and interdisciplinary factors. The CSP which corresponds to whole design task is combined by these CSPs corresponding to sub-tasks, so is the solution space.

As the pretreatment for visual mapping and evaluation for design flow, harmony evaluation is created for two aims. One is to find the constraint conflicts as soon as possible and delimit the conflict area to improve the cooperative design efficiency. The multiform visualization of constraint conflicts can greatly simplify conflict resolving and negotiating. The other one is to evaluate the balance state of the whole system and get the optimal design state.

5.2 Procedure of Harmony Evaluation

For complex constraint information, how to evaluate compatibility is a crucial process in cooperative design. Constraint harmony concept represents the constraint state of cooperative design system. Constraint conflicts can be divided into internal and external conflicts. Harmony also can be divided into local harmony and global harmony accordingly. As Figure 3 shows, each designer including the controller has a system for harmony assessment to give them guidance. The difference mainly focuses on the amount and restriction range of constraint information. The controller owns the entire constraint set, while the designers only keep the relative part of it. The constraint conflicts detected by designers will be transmitted to the controller for integrated analysis. Relative designers evaluate compatibility with corresponding constraints. The conflicts recorded and the analysis results are provided for visualization, and visualization results give the feedback to designers for further coordination.

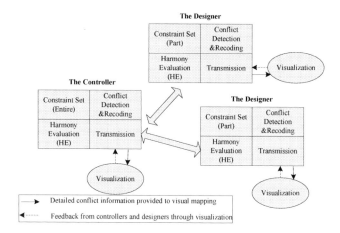

Fig. 3. Procedure of harmony evaluation

The process of Harmony Evaluation can concluded into four main steps:

Step1: Conflict Detection. No matter for the controller or the designer, conflict detection is the first step.

Step2: Conflict Recording. Verify and find the cause of the conflict, and record the detailed conflict information.

Step3: Transmission. Transmit the analysis result to the controller for entire evaluation and visualization.

Step4: Harmony Evaluation. Get the feedback from the controller with the help of visualization results. Then negotiate to delimit the conflict area for conflict resolution to coordinate in cooperative design under the support of visualization as well.

5.3   Constraint Conflict Detection and Visualization

Constraint conflict detection in CIV framework aims to visualize the conflict in different forms. The detection is arranged from two points of view. One is from constraint itself. Interval promulgation algorithm could be adopted to carry this task. The other one is from the attributes of design, such as color, density, material. All attributes are detected one by one. Visualization instances of the two forms are showed in Figure 4.

6 Application of CIV Framework

We have taken direct current motor [13] as the instance for illustration of constraint information visualization in cooperative design. Motor design is divided into several sub-tasks such as main magnetic poles, interpoles, armature and motor base, including electromagnetic and structural design. The controller A manages the CIV flow. The designer B is responsible for armature design while the designer C is for the air gap and main magnetic pole design. The electromagnetic design and structural design in motor design interacts each other. Design parameters mainly follow many industrial constraints. Some constraints are given in the following Table 1.

Table 1. Constraints in direct current motor design

Constraint Parameter	Expression	Constraint Parameter	Expression
Armature outer diameter	D_a	Armature core length	l_a
Number of armature conductor	$N = 2ZuW_a$	Air gap flux density	$B_\delta = \left(\Phi_N \middle/ b_\delta l_a \right) \times 10$
Number of main magnetic pole	$2p$	Armature current	$I_a = (0.93 \sim 0.995)I_N$
Main magnetic pole distance	$\gamma = \pi D_a \middle/ 2p$	Air gap	$\delta = (0.007 \sim 0.009)D_a$
Magnetic pole core length	$l_m = l_a$	Air gap	$\delta \geq (0.3 \sim 0.35)\dfrac{A\gamma}{B_\delta} \times 10^{-4}$
Number of armature slot	Z	Rated current	I_N
Element number of each slot	u	Motor base inner diameter	$D_{ij} = D_a + 2\delta + 2h_m$
Main magnetic pole height	h_m	Motor base outer diameter	$D_j = D_{ij} + 2h_j$
Number of circles of each element	$W_a = N' \middle/ aZu$	Motor base yoke height	h_j
Special current loading	$A = I_a N \middle/ 2a\pi D_a$	Number of armature conductor estimated	$N' = \pi D_a \times 2aA' \middle/ I_a$

During the cooperative design of motor, conflicts of parameters can not be avoidable. We take the conflict on air gap design showed in Figure 5 as examples. The final value of air gap has a profound effect on motor electromagnetic and structural design, such as the motor base inner diameter and air gap magneto motive force. Air gap δ has two constraints $\delta = (0.007 \sim 0.009)D_a$ (1) and $\delta \geq (0.3 \sim 0.35)\dfrac{A\gamma}{B_\delta} \times 10^{-4}$ (2). Designer B gives l_a such a small value that B_δ becomes too large. In order to satisfy constraint (2) δ becomes smaller which does not satisfy constraint (1). So the conflict appears. Designer C discovers the conflict through the local harmony evaluation, then informs the controller this conflict, the controller make use of CIV model and transmits each

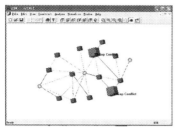

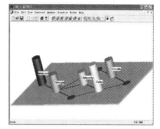

(a)Conflict detection from constraint itself   (b) Conflict detection from attributes

Fig. 4. Visualizations of constraint conflicts

(a) Normal air gap in motor   (b) Abnormal air gap in motor due to conflicts

Fig. 5. Contrast between two design results

designer the visualization of constraint conflict showed in Figure 4(a). Designer B and Designer C delimit the conflict range and cooperate to solve the conflict under the help of visualization. The contrast results of design are showed in Figure 5.

7   Conclusions

In order to detect constraint conflicts early for optimal negotiation and control cooperative design flow efficiently, a concept of CIV and CIV framework are adopted in cooperative design in this paper. Based on the extraction and presentation of constraint information, two key problems are pointed out, which constitute CIV methodology. One is visual mapping including three mapping modes between constraint information and visual forms. The other one is harmony evaluation containing the conflict detection & recording function and the negotiation function interacted with visualization modules. CIV methodology will direct cooperative design research to a new future.

Acknowledgements. The authors are grateful to all the members in VCC (Visualization & Cooperative Computing) division for their efforts and help. This paper is supported by National Nature Science Foundation of China under Grant numbers 60573174 and 60673028.

References

1. Juan, A.C., Stephen, W.D.: Application of Constraint-Based Heuristics in Collaborative Design. Proc. 38th Conference on Design Automation. Las Vegas (2001) 395-400
2. Hu, J., Xiong, G.: Concurrent and collaborative modeling for parameter and tolerance design based on constraints network. Proc. 2003 IEEE International Conference on Systems, Man and Cybernetics. Washington DC (2003) 4678-4683
3. Lottaz, C., Sam-Haroud, D., Faltings, B., and Smith, I.: Constraint Techniques for Collaborative Design. Proc. 10th IEEE International Conference on Tools with Artificial Intelligence. Taipei, Taiwan (1998) 34-41
4. Liu, X., Li, G.L., et al.: Detection & Visualization of Constraints in Engineering Design. Chinese Journal of Scientific Instrument 23(S5)(2002) 84-86 (in Chinese)
5. Liu, X., Shi H., et al.: Visualization of Constraint Information in Cooperative Template. Journal of Computer-Aided Design & Computer Graphics 17(10)(2005) 2334-2338 (in Chinese)
6. Takahashi, S.: A browsing interface for exploring constraints in visualization rules. Proc. 2003 IEEE Symposium on Human Centric Computing Languages and Environments. Auckland (2003) 108-110
7. Zhong, Y., Mueller-Wittig, W., and Ma, W.: A hierarchically structured constraint-based data model for solid modeling in a virtual reality environment. Proc. First International Symposium on Cyber Worlds. Tokyo (2002) 537-544
8. Cruz, I.F., Leveille, P.S.: Implementation of a constraint-based visualization system. Proc. 2000 IEEE International Symposium on Visual Languages. Seattle (2000) 13-20
9. Liu, X., Shi, H., and Chen, X., et al.: Study on visual design environment of cooperative template. Proceedings of the 9th International Conference on Computer Supported Cooperative Work in Design. Coventry, UK (2005) 157-163
10. Liu, X., Shi, H., et al.: Cooperative template mechanism for cooperative design. Proceeding of the International Conference on Computer Supported Cooperative Work in Design (CSCWD'05). Lecture Notes in Computer Science 3865 (2006) 102-111
11. Hamissi, S., Babes, M.: A neural approach for solving the constraint satisfaction problem. Proceedings of 2003 International Conference on Geometric Modeling and Graphics. London (2003) 96-103
12. Fung, S.K.L., Zheng, D.J., Leung, H., Lee, J.H.M. and Chun, H.W.: A Framework for Guided Complete Search for Solving Constraint Satisfaction Problems and Some of Its Instances. Proc. 16th IEEE International Conference on Tools with Artificial Intelligence. Boca Raton (2004) 696-703
13. Shanghai Electrical Apparatus Research Institute: Medium-sized and Pint-sized Motor Design Manual. Beijing: Machine Press (1994) (In Chinese)

Sharing Design Information Using Peer-to-Peer Computing

Phil Thompson, Anne James, and Leonid Smalov

Faculty of Engineering & Computing, Coventry University, Coventry, West Midlands, England, United Kingdom
`p.thompson@www.coventry.ac.uk`,
`a.james@www.coventry.ac.uk`,
`l.smalov@www.coventry.ac.uk`

Abstract. Sharing information between team members and the need to collaborate on design work to ensure that all elements of the design are compatible is essential. The type of information to be shared in a design project takes many different forms which can be stored digitally and processed electronically using all types of digital devices. Peer-to-Peer computing has opened up the possibility for information to be transferred directly between digital devices so that mobile phones, PDA's, networked computers, and other communicable devices could be used to pass information between team members. The use of XML allows information to be held in data structures and these structures can be processed in a peer-to-peer environment using software tools. This paper shows through the creation of a simple prototype and a tool called JXTA from the SUN Corporation how the sharing of data structures using Peer-to-Peer computing can be achieved.

1 Introduction

Traditionally the information exchanged between designers working on a collaborative project could take many different forms including drawings; photographs; text documents; correspondence; sound recordings; film; etc. All that information can now be held digitally and stored on computer files on a variety of different media. For example drawings could be created from a CAD system such as Autocad or text documents could be created from word-processing software such as Microsoft Word. Photographs could have been created in one of a number of different image formats including JPEG, BMP, TIFF, etc. Correspondence will more commonly be held as e-mails or may be paper documents scanned in through a work-flow system and held digitally. The range of devices now available offer flexibility, portability and mobility to the environment in which design takes place. As observed by Raymond Gao [1], "clients for P2P interaction could be devices ranging from a PC, to a UNIX workstation, to a file server, to a mainframe, to a handheld device, i.e. personal digital assistant (PDA), a cell phone, a wristwatch, or even an MP3 player".

If a computer infrastructure to support collaborative working is to be developed the first requirement is that it must be capable of processing many different types of

W. Shen et al. (Eds.): CSCWD 2006, LNCS 4402, pp. 73–81, 2007.
© Springer-Verlag Berlin Heidelberg 2007

digital information. The infrastructure should allow these different types of digital information to be transferred from one member of the team to another as well as provide a repository in which this information can be stored and accessed when required. This requirement is considered in more detail in Section 2.

Large collaborative working projects such as those that develop open source software can involve participants in many different global locations. The use of the Internet for many of these projects has provided a means of achieving physical communication between members and made it easy for new members to join the project. The ease with which this can be achieved makes it possible to have thousands of people working on a project at any one time although because of different time zones synchronous communication may not be possible. With so many people working on the project the range of specialties and experience is increased. Individuals with similar interests may work together or in small sub-groups to develop different parts of the total product. This makes it necessary for information to be shared between them. The usual form of distribution to design team members is from a central repository from which each team member selects the required information. This has the disadvantage of being a "single point of failure" i.e. loss of the central repository means all team members are unable to access information. The second requirement for the collaborative working infrastructure then is the ability for new members to join the project easily, to be able to share information directly between each other without the problem of the single point of failure and to form sub-groups which are be able to work on different aspects of the product design. This requirement is considered further in Section 3.

2 Sharing Digital Information

With a need to share so many different types of information it is necessary to find a way to distinguish between them. The distinction this paper will used is structured, semi-structured and unstructured data. A good definition of structured data is in [2] as "*Information that has been organised to allow identification and separation of the context of the information from its content.*" The best example of this would be a database.

However, as recognised by Halevy et al. (2003) [3], it has frequently been observed that most of the world's data lies *outside* database systems. The remainder would be as data that was unstructured or semi-structured. What then is unstructured data? Weglarz [4] defines unstructured data as "any data stored in an unstructured format at the atomic level". Examples of unstructured data would be bit-mapped and textual objects. Bit mapped objects are audio, video or image files. Textual objects are free text files such as occurs in word processing documents. Weglarz [4] discusses the use of Enterprise Content Management (ECM) for the management of text and the use of textual data mining and analysis but suggests that technologies for the management and interpretation of bit-mapped data are in their infancy.

In his article on content management [5] software, Bourret lists the functions of Content Management Systems as "storing, assembling and retrieving documents from document fragments". He lists the features provided with these systems as, "editors, version control and multi-user access capability". In another article [6] he goes on to describe how these systems are based on two main types of database, the "native XML" and "XML enabled database". The native XML database defines an XML model for the document and uses that model to access all documents of that type. The underlying database in which the actual document is stored can be relational, object or hierarchical in form. The XML enabled database differs from the native XML database in that it is a conventional database with extensions to process XML documents and convert them into its own data types.

In his article, David [7] describes the medium used to store images, videos, audio, animation, graphics, hypertext, hypermedia and data from medical equipment (e.g. MRI scans, x-rays, electro-cardiographs), etc., as a "multimedia database". He categorises multimedia databases of this kind as holding a sub-class of unstructured data called "abstract" data.

Erramouspe [8] introduces a third category of data, semi-structured data. Into this category he puts e-mails and data held in Exchange servers. In the unstructured data category he includes Microsoft Word documents, Excel spreadsheets, Powerpoint presentations and PDF's. He quotes "recent studies" which state that in many enterprise networks, 50% of storage is consumed by unstructured data, 25% is made up of structured data in enterprise databases and the remainder is semi-structured data.

The work of Weglarz [4], Erramouspe [7], David [8] and others have ushered in the terms unstructured, semi-structured and structured. What is required is a means of processing these different type of data through the use of a common format. That requirement can now be met by the use of XML.

The use of XML as a common format to link what has been called the "heterogeneity of data structure" [9], with particular application to Computer Supported Collaborative Design systems is not new. The use of an XML envelope [10] to be used to wrap e-mails held on an XML enabled database has been proposed. This proposal will be extended in this paper to data structures and images reflecting to some degree the various document types used in a collaborative design environment.

3   Peer-to-Peer as a Solution to Collaborative Working

Peer-to-Peer Computing is proposed as a solution to the second requirement of the collaborative working infrastructure mentioned above. Peer-to-Peer networks have scalability which means that it is easy for new peers to join the network. In a conventional client-server network extra resources have to be provided at the server as more and more nodes join the network. In a peer-to-peer network no central server is required each peer brings enough extra resource to support its own membership of the network.

Peer-to-Peer computing also allows shared information to be accessible by other peers directly, without passing intermediary entities [11]. When a new member joins the team information can be sourced from any of the other members. Although this creates data redundancy it does provide an answer to the single point of failure referred to above because no central repository is used for information.

The ability for a group of peers to have a single identity as well as having their individual identity would allow measures to be put in place which would allow members of the design team working together on a particular part of the design to be allocated the group identity. This group identity could be subject to password control if security was required.

4   The Prototype

The Prototype needed to have peer-to-peer capability with the ability to create peer groups and provide the type of XML database discussed above in order to process the various data type discussed above.

4.1   Software

The software used to support the peer-to-peer processing requirements of the JAVA prototype is JXTA [12]. Introduced by Sun Microsystems, Inc., the award winning JXTA technology is a set of open, generalized peer-to-peer protocols that allows any connected device (cell phone to PDA, PC to server) on the network to communicate and collaborate.

The JXTA platform (see Figure 1) [13], is an Application Program Interface (API) which allows the peer-to-peer protocols to be used from an application program giving more flexibility.

Using JXTA, a peer can be set up, other peers can be located, peers can be organised into groups, communication can take place using messages and files can be transferred between them.

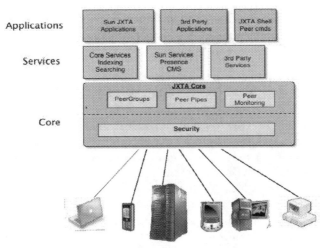

Fig. 1. The JXTA platform API [13]

4.2 Database Management

The database software used will be eXist [14]. eXist is an open source native XML database featuring efficient, index-based XQuery processing, automatic indexing, extensions for full-text search, XUpdate support and tight integration with existing XML development tools. eXist is also implemented in the JAVA language which will make it easy to incorporate it into the prototype. It comes in API form as well as a stand-alone database server. The stand-alone database server will be used to develop the database for the prototype. The API will be used to allow the database to be processed from the programs, which will be used to perform the tests within the prototype.

XML [15] or Extensible Markup Language is used to give meaning to data stored in a file so that a program can process it. A native XML database allows the data in XML files to be queried and updated. XQuery [16] provides a set of commands to allow data in an XML file to be located and accessed. XUpdate [17] provides a set of commands, which allow data in an XML file to be added, changed or deleted. Using XML will allow the prototype to process both structured semi-structured and unstructured data.

4.3 Database Design

The databases will be created using XML files. There will be three databases used for the test. A telephone directory database will be used to exemplify a structured database. A simple XML data structure of record type, forename, surname, two address lines and county will be used. An e-mail database will be used to exemplify a semi-structured database. The email will have a data structure of sender and title and the email will be stored as a .eml file converted into hexadecimal and stored in an XML data element.

4.4 Prototype Environment

A diagram of the test environment for the prototype is shown below in Figure 2. To demonstrate some level of interoperability the computers were initially set up with three different operating systems being Microsoft Windows XP and Microsoft Windows 2000. Also to introduce an element of flexibility testing one of the computers would be a laptop and the other two desktop computers. The three computers were then configured to operate over a private wireless network to isolate them from the other networks in the building. This would provide a suitable connection over which the peer-to-peer network could operate.

One of the computers would be used as a "rendezvous peer". A rendezvous peer in JXTA was necessary to intercept network requests and store the network address of the computer making the request together with its unique peer identification in a table. This table would then be used to propagate the messages from peers to all other peers in the network, which have an entry in the table.

The three computers were then configured to operate over a private wireless network to isolate them from the other networks in the building. This would provide the necessary connection for the peer-to-peer network to operate over.

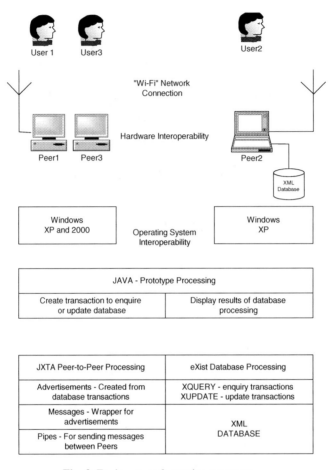

Fig. 2. Environment for testing prototype

4.5   Prototype Processing

A custom JXTA advertisement was designed to hold the transaction for updating the database. The transaction was entered at the originating peer and the transaction details were copied into the prototype advertisement as a database request transaction. The prototype advertisement was then published and the advertisement propagated by the rendezvous peer to all other peers in the network. The transaction was processed by all the receiving peers but only operated by the destination peer. The destination peer then processed the transaction against the database and copied the database details into another prototype advertisement as a database result transaction and directed it back to the originating peer.

The peer processed two types of transaction, used for inquiry or update. The inquiry transaction used eXist API classes embedded in a bespoke JAVA program. The inquiry transaction used XQUERY as its database language and the update transaction XUPDATE. The API supported both of these languages. On receiving the result transaction the originating peer then processed the prototype advertisement and displayed the results getting from the database transaction.

4.6 Results from Prototype

Unstructured data in the form of images was processed by the prototype and it was successfully passed between peers and processed from the database. Semi-structured data in the form of .eml files saved from a Microsoft Outlook e-mail system and structured data in the form of an address record held as a series of elements in an XML database were successfully processed and passed between peers by the prototype.

The XML database used by the prototype was proved to be a good way of storing all types of data. Unstructured and structured data could be processed over a peer-to-peer network in spite of any problem encountered.

5 Observations

The following observations were made as a result of the tests performed with the prototype.

5.1 Peer-to-Peer Processing

The propagating of messages to all other peers in the network was achieved in JXTA by the use of a "rendezvous peer". When a request for information was sent from one peer it was intercepted by the rendezvous peer that held an address table of all the other peers in the network. This address table was then used to send the request to all the other peers. This creates the potential for the problem which true Peer to Peer networks are supposed to avoid, the "single point of failure". Any problem which causes the rendezvous peer to fail stops the transferring of requests to other peers in the network. While it is possible to have more than one rendezvous peer, that would cause other problems with the duplication of requests.

While it was possible to send requests from one peer to another the "telecast" mechanism used by the rendezvous peer in JXTA meant that all other peers in the network also received the request. In a design environment each member of the team would have to decide whether or not this was relevant to them and either store or delete the request. The main problem with this telecasting is that with a large team a processing overhead would be created on the network from the potential surplus of requests.

A further problem concerns the time a request remains active on the network. In JXTA this is handled by the peer who creates the request setting a "lifetime" against the request. When the rendezvous peer receives the request it will continue to send that request to all other peers on the network until the lifetime expires. This creates a number of difficulties. Firstly the peer sending the request has to estimate how long it will be before all interested peers have responded. If it is too short some peers could miss the message and if it is too long then the sending of a request that all peers have already responded to, will create an overhead on the network.

5.2 Database Processing

For the successful management of data held in a database the processing of the database must be guaranteed or at least notification of the failure to process must be transmitted back to the initiator of the processing.

Because processing is asynchronous the request to update may never get to the location of the destination database. If it actually arrives at the location of the database processing may never take place. If processing takes place the results may be sent back but never reach the originator. Even if all these steps are successful and the results get back to the originator, the time taken to complete the steps may mean that the results are already out of date.

The order in which requests are received may not be the same order as they were initiated and this could be significant. For example a request to add data to a database and then subsequently amend the added data may be processed out of order. The amendment would be processed and find no data to amend. The request to add data would be then be processed successfully but the database would not have the latest information. This would cause confusion to the requestor as well as needing a further duplicate amendment to correct the added data.

6 Conclusions

Although the prototype has demonstrated the ability to process database transactions carrying different types of information between peers, the problems identified in this paper would mean that additional work would be necessary to produce an infrastructure suitable for a collaborative design environment.

Members of a design team would only want to see information that is related to them so the telecast method used by JXTA which propagates requests to all peers would require additional processing at each peer to process only requests which are intended for that peer.

The need to keep all design team members updated with certain information could be jeopardized if the lifetime of the database request is not long enough to allow all team members to pick up the updates. Members of a global team could be operating in different time zones which would exacerbate this problem.

The prototype performs well for the transfer of individual pieces of discrete information between peers, particularly if that information has to go to all peers on the network which the telecast scheme supports. However if several pieces of linked information have to be sent to each team member, a satisfactory two phase commit would make it necessary for each piece of information to be sent as separate transactions and then linked again at the receiving peer.

The problem of out of sequence requests should be detected and corrected at the rendezvous peer and should never appear at the peer level. But this problem may have been corrected in following releases of JXTA.

The ability to address peers directly across a network rather than propagating through uninterested peers would considerably reduce the overhead of unnecessary requests and the accompanying performance degradation.

In 2002, Aberer et al. [18] concluded after their research that "considerable research and experimentation remains to make p2p systems feasible for application domains". This research paper has shown that the combination of Peer-to-Peer, database and XML has brought closer that aim although further work will still be needed.

References

1. Gao, R.: Definition of P2P. Peer to Peer Research Group (2003) https://www1.ietf.org/mail-archive/working-groups/p2prg/current/msg2001.html
2. www.agimo.gov.au/publications/2005/04agtifv2/glossary
3. Halevy, A., Etzioni, O., Doan, A., Ives, Z., Madhavan, J., McDowell, L., Tatarinnov, I.: Crossing the structure chasm. Proc. First Biennial Conference on Innovative Data Systems Research. Asilomar, CA (2003)
4. Weglarz, G.: Two worlds of data - Unstructured and structured. DM Review Magazine (2004). http://www.dmreview.com/article_sub.cfm?articleId=1009161
5. Bourret, R.: XML Data Products - Content Management Systems (2000-2003). http://www.rpbourret.com/xml/ProdsCMS.htm
6. Bourret, R.: XML Data Products - Native XML Databases (2000-2003). http://www.rpbourret.com/xml/ProdsNative.htm
7. David, M.: Multimedia database through the looking glass. Miller Freeman Inc (1997). http://www.dbpd.com/vault/9705davd.htm
8. Erramouspe, J.: Unstructured data, roadblock to effective ILM. The Online Storage Network Magazine for IT Leaders (2004). http://www.snwonline.com/behind/unstructured_data_09-06-04.asp?article_id=447
9. Yin, Y., Huang, H., Gu, Y., Wu, W., Zu, X.: Application of XML in Computer Supported Collaborated Design Systems. Proceedings of The 8th International Conference on Computer Supported Cooperative Work in Design. Volume 2. Xiamen, China (2004) 132-135
10. Wang, Y., Chen, G., Dong, J.: DXEC Integrating Database, XML and Email for Collaboration. Proceedings of the 9th International Conference on Computer Supported Co-operative Work in Design. Volume 1. Coventry, UK (2005) 152-156
11. Kelllerer, W.: Dienstarchitekturen in der Telekommunikation – Evolution, Methoden und Vergleich. Technical Report TUM-LKN-TR-9801 (1998)
12. http://www.sun.com/software/jxta/
13. JXTA Programmers Guide. Ver. 2.3. Sun Microsystems Inc (2005)
14. http://exist.sourceforge.net/
15. http://www.w3.org/XML/
16. http://www.w3.org/TR/2005/WD-xquery-20050404/
17. http://xmldb-org.sourceforge.net/xupdate/
18. Aberer, K., Punceva, M., Hauswirth, M., Schmidt, R.: Improving data access in P2P systems. IEEE Internet Computing 6(1) (2002) 58-67

A Technique for Evaluating
Shared Workspaces Efficiency

Antonio Ferreira and Pedro Antunes

Department of Informatics, University of Lisbon, Portugal
{asfe,paa}@di.fc.ul.pt

Abstract. We propose a technique based on human-performance models to evaluate the efficiency of shared workspaces, where individual and collaborative actions are intertwined. We apply the technique to an illustrative case and report that it: 1) facilitates the fine-grained analysis of workspace collaboration; 2) provides time predictions about collaborative actions; and 3) enables quantitative comparisons of alternative designs via multi-dimensional team performance estimates. The technique may be used to complement existing practice and knowledge with the ability to make quick measurements and calculations without users or functional prototypes, thereby enabling faster design iterations.

1 Introduction and Motivation

CSCW usability evaluation is a challenging endeavor for researchers and practitioners because current methods and techniques impose significant constraints motivated by the number of participants in the evaluation processes and by the required control over variables related to the group, the task, the context, and the technologies [1].

In this paper our research interest is in reducing the cost and complexity of evaluating shared workspaces efficiency, thus enabling more design iterations and allowing for the emergence of more successful designs. Collaboration in shared workspaces entails high levels of interdependence and workspace awareness because continuing individual actions often limit the options and affect the outcomes of the other team members, and vice-versa [2]. For this reason, small design decisions (the low-level details of individual and collaborative actions, usually performed in very dynamic contexts) have much greater impact in workspace collaboration than in other contexts, where the focus may be on more abstract activities such as group decision making.

Several techniques from the HCI (Human-Computer Interaction) field—and thus focused on single user interactions—already reduce complexity and give attention to details. For example, the GOMS (Goals, Operators, Methods, and Selection Rules) family of techniques [3] relies on human-performance models to analyze fine-grained usability problems. From these techniques, we are particularly interested in the KLM (Keystroke-Level Model) [4-5], because it is relatively simple to use and has been successfully applied to evaluate the efficiency of many single-user designs [3].

In this paper we propose a technique, based on earlier research on the benefits of using human-performance models [6], to provide additional insights about workspace

W. Shen et al. (Eds.): CSCWD 2006, LNCS 4402, pp. 82–91, 2007.
© Springer-Verlag Berlin Heidelberg 2007

collaboration, not covered by other evaluation techniques. Some advantages of this technique emerge from the following characteristics of human-performance models:

- Afford studying alternative designs without the participation of users or the development of prototypes, which may reduce design time and effort;
- Elucidate the assumed capabilities and mechanisms of the human processing system, which may be instrumental to develop more useable CSCW tools;
- Offer quantitative predictions of human performance, which may be used to make design decisions based on quick measurements and calculations;
- Address the fine-grained details of workspace collaboration, which may be used to optimize overall team performance.

In Section 2 of this paper, we apply our evaluation technique to an example of workspace collaboration, compare two alternative designs, and discuss benefits and limitations; in Section 3 we address related work; and Section 4 concludes contributions of this research and proposes future work.

2 Illustrating Example

The technique proposed in this paper will be described and explained by means of its application to an example of workspace collaboration. The example refers to a collaborative game where multiple players draw either vertical or horizontal connections between adjacent pairs of points in a board. The game is over when the board is filled with connections, but players must observe this rule: if a player, e.g. Sophie, is an expert in drawing vertical connections, then she must consider adjacent pairs of points that contain, at least, one horizontal connection to a third point. The behavior of an expert in horizontal connections, e.g. Charles, is analogous.

For illustration purposes, the board is characterized by a square arrangement of contiguous cells, numbered 1 to 9, and by an initial state that contains at least one horizontal and vertical connection lines (see Fig. 1).

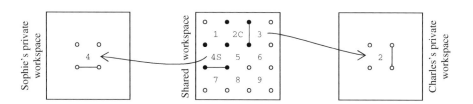

Fig. 1. Cell reservations and ownership letters (2 players shown)

The game features a shared workspace for displaying a public up-to-date view of the board, and private workspaces where players can connect cell points. To simplify our analysis, we restrict player interactions to a mouse with a button.

In order to connect points, players must first reserve the points by selecting and dragging the corresponding cell into the private workspace. Later, the modifications on the cell will be made public when the cell is moved back to the shared workspace.

To minimize inadvertent selections of reserved cells, the shared workspace provides awareness by displaying a letter, next to the cell number, that identifies the current owner (see Fig. 1). Additionally, the collaborative game impedes concurrent reservations of the same pairs of adjacent points. For example, if two players select vertically or horizontally neighbor cells (or the same cell), and simultaneously try to reserve them, then only one player will accomplish the cell reservation, while the other is notified that the cell cannot be reserved.

It is expected that the cells remain reserved for a small amount of time due to the expertise of the players and their eagerness to accomplish the shared goal.

To demonstrate why this case concerns workspace collaboration we can consider that the team must work in harmony in order to quickly connect all pairs of adjacent points: the more horizontal connections exist, the more vertical connections can be drawn, and vice-versa. Conversely, if one player stops drawing connections, the other player will soon also stop. In other words, the actions of the team members (the players) are intertwined, this being a distinctive feature of workspace collaboration [2].

2.1 The Proposed Technique

Step 1: Characterizing goals and actions. The technique begins with the characterization of the collaborative environment in terms of goals and actions. In the collaborative game, players pursue *individual goals*: to draw connection lines as fast as possible. At the same time, they are conscious of team performance towards the *shared goal*: to quickly connect all adjacent points in the board.

Complementarily, team work results from a combination of individual and collaborative actions. *Individual actions* correspond to drawing vertical and horizontal connections, which, due to their similarity, can be generically identified by DRAW. *Collaborative actions* are related to moving a cell from the shared into the private workspace, and vice-versa. These actions, named RESERVE and RELEASE, involve the shared workspace and are required to coordinate work and prevent conflicts.

Step 2: Detailing actions. The technique proceeds with detailed descriptions of the individual and collaborative actions that characterize the collaborative environment. Table 1 shows the details of the actions that players can perform in the game.

Table 1. Individual and collaborative actions

Action	Description
RESERVE (collaborative)	The player: 1) locates a cell in the shared workspace; 2) presses the mouse button over the cell; 3) moves the mouse cursor to the private workspace; and 4) releases the mouse button
DRAW (individual)	The player: 1) locates a cell point in the private workspace; 2) presses the mouse button over the point; 3) moves the mouse cursor to the adjacent point in the cell; and 4) releases the mouse button
RELEASE (collaborative)	The player: 1) locates a cell in the private workspace; 2) presses the mouse button over the cell; 3) moves the mouse cursor to the shared workspace; and 4) releases the mouse button

In a shared workspace, the individual and collaborative actions are entwined and under the control of the CSCW tool, which means that their design can influence individual, and especially, team performance.

Step 3: Predicting execution times. The technique proceeds with an evaluation of efficiency using the KLM (Keystroke-Level Model) [4,5]. In this model an action (e.g., each action in Table 1) is converted into a sequence of mental and motor operators whose execution times have been quantified and validated in psychological experiences [4,7]. An important KLM requirement is that modeling applies to expert error-free behavior only. This is met in the collaborative game since the players are highly trained in drawing connections and in using the shared workspace.

To illustrate the conversion from a detailed textual description into a KLM representation, consider the RELEASE action in Table 1. In steps 1 and 2, player Sophie locates a worked cell in her private workspace; this is converted into the M operator. Then, she moves the mouse cursor over the cell, a P, and presses the mouse button, a K. In step 3 she moves the mouse cursor to the shared workspace, an operation that is translated into a P, without a preceding M since there is no need to find the workspace. In step 4 Sophie releases the mouse button, K. The total predicted time for the execution of the RELEASE action is obtained by adding the individual times of the KLM operators, which for MPKPK gives 1.2 + 1.1 + 0.1 + 1.1 + 0.1 = 3.6 seconds.

Interestingly, all actions in our case are essentially a sequence of MPKPK operators, hence the predicted times are the same. This suggests that the required human skills for drawing a connection between two points are very similar to those needed for moving a cell between workspaces, which seems plausible if we consider Fitts's Law, the sizes of the objects, and the distances between them [4].

The previous time estimates apply to actions as if they were unrelated. To reveal goal achievements—individual and shared—in a collaborative environment we need to realize how work is produced with the CSCW tool. In the next step we will analyze individual behavior and then proceed to an evaluation of team performance.

Step 4: Focusing on the individual goals. In the collaborative game, and given an appropriate cell in the shared workspace, each player carries out individual goals by following one of two possible sequences of actions, shown in Table 2. Sequence S1 corresponds to drawing a single connection in a cell. The sequence of actions S2 applies to cases where two connections can be drawn in the same cell.

Table 2. Sequences for achieving individual goals

S#	Actions	Time (s)	Collaborative	Individual
S1	1) RESERVE 2) DRAW 3) RELEASE	3.6 + 3.6 + 3.6 = 10.8	7.2/10.8 = 67%	3.6/10.8 = 33%
S2	1) RESERVE 2) DRAW × 2 3) RELEASE	3.6 + 3.6 × 2 + 3.6 = 14.4	7.2/14.4 = 50%	7.2/14.4 = 50%

Table 2 is very interesting because it shows that the collaborative actions, RESERVE and RELEASE, are more costly (7.2s or 67% of total predicted time) than the individual action of drawing a connection line, DRAW, that characterizes sequence S1. It is therefore likely that the CSCW designer admits that players will avoid such situation and instead prefer sequence S2, due to its lower collaboration overhead (50%).

Step 5: Focusing on the shared goal. In this step we analyze team performance. We start by defining a *goal unit* as a conceptual metric for assessing progress in terms of the shared goal. In the collaborative game, the shared goal is reached when all line connections have been drawn on the board, which gives a total of 24 goal units.

We continue the analysis with a characterization of the sequences of actions along three dimensions which we think are intrinsic to workspace collaboration. The *productivity* dimension measures the number of goal units produced per time unit. The greater the value, the faster the team may progress towards the shared goal. In single-user software design this dimension measures individual efficiency. However, with workspace collaboration team efficiency cannot be determined by simply combining individual efficiencies; we try to capture this with the other two dimensions.

The *opportunities* dimension is related to the intertwined nature of workspace collaboration: if a team member stops, then soon the team will also halt, eventually never reaching the shared goal. This suggests that collaboration among team members is bound by opportunity dependencies created by the achievement of individual goals. The measurement unit for this dimension is new goal unit opportunities potentially created per time unit. The greater the opportunities, the faster the team may progress.

The *restrictions* dimension reflects a possible negative outcome of coordination in shared workspaces: the prevention of conflicts and duplicate efforts (positive outcomes) may slow down or even impede the work of other team members. Restrictions are measured in inaccessible goal units times the duration of the sequence of actions. This unit of measurement emphasizes fast and unobtrusive execution of individual goals: the greater the restrictions value, the slower the team may progress, because team members will probably spend more time waiting to proceed.

We can now evaluate team performance based on the analysis of the sequences of actions S1 and S2 along the three dimensions (see Table 3). Once more, a goal unit (gu) corresponds to one connection. The main time unit, for convenience, is minutes.

Table 3. Team performance for the initial design

S#	Productivity	Opportunities	Restrictions
S1	1 gu / 10.8 s = 5.5 gu/min	2 gu / 10.8 s = 11.1 gu/min	1 gu * 10.8 s = 0.18 gu.min
S2	2 gu / 14.4 s = 8.3 gu/min	5 gu / 14.4 s = 20.8 gu/min	1 gu * 14.4 s = 0.24 gu.min

The predictions in Table 3 show that S2 is more productive than S1, because S2 takes 14.4s to draw 2 line connections—thus the 8.8 gu/min—in contrast with 5.5 gu/min of S1. S2 also compares favorably with S1 in creating new individual goal opportunities for the other team members: 20.8 versus 11.1 gu/min. The logic behind the number of opportunities for each sequence of actions is illustrated in Fig. 2.

Using sequence S1 only one vertical connection line can be drawn by Sophie in cell 5, which, in the best case, opens two new opportunities to Charles since he will be able to draw two horizontal connections: the top and bottom lines in cell 6. The missing

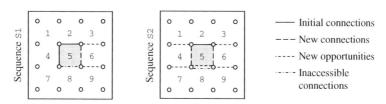

Fig. 2. Productivity, opportunities, and restrictions

bottom horizontal line in cell 5 is *not* an opportunity because it was already available via the left vertical connection in cell 5. Actually, this bottom connection is inaccessible to the other players while Sophie is running s1. In sequence s2 up to 5 opportunities can be created after the left and right vertical lines are drawn in cell 5.

The only dimension where s1 is preferable to s2 is the restrictions to the work of other team members. The lower 0.18 gu.min of s1 versus 0.24 gu.min of s2 is caused by its faster predicted execution time, 10.8 versus 14.4s, since the number of inaccessible goal units during the execution of the sequence of actions is the same in both cases: a single line connection drawing (the bottom horizontal connection in cell 5).

The data in Table 2 and Table 3 provide a basis for doing comparisons with other designs. In the next section we evaluate a design alternative using the same technique.

2.2 Evaluating a Design Alternative

Our design alternative for the collaborative game features multiple cell reservations/ releases, and the display of awareness information while team members *select* cells in the shared workspace. The motivation is twofold: a) the impact of collaborative actions on individual goal execution decreases with the number of connections that can be drawn consecutively; and b) selecting cells in the shared workspace is faster than reserving cells, which means that awareness information will be more up-to-date.

The new features introduce changes in the *collaborative* actions that characterize the work environment: two novel actions are used for selecting single and multiple cells, **SELECT_1** (a simple click on a cell) and **SELECT_N** (a click and drag movement over consecutive cells); additionally, the reservations and releases, **RESERVE_B** and **RELEASE_B**, are now a bit simpler to reflect the fact that players don't need to search for a cell or cells that they have just selected (cell selections always precede cell reservations or releases). Table 4 shows the new KLM models and predicted times.

The data show that the 2.5s of **SELECT_1** is lower than the 3.6s of the previous **RESERVE** action (cf. Table 2), meaning that players should experience less time dealing with coordination conflicts. On the other hand, the time to reserve a single cell

Table 4. New collaborative actions

Action	KLM Model	Time (s)
SELECT_1	MPKK	2.5
SELECT_N	MPKMPK	4.8
RESERVE_B	KPK	1.3
RELEASE_B	KPK	1.3

increases because now it takes a **SELECT_1** followed by **RESERVE_B**, with a total of 3.8s. We consider this tradeoff acceptable because the time to recover from a reservation conflict is, at least, an order of magnitude greater than the extra 0.2s.

In Table 5 we analyze the new sequences of actions for achieving individual goals.

Table 5. New sequences of actions

S#	Actions	Time (s)	Collaborative	Individual
S3	1) SELECT_1 2) RESERVE_B 3) DRAW 4) SELECT_1 5) RELEASE_B	2.5 + 1.3 + 3.6 + 2.5 + 1.3 = 11.2	7.6 / 11.2 = 68%	3.6 / 11.2 = 32%
S4	1) SELECT_1 2) RESERVE_B 3) DRAW × 2 4) SELECT_1 5) RELEASE_B	2.5 + 1.3 + 3.6 × 2 + 2.5 + 1.3 = 14.8	7.6 / 14.8 = 51%	7.2 / 14.8 = 49%
S5	1) SELECT_N 2) RESERVE_B 3) DRAW × n 4) SELECT_N 5) RELEASE_B	4.8 + 1.3 + 3.6 × n + 4.8 + 1.3 = total	12.2 / total $n = 1 \rightarrow 77\%$ $n = 2 \rightarrow 63\%$ $n = 3 \rightarrow 53\%$ $n = 4 \rightarrow 46\%$	3.6 × n / total $n = 1 \rightarrow 33\%$ $n = 2 \rightarrow 37\%$ $n = 3 \rightarrow 47\%$ $n = 4 \rightarrow 54\%$

As expected, if players can *only* select single cells, they will probably prefer reserving those in which they can draw two connection lines using sequence S4, in detriment of S3. This is because in S4 the overhead of collaborative actions, 51%, is lower than the 68% in S3. However, if players see an opportunity for reserving multiple cells at once, then they will likely use sequence S5 when *at least* four connections $(n \geq 4)$ are doable in those cells, because the impact of collaborative actions is *at most* 46%, this being unmatched by any of the sequences S3 and S4.

Table 6 shows the new team performance values afforded by the alternative design, for the sequences of actions **S3**, **S4**, and for three variants of **S5**, which are illustrated in Fig. 3.

The first rows in Table 6 represent the sequences of actions, S3 and S4, which are less restrictive and offer good opportunities, albeit with lower productivity. The last rows describe the more productive variants of sequence S5, but which are the most restrictive and offer only normal opportunities to the other team members.

Table 6. Team performance for the alternative design

S#	Productivity (gu/min)	Opportunities (gu/min)	Restrictions (gu.min)
S3	5.4	10.7	0.19
S4	8.1	20.3	0.25
S5 a)	9.0	18.0	1.8
S5 b)	10.6	17.8	3.4
S5 c)	11.7	19.0	6.2

We end the analysis of the design alternative by noting that the s5 variants in Fig. 3 are ideal cases and that actual team performance depends upon the evolving state of the board. However, an exhaustive analysis of s5 variants is clearly unmanageable. By focusing our attention on ideal cases of s5 we can create a reasonable basis for evaluating and comparing team performance towards the shared goal.

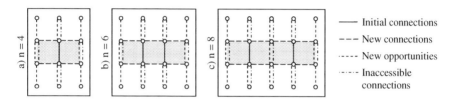

Fig. 3. Analysis of three variants of sequence s5

2.3 Using the Technique to Compare Designs: The Big Picture

We now describe how the proposed technique can be used to compare the two design alternatives. Fig. 4 shows the impact of collaborative overhead in total predicted time versus the proportion of time for doing individual actions. The values are sorted by collaborative overhead to facilitate the detection of the sequences of actions that are more costly to perform in the shared workspace.

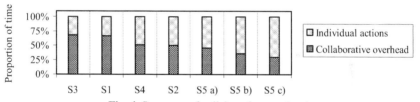

Fig. 4. Summary of collaborative overhead

The data in Fig. 4 show that the two pairs of sibling sequences, s3/s1 and s4/s2, have similar proportions of collaborative overhead, and that the variants of s5 have the best proportions of individual actions in total predicted time. These results seem to indicate that the alternative design is preferable to the first design, even more so because, intuitively, collaborative overhead has a negative effect in team performance.

To show that the intuition is *wrong*—at least in this case—we state this proposition: lower proportions of collaborative overhead for achieving individual goals lead to higher team performance towards the shared goal. Now, consider the succession of s5 variants, with equal ordering in Fig. 4 and Fig. 5. Reading left to right, the proportion of collaborative overhead steadily decreases while the productivity increases in a symmetrical way, the opportunities remain almost constant, and the restrictions raise at a higher rate. So, contrary to the proposition, the lower the proportion of collaborative overhead in the variants of s5 the *slower* the team progresses towards the shared goal because its team members will probably spend more time waiting to proceed.

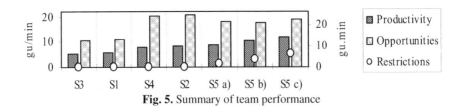

Fig. 5. Summary of team performance

Given this somewhat puzzling scenario the designer must find an optimal equilibrium between individual goals and the shared team goal. Were this equilibrium could be is the subject of further work. At the moment the big picture is still getting clearer.

3 Related Work

The use of human-performance models in the CSCW context is very rare, and mostly inexistent for workspace collaboration. DGOMS (Distributed GOMS) [8] is an extension of GOMS that allows group tasks to be decomposed until individual subtasks are reached. A communication operator is then used to coordinate individual tasks executed in parallel, meaning that this method does not address workspace collaboration, but coordinated work. A similar approach is also suggested in a study of GOMS applied to a team task [9], where several users with individual roles were to monitor a display while coordinating their actions via a shared radio communication channel.

We now refer to three methods developed for CSCW that share our purpose of reducing the complexity and cost of CSCW usability evaluation. They are: Collaboration Usability Analysis (CUA) [10], Groupware Walkthrough [11], and Groupware Heuristic Evaluation [12], and, all based on a common framework called "mechanics of collaboration." It is interesting to contrast the CUA and human-performance model approaches; both analyze tasks via hierarchical decomposition but CUA reduces collaboration tasks to the mechanics performed by users in shared workspaces (such as writing a message or obtaining a resource) while human-performance models decompose tasks at a much lower level of detail, for instance, keystrokes. Single keystrokes are most times unrelated to collaborative work—notably when group decision making is involved—which is a strong argument in favor of high-level approaches such as CUA. However, in this paper we hypothesize that the designer of shared workspaces may find it necessary to optimize the effort applied by users in low-level tasks.

4 Conclusions and Future Work

In this paper we show how an analytical technique that is based on human-performance models and three dimensions of team performance—productivity, opportunities, and restrictions—can be used to inform the design of shared workspaces. We also show how the technique can be used to provide quantitative indications of which design alternatives may be more beneficial to team performance.

In our view, shared workspace designers should complement existing practice and knowledge—based on high-level task analysis or depending on inspections performed by multiple usability experts—with the ability to make quick measurements and calculations about shared workspaces efficiency. Our motivation is based on the century-old need to measure before improving as well as on the evidence that faster evaluation enables more design iterations.

Research described in this paper is a preliminary step in the direction of exploring shared workspaces efficiency with human-performance models. As it is, the technique calls for external validity and more work is needed to better understand how it can be combined with other existing techniques and methods.

Acknowledgments. This work was partially supported by the Portuguese Foundation for Science and Technology (Project POSC/ EIA/57038/2004).

References

1. Fjermestad, J., Hiltz, S.: An assessment of group support systems experimental research: methodology and results. Journal of Management Information Systems 15(3) (1999) 7–149
2. Nunamaker, J., Briggs, R., Mittleman, D., Vogel, D., Balthazard, P.: Lessons from a dozen years of group support systems research: A discussion of lab and field findings. Journal of Management Information Systems 13(3) (1997) 163–207
3. John, B., Kieras, D.: Using GOMS for user interface design and evaluation: Which technique? ACM Transactions on Computer-Human Interaction 3(4) (1996) 287–319
4. Card, S., Moran, T., Newel, A.: The psychology of human-computer interaction. Lawrence Erlbaum Associates, Hillsdale, New Jersey, USA (1983) 259–311
5. Card, S., Moran, T., Newell, A.: The keystroke-level model for user performance time with interactive systems. Communications of the ACM 23(7) (1980) 396–410
6. Antunes, P., Ferreira, A., Pino, J.: Analyzing shared workspaces design with human-performance models. Proceedings of the Twelfth International Workshop on Groupware. LNCS 4154 (2006) 62–77
7. Olson, J., Olson, G.: The growth of cognitive modeling in human-computer interaction. Human-Computer Interaction 5(2&3) (1990) 221–265
8. Min, D., Koo, S., Chung, Y., Kim, B.: Distributed GOMS: An extension of GOMS to group task. Proceedings of the 1999 IEEE Conference on Systems, Man, and Cybernetics. Tokyo, Japan (1999) 720–725
9. Kieras, D., Santoro, T. Computational GOMS modeling of a complex team task: Lessons learned. Proceedings of the 2004 Conference on Human Factors in Computing Systems. Vienna, Austria (2004) 97–104
10. Pinelle, D., Gutwin, C., Greenberg, S.: Task analysis for groupware usability evaluation: Modeling shared-workspace tasks with the mechanics of collaboration. ACM Transactions on Computer-Human Interaction 10(4) (2003) 281–311
11. Pinelle, D., Gutwin, C.: Groupware walkthrough: Adding context to groupware usability evaluation. Proceedings of the SIGCHI Conference on Human Factors in Computing Systems. Minneapolis, Minnesota, USA (2002) 455–462
12. Baker, K., Greenberg, S., Gutwin, C.: Empirical development of a heuristic evaluation methodology for shared workspace groupware. Proceedings of the 2002 ACM Conference on Computer Supported Cooperative Work. New Orleans, Louisiana, USA (2002) 96–105

Robust Data Location Infrastructure in Distributed Collaborative Environment

Wei Ye and Ning Gu

Dept. of Computing and Information Technology, Fudan University,
Shanghai, P.R. China
{weiye, ninggu}@fudan.edu.cn

Abstract. Distributed and real time collaborative applications are developing at a trememdous speed. People now can effortlessly collaborate with each other in a relatively small scale and location. But there are still numerous challenges to extend the application to a large scale, for example, tens of thousands of users distribute all over the world. Effective and efficient data and object location is one of the most critical issues. In this paper, we presented a Resilient Mechanism for Data and object Location and routing (RDLM), a self-organizing, scalable, robust wide-area infrastructure that efficiently routes requests to content in the presence of heavy load and network faults. Simulation experiments show that RDLM has a satisfying performance especially under heavy network traffic.

1 Introduction and Motivation

With the rapid development and wide application of distributed collaborative technology, people now are able to easily collaborate with each other in a relatively small scale and location. But since in today's chaotic network, data and services are mobile and replicated widely for availability, durability, and locality, an effective and efficient data and object location mechanism is essential to extend the application to a large range, like tens of thousands of users distributed in all over the world. This has lead to a renewed interest in techniques for routing queries to objects using names that are independent of their locations. The notion of *routing* is that queries are forwarded from node to node until they reach their destinations. The *location-independent routing* problem has spawned a host of proposals. Many of them are in the context of data sharing infrastructures such as OceanStore [13], FarSite [3], CFS [8] and PAST [9]. To permit locality optimizations, it is important that the routing process use as few network hops as possible and that these hops be as short as possible.

Properties from a location-independent routing infrastructure include:

1. *Deterministic Location*: Objects should be located if they exist anywhere in the network.
2. *Routing Locality*: Routes should have low *stretch*, not just a small number of application-level hops. Sending queries to the nearest copy across the shortest path possible is the ideal.

W. Shen et al. (Eds.): CSCWD 2006, LNCS 4402, pp. 92–100, 2007.
© Springer-Verlag Berlin Heidelberg 2007

3. *Minimality and Load Balance*: The infrastructure must not place undue stress on any of its components; this implies minimal storage and balanced computational load.
4. *Dynamic Membership*: The system must adapt to arriving and departing nodes while maintaining the above properties.

Although clearly desirable, the first property is not guaranteed by existing distributed or P2P systems such as BitComet [2], Gnutella [7] and FreeNet [5].

A simple object location and routing scheme would employ a centralized directory of object locations. Servers would *publish* the existence of objects by inserting entries into the directory. Clients would send *queries* to the directory, which forwards them to their destinations. This solution, while simple, induces a heavy load on the directory server. Moreover, when a nearby server happens to contain the object, the client must still interact with the potentially distant directory server. The average routing latency of this technique is proportional to the average diameter of the network – independent of the actual distance to the object. Worse, it is neither fault tolerant nor scalable, since the directory becomes a single point of both failure and contention.

An alternative solution is to broadcast an object's location to every node in the network. This allows clients to easily find the nearest copy of the object, but requires a large amount of resources to publish and maintain location information, including both network bandwidth and storage. Furthermore, it requires full knowledge of the participants of the network. In a dynamic network, maintaining a list of participants is a significant problem in its own right.

In our solution, we use as a starting point the distributed data structure of Plaxton, Rajaraman and Richa [13], which we will refer to as the PRR scheme. Their proposal yields routing locality with balanced storage and computational load. However, it does not provide dynamic maintenance of membership. The original statement of the algorithm required a static set of participating nodes as well as significant work to preprocess this set to generate a routing infrastructure. Additionally, the PRR scheme was unable to adapt to changes such as node failures. This paper extends their algorithms to a dynamic network.

2 Related Work

Several existing object location schemes exhibit routing locality, including Plaxton, Rajaraman, and Richa (PRR) [13], Awerbuch and Peleg [1], and Rajaraman et al. [14]. All of these provide the publication and deletion of objects with only a logarithmic number of messages and guarantee a low stretch, where stretch is defined as the ratio between the actual latency or distance to an object and the shortest distance. The PRR scheme finds objects with constant stretch for a specific class of network topologies while ensuring that no node has too many directory entries. Awerbuch and Peleg [1] route with within a polylogarithmic factor of optimal for general network topologies, but do not balance the load. Unfortunately, both the PRR and Awerbuch-Peleg schemes assume full knowledge of the participating nodes, or, equivalently, they assume that the network is static. The RRVV scheme balances the load, bounding the space at every node, and while only a polylogarithmic number of nodes need change when a node enters or leaves the network, they also do not give a method to find the nodes that need to be updated.

There is also an abundance of theoretical work on finding compact routing tables [2][9][12] whose techniques are closely related to Tapestry in Oceanstore. In [7], Gavoille provides an overview of routing in distributed networks. A recent and closely related paper is that of Thorup and Zwick [15], who showed that a sampling based scheme similar to that of PRR could be used to find small stretch routing tables and/or answer approximate distance queries in arbitrary metric spaces.

Most of previous recent work focuses on peer-to-peer networks ignore stretch, while Chord [16] constructs a distributed lookup service using a routing table of logarithmic size. Nodes are arranged into a large virtual circle. Each node maintains pointers to predecessor and successor nodes, as well as a logarithmic number of "chords" which cross greater distances within the circle. Queries are forwarded along chords until they reach their destination. CAN [17] places objects into a virtual, high-dimensional space. Queries are routed along axes in this virtual space until they reach their destination. While its overlay construction leverages network proximity metrics, it does not provide the same stretch as the PRR scheme in object location. A recent paper by Li and Plaxton [10] presents a simplified version of the PRR scheme that may perform well in practice. All of these schemes can find objects with a polylogarithmic number of application-level network hops, while ensuring that no node contains more than its share of directory entries. In addition, Chord and CAN have run-time heuristics to reduce object location cost, so they may perform well in practice. Finally, all of these systems support the introduction and removal of nodes.

3   RDLM

3.1   The Key Ideas of RDLM

The crux of our method for data and object location and routing lies in an algorithm for maintaining nearest neighbors in a restricted metric space. Our approach is similar in spirit to that of Karger and Ruhl [9], who give an algorithm for answering nearest neighbor queries in a similarly restricted metric space.

The idea behind the nearest-neighbor algorithm presented here is to find the nearest neighbor by repeatedly finding some node halfway between the current node and the query node. If this is done $log\ n$ times, one finds the closest node. The restricted metric spaces considered in both these papers mean that there is a substantial fraction of nodes at about the right distance, so halving the distance can be implemented by sampling from nodes within the correct radius. The difficulty is maintaining a structure to do the sampling in a dynamic network.

Karger and Ruhl suggested this general approach in [9] and then present a specific data structure to accomplish it. Their data structure uses a random permutation to maintain the random sampling–an approach is reminiscent of the Chord network infrastructure. Our search algorithm also aims to halve the distance at each step, but we build a different data structure with a different search algorithm. In particular, we use random names to build a tree (for load balancing purposes, many trees) on which we search. This set of trees is the same as the set of trees used in the object location system described in this paper, which means that our search algorithm can share the data structure with the object location algorithm.

We also prove that an alternate scheme by Plaxton, Rajaraman, and Richa (called PRR v.0 in Table 1) gives a low stretch solution for general metric spaces. This follows from arguments similar to those used by Bourgain [3] for metric embeddings. In particular, we show that this scheme leads to a covering of the graph by trees such that for any two nodes u and v at distance δ , they are in a tree of diameter δlogn. Indeed, by modifying the PRR scheme along the lines proposed by Thorup and Zwick [15] one can improve the space bounds by a logarithmic factor, but we do not address this issue here.

3.2 The RDLM Infrastructure

The Resilient Mechanism for Data Location (RDLM) is the wide-area location and routing infrastructure. We assume that nodes and objects in the system can be identified with unique identifiers (names), represented as strings of digits. Digits are drawn from an alphabet of radix b. Identifiers are uniformly distributed in the namespace. We will refer to node identifiers as node-IDs and object identifiers as globally unique identifiers (GUIDs). This means that every query has a unique destination GUID which ultimately resolves to a node-ID. For a string of digits α, let } represent the number of digits in that string.

We inherit our basic structure from the data location scheme of Plaxton et al. (PRR) [9]. As with the PRR scheme, each node contains pointers to other nodes (neighbor-links), as well as mappings between object GUIDs and the node-IDs of storage servers (object pointers). Queries are routed from node to node along neighbor links until an appropriate object pointer is discovered, where the query is forwarded along neighbor links to the destination node.

1. Basic location and routing

The core location and routing mechanisms of RDLM are similar to those of Plaxton. Every node in the RDLM network is capable of forwarding messages using the algorithm described in [2]. Each neighbor map is organized into routing levels, and each level contains entries that point to a set of nodes closest in network distance that matches the suffix for that level.

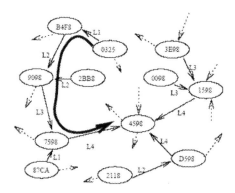

Fig. 1. Plaxton Routing example: Here we see the path taken by a message originating from node 0325 destined for node 4598 in a Plaxton mesh using hexadecimal digits of length 4 (65536 nodes in namespace)

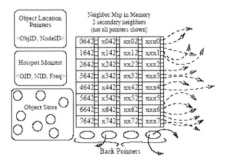

Fig. 2. A node structure: The complete components of a node 0642 that acts as a client, object server, and router. Components include a neighbor map, hotspot monitor, object location pointers, and a store of objects.

As shown in Figure 1, each node also maintains a backpointer list that points to nodes where it is referred to as a neighbor. We use them in the neighbor table generation algorithm, to generate the appropriate neighbor maps for a node, and to integrate it into the distributed collaborative environment. Figure 2 shows an example of a complete node structure.

The RDLM location mechanism is similar to the Plaxton location scheme. Where multiple copies of data exist in Plaxton, each node routed to the root node only stores the location of the closest replica to it. Our solution, however, stores locations of all such replicas to increase semantic flexibility. Where the Plaxton mechanism always returns the first object within some distance, RDLM location provides more semantic flexibility, by allowing the application to define the selection operator. Each object may include an optional application-specific metric in addition to a distance metric. Applications can then choose an operator to define how objects are chosen. For example, in distributed storage architecture, queries can be issued to only find the closest cached document replica satisfying some freshness metric. Additionally, archival pieces issue queries to collect distinct data fragments to reconstruct lost data. These queries deviate from the simple "find first" semantics, and ask RDLM to route a message to the closest N distinct objects.

2. Building the neighbor table

Building the neighbor table is perhaps the most complex and interesting part of the routing process, so we present it first. The problem is to build the neighbor sets. This can be seen as solving the nearest neighbor problem for many different prefixes. One solution is to simply use the method of Karger and Ruhl [9] many times, once for each prefix. This would essentially require each node to participate in O(log n) Karger-Ruhl data structures, one for each level of the neighbor table.

The algorithm we present below has lower network distance than a straightforward use of Karger and Ruhl (although the same number of network hops) and incurs no additional space over the PRR data structures.

Building a Neighbor Table

p **method** ACQUIRENEIGHBORTABLE (*NewNodeName, NewNodeIP, PName, PIP*)
1 α←GREATESTCOMMONPREFIX(*NewNodeName, PName*)
2 *maxLevel*←LENGTH (α)
3 list←ACKNOWLEDGEDMULTICAST [**on** *PIP*] (α, SENDID(*NewNodeIP, NewNodeName*))
4 BUILDTABLEFROMLIST(list, *maxLevel*)
5 **for** *i* = *maxlevel* - 1 **to** 0
6   list←GETNEXTLIST(list, *i*, *NewNodeName, NewNodeIP*)
7   BUILDTABLEFROMLIST(list, *i*)
  end ACQUIRENEIGHBORTABLE

  method GETNEXTLIST (**neighborlist**, *level, NewNodeName, NewNodeIP*)
1 nextList ←Φ
2 **for** n is on **neighborlist**
3   temp←GETFORWARDANDBACKPOINTERS (n, *level*))
4   ADDTOTABLEIFCLOSER [**on** *n*] (*NewNodeName, NewNodeIP*)
5   nextList←KEEPCLOSESTK(temp Ù nextList)
6 **return** nextList
  end GETNEXTLIST

The above algorithms shows how to build neighbor tables. The Acknowledged-Multicast function is presented in [12]. In words, suppose that the longest common prefix of the new node and any other node in the network is α. Then we begin with the list of all nodes with prefix α. We proceed by getting similar lists for progressively smaller prefixes, until we have the closest k nodes matching the empty prefix.

Let a level-I node be a node that shares a length i prefix with α. Then, to go from the level-(i+1) list to the level-I list, we ask each node on the level-(i+1) list to give us all the level-I nodes they know of (we ask for both forward and backwards pointers). Note that each level-I node must have at least one level-(i+1) node in its neighbor table, so following the backpointers of all level-(i+1) nodes gives us all level-I nodes. We then contact these nodes, and sort them according to their distance from the inserting node. Each node contacted this way also checks to see if the new node should be added to its own table. We then trim this list, keeping only the closest k nodes. If k=O(logn), the lists at each level contain exactly the k closest nodes.

We then use these lists to fill in the neighbor table. This happens in line 7 of AcquireNeighborTable. More precisely, recall that level I of the table consists of nodes with the prefix $\alpha_{i-1}oj$, where α_{i-1} is the first i-1 digits of the node's prefix. To fill in level i of the neighbor table, we look in the level-(i-1) list. For $j \in [0, b-1]$, we keep the closest $R(\alpha_{i-1}, j)$ nodes.

Due to the limitation of space, the proofs of correctness of the algorithms are omitted.

3. Fault-tolerant routing

The ability to detect, circumvent and recover from failures is a key goal for distributed collaborative system. Here we discuss approaches to operating efficiently while accounting for a multitude of failures. We address the issue of fault adaptivity by using soft state to maintain cached content for graceful fault recovery, rather than provide reliability guarantees for hard state. This is the *soft-state* or *announce/listen* approach first presented in IGMP [9] and clarified in the MBone Session Announcement Protocol [12]. Caches are updated by periodic refreshment messages, or purged based on the lack of them. This allows to handle faults as a normal part of its operations, rather than as a set of special case fault handlers.

Types of expected faults impacting routing include server outages (those due to high load and hardware/software failures), link failures (router hardware and software faults), and neighbor table corruption at the server. We quickly detect failures, operate under them, and recover router state when failures are repaired.

To detect link and server failures during normal operations, we can rely on TCP timeouts. Additionally, each RDLM node uses backpointers to send periodic heartbeats on UDP packets to nodes for which it is a neighbor. This is a simple "hello" message that asserts the message source is still a viable neighbor for routing. By checking the ID of each node a message arrives at, we can quickly detect faulty or corrupt neighbor tables.

For operation under faults, each entry in the neighbor map maintains two backup neighbors in addition to the closest/primary neighbor. Plaxton refers to these as secondary neighbors. When the primary neighbor ails, we turn to the alternate neighbors in order. In the absence of correlated failures, this provides fast witching with an overhead of a TCP timeout period.

Finally, we want to avoid costly reinsertions of recovered nodes after a failure has been repaired. When a node detects a neighbor to be unreachable, instead of removing its pointer, the node marks it invalid, and routes through an alternate. Since most node and link failures are discovered and repaired in a relatively short time period, we maintain a *second chance* period of reasonable length (e.g. a day) during which a stream of messages route to the failed server, serving as probe messages. Failed messages from that stream are then rerouted to the alternate path after a timeout. A successful message indicates the failure has been repaired, and the original route pointer is again marked valid. To control the probe traffic volume, we use a simple probability function to determine whether each packet routes to the original router, where the probability is a ratio of desired probe traffic rate to incoming traffic rate for this route. If the failure is not repaired in the second chance period, the neighbor is removed from the map, alternates promoted, and an additional sibling is found as the final alternate.

4 Evaluation and Performance Analysis

In this section, we present simulation results demonstrating the benefit of our object location mechanism and how it performs under adverse conditions. We can see that compared to replicated directory servers, RDLM based servers show graceful degradation in both throughput and response time as ambient network traffic increases.

In the experiments shown in Figures 3 and Figure 4, we compared a simplified RDLM location mechanism against a centralized directory server on a 100 node *ns-2* [3] TCP/IP simulation of a topology generated by GT-ITM. We simulated our resilient data and object location mechanism without the benefit of replication from hotspot managers or replicated roots, and assumed negligible lookup times at the directory servers.

In our experiments, we measured throughput and response time to a synthetic query load while artificially generating high background traffic from random paths across the network. The query load models web traffic and is mainly composed of serialized object requests, with 15% of requested objects receiving 90% of query traffic. The background traffic causes high packet loss rates at multiple routers. Because of the inherent replication along nodes between the server and the object root

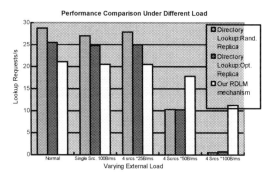

Fig. 3. Performance comparison under different loads

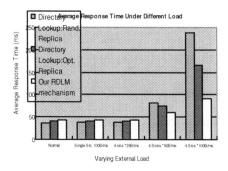

Fig. 4. Response time under packet loss

node, our solution responds to sporadic packet loss favorably with graceful performance degradation, as shown in Figures 3 and Figure 4. Centralized directory servers
become isolated as packet loss increases, and throughput and response time further
degrade due to TCP retransmissions and exponential backoffs.

5 Conclusion

In this paper, we presented a resilient data and object location and routing mechanism
(RDLM) for distributed collaborative environment. It is a self-organizing, scalable,
robust wide-area infrastructure that efficiently routes requests to content in the
presence of heavy load and network faults. While RDLM is similar to the Plaxton
distributed search technique, we have additional mechanisms that leverage soft state
information and provide self-administration, robustness, scalability, dynamic adaptation, and graceful degradation, while eliminating the need for global information and
improving root node vulnerabilities.

RDLM provides an ideal solution for dynamic wide-area object location and routing
that need to deliver messages to the closest copy of objects or services in a location
independent manner, using only point-to-point links without having centralized services,
which will contribute to wider application of large scale collaborative applications.

Acknowledgments. This paper is supported the National Natural Science Foundation of China (90612008); the National Basic Research Program of China (973 Program) (2005CB321905); Shanghai Science and Technology Committee Key Fundamental Research Project (05JC14006).

References

1. Awerbuch, B. and Peleg, D.: Concurrent online tracking of mobile users. Proc. of SIGCOMM 1991. Italy (1991) 221-233
2. Bolosky, W.J., Douceur, J.R., Ely, D. and Theimer, M.: Feasibility of a serverless distributed file system deployed on an existing set of desktop PCs. Proc. of ACM SIGMETRICS 2000. Santa Clara, CA (2000) 34-43
3. Bourgain, J.: On Lipschitz embedding of finite metric spaces in Hilbert space. Israel J. Math 52 (1985) 46-52
4. Castro, M., Druschel, P., Ganesh, A. and Rowstron, A.: Secure routing for structured peer-to-peer overlay networks. Proc. 5th Symposium on Operating Systems Design and Implementation (2002)
5. Clarke, I., Sandberg, O., Wiley, B. and Hong, T.W.: Freenet: A distributed anonymous information storage and retrieval system. Lecture Notes in Computer Science 2009 (2001) 46-66
6. Cowen, L.J.: Compact routing with minimum stretch. Proc. 10th Annual ACM-SIAM Symp. on Discrete Algorithms (1999) 255-260
7. Gavoille, C.: Routing in distributed networks: Overview and open problems. ACM SIGACT News - Distributed Comp Column 32 (1) (2001) 36-52
8. Gopal, B. and Manber, U.: Integrating content-based access mechanisms with hierarchical file systems. Proc. ACM OSDI (1999) 265-278
9. Karger, D. and Ruhl, M.: Find nearest neighbors in growth-restricted metrics. Proc. 34th Annual ACM Symp. on Theory of Comp. (2002) 741-750
10. Li, X. and Plaxton, C.G.: On name resolution in peer-to-peer networks. Proc. Second ACM International Workshop on Principles of Mobile Computing (2002) 82–89
11. Oram, A. (eds.): Peer-to-Peer, Harnessing the Power of Disruptive Technologies. O'Reilly Books (2001)
12. Peleg, D. and Upfal, E.: A tradeoff between size and efficiency for routing tables. Proc. 21th Annual ACM Symp. on Theory of Comp. (1989) 43–52
13. Plaxton, C.G., Rajaraman, R. and Richa, A.W.: Accessing nearby copies of replicated objects in a distributed environment. Proc. 9th Annual Symp. on Parallel Algorithms and Architectures (1997) 311–320
14. Rajaraman, R., Richa, A.W., Vöcking, B., and Vuppuluri, G.: A data tracking scheme for general networks. Proc. 13th Annual ACM Symposium on Parallel Algorithms and Architecture. Crete Island, Greece (2001) 247-254
15. Thorup, M. and Zwick, U.: Approximate Distance Oracles. Proc. 33rd Annual ACM Symp. on Theory of Comp. Hersonissos, Crete, Greece (2001) 183-192
16. Stoica, I., Morris, R., Karger, D., Kaashoek, M.F. and Balakrishnan, H.: Chord: A scalable peer-to-peer lookup service for internet applications. Proc. SIGCOMM (2001) 149-160
17. Zegura, E.W., Calvert, K. and Bhattacharjee, S.: How to model an internet work. Proc. IEEE INFOCOM. Vol. 2. San Francisco, CA (1996) 594-602

Heuristic Frequency Optimizing in GSM/GPRS Networks

Wen Ye, Lei Cheng, Hongxu Cui, and Ju Bu

School of Computer Science and Technology,
Beijing University of Posts and Telecommunications,
Beijing 100876, China
yewen@bupt.edu.cn

Abstract. As an important aspect in GSM/GPRS network optimizing, frequency optimizing is theoretically reduced to the channel assignment problem (CAP). This paper puts forward HFA, an engineering-oriented heuristic CAP algorithm that takes the assignment difficulty coefficient (ADC) and the call priority as heuristics for channel allocation. We introduce the concept of hotspot cells, which has higher priority in channel assignment, and elaborate the rules for calculating channel separations on the basis of radio propagation models and geographical information. HFA is verified by the 21-cell benchmark and has been used to optimize the GSM/GPRS networks in several cities of Liaoning Province. Suggestions are also presented on heuristic assignment of PN offsets in CDMA2000 systems and of scrambling codes in WCDMA systems.

1 Introduction

Frequency optimizing proves to be helpful for improving the utilization of radio spectrum, increasing network capacity and providing services of higher quality in GSM/GPRS networks. It has been an important aspect in network optimizing for *China Mobile* and *China Unicom*, two major mobile operators of China.

Frequency optimizing is theoretically reduced to the channel assignment problem (or CAP for short). CAP deals with allocating channels to the calls in cellular radio networks while satisfying channel reuse constraints, the calls in networks need channels to support their voice or data traffics.

In FDMA/TDMA mobile communication systems, such as GSM/GPRS networks, the term channel means a combination of a carrier frequency and a time slot. In this paper, we assume that all the time slots in a carrier frequency are allocated to the same cell so that a carrier frequency is treated as a channel. We use the words channel, frequency and carrier frequency interchangeably in the rest of this paper. The m channels are numbered 1, 2, . . ., and m with adjacent channels are given consecutive numbers, and denoted as $f_1, f_2, \ldots, f_m$. The channel separation between f_i and f_j is $|j - i|$.

Graph coloring [1-2], simulated annealing [3], neural networks [4-5] and genetic algorithms [6] are proposed to solve CAP. However, these methods are time-consuming to some extent and of higher computational complexities, and thus it is not feasible to apply these approaches to frequency optimizing in extensive GSM/GPRS networks.

W. Shen et al. (Eds.): CSCWD 2006, LNCS 4402, pp. 101–109, 2007.
© Springer-Verlag Berlin Heidelberg 2007

Heuristic CAP algorithms [7-10] are practical and popular approaches to frequency optimizing. The principle behind these algorithms is that channels are allocated to calls in accordance with some heuristics such as the assignment difficulty coefficient ADC in descending orders. However, these heuristic algorithms have some shortfalls when applied in practice. They do not consider priorities among different calls, though some calls may be more important than others in real networks. Moreover, it is difficult to decide the minimum channel separation between any pair of calls in different cells or within one cell. Minimum channel separations are a key point of these algorithms and determined by a variety of factors. Another issue to be addressed is that in practical cellular radio networks, the number of channels able to be distributed is not unlimited. Therefore, with respect to the aim of CAP, allocating a finite set of channels available to as many calls in cells as possible is more reasonable than allotting an unlimited number of channels to calls with minimum number of channels being assigned.

This paper introduces two concepts, the hotspot cell and the call priority, presents the methods for calculating channel separations and proposes an improved heuristic CAP algorithm HFA.

In Section 2, we present the Heuristic Frequency Assignment algorithm HFA, which is verified by the 21-cell benchmark in Section 3. In Section 4, we describe the application of HFA in GSM/GPRS network optimization in the City of Fushun of Liaoning Province. In Section 5, we discuss the heuristic assignment of PN offsets in CDMA2000 systems and of scrambling codes in WCDMA systems. Section 6 summarizes our contributions.

2 Heuristic Frequency Assignment Algorithm HFA

2.1 CAP Model

CAP involves allocating radio channels to the requested voice or data calls in cells. CAP should be subject to three kinds of constraints due to radio interferences, they are:

1. Co-channel reuse constraints, which means that the same channel should not be allocated to some pairs of cells simultaneously in order to avoid cofrequency interferences.
2. Adjacent channel reuse constraints, which means that adjacent frequencies should not be assigned to some pairs of cells simultaneously in order to avoid adjacent frequency interferences.
3. Co-site constraints, which means that for any pair of calls in the same cell, the separation of channels distributed to these two calls should not be lower than a limit.

In a cellular radio network with N cells, these constraints are represented as minimum channel separations between cells in the form of a $N \times N$ channel separation matrix $C=[c_{ij}]$, where $i, j \leq N$. An element $c_{ij} (i \neq j)$ indicates the minimum channel separation required between the channel assigned to a call in the ith cell and the channel assigned to another call in the jth cell; c_{ii} indicates the minimum separation between two channels that are allocated to any pair of calls in cell c_i.

Each cell demands some channels to support the voice or data calls in it. The channel demanding vector R=(r_i), $i \leqslant$ N, describes the channel demand of each cell in the networks, where r_i is the number of channels required by the calls in cell c_i.

Assuming that f_{ik} indicates that the kth channel is assigned to the ith cell, the channel separation constraints can be described as

$$f_{ik} - f_{jl} \geqslant c_{ij}, 1 \leqslant i, j \leq N, 1 \leq k \leqslant r_i 1 \leqslant l \leqslant r_j, (i, k) \neq (j, l).$$ (1)

Given matrix C and vector R, CAP is aimed to minimize the number of channels allocated to the cells under the channel separation constraints. CAP is known to be NP-complete [9].

2.2 Heuristic Frequency Assignment Algorithm HFA

Heuristic CAP algorithms allocate channels to calls in cells in accordance with some orders determined by heuristics.

HFA takes the assignment difficulty coefficient ADC and the call priority as ordering heuristics. The ADC associated with each call is the measurement of how hard it is to find a channel available for this call. The calls with higher ADC have priorities in channel assignment over other calls.

In practical GSM/GPRS networks, some cells are considered as hotspot cells, which may be the cells covering the areas in which government institutions are located, or the cells situated at downtown areas with heavier voice or data traffics. The calls in hotspot cells have higher call priorities and should be allocated channels prior to those in non-hotspot cells.

The idea of HFA is to take the call priority and ADC as heuristics to allocate channels available to calls in an iterative manner. At each iteration, HFA records all calls needed to be allocated in a data structure, named the call list, and sorts these calls at two levels. Firstly, HFA sorts these calls in accordance with their call priorities; then orders the calls of the same call priorities on the basis of the ADC; afterwards, under the constraints specified by matrix C, HFA distributes channels available to as many calls in the ordered call list as possible, according to the orders of these calls in the list.

The priority of each call is an application-specific parameter that is determined in advance and unchanged afterwards. The ADC of each call is initialized and adjusted as follows.

In the first iteration, on the basis of the column wise node-degree ordering [9], HFA defines the initial ADCs for the calls within cell ci as

$$d_i = [\sum_{j=1}^{n} r_j \times c_{ij}] - c_{ii}, 1 \leq i, j \leq N.$$ (2)

For the calls that fail to be allocated to channels in the current iteration, their ADCs are increased by a random number between 0 and 1, while for the other calls, their ADCs remain unchanged.

HFA describes CAP as a 6-tuple CAP (**X**, **H**, **C**, **R**, **P**, **F**) and finds a near-optimal solution as follows.

Input:

X={c_1, c_2,..., c_N}, the cells in the network, where N is the number of cells;

H={h_1, h_2, ..., h_k}, the set of hotspot cells, k < N;

C[N×N], the channel separation matrix;

R[N], the channel demanding vector;

P[m], the call priority vector, where m is the total number of the calls;

F={f_1, f_2,...f_M}, the set of channels available arranged in an ascending order;

Output:

CH={S_1, S_2,..., S_N}, where S_i is the channel sets allocated to cell c_i, $1 \leq i \leq N$.

Procedure:

1. Generate the call list according to **R**.
2. Initialize the ADC of each call in the list as is shown in (2).
3. Sort the calls in the list on the basis of their call priorities and ADCs. The call with higher priority and ADC is arranged nearer to the top of the call list.
4. Allocate channels in vector **F** to the calls in the sorted call list one by one, starting from the top of the list and by means of Frequency Exhaustive Strategy [7] that distributes to each call in the list the *least* possible channel without violating the channel separation constraints.
5. *If* each of the calls in the list has been allotted a channel or the number of iteraions so far reaches its up-bound,
   then output the solution **CH**, exit; *else* continue to step 6.
6. Adjust ADCs of the calls in the list. Go to step 3.

If the number of cells is N, the total number of calls, denoted as m, is

$$m = \sum_{i=1}^{n} r_i = r_A \times N ,$$ (3)

where r_i represents the channel demand of the ith cell, and r_A denotes the average channel demand of all cells. Given |**F**|, the number of channels available, HFA's time complexity is

$$O(m + |\mathbf{F}| + N^2 + m + a \times (m \times |\mathbf{F}| + m))$$

$$=O (N^2 + a \times m \times |\mathbf{F}|)$$ (4)

$$=O(N^2 + a \times r_A \times N \times |\mathbf{F}|) .$$

In GSM/GPRS networks, $r_A \leq 8$, |**F**| is a limited integer. Let b represent an integer that is extremely larger than N, then the time complexity turns to O ($N^2 + b \times N$).

2.3 Application-Specific Considerations

In the algorithms presented in [7-10], the number of channels available in the channel list F is assumed to be not limited. However, the radio channels that can be assigned to calls are limited in practical GSM/GPRS networks. For example, GSM/GPRS 900MHz network in China is specified for uplink operation in the 890~915 MHz band and 935~960 MHz for the downlink, with the channels numbered from 1 to 124.

Therefore, HFA should take as its aim allocating a finite set of channels to as many calls as possible under the channel separation constraints specified by matrix C. HFA evaluates the assignment results by *satisfied ratio*, the percentage of the calls having been distributed channels successfully.

Moreover, in practical GSM/GPRS networks, all the voice and data calls must be allocated the channels they required, though some interference constraints may not be satisfied. The goal of frequency planning and optimizing is to assign a limited number of frequency channels to all the calls in the networks while minimizing constraint violations. HFA can be employed at first to allot channels to as many calls as possible under the separation constraints specified in C; other methods such as constraint relaxation, frequency borrowing/adding and local frequency adjusting are then used to allocate channels to the calls to which HFA fails to assign the channels needed, at the cost of some separation constraints in C being violated.

The separation matrix **C** is the key information for frequency optimization. To calculate the matrix **C**, it is assumed that all the cells in the networks use only the same frequency channel and only co-frequency interferences are considered. For any pair of cells in the networks, the *Carrier to Interference Ratio* C/I between these two cells is calculated on the basis of radio propagation models and geographical information such as terrains along the propagation path between these two cells. This C/I is then transformed into the channel separation between these two cells in accordance with the following rules: (i) if C/I $\geq$ 9dB, the separation is zero; (ii) if -9dB $\leq$ C/I $\leq$ 9dB, the separation is 1 and (iii) if C/I $\leq$ -9dB, the separation is 2.

Furthermore, to prevent co-site interferences, channel separation between any pair of channels allocated to the calls in the same cell is set to 4 or 5 in matrix **C**. To avoid adjacent frequency interferences, the channel separation between any pair of channels allotted to the two calls in two different cells that belong to the same BTS is set to 1 or 2 in matrix **C**.

3 Verifications

The 21-cell cellular network [10] shown in Figure 1 is taken as a benchmark to evaluate HFA. For a cell in the network, the channel separations between this cell and its first-layer adjacent cells is 1, 2 or 3; the separations between this cell and its second-layer or third-layer cells is 1, and the separations between this cell and other cells is 0.

Table 2 illustrates a comparison between HFA and the algorithm in [7] in terms of their performance under different conditions. The co-site channel separation is denoted as A and the channel separation between adjacent cells as B. HFA1 represents the case in which cells 8, 9, 16 and 17 are selected as hotspot cells; and in HFA2, cells 7, 8, 15, 10, 11 and 18 are the hotspot cells. The call priority is 2 for the calls in hotspot cells, and 1 for the non-hotspot ones.

It is observed from Table 2 that the satisfied ratio of HFA decreases a little when hotspot cells are introduced. Hotspot cells impose more constraints on CAP and inevitably result in lower satisfied ratio. However, the performance degrading is not notable and HFA is more feasible to practical networks.

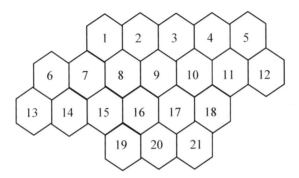

Fig. 1. 21-cell benchmark

Table 1. Channel demanding of cells

cell ID	1	2	3	4	5	6	7
channel demanded	8	25	8	8	8	15	18
cell ID	8	9	10	11	12	13	14
channel demanded	52	77	28	13	15	31	15
cell ID	15	16	17	18	19	20	21
channel demanded	36	57	28	8	10	13	8

Table 2. A comparison of different algorithms in terms of performance

A	B	channels available	satisfied ratio（%）		
			Box [7]	HFA 1	HFA 2
5	1	381	58.63	50.31	51.77
5	2	427	59.25	49.90	53.22
7	1	533	76.72	71.10	71.73

4 Applications in GSM/GPRS Network Optimization

HFA has been applied to frequency planning and optimizing in GSM/GPRS networks in Shenyang, Fushun and Jinzhou of Liaoning Province. Here is an example of optimizing of the GSM/GPRS network in Fushun.

Fushun is a city lying in hilly country and its average height above sea level is about 50m. *China Unicom* GSM/GPRS 900M/1800M network in Fushun covers an area of about 400 square kilometers, in which there exist 7 BSC, 133 BTS, 292 cells/sectors, 514 calls and 29 available channels (ARFCN between 96~124). Among these 514 calls, call priorities 3 and 4 are distributed to the voice calls in the hotspot cells covering the government institutions and several downtown areas, and 2 to the GPRS calls for data traffic in some other areas. Priority 1 is set to the voice and data calls in non-hotspot cells. The channel separation for co-site constraints is 4, and the separation for adjacent channel constraints is 2.

4.1 Frequency Planning

HFA has been used to plan the frequency assignment in the whole network. Out of all 514 calls in 292 cells/sectors, 451 calls are allocated the channels requested, accounting for about 87.8 percent, guaranteeing that no channel reuse constraints and co-site constraints among these 451 calls are violated.

For the calls that fail to be assigned the demanded channels in some local areas, local frequency adjusting is employed. Several channel reuse constraints are relaxed; frequency borrowing and adding are also applied.

By means of these three mechanisms, 29 frequency channels are distributed to each of all the 512 calls in the network, while minimizing the violations of channel reuse constraints and co-site constraints in the network as far as possible.

4.2 Local Frequency Adjusting

Driving tests revealed that there exist severe radio interferences in a downtown area of about 3 square kilometers is higher, because of the dense assignment of a set of frequency channels in the five cells within this area. There are 5 different BTS, 15 sectors and 24 calls in these five goal cells. The co-channel reuse constraint and adjacent channel reuse constraint are 4 and 2 separations respectively. 14 channels are available for the goal cells. In the old channel assignment scheme in Table 3, the channel 121 was allocated several times, resulting in higher co-frequency interferences among cell 2013, 2053, 2583, and 2643, hence the poorer call quality.

To improve the quality of the calls in these five goal cells, 5 idle channels are added into the set of channels available, some constraints are relaxed, and then HFA is re-applied to these goal cells to obtain the new assignment scheme.

In the new scheme, all the calls in these five cells are allocated the channels needed, and the channel separations among these cells are larger. Driving tests in the coverage area of these goal cells show that the co-frequency interferences among these cells are downgraded obviously, and the call quality improves.

Table 3. New vs old schemes of channel assignment

Cell	Channel needed	Old scheme		New scheme	
		BCCH	TRX	BCCH	TRX
2011	1	98		96	
2012	1	102		115	
2013	2	106	*121*	111	119
2051	1	98		115	
2052	2	102	117	101	111
2053	2	106	*121*	98	119
2581	1	97		96	
2582	2	101	117	109	115
2583	2	105	*121*	99	119
2641	1	96		96	
2642	2	100	117	115	124
2643	2	104	*121*	104	109
2721	2	109	113	96	101
2722	2	104	117	107	115
2723	1	107		119	

5 PN Offsets and Scrambling Code Assignment

Our work is aimed at GSM/GPRS networks, which are TDMA mobile communication systems. The principles and methods proposed in this paper can also be used for PN offset assignment in 3G CDMA2000 systems and scrambling allocation in 3G WCDMA systems [11].

In CDMA2000 networks, each cell or sector is allocated a unique short PN code that is called the pilot PN of this sector. Each pilot PN is distinguished by different time shift (or PN offset) and the sectors are identified uniquely by the offsets of the pilot PN associated with them. The number of pilot PN available is limited and less than 512, and in general, also less than the number of sectors in the network, so some sectors in the network may be distributed to the same pilot PN.

To avoid pilot confusion in CDMA2000 networks, allocation of PN offset to each sector depends on many factors, e.g. sector size and propagation delay of radio signals. At least three constraints must be guaranteed, i.e. (i) if two sectors are assigned the same pilot PN, these two sectors must be located away from each other in at least a particular distance called the pilot PN reuse distance, e.g. 64 PILOT INC/4.096 km, where PILOT INC is an engineering parameter whose value is often set as 4 or 6. (ii) if two sectors are geographically adjacent and have overlapping handoff areas, the phase difference between the pilot PNs allocated to these two sectors respectively must be larger than a particular parameter, i.e., the minimum pilot phase difference which is also related to PN INC. (iii) with respect to CDMA handoff, in the handoff area, the phase differences between the pilot PN associated with the primary serving sector and the pilot PNs associated with other candidate serving sectors should not be less than a low-bound.

To assign a finite set of PN offsets to sectors in a CDMA network under the three constraints mentioned above is somewhat homogeneous to frequency allocation in GSM/GPRS networks. This problem can be reduced to CAP and be solved in a heuristic manner similar to HFA proposed in Section 2.2. The assignment difficulty coefficient ADC associated with each sector is defined and used as the heuristics.

How to define and adjust ADC is a key point for a successful heuristic algorithm for pilot PN assignment. ADC depends on the sector size, the path loss of radio propagation, terrains in network coverage areas and search window parameters. Application-specific issues such as hotspot cells or sectors, partition of cell clusters and reuse patterns must also be taken into account in the algorithms.

In WCDMA systems, each sector is assigned and uniquely distinguished by a scrambling code set that consists of one primary scrambling code and 15 secondary scrambling codes. The number of scrambling code sets available in WCDMA networks is 512 and is usually much smaller than that of sectors in the networks. Allotting of same scrambling codes to different sectors may result in scrambling code confusion. Similarly, as to PN offset assignment in CDMA2000 networks, distribution of WCDMA scrambling codes can also be reduced to CAP and conducted in HFA-like heuristic and engineering-specific ways.

6 Conclusions

HFA is a practical and engineering-oriented heuristic solution to CAP and available to frequency planning and optimizing in GSM/GPRS networks. The concepts of the hotspot cell and the call priority are introduced. HFA has been applied to optimize *China Unicom* GSM/GPRS networks in several cities of Liaoning Province in China. Desirable results are obtained and the effectiveness of HFA is verified

There is still much to be done to improve HFA in the future. The performance of heuristic CAP algorithms depends heavily on how to pick up the heuristics for ordering the call list in optimum manners. HFA and other algorithms in [7-10] put emphasis on the adjustment of the assignment difficulty coefficients ADC. More efficient heuristic information for adjusting the ADC is expected and these heuristics should be more application-specific.

HFA cannot automatically partition cells into different clusters that adhere to the frequency reuse patterns for GSM/GPRS network. Only after goal cells are grouped into clusters can HFA be used to allocate channels to the calls in the clusters. Our future work will consider integrating of HFA with auto-partitioning of cells into clusters on the basis of radio channel interferences and geographical information.

Assignment of pilot PN in CDMA2000 systems and allocating of scrambling code in WCDMA system can also be conducted in heuristic and engineering-specific ways.

Acknowledgments. This project is supported by Innofund of Ministry of Science and Technology of the People's Republic of China (02C26211100479) and Co-sponsored Project of the Municipal Commission of Education of Beijing (SYS100130422).

References

1. Sun, C.-W., Wong, W.-S.: A graph theoretic approach to the channel assignment problem in cellular systems. Proc. 45th IEEE Veh. Technol. Conf. Vol. 2. Chicago (1995) 604-608
2. Even, G., Lotker, Z., Ron, D., Smorodinsky, S.: Conflict-free colorings of simple geometric regions with applications to frequency assignment in cellular networks. Proc. FOCS'02. Vancouver, Canada (2002) 691-700
3. Duque-Antón, M., Kunz, D., Rüber, B.: Channel assignment for cellular radio using simulated annealing. IEEE Trans. Veh. Technol. 42 (1993) 14-21
4. Funabiki, N., Takefuji, Y.: A neural network parallel algorithm for channel assignment problems in cellular radio networks. IEEE Trans. Veh. Technol. 41 (1992) 430-437
5. Alabau, M., Idoumghar, L., Schott, R.: New hybrid genetic algorithms for the frequency assignment problem. IEEE Trans. on Broadcasting 48 (2002) 27-34
6. Ghosh, S.C., Sinha, B.P., Das, N.: Channel assignment using genetic algorithm based on geometric symmetry. IEEE Trans. Veh. Technol. 52 (2003) 860-875
7. Box, F.: A heuristic technique for assigning frequencies to mobile radio nets. IEEE Trans. Veh. Technol. 27 (1978) 57-64
8. Thavarajah, A., Lam, W.H.: A heuristic algorithm for channel assignment in cellular mobile systems. Proc. 48th IEEE Veh. Technol. Conf. Vol. 3. Ottawa, Canada (1998) 1690-1694
9. Sivarajan, K.N., McEliece, R.J., Ketchum, J.W.: Channel assignment in cellular radio. Proc. 39th IEEE Veh. Technol. Conf. Vol. 2. San Francisco, CA (1989) 846–850
10. Gamst, A.: Some lower bounds for a class of frequency assignment problem. IEEE Trans. Veh. Technol. 35 (1986) 8–14
11. Laiho, J., Wacker, A., Novosad, T.: Radio Network Planning and Optimization for UMTS (in Chinese). Publishing House of Electronics Industry, Beijing (2004)

Unexpected Exceptions Handling Based on Chinese Question Answering in Collaborative Design

Feng Tian, Renhou Li, Bo Chen, Jiao Ding, and Qinghua Zheng

School of Electronics and Information Engineering, Xi'an JiaoTong University,
Xi'an, ShaanXi Province, P.R. China, 710049
phdfengtian@yahoo.com.cn

Abstract. It has been difficult to handle unexpected exceptions in collaborative design. The expert system based method is extensively used, but it seems mission impossible not to loss some information when storing the expert experience in structured format, and to interact friendly in natural language. Aiming at these, we proposed a knowledge acquisition based approach for unexpected exceptions handling in collaborative design, which enable design engineer to define an exception using natural language, and make expert experience stored in natural language which is zero information loss. In this paper, two methods for mining similar records are proposed, and the performance comparison is shown that our approach is more efficient, extendable and precise.

1 Introduction

Computer Supported Collaborative Design (CSCD) is one of main applications of computer supported collaborative works (CSCW) in engineering design and also one of the core technology of concurrent engineering which providing an environment for collaborative works in enterprise product development. Collaborative design is a group-oriented method with its own characteristics such as group decision-making, document-centered, time-critical, knowledge centered and multi-disciplines involved, therefore researches on exception handling is a hot but difficult topic.

Presently, many collaborative process management systems adopted workflow technology, but research on exceptions handling and evolution of workflow systems are still under investigation. According to the classification of exceptions in workflow systems, exceptions in collaborative design can be classified as Expected Collaboration Exceptions (ECE) and Unexpected Collaboration Exceptions (UCE) [1]. In multiagent systems [1], change is regarded as exceptions to predefined rules. An expected exception can be represented in a predefined agent model or reference, therefore an exception handling agent can capture a deviation from the normal or desired course of events. An unexpected exception is caused by a deviation in the system domain that was not anticipated at modelling time. Moreover, causes of Unexpected Collaboration Exceptions (UCE) are much more difficult to be detected, such as unavailable design results, conflicts within designs, this implies that methods for auto-detecting UCE causes has not been found in available literatures yet, and UCE is handled manually by experts now. However expert experience is always individualistic in nature and

W. Shen et al. (Eds.): CSCWD 2006, LNCS 4402, pp. 110–117, 2007.
© Springer-Verlag Berlin Heidelberg 2007

cannot be easily shared. In additional, it's difficult to store expert experience in structured format without losing some potential helpful information. Hwang [2] mined exception instances to facilitate unexpected exceptions handling in workflow with incorporation of the notion of concept hierarchy, which can only process the formatted data stored in database. Tian et al. [1] suggested that a solution of an exception can be directed by using algorithm of similarity-match based on knowledge, in which expert experience is not clearly present and hard to understand. Both the methods presented in [1] and [2] lose some information during storing data, and need more knowledge about techniques of expert system and machine learning, so that these methods are hard to be used.

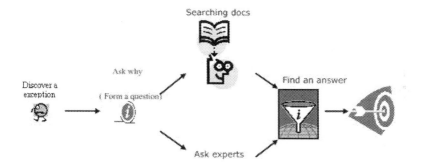

Fig. 1. A normal process of unexpected exceptions handling

In general, shown in Figure 1, a normal process of handling UCE by an expert follows two steps: 1) a question in natural language is formed in a designer's brain according to characteristics of an unexpected exception when detected. 2) According to the question, a set of most likely records is pinpointed from related resources or available experience. So, it is helpful that unexpected exceptions can be handled by a human-like way of thinking and solving problems in our system. Moreover, instances and expert experience of exception handling are described by causality type sentence stored in unformatted text. Obviously, it is helpful to "understand" and use expert experience and Internet resources stored in real natural language. In addition, it is beneficial that technicians and engineers can interact friendly with a system by using natural language, because natural language is user-friendly for engineers, technicians and designers. So a process of unexpected exception handling is quite similar to a question answering system, especially similar to a causality-type one. Based on this idea, combining Natural Language Processing with Information Retrieval, we proposed a Chinese question answering mechanism for handling UCE.

This paper is organized as follows. The first section introduces the previous work and motivation on exception handling in collaborative works. Related works is introduced in Section 2. Section 3 describes our system configuration, flow and approach.

Experiments on retrieval of most likely related exception handling records are shown in Section 4, while this paper is concluded in Section 5.

2   Related Work

Information Retrieval (IR) techniques have been proven quite successful in locating within large collections of documents that are relevant to a user's query. Combining Nature Language Processing (NLP) technology with machine learning technology, question answering technique, which is a typical applications of IR and extensively used to solve many related problems.

Recently, Sosnin [3] introduced question answering mechanism into collaborative works to control and provide design process with suitable information, but not involving exception handling. Aberg [4] used question answering system for knowledge management in personal assistant application, but only English language was supported.

Since Chinese question answering system has just been developed recently and Chinese language has many specific characteristics, the approaches are quite different from that studied and proposed to deal with Western language by researchers. Furthermore, some systems [5-7], for example The Webclopedia [5], support the search based on natural language. The Webclopedia supports English language processing, Chinese is still unsupported now. Huang [7] developed a Chinese question answering system, which emphasized on the problem of solving Chinese text document retrieval and may not suitable for exception handling of causality-type in collaborative works.

3   System Configuration, Flow and Approach

3.1   System Configuration

Our system consists of a case base of exception handling, Internet resources (downloaded from internet), a module of syntax analysis, a library of domain terms and feature attributes, a module of feature matching, a input and an output module for exception handling. The system configuration is shown in Figure 2.

3.2   Flow of UCE Handling

Once an unexpected exception occurred, a designer who discovered it describes the phenomenon and input them into the module of exception description by a question in real language. Combining with the library of domain terms and features, the module of syntax analysis abstracts the syntax, domain range, topic, feature attributes of the exception description, and forms a query understandable for computer. Then after using module of feature matching to retrieve the exception handling case base stored in form of natural language according to the query, a set of most likely records is obtained to direct the locating and handling of this exception.

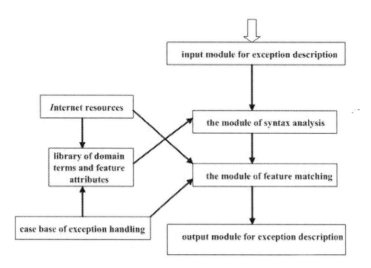

Fig. 2. System configuration

3.3 Module of Syntax Analysis

As we observed it, once an unexpected exception occurred, causality-type questions in natural language is used to enquire experts or search in documents. Causality-type questions always show the style, such as "what", "what is the reason that…".

Natural questions contain interrogative words. Four Chinese interrogative words: "why", "who", "where", "how" are defined. Each interrogative words has a set of words, such as "what", "why" etc, which are of the same meaning. Some co-occurrence patterns and characteristic words in given questions may also reflect the target intention of these questions. Characteristic words are a content part of sentences and co-occurrence patterns are often several concurrent Chinese characters. All of those characteristics are the clues for classifying the question type.

The steps of identifying the question type are as follows: first, to make a shallow parsing based on the words appearing in an original query, including word segmentation and part of speech (POS) tag; second, to identify the question type according to interrogative words. If the given sentence lacks of interrogative word, turn to next step; third, to judge whether co-occurrence patterns exist or not, because co-occurrence patterns are greatly helpful to identify the question type quickly. If the given sentence still lacks of co-occurrence pattern, it just turns to the next step; at last characteristic words and their subsequent words' POS tags will give us some hints to identify the question type.

Therefore, we can analyze a question to know the "real" intention of an exception query, and form a formatted query that most approximate to the intention.

3.4 Extracting Domain Terms and Feature Attributes

Another important problem is to extract feature attributes from the formatted query. Before doing this, a library of domain terms must be built.

Collaborative design is knowledge-central and crossing-discipline. This introduces an important problem that is how to identify a term among different disciplines.

In this paper, a rule-based approach for acquiring key words and thesaurus from the resources downloaded from the web is adopted to build discipline-oriented term library, which give a support for extracting feature attributes. This approach is introduced in [8].

After building the library of domain terms, it is easy to select feature attributes from an exception cause query. What we need to do is that, combining the result of parsing module with the context of domain knowledge involved (discipline, major, topic, etc, seen the detailed in [1]), the rule-based approach is adopted, in which feature attributes are selected from the exception description by Chinese syntax, such as subject, object, attribute and phase.

3.5 Methods for Matching Similar Records

After obtaining the special discipline, major, topic and feature attributes, methods for matching similar records from case base of exception handling and resources downloaded from Internet must be introduced. At present, there are three kinds of IR approaches: 1) statistical (learning) approaches; 2) symbolic (rule- and representation-based) approaches; 3) the mixture ones. Two kinds of approaches, a rule-based and a mixture one, were executed in our system.

Matching similar records has two steps: classifying and pinpointing. The first step is to classify the corpus into causality type or non-causality type, and mark them. The latter is to pinpoint a set of the most likely answers from the marked resource. In our rule-based approach, rule-based method are adopt in the both steps. While, in our mixture approach, a machine learning method and a rule-based method are adopted in the first step and the second step respectively. According to the characteristic of Chinese semantics and syntax, the rule-based method adopted in the second step is the same in both approaches. In rule based approach, the rule based method in the second step is improved from that of the first step by only adding position of speech tag and features words. So, the details of the first step in our system are described in the followings.

A rule-based approach in first step. After analyzing Chinese syntax and ten thousand corpora, a rule-based approach is proposed, in which causality-type question, causality-type statement, first statement in a paragraph and paper title are the key features or clues of describing the causes and solution of exceptions.

So, nine important rules as followings are concluded as follows:

[Rule 1] search causality-type interrogative words, such as "why", "what", "what is the reason that…".

[Rule 2] search result-type words, such as "so", "so as to", "so that".

[Rule 3] search reason-type words that appear after the result, such as "this is because…", "the reason is …", "this is due to".

[Rule 4] search the causality-type phase at same statement, such as "… is caused by …", "… is triggered by …".

[Rule 5] search the causality-type phases appear before results, such as "because", "due to".

[Rule 6] search the result-type combined phases appear at the start and end of a statement, such as "…is the reason that …".

[Rule 7] search the main statement from a paragraph.

[Rule 8] search paper's titles.

[Rule 9] search the causality-type questions that appear at the end of a paragraph.

Using those rules, the exception handling record in natural languages can be analyzed literally in order to match similar records to direct our solution of exception.

A machine learning approach in first step. A machine learning based approach is adopted by the first step of the mixture approach in our system and has three steps: feature analysis, feature abstraction and exception features matching.

The analyzed objects are the same as the rule-based approach: causality-type question, causality-type statement, first statement in a paragraph and paper title, etc. After analyzing the feature of exception handling records in natural language, the feature classification can be concluded as follows:

[Feature 1] one includes causality-type words.

[Feature 2] one includes causality-type phases.

[Feature 3] causality-type feature words composed by two words.

[Feature 4] causality-type feature words composed by three words.

[Feature 5] causality semantic relation combined interpunction with combined phases.

[Feature 6] causality relation among paragraphs.

After determining the features to be extracted, those features are represented by a vector includes 103 dimensions, in which each dimension express a feature with 1(if exist) or 0 (if not exist).

Then after combining attributes extracted by syntax analysis module with statement feature classified by using above features, a set of similar records can be mined from labeled exception handling records. In our system, a perception-based method for mining similar records is introduced in the machine learning based method.

3.6 Exception Location and Exception Handling

After obtaining the mined similar records set, solution of exception is directed. This process is the same as the method in [1].

3.7 An Example

Suppose that an exception occurred that the design of locating a window in a fireproofing wall is not permitted. A natural question "why does locating a window in a fireproofing wall during designing high buildings violate a routine" is inputted to our system by the designer. Then after analysis, the real intention of user is obtained, such as, the topic is high building design, the key attributes are "fireproofing wall" and "locating a window". After mining the documents about law and case base of exception handling, a history record and a national standard rule, the declaration that locating a window in a fireproof wall is forbidden are obtained. So the designer changes the window's location according to the rule. This is our way of helping unexpected exception handling in our system. A screenshot of our system is shown in Figure 3.

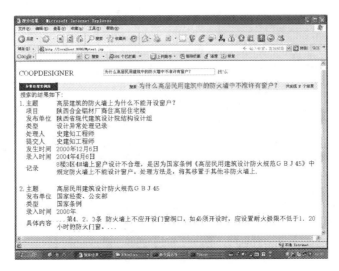

Fig. 3. A screenshot of an interface of an unexpected exception handling in our system

4   Experiments and Discussion

4.1   Experiments

Ten thousands labeled corpora (downloaded from Internet and exception handling history log obtained from ShaanXi Modern Architecture Design Institute) are collected and stored into database as training and testing data set. Two approaches are used and compared. The performance comparison is shown in Table 1.

Table 1. Performance comparison of two approaches

Methods	Precision	Recall	Accuracy
Rule-based	0. 3977	0. 7975	0. 7695
Perception-based	0.8677	0.8868	0.901

4.2   Discussion

As shown in Table 1, it is obvious that the perception-based approach has better performance, higher precision and recall value than that of the rule-based method. Although the rule-based approach is easy to be done, its precision is lower and its extendibility is worse than the perception-based method. The reason for such lower precision is that it is difficult to collect rules for every situation. Based on 103 features, their statistical information, semantic information and the weights of related features, the perception-based method considered synthetically those factors to reduce the serious missing or error. Moreover, some causality sentences are without the rule-like feature, in which situation the feature can be easily identified by the perception based method. In addition, from the view of system maintenance and performance, each rule must program a specific validation procedure, that is, more rules are discovered and added, more programming works are carried out, while the perception based method only extend the feature vector and re-train the perception. So the latter is prospective.

Moreover, Huang [7] declared that average precision and average recall value in their system is about 86% and71% respectively. It is clear that the average recall of our results is better, and even the size of our corpora is larger than theirs.

5 Conclusion

In this paper, an approach for unexpected exceptions handling based on Chinese question answering is proposed in collaborative design. Especially, two methods for mining similar records are introduced. Initial results are discussed.

At present, because it takes two minutes to feedback the searching results (all the code is programmed in Java), there is still many work to improve its efficiency. In the future, the size of term dictionary needs to be expanded and new approaches for pinpointing a set of most likely answers need to be developed. Also, we need to apply our method to other practical cases.

Acknowledgments. This project is supported by the National Natural Science Foundation of China (60373105, 60473136), the Doctoral Program Foundation of the China Ministry of Education (20040698028), the Program of National Tackle Key Problem (2005BA115A01), the Youth Science Foundation of School of Electronics and Information Engineering and Natural Science Foundation of Xi'an Jiaotong University.

References

1. Tian, F., Li, R.: A Multi-agent based Approach for Exception Handling in CSCD. Proc. 9th International Conference on CSCWD. Xiamen, China (2004) 297-302
2. Hwang, S., Ho, S., Tang, J.: Mining Exception Instances to Facilitate Workflow Exceptions Handling. Proc. 6th Int. Conf. on Database Systems for Advanced Applications. Hsinchu, Taiwan (1999) 45-52
3. Sosnin, P.I.: Question-answer processor for cooperative work in human-computer environment. Proc. 2nd Int. IEEE Conf. on Intelligent Systems. Varna, Bulgaria (2004) 452-456
4. Aberg, J., Shahmehri, N.: Collection and exploitation of expert knowledge in Web assistant system. Proc. 34th Annual Hawaii Int. Conf. on System Sciences. Hawaii (2001) 1-10
5. URL: http://www.isi.edu/natural-language/projects/webclopedia /description.html
6. URL: http://trec.nist.gov
7. Huang, G., Yao H.: A system for Chinese question answering. Proc. IEEE/WIC Int. Conf. on Web Intelligence. Halifax, Canada (2003) 458-461
8. Sun, X., Zheng, Q., Wang, Z., Zhang, S.: A Method of special Domain Lexicon Construction based on Raw materials. Mini-Micro Systems (6)(2005) 1088-1092

An Efficient Cooperative Design Framework for SOC On-Chip Communication Architecture System-Level Design

Yawen Niu, Jinian Bian, Haili Wang, and Kun Tong

Department of Computer Science and Technology, Tsinghua University,
Beijing 100084, China
nyw_0629@163.com, bianjn@tsinghua.edu.cn,
{whl01, tk02}@mails.tsinghua.edu.cn

Abstract. In this paper an efficient cooperative design framework is proposed to help SOC designers to construct their desired application-specific communication architectures. The proposed framework makes contributions as follows: (1) it outlines an approach of model refinement from one level of abstraction down to another closer to implementation; (2) it is particularly suitable for complex systems which consist of hundreds of processing elements (PEs) because it adopts a "divide-and-conquer" approach and provides the On-Chip Communication Architecture constructing method for PEs with compatible and incompatible protocols; (3) it can achieve a fine trade-off between system performance and implementation cost through a multi-objectives cost function taking into account of bus widths, bus load, cost for arbitration logic and transducers. The correctness and effectiveness of the method is evaluated through an illustrative JPEG decoder application.

1 Introduction

In order to handle the ever increasing complexity and time-to-market pressures in the design of System-On-Chips (SOCs), the design has been raised to the system level to increase productivity [1]. Meanwhile, Intellectual Property (IP) based design is becoming the dominant design paradigm with the advent of the SOC era. Under this paradigm, the verified system specification is first mapped onto a certain set of pre-design IPs. Then, the SOC designer's task is to construct a communication network and corresponding glue logic to interconnect these IPs to achieve efficient communication performance [2]. Therefore, with the shift from "computation-bound design" to "communication-bound design" [3], in modern distributed embedded systems, especially in real-time applications such as imaging processing, communication performance determined by the quality of interface and the throughput of communication interconnection among various components is often the main bottleneck of the system performance. As the design of efficient communication structures is a time-consuming and error-prone process, system designers rely more and more on sound cooperative design framework and EDA tools.

As a key problem in cooperative system design, automated communication architecture design has received a large body of work. In [2], Hu et al. present a point-to-point

W. Shen et al. (Eds.): CSCWD 2006, LNCS 4402, pp. 118–127, 2007.
© Springer-Verlag Berlin Heidelberg 2007

(P2P) communication synthesis method for SOCs. They take Communication Task Graph (CTG) and IP sizes as input and automatically synthesize a P2P communication network. In [4], Cyr G. et al. propose a complete SOC design method that allows flexibility and rapid integration of communication mechanism by using a standard communication protocol, the VSIA's Virtual Components Interface. The method achieves a good compromise between the two well-known approaches: platform-based and IP assembly. Renner Michael et al. [5] aim at the automated communication synthesis for architecture-precise rapid prototyping of real-time embedded systems. They emulated the complete hardware/software system as an architecture-precise prototype on a real-time platform to verify the derived communication architecture as well as the hardware/software partitioning. Gasteier et al. [6] implemented automatic generation of communication topologies for embedded systems scheduled statically. Given a behavior specification composed of processes that communicate with each other via abstract send and receive functions, a cost-efficient communication topology with one or more buses but no arbitration scheme can be set up for such applications. In [7], Cai and Gajski introduced a design flow and related algorithms to execute the channel mapping for complex systems containing multi-PEs with incompatible communication protocols.

Compared to the above classical approaches of communication synthesis, this paper makes contributions as follows:

1) It outlines the overall cooperative system design framework from the system specification to the OCAs construction. Under the guidance of the proposed framework, SOC designers can synthesis the desired application-specific communication resource by the approach of model refinement from one level of abstraction down to another closer to implementation.

2) It is most suitable for complex systems which contain hundreds of PEs. Through a "divide-and-conquer" approach, it divides all the PEs into multi-clusters according to their communication protocols, and presents the OCAs construction method within cluster and among clusters respectively to deal with both compatible and incompatible communication protocols.

3) It is driven by a multi-objectives cost function which takes into account bus widths, bus load, cost for arbitration logic and transducers to realize a fine trade-off between system delay and implementation cost.

The remainder of this paper is organized as follows. Section 2 presents the system design framework and proposes the related communication synthesis algorithms to automate the key steps. In Section 3, the JPEG decoder application is illustrated to evaluate the correctness and effectiveness of our method. The overall design flow of the framework is demonstrated by this application. Finally, the conclusion is drawn in Section 4.

2   Proposed Design Framework

In this section, we mainly introduce the proposed design framework and related exploration algorithms for the key steps to help designers automate the OCAs construction process. Three common approaches for SOC design are proposed in [8]. To raise the level of system abstraction and provide much design flexibility, we adopt the "synthesis from specification" approach that follows a top-down exploration process.

2.1 System Design Flow

The proposed system design flow is shown in Figure 1. Taking the embedded system specification as input, designers can step by step refine the system model from one level of abstraction down to another closer to implementation.

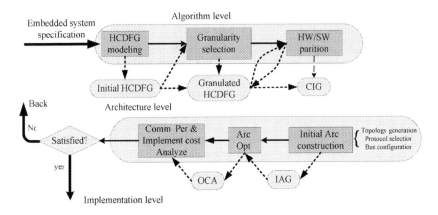

Fig. 1. System design flow

To automate the design process, four inter-models are presented: 1) HCDFG (Hierarchical Control Data Flow Graph [9]) 2) CIG (Communication Information Graph [10]) 3) IAG (Initial Architecture Graph) 4) OCA (output). HCDFG is a golden inter-representation model for embedded system specification. It can be modeled at different granularity level which will result in different design accuracy and exploration time. Designers should choose the proper granularity through the step granularity selection. Taking the granulated HCDFG as input, the HW/SW partition step determines the amount and types of PEs to implement the system, and maps the functions/procedures in the functional model onto selected PEs. Analyzing the partition result, CIG model can be generated through the approach described in [10].

CIG model is the output of the algorithm design level and also the input of the architecture level. In the executive architecture level, the inter-processes communication using abstract send and receive functions in the specification should be replaced by physical communication structure. Figure 2 gives a typical example using the global FIFO communication link to realize the abstract send and receive functions between SW/SW (SW/HW, HW/HW). The wrapper implements the separation of communication and computation.

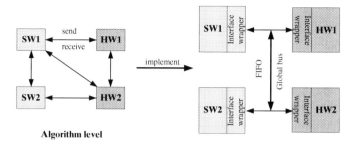

Fig. 2. Use global bus to implement the abstract send and receive functions

To explore and evaluate a great amount of architecture solutions to construct a high performance communication structure, we divide the communication synthesis process into two steps: initial architecture construction and architecture optimization. Initial architecture construction process is to construct the IAG model based on the analysis of CIG. It consists of three sub-steps: interconnection topology generation, communication link protocol selection and bus parameter configuration. Interconnection topology generation is to determine the proper topology structure to interconnect communication resources, while communication link protocol selection and bus parameter configuration are to determine the communication protocol and bus width for each bus (as shown in Figure 3, the rhombuses represents transducer to implement the communication between PEs with incompatible protocols).

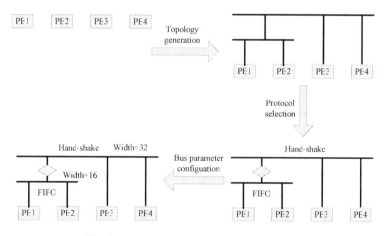

Fig. 3. Initial architecture construction process

As for complex SOC containing hundreds of PEs, the constructed communication structure should consist of complicated hierarchical buses. To improve the system performance and decrease the implementation cost for such applications, the architecture optimization process is introduced. This step aims to adjust the IAG structure to balance the bus load among communication links. Finally, designers should evaluate the optimized OCA to confirm if the solution can satisfy the system constrains and determine whether to go to the implementation level or return back to the proper pre-steps.

2.2 OCAs Construction Approach

As we have discussed the HCDFG and CIG modeling approaches in our previous work [9-10], this section mainly focuses on the architecture level design method taking the CIG as input.

As we know, a complex SOC may contain hundreds of PEs with compatible/incompatible communication protocols. Since transducers should be inserted to implement the communication between incompatible communication protocols, which will greatly increase the data transfer time and also the implementation cost, we take the "divide-and-conquer" approach to deal with such applications in order that we can keep the smallest amount of transducers. First, all the PEs are divided into n clusters according to the PEs protocol compatibility, ensuring that all the PEs in the same cluster have the compatible protocols, while any two PEs in different cluster have incompatible communication protocols. For each cluster, we present the OWC (OCAs within the same cluster) algorithm to construct communication architecture for PEs with compatible protocols. Then, based on the construction result of each cluster, the OAC (OCAs among clusters) algorithm is provided to design the OCAs among clusters with the consideration of incompatible communication protocols. The entire OCAs construction process is shown in Figure 4. Both the OWC and OAC algorithms consist of IAG construction and the OCAs optimization processes.

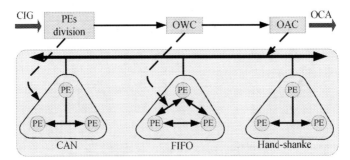

Fig. 4. OCAs construction flow

2.3 OWC Algorithm

OWC algorithm is to construct the OCA within each divided cluster, respectively. In order to achieve a fine compromise between system performance and implementation cost, a multi-objectives cost function taking into account bus widths, probability of bus collision and cost for arbitration logic is constructed in (1).

$$f(solution) = \alpha * \max_{\forall bus_i \in solution} (\sum_{\forall c_j \in bus_i} T(c_j)) + \sum_{bus_i \in solution} Width(bus_i) + n_a * AreaA \qquad (1)$$

The first item in the cost function is to evaluate the system performance. Because the total communication performance is usually dominated by the slowest communication link within the system [6], we evaluate the system performance by the traffic of the bus mapped onto the most data transfers. $T(C_j)$ returns the data transfer times of channel C_j mapped onto bus_i. The second and third items are used to evaluate the system area. $Width(bus_i)$ returns the bit width required by bus_i. Accumulating the bit width of all the buses used gives us an estimation of the required bus area. n_a is the amount of bus arbiters used in the system. When a bus is mapped to more than one channel, a bus arbiter should be inserted. Each arbiter increases the area by $AreaA$. The compromise between performance and area can be controlled by the parameter α.

To prune the exploration solution space, a topology tree is used to represent the generated architecture. The leaf nodes of the tree represent the PEs and the hierarchical nodes represent the buses. Based on the cost function in (1), OWC algorithm first introduces a cluster process to construct IAG, as shown in Figure 5.

```
1  cluser_tree = Initial_tree();
2  Protocl(root) = Protol(v_i);
3  Width(root) = max_data_exchange(v_i, v_j);(∀v_i, v_j ∈ V)
4  cost_current = cost(cluster_tree);
5  Repeat
6      cost_temp_ij = cost_merge(v_i, v_j); (∀v_i, v_j ∈ V)
7      cost_temp = cost_min(cost_temp_ij)
8      if(cost_temp < cost_current)
9          temp_protocol = Protocol(v_i);
10         temp_width=data_change(v_i, v_j);
11         root->remove(v_i);
12         root->remove(v_j);
13         root->addnode(v_i);
14         Protocol(v_i) = temp_protol;
15         Width(v_i) = max{temp_width,
                                 max_data_exchange(v_i, v_j)}:
16         Width(root) = max_data_exchange(v_i, v_j);
17         cost_current=cost_temp;
18         Improved=true;
19     else
20         Improved=false;
21     end if;
22  Until Improved=flase;
```

Fig. 5. OWC algorithm

The OWC algorithm integrates the three processes of interconnection topology generation, communication link protocol selection and bus parameter configuration. It starts from an initial solution of global bus architecture, and then adjusts it by iteratively merging two child clusters. Child cluster means the direct child node of the root. Each child cluster can be a PE or a hierarchical cluster representing bus. At each iteration of clusters merging, the two child clusters that can maximally decrease the cost function are selected to merge, and an additional cluster is generated as their father node. When merging two child clusters, we choose the maximum bit width of the data to be transferred through the merged bus as its bit width so that each data transfer can be finished in one transfer time, and the protocol of either merged clusters as its bus protocol. After each cluster iteration, the bus width of the root should be reconfigured. Until no further decrease can be gained by merging any two child clusters, the cluster algorithm stops. After the clustering process, the optimization process that we proposed in [11] is introduced to adjust the IAG structure through the analysis of bus load, which may enhance the system performance and decrease the implementation cost.

2.4 OAC Algorithm

OAC Algorithm is to construct the OCAs among clusters with the consideration of incompatible communication protocols on the basis of the OWC output. In OAC algorithm, all the n input clusters have incompatible protocols with each other. Taking transducers into account, the cost function of the OAC algorithms can be computed in (2).

$$f(solution) = \alpha * \max_{\forall bus_i \in solution} (\sum_{\forall c_j \in bus_i} (T(c_j)(1 + \beta * n_{c_j}))) + \sum_{bus_i \in solution} Width(bus_i) + n_a * AreaA + n_t * AreaT \qquad (2)$$

n_{Cj} represents the amount of transducers which channel C_j goes through. β is the weight factor to adjust the performance influence by transducers. n_t is the total number of transducers needed. Each transducer is assumed to consume area $AreaT$.

The main distinction between the OWC and the OAC algorithms is the different bus protocol selection strategies. In the OAC algorithms, we select the bus protocol that can minimize the cost function in (2) from the n PE protocols as the initial global bus protocol solution (different from Line 2 in Figure 5). Therefore, n-1 transducers are inserted between the global bus and the clusters with incompatible protocols at first. When clustering two child clusters v_i and v_j, we choose the protocol of the root node as the protocol of the generated cluster (different from Line 9 in Figure 5). By this way, we can ensure that no more transducers are inserted so that we can keep the smallest amount of transducers. As the same as OWC, the optimization process can also be applied in OAC algorithms to optimize the IAG structure.

3 Experiment: JPEG Decoder Application

To illustrate the effectiveness of the proposed design framework, we apply it to a JPEG decoder application. A typical JPEG decoder design flow is illustrated in Figure 6. The three main processes in the JPEG decoder are Inverse Discrete Cosine Transform (IDCT), Inverse Quantization (IQuantization), and Huffman Decoding (HDecoding).

In algorithm level, we model the application in C specification containing 13 inter-communicating functions: main (MP), InitiaLize (IL), MakeBmpHeader (MB),

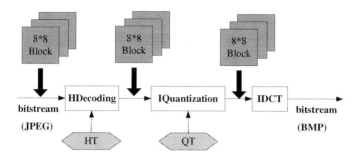

Fig. 6. A typical JPEG decoder flow

Decode (DP), DecodeMCUBlock (DM), HufBlock (HB), DecodeElement (DE), IQTZMCU (IM), IQTZBlock (IB), IDCTInt (II), IDCT(ID), GetYUV (GY) and SaveBmp (SB). According to the system design flow, we first choose functional granularity to model the system specification in HCDFG format (as shown in Figure 7, only the operation nodes are kept for simplicity).

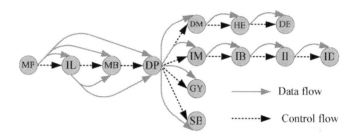

Fig. 7. HCDFG of the JPEG decoder application

Based on the functional granulated HCDFG, the 13 functions should be partitioned and mapped onto proper PEs. From our preliminary analysis on the JPEG decoder, the IDCT (Inverse DCT) transformation is intensive computation and consumes about 70% of the overall software execution time on average. To improve the total system performance, we map the processes II and ID which perform the IDCT operation onto hardware implementation. As for the other functions, we map each of them onto a separate PE. In addition, we map all the variables onto a global memory to simplify the variable-memory mapping process. The mapping result can be shown in Table 1. We also assumed that each PE has a fixed protocol.

According to the partition and mapping results, CIG (Figure 8) can be derived through the approach we proposed in [10]. Based on CIG model, the OCAs construction approach provided in Section 2 are applied to construct the optimized communication architecture (Figure 9, arbitration logic is omitted for simplicity).

Table 1. Mapping result, PE type, PE protocol

PE type	PE protocol	PE name	Func. name	PE type	PE protocol	PE name	Func. name
uP	ColdFire	MP	main	DSP	ColdFire	IM	IqtzMcu
IP	ColdFire	IL	InitianLize	DSP	FIFO	IB	IqtzBlock
IP	ColdFire	MB	MakeBmp	ASIC	Hand-shanke	IDCT	IDCTInt
IP	ColdFire	DP	DecodeProc				IDCT
IP	ColdFire	DM	DecodeMcu	ASIC	Hand-shanke	GY	GetYuv
IP	FIFO	HB	HufBlock	ASIC	Hand-shanke	SB	SaveBmp
DSP	FIFO	DE	DecodeElement	MEM	FIFO	GM	Global variable

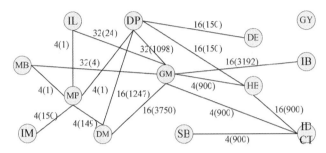

Fig. 8. CIG of the JPEG decoder application

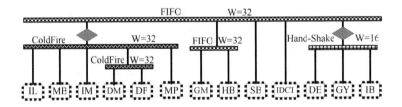

Fig. 9. OCA of the JPEG decoder application

4 Conclusion

In this paper, we presented an efficient cooperative design framework to assist designers to construct the optimized OCAs following the approach of model refinement from one level of abstraction down to another closer to implementation. Besides, we also provided the communication synthesis algorithms to automate the key steps of topology generation, communication link protocol selection and bus parameter configuration. The framework aims at dealing with complex embedded system containing hundreds of components with incompatible communication protocols. Under its guidance, designers can automatically synthesize the desired application-specific communication architectures following the top-down design flow from the very beginning, system specification. The experimental results of the JPEG decoder application demonstrate the correctness and effectiveness of method.

Acknowledgments. This work is supported by National Nature Science Foundation of China under grant numbers 90207017 and 60236020.

References

1. Lukai, C., Gajski, D.: Grouping-Based Architecture Exploration of System-Level Design. Technical Report ICS-TR-00-03. University of California, Irvine (2002)
2. Jingcao, H., Yangdong, D., Radu, M.: System-Level Point-to-Point Communication Synthesis Using Floorplanning Information. Proceedings of the 15th IEEE International Conference on VLSI Design (2002) 573-579
3. Mai, R., Horowitz, M.: The future of wire. Proceedings of the IEEE (2001) 490-504
4. Cyr, G., Bois, G., Aboulhamid, M.: Generation of processor interface for SOC using standard communication protocol. IEE Proc.-Comput. Digit. Tech (2004) 367-376
5. Renner, F. M., Becker, J., Glesner, M.: Automated Communication Synthesis for Architecture-precise Rapid Prototyping of Real-Time Embedded Systems. Proceedings of the 11th IEEE International Workshop on Rapid System Prototyping (2000) 154-159
6. Gasteier, M., Munch, M., Glesner, M.: Generation of interconnection topologies for communication synthesis. Proceedings of the Conference on Design, Automation and Test in Europe. Paris, France (1998) 36-43
7. Lukai, C., Gajski, D.: Channel Mapping in System Level Design. Technical Report ICS-TR-00-03. University of California, Irvine (2003)
8. Gajski, D., Zhu, J., Domer, R., Gerstlauer, A., Zhao, S.: SpecC: Specification language and Methodology. Kluwer Academic Publishers (2000)
9. Qiang, W., Jinian, B.: A Hierarchical CDFG as Intermediate Representation for Hardware/Software Co-design. Proceedings of the International Conference on Communications, Circuits and Systems (2002) 1429-1432
10. Yawen, N., Jinian, B., Haili, W.: CGEM: A Communication Graph Extraction Method Based on HCDFG for Channel Mapping in System Level Design. Proceedings of International Conference on Computer Aided Industrial Design and Conceptual Design (2005) 696-701
11. Yawen, N., Jinian, B., Haili, W., Kun, T., Liang, Z.: SLCAO: An Effective System Level Communication Architectures Optimization Method for System-on-Chips. Proceedings of 6th International Conference on ASIC. Shanghai, China (2005) 114-117

Scenario-Based Design Knowledge Acquiring and Modeling in Collaborative Product Design

Hao Tan and Jianghong Zhao

State Key Laboratory of Advanced Design and Manufacture for Vehicle Body,
Hunan University, 410082 Changsha, China
hao.tan@163.com, zhaomak@126.com

Abstract Collaborative product design is a typical complex problem-solving process where designers' knowledge and expertise are always tactic and implicit. This paper depicts the concept of design scenario and the scenario-based design knowledge acquiring in a cognitive approach. Through a cognitive experiment based on protocol analysis and sketch analysis in terms of scenario-based collaborative product design, a model of scenario-based knowledge acquiring in product design is proposed. The model includes two types of spontaneous design knowledge acquiring method - concept-driven knowledge acquiring and data-driven knowledge acquiring, which indicates that design knowledge acquiring is a process of scenario moving. On the basis of the model, a scenario-based computer aided product design system CBID is developed to improve the ability and quality of collaborative product design of seven Chinese corporations.

1 Introduction

Product design is a problem-solving process where designer's knowledge and expertise are employed. However, design knowledge and expertise are always tactic and implicit; and even experienced designers cannot be clear what kind of expertise they use in designing and how [1-2]. This has been one of the major problems in the design community, especially in collaborative product design.

Meanwhile, case-based reasoning (CBR) is a research paradigm that uses design cases for solving a new problem from previous design experience by analogical reasoning [3-5]. From knowledge representation and problem-solving patterns, case-based reasoning is very similar to the cognitive processing and thinking model in product design [6-8]. In CBR, knowledge representation ties to a scenario or context and records knowledge in an operational level, which can represent tactic and implicit knowledge effectively and be fit for a collaborative design environment.

This paper aims to examine the design scenario, design knowledge and a scenario-based cognitive model of knowledge acquiring in product design and builds a computer aided collaborative product design system. In the following sections, the concept of design scenario and design knowledge is introduced. Then, from a cognitive design experiment and its analysis, this paper presents a model of knowledge acquiring in scenario-based product design and the application—CBID, a scenario-based computer aided collaborative design system.

W. Shen et al. (Eds.): CSCWD 2006, LNCS 4402, pp. 128–138, 2007.
© Springer-Verlag Berlin Heidelberg 2007

2 Design Knowledge and Design Scenario

2.1 Design Knowledge

Modern design is based on design knowledge, which is considered as the knowledge of building product [9]. Product design is a process of knowledge transformation from the interpreted initial state into the requirement-matching state or goal state [10]. In the initial state, design knowledge is retained in the heads of collaborative designers [11] and represents as implicit design knowledge such as a fluid mix of designer's experience, value and intuition. And in the goal state, design knowledge is retained in design solution (product) and represents as explicit design knowledge such as the product function, structures, and so on. The two states produce a product knowledge transformation cycle in which design knowledge is used to create products; products and their usage are evaluated to build design knowledge, as shown in Figure 1. From knowledge transformation, the implicit design knowledge changes to explicit and the designer's experience, value and intuition change to product function, structures, etc.

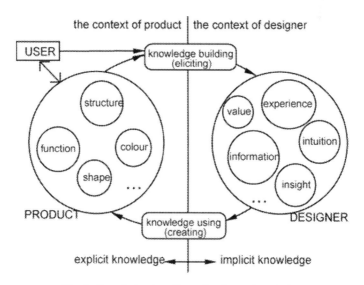

Fig. 1. Knowledge transformation in product design

2.2 Design Scenario

The concept of "design scenario" has been proposed in the field of situated cognition studies, which assume that a better understanding of design involves the study of designers and their environments as integrated systems [12]. The term "design scenario" has multiple meanings, which we can relate systematically by a framework of three levels commonly used to describe design knowledge: background, implicit and explicit. The three levels of scenarios are considered as the three stages of problem solving: problem scenario, solving scenario and solution scenario. The first level of design scenario is problem scenario that emphasizes design problem and the other contextual and restricted knowledge. Problem scenario is the starting state of the design process, and in which design knowledge represents as background knowledge. The second level is solving scenario and relates design cognition to a design process which is a transition from problem to solution and represents as a procedural scenario. Design solving knowledge is a typical implicit knowledge and the means or methods to achieve design solution and the set of reasoning steps to solving design problem are main parts of design knowledge in the scenario. And the third level is solution scenario that focuses on design solution, which includes product function, structure mechanism and other physical coordinates and represents as explicit design knowledge. Therefore, a design scenario is the part of the world or context which a product and design process are exposed to, interacts with them and as a consequence causes a change in the product or process.

In case-based reasoning, design scenarios build up cases, which are considered as a carrier of implicit and explicit design knowledge from the three levels. While designing, designers acquire knowledge from design cases or design scenarios, and analogy from the old cases to a new one. At the same time, design knowledge transforms from an inner state to an outer state.

3   A Scenario-Based Knowledge Acquiring Cognitive Experiment

The purpose of the experiment was to understand the knowledge acquiring methods and process in scenario-based collaborative product design.

3.1   The Design Problem

Designers (subjects) were requested to design a typical industrial product—numerical control machine tools (NC machine tools) in the experiment. About 1500 NC machine tools cases were available to designers and the subjects finish the form design and the arrangement of doors, windows, handles and display-control panels.

3.2   Methods

Protocol analysis and sketch analysis were used to investigate the cognitive actions of the subjects.

Protocol analysis is a major technique to examine cognitive process in psychology and design studies [13-14]. In the protocol analysis, subjects were asked to report concurrently what was going on in their minds. Meanwhile, the whole design process was also recorded by video/audio to gain more detailed information. Protocol analysis can describe design, knowledge acquiring processes and the contents of what designers see, attend to, think of and retrieve while designing.

Sketch analysis is a macroscopic method to study designers' sketches. And there are many analysis strategies to analyze the sketches [15-16]. In the experiment, sketch analysis was adopted to identify the design knowledge and its transformation model in a collaborative product design by sketch similarity analysis.

3.3 The Process

There were two stages in the experiment: the first stage held in Hunan University China and the second stage held in 7 key NC machine tools corporations in China. There were 15 designers with at least 5 years experience on NC machine tools design participated in the experiment as subjects [17]. A warm-up session was given to all subjects for familiarizing the experiment process. Then subjects were asked to finish a design of NC machine tools with another designer. The information about the NC machine tools was explained to all subjects before the design. Video/audio recorders recorded the whole process of the experiment. After the subjects finished the design task, they were asked to fill up a questionnaire as the retrospective supplement of the protocol reports.

3.4 The Analysis

In the experiment analysis, protocol reports were coded and analyzed. Firstly, as a scheme for coding designers' protocol reports [18], the level of abstraction of design problem was coded and a six point scale, 0 to 5, was adopted to represent the levels of problem abstraction from system problem to detail problem and design basic require-ments. Secondly, the design scenarios, knowledge acquiring methods (design strategy) and the design objects were investigated in different design stage. Table 1 shows some outcome of the protocol report coding. Sketch analysis focused on the similarity be-tween the chosen case and the final design. Figure 2 is a 5-point similarity scale built to evaluate the similarity. The similarity level represents the situation of knowledge transformation.

Table 1. Protocol analysis of a designer (part). CO=Consulting External Information, PS=Proposing a Solution, EV=Evaluating a design, AN=Analyzing a Proposed Solution, Sca=Scale, Out=Outline.

No.	Levels of problem abstraction	Design strategy	Design objects	Protocol report description
15	3	PS	Out	Drawing the outline from top view.
16	2	EV	Out	Evaluate the outline, and be not very satisfied.
17	2	CO	Out	Consider the reason of dissatisfaction.
18	3	AN	Sca	Analysis the width of the NC machine tools.
19	0	CO	Out	Search new case to meet width.

Fig. 2. 5-point similarity scale

By analysis of the level of abstraction of design problem domain and the design strategy in protocol reports coding table, the experimental analysis or experiment is found that the design knowledge acquiring is a process of moving from one scenario to another or from one case to another. Two types of spontaneous design knowledge acquiring methods in product design: concept-driven acquiring and data-driven acquiring were identified. In concept-driven knowledge acquiring, design knowledge is acquired to define the source-target problem domain and make the implicit design problems explicitly, while in data-driven reasoning, design knowledge is used to solve the detailed design problems only in target problem domain. Table 2 illustrates the differences of concept-driven and data-driven in terms of the level of design problem, the cognitive patterns, the strategies of knowledge acquiring and the knowledge attribute.

Table 2. Differences between the two methods of knowledge acquiring

	Concept-driven	Data-driven
Level of Problem	System	Detail
Cognitive patterns	Top-down	Bottom-up
Strategy of knowledge acquiring	Explore knowledge	Directly gain knowledge
Knowledge attribute	Implicit	Explicit

4   A Model of Scenario-Based Knowledge Acquiring in Collaborative Product Design

From the design experiment analysis, the theory of collaborative design and the research in case-based reasoning [19], the study develops a model of knowledge acquiring in scenario-based product design, which includes design knowledge scenario model and scenario-based knowledge acquiring in collaborative product design.

4.1   Design Knowledge Scenario Model

Design knowledge scenario model as shown in Figure 3 is a hierarchical network which includes three basic scenarios: problem scenario, solving scenario and solution scenario. Each basic scenario includes different nodes which represent the structure of the scenario as index-value pairs. Meanwhile, a design case is composed of the corresponding nodes in the hierarchy of the design scenario. That is to say a design case is represented by the corresponding nodes of the three levels of design knowledge scenario. Figure 3 also shows that a design case is problem-solving process which is indexed with the problem scenario, solving scenario and solution scenario. Therefore, by design scenario, knowledge can be retained in design cases and be acquired by designers easily.

Design problem scenario consists of design goals and constraints defined by statements – usually a design brief. From the experiment, a design problem index has been

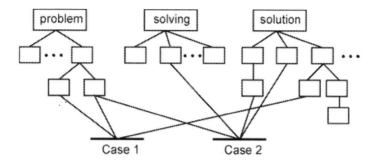

Fig. 3. Design knowledge scenarios

constructed and the membership [16] between the index and the design problem description has been gained by semantic computing [17], some examples are shown in Table3. Design problem index and its membership build up design problem scenario.

Table 3. Some of the membership value of design problem index with the design problem description (NC Machine Tools: N084B)

Design problem index	Problem-description(statements):N084B Display-control panels are the left of the door. A big and wide window which can be easy to open and observe. Pay much attention to the bottom of the door which should be easy to maintain.
Production	0.00
Maintain	0.79
Ergonomics	0.67
Layouts	0.47

Design solving scenario is a kind of procedural design knowledge scenario and it can be considered as pairs of verb and noun which can represent procedural knowledge well. Verb illustrates the reasoning process and noun is the object of designing. As the level of innovation, three verbs are defined in the study, which are "keep", "modify" and "create" from the design problem description that means copy outcome, adapting methods and create products. From the protocol analysis(see Table 1), 13 nouns were defined as design objects, which are colour, style, shape, position, function, PP (process planning), etc.. Design solving scenario can be defined as a matching matrix. For example, a NC machine tools design solving can be represents as below:

$$Cv = \begin{cases} Cv_{1n_1} & Cv_{1n_2} & Cv_{1n_3} & ... & Cv_{1n(j-1)} & Cv_{1n_j} \\ Cv_{2n_1} & Cv_{2n_2} & Cv_{2n_3} & ... & Cv_{2n(j-1)} & Cv_{2n_j} \\ Cv_{3n_1} & Cv_{3n_2} & Cv_{3n_3} & ... & Cv_{2n(j-1)} & Cv_{3n_j} \end{cases} \tag{1}$$

Where rowCv represents verb, colCv represents noun.

Design solution scenario is a carrier of explicit knowledge, which is a description of design outcome and consists of function attributes and physical attributes.

Function attributes can be seen as one abstract representation of physical attribute.

A design solution includes different functions. Functions can be represented as the decomposition of function and the logic connection in functions, as shown following:

```
Function
 Factors: [M] // the serial number of function
 Description :{
          DF_father:[ System Function]
          DF_son:[Sub-function k]
 //decomposing of function
          LF_M [be caused by]
          LF_K [be reinforced with]
 // logic connection in functions
          }
```

Physical attributes representation is a representation of the final form, shape, structure etc. which can be simplified as geometric description. As shown in Figure 4, a CNC lathe left outline can be represented as 9 points $(S_1, S_2, \ldots, S_7, S_a, S_b)$ and their position and attribution.

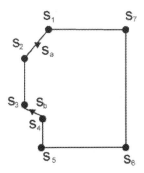

Fig. 4. Physical attribute representation of a CNC lathe's left outline

4.2 Design Knowledge Acquiring

Design knowledge acquiring is a process of scenario moving and the most matching scenario can be found by contrasting and comparing the similarity of the two scenarios that new knowledge are acquired or generated by analogy with the most matching scenario. The scenario-based knowledge acquiring includes the two types of spontaneous design knowledge acquiring method: concept-driven knowledge acquiring and data-driven knowledge acquiring, as shown in Figure 5.

Concept-driven knowledge acquiring starts at a problem scenario. When the designer faces a new problem P_n, he/she can input the problem and find a similar case problem Pi by computing the membership matrix (see Table 3), till the function:

$$\frac{\mu_{pn}(f_n)}{\mu_{pc}(f_c)} \xrightarrow{\text{max}} 1 \tag{2}$$

Where $\mu_{pn}(f_n)$ is the membership value matrix of P_n and $\mu_{pi}(f_i)$ is the membership value matrix of P_i.

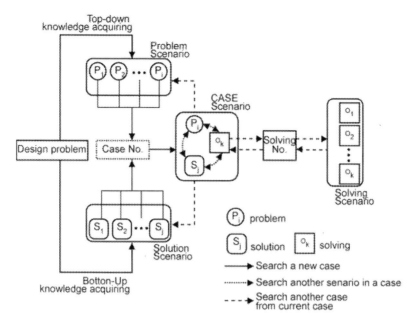

Fig. 5. Scenario-based design knowledge acquiring

Data-driven knowledge acquiring starts at a problem solution. According the designer's expectation of the design solution, he/she can find the most matching design solution and its function attributes and physical attributes. The arithmetic of similarity is showed as Eq. (3).

$$sim = \sqrt{\sum_{j \in I} |\frac{S_j}{S_n}|^2} \qquad (3)$$

Where *sim* is the similarity of cases, S_i is physical and function attributes factors of a case in database and S_n is the desired ones.

The two types of design knowledge acquiring methods can gain the most matching past design scenario and gain the most matching design case. And designers can find the other scenario in the design case such as solving scenario and gain more detailed knowledge.

But the carrier of a design scenario is limited and in collaborative product design, the designer always uses knowledge from different scenarios of other cases. Therefore, even finding the most matching design scenario or case, he/she can still acquire knowledge in other design case and the different scenario to help finish the design task, which is from one case scenario to another (see Figure 5).

5   CBID – An Application Case

On the basis of model of scenario-based knowledge and acquiring in product design and the theory of case-based reasoning, a scenario-based computer aided product

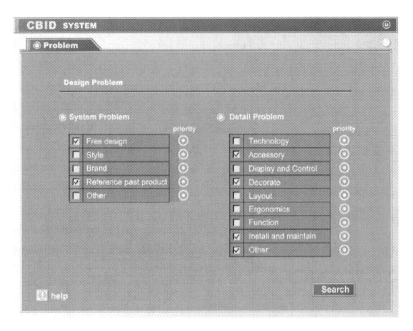

Fig. 6. Problem index in CBID

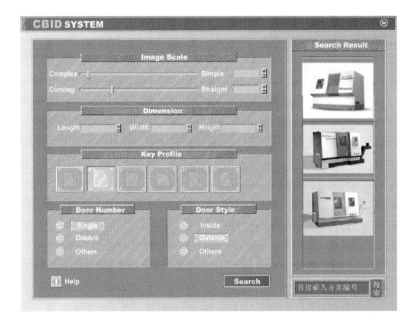

Fig. 7. Solution index in CBID

Fig. 8. A design expression of CK1440 NC machine tool

design system – CBID was developed. There are 4 functional modules in CBID: index, reuse, modify and retain according to the process of case-based design. Two knowledge acquiring methods – problem index (concept-driven) and solution index (data-driven) are applied in index module of CBID (Figure 6 and Figure 7). Designer can index the most matching design scenario and gain the reasonable case while using CBID. And in the reuse, modify module, designer can acquire more detailed knowledge such as design solving knowledge and the design scenarios of other design cases by re-index from the current design case or scenario, which help designer finish the whole design works. If designers finish their works, a build-in submission tool can be used in retain module. Designers can download the data and save data in the database of the system as a new case.

CBID has been adopted in seven key NC machine tools corporations in China and improved the ability and quality of product design of these corporations. Figure 8 is one of the design expressions by using CBID.

6 Conclusion

The paper discusses the scenario-based design knowledge acquiring and application in collaborative product design. From the cognitive experiment, the scenarios and two types of spontaneous design knowledge acquiring methods - concept-driven and data-driven - were identified and a model of scenario-based knowledge and acquiring in product design is proposed. The results of this study indicate that scenario-based design knowledge acquiring is a reasonable way to acquire and accumulate design knowledge and solve the design problem, which could be a phenomenon that can be implicated in other non-rule-based problem solving processes.

However, the arithmetic of knowledge acquiring in product design is not the same as the one in the engineering domain. For example, the reusability of previous design cases is enhanced in terms of inspiring a new design ideas based on the design strategy and knowledge-acquiring model. More researches are needed in the field of design knowledge representation and the arithmetic of knowledge acquiring in the product design domain.

Acknowledgement. This research is supported by the National Basic Research Program of China (Grant No. 2004CB719401) and Key Project of National Science Foundation of China (Grant No. 60635020).

References

1. Owen, C.L.: Design research: building the knowledge base. Design Studies 1(19)(1998) 9-20
2. Tan, H. and Zhao, J.: Knowledge-Based Design Innovation: A Method to Generate New Knowledge in Design. Proceeding of 7th Generative Art Conference GA2004. Italy (2004) 65-67
3. Maher, M.L. and Pu, P.: Issues and Applications of Case-Based Reasoning in Design. Lawrence Erlbaum Associates, New Jersey (1997)
4. Kolodner, J.: Case-based reasoning. Morgan Kaufmann, Los Altos, USA (1993)
5. Ling, W., Yan, J., Wang, J. and Xie, Y.: Case Based Conceptual Design. Chinese Journal of Mechanical Engineering 17(1)(2004) 73-77
6. Zhao J.: The meanings of design. Hunan University Press, China (2005)
7. Heylughen, A. and Neuckermans, H.: A case base of Case-Based Design tools for architecture. Computer Aided Design (33)(2001) 1111-1122
8. Pal, S.K. and Shiu, S.: Foundations of Soft Case-Based Reasoning. Wiley-InterScience Publication, New York (2004)
9. Sakol, T. and Keiichi, S.: Object-Mediated User Knowledge Elicitation Method. Proceedings of the 5th Asian International Design Research Conference. Seoul, Korea (2001) 45-48
10. Tan, H. and Zhao, J.: Knowledge Transformation in Conceptual Design: An Approach to Build a Model of CAID Knowledge System. Proceeding of De Identite Conference, Italy (2004) 32-36
11. Wallace, K.: Capturing, storing and retrieving design knowledge in a distributed environment. Proceedings of the 9th International Conference on CSCWD. Xiamen, China (2004) 1-10
12. Chiu M.L.: Design moves in situated design with case-based reasoning. Design Studies 24(2003) 1-25
13. Ericsson and Simon: Protocol Analysis (Revised Edition). MIT press, Massachusetts (1993)
14. Gero, J. S. and NeillKey, T. M.: An approach to the analysis of design protocols. Design Studies 19(1998) 21–61
15. Kavakli, M. and Gero, J. S.: The structure of concurrent cognitive actions: a case study on novice and expert designers. Design Studies 23(2002) 25–40
16. Hsiao, S.W. and Chou, J.R.: A creativity-based design process for innovative product design. International Journal of Industrial Ergonomics 34(2004) 421–443
17. Myers, A. and Hansen, C.: Experimental Psychology (3rd Edition). Brooks/Cole Publishing Company, CA (1992)
18. Suwa, M., Purcell, T. and Gero, J.: Macroscopic analysis of design processes based on a scheme for coding designers' cognitive actions. Design Studies 19(1998) 455–483
19. Aamodt, A. and Plaza, E.: Case-Based Reasoning: Foundational Issues, Methodological Variations, and System Approaches. AI Communications 7(1994) 39-59

A Framework for Sketch-Based Cooperative Design

Wei Jiang and Zhengxing Sun

State Key Lab for Novel Software Technology, Nanjing University,
Nanjing 210093, P.R. China
szx@nju.edu.cn

Abstract. This paper presents an application framework for constructing sketch-based cooperative design (especially for distributed conceptual design) tools. Three key issues are addressed: (1) how to represent and store sketch document; (2) how does the system infer the designers' intention and help them to complete the design process; (3) how to implement the communication between the client and the server. Solutions to these problems are proposed in this paper. The framework has been implemented and tested on a variety of applications, for example, cooperative UML diagram design. The primary experiments demonstrate the efficiency of the proposed framework.

1 Introduction

Conceptual design is the early stage of a product design process, which focuses on creation and innovation. During this stage, ideas are uncertain and unfinished, and designers do not need to consider too much about the detail. The designers need to find possible solutions as soon as possible, and they produced many sketch documents to communicate with self or others [1]. Sketching is a natural input modality, which helps designers in conveying ideas and guides their thinking process by aiding short-term memory and helping to make abstract problems more concrete [2]. However, conventional CAD tools usually require complete, concrete and precise definitions of the geometry information, which is only available at the end of the design process. Therefore, they are not fit for the conceptual design process in which a great many of sketch documents are generated [2].

Complicated conceptual design usually involves geographically distributed participants. Currently, such kind of design process relies on some conventional synchronized media like audio and video, and some other asynchronous tools such as E-mail. However, these tools do not support the participants to simultaneously create, modify, or view a shared design model in the form of freehand sketch with other participants of the design team.

This study investigates sketching as the input modality in distributed cooperative design, while cooperative designers sketch out their ideas in their own user interfaces and coordinate with each other through a cooperative design server. As a result, distributed designers can exchange ideas in a sketch form in a virtual design environment.

In this study, we have proposed an application framework for sketch-based cooperative design systems. Three fundamental problems arise in developing the framework: (1) How to represent and store the sketch documents, which are produced

W. Shen et al. (Eds.): CSCWD 2006, LNCS 4402, pp. 139–148, 2007.
© Springer-Verlag Berlin Heidelberg 2007

by a design team? (2) How does the system know designers' intention and help them to accomplish the design tasks without any interruptions? (3) How to implement the communication between the client and the server?

The solutions to these problems are proposed in this paper. For the first problem, an XML-formatted layered sketch document format is used to represent freehand sketch documents. For the second problem, we have built a sketch recognizer in the application framework, which uses a primitive-based sketch recognition algorithm to recognize the designer's input and gives useful guidance to the designer. For the third problem, we used hybrid system architecture and an event-based model to facilitate the communication.

The rest of the paper is organized as follows. First, we describe some related works on sketch-based user interface both in single-user and multi-user applications. Next, we address the application framework and discuss the key issues mentioned above in detail. Then we describe the implementation of the framework and an experimental prototype for cooperative UML class diagram design. Finally, we make a conclusion and identify some future directions.

2   Related Work

Sketch-based user interface draws a lot of attention in the past decades. A number of academic prototypes and commercial products have been developed. Alvarado [3] proposed ASSIST which uses sketch-based interface to support mechanism design. Hong and Landay [4] developed SATIN, which is a toolkit to support the creation of pen-based applications. Landay and Myers [5] introduced an interactive sketching tool called SILK, which helps designer to sketch out user interfaces. Most of current works on sketch-based user interface focus on sketch recognition and most of them are designed for single-user use. In our previous study, a sketch-based graphics input system for conceptual design, named magicsketch [2], has been developed. A set of sketch recognition methods have also been proposed, especially for complicated sketch recognition (based on Spatial Relationship Graph [6], Sketch Parameterization [7], Dynamic Programming [8] and Dynamic user modeling [9]) and user adaptation (based on Support Vector Machine [10], Hidden Markov Model [11] and Bayesian Networks [12]).

To date, a few works have introduced freehand sketching in cooperative design. NetSketch [13] is a sketch-based application, which supports cooperative conceptual design. However, there is a limitation of the graphical shapes that can be created in sketch. Furthermore, NetSketch uses a peer-to-peer network topology and cannot guarantee the consistency among all users. Zhe et al. [14] describe a sketch-based interface for collaborative 3D conceptual design. Using the Web-based system, designers can rapidly and easily create, and edit a 3D design geometric model. Their work focuses on 3D geometric modeling and simulation. However, different works focus on their own requirements. Research in this field is still emerging and there are no mature models and standards at hand. Most of current researches just support a few simple freehand shapes and only a few design works can be done by sketch. Therefore, the sketch-based cooperative design tasks in real world require broader capabilities than are provided by most of current available applications.

3   Sketch-Based Cooperative Design

Before a cooperative design session starts, distributed participants connect to a fixed server and then start a new drawing session. Then they begin to draw sketches on their own user interfaces as they do on physical paper. The server side controls the design team to work smoothly and effectively. This section presents an overview of the application framework and some key issues.

3.1   Framework Overview

The framework is based on Client/Server model. There are mainly three kinds of architectural alternatives for constructing CSCW system: centralized approach, replicated approach, and hybrid approach. We use a hybrid approach, which benefits from both centralized and replicated approach. Each participant contains a copy of the whole design document that is to be collaborated on. Therefore the network traffic is reduced and the designer can work effectively without be interrupted by network communication. The server side uses a central control process for synchronization and for mediating users' potentially conflicting requests.

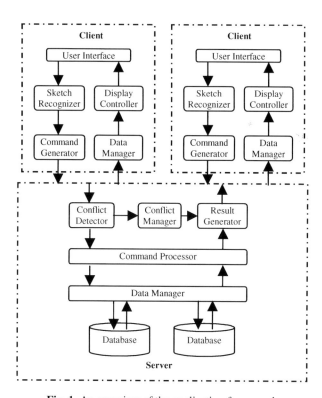

Fig. 1. An overview of the application framework

Figure 1 is the functional diagram of the application framework. As we can see from this figure, a client side is composed of five modules: UI (user interface), sketch recognizer, command generator, data manager and display controller. UI contains a draw panel for the designer to draw and view sketches. Sketch recognizer recognizes the designer's input. It is a fast and simple approach to identify multi-stroke geometric shapes, which will be described later. Once the inputting sketch is recognized, the command generator will generate a proper command and send the command to the server side. The data manager module retains the latest local design data (maybe different from the latest sketch data in the server side) and provides the basic functions on the sketch data (such as add stroke). The server responds the user's command and returns the result to the client side. Then data manager updates local sketch data. Finally, the display controller displays the latest modification according to the results. The display controller also supports different view for different designer, which is very helpful for cooperative design work since different designers may in charge of different parts.

The server architecture is also shown in Figure 1. It also contains five modules: conflict detector, conflict manager, command processor, data manager and result generator. At first, the command sent by a client side is dispatched to the conflict detector. The conflict detector parses the command and determines the objects to be operated and the designer's intention. Then it looks up current designer's privilege and the state of the objects and decides whether the command is legal. If the command is an illegal one, which means it may lead confliction; the conflict manager module will process the command and return results to result generator module. In the other way, if the client user's command is a legal one, the command processor will execute it (add new objects or make some modifications use data manager module). The data manager in server side is similar to the one in the client side. However, it retains the latest design data. Finally, the result generator generates the result and sends the result to proper client side(s).

3.2 Sketch Document

As we mentioned in the first section, while using sketch-based interface in cooperative design systems, a fundamental problem is how to represent sketch data. Recently, ink-based document format draws lots of attention in both academics and industries, and several standards have been proposed, such as JOT [15], UNIPEN [16] and InkML [17]. Although these standards are very capable for storing ink-based data, they cannot be applied into CSCD system directly. A designer cares about both the low-level raw sketch data (such as points in a graphical shape) and the high-level semantics (such as what a sketch represents and what components it contains). As a result, we proposed a layered document format named Sketch Document, which will be described below.

At first, we will introduce some basic concepts for representing sketch data. *Sample Point* indicates the point captured by an input device. It is parameterized as (x, y, p, t), where x and y refer to the coordinates of the point, p represents for the pen pressure, and t is for the timestamp. *Stroke* is consisted of a set of sample points captured by a device from pen-down to pen-up events. A *Primitive* is a predefined geometric shape (such as line segment, arc segment and ellipse), which is extracted from strokes by stroke segmentation. *A Sketch Component* is a domain-related visual object (such as a resistance in a circuit diagram and a class symbol in a UML diagram), which contains certain semantics and is meaningful to participants. *Sketch Document* represents the entire design document, which contains a number of sketch components. For example, a UML class diagram in the form of freehand sketch, which consists of a set of class, interface, and arrowhead line symbols. All sketch document instantiations are finally XML-formatted.

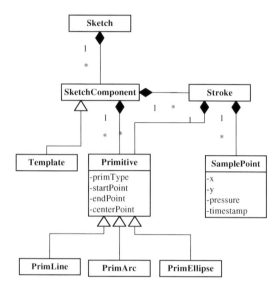

Fig. 2. Sketch document data structure

Figure 2 lists the data structures mentioned above and indicates the relationships between them. As a result, a sketch document is organized in a layered structure. From the bottom up, the layers are raw sketch data, semi-raw sketch data, recognized sketch components and sketch semantics. Raw sketch data refer to the sample points in the strokes captured by the input equipment. Semi-raw sketch data refer to the primitive shapes extracted from the stroke. Recognized sketch component refers to finished sketch component. Finally, sketch semantics refers to some high-level information of the sketch document, such as sketch category, author name and create date.

3.3 Sketch Recognizer Module

Sketch recognizer is an important module in our proposed framework, which infers designers' intention and helps them to accomplish the design tasks. Furthermore, the sketch documents need to be formalized into detailed design documents, and a sketch recognizer will avoid the tedious work of moving the initial freehand sketches to accurate design files (such as CAD files).

We have developed a set of sketch recognition algorithms in our previous research. We choose a primitive-based algorithm that the inputting strokes are first decomposed into basic geometric primitives (ellipses, line and arc segments). Then the primitives are assembled into a graphical structure, which encodes both the intrinsic attributes of the primitives and their relationships. Sketch recognition is accordingly formulated as a template-matching problem.

Figure 3 shows the framework of the recognizer. First, the primitives of sketch are recognized in the primitive recognition stage. Then the feature vector of a sketch is extracted in order to construct the vector-model. In our study, features are refined into two categories: edge feature and spatial relationship feature. The edge feature represents statistical primitive information of a sketch, such as the number of line segments. The relationships between two primitives (such as parallelism, intersection and tangency) are also considered in our approach. We combine the edge feature and spatial relation feature together into a multi-dimensional feature vector. During the template matching stage, the recognizer calculates the similarity between a given sketch and each standard shapes in a domain-specific shape library which results in an objects set, based on the vector-based model. We employ Euclidean distance for matching. Finally, the recognizer returns the recognition result to user.

Fig. 3. Framework of the sketch recognizer

3.4 Event-Based Model for C/S Communication

In this section, we will discuss the communication between the client side and the server side. As we mentioned before, each client side contains a copy of the whole sketch document data. Once a designer makes a modification to the sketch document, the client only sends the corresponding data (including the action type and the graphical object to be modified) to the server.

We have introduced the event-based model in the framework. Each command generated by the command generator module in the client side is regard to be an Event. There are mainly two types of Events: One is for control, such as logging in to a server and logging out the server; the other is for data modification, such as adding a simple stroke to the sketch document, and removing a stroke from the document.

```
<?xml version="1.0" encoding="gb2312" stand-
alone="no"?>
<SketchDesignEvent>
  <Author>user</Author>
  <Type>ADD_STROKE</Type>
  <Arguments>
     <ComponentID>12</ComponentID>
     <Sample-
Points>(1,1,0,1);(3,4,0,1)<SamplePoints>
  </Arguments>
</ SketchDesignEvent >
```

Fig. 4. A simple event: an operation of adding a single stroke

We construct a unified XML-based format for both of the two types of events. Each XML-formatted event has an "Author" element to indicate designer ID, a "Type" element to indicate event type, and an "Arguments" element to list corresponding parameters. Figure 4 gives a sample Event, which is designed for adding a stroke to a sketch component. We can see that the client side sends only the additional stroke data and the sketch component ID to be modified to the server side.

4 Implementation and Evaluation

We have implemented the application framework as a middleware for sketch-based cooperative design applications. It is implemented in Java, a network programming language, which is platform-independent and fit for distributed cooperative work. Moreover, we can easily use Java Applet to implement a Web-based CSCD system.

We have also implemented a prototype system for cooperative UML class diagram design to evaluate the framework. Consider a scenario in customized software design, software developers and customers need to discuss about the requirements in the early stage of the development, and they need to meet together and draw some UML diagrams. However, in many cases, the software developers and the customers are at physically separate locations. The prototype system is designed for such cases.

Figure 5 shows a cooperative UML class diagram design process done by two designers (User A and User B). Each designer sketches in his own UI, and he can watch the other user's input via the design server. In Figure 5(a), User A began to draw sketches in his own UI and he drew a class. After he had finished the class element, the recognizer recognized the sketch as a class. The client side sent an "Add Component" event to the server. The server adopted the addition to the main sketch document and broadcast the modification information to both of the two clients. Then both of the two users could see the newly added standard class element (a standard class symbol shown in Figure 5(b)). In Figure 5(b), User B started to draw an interface element. As the design session was going on, in Figure 5(c), User A drew an implementation line between the existed class and interface elements. In Figure 5(d) and Figure 5(e), User B drew a sub-class extended from the first class element. Finally, the two users finished the class diagram design (Figure 5(f)).

As we mentioned in Section 3, each client side contains a display controller module, with which each designer can get their own view of the same document. Figure 6 gives an example. User A and B have their own views of the document, which are different from each other. However, both views correspond to exactly the same sketch document on the server.

As we can see from the experimental design session, the prototype system is valuable for cooperative design in practice. Moreover, by using our proposed application framework, distributed designers can obtain the benefits of freehand sketching in the cooperative design, which is seldom supported by current design tools. Although the case we used for testing is simple, we can easily extend the design tool to more complicated cases, for example, by extending the shape library in the recognizer module.Compared with other cooperative design tools, such as NetSketch [13], which also

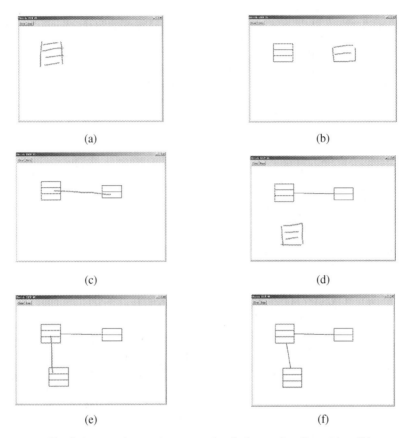

(a)   (b)

(c)   (d)

(e)   (f)

Fig. 5. An experiment of a cooperative design session (from (a) to (f))

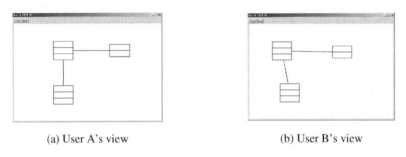

(a) User A's view   (b) User B's view

Fig. 6. Two different designers' views of the same design

support sketching interaction, the hybrid architecture and event-based communication mode are more suitable for sketch-based cooperative design and can easily satisfy multi-designer application requirement. The hierarchical sketch document model facilitates the representing and storing designers' ideas in the form of sketch.

Furthermore, the recognition algorithm used here is more complicated which can recognize more sketchy shapes.

5   Conclusion and Future Work

Sketching is a nature way for visual thinking and communication. A great number of sketch documents are generated in product design processes. This paper studies the sketch-based interface in computer supported cooperative design, especially in distributed cooperative design, where participants are geographically distributed and they use physical pencil and paper to discuss the design. In this study, we have considered the fundamental problems and developed an application framework for sketch-based cooperative design.

We proposed a novel layered sketch document format that is capable for storing and modifying sketch-based document. The sketch data representation is XML formatted and can be easily exchanged in different platforms.

A similarity-based sketch recognizer is used in the system to infer users' intention and transfer the sketch document directly into formalized design files, which helps designers complete their design work.

The distributed architecture can easily support a group of users (two users or above) to draw sketches in a common virtual drawing space. The event-based model facilitates the communication between a participant and the server.

The framework has been implemented as a middleware for sketch-based cooperative design applications. We have also implemented a prototype system based-on the proposed application framework for cooperative UML diagram design and have obtained satisfactory results. As we can see from the experiment, our proposed framework is valuable for cooperative design, and designers will be able to obtain the benefits of freehand sketching, which are seldom supported by current CAD tools.

However, some problems still have not been solved yet, such as date consistency problem in the cooperative design process. We plan to use a locking strategy in which a user needs to apply the lock at first and unlock it at the end.

We have just tested the framework in a local network with only a few clients (up to four), and the experiments showed that there is no network overload problem in such cases. However, further experiments are needed to evaluate the framework with more clients on the Internet.

Acknowledgments. This paper is supported by the National Natural Science Foundation of China (Grant No. 69903006 and 60373065) and the Program for New Century Excellent Talents in University (Project No. NCET-04-0460).

References

1. van Dijk C.G.C: New insights in computer-aided conceptual design. International Journal of Design Studies 16(1) (1995) 62-80
2. Sun, Z., Liu, J.: Informal user interfaces for graphical computing. LNCS 3784 (2005) 675-682

3. Alvarado, C.: A Natural Sketching Environment: Bringing the Computer into Early Stages of Mechanical Design. Master Thesis. MIT, USA (2000)
4. Hong, J.I., Landay, J.A.: SATIN: A toolkit for informal ink-based applications. Proceedings of the ACM User Interfaces and Software Technology (2000) 63-72
5. Landay, J.A., Myers, B.A.: Sketching interfaces: Toward more human interface design. IEEE Computer 34(3) (2001) 56-64
6. Xu, X., Sun, Z., et al.: An online composite graphics recognition approach based on matching of spatial relation graphs. IJDAR, 7(1) (2004) 44-55
7. Sun, Z., Wang, W., Zhang, L., Liu, J.: Sketch parameterization using curve approximation. LNCS 3926 (2006) 334-345
8. Sun, Z., Yuan, B., Yin, J.: Online Composite Sketchy Shape Recognition Using Dynamic Programming. LNCS 3926 (2006) 255-266
9. Sun, Z, Li, B., Wang, Q., Feng, G.: Dynamic User Modeling For Sketch-Based User Interface. LNCS 3942 (2006) 1268-1273
10. Sun, Z., Liu, W., Peng, B., et al: User adaptation for online sketchy shape recognition.LNCS 3088 (2004) 303-314
11. Sun, Z., Jiang, W., Sun, J.: Adaptive Online Multi-Stroke Sketch Recognition based on Hidden Markov Model. LNAI 3784 (2005) 948-957
12. Sun, Z., Zhang, L., Zhang, B.: Online Composite Sketchy Shape Recognition Based on Bayesian Networks. LNCS 4222 (2006) 506-515
13. LaViola, J.J., Holden L.S., Forsberg, A.S., et al.: Collaborative Conceptual Modeling Using the SKETCH Framework. Proceedings of the International Conference on Computer Graphics and Imaging (1998) 154-158
14. Zhe, F., Oliveira, M.M., Chi, M., Kaufman, A.: A Sketch-Based Interface for Collaborative Design. Proceedings of Eurographics Workshop on Sketch-Based Interfaces and Modeling (2004) 143-150
15. JOT: A Specification for an Ink Storage and Interchange Format (1993). URL: http://hwr.nici.kun.nl/unipen/jot.html
16. Guyon, I., Schomaker, L.R.B.: UNIPEN: Project of Data Exchange and Recognizer Banchmarks (1993). URL: http://hwr.nici.kun.nl/unipen.
17. Chee, Y.M., Magana, J.A., Franke, K., et al.: Ink Markup Language. W3C Working Draft (2004). URL: http://www.w3.org/TR/2004/WD-InkML-0040928

Supporting Self-governing Software Design Groups

Adriana S. Vivacqua[1,3], Jean-Paul Barthès[3], and Jano Moreira de Souza[1,2]

[1] COPPE/UFRJ, Graduate School of Computer Science
[2] DCC-IM, Institute of Mathematics
Federal University of Rio de Janeiro, Brazil
{avivacqua, jano}@cos.ufrj.br
[3] Heudyasic, Université de Technologie de Compiègne, Compiègne, France
barthes@utc.fr

Abstract. In decentralized projects, several organizations come together to work on a joint project. Increased networking and distribution have facilitated their implementation. Common practices, such as subcontracting and consulting, sometimes lead to the creation of more flexible, less hierarchical structures. Partners are often considered as peers and the group has the flexibility to restructure itself according to its needs. In this paper, we present a conceptual framework for supporting decentralized groups using agent technology. This framework was developed based on a study of a decentralized group involved in a software research, design and development project. In our observation, a great amount of time is spent with articulation and maintaining partners up-to-date, which suggests that appropriate awareness support might facilitate the group's activities. We define the necessary modules and a specific agent architecture to support these groups.

1 Introduction

Networking technologies are quickly becoming ubiquitous, and organizations have become increasingly reliant on these technologies to achieve their goals. Recent studies have shown increased adoption of virtual teams, where individuals collaborate using only computer-mediated tools [7].

Similar work arrangements have been emerging between organizations: the European Union, for instance, has been funding research projects where partners from several different countries collaborate towards a common goal. The structure of these projects is much more egalitarian than that found in formal organizations: participants treat each other as peers, with only a loose coordination structure to oversee the work. Partners negotiate several aspects of the work prior to undertaking it and they are all accountable for the outcome of the project. Work subdivision, coordination, determination of overlaps and interfaces are some of the aspects that come into play.

In this paper we analyze the work performed by one such group, researching and designing a technical solution to a given problem. Given the open-ended nature of the work, certain aspects had to be discussed and agreed upon by the group. The group refined the initial proposal and project vision, designed the solution and chose

W. Shen et al. (Eds.): CSCWD 2006, LNCS 4402, pp. 149–159, 2007.
© Springer-Verlag Berlin Heidelberg 2007

appropriate technologies. In this analysis, we focus on the extra work necessary for the group to accomplish its goals, and what tools could provide group support.

The official tools available to the group were a website and a forum. However, group members frequently resorted to parallel media to exchange information and resources. Some of the specific group processes, especially those involving negotiation, decision-making and articulation of efforts were very poorly supported. As a result, quite a bit of discussion time was spent on these activities.

In the following sections, we briefly summarize the background theories that guided our observations (Section 2), followed by a brief description of our case study in Section 3. In Section 4, we present the requirements for support of self-governing groups and a brief discussion of how Software Agent Technology could support it, and in Section 5 we summarize other research and how it relates to ours.

2 Background Theory

Organizations are composed of networks of actors and relations between these are subject to constant renegotiation. The organization provides structures and regulations, but functions as a result of actors' interactions and relations [2]. Thus, an organization can be seen as a coalition of individuals motivated by particular interests, who must negotiate and organize themselves to attain their goals, while still helping the organization achieve its own goals. The formal organization provides a governance structure that influences the behavior of individuals and collectives [15]. The "organizational interests" follow those of members of the organization and of external stakeholders. Thus, work happens through the establishment of cooperative work arrangements that emerge as a response to unforeseen requirements and dissolve when they are no longer necessary. These arrangements are organized according to a need, but follow established patterns [2].

According to these views, work is the result of negotiations between actors. In the extreme case, where there is no overarching organization to provide rules and guidelines for interaction, actors have to create their own, negotiating agreements and duties. This task becomes harder the more differentiated and more numerous the members of the group. Collaboration also becomes harder with distance: distributed groups tend to change their organization and task distribution to reduce coupling of the non-collocated members, to reduce the group's articulation needs [12]. This leads to a decrease in involvement with the project, as members that do not communicate very often are not kept up-to-date of the latest evolution in other teams' designs, and that increases fragmentation in the group, which usually leads to poorer results [6].

People often alternate between individual and shared work, and between loosely and tightly coupled collaboration [5]. In these situations, primary support should focus on the individual work and collaboration support should then be added to the personal workspace, enabling the shift towards collaborative work when necessary [13]. Awareness of current and past efforts is essential in these cases, as individuals work on shared artifacts at different points in time [4].

Awareness is knowledge about a dynamic environment that must be maintained as the environment changes. This knowledge is created through interactions with the environment [5]. Situation awareness involves perception, comprehension and prediction of future states of relevant elements of the environment. Awareness facilitates collaboration by simplifying communication and coordination, allowing better management of coupling and determination of the need to collaborate.

Most awareness support systems fall into one of two categories: they're either subscription systems, where users must actively subscribe to certain events to be notified when they happen, or they're media based information dissemination systems, which distribute information that goes through a given channel (video, chat windows, etc.). This second type of system has the potential to bring to the user information that isn't of interest, because it performs no content analysis to check whether the information falls into the user's attention focus. Systems such as Portholes [3], which distribute video based information, or CommunityBar [10], which distributes information going through video, chat, sticky notes and other media elements fall into this category and, while useful, have the potential of generating unwanted information. The first type of system, while allowing the user to set preferences regarding events that are to be monitored, usually requires quite a bit of configuration, which must be updated as users' interests change. Depending on the speed of changes in the environments and the users' work rhythm, there may be a constant need for reconfiguration, demanding more work form the users. The Doc2U [11] system falls into this category: it enables the user to determine what he or she wants to be informed of during collaborative editing. However, it requires that users be logged onto a particular editing environment and configure it to so that they might know who else is working on that same document.

3   Software Design in a Distributed Group

Software design is an activity where several different solutions are possible for any given problem. It involves decisions regarding approaches and technologies, and making a number of choices that impact the final product to be built, with each choice having a certain impact on modules and individuals. The project under study is one among many efforts being funded by the European Union (EU). As such, it involves a number of teams from different countries, who must work together to deliver the final product.

3.1   Project and Participants

The project concerns research and development of eGovernment solutions. It focuses on the creation of flexible and interoperable tools to support eGovernment services, and on the study of new technologies that can be applied to this problem. A number of partners from different countries are involved, with "technical partners" being directly involved in the research, design and development of working prototypes. The project's initial lifespan is 4 years. Technical partners perform requirements analysis for pilot regions and work towards the design of an appropriate solution to the problem. Development follows the open source model.

This project involves several collaborators working from different locations and exchanging information as necessary. Despite frequent meetings, partners have difficulty coordinating work, exchanging ideas and keeping abreast of each other's activities. We analyzed the interactions between the technical partners, as they were more closely involved with the design and development of the system at hand. We classified the types of interactions to elicit what types of tasks were being undertaken and how much time was being spent on them.

3.2 Group Structure

At an initial stage, partners had to refine the definition of what was to be built, since the project had been defined in loose terms and without a formal specification. At this moment, an initial architecture was proposed and tasks were subdivided between partners. Assignment to different initiatives was spontaneous, and partners chose according to their preferences and skills. Work was subdivided into packages, with different partners being involved in each one, and different partners assuming the coordination role for different packages. Thus, coordination duties rotate between partners, and the extra work involved is spread around. The package coordinator is in charge of preparing progress reports, deliverables and any additional documentation that is to be sent to the European Commission (EC) review board.

Partners have relative freedom to decide how to carry out their business, how to organize and how to divide their work amongst themselves. They treat each other as equals and coordinate with each other to get work done. This generates a number of difficulties and a huge quantity of additional work, as there is no central system or entity to perform all the coordination activities. A mutual understanding that the project must be completed at a given date drives partners to orchestrate their efforts to achieve the shared goals.

Additionally, teams from the different organizations are often engaged in multiple tasks at a time, some related to the project and others unrelated. These partners must manage constraints and interdependencies arising from the existence of different foci, including possible inconsistencies and conflicts of interest arising from these multiple goals.

Partners have at their disposal a website where project related documents are stored. Deliverables, project specifications and plans are posted to the website. On the same website there is a private threaded forum for partners only where discussion can be carried out. Interaction on the forums becomes public to all partners. The website is used primarily to store public documents. It is a public, central, repository of data and information about the project and provides a means for interaction between partners. This is the tool officially provided for the project, but partners use whatever other tools they need to accomplish their goals (email, messenger, IRC, word, excel, etc., plus specific tools for coding, modeling, analysis, etc.).

3.3 Interaction Patterns

We analyzed a year and five months worth of interactions on the forum, two meetings over IRC and one face-to-face meeting, to verify how the group's time was being spent. Most of the discussions (39%) on the forum concerned scheduling meetings (arranging dates and locations, providing instructions on how to get there, etc.). The second most frequent thread type (28%) were requests for contributions, where the coordinator for a certain package solicits that all partners send in their portions of the work, so that a consolidated report may be generated. Planning threads involving

work subdivision, task assignment, deciding on deadlines, determination of interdependencies, and revising project plans were the third most frequent topic (15%).
Technical discussions come in fourth place (11%) with status reports, announcements
and reminders forming up the rest of the activity. Message distribution can be seen in
Table 1. If we consider planning, scheduling, announcements and reminders as an
organizational category, it becomes clear that more than half the discussion time is
spent with articulation work (403 messages or 57%).

Table 1. Forum message distribution

Message Type	Number of Messages	Percentage
Scheduling	278	39,27%
Request for Contributions	198	27,97%
Planning	108	15,25%
Technical Discussions	76	10,73%
Status Reports	31	4,38%
Announcements	13	1,84%
Reminders	4	0,56%
Total	708	100

Synchronous meetings involved more technical discussion than planning and
scheduling, although there was always some of each involved. During the face-to-face
meeting, 10 discussions were technical versus 7 involving planning and, on the online
meetings, 9 discussions were technical, 4 were planning and 2 were scheduling. In
total, 19 discussions concerned technical matters and 13 were organizational.

During the synchronous meetings, members exchanged information and made arrangements for further, "offline" cooperation in parallel conversations. Group members
clearly preferred synchronous meetings for technical discussions, as these enabled
partners to give and receive immediate feedback, thus speeding up the discussion. On
the forum, messages sometimes took a couple of days to be answered.

The group had difficulty coordinating its efforts and maintaining awareness of each
other's activities and of the overall evolution of the project. Furthermore, partners
often collaborated outside the shared project space, thus leaving out other partners
who might also be interested on the aspects at hand and able to contribute ideas and
suggestions to the topic.

The fact that the group is self-organizing suggests that there is a need for tools to
support this flexibility in work configurations. These tools should allow partners to
establish the tasks to be undertaken during the project, determining their interdependencies and who will be in charge of each task. Additionally, tools should also allow
the group to alter these task configurations and validate task outcomes.

In a situation such as the one described, groupware should be organized around individuals working independently rather that in shared applications or documents. The
system should provide the necessary support for individuals to collaborate: becoming

aware of each other and of each other's work; lightweight means of initiating interactions and the ability to move into closely-coupled work if necessary [6].

4 Support for Self Governing Groups

The group spends a large amount of time on organizational issues, most of which are resolved after extensive negotiation which takes quite a while get resolved. Thus, there is a need for articulation support at a basic level, so that group members' time may be better spent, pursuing their work. With this in mind, and the fact that most of the actual work is done individually and then reported to the group, we conceived of a framework to support self-governing groups.

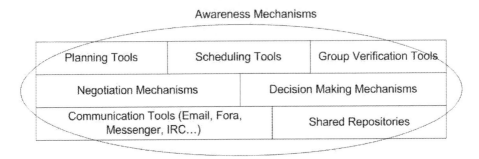

Fig. 1. lements necessary for Self-Governing Support

The base layer is composed of communication mechanisms and shared repositories, on top of which stand negotiation and decision making mechanisms, since these activities permeate all of the group's activities. At the topmost layer stand more specific tools for Planning, Scheduling and Validation, all performed by the ensemble. Awareness mechanisms permeate the whole architecture. The basic framework is composed of eight modules (Figure 1). They are described in the following:

- **Communication:** These are the standard communication media users have at their disposal. In our case, these were email, IRC, the forum and messenger systems. Communication tools should be integrated with other tools in order to better support the emerging work arrangements.
- **Shared Repositories:** Shared repositories hold the group's work and history, including documents and other artifacts produced by the partners and the history of interactions and decisions made, so that it can be referred back to. Metadata such as authorship and alterations would provide object histories and facilitate the implementation of awareness mechanisms.
- **Negotiation:** Negotiation plays an important part in self-organizing groups, as they design their work arrangements [2]. Partners come into the project with different interests and try to make the most beneficial arrangement possible for themselves. Facilitating negotiation would speed up discussion and allow the group to concentrate on technical issues and the work at hand.

- **Decision-Making:** Mechanisms to simplify decision-making would help the group focus on the work at hand. These mechanisms should also enable rationale capture, so that the group can understand why decisions were made. Additionally, decisions are not static, and can be revised, so the ability to "undo decisions" should be provided, with appropriate tracing and logging.

- **Planning:** A large amount of time is spent on planning, which should be better supported by computational tools. Tools should enable the definition of the work to be done, division into activities, determination of interdependencies, and assignment of tasks and roles. The group plan is the result of a collective decision and should be available to all partners, who should be able to report on progress through these same tools. In this fashion, inconsistencies or overlaps could be more easily detected. Awareness of local environments (holidays, vacations, etc.) enables the group to adjust expectations accordingly.

- **Scheduling:** Meeting scheduling is basically a constraint satisfaction problem, which can be supported by computational tools and even partially automated. The discussion on agenda items involved mostly negotiation and decision making by the group, which could be supported by the underlying layer of negotiation and decision making mechanisms.

- **Group Verification:** Specific tools should support group checking, review and approval of tasks and deliverables, and enforcement of deadlines. This would enable the group to better control and check the work in progress, making sure it is acceptable to all involved.

- **Awareness:** These mechanisms distribute knowledge of the work environment among all partners. They are important because they enable the maintenance of a certain level of conscience of how the project is progressing; who is doing what; who is interacting with whom; who has worked on a certain part of the project since a certain date; etc. This enables group members to better understand the working environment and to adjust their own work according to the situation, enabling the group to better function as a coherent unit [5]. Synchronous and asynchronous awareness should be maintained. The former concerns what is happening at the moment, and enables the partners to act on the spot (for instance, joining a discussion or correcting incorrect assumptions on his/her work). Asynchronous awareness concerns mostly shared resources (e.g., who has worked on what, what have they done, what have people been talking about, etc.) What information should be provided, whom it should be provided to and how, varies according to the situation.

Specific contextual elements need to be taken into account for each of the modules, and should be developed based on each group's work patterns and needs. Indicators need to be selected and treated accordingly: too much time spent on a negotiation or discussion might indicate dissent or polarized points of view. In this case, the system itself could propose different group dynamics, to enable the group to focus and reach consensus more easily. Additionally, time spent in negotiations or decision making, for instance, might be reduced if a group is reminded of deadlines that need to be met and of the specific impact of given decisions. Presenting the rationale for earlier (and similar decisions might also help a group focus and act consistently throughout a project.) Even though they will apply to many groups, these conditions and actions need to be determined when the group is first studied, and there should be means to enable the system to automatically adjust to the groups patterns of interaction.

4.1 Technological Perspective

Since partners are independent actors involved in several projects, it makes sense to have systems running on each partner's end and communicating with each other as necessary (possibly posting copies of these communications to central repositories).

Due to its proactive behavior, agent technology can provide adequate support for this framework. By enhancing a user's desktop with agents to perform most of the services, these could, in parallel, propagate information and contribute to the orchestration of the group's efforts, as proposed by [18]. For instance, scheduling could be almost completely done by agents on behalf of the user: agents can elicit preferences from the user and automatically negotiate with each other the most appropriate dates, presenting a few final options for user decision and confirming each user's presence. An agent could then collect the replies, build a list of participants and send directions created by the host user to those who will be present. Other research has proposed agent applications for determining opportunities for collaboration [18].

Agents can interact with the operating system to elicit task information, calling system functions. Interacting with specific applications requires specialized programming. This can be accomplished through the use of libraries (e.g., JACOB to interface with MS office applications from Java programs), or by reading local files. Analyzing email is possible either by instrumenting the server or reading local logs on the client. This means that the framework should include a basic service layer, with specialized agents to interface with each of the applications. Communication can be obtained from for a, messenger and email logs, topics of ongoing work from text files created or edited by the user, topics of interest or study from pages surfed by the user and recommendations or shared work from links and files sent to the user by his or her acquaintances. This information can then be passed up one level, to agents that reason about it and decide what information to distribute based on system specific rules, and then up one level to appropriate display and interaction mechanisms, which enable user interaction with the system and with each other. This three-layered architecture (data collection-reasoning-display) should support most awareness applications.

Thus far, our research has focused on the awareness mechanisms needed to support collaboration. Given that much of the work is undertaken via email and file exchange, an agent analyzes local emails logs to check (1) for the occurrence of cooperative activity (and with whom) and (2) for the existence of shared objects or resources. The reasoning agent receives email data collected from the logs and uses statistical measures to determine where the user is directing his or her attention. Ongoing ties with other individuals are established through a structural analysis of email: the FROM, TO and CC fields establish who is working with whom, building an egocentric, interaction based, social network [9]. Attachments are files usually shared for revision or addition of contributions, and embody collaboration. Once a file has been sent, access to it can be tracked and other users involved with it can be informed. A desktop agent periodically checks the operating system for access to shared resources and notifies their owners when resources have been manipulated.

At a second stage, content analysis is used to infer what themes are related to the group's collaborative activities. An analysis of the content of interactions elicits he shared context between two individuals. Local agents can match (using information retrieval techniques) these themes to ongoing individual work (e.g., if one of the users is surfing the web researching a topic related to the shared project, the links found can be relayed to others). Individual work related to shared themes can be relayed to other group members. Additionally, the agents can post messages exchanged by sub-groups to shared repositories where other group members can check them. This transparency of interactions can help members become aware of ongoing collaborations and the work of the rest of the group, and understand the reasoning behind decisions and choices made.

Many other inference possibilities exist: an agent could, given the normal time spent on discussion, check to see if a discussion is taking too long, and what could be done about it. Each member's participation level in each discussion indicates their interest or commitment to the particular topic under discussion. This allows an agent to rout information appropriately, prioritizing certain threads. With appropriate text processing, it might be possible to determine if discussions are highly polarized or not, and to suggest the application of group techniques to help the group focus and reach their goals (e.g., anonymized brainstorming, voting, etc.).

An associated problem is the quantity and display of this awareness information. There is a need for better ways to display information that provide each user with the relevant information at an appropriate level of granularity. Hence, agents need to have filtering or consolidating capabilities (for instance, displaying only the conclusions of a conversation, instead of the whole interaction.) There are different display possibilities for awareness information, but they should be unobtrusive and allow perception of cues through secondary channels. Our prototype interface shows a list of users and their activities, in a modified messenger interface. Users' avatars are color-coded to represent activities that are more relevant to the user, and a list of relevant activities is shown below each user.

5 Final Considerations

In recent years, organizations have been changing their way of conducting business. Traditional, centralized, design is no longer sufficient to handle the highly dynamic environments in which they operate [17]. Our observation of a loosely structured collaborative group helps the definition of requirements and needs specific to these types of groups. In decentralized settings, even with appointed coordinators a democratic scheme may surface, with members discussing decisions or problems and deciding as a group on the directions of the project. While this generates decisions that are most likely to be embraced by the group, it also creates additional overhead.

Given the underlying interdependence, workers have to articulate (i.e., divide, allocate, coordinate, schedule, interrelate, etc.) their activities. Cooperative work formations emerge because actors cannot accomplish certain tasks individually [15], and organizations provide these actors with a relatively stable pattern of cooperative arrangements and structures to regulate members' diverse interests.

Studies have shown that even in shop floor environments, actors have control over job allocation and day-to-day production planning and control, superseding predetermined plans and schedules set up by the organization [2]. These self-governing groups have the freedom to adapt their behavior according to circumstances or unforeseen events, using the plans as a guideline towards work completion. These observations echo our perception that groups often function in a loose, open-ended way. Individuals must adjust and self organize to remain productive.

However, groups in the former studies had a predefined structure that had to be adhered to and a well-defined goal to reach, with pre-defined tasks to perform. In addition, individuals were collocated, which facilitated maintenance of awareness. In our case, there are no underlying structures, and even though there is a partner who is the appointed coordinator, members treat each other as equals and negotiate most decisions. Distance becomes an additional complicating factor. Many aspects of the project itself had to be negotiated, such as deliverables and task subdivision, which meant the group's effort included much more work than developing the system (as predicted in [15]).

A study of Free/Open Source Software (F/OSS) environments reports several instances of negotiation related to problem solving in bug reports. Developers discussed items such as the nature of the problems reported, how to solve these and who was responsible for them [14]. The F/OSS environment is very similar to the one we studied, except that, since all participants are volunteers, there are fewer commitments, deadlines and dates that need to be adhered to and overall lower accountability for the final product.

To function well in a group, workers must maintain awareness of three different aspects: of the possibility of collaboration, of the aims of the collaboration and of the process of collaboration [8]. They do that by observing exchanges between others and exchanging information as needed. In shared workspaces this is easier to achieve, not so in distributed environments. It has been shown that awareness enables individuals to better adapt their own behavior to fit group needs, intervening when necessary, exchanging information or adjusting one's own individual work.

In this paper we present a framework and a set of requirements to support the basic needs for a self-governing group. While the study itself was based on a software development project, we believe this framework will hold for other types of project. The modules in this framework concern the additional work that must be undertaken by the group, rather than tool support for specific functions related to the work being undertaken. Ideally, these would be integrated, so that work information could be more easily propagated between group members.

Acknowledgments. This research was partially funded by CAPES and CNPq grants. We thank the group involved in the study for their support.

References

1. Bernoux, P. : La Sociologie des Entreprises. Éditions du Seuil, Paris (1999)
2. Carstensen, P., Schmidt, K.: Self Governing Production Groups: Towards Requirements for IT Support. Proceedings of the Fifth IFIP International Conference on Information Technology in Manufacturing and Services (BASYS'02). Cancun, Mexico (2002)

3. Dourish, P. and Portholes B.S.: Supporting Awareness in distributed Work Group. Proceedings of the 1992 ACM Conference on Human Factors in Computing Systems (CHI'92). Monterey, CA (1992) 541-547
4. Edwards, K., Timewarp M.E.: Techniques for Autonomous Collaboration. Proceedings of ACM Conference on Human Factors in Computing Systems (CHI'97). Atlanta, GA (1997)
5. Gutwin, C., Greenberg, S.: A Descriptive Framework of Workspace Awareness for Real-Time Groupware. Computer Supported Cooperative Work 11(2002) 411-446
6. Gutwin, C., Greenberg, S., Blum, R., Dyck, J.: Supporting Informal Collaboration in Shared-Workspace Groupware. The Interaction Lab Technical Report HCI-TR-2005-01. University of Saskatchewan, Canada (2005)
7. Hertel, G., Geister, S., Konradt, U.: Managing Virtual Teams: A review of current empirical research. Human Resource Management Review 15 (2005) 69-95
8. Leinonen, P., Jarvela, S., Hakkinen, P.: Conceptualizing the Awareness of Collaboration: A Qualitative Study of a Global Virtual Team. Computer Supported Cooperative Work 14 (2005) 301-322
9. McCarty, C., Bernard, R.: Social Network Analysis. In: Christensen, K. and Levinson, D. (eds.): Encyclopaedia of Community: From the Village to the Virtual World. Thousand Oaks, CA: Sage (2003)
10. McEwan, G. and Greenberg, S.: Community Bar: Designing for Awareness and Interaction. Proceedings of ACM Conference on Human Factors in Computing Systems (CHI 2005). Portland, Oregon (2005)
11. Morán, A.L., Favela, J., Martínez-Enríquez, A.M. and Decouchant, D.: Before Getting There: Potential and Actual Collaboration. Proceedings of the 2002 International Workshop in Groupware (CRIWG 2002). Berlin: Springer-Verlag (2002)
12. Olson, J., Teasley, S.: Groupware in the Wild: Lessons Learned from a Year of Virtual Collocation. Proceedings of Computer Supported Cooperative Work 1996 (CSCW'96). Cambridge, MA (1996)
13. Pinelle, D., Gutwin, C.: A Groupware Design Framework for Loosely Coupled Groups. Proceedings of European Conference on Computer-Supported Cooperative Work (ECSCW'05). Paris, France (2005)
14. Sandusky, R.J., Gasser, L.: Negotiation and the Coordination of Information and Activity in Distributed Software Problem Management. Proceedings of GROUP'05. Sanibel Island, FL (2005)
15. Schmidt, K., Bannon, L.: Taking CSCW Seriously: Supporting Articulation Work. Computer Supported Cooperative Work 1(1)(1992) 7-40
16. Schmidt, K.: The Organization of Cooperative Work: Beyond the Leviathan Conception of Cooperative Work. Proceedings of Computer Supported Cooperative Work (CSCW'94). Chapel Hill, NC, USA (1994)
17. Shen, W. (eds.): Special Issue on Collaborative Environments for Design and Manufacturing. Advanced Engineering Informatics 19 (2005) 79
18. Tacla, C. Barthès, J.P.: A Multi-Agent System for Acquiring and Sharing Lessons Learned. Computers in Industry 52 (2003) 5-16
19. Vivacqua, A.S., Moreno, M, Souza, J.M.: Using Agents to Detect Opportunities for Collaboration. In: Shen, W., et al. (eds.): Computer Supported Cooperative Work in Design II (CSCWD 2005), LNCS 3865. Springer Verlag Berlin Heidelberg (2006) 244-253

Enhancing Support for Collaboration in Software Development Environments

Arnaud Lewandowski and Grégory Bourguin

Laboratoire d'Informatique du Littoral (LIL),
Maison de la Recherche Blaise Pascal
50 rue Ferdinand Buisson, BP 719
62228 Calais Cedex, France
{lewandowski, bourguin}@lil.univ-littoral.fr

Abstract. Many studies have shown that collaboration is still badly supported in Software Development Environments (SDEs). This is why we try to take benefits from a theory developed in Social and Human Sciences, the Activity Theory, to better understand the cooperative human activities in which SD is realized. This paper particularly focuses on the experience crystallization principle to propose new solutions while enhancing the support for collaboration in the widely used Eclipse IDE.

1 Introduction

Over the past years, many studies have shown that collaboration is still badly supported in Software Development Environments (SDEs). Recently, many propositions have been made to enhance the support for this particular dimension in existing or new tools. These new propositions take benefit from an approach largely developed in the frame of the CSCW (Computer Supported Cooperative Work) research field: using theories developed in Social and Human Sciences (SHSs) to better understand the cooperative human activities in which SD is realized. One of these theories that has a wide audience in CSCW is the Activity Theory (AT). AT has recently been used to propose better computer support for design activities and has also provided very interesting results for studying SDEs [3]. However, we believe that this theory still has not delivered all its secrets as for helping us to better understand how to support software development.

Starting from this assumption, we will first summarize the main issues that have already been identified for creating collaboration-aware SDEs. After a brief presentation of the AT, we will particularly focus on the issues highlighted by using it. This study will lead us to propose a new focus that still has not really been taken into account in the design of SDEs. Finally, we will show our proposition trying to support the identified properties in a widely used SDE.

W. Shen et al. (Eds.): CSCWD 2006, LNCS 4402, pp. 160–169, 2007.
© Springer-Verlag Berlin Heidelberg 2007

2 Supporting Collaboration in SDEs

2.1 General Issues

Adding collaboration support in SDEs means more than providing additional communication tools [20]. Even if efforts have been done to improve collaboration support, some collaborative aspects are still missing. For example, most Integrated Development Environments (IDEs), such as the widely used Eclipse, focus on code-producing activities, considering them as 'individual' activities in the development process. The collaborative support is then generally limited to the use of a common repository — such as CVS — that supports documents sharing, but not the collaboration between developers [18]. In other cases, some collaboration support is provided, but is still disconnected from the development process: collaboration is supported by adding communication functionalities, without really connecting this dimension to the main activity. This is for example the case when a synchronous discussion tool is simply plugged into the environment. A real support for collaboration in SD supposes that the environment should be able to support this activity as a whole. Collaboration is a constituting part of the global activity, not an aside one. Thus, the tool we want to build can be called an integrated collaboration environment, as proposed by Sarma [23]. However, it clearly seems that such environments are currently very rare and research in this area is still in progress [5][24].

Tailorability is also a well-identified requirement for SDEs. Many empirical studies [8][11] and theoretical research [21] have demonstrated that human activity, and then SD, is reflective in the sense that the users needs emerge during their activity. In SD, this continuous evolution may for example affect the development process that has to change in order to take care of unexpected events [14]. Considering this issue, many workflow solutions have already been largely criticized for their rigidity [1]. The set of tools involved by the users may also evolve and we can notice that most of the widely used solutions are faced with this problem [16]. For example and even if they propose useful tools, Web portals like SourceForge integrate several components intended to support collaboration through the development process, but the tailorability of such environments is in most cases reduced since the available tools are defined a priori. The dynamic integration of new tools by end-users is generally not possible. One commonly accepted generic solution for such tailorability is to propose reflective properties in SDEs, thus allowing for example the dynamic redefinition of the enacted process model, or the dynamic integration of tool components. However, if tailorable solutions like Eclipse (URL: http://www.eclipse.org/) exist, none of them actually supports all the identified issues, and research on how to improve tailorability in collaborative SDEs is still an on-going work [12][14][25].

2.2 The Activity Theory

We have presented some results coming from a general state-of-the-art in the SDEs field. These results, mainly coming from empirical studies, highlight what should be done to improve collaboration support in SDEs. Moreover, we strongly believe that studying these results about SD activity by using theories coming from the SHSs, like the Activity Theory (AT), can help to better understand these requirements. We will now briefly introduce the basic concepts of AT, but one can refer to [4][10] to get further information.

The AT takes the activity as the basic unit for analyzing human activities. The basic structure of an activity proposed by Engeström [10] presents the human activity as an interdependent system involving a subject that realizes the object of the activity, and the community of subjects who are concerned with this realization. Relations between the subject, the object and the community are mediated. In particular, the subject uses tools to realize the object of the activity. Rules determine what means belonging to the community, and a division of labor describes how the members of the community share the work up. Furthermore, activity is dynamic and continually evolves during its realization. For example, subjects may transform the mediating elements as new needs emerge in response to contradictions that rise between elements of the activity. Activity dynamics have been classified by Bardram [2] in three levels: the coordination level, where subjects concentrate on performing basic actions; the cooperation level, where subjects effectively act cooperatively towards their object; and the co-construction level, where subjects re-conceptualize their activity. Finally, subjects themselves evolve during the activity by acquiring skills and developing some experience about its realization. Thus, when subjects transform the elements participating in their activity, their experience is crystallized in these elements. This experience, written in the transformed artifacts, becomes available for others that reuse them in other activities.

2.3 Previous Studies Using AT

Many studies have already been conducted by using AT in the field of software development. For example, in [9], de Souza and Redmiles use the AT to study collaboration in a particular software development activity. They focus on the many contradictions rising inside such an activity and underline how these tensions have an impact on the other elements constituting the activity, or even on the other connected activities. For example a change in the source code may make the documentation out-of-date. This is what they call an inconsistency. They also show how multiple instances of an activity can increase the number of inconsistencies, e.g. when several developers simultaneously check-in the same part of code on the common repository. It is interesting to note that contradictions inside and even between activities hold a strong place in SD. Moreover, this "focus on identifying tensions and conflict is useful for highlighting areas where software tools and practices might be improved" [9]. These considerations help to better understand the above-mentioned issue about the need to support the SD activity as a whole: in order to manage the tensions existing between several activities, we should support the global activity they belong to.

Korpela et al. propose a framework to study information systems development as "a real-life work activity in context" [17]. They consider the development activity as part of a network of activities, taking care of others activities (such as the company's organizational management) and the way they are connected together. This framework is basically intended to describe information systems development. However, the concept of activity network, originally proposed by Kuutti [19], remains very interesting and can be useful to manage the contradictions emerging between activities during the development process.

Barthelmess and Anderson [3] use the AT to undertake a full analysis and evaluation of Process-Centered Software Development Environments (PCSDEs). The study is conducted by analyzing how these environments support the three levels defined by Bardram, i.e. coordination, cooperation, and co-construction. They underline that PCSDEs aim at supporting collaborative activities by providing support for division of labor through enactment of process models. However, "this emphasis on software process can result in 'blindness' with respect to other important aspects of work, in particular collaboration" [3]. Actually, even if they provide a good support at the coordination level, PCSDEs suffer from their production-oriented philosophy and present a serious lack of adequate support for cooperation, and then also limit the support for co-construction: existing PCSDEs limit the co-construction support to the reconceptualization of process models. Unfortunately, co-construction may also imply the reconceptualization of the whole activity structure through cooperation between subjects: co-construction needs then a good support for cooperation.

These studies point out some important aspects of software development activities. Supporting these dimensions in SDEs is important and remains a non-trivial work. Moreover, we have been working for years in the CSCW research domain by using the AT [6-7]. We have identified some other properties that have not really been taken into account in developing such systems. We will then now introduce these results that we want to add in the issues for creating better SDEs.

2.4 Adding Our Experience

We have been working in the field of CSCW for the last years [6] and we also have identified the need for better supporting co-construction through cooperation between subjects. The approach we have developed has been synthesized under the co-evolution principle that we have defined in [7]. Co-evolution emphasizes the fact that human activity is reflective in the sense that any (cooperative) activity is closely linked to a (cooperative) meta-activity where the subjects co-construct their environment in response to contradictions emerging during the core activity. Then, the Activity Supports (AS) we create aim at supporting domain-specific activities, and also their closely related cooperative meta-activities.

Today, we apply the co-evolution principle in creating SDEs and the techniques we have used, even if a little different, are close to those we have just presented in other SDEs: for example, tailorability at the process level is realized by providing computational reflective properties and a particular process meta-model that allows the subjects to create/transform their own process models. In our case, the process meta-model is mainly inspired by the AT and is called a Task: i.e. an Activity model [20]. A task specifies the Roles of the subjects, thus defining how they can (or have to) use the Resources involved in the activity. Some of these Resources are meta-tools allowing the (re)definition of the task. One difference between our approach and the others is that we have developed a minimal kernel introducing a recursive approach in which the meta-tools are used in cooperative (meta-)activities that are defined in (meta-)tasks.

Then, in our approach and according to the co-evolution principle, co-construction is realized during cooperative (meta-)activities themselves managed by particular and tailorable process models.

However, and as we would not have the space here to present all the differences between our realization and the others, we have decided to present in the rest of this paper a particular aspect of the co-evolution that has not been brought to the fore in other approaches. This work takes its roots in a fundamental idea developed in the AT while emphasizing the cultural and historical dimensions of human activity: the crystallization of the subjects experience inside their developed artifacts. We have briefly introduced how the subjects experience can crystallize at the end of Section 2.2. We will now present how this can happen in the SDEs we build.

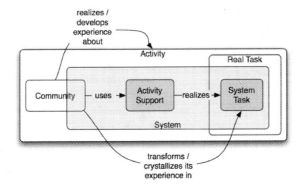

Fig. 1. Crystallizing subjects' experience

This mechanism is illustrated in the Figure 1. The community of subjects realizes an activity in the real world. This activity is supported by the system. The System Task is the part of the real task that has been specified inside the system to create an Activity Support (AS). The community acquires some experience while performing its activity. Making the System Task evolve can make this experience explicit through the system. For example, an evolution in the division of labor in the real activity may result in a new set of roles specified in the system task and that will affect the corresponding AS. This new evolved task corresponds to a new AS model that can also be instantiated for another community. The crystallized experience developed during an activity can then be transmitted through the tailorable system, thus supporting the experience crystallization and sharing through developed artifacts.

One can notice that this property seems at least partially supported by any system proposing tailorability by such a model-driven approach. However, our work goes a little further because we try to really merge the results coming from the AT and the computational techniques used to support human activities. Tailorability in a cooperative and shared system poses the problem of stability. Of course, there is a stability problem from the computer system point of view: a reflective system is not easy to maintain, and access to reflection should be controlled, as stated in the Open

Implementation proposed by Kiczales [15]. But we focus here on stability issues from the human point of view. Considering the AT, we believe that the subjects have to understand their system before to make it evolve. However, subjects will not be able to understand a continuously changing system. This is why evolution should only happen after stable phases and in a cooperative meta-activity where subjects may for example negotiate this evolution. Moreover, we cannot talk about experience crystallization if no experience has been developed. This is why, even if we believe that the use of shared model transformation is interesting for crystallizing and sharing experience, a model should also only evolve after discussion about an evolved prototype. With such a prototyping approach, subjects will be able to test new solutions before really modifying the system model. Following this idea, we now present how we have started to support this co-evolution principle in CooLDev.

3   CooLDev: Collaboration Under Eclipse

In the previous parts of this paper, we have identified issues to improve collaborative support in SDEs. We have underlined that SDEs should consider the global activity as a whole, be tailorable in a cooperative fashion, and take benefit from experience developed during the activities they support. We think that even if most currently used SDEs do not well support the collaborative dimension of SD activities, an appropriate approach would be to enhance one of these SDEs. This is exactly what we have done by extending the Eclipse platform in the CooLDev (Cooperative Layer for software Development) project.

3.1   The Eclipse Platform

Eclipse is an open-source generic platform based on a powerful integration framework that supports the dynamic discovery, installation and activation of plug-ins. In other words, this kernel manages and controls a set of integrated tools working together to support specific tasks. Thus, our choice has mainly been driven by the fact that Eclipse has been conceived in terms of tailorability. The subject can adapt the environment according to his emergent needs by dynamically integrating tools made available on the network. In a few years, Eclipse has grown very quickly due to the great amount of developers using it, and making it evolve.

However, regarding the collaborative dimension of software development, Eclipse still presents some drawbacks. Indeed, like other IDEs, collaboration support is limited to the use of a common repository such as CVS. Developers using the platform have been faced with this limitation and, as a result, some collaborative plug-ins have been produced [13][22]. However, and even if needed, this kind of extensions providing collaborative functionalities like an IRC does not tend to consider the cooperation at a global level. Eclipse has not been designed in that orientation, and for example, it does not propose a role notion managing the status of a user in the global cooperative activity. As a result, each subject has to integrate the tools (plug-ins) he needs, and to configure them himself according to his role in the real supported activity.

3.2 Introducing Global Collaboration

In Section 2, we have mentioned that some researchers already try to support this kind of global collaboration in Eclipse. This is particularly the case in Jazz [13] where many existing plug-ins have been enhanced. Our approach is different because we do not modify existing plug-ins: we propose a context for their execution.

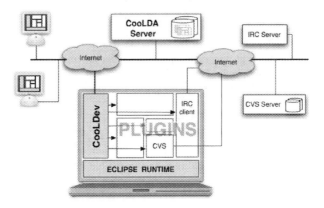

Fig. 2. CooLDev's architecture

We consider that each plug-in supports a particular activity like coding, merging different sources, or even chatting. In this approach, supporting the global activity means supporting the links existing between these (sub-) activities, i.e. managing the inter-activities [20]. This is mainly inspired by the above-mentioned work (see Section 2.3) of Kuutti [19] about relations between activities. To achieve this, we propose a plug-in called CooLDev whose role is to articulate the other plug-ins in the context of global cooperative activities. CooLDev's architecture is presented in Figure 2. After a basic identification phase, CooLDev retrieves on the CooLDA server the activities the subject is involved in, and configures his environment according to his role(s): subjects playing the same role retrieve an instance of the same CooLDev's perspective that will configure properly the user's environment. Moreover, CooLDev uses Java introspection mechanisms to dynamically retrieve public methods provided by the other plug-ins and to pilot them in response to activity state changes as defined in the task (activity model) that is running on the CooLDA server. These mechanisms are further described in [20] and we will now particularly focus on how experience can be crystallized and shared in CooLDev.

3.3 Experience Crystallization

A first look at Eclipse shows that the concept of experience crystallization, even if not clearly identified, seems to be in tune with Eclipse perspectives. A perspective corresponds to a particular point of view on the working environment (and the activated plug-ins) during the realization of a task. It manages the plug-ins activation and arrangement at the user interface level. Eclipse lets the subject create and modify his own perspectives, thus saving his preferences for a task. From our viewpoint, the perspectives mechanism provides a powerful mean to crystallize some experience. However, this experience is not intended to be shared by users. Even if some people may work with the same perspective because it has been packaged with a specific plug-in, nothing is provided for sharing perspectives in the context of a particular global, evolving and cooperative activity. As a first step in trying to better manage some experience crystallization and sharing through CooLDev, we have developed some basic features over the perspectives mechanisms.

CooLDev associates roles in a given activity with particular perspectives. When a subject joins an activity, he retrieves a perspective instance that is defined according to his role. However, all the subjects playing the same role may not share exactly the same perspective since we let them adapt/modify it according to their role and emerging needs. These instances, originated from the same role model, can then evolve and be considered as prototypes reflecting the subject's experience he has developed while playing his role. We then have developed a plug-in allowing subjects to share their perspectives. This feature is presented in figure 3. The view we developed shows the perspectives shared with others, and allows the users to test these shared perspectives . Finally, CooLDev allows generalizing a perspective at the task level, i.e. in a role model, for example after some negotiations between the subjects. Following the co-evolution principle, this form of co-construction helps the subjects to develop a real experience that is written into the perspective prototype. This experience can be crystallized in the model that can benefit to the subjects playing this role, and can be re-used later in similar activities. This demonstrates how a community of developers can make their environment co-evolve by sharing their experience. As CooLDev also supports transformations of the whole activity (process) model, we are currently extending this prototype-based approach to support experience crystallization in the other AS elements.

Fig. 3. Zoom on the shared perspectives view

4 Conclusion

In this paper, we have shown that Software Development (SD) activities still need better computer supports. Indeed, SD is nowadays an intrinsically collaborative activity. The software development research field has identified some issues to improve collaboration supports in SDEs. We have presented those that we find most important. Furthermore, the Activity Theory highlights these issues by explaining the basic mechanisms ruling every human activity. In our words, these issues are synthesized in the co-evolution principle where computer tools should be tailorable while supporting their co-construction through cooperative meta-activities. We have presented how these identified issues can be taken into account and we have particularly focused on an aspect of human activity that has still not well been identified and supported in SDEs: the subjects experience crystallization and sharing. We have developed this concept in the CooLDev environment that tends to manage SD activities at a global level, while supporting experience crystallization and sharing in and through the system. CooLDev is implemented over the widely used Eclipse platform. Currently, this proposition is still a prototype. Nevertheless, the basic presented features helped us to verify the feasibility of our approach and to illustrate how we can support some co-evolution through experience crystallization and sharing inside the platform.

We are pursuing our efforts in order to improve these mechanisms. We are particularly working on extending existing component models to provide a higher abstraction level that will ease introspection for the dynamic and fine integration of plug-ins in supported activities. Finally, a next step will include conducting evaluations of our approach by experimentations in real situations. We plan to test the platform in the context of a real commercial development team, which already uses an Eclipse compatible tool and is faced with the issues presented in this paper.

Acknowledgments. The authors want to thank the organizations supporting this work, in particular, the French Research Ministry for the ACI Jeunes Chercheurs CooLDev, and the TAC (Advanced Technologies for Communication) program financed by the Région Nord/Pas-de-Calais and by the French State in the framework of the NIPO/MIAOU and the EUCUE projects.

References

1. Agostini, A., de Michelis, G.: A light workflow management system using simple process models. Computer Supported Cooperative Work 9(3-4) (2000) 335-363
2. Bardram, J.E.: Designing for the dynamics of cooperative work activities. Proc. 1998 ACM Conference on CSCW. Seattle, Washington, USA (1998)
3. Barthelmess, P., Anderson, K.M.: A view of software development environments based on activity theory. Computer Supported Cooperative Work 11(1-2) (2002) 13-37
4. Bedny, G., Meister, D.: The Russian Theory of Activity, Current Applications to Design and Learning. Lawrence Erlbaum Associates (1997)
5. Booch, G., Brown, A.W.: Collaborative development environments. Advances in Computers 59 (2003)
6. Bourguin, G., Derycke, A.: A reflective CSCL environment with foundations based on the activity theory. Lecture Notes in Computer Science 1839 (2000) 272-281

7. Bourguin, G., Derycke, A., Tarby, J.-C.: Beyond the interface: Co-evolution inside interactive systems - a proposal founded on activity theory. Proceedings of the IHM-HCI 2001. Lille, France (2001) 297-310
8. CubraniC, D., Murphy, G.C., Singer, J., Booth, K.S.: Learning from project history: a case study for software development. Proceedings of the 2004 ACM conference on Computer supported cooperative work. ACM Press, New York, NY, USA (2004) 82-91
9. de Souza, C.R., Redmiles, D.: Opportunities for extending activity theory for studying collaborative software development. Workshop on Applying Activity Theory to CSCW Research and Practice, in conjunction with ECSCW 2003. Helsinki, Finland (2003)
10. Engeström, Y.: Learning by expanding. Orientakonsultit, Helsinki (1987)
11. Folcher, V.: Appropriating artifacts as instruments: When design-for-use meets design-in-use. Interacting with Computers 15(5) (2003) 647-663
12. Grundy, J., Welland, R., Stoeckle, H.: Workshop on directions in software engineering environments. SIGSOFT Softw. Eng. Notes 29(5) (2004) 1–3
13. Hupfer, S., Cheng, L.-T., Ross, S., Patterson, J.: Introducing collaboration into an application development environment. Proceedings of the 2004 ACM conference on Computer supported cooperative work. ACM Press, New York, NY, USA (2004) 21–24
14. Kammer, P.J., Bolcer, G.A., Taylor, R.N., Hitomi, A.S., Bergman, M. : Techniques for supporting dynamic and adaptive workflow. Computer Supported Cooperative Work 9(3-4) (2000) 269-292
15. Kiczales, G.: Beyond the black box: oOpen implementation. IEEE Software 13(1)(1996) 8-11
16. Koch, T., Appelt, W.: Beyond web technology - Lessons learnt from bscw. Proceedings of the 7th Workshop on Enabling Technologies. Washington, DC, USA (1998) 176-181
17. Korpela, M., Mursu, A., Soriyan, H.A.: Information systems development as an activity. Computer Supported Cooperative Work 11(1-2) (2002) 111–128
18. Krause, R.: CVS: an introduction. Linux Journal (87)(2001) 3
19. Kuutti, K.: Notes on systems supporting "organisational context" - An activity theory viewpoint. In: Bannon, L., Schmidt, K. (eds.): Issues of Supporting Organisational Context in CSCW Systems. COMIC Deliverable 1.1, Lancaster University, Lancaster (1993)
20. Lewandowski, A., Bourguin, G.: Inter-activities management for supporting cooperative software development. Proceedings of the 14th International Conference on Information Systems Development (ISD'2005). Vol. 1. Karlstad, Sweden (2005) 155-168
21. Rabardel, P.: From artefact to instrument. Interacting with Computers 15(5)(2003)641-645
22. Ripley, R.M., Yasui, R.Y., Sarma, A., van der Hoek, A.: Workspace awareness in application development. Proceedings of the 2004 OOPSLA Workshop on Eclipse Technology eXchange. ACM Press, New York, NY, USA (2004) 17–21
23. Sarma, A., van der Hoek, A., Cheng, L.-T.: A need-based collaboration classification framework. Proceedings of the 1st Workshop on Eclipse as a Vehicle for CSCW Research. Chicago, USA (2004)
24. van der Hoek, A., Redmiles, D., Dourish, P., Sarma, A., Filho, R.S., de Souza, C.: Continuous coordination: A new paradigm for collaborative software engineering tools. Proceedings of the Workshop on Directions in Software Engineering Environments. Edinburgh, UK (2004) 29–36
25. Webster, M.: An end-user view of the collaborative software development market. Market Research Report, IDC 30608 (2003). URL: http://www.collab.net/

A Strategic Approach Development for a Personal Digital Travel Assistant Used in 2008 Olympic Game

Lai-Chung Lee[1] and Whei-Jane Wei[2]

[1] Department of Industrial Design, National Taipei University of Technology,
1 Chung-Hsiao East Road, Section 3, Taipei, Taiwan
f10666@ntut.edu.tw
[2] Taipei Municipal University of Education
1 Ai-Kuo West Road, Taipei
Taiwanprofewei@yahoo.com.tw

Abstract. The study was to develop a strategic approach by which designers can identify what 2008 Olympic game travelers require for a personal digital travel assistant (PDTA) and how the user requirements can be met in the new PDTA product. To achieve the purpose, the researchers organized two teams co-working across two countries. Beijing Team comprised a professor, three observers, and fifteen travelers including two subjects observed by three observers. Taipei Team was composed of another professor, two designers and twelve subjects using brain storming to predict consumers' requirements for a PDTA. The procedures of the study included technical trial between two sites, scenario approach for briefing, a field trip for concept development according to user requirements observed throughout the travel, and a computer mediated communication between two sites for concept refinement. The findings include a strategic approach developed. It could be applied into any new product development based on user requirements.

1 Introduction

A strategic approach can be defined as a more integrative way to make a better decision toward the maximum of benefits. A strategic approach enables experts in two sites to work together in order to create synergy, develop a common vision and objectives, make agreement on priorities, and identify problems and barriers at an early stage. Asian Development Bank (ADB) had adopted a strategic approach to assist its developing countries by helping them apply Information and Communication Technology (ICT) into the economic development [1]. It is the rationale for conducting this study that the researchers apply computer-mediated communication (CMC) and scenario approach in developing a strategic approach to help Beijing and Taipei experts work together. In this case, Beijing site will benefit the skills of CMC and scenario approach; while Taipei site can create a niche market of PDTA in Beijing for 2008 Olympic Game. With such a strategic approach, both sites create synergy and develop a common vision and objectives.

W. Shen et al. (Eds.): CSCWD 2006, LNCS 4402, pp. 170–177, 2007.
© Springer-Verlag Berlin Heidelberg 2007

To achieve the purpose of the study, four questions are proposed to be answered:

Q1   What is the model of strategic approach across countries based on scenario approach and CMC?

Q2   How did the underlying scenario approach and CMC be integrated into a strategic approach?

Q3   Are there any problems to the strategic approach?

Q4   According to Q3, what are the solutions to the problems?

2   Literature Review

2.1   Scenario Approach

By definition, scenario approach is a method used to combine story description techniques and visual communication to promote discussion on user requirements. The story description techniques are to predict user requirements from three macro-perspectives of society, economy and technology. Meanwhile, participants will further predict and describe user profiles and their requirements from the micro-perspectives in terms of who, when, where, what, why and how. The visual communication requires text and pictures for a clearer communication.

Theoretically, Peters [2] indicated that there were five steps to build up scenarios: choose the area of investigation, establish the vectors of change, prepare the team, develop antithetical outcomes and identify scenarios via comment themes. It is essential to plan, understand, discuss and identify the key themes that will generate new concepts. For example, IDEO, one of the well-known product design consultancy in USA, emphasized that product innovation precedes a cyclic loop including understanding, observation, visualization, evaluation and refinement [3]. The product innovation process may go several rounds throughout this loop and then finally the innovative concepts will come out for further implementation. Kelley suggested that the IDEO design team should observe how consumers used the related products and listened to their comments before IDEO developed the new product concepts [4].

2.2   Computer-Mediated Communication (CMC)

CMC was applied in distributed group communication. The definition of distributed group communication refers to providing an infrastructure for site to site communication [5]. From the product design perspectives, the distributed group communication was a process illustrating how a design project was executed at a distance.

Taylor and O'Connor [6] indicated that concurrent engineering activities required CMC that facilitated their work. Such detailed usage information derived from CMC was in need to be gathered and collected for further analysis such as email, newsgroup posting, web page hit and data transfer. Even though the team members employed an assigned task of team goals, the participants may suffer from their unfamiliarity of facilities while they were executing their tasks. To avoid such difficulty, the training and well preparation were needed in distributed groups [7]. Sufficient preparation seems likely to conduct the successful outcomes during the design stage.

Much literature defined the tools for CMC as electronic mail and computer conferencing [8-9]. CMC in the office was considered as a 'social-technical system', because the acceptance and successful use of CMC for organizational communication were affected by the characteristics of the users, the group and organization as well as their process [10]. Regarding the tools for collaborative engineering, technologies used in CMC include electronic mail, voice mail, videoconferencing and teleconferencing [7][11]. D'Ambra et al. [11] thought that bulletin board and group decision support systems should be included in CMC. Mills [12] pointed that CMC included email, bulletin board, groupware, user net news, chat, file transfer, Web documents and desktop videoconferencing. In this study, CMC was concentrated on video conferencing and data conferencing.

2.3 A Strategic Approach

For a strategic approach, scenario approach and CMC were integrated in this study. Scenario approach was employed to describe user profiles and their requirements through distributed group communication. The distributed group communication was to imagine and predict user's situations and propose their macro perspectives and micro perspectives. An observation plan was followed. The researcher observed two potential users who might participate in 2008 Olympic Game about their activities of an 11-days tour in Beijing. The macro perspectives considered three dimensions on social, economy and technology including positive and negative issues. The micro perspectives were to think about whom the target users of PDTA were and what the functions of PDTA should have. Afterwards, observation took place in Beijing. The researcher selected two potential users who might participate in 2008 Olympic Game. They were on a tour in Beijing. The traveling events were observed including currency exchanges, shopping, picture taking and so on. Incidents and reactions were also observed and recorded. Data collection was completed throughout the 11 days. The final stage is to identify the top theme when we generate the outcomes for the users in the future.

3 Experiment of a Strategic Approach

The methodology of the study includes an experiment and observation. The experiment was to distribute six participants in an Internet environment. Data analysis of the study included qualitative analysis and quantitative analysis. Figure 1 indicated how the infrastructure for a distributed group communication was set up each site.

The experiment took place in the e-learning laboratory with concentration on the distributed group communication. Three participants were involed each site including two designers and one observer. Two senior designers were in Taipei and two junior designers were in Beijing. The senior designers were graduate students from the Graduate Institute of Innovation and Design in National Taipei University of Technology. The junior designers were undergraduate students from the Mechanical Engineering Department at University of Science and Technology in Beijing. Four designers communicated one another through Internet system with xDSL connection. The observer each site was also a facilitator. On videoconferencing, each observer was in charge for videotaping and meanwhile also responsible for problem solving including hardware and software issues.

Data was collected through videoconferencing and data-conferencing both sites. The videoconferencing employed a Polycom ViaVideo desktop conferencing system.

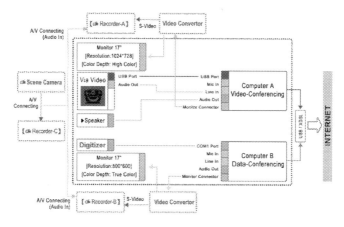

Fig. 1. An infrastructure for a distributed group communication

The data-conferencing applied an OneSpace Server system to upload and download computer-aided design files. Besides, all participants' data including note-making and video taping were also collected and analyzed. The instrument for data collection was the descriptive observation record sheet designed by the researchers. With the descriptive observation record sheet, all of the meeting transcripts were collected and analyzed. Inter-Rater Reliability and Constructive Validity were applied in the study.

4   Results of Experiment and Discussion

For research question Q1, what is the model of a strategic approach in distributed group design across countries based on scenario approach and CMC? A model of a strategic approach in distributed group design across countries was proposed in Figure 2.

To develop a model of strategic approach in distributed group design across countries, first of all, it was in need to organize a core team and exterior/outsourcing team shown as Figure 2. By the way, a technical trial between two sites was well settle down. The core team, secondly, applied a scenario approach for design briefing and concept development. The exterior/outsourcing team, thirdly, brought the concepts developed in mind with them and moved onto travelling. And meanwhile, two of them were observed throughout the filed trip for facts found with concentration on the user requirements for the PDTA used in the coming 2008 Olympic Games in China. Fourthly, the user requirements were proposed and discussed between two team members through CMC. Finally, the ultimate goal of PDTA concept refinement was presented by the distributed groups.

In terms of Q2, how did the underlying scenario approach and CMC be integrated into a strategic approach? A strategic approach in product development stages was further analyzed in Table 1. Table 1 indicated that ViaVideo media was in need before, during and after the meeting and meanwhile ViaVideo media was used throughout four stages of product design. The media of OneSpace Adviser was only in need during the meeting at three stages of scenario description, concept development and concept presentation. The findings showed that the use of OneSpace Adviser would replace many functions of ViaVideo media.

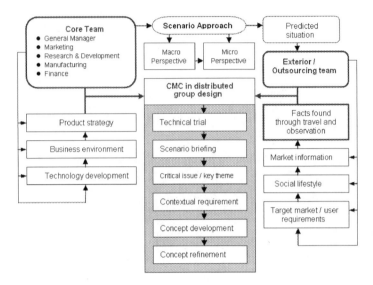

Fig. 2. A model of strategic approach in distributed group design across countries

Table 1. A strategic approach in product development stages

stages / CMC Media / procedure	Scenario and planning			Design Briefing			Concept Development			Concept Refinement		
	B	D	A	B	D	A	B	D	A	B	D	A
ViaVideo R3.0												
Video & audio		•			•			•			•	
Audio only		•										
Snap shot		•			•			•				
Video mail			•			•		•		•		
Application sharing												
Chat												
Whiteboard		•			•			•				
File Transfer Protocol		•		•	•							
OneSpace Adviser V11.0A												
3D Models								•			•	
Documents and Drawing												
Meeting Notes												
Markup		•						•			•	
Chat												
E-mail												
E-mail	•		•	•		•	•		•	•		

Key: B= before the meeting, D= during the meeting, A=after the meeting.

Regarding Q3, are there any problems to the strategic approach? Findings of the study indicated that there were several problems of the CMC usage. During the meeting, the video conferencing was sometimes broken down due to the CMC problems. Two causes of breakdown were found including operational issues and CMC Tools issues. Operational issues regarded participant's behaviors such as inappropriateness of video camera adjustment or argument due to different viewpoints. CMC Tools issues related to interference due to low speed transmission of broad width. The occurrence of breakdown was caused by video and audio, application and Internet connection. Video and audio breakdown related to a short break due to the disconnection. Audio disconnection would cease the communication but the communication could still continue if there was a video disconnection. Normally, the application and Internet breakdown will stop the communication and it was in need of repair.

In terms of the phenomena of CMC, some features should be further discussed in details. For example, the image of remote side gesture would exceed the video screen due to the screen size. Finally they would realize that this gesture did not be seen by the other side designers (see Figure 3).

Fig. 3. The remote side video gesture was out of video screen

During the meeting, designers might be off-task and became out of attention due to the long period of remote discussion. The possible causes of such an ineffective conference were lack of preparation, uncertain decision and so on. In this case study, we did not employ the broadband facility, both side of designers were waiting for the data transmission while sending concept images. The time remaining might extend the period of conference that face-to-face meeting would not occur.

Fig. 4. Designers express ideas with artifacts close to camera

Designers might use artifacts to clearly express the designer's ideas about what he/she concerned about. For example, the Taipei side designers would take his mobile phone very close to the ViaVideo camera so that he could clearly point out the texture printed in his mobile phone (see Figure 4).

In terms of Q4, what are the solutions to the problems previously described? According to the findings of the study, the solutions to the problems were proposed in terms of the guidelines of CMC usage. The guidelines were required for facilitating the effectiveness on distributed group communication. The guidelines of CMC usage included two parts. Part A was for users and tasks as follows:

1. To identify the goals of collaborative design and to build up common ground.
2. To plan project procedures with operational guidelines.
3. To arrange the task of the mediator.
4. To familiarize what and know how to apply the scenario approach.
5. To organize interdisciplinary team members.
6. To implement electronic management of the project data.
7. To communicate with the same terminology.
8. To channel informal or alternative communication.
9. To facilitate group communication with visualized story board.
10. To propose a non-participatory observational plan.
11. To collect data through triangulation.

Part B of the guidelines of CMC usage was concerned about the CMC tools. The guidelines were given below:

1. To concern user friendly applications.
2. To upgrade the monitor resolution for better quality of visualized data.
3. To enlarge the image of video conference.
4. To provide medium-mechanism combination shifts.

5 Conclusion and Implications

To meet user requirements for the PDTA used in 2008 Olympic Games, the researchers developed a strategic approach based on the theory of scenario approach. Accordingly, the macro and micro perspectives were generated. The study found that some factors needed to be considered in distributed group design. The guidelines of CMC usage were developed. For example, CMC users required to familiarize the scenario approach for user requirements. Also, distributed group members required to facilitate group communication with visualized story board.

According to Table 1, the study concluded that the use of OneSpace Adviser would replace many functions of ViaVideo media. There are unavoidable technological problems such as broad width derived from videoconferencing facilities. The possible solutions to the problems were proposed that it was in need of at least 512 MB xDSL broadband for each site.

To guide the distributed group design work, findings indicated some key issues on how to identify the collaborative goals, how to build up common ground, how to apply observation in scenario approach, how to arrange the mediator's tasks in both sites, how to coordinate interdisciplinary team work, how to make the project data electronic, how to communicate with the same terminology between countries. These issues were the key findings for the distributed group team work. The study suggested that designers should follow up the proposed guidelines to prevent from problems. For instances, the study found that the incompatible application was a problem. The reason was that OneSpace Adviser and NetMeeting did not support other file formats while importing a file into the whiteboard. It was a sort of non user-friendly application problem that might confuse users during the videoconferencing. Besides, in the concept refinement stage, the designers could not display the completed storyboard due to the limitation of screen size and monitor resolution. Although the conference platform provided the mechanism of CMC tools, designers sometimes did not follow up the guidelines on how to use CMC tools that was the problem. Concerning implications for follow up study, we will apply this model in heterogeneous group members such as manufacturing, outsourcing design experts from target markets or in other countries. Regarding implications for practice, the strategic approach model can be applied in workshop provision for problem solving by using the strategic approach model proposed in this study including processes of diagnosing situation, establishing goals, considering treatment options, choosing the best treatment, implementing the treatment, reviewing the outcome, and modifying the treatment plan in the light of the review.

References

1. Asian Development Bank: A Strategic Approach for Information and Communication Technology. Asian Development Bank, Philippines (2003)
2. Peters, G.: Beyond the Next Wave: Imaging the Next Generation of Customers. Pitman Publishing, London (1996)
3. Kelley, T., Littman, J.: The Art of Innovation: Lessons in Creativity from IDEO. America's Leading Design Firm, Currency (2001)
4. Kelley, T.: Design for Business: Consulting for Innovation. Design Management Journal (1999) 30-34
5. Chiu, M-L.: An Organizational View of Design Communication in Design Collaboration. Design Studies 2 (2002) 187-210
6. Taylor D., O'Connor, K.: Experiences with Remote Collaboration for Concurrent Engineering. Proc. IFIP WG5.2 Workshop on Formal Aspects of Collaborative CAD. Sydney (1997) 30-47
7. O'Hara-Devereaux, M., Johansen, R.: Globalwork: Bridging Distance, Culture, and Time. Jossey-Bass, San Francisco (1994)
8. Walther, J. B., Anderson, J. F., Park, D. W.: Interpersonal Effects in Computer-Mediated Interaction: A Meta-Analysis of Social and Antisocial Communication. Communication Research (1994) 460-487
9. Steeples, C., Unsworth, C., Bryson, M., Goodyear, P., Riding, P., Fowell, S., et al.: Technological Support for Teaching and Learning: Computer Mediated Communications in Higher Education. Computer and Education (1996) 71-80
10. Hiltz, S. R., Johnson, K.: User Satisfaction with Computer-Mediated Communication Systems. Management Science (1990) 739-764
11. D'Ambra, J., Rice, R.E., O'Connor, M.: Computer-Mediated Communication and Media Preference: An Investigation of the Dimensionality of Perceived Task Equivocality and Media Richness. Behaviour and Information Technology (1998) 164-174
12. Mills, A.: Collaborative Engineering and the Internet. Society of Manufacturing Engineers Michigan (1998)

A Distributed M&S Environment for Multidisciplinary Collaborative Design of Virtual Prototyping

Heming Zhang[1], David Chen[2], and Hongwei Wang[1]

[1] CIMS-ERC, Tsinghua University, Beijing 100084, China
hmz@mail.tsinghua.edu.cn
[2] LAPS, University Bordeaux 1, 351 Cours de la libération, 33405 Talence cedex, France
david.chen@laps.u-bordeaux1.fr

Abstract. This research focuses on a multidisciplinary collaborative modeling and simulation (M&S) approach for virtual prototyping. The design of complex product is supported by this approach in the distributed network environment. HLA and web services technologies are employed in our approach for interoperability and reusability of the M&S system. A HLA and web services based framework to support multidisciplinary M&S and its key technologies are presented. A consistent modeling method is studied. The interoperability issue of this approach is also discussed. A typical application demonstration of multidisciplinary collaborative M&S for the virtual prototyping of locomotive development is introduced. The demonstration of prototype system shows that HLA and web services are effective infrastures for collaborative M&S and they are promising for a new paradigm for collaborative design of complex product.

1 Introduction

A complex product is usually concerned with multidisciplinary knowledge, such as aerospace vehicle, locomotive, automobile, robot, etc. The design and development of such product is multidisciplinary in nature. It is necessary to consider the design problem globally and take various aspects into account in current industrial context. To analyze a complex product accurately, not only all of the single disciplinary problems, but also the interactions among different disciplines should be simulated in high fidelity. As a single simulation application cannot analyze the multidisciplinary behavior of a complex product comprehensively and accurately, it is an effective means to adopt multidisciplinary collaborative simulation, which combines different disciplinary models and simulation tools together, and also facilitates greater communication and cooperation among different development teams.

The virtual prototyping (VP) is a digital design method and technology, which is based on modeling & simulation of various engineering disciplines and can synthesize different elements in the early design stage [1]. It is concerned with many elements to implement multidisciplinary collaborative simulation for a complex product in the whole engineering lifecycle, such as simulation federation integration, model transform, service encapsulation, simulation run-time management, integrated supporting environment, etc. The systematic viewpoint and approaches should be applied.

Interoperability between distributed and heterogeneous design teams and simulation tools is an important issue to develop collaborative design. Most of the software

W. Shen et al. (Eds.): CSCWD 2006, LNCS 4402, pp. 178–187, 2007.
© Springer-Verlag Berlin Heidelberg 2007

applications were in many cases not designed to interoperate with others. Moreover, in the context of multidisciplinary collaborative design, interoperability is not only a software and IT technology problem; it also implies support of communication and transactions between different designers/teams that must be based on shared business and technical references, with its underlying semantic, syntactic and organizational barriers to overcome to achieve interoperability. Within the frame of European research framework, Three main research domains that address interoperability issues were identified, namely: (1) Enterprise modeling dealing with the representation of the inter-networked organisation to establish interoperability requirements; (2) Architecture & Platform defining the implementation solution to achieve interoperability; (3) Ontologies addressing the semantics necessary to assure interoperability [11]. It is considered that combining the knowledge of the three domains contributes to solving interoperability problems.

2 Architecture of Distributed Collaborative Environment for VP

The multidisciplinary character of design and development for a complex product has at least two dimensions. On one hand, the development of design models and methodologies must take into account the achievements of various scientific disciplines such as engineering science, cognitive psychologies, mathematics, cybernetics, and social sciences etc. On the other hand, the design of complex product should consider multidisciplinary collaboration among various engineering domains, e.g. mechanical, kinematics, dynamics, control and electronics, etc. The architecture of virtual prototyping for complex product development to meet multidisciplinary modeling and collaborative simulation in the distributed network environment is shown in Figure 1.

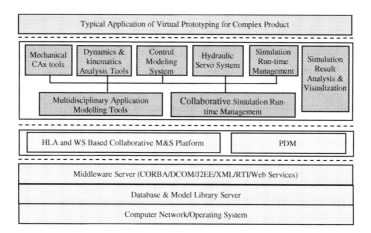

Fig. 1. Architecture of distributed collaborative environment for VP

There are principally four layers in the architecture of distributed virtual prototyping environment.

(1) **The application layer.** Approaches supporting multidisciplinary, concurrent and collaborative development for complex products are provided in this layer. Through the computer network and facilities of this layer, IPTs that possess all kinds of data and supports their cooperative work and innovation are connected.

(2) **The multidisciplinary application tools layer.** This layer consists of tools such as mechanical CAx tools, the kinematics & kinetics analysis tools, control modeling tools, hydraulic servo system, simulation run-time management and result analysis tools, etc. The models and simulation result for the virtual prototyping of a complex product are constructed through these tools.

(3) **The collaborative simulation platform layer.** The platform is mainly based on HLA (High Level Architecture) and Web Services. It provides a collaborative simulation environment and efficiently integrates the modeling, simulation running and evaluating tools to achieve synchronized execution and real-time interaction for multidisciplinary models. It can also manage the product data, simulation models and related processes in a smaller granularity, and integrates with the PDM system.

(4) **The infrastructure layer.** This layer consists of corresponding standards and technologies that enable interoperability and semantics among simulation federates. It is the basis of the collaborative design environment of complex product. In this distributed information integration and sharing mechanism, different applications are encapsulated according to HLA and Web services paradigm.

3   A Consistent Modeling Framework for Collaborative Design

HLA is initiated by the US Department of Defense (DOD) to promote the interoperability between diverse simulations and improve the reusability of legacy models. HLA is adopted as IEEE Standard and HLA based simulation develops tremendously in both military and civilian simulation.

HLA provides a specification and a federation development process to support the distributed collaborative modeling and simulation. To simplify modeling processes in complex product development and to reduce developing complexity for distributed simulation systems, a multidisciplinary consistent modeling approach is proposed as shown in Figure 2, which consists of five phases: (1) Conceptual modeling; (2) High level modeling; (3) Domain modeling; (4) Domain model transformation and metadata modeling; (5) Federation integration. According to characteristics of complex product development, the structure of collaborative simulation system can be established [6].

(1) In the conceptual modeling process, the component members, related domains, scenario of the multidisciplinary modeling and collaborative simulation system is constituted for a complex product development.

(2) In the high level modeling process, according to the HLA-based modeling, the simulation object model (SOM) and the federation object model (FOM) are designed. In this phase, the interactive information among SOMs and the content of FOM (such as object classes, interaction classes, attitudes and parameters) are defined. For the

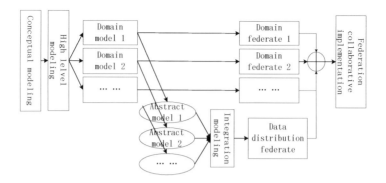

Fig. 2. Multidisciplinary consistent modeling processes for collaborative design

aim of high flexibility, it is necessary to define some dynamic attributes for each domain object and utilize XML for the interaction information of dynamic attributes.

(3) In the domain modeling phase, all the domain models are constructed by the IPTs of different disciplines through commercial software tools.

(4) In the phase of domain model transformation and meta data modeling, the input and output interfaces of each model, meta-data of domain model are established. The domain model transformation is implemented through the adaptor paradigm which encapsulates the domain model details. The meta-data of domain model is based on pre-defined XML template which includes function, input and output interface information of the domain model.

(5) In the phase of federation integration modeling, it is necessary to establish input and output matching relations between different domain models and form a simulation federation model for the collaborative simulation implementation.

4 Key Technologies

4.1 A HLA and WS Based Framework for Distributed M&S Environment

HLA provides a specification and a common framework for distributed collaborative modeling and simulation. Through the HLA adaptor, simulation modules can join the HLA federation of a simulation application. However, current available HLA implementations only support local area network (LAN) distributed modules of simulation, which is a barrier for modern product development. The rules of the HLA restrict federates to sharing FOM data via the federation's RTI, but do not preclude sharing data with other software or other federations by means of a web services offered or called through the RTI [2-3]. Consequently, we propose such a framework that combines HLA and web services (WS), as shown in Figure 3. In the framework [5], the web-based technology is used to provide the remote communication with the user clients, while HLA is primarily for the simulation traffic.

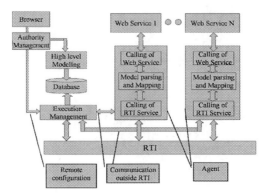

Fig. 3. A web service and HLA based framework

This framework of multidisciplinary modeling and collaborative simulation for complex product has advantages as follows:

(1) It provides a highly distributed simulation environment. We can execute collaborative simulation in Wide Area Network (WAN).

(2) The SOAP protocol is an open standard. There are publicly available implementations of SOAP, which reduces the implementation cost of simulation system.

(3) The SOAP protocol can be implemented in safe network protocol. It can be implemented by simple HTTP protocol, which eliminates the disturbance of the firewall in simulation execution.

(4) Legacy modeling and simulation software tools can be wrapped or reconstructed, so as to be integrated in the simulation application.

(5) The whole simulation system is controllable. From high level modeling to simulation execution, all the stages are managed and integrated through network centric information platform.

4.2 Model Transformation

The interoperability strategy in HLA is realized by defining Federation Object Model (FOM). FOM is common to all federates of the federation. The rules of HLA restrict federates to sharing FOM data via RTI. It is necessary to transform the model between the model data and FOM data [4]. We introduce the concept of adaptor, which is a glossary of software design pattern, to the collaborative modeling and simulation system. HLA adaptor wraps the model and makes it HLA compatible. Real-time message interaction is through calling RTI service and RTI callback. This mechanism is implemented by RTI through two ambassador paradigms: RTIAmbassador and FederateAmbassador. The structure of HLA adaptor is shown in Figure 4.

The adaptor consists of two parts: model transform and simulation time advance. The model transform facility consists of three parts, i.e. model operations, data map between model and FOM, the maintenance work of interactions with other federate. Time advance facility guarantees the synchronization of simulation execution.

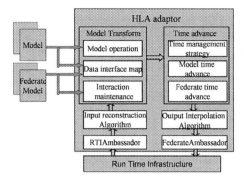

Fig. 4. The structure of HLA adaptor

There are several ways for HLA adapters to deal with component models. One is utilizing the APIs (Application Programming Interfaces) provided by simulation packages. Some commercial packages, such as MATLAB, provide a comprehensive API library for users to call interactive functions from programs in some programming languages.

Some simulation packages do not provide APIs, for example ADAMS. It can create a user's library of executables which include custom subroutines wrote in FORTRAN. As ADAMS runs with this library, the commands from HLA adapters will be executed.

4.3 Service Encapsulation

Web service is a self-contained, self-describing unit of modularity for publishing and delivering XML-based digital services over the Internet. Web services are consumed by the accepting and returning messages, which encoded in XML [7].

There are many ways to implement web service, for example FTP, HTTP, SMTP. Web service provides a powerful approach that enables integration of distributed computational resources through open standardized protocol. A highly distributed collaborative simulation system can be built in a service-oriented environment through encapsulation of enterprise resources. The structure of service encapsulation is shown in Figure 5.

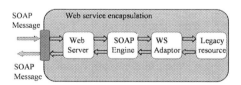

Fig. 5. The structure of web services encapsulation

Four pars are necessary for a Java web services encapsulation:

(1) A web server, the container for the HTTP requests, responses and SOAP engine.

(2) The SOAP engine provides a mechanism for SOAP message, XML serialization and de-serialization [8].

(3) WS adaptor. It is the interface between legacy resource and SOAP engine. A WS adaptor has something in common with the HLA adaptor. It gets data from legacy resource and serializes it in XML stream format. It de-serializes the XML stream and puts the data to legacy resource.

(4) Legacy resource. It is the components of simulation. In real simulation system, legacy resource can be either a standalone software tool or a simulation system.

4.4 Web Services Adaptor

WS adaptor is a coordinator between SOAP engine and legacy resources. Thus it must implement the bi-directional interface to SOAP engine and legacy resources. The structure of a Java-based WS adaptor is shown in Figure 6.

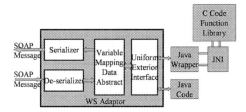

Fig. 6. The mechanism of web services adaptor

The WS adaptor exchanges data with SOAP engine through serialization and de-serialization. It provides several functions which seamlessly link the legacy resource through variable mapping and a uniform exterior interface. The uniform exterior interface links the C functions and libraries through JNI and transforms the data into Java type or object classes. It serializes the Java object as SOAP message and returns the message as response. Thus the service consumer can get access to the legacy resources in a highly distributed environment.

4.5 Some Interoperability Issues

The interoperability issue must be taken into account. Interoperability is defined as the ability for two (or more) systems or components to exchange information and to use the information that has been exchanged [9]. Main barriers to interoperability are syntactic and semantic mismatches between software tools and applications. For example, although many systems and applications speak XML, their data models and schemas are often quite different. The definition of common concepts such as 'product' or 'part' may vary greatly among applications. Another obstacle is the lack of standards in a number of cases, for instances for describing and orchestrating design process flows across multiple design teams [10].

From the interoperability point of view, in [12], some interoperability issues within the HLA framework are discussed:

- Interoperability between different simulation models
- Interoperability between different off-the-shelf simulation packages
- Interoperability between software systems within enterprises and off-the-shelf simulation packages (e.g. for test scenarios of controlling systems)

- Monitoring of a distributed scenario
- Data exchange and configuration

Use semantic annotation technique and ontology to allow mapping between different data models having different semantics, to detect semantic conflicts and reconciliate semantic mismatch.

It has been considered that XML based approaches provide the best hope to achieve data and application interoperability. However, current XML technology still lacks semantic power. Ontologies, tightly connected with the XML solutions, will play a major role in the future platforms for software interoperability. Some requirements [11] refer to how data structures are managed inside the application (database, flat files, XML). For example, in a data exchange transaction all data harmonization and mapping activities shall be performed at the origin of the transaction. There is also a demand to preserve sartorial standards for product data management, and use general standards for other data management (process, commercial and knowledge data). Ontology must not be information technology dependent. A suitable mechanism for reconciling semantic mismatch, between software applications that need to cooperate, should be developed. There is great variety of IT architectures and platforms as well as emerging De facto standards in this area. However there is a lack of interoperability between different architectures/platforms. For example, it is not clear how the platform using the web services paradigm would relate to and interoperate with architectures and platforms developed with reference to other paradigms [10].

According to [12], main limitation of HLA based simulation approach is the missing of standardization. Standards are needed for:

- Exchange Object Structure: Description of the objects exchanged within a distributed environment (potential base: ebXML).
- Federate Configuration File format: Reduces reprogramming effort for simulation tool interfaces in an HLA RTI environment. Different approaches have to be synchronized in this field.
- Ownership Mechanism: Incompatible approaches to adapt the HLA ownership mechanism for industrial usage.
- Generic Adapters: Interfaces to adapters should be standardized in order to reduce the investment for distributed simulation environments.

5   A Case Study of Locomotive Development

The development of locomotive is seen as a key technology for the successful implementation of this railway network. The development of locomotive corresponds to multi-disciplines. In order to consider design problem globally at the early design stage, it is necessary to implement the collaboration simulation. In this case, the aim of collaborative simulation is to get the dynamic responding data when the locomotive moves with different velocities on curve of railway at different radii. The design of locomotive multi-body dynamics system is depended on the control model. The federation model consists of three domains principally, i.e. the mechanical multi-body dynamics model, the control model and the hydraulic servo model of the locomotive. The interaction among various domain models is shown in Figure 7.

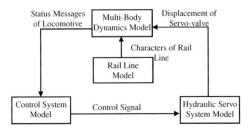

Fig. 7. Interactions among various domain models

Fig. 8. The tilting curve of locomotive body in simulation

We accomplished the multidiscipline modeling and collaborative simulation of locomotive development in a distributed simulation environment. The mechanical system of the locomotive was built in ADAMS, the control system was built in MATLAB and the hydraulic servo system model was built in Hopsan. After running of the collaborative simulation federation, the results can be utilized for evaluation. The result in Figure 8 shows that the locomotive body gets stable very soon.

6   Conclusions

The design and development of a complex product usually includes multidisciplinary knowledge. In order to consider the design problem globally and take various aspects into account in the early design stage, it is an effective means to adopt multidisciplinary collaborative simulation. In this paper, the architecture of collaborative modeling and simulation for the virtual prototyping of complex products is presented primarily. An approach of multidisciplinary modeling towards HLA-based distributed collaborative design is studied. A HLA and web services based framework and its key technologies of the distributed network environment to support multi-disciplinary M&S is discussed. A typical application demonstration of multidisciplinary collaboration simulation for the virtual prototyping of locomotive development is introduced. Our future work is concerned with the implementation of web based collaborative simulation platform, which supports the disciplinary knowledge exchange.

Acknowledgement. This paper is supported by the National Natural Science Foundation of China (Grant No. 60674079), the National R&D High-Tech Plan (863 Program) of China and the Key Laboratory of Beijing Simulation Center (Grant No. B0420060524).

References

1. Xiong, G., Li, B.: Virtual Prototyping Technology. Journal of System Simulation 13(1) (2001) 114-117
2. Blais, C., Brutzman, D., Drake, D.: Extensible Modeling and Simulation Framework (XMSF). 2004 Project Summary Report. Naval Postgraduate School, Monterey, California (2005)
3. Morse, K., Drake, D. and Brunton, R.: Web Enabling HLA Compliant Simulations to Support Network Centric Applications. Proceedings of the 2004 Symposium on Command and Control Research and Technology. San Diego, CA (2004)
4. Jian, J., Zhang, H., Guo, B., Wang, K., Chen, D.: HLA-based Collaborative Simulation Platform for Complex Product Design. Proc. 8th International Conference on Computer Supported Cooperative Work in Design (CSCWD 2004). Xiamen, China (2004) 462-466
5. Wang, H., Zhang, H.: Framework Of Web Service And HLA Based Collaborative Simulation System. Proc. Int. Conf. on Advanced Design and Manufacture. Harbin, China (2006) 477-481
6. Wang, K., Zhang, H.: Web Service And HLA Based Collaborative Modeling and Simulation for Complex Product Design. Proc. of the Int. Conf. on Advanced Design and Manufacture. Harbin, China (2006) 551-555
7. Buss, A., Ruck, J.: Joint Modeling And Analysis Using XMSF Web Services. Proceedings of the 2004 Winter Simulation Conference. Washington D.C. (2004) 1032-1038
8. Apache SOAP. URL: http://ws.apache.org/soap/
9. IEEE: IEEE standard computer dictionary: A compilation of IEEE standard computer glossaries (1990)
10. Chen, D. and Doumeingts, G.: European Initiatives to develop interoperability of enterprise applications - basic concepts, framework and roadmap. Journal of Annual Reviews in Control 27(2) (2003) 151-160
11. IDEAS (EU–IST–2001–37368): Interoperability Development for Enterprise Application and Software – Roadmaps. Description of Work (2002)
12. Jaekel, F.-W.: Distributed Federated Simulation of Supply Chains. In: Chen, D. (eds): Network of Excellence D6.1: Practices, Principles and Patterns for Interoperability. EU (2005)

A Development Framework for Virtools-Based DVR Driving System

Xunxiang Li[1,2,3], Dingfang Chen[1,4], Le Wang[1], and Anding Li[1,2]

[1] Wuhan University of Technology, Wuhan, P.R. China
lixunxiang@163.com
[2] Huangshi Institute of Technology, Huangshi, P.R. China
[3] Sanming College, Sanming, P.R. China
[4] Lab of Intelligent Information Processing, Institute of Computing Technology
Chinese Academy of Sciences, Beijing, P.R. China

Abstract. The multi-client technique framework is an essential mechanism of the Distributed Virtual Reality (DVR) driving simulator, which supports remote network real-time interaction and cooperation. As one of the excellent Virtual Reality software Development tools, Virtools is remarkable for its strong capability of interaction. Through an in-depth study on Virtools, the authors have developed a distributed driving simulator system based on the 3D engine, and studied the distributed network system with a real case. At the same time, some key issues for Distributed Virtual Reality of the Virtools-based platform, such as real-time prediction and dead reckoning, have been discussed in the paper.

1 Introduction

The various virtual environments which are located in different places can interact with others and share information through Distributed Virtual Reality (DVR) network system supporting remote network real-time interaction and cooperation [1] . Since DVR involves many scientific fields, as well as its tremendous tech and application potential, it has become an important research branch of Computer Graphics domain. Now, distributed techniques have been widely used, especially in new generation network game platform.

According to the number of the shared application system running in distributed environment, DVR system can be divided into central structure and duplicate structure. In central structure mode, central server runs a multi-client shared application system. The role of Central server is to manage the I/O operation of various clients and allow information communion among them. In duplicate structure mode, each client duplicates the content of central server, so all of them have a share of application system. Central server receives information from the application system of clients, and transfers the information to each of them, while the application systems do essential computations and generate necessary outputs [2].

The DVR driving simulator system [3] which the authors have developed adopts the duplicate structure. Among several distributed techniques carefully studied, Virtools Dev, the virtual reality software development package, is deemed to have the capability to implement DVR driving effectively.

W. Shen et al. (Eds.): CSCWD 2006, LNCS 4402, pp. 188–196, 2007.
© Springer-Verlag Berlin Heidelberg 2007

2 The Structure of DVR Driving System

2.1 Introduction to Virtools

Virtools Dev provides a development environment for building interactive 3D applications, and more than 600 kinds of reusable behaviors in the form of Behavior Building Blocks (BBs) that allow users to create almost any type of content through a simple, graphical interface. This makes the development of complex 3D interactive applications quick and effective. And the 3D engine has been certificated by Microsoft XBox system [4].

The application of the DVR driving system involves Virtools Dev, and distributed modules of Virtools Server.

2.2 The Network Modules of Virtools

Virtools Server contains the network modules of Virtools, which help users develop 3D interactive contents for internet and intranet utilization effectively by a network engine. Users can manipulate databases and exchange data easily through accessing the server.

Virtool Server contains two types of multi-user on-line server, independent network server and peer-to-peer intranet server. Users implement all necessary functions by Building Blocks without considering any problem of network itself.

Before running the executive files, Virtools Server allows users to download interactive components (including interactive modules, media data and databases, etc.) and to local computer by Virtools Web Player.

Virtools Server provides four modules as follows:

- Multiuser Module
- Download Component Module
- Download Module
- Database Module

All modules are independent. They share the data in server, and can be called separately, or be invoked by different threads simultaneously. The authors apply the Multiuser Module chiefly to construct DVR driving platform.

2.3 Multiuser Module

Multiuser Module is the key to implement distributed technique in Virtools. It provides a simple but highly-efficient way to create multiuser Virtools composition files (VMO/CMO) using the classical client-server structure and the standard networking protocol - TCP/IP. Multiuser Module allows the client composition to join a session hosted by a Server. Virtools Multiuser Module provides easy management of users, network messages, and distributed objects. It contains two fundamental steps to create a session.

Creating a Session. A client must first start a session using the Create Session BB. The client who creates the session is known as the session master and can perform certain operations that ordinary users cannot. Before joining the session, other clients must get a Session ID as well as a password if the session master has specified one. A client can choose to leave a session at any time (using the Leave Session BB). Note that if the session master leaves a session, the session is destroyed immediately afterwards.

Configuring Virtools Server Controller. You should open the Multiuser module configuration window of the Virtools Server Controller to create a session type, then name it and set the relative properties.

2.4 The Technical Framework of DVR Driving System

The Development of DVR driving system involves five modules as follows:

- Server
- Session
- Clients
- Network Messages
- Distributed Objects

Server. The Virtools Multiuser Pack is client-server based technology. All communication between clients (users) must pass through the server. Therefore, server is a basic requirement for any Virtools Multiuser application. The Virtools Multiuser Pack supports two types of servers: Behavioral Server and Peer Server.

Session. A session is a basic organizational element for multiuser applications. A session is simply a virtual space within which an instance of an application takes place. Each instance of a session has a unique identifier, the Session ID.

Each instance of a session uses universal time, unique to that particular session and identical for all users, to synchronize actions between clients. Universal time is recorded using a new type called Multiuser Time, designed for timekeeping over long periods.

Clients. To remain as open and generic as possible, a Virtools multiuser client has just two defining parameters: user name (in the form of a string) and user ID (in the form of an integer).

A client must set a user name before it can join or create a session. A client can subsequently change the user name. The Set User Name BB is used both to set the user name and to modify it.

Two or more clients may have the same user name as it is the user ID that is used to manage clients. On entering a session, a client needs to get information about the other clients of the session, and the clients need information about the client that has just joined. The Get Incoming User BB is used in both cases. The Get Outgoing User BB is used to detect when a client leaves a session.

Network Messages. Network messages are the principal way of communicating between clients. Network messages are very similar to messages in Virtools Dev. As in Virtools Dev, all messages are of a certain type: the default types are OnClick and

OnDblClick. Two different communication methods are available for sending a particular message type:

- Reliable communication: The network message is sent by TCP; transmission is "guaranteed" and the order of messages is preserved.
- Non-reliable communication: The network message is sent by UDP; transmission is faster but there is no guarantee that the message will be delivered or that messages will arrive in the correct order.

Distributed Objects. Distributed objects are another mechanism to send information between clients. A distributed object is an object whose state is spread along the network to all clients [5-6].

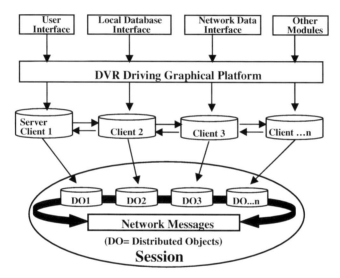

Fig. 1. The technical framework of DVR driving system based on Virtools

There is a one-to-one relationship between BeObjects and distributed objects - a distributed object can only ever be attached to one BeObject. Distributed objects can only be manipulated by one client at a time, who is said to be the owner of that object. However if a client releases an object, this object is free and is available for other clients to take ownership and control. A client can be owner of several distributed objects at the same time. Figure 1 shows the technical framework of DVR driving system based on Virtools.

3   Development of DVR Driving System

The application of DVR driving simulator contains three principal components: scene modeling, Virtual Reality interaction and distributed network techniques. Figure 2 shows the developing process of the DVR driving simulator system.

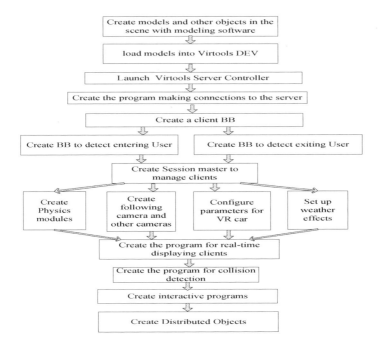

Fig. 2. Developing process of DVR driving simulator

3.1 Construction of Server and Session

Loading and Configure. Scene and car models should be loaded into the Virtools Dev Development platform firstly; next, run the Virtools Server Controller; and then configure IP, port, timeout limit and thread number for the host acting as a session master.

Afterwards, create a session type in the Multiuser Module, then make connections to the server through the Connect To Server BB to get the connection ID, client ID and available session type list. The client who creates the session is the session master. And other clients joining the session play roles as the Distributed Objects. At last, choose one of the pre-created cars for driving.

Connecting a pre-created Distributed Object to the selected car. The requests to join the session can be detected by means of real-time prediction. When a client joins a session, the existing clients will receive messages about it. The messages contain its position, orientation and the other information. And the existing clients can see the new client and observe its behaviors. At the same time, the new client will receive information of the existing clients, and see the other distributed objects-cars. Using the Get Incoming User BB, The existing clients in the session can get the username and ID of the new client. Meanwhile, the BB will return all information of the existing clients in the session.

3.2 Management of the Distributed Objects in the Session

Using the Lock Session BB and Unlock Session BB, a session can be open or closed. The Remove User BB helps to remove a user from the current session. And the leaved distributed objects can be detected with the Get Outgoing User BB. A client can leave a session at any time. Soon after that, the other clients in the session will detect one of the distributed objects disappeared, and delete its instance from the scene. In this way, it will not occur that the instance-car is still in the scene after the client leaved. Note that if the session master leaves a session, the session is destroyed immediately afterwards and all the other clients will be forced to exit from the virtual scene.

Fig. 3. Session: Client 1_BlueCar. Chat mechanism can be created to send messages to all clients. This figure shows that message appears above the car (avatar of the client) that sent it.

Fig. 4. Session: Client 2_GreenCar. As it appears in a 3D front, other clients of the scene can see the messages in all directions.

Chat mechanism can be created to send messages to all clients, as well as choose clients to receive messages from a pre-setting list. The message appears above the car (avatar of the client) that sent it. As it appears in a 3D font, other clients of the scene can see the messages in all directions. Figure 3 and Figure 4 show an example.

3.3 Establishing the Car Engine and Configuring Its Parameters

Car models are created by other 3D modeling softwares, while the process is not discussed here. The following introduction stresses on how to establish the car engine, as well as how to configure its parameters and how to manipulate it in the Virtools Dev. Although Virtools provides the function to add lights and textures to the car, what's more important is to establish the car engine with its Physics Car BB. Three arrays of the car engine should be created with Physics Car BB, and if necessary, various types of car can be simulated by configuring their principal parameters differently. The three arrays respectively are Body Parameters, Engine Steering Parameters, and Wheel-Suspension Parameters. The Body Parameters include mass, friction factor, flexibility, moment of inertia, speed attenuation factor and other parameters of the car; the Engine Steering Parameters involve the drag-force, minimal and maximal rotating speed, maximal speed, level-switch and so on; the Wheel-Suspension Parameters is related with parameters of four wheels, such as mass, friction factor, flexibility, moment of inertia, speed attenuation factor, rotating speed attenuation factor, etc. Various cars with different performance can be simulated exactly by the three arrays. The Switch On Key BB and Physics Car BB are used to implement the manipulation of the car, such as forward, backward, turn, level-switch, and so on.

The collision detection between cars can be solved with the following steps. Create an array or a group; and add the real-time distributed objects to it next; then declare the members of the array or group as a physical collision objects; after that, configure relative parameters such as collision radius, precision; finally, the collision of the cars can be simulated. In this way, the turnover scene of two collision cars with high speed will be shown vividly.

Create another type of distributed objects in the scene, a cubic warehouse for cars. When a user drives into the warehouse, an elevator runs, and sends the car to the right place. Other distributed objects, such as stubs or stones, can also be defined in the scene. Users can make collision with them to simulate the collision effects, at the same time, another type of distributed objects have been created.

3.4 Distributed Real-Time Prediction Technique

If the server or the existing clients detect a new client, two methods can be adopted to get status of the new client joining into the scene, which contains position, shape, volume, orientation, speed and so on.

Using Network Messages. Add network messages to the distributed application of a local client. That is, once a client joins the scene of a distributed application, a distributed object is created for it in the local host, and avatar of the client is attached to the distributed object. At the same time, the messages are sent to the other clients through network messages to notify the new client joins. After server and the existing clients receive the messages, the code to detect the new client is called to get its status such as position, orientation, speed etc. And the status will be refreshed periodically. In this way, the behaviors of all distributed clients, in the form of avatars, can be simulated in the same scene effectively.

When a distributed client leaves, it can be detected by the application of local host, so the network messages are not sent. Once local host finds a client left, the avatar of it will be destroyed at once. Note that the piece of code should be executed every cycle to detect the destroyed distributed objects.

Using a cycle program to detect distributed objects directly. A cycle program can be used to detect distributed objects in the development of distributed application. When a client joins the distributed scene, the program to detect distributed objects will find the new client. In this way, the existing clients create avatars for the new client, get the status of it and refresh the status periodically. The process to detect a distributed client left is the same as the method just mentioned.

3.5 Dead Reckoning Technique

Dead reckoning is the name of a technique used to predict a future value based on the previous two or three values. Dead reckoning therefore allows clients to update (predict) the value of properties for a distributed object even if no update has been received. In this way, it is possible to keep distributed objects up to date for all clients without having to send updates at each frame, thus the running of distributed application will be more effective.

Dead reckoning is essential for movement. For example, a client moves an object about locally and sends the object's new position out onto the network at every frame. However it cannot be guaranteed that all the other clients will have a new updated position every frame. Any client that misses updates at any regularity will not be able to move the distributed object smoothly at each frame, but will be forced to 'catch up' between frames –resulting in jerky, irregular (not to say unnatural) movement.

Here dead reckoning for a vector is illustrated. With three given positions for an entity, it is possible to predict where the entity will be in the near future. That is: given three positions P0, P1 and P2 and their associated times T0, T1 and T2, the object's speed and acceleration can be calculated at P2. This allows a convergence point Pc to be calculated at a certain time Tc=T2+(T2-T1). Figure 5 illustrates what happens.

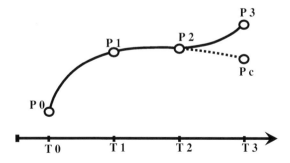

Fig. 5. Dead Reckoning. Given three positions P0, P1 and P2 and their associated times T0, T1 and T2, the object's speed and acceleration can be calculated at P2.

By sending regular updates, such as at 100ms intervals, of an object's position , the prediction can be very effective. However, thanks to dead reckoning, the client that controls (owns) the object may not even need to send an update at every interval (e.g. every 100ms).The client controlling the object performs the same dead reckoning calculation as the other clients out on the network. If the difference between the object's real position and dead reckoned position is very small, then the client does not actually need to send out an updated position.

For example, P0, P1 and P2 are the last three known positions for an object. Pc is the point of convergence. As T3 approaches, the object's real position P3 is compared to the position calculated Pc. If the level of error is below a certain level, then no update is sent.

4   Conclusions

DVR technique is always the key and difficult point in system development. Though it can be implemented in many ways, the most promising approach is to find out a comprehensive platform on which to develop, use and maintain distributed technique more effective and reliable. In order to fulfill the requirements of distributed technique in a virtual driving system, the authors find it more flexible and extensible to develop the system with Server and Multiuser modules of Virtools. The research result shows that programmers and 3D designers can collaborate well with each other through intuitional graphical interfaces and modular script programming mode so as to reduce the development cycle time and improve the executive efficiency of the program.

References

1. Yang, C., Chang, M., Xiao, R.: Research on Implementation of Distributed Virtual Reality System InteVR1.0. Journal of Engineering Graphics (2004) 77-84
2. Li, D.: Distributed Virtual Reality System. Journal of Ili Teachers' University (2004) 65-67
3. Chen, D., Li, X., Li, W.: Investigation of Vehicle Driving Simulator by Distributed Virtual Reality Technology. Journal of System Simulation (2005) 347-350
4. Liu, M.: 3D Game Designer Bible - Virtools Dev. Sichuan Publishing Group, Chongqing, China (2005) 3-15
5. Gao, S., Chen, D.: The Research on the Distributed Virtual Design/Manufacture System Based on the Multi-Agent. Computer Engineering and Applications (2002)
6. Li, W., Wang, Q., Chen, D.: Constitution of VR design environment and Development of OpenGL and VRML. Journal of Engineering Graphics (2000) 1-5

A New Method for Customer-Oriented Virtual Collaborative Design with VRML Product Model

Lianguan Shen, Wei Zhao, Mujun Li, and Jinjin Zheng

Department of Precision Machinery and Precision Instrumentation
University of Science & Technology of China
Hefei, Anhui 230026, China
lgshen@ustc.edu.cn

Abstract. A web-based customer-oriented virtual collaborative design system has been established. The system, using VRML product model as the inter-medium, provides customers and enterprise designers with a new and interactive way to discuss and improve the product design to satisfy the requirements of the customers. The relevant key technologies, such as pretreatment of VRML file and Reloading Model File, online design, alternating operation of the model and synchronous display, are introduced.

1 Introduction

The competition of the market continues to demand companies to develop and manufacture more individualized and diversified products to meet customer's requirements. It is very important to respond to the market quickly in terms of acquiring personalized information from the customers and providing them with many choices. A web-based virtual design environment, as shown in Figure 1, is created to allow the customers to collaborate with the product designer real-time, so that the customers' feedback can be incorporated into the designs instantly.

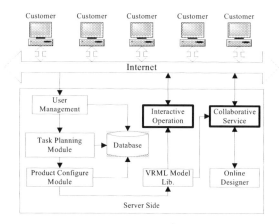

Fig. 1. System framework

W. Shen et al. (Eds.): CSCWD 2006, LNCS 4402, pp. 197–206, 2007.
© Springer-Verlag Berlin Heidelberg 2007

Virtual reality technology provides people with new, exciting and interactive ways to show the product models. VRML (Virtual Reality Modeling Language), as the first international standard of virtual modeling on the internet, is widely used for its open and platform-independent features [1]. VRML provides a minimum set of geometric modeling features and contains numerous features far beyond the scope of a modeling language. But the VRML models created by a 3D modeling software are static. To make them interactively operable, the static models must be enhanced. For example, in order to catch the vision of the product models, some parts in the virtual models need to be hidden or disassembled, colors of certain parts should be changed when the customer requires, and so on.

A new node database is developed to make VRLM models interactive for customers.

2   Product Configuration Module

2.1   Creation of the VRML Product Model

The VRML model is created in an ubiquitous 3D solid modeling software. In the system a Modeling Driving Module (MDM) is developed to monitor the instructions of modeling and correlative parameters, and then drive the 3D modeling software to update the product prototype and export a new VRML model. Figure 2 shows the workflow of the Modeling Driving Module.

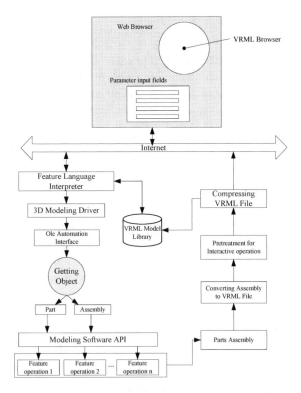

Fig. 2. The workflow of the Modeling Driving module

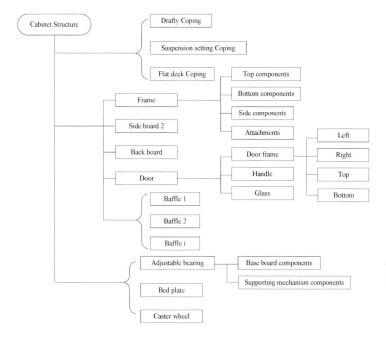

Fig. 3. Product Structure Tree of a cabinet

As the precondition, the enterprise designer should create a parametric prototype of the product previously and construct a Product Structure Tree in the product configuration file in feature language [2-3]. Figure 3 is an example which shows the tree structure of an instrumentation cabinet. The designer should release some optional parameters of certain components or assembly for customers to customize the product, such as style, length, width, height and color, etc.

According to the assembly relationship of the parts, every part is located in corresponding node on the tree. Each of them is assigned an identifiable name and its constraints necessary for assembly relation. The Product Structure Tree is the foundation of pretreatment VRML file and interactive operation.

As shown in Figure 2, after receiving the parameters submitted by customer on the enterprise's website, the Feature Language Interpreter (FLI) of MDM on the server side is activated. Then FLI matches the received parameters with the related parameters in the product configuration file, and then searches in the VRML model library to find if there is a VRML model with the same parameters. If the returned value is false, the 3D modeling driver is activated, it calls the 3D modeling software through the OLE Automation interface to implement feature operation on the parameterized prototype of the product [4]. After reassembling the new parts and creating a new VRML model, MDM compresses and sends it to the customer immediately. At the same time, a copy of the VRML model is stored to the VRML model library for the next reservation.

If the returned value is true, it means that there is a VRML model with the same parameters in the VRML model library. Then MDM sends the model to the customer directly. In such way, the time of modeling can be saved.

All the procedures are completed automatically by MDM without interference from enterprise designer.

2.2 Pretreatment of VRML Model File

A node database created from Product Structure Tree records the node's information of the VRML model. It is shown in Table 1. Every node has an identifiable ID. The node name, its maneuverability and the corresponding relationship of all nodes are also defined in Table 1. For example, switch nodes are defined to hide or show some special parts, and color nodes are defined to change the surface color of the selected parts, etc. [5-6].

Table 1. Node Database

ID	Parent	NodeName	Operation
1_	0_	Side_1	1
2_	1_	Color_1	0
3_	0_	Side_2	1
4_	3_	Color_2	0
5_	**0_**	**Top**	1

Two more important nodes must be inserted to the VRML file. They are ProximitySensor ("PS") Node and ViewPoint ("VP") Node. The PS node can perceive the change of the view point of the VRML model in the browser. It can then output a group of double-precision type parameters, which the VP node then uses to change the view point of the model in the browser. The codes are as following:

```
DEF VP Viewpoint{position 0 0 4 orientation 1 0 0 0}
DEF PS ProximitySensor{size 999 999 999 center 0 0 0}
```

Figure 4 presents the exhaustive logic relationship between the database and the inserted nodes.

3 Interactive Operation

On the client-side, after logging into the virtual design website of the enterprise, the customer can choose the style of the parts and input the product size, shape parameters, such as height, width, style and color of the parts, etc. Then he submits the data to the server. A processed VRML model would be created and be downloaded from the server automatically, and then it shows in the Cortona browser in the webpage of the client-side. The Cortona browser is a kind of VRML browser, Ubiquitous tools such as Visual Basic and Visual C++ can communicate with special nodes of VRML model through the intrinsic engine of Cortona VRML Browser.

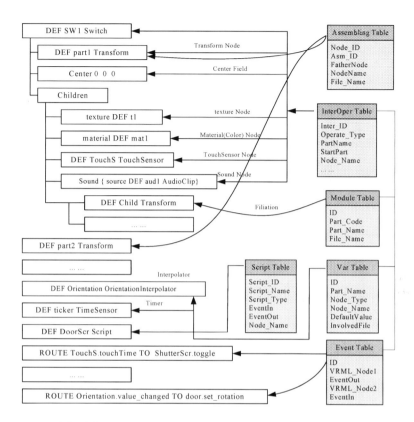

Fig. 4. Logical relationships between inserted nodes in database

In order to show the details, the VRML model should enable interactive operations, such as hiding or disassembling, changing color or performing customized animations (such as opening or closing the instrumental cabinet door as shown in Figure 5), in addition to standard operations, such as moving, rotating and scaling.

Therefore, some special controls should be set on the web page to communicate with the inserted nodes of the VRML model file. These controls are associated with a series of VBScript or JavaScript embedded in the webpage code [7-9]. As an example, the following pseudo-code segment illustrates the example of hiding or showing the door of the instrumental cabinet model.

```
function Hidedoor()
{
Cortona1.Engine.Nodes('DoorBoard').Fields('whichChoice')=-1;
}
<input type="button" value="hidedoor"
    name="HidedoorBtn" onclick="Hidedoor()" >
```

In this example, the Switch Node names "DoorBoard" has been inserted into the VRML file by the auto processing module on the server-side. This type of node has a "whichChoice" field. If the value of "whichChoice" is set to 0, the geometry information included in the switch node can be seen in the Cortona Browser. This information will be hidden if the value is set to -1. While clicking the "HidedoorBtn" button in the web page, the function named "Hidedoor()" will be called, and then the engine of the Cortona browser responds to find the "DoorBoard" node. After the function being executed successfully, the door of the instrumental cabinet model is hidden.

Here is another example of customized animation for opening or closing a door. The scripting is inserted in the VRML file, but not in the web page [10-11].

```
ROUTE TouchS.touchTime TO ShutterScr.toggle
ROUTE ticker.fraction_changed TO ShutterScr.set_fraction
ROUTE ShutterScr.fraction_changed TO Orientation.set_fraction
ROUTE Orientation.value_changed TO Tdoor.set_rotation
```

Here, "TouchS" is defined as a TouchSensor Node, when the mouse cursor moves onto the part included in such node, the TouchSensor can perceive and activate sequential animations. "Ticker" and "ShutterScr" are customized scripts (like sub functions) that define the rules for a high reliability of the animation. "Orientation" is defined as an OrientationInterpolator Node which defines every step of the animation, and "Tdoor" is a Transform Node that includes the geometry information of the instrumentation cabinet's door.

When the Touch Sensor of the cabinet is clicked, the door will be opened or closed automatically (see Figure 5).

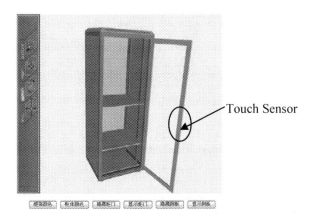

Fig. 5. Opening and closing the door

4   Collaborative Discussions

4.1 Synchronous View

When a customer is interested in a certain product and the information presented in the web page is not sufficient, the customer can request a collaborative discussion with the online designer of the enterprise via the web page. Here the collaboration has two meanings: the customer and designer operate the same VRML model of the product and the state of the model always keeps same in both Cortona browsers.

The function is realized by processing the PS node and the VP node. The PS node is defined as the ProximitySensor Node. This node can perceive the actions of mouse and output a group of 7 double-precision numbers which describe the position and orientation of the model. The group of numbers can be acquired through the engine of the Cortona Browser. The VP node is defined as the Viewpoint Node, and it also has a group of 7 double-precision parameters correlative with the PS node. These parameters can be evaluated to change the position and orientation of the viewpoint of the VRML model. The change of viewpoint creates the illusion that the VRML model changes its position and orientation. That is to say, if the PS node's parameters from the Cortona Browser of one side of the collaborators are continuously monitored by the VP node's homologous parameters of the Cortona Browser of the other side via internet, the frames of the VRML model of the two sides will always look the same while the minimal data transfer delay is ignored. It works smoothly when the sample interval of the PS node's parameters set to approximately 200ms.

To facilitate efficient collaborative discussion, both the customer and the developer should be able to operate the model. To avoid conflict, an arbitration mechanism must be established. In this paper, a "Raising Hand" method is represented as shown in Figure 6. The super user (for example, the enterprise designer), has access to arbitration. Every user can raise hand to request access but only one user can get the access at a time. The operation information of the current controller will be sampled and sent to other clients. In the case, it is actually a half-duplex system.

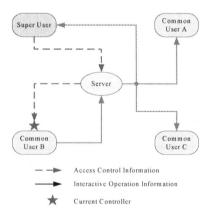

Fig. 6. Raising Hand method

4.2 Collaborative Operation

The current controller can operate special parts besides change their position and orientation. Regarding disassembling certain part and changing its color are as examples here: every part is created separately by the modeling system and the geometry information of all parts is detached with each other. Every part can be included in one or more special nodes. We can define a color node "Cdoor" which encloses the door's geometric entity of the instrumentation cabinet model. The door's color would be set by changing the parameters (such as diffuseColor, emissiveColor, etc) of the color

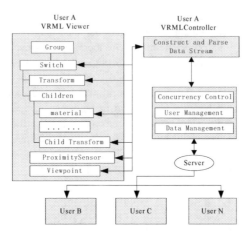

Fig. 7. Flow of collaborative operation

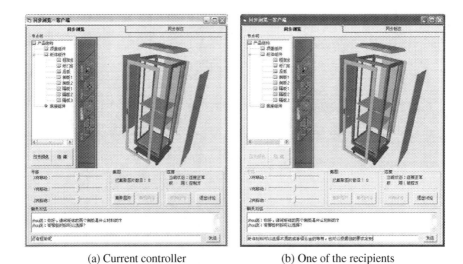

(a) Current controller   (b) One of the recipients

Fig. 8. Snapshot of collaborative discussion

node. In like manner, a transform node "Tdoor" which has three parameters is defined to change the position of the door. To disassemble a VRML model is equally to move each part to a proper position. Figure 7 shows the workflow of collaboration discussion.

A Treeview control is set for user to select the part which he wants to operate on. The tree is built based on the database which is created by auto processing model on the server-side, and it contains all operable nodes which are inserted into the VRML model file. When the current controller clicks any node to do corresponding operation, the operation information is sent to other sides of the collaboration partners immediately through the Internet. The customers also can communicate with the designer by typing or talking in the system. Figure 8 shows a snapshot of collaborative discussion scene.

4.3 Reloading Model File

During our research, an unexpected phenomenon occurred. The current controller's VRML Browser would be out of synchronization with others' browsers when he lost the control right and started to receive the collaborative data from the new controller. We also found that the parameters of the PS node were changed, but the VP node's parameters remained the same in the current controller's VRML Browser when the posture of the model was changed by the new controller's mouse actions. But the PS node's and VP node's parameters in the other users' VRML Browsers (its model did not operated directly by mouse) kept the same with the new controller's at any time. In this case, the disorder of parameters of the PS node and the VP node made the last controller out of synchronization with the others.

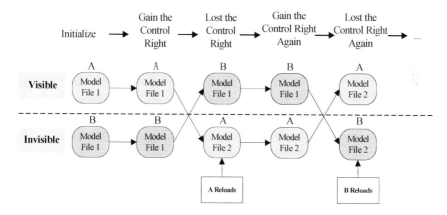

Fig. 9. Method of reloading model file

To solve the problem, a method named "Reloading Model File" is developed. Its core idea is to accord the parameters of the PS node with the VP node.

Figure 9 shows the principle of the "Reloading Model File" method. In the collaborative discussing module, two VRML Browsers A and B are superposed in every client browser. They both load the same VRML model, but only one browser is visible and the other one is hidden.

To keep synchronization the following three processes are adopted:

1. Initialization. Two copies of the current operated model file are loaded to the Browser A and B.

2. When a user becomes the current controller, he does interactive operations on the model in the visible browser A, and his invisible browser B receives the collaborative data at the same time.

3. Once the current controller loses control access, the browser A is hidden and the browser B becomes visible to replace browser A to take part in the collaborative discussion. In order to smooth the switch of the two browsers at the next time, the browser A reloads a copy of the model file immediately and receives the collaborative data to adjust the posture of the model too.

The "Reloading Model File" method is proved to be able to solve the outer-sync problem sufficiently.

5   Conclusion

An approach of interactive operation of VRML product model is presented. Key technologies, such as defining proper nodes, auto processing the VRML model file and inserting customized VRML scripting, are introduced.

A method of realizing collaborative discussion is also described. It provides a cooperative virtual product design environment by showing products to customers vividly and gathering feedbacks to product designers in real-time. The "Raising Hand" method is developed to ensure reliable collaboration discussion between the customers and enterprise designers.

Acknowledgments. This project is supported by the Anhui Province Natural Science Fund (Grant No: 03044106), the National Science Foundation of China (Grant No: 60473133), and "Hundred Talent Project" of Chinese Academy of Sciences."

References

1. Hideyuki, A., Akihiro, K.: Study on the collaborative design process over the Internet: a case study on VRML 2.0 specification design. Design Studies 19(3)(1998) 289-308
2. Lee, J.Y., Kim, H., Kim, K.: A Web-enabled approach to feature-based modeling in a distributed and collaborative design environment. Concurrent Engineering Research and Applications 9(1)(2001) 74-87
3. Zhou, Z., Li, X., Shen, L.: Research of Web-based collaborative modeling using layered feature language. Proceedings of IE&EM'2002 & IceCE'2002. China Machine Press, Beijing (2002)
4. Jiang, H., Li, Z., Xing, Q.: Tutorial for Customization of Solidworks 2003. Pub. House of Electronics Industry, Beijing (2003)
5. Zhou, Z., Li, M., Zhao, W., Shen, L.: Methods of Deal with Real-Time VRML Modeling for Interactive Browse on the Web-based Virtual Design. Journal of Computer-Aided Design & Computer Graphics 6(2005) 1371-1377
6. The web3D Consortium (1998). The Virtual reality modeling language. URL: http://www.web3d.org/specifications/vrml97
7. Zak, D.: Programming with Microsoft Visual Basic 6.0. Pub. House of Electronics Industy, Beijing (2002)
8. VRML Automation in Cortona VRML Client. URL: http://www.fit.ac.jp/~araya/vrml20/sample/VrmlAutomation/
9. Belfore II, L.A., Chitithoti, S.: An interactive land use VRML application (ILUVA) with servlet assist. Proceedings of IEEE Winter Simulation Conference (2000) 1823-1830
10. Liang, J.S., Pan, W.: The research of Web-based 3D interactive technology for conceptual design system. Proceedings of the 9th International Conference on Computer Supported Cooperative Work in Design. Coventry, UK (2005) 611-616
11. Wang, H., Xie, X., Huang, Z.: Collaborative and interactive room design on the web. Proceedings of the 7th International Symposium on Parallel Architectures, Algorithms and Networks (2000) 238-245

Development of a Design Supporting System for Press Die of Automobile Panels

Sang-Jun Lee[1], Keun-Sang Park[2], Jong-Hwa Kim[3], and Seoung-Soo Lee[3]

[1] Dept. of Automobile, Dongeui Institute of Technology, Busan, South Korea
leesj@dit.ac.kr
[2] Dept. of Industrial Engineering, Konkuk University, Seoul, South Korea
ergpark@konkuk.ac.kr
[3] CAESIT, Konkuk University, Seoul, South Korea
jhkim@konkuk.ac.kr,
sslee@konkuk.ac.kr

Abstract. This paper presents the development of a design supporting system for press die of automobile panels. The proposed system supports the design process of press die efficiently and systematically by utilizing standard data, and reflecting knowledge of press die design collected and accumulated through the interviews with design specialists working in a Korean motor company. This paper illustrates a methodology for systematic press die design, automatic checking of dimensions and implementation.In addition the rule-based design system is developed based on the product data. All components of the press die are regarded as product data and the components are regarded as the unit of press die. Parametric design using knowledge base and standard database is introduced to make it easier to deal with the complicated design knowledge easily. For implementation, the rule-based design system is programmed with C++ and Motif and the system can be linked with CATIA.

1 Introduction

Reducing manufacturing cycle time is an important issue in the recent automobile industry with changing customer needs. Although the industry has adopted various new technologies such as CAD/CAM and factory automation, the results do not meet the expected level. The main reason is that the new technologies must be adapted to the industry's own know-how and knowledge workflow, as well as administrative traits of a particular company. [1]

In designing and manufacturing of trim die and draw die, the variety of car panel shapes and the complexity of the structures complicate the problem even more. A lack of consistency in the design may cause weak relationship between the design and manufacturing, and presents difficulties in finding out the errors of designer. Due to these problems, a lot of time and resources are wasted. [1]

In spite of the variety and the complexity of the car panel structure, some consistencies can be found in the rules, knowledge and the methods of design, although they are redundant sometimes. [2-3]

W. Shen et al. (Eds.): CSCWD 2006, LNCS 4402, pp. 207–216, 2007.
© Springer-Verlag Berlin Heidelberg 2007

Hence, it is helpful to develop a design supporting system for trim die and draw die. The design supporting system can be developed by systematically converting the regulation of the design characteristics and the know-how's of design specialists into the decision rules and knowledge bases. [4]

2   The Current Design Process

Since the dies are essential tools in manufacturing the body panel of an automobile, the design processes and the process plans of the dies determine the cost, quality, processing time and even the safety factors. [5]

In the stamping process many kinds of dies such as draw dies, trim dies, flange dies, cam dies, flanking and piercing dies and progressive dies are used. Among them the trim dies are used in the shear forming pressing process which cuts and removes the panel material by the force of fracture made with cast iron or steel die. [1] The main functions of the trim die are as follows: 1) trimming to cut the boundary of a body panel, 2) removing the scraps, 3) piercing to make holes on a body panel.

Until now, these three processes were performed manually due to the complexity of rules to determine various design variables even if the designers are experts of commercial CAD system. They use approximate work-piece sizes and tentative methods, and relied on past experience to layout the die sets. Also the resulting designs are prone to errors since it is difficult to figure out 3D free surface from the 2D draft and it is very complicated task to calculate the angles of normal and tangent vectors of the trim line and the heights of the inner shapes. To facilitate the die design process and perform the above three processes in a single step a design supporting system is proposed.

The draw die process is to force the flat blank into a cavity of the required shape, and at the same time to confine the metal between the drawing surfaces which is forced to change its form from a flat blank to the desired shape. This process is dependent on the thickness of the metal, depth of the draw, and height of the flange to be formed.

Specification of the die for a particular application must be governed by the engineer who has sufficient experience and knowledge about the operation and construction of the various die shapes. In the designing process of draw dies, the designer examines whether the panel geometry data has defects or not. If there is a defect, it should be rearranged. After this process, the designer points out the punch profile and blank curve among the surfaces and curves which consists the geometry of the panel.

The first step is to determine die face, offset line, design of wear plate, block lifter and gauge. Next important step is to determine the size and layout of die set. [1] Finally, several components such as balance block, cushion pin, and rib, etc. are designed.

3 Development of Design Supporting System for Press Die

In developing the design supporting system the following criteria must be satisfied. First, the design process should be carried out according to the standardized design work flow. Second, the design variables are determined by the rules of design processes. Third, the complex geometry can be checked automatically.

For embodiment, the design rule base is programmed using CATGEO, CATMSP in the CATIA version 4.2.1. [13] The program is developed on IBM RS/6000 with C++ and IUA for GUI. The design rules and knowledge are collected by the interviews of design specialists in the press engineering department of H Motor Company.

The configuration of the system is presented in Figure 1.

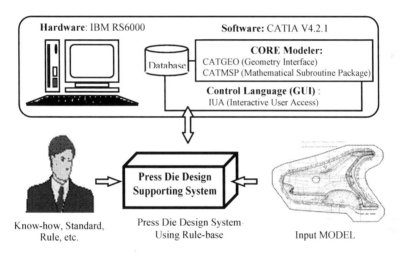

Fig. 1. Schematic configurations of the developed design system for press die

3.1 The Structure of the Design Supporting System for Press Die

The design supporting system for trim die and draw die design consists of the user interface module, the design process module, and the rule-base module. The user interface module helps to design the press die easier and faster. The design process module controls the input data and the data generated at a design stage so that they can be stored or retrieved systematically. The rule-base module helps representing the know-how of design specialists and design rules of the automotive industry. The structure of the developed system is shown in Figure 2. [6]

The proposed system enables the design process to be dialogical one and checks the errors in user input to prevent a failed design. Hence, the system can be used as an error checking tool as well as design tool.

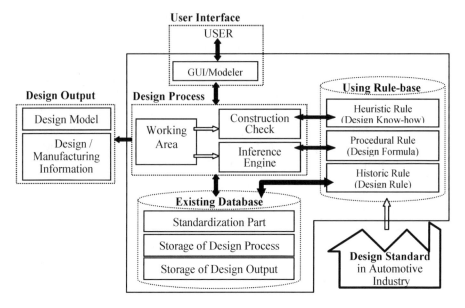

Fig. 2. Schematic diagram of rule-based system for press die design developed in this system

3.2 Representation of the Design Rules

When designing a panel with prismatic shapes and complicated structure, the resulting design tends to be different from the original design or even faulty even if the same design conditions and design processes are applied. However, no one can clear out the reason due to the inherent complexity of design rules and structure. [6-7] Therefore, it is important to establish robust design system which can give us consistent results especially when designing and manufacturing complex products.

To establish robust design system it is necessary to standardize the design process by extracting the design methods and rules through the careful analysis of design processes and variety of special features included in the design process. [8]

In developing the press die design system, the design processes and the design rules are standardized by gathering information and know-how from the specialists and then storing them in a database to retrieve the information whenever necessary. [4] The design rules are implemented in three groups:

1) **Historic Rule:** general design knowledge, features of design method for each component, selection of die type, selection of material for each component according to the shapes, maximum (or minimum) size of each component, location of each block, bolt location and the number of jig parts in each component, positioning dimension, the number and designing position of reinforcing rigs, etc.

2) **Heuristic Rule:** includes design method and know-how of the design specialists, location of each component in trim line and draw die shape, position decision factor, prohibition section of component separation, machining margin, method of pierce separating, width margin of scrap cutter, location of block, etc.

3) Procedure Rule: calculation of dimension according to the design formulation, design rule, mutual relation between the component's height and width, separation length between each component, calculation of height between each component, etc.

The proposed design system has many advantages: The designer dependency can be reduced by saving the special know-how and experiences related to the design. The new design of an object is corresponded quickly by storing the past design rules in the rule base. [9] Also, modification and maintenance can be done easily.

3.3   The Process of Design Shape in Trim Die Design

To design a block in the quadratic domain the position and dimension of the block are determined by the face surface of the product included in the block feature using the enumerating method implemented in the design rule base.

The dimension of a block is determined in the sequence of width, height, and length after the designer sets the check gap of height in the shape.

When the designer decides the trim line and the start point, the positions of the blocks and the block widths are determined first. The positions and widths of the blocks can be calculated by dividing the trim line into equal parts by the check intervals determined with several rules. Then the block heights bounded by the maximum heights (obtained by the shape checking routine) are calculated so as to minimize the machining volumes. Finally, the length of the block is determined using the width and the height of each block considering the size tolerance and weight of each block.

The system stores shapes and parameters of the resulting design as a feature information in the database so that the system can extract those information in case of designing a trim die with similar shapes and parameters. [10-11]

3.4   The Process of Design Shape in Draw Die Design

The next step is to arrange the block using grid line in 2D according to the design rules as mentioned before, and to select rule-base data management method in order to decide the draw die type by die size and body panel shape.

There are four major functions in draw die design system. They are 1) selection of components and their dimension and shapes from standard database, 2) determination of layout position, 3) construction of the relations among the components and geometries, and 4) modification of the parts and die size from the past design. These programs cover four different types of draw dies; three single action type (transfer, tandem, and cross bar) and one double action type.

Before deciding the height of components feature, user must decide shape checking interval of draw die in the product surface feature and divide surface shape and height of draw die according to the selected checking interval. Positioning of each component is decided by this divided point and an intersecting point on 2-dimensional die shape.

The feature information of each components generated as a result of design and design parameters are stored in database and the system can retrieve the data in case of designing draw die with similar features and parameters to save time repeating the same design work. [10-11]

3.5   Display of Design Information

The proposed system controls product design process in a viewpoint of design administrator and provide 2D user-interface to support the detailed concept design with automatic

3D component calculation. Moreover, the system can provide user-friendly interface with graphics and charts and check design error caused by blunders in design step.

The system shows the design rules and design methods on the system-display panel and they can be corrected automatically using the built-in tool which can induce design data control module with design-object, design process and user-interface. [10-11]

Also the shape and size of the designed block are illustrated as a 3D shape with the material table that includes all the necessary information in the design and production step so that the design results can be passed directly to the production step.

4   An Example

In this section, an example is presented to demonstrate the effectiveness of the "Design supporting system for press die" using the solid model of a panel in CATIA

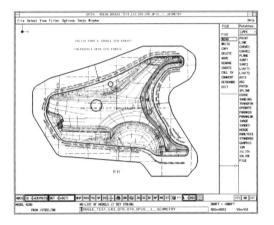

Fig. 3. The shape of Quarter outer panel as input model

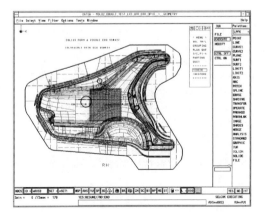

Fig. 4. Height definition of panel using "CHECK" menu

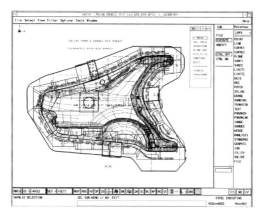

Fig. 5. 2D shape of designed trimming block

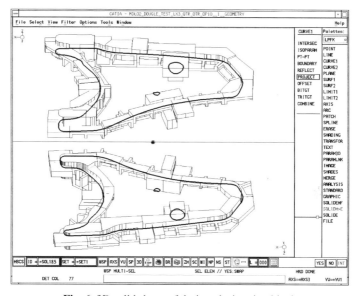

Fig. 6. 3D solid shape of designed trimming block

environment. [13-15] The selected model is the "quarter outer panel" of an automobile, which is designed and produced at the H motor company.

The feature windows displayed during the execution of the proposed system are illustrated in Figure 3 through Figure 6. Also the materials table created after the final design is shown in Table 1. The materials table is automatically created with the name of "PARTLIST".

The design of draw die includes a lot of variables depending on the design conditions and much of the design process is not standardized yet. This makes the designer to select a particular method in the design process sometimes.

Figure 7 shows the feature windows, showing automated execution of draw die design with double action among the press die design process.

Table 1. Part-list output of designed trimming block

```
|        << Output PARTLIST1 of STEEL L/O program >>       |
|Code No.:        |CAR:          |Goods:           |SHT:    |
|SHT No.:         |part no. :          |part name :        |
|BLOCK No.  | Type |material |  SIZE(WxLxH)  |   REMARK     |
|     1     |Upper  | KY870A  | 340  110   65|   FMC        |
|     2     |Up  S/C| 23F85   | 245  170   50|              |
|     3     |Dn  S/C| 23F85   | 250  105  105|              |
|     4     |Upper  | KY870A  | 380  115   90|   FMC        |
|     5     |Upper  | KY870A  | 300  110  100|   FMC        |
|     6     |Upper  | KY870A  | 400  150   80|   FMC        |
|     7     |Upper  | 23F85   | 215  175   65|              |
|     8     |Upper  | 23F85   | 235  165   70|              |
|     9     |Upper  | KY870A  | 435  140  150|   FMC        |
|    10     |Up  S/C| 23F85   | 210  130   65|              |
|    11     |Dn  S/C| 23F85   | 230  105   55|              |
|    12     |Upper  | KY870A  | 350  120   70|   FMC        |
|    13     |Down   | KY870A  | 420  105   65|   FMC        |
|    14     |Down   | 23F85   | 320  125  125|              |
|    15     |Down   | KY870A  | 295  105   95|   FMC        |
|    16     |D      |         | 280  115   95|              |
|    17     |       |         | 325  330  200|              |
|                                                           |
|         Upper | KY870A  | 2     |              |   FMC        |
|     6     |Up  S/C| 23F85   | 200        55|              |
|     7     |Dn  S/C| 23F85   | 195  105   50|              |
|     8     |Upper  | KY870A  | 465  150   60|   FMC        |
|     9     |Upper  | KY870A  | 385  180   60|   FMC        |
|    10     |Upper  | KY870A  | 440  210   60|   FMC        |
|    11     |Upper  | KY870A  | 315  245   60|   FMC        |
|    12     |Down   | KY870A  | 230  160  100|   FMC        |
|    13     |Down   | 23F85   | 375  160  195|              |
|    14     |Down   | KY870A  | 405  220   85|   FMC        |
|    15     |Down   | KY870A  | 460  145   60|   FMC        |
|    16     |Down   | KY870A  | 355  140   65|   FMC        |
|    17     |Down   | KY870A  | 320  115   60|   FMC        |
|    18     |Down   | 23F85   | 285  240   55|              |
```

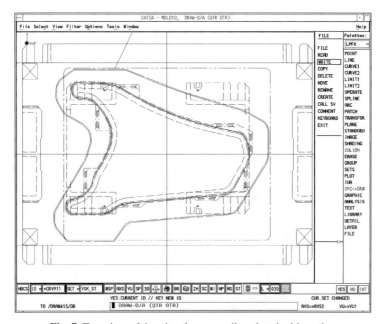

Fig. 7. Top view of drawing for upper die using double action

5   Conclusion

In this paper, a design supporting system for press die is developed. The main features of the developed system are as follows:

1) The number of errors due to the complexity of geometry can be reduced and prevented. Also design accuracy is improved by managing geometrical data mathematically.
2) The feature information of a design can be used as manufacturing information such as orders for raw materials. This can shorten the time for designing and manufacturing.
3) Beginners can design dies by modifying the design rules and the design knowledge standardizes simple operations and the design process for the specialists. Furthermore, a domestic design system fits to domestic conditions. [13-15]
4) Since information of the design feature is represented in a 3D solid feature, it takes enormous memory and handling time.
5) The knowledge and design rules are not perfect. Thus, some of them are not considered in the design process.

Although the proposed design system has some drawbacks and is not perfect, the design system improves accuracy and saves the time for calculating the complex geometry data of inner shape in the shape gauge compared to the manual method. [4][6]

In addition, the information generated in design stage is passed to manufacturing stage so that the efficiency of production is improved. The developed system is currently used for the trim die and draw die design process in the press department of the H motor company.

References

1. Jeong, H.Y.: A Fundamental of Press Die Design. Press Engineering Department of Hyundai Motor Co. (1996)
2. Durkin, J.: Expert Systems - Design and Development. Prentice Hall Int'l, Inc. (1994)
3. Coyne, R.D., Rosenman, M.A., Radford, A.D., Balachandran, M. and Gero, J.S.: Knowledge-based Design Systems. Addison-Wesley Publishing Co. (1989)
4. Batini, C., Ceri, S. and Navathe, S.B.: Conceptual Database Design. The Benjamin/Cummings Publishing Co. (1992)
5. Serrano, D. and Gossard, D.C.: Tools and Techniques for Conceptual Design. In: Tong, C. and Sriram, D.(ed.): Artificial Intelligence in Engineering Design. Academic Press Inc. (1992)
6. Cha, J.H. and Yokoyama, M.: A Knowledge-Based System for Mechanical CAD. Proc. ICED'95 (1995) 1382-1386
7. Jee, H.S., Kim, T.S. and Lee, S.J.: A Standard Feature Based Mold Design System for CAD/CAPP Interface. Proc. 7th IFAC Symposium on INCOM'92 (1992) 152-157
8. Lee, S.J., Lee, S.S., Kim, J.H. and Kwon, Y.J.: Development of Automated Generation Algorithm for Skipped Surface in Die Design. Proc. Int. Conf. Computational Science and Its Applications (ICCSA2006). LNCS 3984 (Part V) (2006) 503-511

9. Research of a CAD System of Drawing Die Based on Software Engineering. Mechanical Science and Technology 23(6) (2004) 720-722

10. Corbett, J., Dooner, M., Meleka, J. and Pym, C.: Design for Manufacture. Addison-Wesley Publishing Co. (1991)

11. Jeoung, H.S., Lee, S.S.: Automatic Design Supporting System for Automobile Stamping Tool. Journal of the Korean Society of Precision Engineering 19(8) (2002) 1225-9071

12. Park, C.H. and Lee, S.S: A Design of Press Die Components by Use of 3D CAD Library. Transactions of the Society of CAD/CAM Engineers 9(4) (2004) 373-381

13. CAD Software: CATIA-Mold and Die Machining Assistant. Dassault System Co. (1996)

14. CAD Software: Computer Aided Die Engineering (CADE). Kelton Graphics Co. (1996)

15. CAD Software: devis-VAMOS. Debis Systemhaus Industrie (1994)

An Agent-Based Collaborative Enterprise Modeling Environment Supporting Enterprise Process Evolution

Wenan Tan[1,2], Ruibin Chen[1], Weiming Shen[2], Jianming Zhao[1], and Qi Hao[2]

[1] Software Engineering Institute, Zhejiang Normal University
Jinhua, Zhejiang, P.R. China 321004
{jk76, chenruibin, zjm}@zjnu.cn
[2] Integrated Manufacturing Technologies Institute, National Research Council of Canada
800 Collip Circle, London, ON Canada N6G 4X8
{weiming.shen, qi.hao}@nrc.gc.ca

Abstract. This paper presents an evolutionary approach to dynamic enterprise process modeling and its supporting development environment. A dynamic enterprise process collaborative modeling framework is proposed for enterprise process evolution. Zero-time enterprise modeling using components assembly technologies and layered complex enterprise processes modeling approaches are discussed. Based on an autonomous agent development environment, an agent-based enterprise collaborative modeling environment was implemented which had integrated some of software resource agents wrapped from the main function modules of EPMS (enterprise process modeling system) to validate the proposed evolutionary approach.

1 Introduction

Global competition and rapidly changing customer requirements have resulted in great changes in the way enterprises do business. Enterprises must dynamically reengineer and improve their business processes to meet the changes. Enterprise dynamic modeling and optimization technology has been the recent research focus in the development of flexible enterprise systems.

There have been significant research efforts aiming at improving business process performance such as PDCA (Plan-Do-Check-Act) [1], IDEAL (Initiating-Diagnosing -Establishing-Acting-Learning) [2], QIP (Quality Improvement Paradigm) [3], and CMM (Capability Maturity Model) [4]. Some of Chinese scholars also have worked on enterprise modeling, system integration theories, methods and tools. Prof. Fan and his colleges from Tsinghua University presented an enterprise modeling architecture and focused on ERP system development based on workflow [5]. The process engineering theory group led by Prof. Zhou from software engineering institute, Beihang University, has researched in software process and enterprise process technologies, and has developed an enterprise process modeling system named EPMS [6].

As we know, multi-agent systems (MAS) can provide a cooperative environment for sharing design information, data, and knowledge among the members of a distributed design team. In agent-based collaborative design systems, intelligent software agents have mostly been used to enable cooperation among designers and to provide

W. Shen et al. (Eds.): CSCWD 2006, LNCS 4402, pp. 217–226, 2007.
© Springer-Verlag Berlin Heidelberg 2007

wrappers to integrate legacy software tools. Shen et al. [7] discussed the issues in developing agent-oriented collaborative design systems and gave a review of significant, related projects or systems.

In this paper, agent- and Web-based techniques are adopted to develop complex enterprise models and implement a collaborative enterprise process modeling environment. The rest of the paper is organized as follows: Section 2 introduces an evolutionary enterprise process modeling methodology; Section 3 discusses the realization of a collaborative enterprise modeling environment using multi-agents; Section 4 gives the conclusion.

2   An Evolutionary Enterprise Process Modeling Methodology

2.1   Dynamic Enterprise Processes Collaborative Modeling

The concept of enterprise process framework is proposed by Peter et al. in the 2nd International Conference on the Software Process in 1993, and a series of process engineering concepts were defined [8]. Many scholars have studied and improved them, and some new relative concepts are proposed and improved such as business process reengineering, business process improvement, process engineering, workflow management coalition [9-12]. We have improved the framework of evolutionary enterprise modeling and proposed dynamic enterprise process collaborative modeling framework as shown in Figure 1.

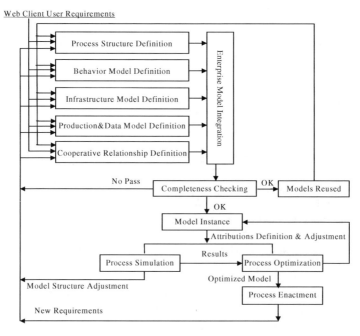

Fig. 1. Schematic representation of enterprise collaborative modeling process

Process is a partial-order set of logical related activities for accomplishing special objectives or tasks. In the proposed framework, an enterprise model can be described from *process model, behavior model, infrastructure model, cooperation model* and *information model*. All these models from different perspectives can be built independently. Adaptive process engineering would seamlessly integrate all these different perspectives into a unified enterprise model. Only enterprise processes that pass completeness checking can be instanced for process simulation.

Process simulation is a virtual execution of the enterprise process model that aims for diagnosing business processes, analyzing system performance under different load conditions, predicting the impacts of organizational changes, and exploring new business opportunities. *Process optimization* is an iterative optimization process of multiple process simulations. The optimization model is controlled by a goal-search algorithm under enterprise decision model for continuous business process improvement. *Process enactment* is the real execution of an enterprise process model in an organization. Only the optimized enterprise process model will be used for process monitoring and control. During process enactment, some new requirements will be fed back to process definition stage if a change is detected and the process needs to be improved. All these iterative steps form the lifecycle of enterprise process evolution.

2.2 Zero-Time Enterprise Modeling Using Components Assembly Technologies

For customized enterprise modeling, an enterprise model framework based on industrial reference model and common components must be built at first. An enterprise model should describe enterprise information as much as possible to automatically support the application software construction [13]. An enterprise model architecture Evolved from COSMOS and SADT model [14], was proposed based on CIMOSA reference model (as shown in Figure 2). In the view-dimension, an enterprise can be effectively described from five aspects: process, infrastructure, behavior, cooperation and information. According to the generality of enterprise model, there are three kinds of models including general component base, industrial reference models and customized models. In the lifecycle dimension, system engineering is divided into four stages: planning, design, implementation and maintenance. Every stage needs the supports of corresponding techniques such as process definition, simulation and optimization.

In order to implement zero-time enterprise modeling, a general component base and a reference model of applicable industrial sectors should be built up. Customization modeling is a rapid process of the inheritance and derivation of some components in the common component base or the reference model. During the modeling process, some information also needs to be appended and some character parameters might be modified. So, a customized model will have better quality and shorter definition duration. In the generality dimension, Figure 2 illustrates how to rapidly define a customized model from general components, as well as how to abstract common industrial features from the particular enterprise models so as to build a general component base and the industrial reference model. The two processes are very important. On one hand, the larger the component base, the more components can be provided for the construction of customized models. On the other hand, the more the customized models, the more the models can be obtained for component abstraction.

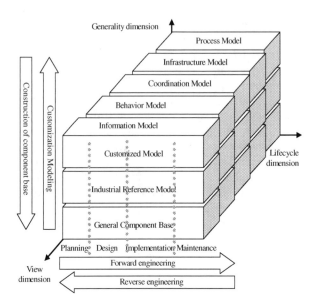

Fig. 2. Framework of zero-time enterprise modeling

In the lifecycle dimension, Figure 2 also illustrates two approaches similar to software engineering. Forward engineering is a process of customized model construction that goes from planning, via design and implementation through to maintenance stages. It needs the supports of enterprise dynamic modeling technologies such as process definition, process simulation, process optimization and process enactment. Reverse engineering modeling is a reversed process that can be used to analyze an existing enterprise system, abstract its model, find defects in the present processes and reengineer enterprise processes. In reverse engineering, all applications can be mapped back to higher-level design abstractions. And these design abstractions also can be mapped back to the conceptual business models to provide extremely useful trace-ability. Reverse engineering is very important for enterprise business process reengineering and enterprise evolution.

2.3   Layered Complex Enterprise Process Modeling

The object-oriented modeling (OOM) has fully demonstrated to be an effective technique for modeling complex systems. Complex enterprise modeling, as the key in building an enterprise information system, is an abstract description of enterprise requirements elicited from the analysis done by software suppliers and the enterprise-itself. Abstraction and decomposition are two kinds of valuable techniques in complex process modeling. Figure 3 illustrates that a lower level model is a decomposition of a certain composite activity in its upper level. Therefore, we can also use a special composite activity to delegate the abstraction of lower level model.

In addition to the proposed theory and methodology, software development tools are also necessary during complex enterprise modeling. Only the organization and

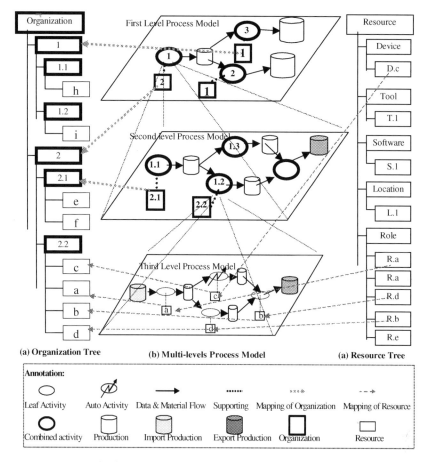

Fig. 3. Layered complex enterprise process modeling

resource defined in infrastructure model can be referred to process modeling. An infrastructure model includes organization model and resource model built in tree structures. They connect with process model via a mapping function. Process simulation and optimization can be used to analyze the distribution and efficiency of resources for organization adjustment and resource configuration optimization. These development tools, which are suitable for business process reengineering, will be introduced in the following section.

3 Agent-Based Realization of Enterprise Collaborative Modeling Environment

3.1 AADE: Autonomous Agent Development Environment

AADE is an engineering-oriented agent framework developed by Integrated Manufacturing Technologies Institute, National Research Council of Canada. AADE provides agent-based engineering application development with reusable agent-oriented classes. The current version of AADE only implements a semantically closed agent community in which all agents can communicate with each other using a dedicated content language expressed in XML.

AADE has developed a generic agent model that includes all fundamental functions common to all agents in the same FIPA agent community, such as agent registration, naming, communication and interaction capabilities. Application-specific agents can be constructed by customizing the interfaces provided by the generic agent model, including a *User Interface* that can be implemented for some agents to show its running state, incoming and outgoing messages, and so on to the human users; an *Application Interface* that can connect an agent to other legacy applications in non-agent systems; and a knowledge-base that can be specified for the agent to obtain certain problem solving skills.

3.2 Agent-Based Enterprise Collaborative Modeling Environment (AECME)

The architecture of AECME based on the AADE framework is shown as Figure 4, which includes Engineering management, Job management, User management, Engineering data management and System integration with different kinds of enterprise modeling software tools such as process definition, simulation, optimization and enactment software tools wrapped from the main functions of EPMS developed by the Software Engineering Institute in Beihang University, China [11].

e-Engineering Server Agent (ES Agent) is the gateway that users must get through to define, manage, and monitor the information about a enterprise modeling project and its affiliated business jobs. When a job starts running, the ES agent will generate a job agent dynamically. A job agent is dismissed by the ES agent after the job finishes.

Engineering Data Management Agent (EDM Agent) has the knowledge of database location, connection configuration, engineering file directories, and location and configuration of FTP server, etc. It handles all manipulations of engineering data related to the enterprise model. Jobs and tasks are handled in the EDM Agent too. EDM contains two main function modules: visual process modeling language (VPML) based on object management system (OMS) and the access control of engineering files and RDMS.

Job Agent (JA) communicates with EDM agent for storing and retrieving job data and engineering files; with the DF agent for a list of matching engineering resource agents; and with the resource agents for conducting negotiation-based task allocation.

Directory Facilitator Agent (DF Agent) has all the registration service functionalities for other agents to reside in this multi-agent system; keeps up-to-date agent registration and informs all registered agents with updated registry; and provides lookup and matching-making services to job agents.

Monitoring Agent (MA) is specially designed to facilitate the monitoring of agents' behaviors in the multi-agent system. In a distributed multi-agent system, because information is distributed and controlled by each individual agent, it is necessary to have an agent that could accumulate information from various resources when required. Through this monitoring agent, dynamic "condition" of the system, the behavior of this multi-agent environment as well as all individual agents can be conveniently monitored or reviewed through a graphical tool.

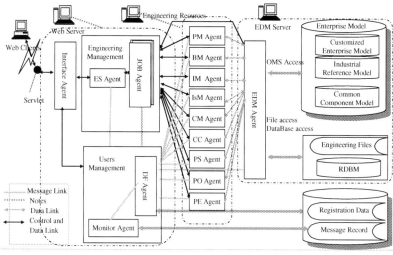

Where Process Modeling (PM Agent), Behavior Modeling (BM Agent), Information Modeling (IM Agent), Infrastructure Modeling (IfM Agent), Cooperative Modeling (CM Agent), Completeness Checking (CC Agent),Process Simulation (PS Agent), Process Optimization (PO Agent), Process Enactment (PE Agent), Visual Process Modeling Language based on Objects Management System(OMS Agent), Directory Facilitator (DF Agent), Engineering Server (ES Agent), Engineering File & Data Base Management (EDM Agent).

Fig. 4. Architecture of ACEME

Interface Agent (IA) is the Web-based user interfaces for user requests to enter the agent system. Several Servlets are responsible for receiving these requests to the Web server. The IA catches the user requests from Servlets, translates the requests to messages, and initiates corresponding conversations to related agents. Similarly, IA creates updates to user interfaces based on the replies from agents.

Engineering resource agents such as PM, BM, IM, CM, IfM, PS, PO, and PE agents are the actual engineering problem-solving agents. They not only carry out the communication, negotiation functions on behalf of the engineering software, but also execute the execution thread to do the related model definition, analysis, simulation, optimization or enactment based on the OMS-Based VPML [6]. In this collaborative enterprise modeling, five models built up by PM, BM, IM, CM and IsM agents could automatically run the syntax and semantic completeness checking and be integrated to a unified model by the PM agent. We want to address each of these agents as below:

Process Modeling (PM Agent) is a graphical editor with the capability of syntax and semantics checking for enterprise process structure definition. According to project management protocol and task assignment, it supports layered visual process modeling, and provides plentiful primitive notations such as activity, production, message, role, machine, and the connections between them, such as data flow charts.

Behavior Modeling (BM Agent) is a window-based editor for every activity's behavior function presentation in Java code. For the human-machine interaction activities, we need to define the interface such as window 2000-based menu (for combined activity), some sheets and buttons (for end activity), and their functions, as well as some of computation algorithms for automatic batch activities.

Information Modeling (IM Agent) is the definition of production, message and various variables, such as conventionality variable and Class definition user itself. It is usually used for the features description of all kinds of primitives defined in the process model. Some of them will be used as parameters of process model for process optimization or as information resource for decision support in process enactment.

Infrastructure Modeling (IsM Agent) is responsible for the definition of organizations and resources within an enterprise. Organization and resource model can be defined in a tree structure. In an organization, some items need to be presented such as the upper-level organization which contains lower-level organization and resources. We usually define a enterprise resource model from its role, machine, location, tool and soft-resource (including software resources and patents etc.).

Cooperation Modeling (CM Agent) is responsible for the definition of collaborative schedule rules which includes eight kinds of schedule strategies such as HPFS (Highest Priority First Serve), MSFS (Minimum Slack time First Serve), FCFS (First Come First Service), SIRO (Service In Random Order), SOT (Shortest Operation Time), LOT (Longest Operation Time), LRPT (Longest Remaining Processing Time), SRPT (Shortest Remaining Processing Time).

Process Simulation (PS Agent) is an actual engineering problem-solving agent for diagnosing business processes, analyzing system performance under different load conditions, predicting the impacts of organizational changes, and exploring new business opportunities. It can provide immediate feedback to decision-makers on how certain combination of changes will affect process costs and profits, and dynamic information about the activity flow, product flow, personnel flow, resource flow, cost flow etc. Using these information, managers can identify the key impacts of a BPR project upon the organization in order to reduce cycle time, increasing customer focus, increasing productivity, and improving quality [16].

Process Optimization (PO Agent) is a process model parameters optimization tool using a FR-TS algorithm [17] combined by Fletcher Reeves method and Tabu search method, where Fletcher-Reeves method is used to obtain a set of local optimal solutions, and Tabu search algorithm is used to discover feasible solutions in undiscovered areas. The two methods will be alternately iterated many times so as to get the set of global optimum solutions. The outputs of PO are a set of optimized models and a recommended model to assist the decision-makers.

Process Enactment (PE Agent) is an actual engineering problem-solving agent for enterprise process enactment. It executes the selected optimum enterprise process model for process monitoring and control, and provides a task-table orderly storing tasks according to the priority and urgency to assist each role-user work [17]. During process operation, some new requirements will be fed back to PM if a change is detected and process needs to be improved.

3.3 Implementation and Consideration

Process is a partial set of business activities with the relative resource supports, inputs, outputs, and controls. Process model is the key enabler of enterprise model in ACEME. Here, we focus on discussion of process model design for collaborative modeling. Other parts about PS, PO, PE agents can refer to references [16-17]. Figure 5 illustrates a meta-model of enterprise process modeling using UML. Enterprise

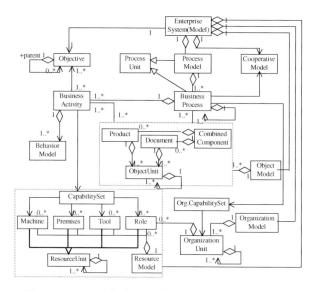

Fig. 5. Meta-model of enterprise process modeling system

system/model contains process model, behavior model, object model, resource model, organization model, and cooperative model. Enterprise process model is usually composed of many business processes, which contain some sorted business activities supporting by a set of resources (classified by machine, premises, tool, role). In process simulation and enactment, activities scheduling and resources allocation is controlled by the specific cooperative rules defined in the cooperative model.

The proposed environment has been implemented on a network of PCs with Windows 2000/XP and Linux operating environments as well as SUN workstations with the SUN UNIX operating environment. Java is the primary programming language for system implementation. Most of engineering resources such as PS, PO and PE programmed by VC++6.0 are also integrated as wrapped legacy systems. All agents are implemented on AADE. The EDM agent is used to integrate OMS as the primary database and MySQL™ as secondary storage for the entire system. Server side modules are implemented on Apache™ and Tomcat™.

4 Conclusions and Perspectives

This paper presents an evolutionary enterprise process modeling methodology from the concepts of enterprise process evolution, technology to complex enterprise modeling. Based on AADE, an agent-based enterprise collaborative modeling environment is being implemented. Some of resource agents are wrapped from the main functions of EPMS developed by the Software Engineering Institute at Beihang University, China. It is our future R&D work to develop an agent-based service-oriented integration framework which will improve the process simulation algorithm in the PS agent for the cooperative simulation of complex enterprise processes.

Acknowledgements. This work is partially supported by the Key Research Foundation for Zhejiang Education of China (Grant No. 20060491).

References

1. Shewhart, W.A., Van, D.: Economic Control of Quality of Manufactured product. Nostrand, New York (1931)
2. Deming, W.E.: Out of Crisis. MIT Press, Cambridge MA (1986)
3. McFeely, B.: IDEAL: A User's Guide for Software Process Improvement. CMU/SEI-96-HB-001. Carnegie Mellon University, Pittsburgh, PA (1996)
4. Bate, R., Kuhn, D., Wells, C. et al.: A Systems Engineering Capability Maturity Model. CMU/SEI-95-MM-003. Carnegie Mellon University, Pittsburgh (1995)
5. Fan, Y., Wu, C.: Research on Integrated Enterprise Modeling Method and the Support Tool System. Computer Integrated Manufacturing Systems 6(3)(2000) 1-5
6. Zhou, B., Zhang, S.: Visual Process Modeling Language VPML. Journal of Software 8 (1997) 535-545
7. Shen, W., Norrie, D.H., Barthès, J.P.: Multi-Agent Systems for Concurrent Intelligent Design and Manufacturing. Taylor and Francis, London, UK (2001)
8. Feiler , P.H., Humphrey, W.S.: Software Process Development and Enactment: Concepts and Definitions. Proc. 2nd International Conference on Software Process (1993)
9. Hammer, M., James, C.: Reengineering the Corporation: A Manifesto for Business Revolution. HarperCollins Publisher Inc. (1993)
10. Grady, R.B.: Successful Software Process Improvement. Hewlett-Packard, America (1997)
11. Zhou, B., Xu, H., Zhang, L.: The principle of process engineering and introduction to process engineering environments. Journal of software 6 (1997) 519-534
12. David, H.: The Workflow Reference Model. Workflow Management Coalition (1994)
13. David, A.T.: Business Engineering with Object Technology. John Wiley & Sons (1995)
14. Yeh, R.T., Mittermeir, R.T.: A Commonsense Management Model. IEEE Software 6 (1991) 23-33
15. FIPA Specifications. URL: http://www.fipa.org/specifications/index.html
16. Tan, W., Zhou, B., Zhang, L.: Research on the Flexible Simulation Technology for Enterprise Process Model. Journal of Software 12(7) (2001) 1080-1087
17. Tan, W., Tang, A.: Research on the Dynamic Optimization Technique for Enterprise Process and the Integrated Support Tool. Computer Integrated Manufacturing Systems 9(2) (2003) 137-142

3D Product Configuration for e-Commerce: Customer-Oriented Advisory Helper of Co-assembler

Sophia M.K. Soo, Stephen C.F. Chan, and Vincent T.Y. Ng

Department of Computing, Hong Kong Polytechnic University, Hong Kong
csschan@inet.polyu.edu.hk

Abstract. The Co-assembler is a customer-oriented collaborative product configuration system, which guides and advises customers to configure their products according to their needs. The system aims to capture customers' needs and convert them into technical specifications, helping facilitate e-commerce for enterprises. In this paper, we focus on discussing the subsystems that apply expert design knowledge and artificial intelligence to assist customers in choosing suitable forms, sizes, styles, colors and product configurations.

1 Introduction

Online product configuration tools allow web users to customize their products over the internet. The tools enable the web users to personalize their products, help enterprises in capturing customers' needs, bridge the gap between customers' desire and designers' interpretation, and enrich the services of e-commerce.

Today, a range of software packages is available to help enterprises in embedding the configuration services in their websites. For example, X-Configurator [22] helps in developing the website to configure computers, software, mobile accessories, etc. ProductCart [16] can be used for computers, gifts, clothes, etc. Contract Furniture [5] focuses on furniture products.

Depending on the type of product, the configuration services can simplify the selection of options. For example, users can select the PC components in web-based computer stores. It can be a straightforward selection among a limited set of choices, for example, users can select from among a given set of colors for clothes. In the case of Co-assembler, the services can customize the appearances, forms and spatial relationships of 3D products. Many 3D product configuration services exist in the web, for example, Nokia [14] has used 3D product demonstrators to display mobile phones of different colors. Toyota [19] has displayed 3D virtual cars showing different types of wheels and accessories. IKEA [6] offers a planner service in which the office layouts can be planned and then used to generate 3D models. IKEA [7], too, offers combinative parts for building customized furniture.

Many product configuration tools focus on showing the products with alternative features or combinations, allowing users to choose from the set of available choices. However, customers who use the tools are not necessarily expert designers and they many not even have very concrete ideas about what they want, how to describe it, how to specify it, or how best to configure it.

W. Shen et al. (Eds.): CSCWD 2006, LNCS 4402, pp. 227–236, 2007.
© Springer-Verlag Berlin Heidelberg 2007

In this paper we discuss Co-assembler, a real-time collaborative 3D product assembly system that automates many of its processes, allowing casual customers to
interactively configure products over the Internet. Co-assembler includes advisory
helper modules based on a body of expert design knowledge which can provide customers with suggestions and feedback on their design choices. This paper focuses on
the advisory helpers to support the customers in their design decisions. Co-assembler
incorporates two assembly-specific archival and data transfer formats – Assembly ML
and Parametric Product ML. It also facilitates collaboration with client/server collaborative architecture. They were described in our previous papers (Chan et. al [4],
Soo & Chan [17], and Chan & Soo [18]). To demonstrate the functionalities of Co-
assembler, we use the target application scenario of an office furniture store that allows customers to select features of its furniture online.

The rest of this paper is organized as follows. In Section 2 we discuss the related
work. In Section 3 we describe Co-assembler's system configuration and architecture.
In Section 4 we describe the interactive interface of Co-assembler. In Section 5 we
offer our Conclusion and an outline of future work.

2   Related Work

Central to the Co-assembler design is that users should perceive it as simple and user-
friendly, that users of Co-assembler should be satisfied with their ultimate design
outcomes, and that it should allow real-time collaboration.

Four issues are thus of particular importance in its design: first, the manipulation of
scene graphs; second, the way that users manipulate and assemble objects, which may
be either manual or semi-automatic; third, user design assistance to support user design choices; and finally the design operations that allow collaboration by providing
real-time feedback.

Scene graphs are widely used in web-based graphics to represent 3D objects and
environments. Manipulation of scene graphs involves representing, rearranging, and
recording the hierarchical nodes in a tree-based structure. Blanchebarbe et al. [1]
discussed how 3D models could be built up from primitive objects, and how 3D models could be described and recorded in an XML-based data format. Lescinsky et al.
[11] described how 3D objects can be rearranged without altering their overall appearance. The underlying geometries of Co-assembler were represented using scene
graphs and similar 3D object manipulation mechanisms.

The tools that are currently available for use in web-based design and assembly
generally use either manual or semi-automatic approaches. Manual approaches include Xu et al.'s [23] preliminary tool for assembling solid models. This tool defined
modeling operations such as Boolean operations (union, intersection, subtraction),
rotation, scaling and translation but these operations required the user to move and
manipulate 3D objects. BEAVER [15], is a web-based tool for interactively assembling virtual furniture that takes a semi-automatic approach in which users manipulate
3D objects using a mouse. Assembly is further supported by constraints such as a
simple snapping mechanism that positions objects within certain ranges. Co-
assembler significantly improves on both of these approaches in that it offers the

choice of a completely automatic design and assembly or the user may choose a semi-automatic or even completely manual mode.

To more effectively incorporate customer needs and tastes, Miyakawa et al. [13] used a database of traditional Japanese motifs and styles that users could access to customize a room to their tastes. It retrieved design images, and the color, shape, pattern of the images. Some recent research has attempted to extend this technique to the Internet. Co-assembler addresses this issue by providing design helpers that provide customers with guidance in their design decisions.

The issue of collaboration was addressed by Wang et al [20], who investigated the information communication model for consumers to participate collaboratively in conceptual design. Jiang et al. [10] described an e-service that incorporated customers, manufacturers and suppliers in manufacturing parts. Wang et al. [21] described the collaborative techniques for assembling and disassembling products such as the event-based collaborative communication protocol. Li et al. [12] designed an assembler that synchronously modified different parts of a model, focusing on developing the representation and the constraints on collaborative assembly. In an earlier paper Chan et al. [3] discussed in detail a real-time collaborative design which described a network infrastructure for supporting real-time collaborative solid modeling (CSM) on the Internet. Co-assembler takes this earlier design approach and features that allow products to be virtually assembled collaboratively in a web-based environment.

3   System Configuration and Architecture

Figure 1 shows the three-layer client architecture comprising first, an Interactive Interface layer, second, an Assembler Layer containing two sub-layers, a composer sub-layer and a parametric sub-layer, and third, a Data File Layer. In this paper we focus on discussing the Inter-active Interface layer that enables customers to input choices, preferences and personal data.

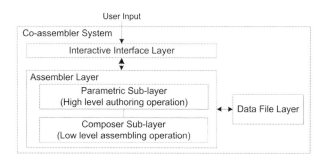

Fig. 1. Three-layer client architecture

4   Interactive Interface Layer

The Interactive Interface Layer contains a four-step product construction procedure to guide customers. Each step is accompanied by design helpers to assist customers make design decisions, using knowledge of customer needs and expert knowledge to suggest design solutions. Customers can examine the furniture in a realistic virtual furniture showroom. In the sub-sections, we first describe the format, size, style, and color/materials modules (helpers) and their operations. We then describe the functionalities of the Virtual Show Room.

4.1   Form Recommendation Module

The form recommendation module helps customers select different types and forms of products. When customers look for furniture, they often start by searching through existing furniture models. If they find something that is not ideal but close enough, they may then try to make modifications to the existing model. The form recommendation interactive interface contains four "areas", CATALOGUE, TYPE, SHAPE and RECOMMENDATION to guide customers step by step.

4.2   Size Recommendation Module

The size recommendation module suggests configurations based on size relevant to the following considerations:

- Size of user: For example, a tall person may need a higher desk.
- Size of related objects: For example, a bookcase may need shelves of different heights for different sizes of books.
- Size of room and other furniture: For example, a movable drawer unit under a desk must be lower than the height of the desk.
- Number of users: For example, the size of a dining table corresponds to the num-ber of diners.

Chiara et al. [2] formularized a method for determining common furniture dimensions. Figure 2 shows the appropriate height of a desk can be calculated by the user's height, user's height level (UHL) and desktop level (DL). The standard length of a desk can be affected by the size of a monitor. A desk may need to be wide enough for a PC case. The thickness of a desk may be determined by its width.

Figure 3 shows a screenshot from the size recommendation interactive interface. It contains three "areas", IMPACT FACTORS, LEVEL DETERMINATION, and DIMENSIONS. To design a bookcase, the customer begins by clicking the **Recommend** radio button in the IMPACT FACTORS AREA, which actives the impact factors for determining the bookcase dimensions. The factors - customer's height, house height, **Top Reach** and **Place On** should be input. **Top Reach** determines the height of the bookcase. The **standing-hand** option means the customer can reach the highest level of a bookcase while standing. The **sitting-hand** option means the customer can reach the highest level while sitting. The **ceiling-level** option means that the bookcase be as high as the ceiling. The **Place On** factor defines the location of a bookcase - the bookcase can be placed on the floor or on top of a desk. Then, the number of shelves required and information such as the size of books to be placed in the shelf should be set in the LEVEL DETERMINATION AREA. Finally, customers can then click on the **Build** button in the DIMENSIONS AREA to have the system calculate the proper dimensions of the bookcase. The virtual bookcase will then be created automatically.

Desk Height = U * DL / UHL

Where   U = User Height
        UHL= User Height Level
        DL = Desktop Level

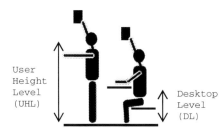

User
Height
Level
(UHL)

Desktop
Level
(DL)

Desk Length
1. with LCD monitor = 60 cm
2. with large monitor = 90 cm

Desk Width
1. with main case on top = 150cm
2. without main case = 180 cm

Desk Thickness
1. If desk width > 170cm,
            Thickness = 5 cm
2. If 120cm<desk width<170cm,
            Thickness = 3 cm
3. If desk width < 120cm,
            Thickness = 2 cm

Fig. 2. Calculation of the height, length, width and thickness of the desk

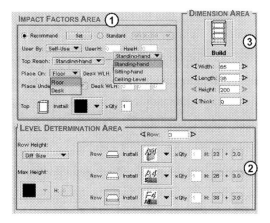

Fig. 3. A screenshot of the size recommendation interface using a bookcase for demonstration

4.3 Style Recommendation Module

Style and material configuration provides components with styles and materials for customers to select and configure the products.

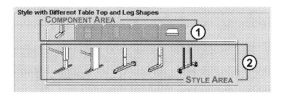

Fig. 4. A screenshot of the style recommendation interface using a desk leg for demonstration

Figure 4 shows a screenshot from the style configuration interactive interface. It contains two "areas", COMPONENT and STYLE. To configure the style of desk legs, customers click on the legs icon in the COMPONENT AREA. Then, a set of desk legs with different styles will be displayed for selection in the STYLE AREA. Their selections will automatically be reflected in the virtual desk. The procedure for changing the styles of other components is basically the same as that for the desk legs.

4.4   Color and Material Recommendation Module

Casual customers may not possess expert knowledge of design and aesthetics. The color and material recommendation module suggests various combinations of colors and materials for furniture according to customers' desires.

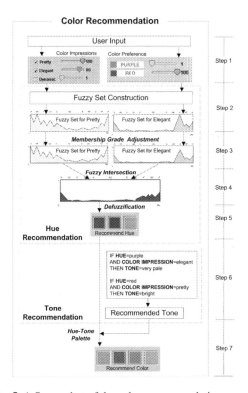

Fig. 5. A Screenshot of the color recommendation process

Figure 5 shows the flow of the color recommendation process. Note that in this recommendation process, color is described in terms of two attributes – hue and tone – and supported by fuzzy logic. The color recommendation process begins with the customer being asked to specify two color impressions and a color preference as the inputs. Each input is quantified by a value, which we called the *favorite value* (degree of significance). The color impression represents the effect or feelings projected by the furniture, e.g., pretty, elegant, dynamic, pure, mild, antique, cheerful, casual and peaceful. The color preference is the choice for a specific color under the selected impression (favorite or preferred color). After these choices are made, fuzzy sets are created for each color impression in the hue recommendation. The fuzzy sets then pass through a sequence of processes including membership grade adjustment, fuzzy inter-section and de-fuzzification. The final fuzzy sets eventually generate the hues. The resulting hues will be inputs into the tone recommendation which is used to generate the tones using fuzzy IF-THEN rules. Finally, a color palette, which is adopted from I.R.I [8], is used to determine the colors according to the generated hues and tones. It employs ten hues and eleven tones to form various colors. The color recommendation process will recommend a maximum of five color combinations. Figure 6 includes the color recommendation with an example. A customer chooses furniture and then inputs two color impressions – PRETTY and ELEGANT with *favorite values* 100 and 80 respectively, and one color preference – RED with *favorite value* 100.

Figure 6 illustrates the process flow of the material recommendation. Material recommendation module suggests materials for the major components of the furniture such as a desk top. We make use of the rules from the Japan Tis Institute [9] that matches the materials of the major components to the color tones of the accessory components. The most suitable materials for the major components are derived based on the tones generated from the color recommendation.

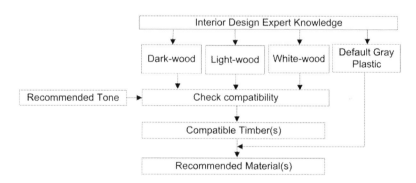

Fig. 6. The flow of the material recommendation

Figure 7 shows a screenshot from the color and material recommendation interactive interface. It contains four "areas", IMPRESSION, PREFERENCE, ADVICE, and OUTPUT. To select the overall color and materials, the customer first inputs two color impressions and the corresponding favorite values in the IMPRESSION AREA. The customer then inputs a color preference and a favorite value in the PREFERENCE AREA. The customer can obtain advice by clicking the **Get Advice** button in the ADVICE AREA. This will cause different recommended combinations of colors and materials to be recommended in the OUTPUT AREA. By clicking on the buttons in the OUTPUT AREA, customers can make the recommended colors and materials automatically map onto the constructed furniture.

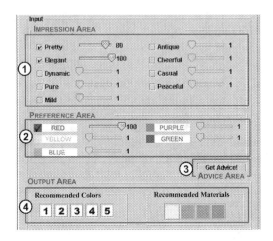

Fig. 7. A screenshot of the color and material recommendation interface

4.5 The Virtual Show Room

Co-assembler provides customers with a virtual environment to view and interactively try out their tailor-made furniture, as shown in Figure 8. To provide scale, the virtual show room features a 3D model of a person of the customer's height (Figure 9).

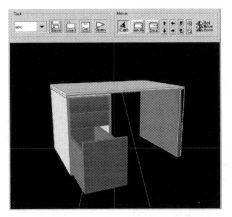

Fig. 8. Constructing desk in the virtual environment

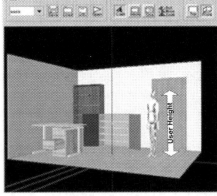

Fig. 9. Virtual show room

5 Conclusion and Future Work

We have described a framework for a real-time collaborative interactive 3D assembler system on the WWW, Co-assembler. The Co-assembler has been implemented with an initial prototype of a virtual furniture store. The interactive interface with the advisory helpers has been described to support the customer-oriented product configuration. The methodologies allow web customers to customize and build made-to-order products. In future work we will need to further analyze the relationships between customers' needs and products, study the coupling between different functional regions, and apply the system to different areas of e-commerce. We will also need to enhance the flexibility and expansibility of the framework to accommodate changing fashions and tastes.

Acknowledgments. This project was partially supported by the Hong Kong Polytechnic University Research Grant GU-047.

References

1. Blanchebarbe, P. and Diehl, S.: A Framework for Component Based Model Acquisition and Presentation Using Java3D. Proceedings of Sixth Symposium on Web3D Technologies. Paderbon, Germany (2001) 117-125
2. Chiara, J.D., Panero, J. and Zelinik, M.: Time-Saver Standards for Interior Design and Space Planning. McGRAW-HILL Int. Editions (1992)
3. Chan, S.C.F. and Ng, V.T.Y.: Real-Time Collaborative Solid Shape Design (RCSSD) on the Internet. Concurrent Engineering: Research and Applications 10(3)(2002) 229-238
4. Chan, S.C.F., Soo, S.M.K. and Yu, K.M.: Customer-driven Collaborative Product Assembler for Internet-based Commerce. Concurrent Engineering: Research and Applications 14(2)(2006) 99-109
5. Contract Furniture. TechniCon Systems, Inc.
   URL: http://www.technicon.com/industry_furniture.html
6. IKEA.: IKEA Office Planner. IKEA United Kingdom.
   URL: http://www.ikea.com/ms/en_GB/rooms_ideas/office/office_planner.html
7. IKEA.: International IKEA System B.V. URL: http://www.ikea.com
8. I.R.I.: I.R.I Color Design Inc.
   URL: http://www.iricolor.com/04_colorinfo/sensetest.html
9. Japan Tis Institute.: Home Color Design: Color Coordination for Interiors. Graphic-sha Publishing Co., Ltd., Tokyo, Japan (1991) 14-33
10. Jiang, P.Y. and Zhang, Y.F.: Visualized Part Manufacturing via an Online e-Service Platform on Web. Concurrent Engineering: Research and Applications 10(4)(2002) 267-277
11. Lescinsky, G.W., Touma, C., Goldin, A., Fudim, M. and Cohen, A.: Interactive scene manipulation in the Virtue3D system. Proceedings of Seventh Symposium on Web3D Technologies, USA (2002) 127-135
12. Chen, L., Song, Z. and Feng, L.: Internet-enabled real-time collaborative assembly modeling via an e-Assembly system: status and promise. Computer-Aided Design 36(9)(2004) 835-847
13. Miyakawa, A., Sugita, K. and Shibata, Y.: Construction of the Traditional Crafting Search Engine Using Kansei Information Processing. Proceedings of the sixth Int. Workshop on Multimedia Network Systems and Applications (2004) 50-55
14. Nokia. URL: http://www.nokia.com
15. Nousch, M. and Jung, B.: CAD on the World Wide Web: Virtual assembly of Furniture with BEAVER. Proceedings of the Fourth Symposium on Virtual Reality Modeling Language. Paderborn, Germany (1999) 113-119
16. ProductCart. Product Configurator.
    URL: http://www.earlyimpact.com/productcart/build_to_order/product-configurator.asp

17. Soo, S.M.K. and Chan, S.C.F.: Interactive 3D Product Assembler for the WWW : A case study of a 3D furniture store. Proc. Int. Conference on Enterprise Information Systems (2004)
18. Soo, S.M.K. and Chan, S.C.F.: Real-time collaborative 3D product assembler for internet-based manufacturing. Proceedings of the 11th Int. Conference on Concurrent Engineering (2004) 419-425
19. Toyota. Toyota Motor Corporation.
    URL: http://www.toyota-europe.com/goodies/index.html
20. Wang, C.H., Chu, W.H. and Chou, S.Y.: Interpreting Customer Needs in Collaboration-A Qualitative Realization Process for Conceptual Design. Proceedings of the eleventh Int. Conference on Concurrent Engineering (2004) 411-418
21. Wang, J., Liu, J. and Li, S.: Collaborative assembly/disassembly on the Web. Proceedings of the 11th Int. Conference on Concurrent Engineering (2004) 425-430
22. X-Configurator. Qualiteam: e-business software.
    URL: http://www.x-cart.com/product_configurator.html
23. Xu, T.H., Lin, Y.J. and Chan, C.C.: A web-based product modelling tool – a preliminary development. Int. Journal of Advanced Manufacturing Technology 21 (2003) 669-677

A Reusable Design Artifacts Managing Framework for e-Business Systems

Hwa Gyoo Park

Department of Electronic Commerce and U-healthcare, Soonchonhyang University
646, Shinchang, Eupnai, Asan, Choongchung Nam-Do, 336-745, Korea
hkpark1@sch.ac.kr

Abstract. Recently, as the requirements of e-business are evolving, and the domain complexity is increasing, the practical use of component is growing in the e-business applications. By enhancing flexibility and maintainability, the component management framework can potentially be used to reduce system development costs, assemble systems rapidly, and relieve the spiraling maintenance burden for supporting the evolution of e-business. In this paper, we propose a component-driven development framework named EbizCom. The EbizCom provides a plug-and-play component-oriented development environment for e-business systems.

1 Introduction

The web has become a ubiquitous environment for application development [1]. Recently, many organizations have attempted to build e-business systems to harness all business information and assets into access to all partners in a given business community within a multi-channel distribution network, including producers, distributors, dealers, service groups, and end consumers [10][19]. However, e-business requirements continuously change to adapt a community strategy [17]. Increasingly, it becomes more important than ever to implement and maintain the components [1][3][16].

The component-driven development approach includes a variety of benefits: reusability, rapid development, cost effectiveness, and better and more dynamic service [4][5]. Accordingly, these advantages can provide a flexible environment that caters to dynamic change [9]. For that mechanism in our architecture, we used a component approach in which the conceptual artifacts of analysis were adapted to the technical artifacts. The analysis results can be transformed effectively and consistently into reusable component units in implementation via design works. Though the object-oriented approach brought about a major revolution from traditional software development, the promise of being able to reuse large-scale codes has not become a reality [2][11][18].

2 Form of Components for e-Business

The proposed approach is component-oriented [4][9] for e-business systems. Once components are defined, they can help reassemble the web-enabled e-business systems rapidly and reduce the spiraling maintenance burden [14-15].

W. Shen et al. (Eds.): CSCWD 2006, LNCS 4402, pp. 237–246, 2007.
© Springer-Verlag Berlin Heidelberg 2007

These benefits can be enhanced if the components can be used for any specific technical platforms or component integration technologies [5][13]. Our component concept attempts to respond to evolving e-business systems through quick modifications as well as plug-and-play compositions and reusability [3][7]. The principle of component technology enabling the standard engineering software permits artifacts from other manufacturers [6][8][12]. In EbizCom, the business components and their control functions relationship is depicted as shown in Figure 1.

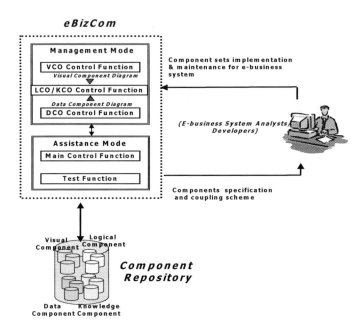

Fig. 1. Components and control functions relationship in proposed framework

2.1 Business Component

Business component (BCO) represents logical reusable components. In our architecture, there are four logical components as follows:

- VCO (Visual Component): A navigational primitive that will be implemented as a screen interface; it can become a whole or partial interface.
- LCO (Logic Component): An encapsulated non-expertise component that will be implemented according to the component view responsibilities; invoked from a screen or dialogue unit; may become a whole or partial view responsibility. The LCO refers to programs performing application logic and method.
- KCO (Knowledge Component): An encapsulated expertise component dealing with knowledge-required intelligence action, which will be implemented according to the component view responsibilities. KCO encapsulates rules, meta-rule, and reasoning elements ([3]).
- DCO (Data Component): DCO corresponds to a data attribute set or relational table.

2.2 Service Component

The service component (SCO) is for the support component editing and execution. The SCO is a core component, which have a role of supporting component framework. It is a standardized interface for linking components, and services are an elementary part of open programming environments. The component is implemented to manipulate the components, attributes and methods. It acts as suggested system servers. Figure 2 depicts the proposed EbizCom framework. It shows the four layers of infrastructure, component, framework, and e-business applications.

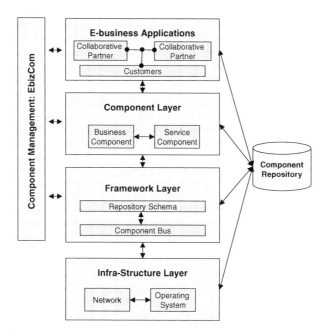

Fig. 2. Illustration of component-oriented e-business system layers and EbizCom

3   Component Management Framework: EbizCom

The component management mode is composed of three sub-modes; VCO control function, LCO/KCO control function, and DCO control function. The assistance mode is composed of two functions: main control and testing functions.

3.1 Management Mode

DCO Control Function. The EbizCom adopts the component model for data modeling. If an object-oriented database is used, these DCOs can be transformed directly. However, in many real-life projects, relational database are widely used. Therefore, the transformation of the DCOs into relational schema may be required to form a relational table in DCO control function. Designers require guidelines for this transformation. By using these rules, a physical database is generated automatically from the DCOs via the DCO control function. This function is for implementing physical data schema, and this schema is tightly coupled with the entire screen and business logics to form a composite component set for a task in an e-business application.

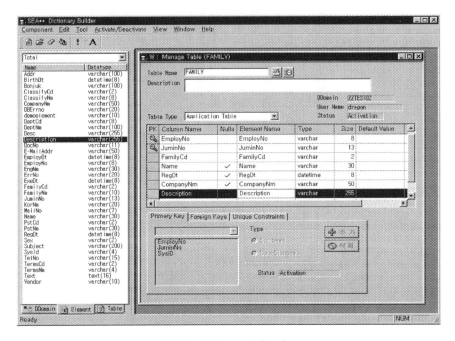

Fig. 3. DCO control function

VCO Control Function. It is for creating, editing, or modifying user interfaces: screen and dialogue. Through the VCO control function, user interfaces (UIs), and the navigation flow of one UI to another are defined according to their navigational paths. The VCO control function specifies and implements and manages UI components. A UI is a screen or dialogue having information and navigational guide. UIs are designed for customers to obtain necessary information as they want. A UI specification may be composed of one or several VCOs. However, we mapped a VCO into a UI in this paper.

The VCOs may be enhanced through additional efforts by developers and graphic designers on the basis of the corresponding simulation and specifications, using the test browser. Figure 4 shows a VCO in a screen type, how customers choose desired design.

LCO/KCO Control Function. The LCO/KCO can be converted into a program or method using the LCO control function. The DCO refers to a data attribute set or relational table. The LCO controls the DCOs through the functions of the VCOs. The association relationship is one-to-one (1:1) between the VCO and the DCO and one-to-many (1:N) between the VCO and the LCO. For example, a VCO may be linked with more than one LCO. A complete component set consists of a set of components that are mapped to the corresponding component view.

3.2   Assistance Mode

Main Control Function. In the system, if some components in terms of VCO, LCO, KCO, NCO or DCO artifacts, such as screen, dialogue, knowledge, program, method, or data should be searched and reported, it is not easy to find all the component types related to the task unit in a short time. Accordingly, the search sub-function can play a critical role in maintaining components.

The mode is developed for the purpose of direct maintenance of components by using the meta-schema stored in a repository. The drill-down search derives nested attributes from the selected attributes, and the query is based on the attributes chosen from the latest nested ones. The keyword search gets an input word, and finds components related to the word. As a search result, component indexes and titles are listed, and then if a user selects a component, results can be reported on the main editor depending on the reporting domain chosen.

Test Function. The test function checks the completeness and robustness to each component before releases it. The browser has the function detecting errors of component sets forming a navigational transaction based on LCO, KCO, DCO, and VCO.

The following figures (Figures 4-7) show the screenshots of VCO, LCO/KCO, main control and test functions. And the functions of each mode are summarized in Table 1.

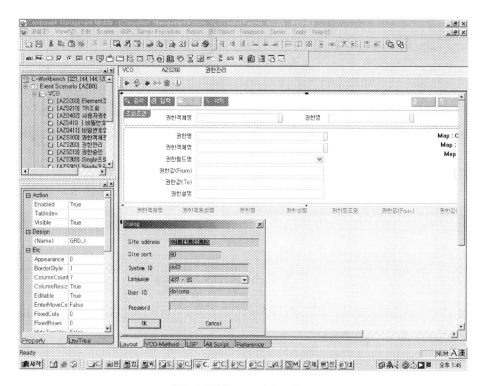

Fig. 4. VCO control function

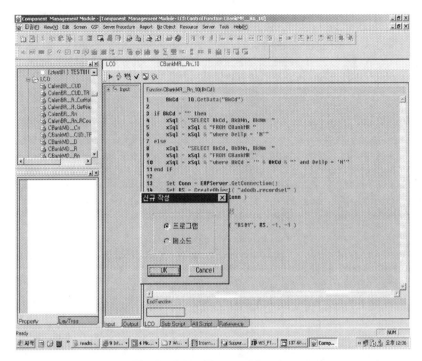

Fig. 5. LCO/KCO control function

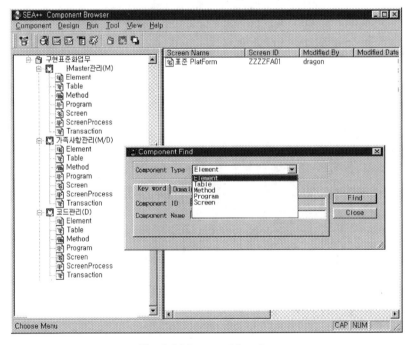

Fig. 6. Main control function

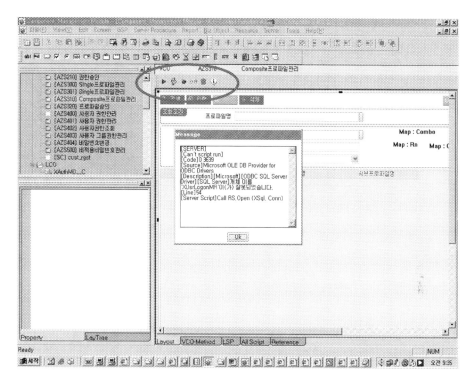

Fig. 7. Test function

Table 1. A summary of EbizCom functions and descriptions

Mode	Function	Description
Management	VCO Control	-Define user interface element -Define types of user interface -Generate user interfaces such as screen or dialogue
	DCO Control	-Define data element -Define table component -Generate physical database schema for target DBMS
	LCO/KCO Control	-Define types of logics -Develop a program, method, or knowledge
Assistance	Main Control	-Drill-down and drill-up searches -Store components in meta-schema and manage instances for meta-schema -Present a bird's eye view of application project resources
	Test	-Simulate implemented component to check the completeness and robustness before releasing it

A Case Implementation. The implementation constructs a physically running e-business system (Figure 8). The company in this real-life case produces elevators and escalator systems for the commercial sector. By working in close cooperation with international partners and developing in-house technology, the company has become a major supplier of passenger elevators, escalators and moving walkways. The company is participating in e-business to share product designs, procurement plans, manufacturing schedules, distribution activities, and transportation movements. The proposed framework is applied to this company to enhance modeling reusability, scalability, and rapid modeling the system.

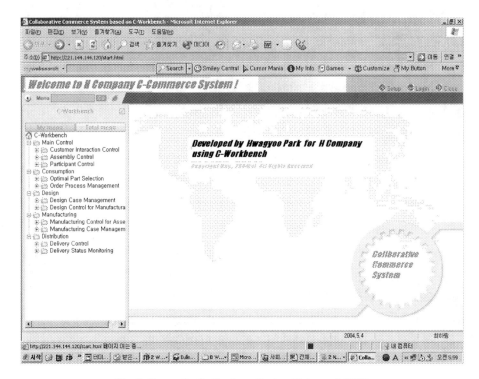

Fig. 8. Screen for "e-Business System Entrance" VCO

All of the artifacts during the design phase should be mapped to physical components. Using EbizCom, developers could transform the DCO, VCOs, LCOs and KCOs into physically running components such as a database schema, user interfaces, and program logics, respectively. To construct the system more than 150 VCOs, 195 LCOs, 30 KCOs and one DCO were built. To support interoperability in a heterogeneous environment, the system was based on DCOM [3][11]. Each component was packaged as an independent piece of code that could be accessed by remote clients via method invocations. The broker establishes the client–server relationships between the components.

To log on to the e-business system, each stakeholder's information is required such as customer identification, password site address, port number, system for DBMS, and language type, menu name. Currently, Korean, Japanese, and English languages are supported for multi national stakeholders [20].

Depending on the user information, his or her available menu functions area restricted based on a role-driven access control security policy. For example, users on consumption side can perform on their role domain, and partially check up permitted data, information, and expertise of other role domains. If a design engineer on consumption side requires information on the type of escalator and parts to be designed, the engineer can access and generates a possible design along with complete technical specifications. If required, on-line visual communication function can be used for being consulted with agents on the design stakeholder side. The engineer also can check each part's dependencies and alternative fittings to see if its specifications are geometrically and technically permitted for a target escalator type. This process is performed by the use of design and cluster codes. The representation of design geometry, including ideal tolerance geometry and geometric accuracy is considered internally. The parts relations between design and geometric descriptions are described as LCO programs. The most effective design for selected gearbox is found by the optimization search method.

By adopting the e-business system, the company and the partnered stakeholders can share information from a variety of sources. It works as a secure portal that enables the stakeholders' collaborations. The author believes that the system can be applied to other virtual enterprise applications.

4 Conclusion

Industrial enterprises are currently faced with fundamental changes in the overall application framework. Aggressive early adopters are now leveraging the Internet for a far more strategic advantage. These companies are participating in e-business to share product designs, procurement plans, demand forecasts, manufacturing schedules, distribution activities, and transportation movements. The proposed framework attempts to develop an e-business system based on component-driven development framework perspective to enhance modeling reusability, scalability, and rapid modeling the system. These results will enable the practice of e-business, and consequently help increase system development capability and quality, reduce development cycle time and cost, and hence increase product marketability.

The proposed framework will continually be improved to facilitate the all aspects of components construction and maintenance supports. One of the directions is to accommodate components from other architecture such as Enterprise JavaBeans, DCOM, and CORBA in implementing the collaborative e-business systems. Furthermore, the author will consider strategic aspects toward organizational memory because they are a major source of organizational asset in the applications.

References

1. Frederic A.H.: Mobile Web Services. Wiley (2006)
2. Bock, C. & Odell, J.J.: A more complete model of relations and their implementation: Roles. Journal of Object-Oriented Programming 11(2) (1998) 51-54
3. Chen, Y. & Liang, M.: Design and implementation of a collaborative engineering information system for allied concurrent engineering. Int. J. CIM 16 (2000) 9-27
4. D'Souza, D.F. & Wills, A.C.: Objects, Components and Frameworks with UML. Addison-Wesley, Reading, MA (1998)
5. Eddon, G. & Eddon, H.: Inside Distributed COM, Microsoft Press (1998)

6. Elmasri, R., Weeldreyer, J. & Hevner, A.: The category concept: an extension to the entity relationship model. Data & Knowledge Engineering 1(1) (1985) 75-116
7. Ginige, A. & Murugesan, S.: Web engineering: An introduction. IEEE Multimedia 8(1) (2001) 14-18
8. Gottlob, G., Schre, M. & Ock, B.R.: Extending object-oriented systems with roles. ACM Transactions on Information Systems 14(3) (1996) 268-296
9. Henderson, P. & Walters, R.: Behavioral analysis of component-based systems. Information and Software Technology 43 (2001) 161-169
10. Holsapple, C.W. & Singh, M.: Electronic commerce: definitional taxonomy, integration, and knowledge management. Journal of Organizational Computing and Electronic Commerce 10(3) (2000) 151-164
11. Jacobson, I.: Object-Oriented Software Engineering: A Use Case Driven Approach. Addison-Wesley (1995)
12. Kunda, D. & Brooks, L.: Assessing organizational obstacles to component-based development: A case study approach. Information and Software Technology 42(2000)715-725
13. OMG CORBA. URL: http://www.omg.org
14. O'Brien, A.: An intelligent component model for building design. Proc. Second European Conference on Product and Process Modeling in the Building Industry (1998) 7-12
15. Rosenman, M.A. & Wang, F.J.: CADOM: a Component Agent model based Design-Oriented Model for Collaborative Design. Research in Engineering Design II (1999) 193-205
16. Sessions, R.: COM and DCOM: Microsoft's Vision for Distributed Objects. Wiley, New York (1998)
17. Shin, K. & Lim, C.S.: A reference system for Internet based inter-enterprise electronic commerce. The Journal of Systems and Software 60(3)(2002) 195-204
18. Senghyung, K.: Java Programming & Components, Freetech (2006)
19. van der Aalst, W.M.P.: Process-oriented architectures for electronic commerce and inter organizational workflow. Information Systems 24(9)(1999) 639-671
20. Zongmyung B.: Ubinet Component Software: SAFE ERP. Ubinet (2006)

Research on Hybrid Distributed Manufacturing Execution System in Multi-location Enterprises Environment

Xiaobing Liu, Hongguang Bo, Yue Ma, and Qiunan Meng

CIMS Centre, Dalian University of Technology,
Dalian 116023, China
xbliu@dlut.edu.cn, bohongguang@sohu.com,
mayue_dalian@sina.com, code_name@163.com

Abstract. Hybrid distributed manufacturing execution system (HDMES) can be widely considered as a typical case of complicated application system. In this paper, the management characteristics of a multi-location special steel enterprises are analyzed; the flat-style management pattern system architecture for Special Steel Enterprises Information System (SSEIS) is constructed and the hardcore functional structures of HDMES—planning and scheduling system and material flow tracking system are brought about. This paper proposes the usage of applied information models to support the distributed product manufacturing process. On the basis of the corresponding relation between production number and contract number, the contract-tracking model is proposed. Based on the grouping of products with similar attributes, the material balance model is put forward. This system is developed based on J2EE and its interrelated modules work dynamically and systematically in Web environment.

1 Introduction

As the support industry of a civil economy, special steel enterprise provides the primary materials for machinery, automobile, construction and other industries [1]. Situated in the environment of global markets and increasing customized orientation, modern special steel enterprises are impelled to seek new paradigms, such as concurrent engineering, lean production, agile manufacturing, business reforming, business incorporating and corporation annexing. Multi-location special steel enterprises are brought. A multi-location special steel enterprise is a permanent organization of inner companies that come together to share costs and skills to address business opportunities that they could not undertake individually [2]. On the one hand, sub-plants (sub-bases) in a multi-location special steel enterprise will keep their independence and autonomy. On the other hand, they will contribute their core competencies to the wholeness of multi-location special steel enterprise. Through the combination of the core competencies of sub-plants, the distributed multi-location special steel enterprise may become a best-of-everything enterprise. Nowadays, the distributed multi-location special steel enterprise is considered as one of the most promising paradigms for the future enterprises.

W. Shen et al. (Eds.): CSCWD 2006, LNCS 4402, pp. 247–256, 2007.
© Springer-Verlag Berlin Heidelberg 2007

Today, many manufacturing enterprises utilize manufacturing execution systems (MES) to deliver information to optimize production activities from order booking through design, production, and marketing to realize the agile manufacturing enterprise. The MES evolution is composed of traditional MES phase, integrated MES phase and distributed MES phase. An integrated MES may have more advantages than traditional MES, such as a single-logic database, rich functionality, well-integrated applications, and a single model of factories, products, and manufacturing processes. However, integrated MES is sometimes regarded as monolithic, insufficiently configurable, and difficult to modify. In order to solve the problem of the dichotomy between the traditional MES and integrated MES, the concept of the distributed MES has been proposed in 1996 [3]. With the distributed MES, each application can be both a self-sufficient single-point solution, and can be integrated into a larger suite of products. Therefore, the distributed MES offers an open, modularized, configurable, distributed, and collaborative environment such that rapid implementation, complexity reducing, agility, cost-effective integration, easiness of use, and ownership cost reducing may be achieved.

A multi-location special steel enterprise production management system is a representative hybrid distributed manufacturing execution system. In the hybrid distributed manufacturing execution system for a special steel enterprise, planning and scheduling problems and material tracking problems have been considered the typical hybrid distributed computing problems, and they have been drawn as wide attention of the production and operations management researchers as many other manufacturing industries.

2   Production Management Characteristics for SSE

Multi-Location Special Steel manufacturing enterprises are being forced into greater collaboration with customers, suppliers and inner sub-plants in order to produce quality products in smaller batches, shorter lead times and with greater variety. Accordingly, the tasks of design and implementation for the multi-location special steel enterprises-oriented manufacturing execution system must be conducted in these distributed sub-plants across traditional organizational boundaries. Special steel product has the features of multi- variety, diversification and small batch. The make-to- order (MTO) production positioning strategy is widely adopted by special steel enterprises in order to supply their products in short time, high quality, low cost and good service to meet the needs of the market. Controlling the expenses and cost is core target for improving competition abilities of any enterprises. Continuous casting and hot rolling technologies are developed and can save energy consumption in the production process from hot steel to slab.

Due to the differences in the production processes of Continuous casting-cold charge rolling (CC-CCR), Continuous casting-hot charge rolling (CC-HCR), Continuous casting-direct hot charge rolling (CC-DHCR), Continuous casting-hot direct rolling (CC-HDR) [1], the production planning and scheduling problems and material tracking problems in these processes are also different. Continuous casting and hot rolling which are integrated into a single entity conform to the unified overall production plan and the steel rolling mill can no longer roll slabs simply according to the sequence from wide to narrow. Instead, it must observe the scheduling from steel making to continuous casting. Planning and scheduling, material tracking in the integrated process are the combined lot scheduling and tracking problems integrating multiple production stages.

Mould casting and cold rolling technologies are still used in some sub-plants (sub-bases, companies) of the multi-location special steel enterprise. In the traditional steel making (SM), mould casting (MC) and cold charge rolling (CCR) process, the SM, MC and CCR belong to different plants which execute production planning and material tracking management independently.

3 Using Structure of Multi-location SSE- Oriented HDMES

Operation of hybrid distributed manufacturing execution system for multi-location special steel enterprise production is a challenging and difficult task. Advanced and practical planning and scheduling system and material tracking system are characterized by promotional demands, which take a toll on the target production management as well as result in improving production process automation, reducing product cost and enhancing customer service. To cope with the challenges of raising production efficiencies and reducing inventory costs, organizations between different corporations or inner current enterprise cannot rely solely on isolated changes to specific parts of the supply chain, like suppliers or distributors, but instead depend critically on the relationships and interdependences among different organizational units. The production management and control pattern are analyzed, supply chain management (SCM), custom relation management (CRM), process control system (PCS) are adopted in this brand-new manufacturing execution system.

According to the characteristics, production organizing architecture of the multi-location special steel enterprise, hybrid distributed manufacturing execution system is presented, which includes central MES and distributed MES and comprises all the production operation processes, such as production cost management, contracts management, central material preparing management, central planning and scheduling management, process route management, quality management, sub-plant ability balance controlling, sub-plant material require plan, sub-plant daily production plan, sub-plant material tracking controlling and etc [4]. In order to integrate and optimize the whole production management, the system should be duly regulated executing function and controlling strategies, it contains all the elements of the production process, such as production planning, production scheduling, etc., and it must regard receiving feedback information from material flow as determining basis. Other data information of equipment states, quality management and professional process etc. are important reference for production organization. Interrelation and corresponding mode of the mentioned agents is illustrated in Figure 1 [5].

Special steel enterprise has the feature of dense capital and it is an important target to arrange the equipments at the best ability in making production plan. According to

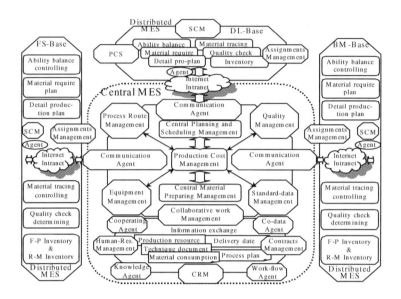

Fig. 1. HDMES Integrated framework [5]

orders and market prediction, the ability of equipments and units and production efficiency of different kinds should be taken into account to confirm the production procedure at the best profits. The production of rolled steel is a continuous sequence, and
the output is comparatively stable. It is difficult and unpractical to change the purchasing plan and production plan to meet the change of orders. It has to adjust its
production according to many factors, such as, orders, economical batches, and market predictions. Distributed production plan model is adopted to mark out the dynamic
production process and deploy material, equipment, human resource etc. Multi-closed
loop control technique is exerted between plan and material flow information; it
makes production program flat and stable [6]. Combining operation features of iron
and steel factory, production plan model for this enterprise is formed as shown in
Figure 2.

Product cost is an important economic index in reflecting the operation of special
steel enterprise generally. Combined with production plan and control is beneficial to
the unification of material flow and capital flow. Cost management is also a combination of plan, control and analysis of occurrence to implement the functions of prediction, plan, decision-making, control, analysis and check for the cost, which can
reduce the non-profit business operations, decrease production cost and raise competitive ability [7]. While extensive work has been fulfilled in developing effective data
models, more effort has been performed in perfecting the manufacturing model of
multi-location special steel enterprises. Different approaches used to model various
aspects of manufacturing processes are reviewed and found, and an approach based on
scheduling rules, multi-agent technique, distributed control, multi-closed loop control
and user cooperation is presented to solve the distributed planning and scheduling

problem. It hierarchically decomposes the large-scale planning and scheduling problem into the planning level problems, the scheduling level problems and material tracking feedback level problems. Relatively, material flow tracking model based on furnace number and production batch is also given, which can distinguish the identical batch material with the same attribute.

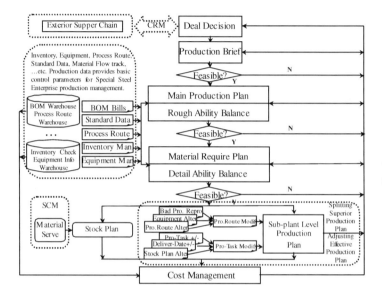

Fig. 2. HDMES Integrative Planning and Scheduling Model

Cost management adopts standard cost mechanism and the cost calculation mode in full. ABM (Activity-based management) [8] is adopted inner the branch factory and Settle account passed to the next machining factory adopted between the branch factories. ABM has the following steps: 1) ascertaining and sorting all the resources related to cost management, then compiling cost subject; 2) ascertaining all the processes in the production; 3) relating the corresponding resources to the process; 4) according to the production plan, relating the process to the product; 5) based on the above steps, the managers can find the process exhausting resources with no increment value. Product cost is obtained by using ABM method in one factory and will be passed to the next factory as raw material price according to the production plan, till the end of production.

4   Design of Software Platform for HDMES

To build the distributed and integrated system effectively and quickly, the system is designed and developed according to object-oriented method and concurrent engineering concept. Acquirement of domain knowledge and requirement, Object-oriented

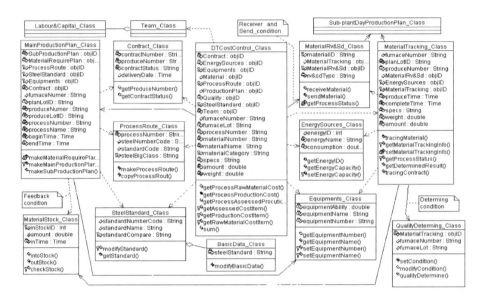

Fig. 3. Software class chart of HDMES platform

analysis, Object-oriented design, system model constructing by UML, system implementation and system testing are necessary. A typical Software class chart for HDMES is shown in Figure 3.

It is well known that MES is composed of several functional modules that handle specifics, e.g., planning, material, cost, equipment. The abstract object model is constructed through them as in Figure 4. The four key elements of a factory are planning, material, equipment, and work-in-process (WIP). Each element is controlled by its specific managing cells. The contract management module dispatches orders to the production. The planning and scheduling sub-system dispatches jobs to material tracking sub-system, WIP management module, etc. In production process, the actual production information is responded to pre-level module and pre-level module will adjust output parameters.

The basic run-time undertaker of the functional module is working-agent manages/uses agent-configuration that consists of CORBA&RMI/Local-Interface, Security-Mechanism, Local-Database, and Knowledge-Base. By inheriting Basic-Agent, a functional module can possess all the characteristics of the Basic-Agent. CORBA&RMI/Local -interface is designed for constructing a communication infrastructure and achieves the collaboration platform. In order to establish secure communication, the Security-Mechanism is created for handling all the operations of security. Knowledge-Base constructs a search engine for searching desired services and a reasoning mechanism for exception diagnosis. The Local-Database sets the connection of database for Security-Mechanism and Knowledge-Base to access the database. Using Local-Database the function-Agent can maintain autonomous properties and necessary information. The function-Agent owns Basic-Agent to communicate with other agents by CORBA&RMI/Local -Interface.

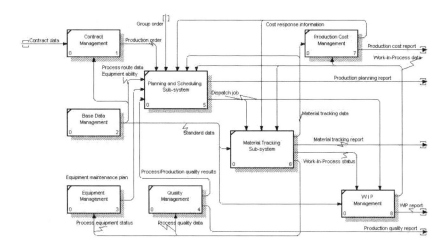

Fig. 4. Defining HDMES system interfaces

In each local agent-working environment, agents at the four levels interact with each other to address activity precedence arrangements and activity-resource assignments [9]:

1) Interactions between distributed MES agent (Sub-Base agent) and activity agents realize macro-management of the multi-location special steel enterprise. Activity agents receive directions and guidelines from the distributed MES agent. Besides, activity agents corresponding to interface activities also interact with the central MES agent to send (receive) messages to (from) the outside world.

2) As activities of the sub-base production process are interrelated, activity agents in the local MES interact with each other to implement smooth and efficient activity advancements while satisfying activity precedence constraints.

3) According to certain optimization rules, activity agents assign their activities to appropriate role agents, which further assign the activities to appropriate resource agents. Therefore, resource agents that are most competent for performing activities are organized and coordinated to execute the sub-base production. Since one or more optional resources available can fill one role during the production process, the role-based activity-resource assignment has high flexibility.

4) Resource agents are actual performers of various activities of the special steel production process. They will feed back real-time information about activity execution upward level by level: from resource agents to role agents, and further to appropriate activity agents, and finally to the member enterprise agent. Along with the feedback are analyses of activity execution status and corresponding adjustments performed by role agents, activity agents and the member enterprise agent, such as activity resource reassignments, activity replanning. All adjustments along with the feedback are dedicated to completing activities as scheduled. In this way, the multi-location SSE can monitor and control the sub business process execution in a real-time fashion. When

required, the member enterprise will interact with other member enterprise agents to implement activity adjustments and/or resource sharing, as discussed before.

In Figure 5, we illustrate interactions among the multi kinds of agents in the agent-based multi-location enterprise model [10].

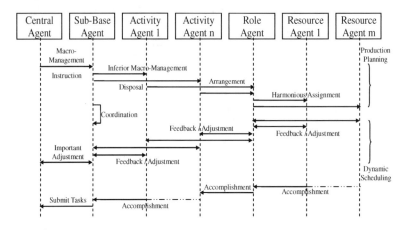

Fig. 5. Interaction among agents in HDMES model

The multi-location special steel enterprise-oriented hybrid distributed manufacturing execution system includes the following modules: contact management, quality management, basic data management, central and distributed production management, distributed material tracking management, equipment management and cost management. The sub-systems share the data and information to optimize the behaviors and processes.

CORBA and RMI technologies are adopted to integrate legacy system deployed on other platforms to share the information between the systems. In order to raise programming efficiency and transplant the components to the utmost extent, we work out three-tier software architecture shown in Figure 6, which contains presentation tier, business logic tier and basic information tier. J2EE technology is adopted to develop the system based on B/S, which is put forward by Sun Micro system Company. J2EE technology can be used across various platforms and has a good mechanism to develop a scalable, flexible, distributed, reconfigured and easy-maintained business application and can integrate the legacy systems [11]. The programmers can concentrate their attention on the business behaviors to shorten development time and develop the system with high efficiency.

The Presentation Tier is to interchange the information between users and the system by using Internet explorer, provide the systematic information for the users and accept the requests from the users. The Business Logic Tier is the main body of the system, accepts the information from presentation tier and accesses the corresponding methods to deal with it by using Servlet/JSP technologies. Servlet can deal with the information from the users and return the results to the presentation tier in the form of JavaScript. This tier also encapsulates the business logic behaviors by using EJB, such as working out the techniques, production plan, and management of equipments and so on. The Basic Information Tier contains the database system and legacy systems. Database system is responsible for the maintaining of data, such as standards, techniques, states of equipments and etc.

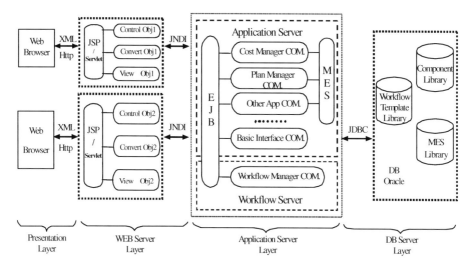

Fig. 6. Software structure of HDMES Platform

5   Implementation Summary and Conclusions

The applied research project was implemented in a particular manufacturing enterprise with hybrid production processes and multi-location production plants. The HDMES framework methodology was adopted to develop the enterprise production management system and the implementation result is considered to be feasible. Table 1 gives a comparison in order to justify the methodologies discussed.

Table 1. Comparisons between Traditional/Integrated/HD MES

	Traditional MES	Integrated MES	HDMES
System architecture	Centralization	Distributed	Distributed OO
Reusable/flexible	Low	Middle	High
Open interfaces	No	Yes	Yes
Modularization	Low	High	High
Recursive development	No	Yes	Yes
Interoperability	Low	High	High
Configurability	Low	High	High
Implementation time	Long	Long	Short
Maintainability	Difficult	Easy	Easy
Security certification	No	No	Yes
Failure recovery	No	No	Yes

The system is deployed and applied in a multi-location special steel enterprise - Dongbei Special Steel Group to solve some current problems cumbering the progress. Through comparing the corresponding parameters during 2004 with the ones during 2003, we can find that 20% of due date is shortened, 8.6% of making product storage is reduced, 10% of interior manufacturing cycle is saved, and 25% of disposing quality dissent cycle is cut. It is confirmed that the system is beneficial for the enterprise to arrange the relationship of the departments and raise its core competitive ability. The implementation results for Dongbei Special Steel Group show the system is feasible and valid.

Acknowledgments. This work was partially supported by NSFC (70572098) and NHTDP for CIMS (2002AA412020 and 2003AA414044).

References

1. Tang, L., Liu, J., Rong, A., Yang, Z.: A review of planning and scheduling systems and methods for integrated steel production. European Journal of Operational Research 133 (2000) 1-20
2. Camarinha-Matos, L.M., Afsarmanesh, H.: The virtual enterprise concept. Proc. of the PRO-VE'99. Porto, Portugal (1999) 3–14
3. Hino, R., Moriwaki, T.: Decentralized scheduling in holonic manufacturing systems. Proceedings of the 2nd International Workshop on Intelligent Manufacturing Systems. Leuven, Belgium (1999) 41-47
4. Gershwin, B.S.: Hierarchical flow control, a framework for scheduling and planning Discrete Events in Manufacturing System. Proc. of the IEEEWE 77(1)(1989) 195-209
5. Frankovič, B., Fogel, J.: Solution of Job Scheduling Problem in Multi Part Production System. IFAC Conference MCPL. Grenoble (2000)
6. Park, B.J., Choi, H.R., Kim H.S.: A hybrid genetic algorithm for the job shop scheduling problem. Computer & Industrial Engineering 45 (2003) 597-613
7. Feng, Y., Yan, H.: Optimal Production control in a Discrete Manufacturing System with Unreliable Machines and Random Demands. IEEE Transactions on Automatic Control 45(12)(2000) 2280-2296
8. OuYang, Q., Wan, S.: Cost Accounting. Dongbei University of Finance & Economics Press (2003) 30-33
9. Aerts, A.T.M., Szirbik, N.B., Goossenaerts, J.B.M.: A flexible agent-based ICT architecture for virtual enterprises. Computer in Industries 49(3)(2002) 311–327
10. Thoben, K.D., Jagdev, H.S.: Typological issues in enterprise networks. Production Planning and Control 12(5)(2001) 421–436
11. Roman, E.: Mastering Enterprise JavaBeans. 2nd edn. John Wiley & Sons, New York (2002)

A Location Method for the Outdoor Mobile Robot Based on GPS/GIS/GPRS

Minglu Zhang, Feng Cui, and Dapeng Zhang

School of Mechanical Engineering, Hebei University of Technology,
Tianjin 300130, China
cfpaper@163.com

Abstract. To improve GPS (Global Positioning System) location precision for the mobile robot, a location method based on GPS/GIS (Geographic Information System)/GPRS (General Packer Radio Service) is proposed. Through analysing GPS data structure, longitude and latitude of the robot can be extracted from GPS data stream. The GPRS module which supported AT commands is used to connect onboard computer on Internet for transmitting these location data and telecommands between the mobile robot and the control center. GIS software is programmed using VC++ and Mapinfo Professional to convert longitude and latitude of the robot into exact positions in the electronic map. A quick map matching solution based on credibility algorithm is added to the electronic map, and its algorithm is described in detail. Experiments show that location error of this method is less than 5m which is better than that of a single GPS receiver.

1 Introduction

Currently, GPS is widely used to locate mobile robots outdoors. The mobile robot can locate itself around the globe by a GPS receiver if more than four GPS satellites are detected. Because GPS supplies poor location precision for the civil use, many methods are adopted to enhance location precision, such as DGPS (Differential GPS) [1], GPS/DR (Dead Reckoning) [2], GPS/INS (Inertial Navigation System) [3], Kalman filtering [4] and so on. DGPS is the most common way. But DGPS need establish a difference datum station and purchase radio stations for transmitting GPS data. It is very expensive to locate single robot. Furthermore, above mentioned methods can only get the longitude and latitude of the robot's current position so that operators have not known the corresponding place of the robot in the map yet. On the other hand, good communication mode should be selected to ensure real time of location. Reference [5] adopts SMS (Short Messaging Service) in stead of radio station to transmit position data. Although this way decreases communication equipments cost, its transmission velocity is slower than radio. As we know, SMS has 6s transmission delay and can not send multimedia information. Especially, when GSM network has full load, transmission delay becomes worse. So, it may lead to inaccurate location when the robot is moving at a higher speed. WLAN (wireless LAN) [6] has high

W. Shen et al. (Eds.): CSCWD 2006, LNCS 4402, pp. 257–266, 2007.
© Springer-Verlag Berlin Heidelberg 2007

speed to transmit multimedia data, but it can not be applied in long distance communication because its effective communication distance is no more than 100m.

In order to solve above problems, this paper puts forward the location method for mobile robots based upon the GPS/GIS/GPRS technologies. Electronic map is used to convert longitude and latitude of the robot into exact position of the map. Meanwhile, a map matching method based on credibility algorithm is added into the electronic map to enhance location precision. It requires little computation time and helps operators directly see the exact position of the robot and which road the robot is moving on. Its location precision is much higher than that of location of single GPS receiver apparently. GPRS network is adopted to transmit location messages and photos between the robot and control center. Comparing with SMS mode, GPRS mode has many advantages, such as high speed, low cost and supporting TCP/IP protocol. Through GPRS network, the robot can connect Internet to send multimedia information to operators and operators also can control the robot via Internet. This paper is organized as follows. Section 2 introduces design of the system. Section 3 describes extracting and transmitting of GPS messages. Section 4 describes map matching method based on credibility algorithm in detail. Some experiments results are shown in Section 5. Section 6 closes the paper with some brief concluding remarks.

2   Constitution of the Location System

Structure of the system is shown in Figure 1, and its working flow is introduced as follows. The mobile robot is equipped with a GPS receiver, a GPRS module and an onboard computer. As long as the GPS receiver works, it will receive and calculate the positioning data and transmit them to the onboard computer through the serial port constantly. Longitude and latitude are contained in these data, but they cannot be utilized before classification and extraction by the GPS data extraction program. Then, longitude and latitude are sent out by GPRS module. These extracted data will flow in two directions. One flow is sent to operators' mobiles by SMS mode. The other flow is connected to Internet via GPRS network and sent to the control center's GIS serve which installs GIS software programmed by VC++ and Mapinfo Professional. In this GIS software, Mapinfo Professional is responsible for establishing electronic map and managing space data and property data of the map; VC++ is used to establish the customer interface and complete tasks of coordinate transformation, Gauss projection, map matching in turn when longitude and latitude of the robot are received. After above steps, the exact position of the robot is displayed dynamically in the electronic map. Meanwhile, operators can realize teleoperation function to the mobile robot by human-computer interface or mobiles, for example, to cut off the electricity of robots, drive robot's cameras to shot the scene and return photos, change the walking direction of robots and etc. When the robot finds something wrong with itself, it will inform operators of necessary maintenance.

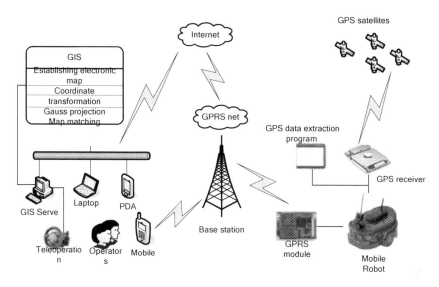

Fig. 1. Constitution of the mobile robot's location system

3 Extracting and Transmitting GPS Data

3.1 Extracting GPS Data

As long as the GPS receiver begins to work, GPS messages will be received and sent to the serial port of the onboard computer all along. We use Win 32 API which is encapsulated in VC++ to develop the serial port communication program between Microsoft Windows and the GPS receiver. Because hardware ports can not be controller directly in Windows and all ports are considered as files, the serial port should be opened by file form and made corresponding parameters setup. The communication parameters of the GPS receiver are as follows: 4800bit/s communication frequency, 8 bit data information, 1 bit stop information, non-parity. Asynchronous serial communication is applied in the process of GPS data collection. After opening and setting the serial port, event burst mode is used to receive and deal with data. The GPS data adopt NMEA0183 protocol. Similar to other communication protocols, to extract GPS data should know its frame structure firstly. GPS messages are data streams which are composed of short sentences in ASCII form. Every short sentence includes three parts --frame header, frame trailer, and intra frame. The frame header determines the structure and content of the data frame. Frame header of each sentence is different, such as, "$GPGGA", "$GPGSA", "$GPGSV" and "$GPRMC". Usually, the location data we care for, for example, latitude, longitude and time, are acquired from "$GPRMC". Because each data segment in frames are divided by commas, generally the searching of ASCII code "$" is used to judge whether it is frame header in the process of dealing with buffer storage data. The positioning parameters handled at present are determined by identifying the category of frame header and by calculating the number of commas, and then measures are taken accordingly.

In the experiment, the results got by using GPS receiver are as follows:

```
$GPRMC,022426,A,3910.6678,N,11709.5870,E,001.9,336.9,151005
,013.6,W*61
```

Data indications are shown in Table 1.

Table 1. Data indications of GPS messages

$GPRMC	Recommended Minimum Specific GPS/Transit Data
022426	UTC_TIME, HHMMSS
910.6678	Latitude
N	North latitude
11709.5870	Longitude
E	East Longitude

3.2 Transmitting GPS Messages

Establishing GPRS Communication Link. GPRS is developed from GSM. Comparing with transmission velocity of GSM 9.6 kbps, the highest transmission velocity of GPRS can reach 171.2kbps. So, GPRS network ensures good performance of real time for transmitting location messages. After longitude, latitude and time are extracted, the GPRS module will connect onboard computer on Internet for transmitting these location data and telecommands between the mobile robot and the control center. Establishment of GPRS communication link has two steps: GPRS attach and PDP context activate. The detailed process is as follows. (1) The onboard computer of the robot sends AT commands to GPRS module for requesting to activate IP. The commands contain APN (Access Point Name), QoS (Quality of Service). (2) The GPRS module sends LCP (Link Control Protocol) data frame to setup network and negotiate parameter. After parameter negotiation, user identification will be completed by PAP (Password Authentication Protocol) and user ID and password will be saved. (3) The GPRS module sends IPCP (Internet Protocol Control Protocol) data frame to request assigning IP addresses dynamically. SGSN (Serving GPRS Support node) send requisition for activating PDP (Packet Data Protocol) context. (4) DNS (Domain Name Server) parses APN by SGSN request and gets IP address of GGSN (Gateway GPRS support node) corresponded to APN. SGSN sends PDP context requisition to the selected GGSN. GGSN identifies user and assigns IP addresses dynamically for the user. Then, SGSN return a success message of PDP context establishment. (5) SGSN sends an activating PDP message and assigns IP addresses dynamically for the GPRS module through IPCP configuration.

Using AT Commands Transmitting GPS Messages. AT command set is responsible for establishing communication link which connects onboard GPRS module of the robot and GIS serve or operators' mobiles. The "AT" or "at" prefix is set at the beginning of each command line. AT commands mainly include following functions: setup GPRS communication parameters, attach and detach GPRS connection, send and receive SMS, activate and deactivate TCP connection, send and receive TCP messages, send and receive UDP messages, and so on. Table 2 lists the corresponding instructions.

Table 2. Functions of AT commands

AT commands	Functions
AT+CGDCONT	Define PDP Context
AT+CGATT	GPRS attach and detach
ATD*98#	Request GPRS IP service
AT+CGDSTIP	Setup aim IP address
AT+CGDSTPT	Setup aim port number
AT+CGSTCPINIT	initialize
AT+CGRGST	register
AT+CGDS	Send data
AT+CGDR	Read data

4 Map Matching

To enhance location precision, map matching based on credibility algorithm is applied in this paper. First, in order to attain the accurate result of map matching, three factors should be taken into account.

(1) The distance element. The distance between the robot's position obtained from the GPS receiver and its projected position on the road should be small.

(2) The direction element. The shape of the road where the robot is moving on should be similar to the trajectory of the robot's position.

(3) The continuous element. When the robot is moving on a road, it cannot jump to another road, so it can never change the road unless it goes through a junction [7].

Considering the above discussions, the normalization distance between position estimate point $\hat{P}^k$ and candidate road i can be defined as:

$$D_i(k) = \frac{1}{\left\| \hat{P}^k - \hat{P}_i^k \right\|^{-1} + 1} . \tag{1}$$

where $D_i(k) \in [0,1]$. $\hat{P}_i^k$ is the projected position of $\hat{P}^k$ in the road.

As for the direction element, the direction for each road may not be uniform because every road may contain many segments. The direction deviation of the normalization is defined in the following way.

$$\theta_i(k) = \frac{1}{\Delta \psi(k)^{-1} + 1} . \tag{2}$$

where $\theta_i(k) \in [0,1)$.

$$\Delta\psi = \begin{cases} \left|\psi_p - \psi_i\right| & \left|\psi_p - \psi_i\right| \prec 180° \\ 360 - \left|\psi_p - \psi_i\right| \end{cases} . \tag{3}$$

ψ_p is the angle between line $\hat{P}^k \hat{P}^{k+1}$, which is connected by two neighboring position estimate points $\hat{P}^k$ and $\hat{P}^{k+1}$, and the north direction.

ψ_i is the angle between line segment $A^j A^{j+1}$ (j=0,1,..., $n_A - 1$) on the i road and the north direction, meanwhile A^j and A^{j+1} are the two ends for the i road and the corresponding line segment of the line $\hat{P}^k \hat{P}^{k+1}$. The map-matching credibility of i road and kth step can be defined based upon the two elements such as distance and direction:

$$C_i(k) = f(D_i(k), \theta_i(k)) . \tag{4}$$

Considering the continuous factor, $C_i(k+1)$ is defined as follows:

$$C_i(k+1) = f(D_i(k+1), \theta_i(k+1)) + \gamma \cdot C_i(k) . \tag{5}$$

where $\gamma > 0$. f is a linear combination of the distance factor and the direction factor. At the kth step, if

$$C_i(k) = \max\{C_n(k) \mid n = 1,2,..., N\} \geq C_T . \tag{6}$$

the road i is the right matching result.

C_T is a threshold value of credibility. To be effective, credibility value should meet the following criteria.

$C(k)$ should maintain a certain value and should be less affected by the noise of the navigation filter.

$C_i(k)$ of the true road should be distinguished distinctly from those of other roads.

The function f is defined as follows:

$$f(D_i(k), \theta_i(k)) = \alpha \cdot D_i(k) + \beta \cdot \theta_i(k) . \tag{7}$$

where $\alpha > 0, \beta > 0$.

To satisfy the first requirement, γ should be selected between 0 and 1 so that the credibility value has a finite steady-state value. The steady-state value C_s is

$$C_s = \frac{1}{1-\gamma}(\alpha \cdot D + \beta \cdot \theta) . \tag{8}$$

The mean and the variance of C_s are given by

$$E[C_s] = \frac{1}{1-\gamma} (\alpha \cdot E[D] + \beta \cdot E[\theta]) \ . \tag{9}$$

$$\mathrm{var}[C_s] = \frac{1}{(1-\gamma)^2} (\alpha^2 \cdot \mathrm{var}[D] + \beta^2 \cdot \mathrm{var}[\theta]) \ . \tag{10}$$

where $E[D]$ and $\mathrm{var}[D]$ are the expectation and the variance of $D_i(k)$, respectively. $E[\theta]$ and $\mathrm{var}[\theta]$ are the expectation and the variance of $\theta_i(k)$, respectively.

As mentioned above, γ should be selected between 0 and 1. If γ is close to 0, the credibility will be sensitive to noise. If γ is close to 1, the credibility will show a slow response. α should satisfy $\alpha > \beta$ so that much weight would be imposed on $D_i(k)$, as $\theta_i(k)$ would not make a critical contribution to making $C(k)$ of the true road distinctive because the shapes of most roads are similar.

The threshold value C_T can be decided by examining the probability distribution of C_s or through computer simulations. If the probability distribution is known, we can decide C_T with a desired probabilistic accuracy. However, it will be conservative as several assumptions are required to calculate the probability distribution function of C_s. It is more practical and efficient to use computer simulations. By evaluating the performance of different threshold values in simulations, an appropriate threshold value can be decided.

The credibility of two paralleled road are simulated, shown in Figure 2, one road is the walking road for the robot, the other road is the paralleled road which is 20m in distance, the error of position estimate is 10m, taking $\alpha = 2$, $\beta = 1$, $\gamma = 0.5$. The credibility for the right walking road is 0.77, whereas the credibility for another road is 0.32. The threshold value of credibility C_T is easily determined by the simulating results. Map matching can be implemented based upon the above calculations. First we initialize credibility C_i ($i = 1,2,...,N$), N is the candidate road number which is expected to match at present. The credibility C_i is calculated for every candidate road after the position has been estimated. If the maximum is bigger than the credibility threshold value C_T, it means the right matching road is found, the position estimate point is projected on this matching road. Otherwise the present point is not matched; the calculation for the following point is implemented. After the right matching road is found, the unmatched location point should be matched in a remedial way. The credibility calculation to every position estimate point on the matching road is implemented. If it no longer meets the condition that the credibility is bigger than the threshold value, the present position estimate point may be transferred to another road, the credibility of each new road which may be matched will be calculated.

Figure 3 indicates the simulating result of map matching credibility when the robot passes the road cross. The position estimate error is 10m, and the moving speed of the robot is 1m/s. The experimental result displays that the exact and stable matching result can be obtained by utilizing the map matching method of the credibility.

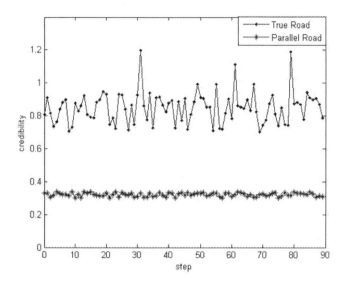

Fig. 2. Simulation result of true road and parallel road

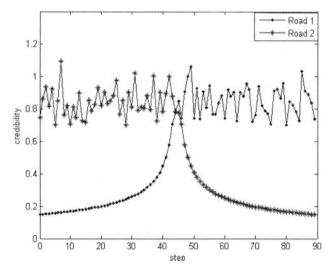

Fig. 3. Simulation result when the robot moves through a junction

5 Experiments

We have conducted a great deal of experiments on campus. The experiment area has several cross roads, teaching buildings, trees and grassland. The GPS signal can be well received in this area. The width of each road is about 5-10 m or so. The moving speed of the robot is 1m/s. After measuring position of the robot when it is moving, we can find deviation between ground truth and estimated position is no greater than 5m. The track which has been matched with the map is illustrated in Figure 4. The robot's track displayed in the electronic is consistent with the real track of the robot. Because the location data is transmitted via GPRS, limit of transmission velocity determines that the robot can not return every longitude and latitude received from the GPS receiver. We set sampling period as 2s. In every sampling period, the mobile robot returns its position to the GIS serve once, so the robot's GPS track is discrete points set. We can see the longitude and latitude in status bar. Because GPRS network has a little data delay sometimes, arrangement of position sampling points is not symmetrical. From Figure 4, we can see that the robot's position is adjusted repeatedly when the robot turns around the corner. This indicates that the credibility values of two paths are very near. As the robot gradually turns, the system locates the robot on another path. Experiments show that the deviation between the track from the electronic map and the real track of the robot is no more than 5m, which is caused by the GPS' error and imprecision of the electronic map.

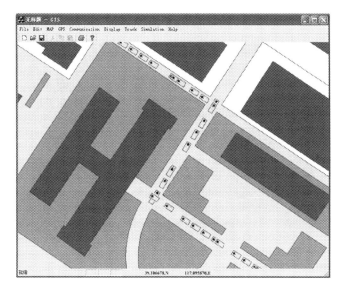

Fig. 4. The mobile robot's track after map matching

We can use GPRS module to transmit all kinds of controlling instructions to the robot, and the robot will implement these orders immediately. For example, we can use joystick to control moving direction of the robot. When the "stop" instruction is transmitted, the robot will stop moving forward until it receives the "start" instruction. When the "taking photo" instruction is transmitted, the robot automatically drives its camera to take photos on the scene. Considering the safety factor, these telecommands should not be sent when the mobile robot beyond our ken.

6 Conclusions

Location method of the mobile robot in this paper has fully presented GPRS network's advantages, such as high speed, easy operation, good reliability and etc. Moreover, map matching technology brings better position precision than that of single GPS receiver. Experiments prove this location platform is feasible.

Meanwhile, this system also can be further improved, for example, a rapid updating system of the GIS database, a new method of searching the shortest route, SLAM (simultaneous localization and mapping), and so on. In addition, the system can be utilized in vehicle monitoring and anti-theft system if it is improved slightly. It has a great market potential and developing prospect.

References

1. Zhang, Y., Bartone, C.: A general concept and algorithm of projected DGPS for high-accuracy DGPS-based systems Navigation. Journal of the Institute of Navigation 51(4) (2004) 293-300
2. Yang, Z., Yu, D., Sun, J., Zhang, B.: Study on the data fusion and integration technology for GPS/DR integrated navigation in urban traffic flow guidance system. Proc. 8th Int. Conf. on Applications of Advanced Technologies in Transportation Engineering (2004) 401-405
3. Sharaf, R., Tarbouchi, M., El-Shafie, A.: Real-time implementation of INS/GPS data fusion utilizing adaptive neuro-fuzzy inference system. Proc. Institute of Navigation 2005 National Technical Meeting (2005) 235-242
4. Jwo, D.J., Chang, C.S., Lin, C.H.: Neural network aided adaptive kalman filtering for GPS applications. IEEE International Conference on Systems, Man and Cybernetics 4(2004) 3686-3691
5. AlBayari, O., Sadoun, B.: New centralized automatic vehicle location communications software system under GIS environment: Research articles. International Journal of Communication Systems 18(9)(2005)
6. Uusisalo, J., Raneda, R.A., Vilenius, A., Huhtala, J.M., Kalevi, J.: Wireless starting system and emergency stop for teleoperated hydraulic mobile machine. Proceedings of IMECE04. Vol. 11. Anaheim, California, USA (2004) 165-173
7. Kim, S., Kim, J.H.: Adaptive fuzzy-network-based C-measure map-matching algorithm for car navigation system. IEEE Transactions on Industrial Electronics 48(6)(2001)432-441

A Unified Bill of Material Based on STEP/XML

Shifan Zhu, Dongmei Cheng, Kai Xue, and Xiaohua Zhang

College of Mechanical and Electrical Engineering,
Harbin Engineering University, P.R. China
zhushifan@hrbeu.edu.cn

Abstract. Bill of Material (BOM) is of a great importance in the dynamic allied enterprises during the product life cycle. A unified BOM method was proposed in the paper in order to bridge the gap between the different forms of BOM. After analyzing the information flow from engineering BOM to manufacturing BOM, the system framework was established based on STEP and XML standards which can secure the product data's uniformity in a collaboration environment; and the implementing method and platform are also introduced. A case study has been conducted and shown that it is reasonable and feasible to tackle the multi-view issue of BOM and provide the integrity, conformability and instantaneity of product data.

1 Introduction

With the rapid development of science and technology, especially the information technology, the market has become international and has been more and more knowledge-based. In the mean time, customer's needs have lend itself to a greater diversity, therefore the mass customization, which is the new frontier in business competition and the new paradigm of design and manufacturing, is inevitable [1].

In order to respond the change of the market quickly, to shorten the lead-time, and to provide better services, more and more enterprises are adopting advanced design and manufacturing technologies, such as web-enabled collaborative environment [2].

However, the works to be done, such as information integration, have to be based on the present systems, not from scratch. The key characteristics are the integration of geographically distributed and heterogeneous systems. A variety of techniques go a long way towards solving these problems. Bill of material (BOM) is one of them, and is of a great importance in the computer integrated manufacture systems (CIMS).

Before an item can be assembled or manufactured, any good manufacturing system needs to know what items are used in the manufacturing process and what quantities are required. What is needed is a complete list of all the parts that make up the whole product or the materials needed. Such a list is so called a BOM. It provides a comprehensive set of features in three important manufacturing categories: bill of materials, production routings and product costing. Hence, it will help to define, manage, and analyze the products an enterprise produces [3].

As the basis of production planning and scheduling, BOM data are widely used in product data management system, computer aided process planning and enterprise

W. Shen et al. (Eds.): CSCWD 2006, LNCS 4402, pp. 267–276, 2007.
© Springer-Verlag Berlin Heidelberg 2007

resource planning (ERP). Realizing the need of manufacturing information sharing, the integration of these heterogeneous and geographically distributed systems is of necessity.

2 Literature Review of BOM

BOM is not a new concept and there is a rich R&D literature. In 1988, Garwood, D. had pointed the importance of BOM application as 'The bill of material is the Achilles heel of making our factories more competitive' [4]. Many research interests had been focused on BOM in the ERP system, material requirement planning system (MRP) and manufacturing resource planning system (MRP II) all the time. According to Erevelles et al., they addressed the integration of PRP-based manufacturing system software with supervisory control software [5]. A BOM, oriented class-based storage assignment method for automated storage and retrieval system, was feasible to be integrated into a CIM system [6].

On a large heterogeneous platform for collaborative and integration over internet, the web collaborative environment should have the following characteristics: scalability, openness, resource accessibility and inter-operation, legacy code reusability and artificial intelligence [7]. Recently, ERP systems available in the market have made progress in shifting to Internet platform and had added some web-based application modules [8-10]. A set of web-based collaborative design, production planning and management tools were established on the Internet/Intranet, and a novel concept of dynamic BOM was developed [11]. By means of case-based reasoning algorithm, a new BOM was constructed in the design of product variation and customization [12]. However, this method, carried out on the company premises, was not fit for the web-enabled collaboration environment.

BOM now has many applications in virtual enterprises or dynamic allied enterprise [13]. If the nuts and bolts of BOM applications are investigated, it shows its pros and cons. The main problems are as follows.

BOM is more scattered, lack of comprehensive, total and systematic methods, thus its integrated framework has not been established.

The focuses of BOM at different stages of the product lifecycle are much different. For instance the production stage involve the Engineering BOM (EBOM), the Process BOM (PBOM) and the Manufacturing BOM (MBOM). The data exchanges among them need deeper researches.

There are all kinds of BOMs with multi-views in every department of enterprises. The overlapping and adjusting of BOM data in these sections will cause data inconsistency issues.

In this paper, the fundamentals of transferring of BOMs at the different product lifecycle stages are analyzed, and then the framework of Unified BOM (UBOM) was set up in dynamic alliance's enterprises environment. The case study conducted has shown that this method is reasonable, feasible and reliable.

3   The UBOM Architecture

3.1   Demand Analysis

BOM should have following characteristics in a networked manufacturing environment.

Flowability: In the production process, the BOM data need constantly adjusting; thus the information flows are ubiquitous. The BOM data flows are a dynamic process.

Instantaneity: If the BOM data in a single level change, the multi-level BOM data should be changed immediately. Instantaneity is more important in dynamic allied enterprises environment, preventing information from being held up.

Connectivity: The data in different sections are in different types and data format, but there are close relationships between them. It is necessary to integrate all kinds of manufacture information into a unified form and to manage it.

During product lifecycle, BOM is applied in nearly all departments, such as engineering, processing, manufacturing, planning, purchasing, sale, and financial department. Frequently, there is no unified design and management standard; in fact every department customizes various kinds of BOM according to the demand of its department. Except EBOM and PBOM, other various kinds of BOMs are set up manually. Accordingly, it is hard to maintain the conformability of the data between every BOM. This issue has become a bottleneck in the product development, manufacture and management. This will also increase the cost of manufacturing and lead-time.

In many small and medium sized enterprises, dynamic alliance has been being formed in the intensely competitive market. In order to guarantee the integrality, correctness and conformability of BOM information, the UBOM model is proposed in the following sections.

3.2   Modeling of the Whole Framework

Product configuration, in the networked manufacture environment, is to assemble series of interrelated parts according to the specific subassembly relations, and then assemble subassemblies and parts into a product [14]. For example, product structure tree is generated by means of the detailed part list of the product and the assembly chart of the product system. All data of the product lifecycle is to be extracted, classified and managed in our research project. The collaborative system framework is shown in Figure 1.

The data warehouse provides the basic supports to the product structure configuration. Based on the BOM as the organizing core, product entities and their relations are maintained and managed; and then the transformation from MBOM to EBOM is implemented and furthermore the data exchanges among the dynamic allied enterprises are carried out.

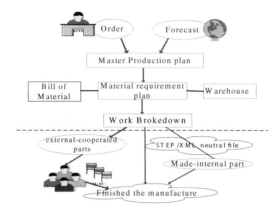

Fig. 1. The Web-enabled manufacture framework

EBOM, which reflects the product structure, is one form of BOM that is widely used in material requirement planning and manufacture resource planning. EBOM is also the foundation of other BOM form of a product. PBOM is used on the stage of processing of parts, which reflects the product assembly structure and sequences. MBOM includes all material items that are necessary in the manufacture of the product [15]. The relationships among EBOM, PBOM and MBOM are clearly illustrated in Figure 2.

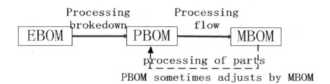

Fig. 2. Relationships among the BOMs

From the materials item point of view, EBOM has provided the basic materials needed in a product, and it is the base of process breakdown of PBOM. As a result, the material items in an EBOM will inevitably exist in the relevant PBOM and MBOM, and these material items are not changed with the BOM structure. On the other hand, from the changes of product structure point of view, the process structure derived from PBOM is broken down based on EBOM. The process structure, which comes from the breakdown of the manufacture structure in MBOM, is gotten through rebuilding the relations of the manufacture structure according to the process flows.

That is to say, from the aforementioned analyses, EBOM is the foundation of PBOM, and PBOM is the foundation of MBOM. The most important issue is that the relationships between different BOMs are dynamic and not static, because it is dynamic linkages between process breakdown, process flow and design of subassemblies and parts.

EBOM, PBOM and MBOM exist in the single source of product data, and the relevant information of the product must be managed based on BOM. The data in

PBOM should change not only with the change of EBOM, but also with the condition of manufacture in assembly design process.

The processes from EBOM to PBOM, then to MBOM, in short, are dynamic. The maintenance of the data conformability becomes particularly difficult, since the data exchange take place continuously. The conformability problem is tackled by adjustments, thus the revise of the original design will bring about some effects on the structures of PBOM and MBOM.

3.3   Implementation Method

Data Format and Modeling Language. STandard for the Exchange of Product model data (STEP) is a series of ISO standard, which describes how to express and exchange the product information; and the neutral mechanism was proposed to deal with multi-vendor or heterogeneous CAD/CAM systems. STEP is the key international product data technology that effectively enables interoperability, supply chain integration, web-based collaboration and life cycle management. It enables manufactures to achieve higher levels of quality and productivity while reducing the cost and time-to-market.

Today STEP use is growing through the world within many industrial sectors, including aerospace, automotive, shipbuilding, electronics, process plants and construction. It has been proved that STEP technology provides a successfully systematic approach for clients to share product data in heterogeneous systems.

However, in the early stages of development of STEP, Internet technology is still in its infant period, less attention had been paid to the data exchange and communication through Internet for the collaborative design and manufacture development. Thanks to the eXtensible Markup Language (XML) drawn up by W3C (World Wide Web Consortium), it is an ideal data format for supporting the deployment of product data on the Internet [16].

Giannini illustrated a product-modeling tool, named product manager, to support SMEs collaborating in design of a unique final product [17]. But, this product manager includes all and only those concepts pertaining to the description of the product. Deshayes developed a collaborative system for cutting data management based on STEP methodology [18]. Yeh and You implemented a pilot system for STEP-based product data exchange between and within enterprises [19]. The system incorporates engineering information in the design and manufacturing stage and guarantees the consistency of the product data exchange and sharing. Chao and Wang suggested a framework which consists of four parts: client databases, an index sever, a CAD data format translator, and a file sharing control model [20]. Zhang [21] proposed an Internet based STEP data exchange framework for virtual enterprises. The basic operations are: upload the data file from the client to the sever end via Internet; exchange the input data file into output data file at the sever end; and download the output file from the server end to the client end via the Internet. The system is composed of translator components, system WebPages, operation controller, and components index. The system WebPages are the interactive interfaces for users and/or clients.

The XML solution of STEP technology has many advantages, such as easier to read and check, to expand and interact. Chan et al. constructed a way of automated conversions from STEP into XML, and carried out the exchange of STEP data through XML-based mediator architecture [22].

In this research, XML is applied to express the networked manufacture information; and the rules of mapping of STEP and XML are established. The STEP and XML methodology will provide a successful systematic approach for clients to share product data in networked manufacturing environment.

Implementation Process. Product structure and BOM are of a great importance in organizing product data, and are such key data that they are the basic form of data transmission in different departments and different workflows in dynamic allied enterprises. BOM is the golden bridge between departments, such as engineering department and managerial department; in the meanwhile, it is the most important interface among CAD systems, and computer aided process planning, product data management and enterprise resource planning. Figure 3 shows the parts' classification and relations in the information management system.

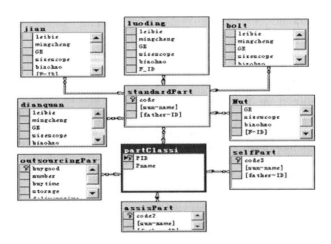

Fig. 3. Parts' classification and relations

The use of the standard parts can be accessed directly through the standard parts database in accordance with the customer's requirements, and a partner in the dynamic allied enterprises through a supplier selection process provides bought parts. The product structure and other product data are transformed through Internet by way of physical file with neutral format based on the STEP and XML standards, and then transferred into data format conformed with Application Protocol 238 of STEP. If the order and other demands change, the adjustments can be directly completed in the database, thus to timely maintain the conformability and effectiveness among the allied enterprises.

In the converting system from EBOM to MBOM, the product structure tree is established according to the EBOM information derived from Product Data Management System (PDMS). The terminal users can add middleware, modify the hierarchical relations of product tree and adjust the assembly sequences and assembly data, finally all these data can access into Enterprise Resource Planning System (ERPS), as shown in Figure 4.

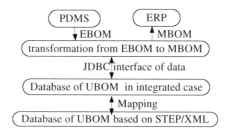

Fig. 4. UBOM model on STEP/XML

Java Sever Page (JSP) and Servlet technology, which provide a simple programming vehicle for displaying dynamic content on a Web page, are adopted in our system, and the operation system at client end is Window 2000. SQL Server 2000 is used at background, which feature the management of database multi-security and reliability.

J2EE (Java 2 Platform, Enterprise Edition), a platform for building Web-based enterprise applications, having been selected as the development and management tool of application programs at the user end, the system is marked by the object oriented, distributed and event-driven features. The interface was Java Data Base Connectivity (JDBC) between application program and network database management system, because JDBC lets Java applications access a database via the Structured Query Language (SQL), and Java interpreters (Java Virtual Machines) are available for all major client platforms, these allow a platform-independent database application to be written. The data drive of the system adopted ADO (Active Data Objects) database engine that is typically used for storing data in the client end. These make the system open and flexible scenarios [23].

4   A Case Study

The application of the prototype networked dynamic UBOM-based STEP/XML is illustrated using a simple production-planning example gleaned from a numerical control manufacturing company. The BOM structure of product is depicted in Figure 5. As it shows, these products share some components.

The UBOM has offered the unified management of the products data; the pars of the product are classified whatever styles belong, standard parts, bought-in parts or made-internal parts. By means of the method describing in the previous section, information can transmit in the form of AP238 to the numerical control lathe and realize the processing of the low-speed axle finally.

The structure and content of product BOM are dynamic in application. Therefore in order to support information flowing among the networked allied enterprises, the information management of enterprises must meet the following requirements: to keep the product data conformability in product lifecycle, to offer the necessary network safety measurements, and to keep the relative independence of enterprises in every alliance if need.

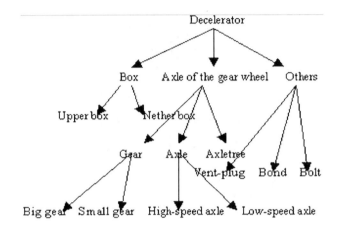

Fig. 5. BOM structure of the finished products involved in the example

According to the requirements mentioned above, the networked manufacture platform was set up by applying management techniques associated with BOM to organize the information in the allied enterprises. The information is all organized on the basis of the product structure tree.

The interface of the case study can be browsed in Microsoft Internet Explorer as shown in Figure 6. The case study shows that the proposed UBOM model can manage the whole product manufacturing data systematically and authorities with different level to guarantee the data security.

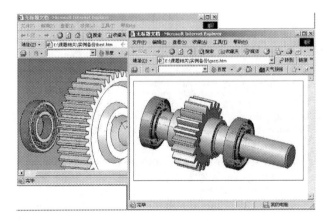

Fig. 6. An interface of the case study

5 Concluding Remarks

The UBOM model proposed is applicable in different departments in the dynamic allied enterprises, and in the meantime, it guarantees the integrity, conformability and instantaneity of product data.

The UBOM is based on STEP/XML standard in the implementation. STEP methodology tackles the data exchange issue of heterogeneous system, and XML provides a good way to deal with distributed system in web environment.

The case study had shown that the implementation methods were reliable and feasible for utilization on the platform selected, and it provided an excellent solution to dynamic allied enterprises.

With the increasing popularity of XML on the Internet, mapping STEP data into XML seems a logical way to make STEP data accessible through the Internet. Future work will focus on developing the mapping tools to combine the rich semantics of STEP and the wide adopted XML technology.

Acknowledgments. The authors are grateful for the support received from the Research Foundation of Harbin Engineering University, P.R. China (Grant No. HEUF04095).

References

1. Pine, J.: Mass Customization. China People's University Press, Beijing (2000) 95-108
2. Su, D.: Web-enabled Collaborative Design and manufacture. Nottingham Trent University, Nottingham, UK (2005)
3. Tatsiopoulos, I.P.: On the unification bills of materials and routings. Computers in Industry 31(1996) 293-304
4. Garwood, D.: Bill of Materials: Structured for Excellence. Dogwood Publishing Co. Marietta, GA (1988) 45
5. Erevelles, W. and Aithal, S.: Development of an interface between a supervisory shop controller and MRP system in a CIM environment. Journal of Materials Processing Technology 61(1996) 120-123
6. Hsieh, S. and Tsai, K.: A BOM Oriented Class-based Storage Assignment Method in Automated Storage/Retrieval System. International Journal of Advanced Manufacturing Technology 17(2001) 683-691
7. Li, J., Su, D., Henshall, J.L. and Xiong, Y.: Development of a Web-enabled Environment for Collaborative Design and Manufacturing. Proc. 8th International Conference on Computer Supported Cooperative Work in Design. Xiamen, China (2004) 540-545
8. Yen, D., Chou, D., and Chang, J.: A synergic analysis for web-based enterprise resource planning system. Computer Standards and Interfaces 24(4) (2002) 337-346
9. Gupta, A.: Enterprise resource planning: The emerging organizational value systems. Industrial Management and Data Systems 100(2000) 114-118
10. Holland, C. and Light, B.: A critical success factor model ERP implementation. IEEE Software 16(3) (1999) 30-36
11. Xiong, M., Tor, S., Khoo, L., Chen, C.: A Web-enhanced dynamic BOM-based available-to-promise system. International Journal of Production Economics 84 (2003) 133-147

12. Tseng, H., Chang, C., and Chang, S.: Applying case-based reasoning for product configuration in mass customization environment. Expert Systems with Applications 29 (2005) 913-925

13. Xiong, M., Tor, S., and Khoo, L.: A Web-enhanced dynamic BOM-based available-to-promise system. International Journal of Production Economics 84 (2003) 133-147

14. Ji, G., Gong, D., and Freddie, T.: Analysis and implementation of the BOM of a tree-type structure in MRPII. Journal of Materials Processing Technology 139 (2003) 535-538

15. Wang, Y.: Research of unified BOM model based on STEP and information integration of PDM/ERP. Kun Ming Technology University, China (2004)

16. Fan, Y. and Li, J.: Enterprise integration and Technology of integrated platform. China Machine Press, China (2004) 105-111

17. Giannini, F., Monti, M., Biondi, D., Bonfatti, F. and Monari, P.D.: A modeling tool for the management of product data in a co-design environment. Computer-Aided Design 34(14) (2002) 1063-1073

18. Deshayes, L.: Collaborative System for Cutting Data Management Based on STEP Standard. Concurrent Engineering: Research and Applications 11(1) (2003) 27-36

19. Yeh, S. and You, C.: Implementation of STEP-based product data exchange and sharing, Concurrent Engineering: Research and Applications 8(1) (2000) 32-41

20. Chao, P., Wang, Y.: A data exchange framework for net worked CAD/CAM. Computer in Industry 44(2001) 131-140

21. Zhang, Y., Zhang, C., and Wang, H.P.: An Internet based STEP data exchange framework for virtual enterprise. Computer in Industry 41(1) (2000) 51-63

22. Stephen, C.F.: Exchange of STEP data through XML-based mediators. Concurrent Engineering: Research and Applications 11(1) (2003) 55-64

23. Chung, Y. and Fischer, G.W.: A conceptual structure and issues for an object-oriented bill of materials data model. Computers and Industrial Engineering 26(1994) 321-339

In-Process Monitoring of Dimensional Errors in Turning Slender Bar Using Artificial Neural Networks

Rongdi Han, Bodi Cui, and Jianliang Guo

Department of Mechanical Engineering and Automation, Harbin Institute of Technology
Harbin 150001, Heilongjiang Province, P.R. China
cbd08007@yahoo.com.cn

Abstract. Dimensional error is one of the most important product quality characteristics during slender bar turning operations. In this study, artificial neural network was employed to investigate the dimensional errors during slender bar turning process. A systematic method based on neural network modeling technique and statistical tool was designed to select the input parameters of the monitoring model. The average effect of each candidate machining factor and sensed information on the modeling performance was determined. Then, the monitoring system was developed to perform the in-process prediction of dimensional errors. Experimental results showed that the proposed system had the ability to monitor efficiently dimensional errors within the range that it had been trained.

1 Introduction

Intense international competition requires higher productivity and quality of products in modern manufacturing. For improving product quality, estimation system of machined parts quality was employed and integrated into turning processes. Dimensional deviation, especially for slender bar turning, is one of the most specified customer requirements. Various approaches have been proposed to estimate dimensional errors [1-4].

In the past decade, due to the powerful non-linear mapping ability, a large number of researchers reported application of artificial neural network in predicting the machined parts quality [5-8]. Azouzi et al. proposed a neural network model based sensor fusion to evaluate surface roughness and dimensional deviation during turning [9]. The results showed that neural network models were more accurate than regression analysis models that were developed for comparison purposes. Suneel et al. developed a neural network predictive model of dimensional and form accuracy to correct the CNC code [10]. Significant improvement in dimensional accuracy of parts was seen in their study. Li developed a radial basis function neural network model to predict cutting-force-induced errors during turning operations based on the estimated cutting forces [11].

However, fewer attentions were paid on the slender part machining. The approaches about the turning of non-slender bar are not well suited for the case of slender bar. During slender bar turning, the deflection of part is the main source of dimensional

W. Shen et al. (Eds.): CSCWD 2006, LNCS 4402, pp. 277–286, 2007.
© Springer-Verlag Berlin Heidelberg 2007

errors, while the deflections of part holder and tool holder have important contribution to dimensional errors in the non-slender bar turning. Risbood et al. developed a neural network model to predict dimensional deviation by measuring cutting forces and vibrations during the slender bar turning [12]. Nevertheless, the error in prediction was quite higher and the range of part dimension was not wide.

In the present work, neural network model was proposed to monitor the dimensional errors in slender bar turning process. The input parameter selection procedure, combining the neural network modeling technique and statistical tool, was design and implemented to determine the optimal input parameter combination of the in-process predicting model. The cutting force components were measured as real-time sensed information. For including the effect of part stiffness on dimensional errors, the diameter and the ratio of length to diameter of the machined parts were considered as independent input parameters of the predictive model. The model was trained within a wide range of cutting parameters and part dimensions. Experiments were conducted to assess the performance of the developed model.

2 Experiment Design

The training data and testing data were collected from experiments. For minimizing the number of experiments, orthogonal array was used here for the design of experiments. Table 1 listed the values of the five-factor three-level design. The ranges of machining condition were selected from the recommendations given by tool manufacturers and machining data handbook.

Table 1. Experimental factors and levels for training data

Parameters	Symbol	Unit	Values of levels		
Cutting speed	v	m/min	30	45	60
Feed	f	mm/rev	0.1	0.15	0.2
Depth of cut	a_p	mm	0.1	0.2	0.3
Diameter	D	mm	20	25	30
Slenderness ratio	L/D		10	20	30

Machining experiments were conducted on CA6140 lathe. C45 steel workpiece was turned with P10 inserts. The material characteristics of the workpiece used in this work were listed in Table 2. The cutting tools employed had the following geometrical parameters: tool cutting edge angle, $\kappa_r = 75°$; tool orthogonal rake angle, $\gamma_0 = 18°$; tool orthogonal clearance angle, $\alpha_0 = 3°$ and tool cutting edge inclination angle, $\lambda_\sigma = 5°$. Coolant was present in all the experiments.

During machining experiments, three components of the cutting forces were measured using a piezoelectric tri-axial dynamometer (KISTLER 9257B). Signals from the dynamometer were conditioned through charge amplifiers with inbuilt low-pass filters of 650 Hz cut-off frequency. Using a 16-channel A/D converter

Table 2. Material characteristics of the workpiece

Young's Modulus of elasticity	$E=2.13\times10^5$MPa
Tensile strength	$\sigma=598$MPa
Density	$\rho=7.85\times10^3$Kg/m^3

(PCI 8310), the samples of cutting force were collected into personal computer. Schematic diagram of the experimental set-up was shown in Figure 1. The dimensional errors of the machined parts were measured by micrometer. For a chosen axial location, three readings were recorded by orienting the instrument at intervals of about 120 degrees. The average of three readings was used as dimensional error of the measured location.

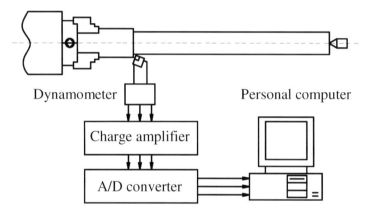

Fig. 1. Schematic diagram of the experimental set-up

3 Input Parameter Selection for Monitoring Networks

3.1 Proposed Method for Input Parameters Selection

The basic idea behind the proposed procedure is to select the input parameters for neural network model by minimizing the modeling error on dimensional errors. For this aim, neural networks were designed with a different set of input parameters selected based on orthogonal array. Each candidate machining factor was considered as one parameter with two levels: Present or Not among the set of input parameters. Thus, the effect of every factor on the modeling performance can be computed as

$$\text{Effect of a factor} = (\text{Average performance at level Present}) - (\text{Average performance at level Not}). \tag{1}$$

For a given factor, if the value of the factor's effect is positive, then the presence of this factor in input parameter set can improve the performance of the real-time predictive model. And if the value is negative, then the presence of this factor can deteriorate the modeling performance. Finally, only the factor that can improve the predicting performance is selected as the input parameter of the predictive model.

3.2 Application of the Proposed Method

In order to include the effect of part stiffness on dimensional errors, the diameter and the ratio of length to diameter of the machined parts were considered as independent input parameters of the developed models in this study. The other factors considered were the feed rate, the cutting speed, the cutting depth, the three cutting force components and the axial cutting distance. The cutting distance was expressed by the ratio of the axial cutting distance from headstock (z) to the length of the machined part (L) here.

Models 1 through 16 were designed based on nine-factor two-level design to determine the input parameters. As shown in Table 3, the "1" and "0" indicate, respectively, whether the factor is input to the network model or not.

Table 3. The designed models and their performance for input parameters selection

No.	Input parameters									Network Performance	
	v	f	a_p	D	$\dfrac{L}{D}$	F_t	F_r	F_a	z/L	Correlation	Epochs
1	1	1	1	1	1	1	1	1	1	0.6551	71
2	1	1	1	1	1	0	0	0	1	0.7993	45
3	1	0	1	0	1	0	1	1	0	0.5433	88
4	1	0	1	0	1	1	0	0	0	0.4311	118
5	1	0	0	1	0	0	1	0	1	0.3802	199
6	1	0	0	1	0	1	0	1	1	0.3800	136
7	1	1	0	0	0	1	1	0	0	0.3538	1282
8	1	1	0	0	0	0	0	1	0	0.3403	2034
9	0	0	0	1	1	0	0	0	0	0.7045	266
10	0	0	0	1	1	1	1	1	0	0.7945	271
11	0	1	0	0	1	1	0	0	1	0.8753	184
12	0	1	0	0	1	0	1	1	1	0.9304	110
13	0	1	1	1	0	1	0	1	0	0.3374	788
14	0	1	1	1	0	0	1	0	0	0.3507	1063
15	0	0	1	0	0	0	0	1	1	0.4994	2438
16	0	0	1	0	0	1	1	0	1	0.4764	1139
17	0	0	0	0	1	0	1	1	1	0.7206	106
18	0	1	0	0	1	0	1	0	1	0.8224	142

In order to reduce the effect of the network architecture on parameters selection, five different networks were used to perform the parameter selection. The first three networks had one hidden layer with 3, 5 and 7 neurons in hidden layer respectively. The other two networks had two hidden layers with 5 and 10 neurons in each hidden layer respectively. Further, the performance of each network was examined based on the correlation coefficient between the network predictions and the experimental values using testing dataset. For a given set of input parameters, the maximum of correlation coefficients produced by these five networks was used to represent the performance of the corresponding input parameter set.

For this study, standard multilayer feedforward neural network was designed with MATLAB. The networks were trained with Levenberg-Marquardt algorithm. This training algorithm was chosen due to its high accuracy in similar function approximation. At the same time, this algorithm appears to be the fastest method for training moderate-sized feedforward neural networks (up to several hundred weights) [13]. In order to improve the generalization of neural network, Bayesian regularization was used in combination with Levenberg-Marquardt algorithm [14]. For all networks tangent sigmoid transfer function and linear transfer function were used in the hidden and output layer, respectively.

During training process of a neural network, the higher valued input variable may tend to suppress the influence of smaller ones. To overcome this problem, the input and output dataset were normalized within the range of ±1. The normalized value (x_i) for each raw input/output dataset (d_i) was calculated as

$$x_i = \frac{2(d_i - d_{min})}{d_{max} - d_{min}} - 1 \; , \tag{2}$$

where d_{max} and d_{min} are the maximum and minimum values of the raw data.

The performance of each set of input parameters was given in Table 3. The best result can be observed with the model 12, and the training of this neural network can be achieved quickly. The average effect of each factor was calculated and listed in Table 4. The result showed that the factors that could reduce the prediction errors were the feed rate, the slenderness, the radial cutting force component, the axial cutting force component and the cutting distance. It could be seen that this result was consistent with model 12 in Table 3. Hence, these five parameters provided the best combination to predict dimensional errors during slender bar turning process.

Table 4. Average effect of each factor on the predicting system performance

v	f	a_p	D	L/D	F_t	F_r	F_a	z/L
-0.1357	0.0541	-0.0833	-0.0060	0.3269	-0.0298	0.0146	0.0136	0.1426

For slender bar turning, the deflection of the machined part under cutting force is the main source of dimensional error. Further, the deflection, which is not uniform along the tool path, makes the dimensional error change along the tool path. Therefore, it is reasonable that the slenderness and the cutting distance carry the important information about the state of the slender bar turning operation. With regard to the sensed information, it is obvious that the radial cutting force component plays a dominant role in determining dimensional errors. At the same time, the axial cutting force component is recognized to have a significant effect on dimensional errors in turning, and the effect of the tangential component is slight [15]. To check the effect of the feed rate and the axial cutting force component, model 17and 18 were trained with the feed rate and the axial cutting force component omitted respectively. As it can be seen in Table 3, the predicting performance became poor.

4   Artificial Neural Networks Modeling of Dimensional Errors

4.1   Training of Neural Networks

The input parameters of the predicting network had been determined by the aforementioned procedure. However, the accuracy of the model 12 in Table 3 was not satisfying. The correlation coefficient was only 0.9304, and the maximal prediction error was 20.5 micron. Thus, another training dataset, consisting of 20 training data obtained randomly, was used to improve the modeling accuracy.

The network architecture or features, such as number of layers and neurons, are very important factors that determine the functionality and generalization capability of the trained network. Hence, different networks with one or two hidden layers and different number of neurons in hidden layers were considered to determine the optimal network architecture. In general, the networks had five neurons in input layer, corresponding to each of the five cutting factors and one neuron in output layer, corresponding to the dimensional errors.

4.2   Testing of Neural Networks

The considered networks were examined based on the correlation coefficient between the network predictions and the experimental values using testing dataset, and the performance was listed in Table 5.

Table 5. Performance of different networks examined by testing dataset

No.	Networks architecture	Performance of the trained networks		
		Correlation coefficient	Maximal prediction error (micron)	Epochs
1	5×3×1	0.9685	9.1305	117
2	5×4×1	0.9783	6.4126	292
3	5×5×1	0.9489	-8.2504	202
4	5×6×1	0.9686	10.9296	124
5	5×7×1	0.9492	-7.7746	183
6	5×10×1	0.9681	7.0077	312
7	5×15×1	0.9621	-6.2383	254
8	5×5×5×1	0.9702	-7.4470	137
9	5×10×10×1	0.9711	6.9879	136
10	5×15×15×1	0.9692	-7.3528	118

Results showed that the network 2 gave the best performance for predicting dimensional errors. The correlation coefficient was heightened to 0.9783, and the learning speed was quick. The comparison between experimental results and network predictions showed that the maximum of the prediction errors was 6.41 micron, and 90% of the testing data had the prediction errors ranging between ±5 micron. Also, the increase in the number of neurons in hidden layer and the hidden layer had no improvement on the performance of the networks. Thus, the network with one hidden layer and four neurons in hidden layer was chosen as the optimum network to predict the dimensional errors. The topology of the network was described in Figure 2.

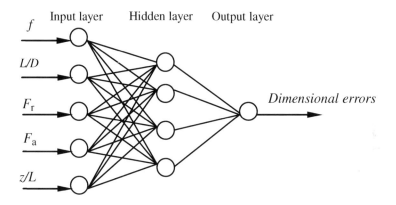

Fig. 2. Neural network used in real-time predicting dimensional errors

5 System Implementation and Experimental Results

Experiments were carried out to test the performance of the in-process monitoring system. In order to reduce the computation time, the model developed by MATLAB was rewritten by C++ programs. The driver file of the A/D converter was called by the present program to obtain the real-time samples of cutting force components. The neural network model used the samples to perform the on-line prediction of dimensional errors during the slender bar turning process.

The experiments were performed under two different cutting conditions, which were not used in training the neural networks, to verify the accuracy and generalization of the present models. The cutting conditions were shown as

    i. $v=35$m/s, $f=0.12$mm/r, $a_p=0.15$mm, $D=22$mm, $L/D=27$;
    ii. $v=56$m/s, $f=0.18$mm/r, $a_p=0.25$mm, $D=26$mm, $L/D=18$.

In order to validate the selection procedure further, the developed models in Table 3 were used to predict the dimensional error in turning process. The model 2 and 9 were ignored because the sensed information was not employed in these two models. The maximal prediction errors were shown in Table 6. It was still the model 12 that produced the best results.

Table 6. The maximal prediction error of the designed model for in-process monitoring

Model	Machining parameters	
	Cutting condition i	Cutting condition ii
1	25.5199	-19.2516
3	-23.8526	-21.7674
4	-32.6250	-26.5159
5	-26.3169	-26.1475
6	-27.2109	25.7650
7	-21.3111	28.1953
8	-28.6853	31.7798
10	-19.2284	-24.7125
11	-19.6664	15.6232
12	17.9484	-13.4151
13	-23.0133	28.1767
14	-22.7519	27.8138
15	-20.9132	20.2976
16	-21.4776	21.4999
17	20.1420	18.2260
18	21.2974	14.9421

The final neural network model retrained in section 4 was adopted to monitor the dimensional errors. The predicted and measured dimensional errors were compared in Figure 3(a) and Figure 3(b). It could be seen from the figures that the neural network model provided satisfying accuracy in predicting dimensional errors. The prediction error was within 8 micron.

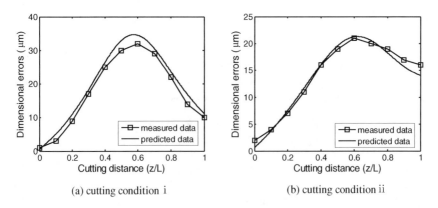

(a) cutting condition i   (b) cutting condition ii

Fig. 3. Comparisons between predicted and measured dimensional errors during in-process monitoring process

6 Conclusions

The objective of this study was to develop an in-process neural network model in monitoring dimensional errors during slender bar turning operations. The input parameter selection method, combining the neural network modeling technique and statistical tool were designed and implemented to determine the optimal input parameter of the in-process predicting model. The average effect of each candidate machining factor and sensed information on the modeling performance was determined by the proposed method. The results show that the feed rate, the slenderness, the radial cutting force component, the axial cutting force component and the cutting distance provide the best combination to predict dimensional errors during slender bar turning process.

Experiments were carried out to support the developed in-process monitoring system. The results show that the developed system has the ability to predict accurately dimensional errors within the range that it has been trained. The error in prediction is within 8 micron.

References

1. Yang, S., Yuan, J. and Ni, J.: Real-time cutting force induced error compensation on a turning center. International Journal of Machine Tools and Manufacture 37(11) (1997) 1597-1610
2. Mayer, J.R.R., Phan, A.-V., Cloutier, G.: Prediction of diameter errors in bar turning: a computationally effective model. Applied Mathematical Modeling 24 (2000) 943-956
3. Gi-Bum J., Dong H.K., Dong Y.J.: Real time monitoring and diagnosis system development in turning through measuring a roundness error based on three-point method. International Journal of Machine Tools and Manufacture 45(2005) 1494-1503
4. Shunmugam, M.S.: On assessment of geometric errors. International Journal of Production Research 24 (2) (1986) 413-425
5. Zhang, H.C., Huang, S.H.: Artificial neural networks in manufacturing-a state of the art survey. International Journal of Production Research 33 (3) (1995) 705-728
6. Suneel, T.S., Pande, S.S. and Date, P.P.: A technical note on integrated product quality model using artificial neural networks. Journal of Materials Processing Technology 121(2002) 77-86
7. Özel, T. and Karpat, Y.: Predictive modeling of surface roughness and tool wear in hard turning using regression and neural networks. International Journal of Machine Tools and Manufacture 45(2005) 467-479
8. Ezugwu, E.O., Fadare, D.A., Bonney, J.: Modeling the correlation between cutting and process parameters in high-speed machining of Inconel 718 alloy using an artificial neural network. International Journal of Machine Tools and Manufacture 45 (2005) 1375-1385
9. Azouzi, R., Guillot, M.: On-line prediction of surface finish and dimensional deviation in turning using neural network based sensor fusion. International Journal of Machine Tools and Manufacture 37(9) (1997)1201-1217
10. Suneel, T.S. and Pande, S.S.: Intelligent tool path correction for improving profile accuracy in CNC turning. International Journal of Production Research 38(14) (2000) 3181-3202

11. Li, X.: Real-time prediction of workpiece errors for a CNC turning centre, Part 4. Cutting-force-induced errors. International Journal of Advanced Manufacturing Technology 17(2001) 665-669
12. Risbood, K.A., Dixit, U.S., Sahasrabudhe, A.D.: Prediction of surface roughness and dimensional deviation by measuring cutting forces and vibrations in turning process. Journal of Materials Processing Technology 132(2003) 203-214
13. Demuth, H., Beale, M.: Neural Network Toolbox User's Guide. Version 4. The Mathworks Inc. (2000)
14. Foresee, F.D. and Hagan, M.T.: Gauss-Newton approximation to Bayesian regularization. Proceedings of the 1997 International Joint Conference on Neural Networks (1997) 1930-1935
15. Mayer, J.R.R., Phan, A.V. and Cloutier, G.: Prediction of diameter errors in bar turning: a computationally effective model. Applied Mathematical Modeling 24 (2000) 943-956

Approach to Extended CSCW Design Based on Embedded Korean Sign Language Recognizer

Jung-Hyun Kim and Kwang-Seok Hong

School of Information and Communication Engineering, Sungkyunkwan University, 300,
Chunchun-dong, Jangan-gu, Suwon, KyungKi-do, 440-746, Korea
kjh0328@skku.edu, kshong@skku.ac.kr

Abstract. In this paper, we suggest and describe an approach to the design of extended CSCW architecture, based on the embedded KSL (Korean Sign Language) recognizer. Our approach is important for deaf person's decision-making and Human-Computer Interaction (HCI) in the CSCW domain. Accordingly, we implement the WPS (Wearable Personal Station)-based embedded KSL (Korean Sign Language) recognizer, that can support clear communication between the hearing-impaired and hearing persons, and then describe and estimate the applicability with 3 items (interaction, visualization and coordination), as basic functional criteria and requirements for a CSCW system. The suggested CSCW architecture provides a wider range of personalized and differentiated information more effectively in brainstorming sessions, and the user need not be constrained by the limitations of a particular interaction mode at any given moment because of the WPS can guarantee the mobility of the embedded KSL recognizer.

1 Introduction

CSCW (Computer Supported Cooperative Work) is a generic term, which integrates the understanding of the way people work in groups, with the enabling technologies of computer networking, associated hardware, software, services and other techniques. In addition, it's used mainly in academic research circles to encapsulate the use of computers (and telecommunications) by groups of people working together. So, CSCW is the human activity of working together using technology, to help group processes - information exchange, information sharing, discussion, joint authorship of texts, decision making, and so on. CSCW researchers study how people work in groups and how the computer can best be applied to support their work [1-2]. If we ook at CSCW systems from the viewpoint of applications, we notice that certain tasks are present in a generic method such as brainstorming, to generate ideas, structure these ideas, and evaluate them in many application scenarios [3]. The concept of co-operation is often used in relation to the concepts of coordination and communication. First, the splitting of a cooperative task into independent subtasks naturally leads to the need for coordination. Then, communication can be defined as a process by which information is exchanged between individuals through a recognition system of symbols, signs, or behaviors. In other words, traditional CSCW systems for cooperation

W. Shen et al. (Eds.): CSCWD 2006, LNCS 4402, pp. 287–296, 2007.
© Springer-Verlag Berlin Heidelberg 2007

and HCI in distributed computing environments are used in various domains such as videoconference, messaging (instant messaging, e-mail) and collaborative software, including groupware and dialog systems. There has been much research on dialog applications and tools for the CSCW system, because they can be used in communication, co-design, and education. Nevertheless, as traditional and existing applications do not sufficiently consider human's physical restrictions and dialog components between hearing-impaired and hearing persons, they are not flexible and effective as a system architecture and user interface for CSCW. Above all, the hearing-impaired can not only present their intention and idea freely, but also find it impossible in understanding and learning spoken language in information interchange or communication domains for CSCW. Sign language used by the hearing-impaired, is very difficult and time consuming to represent and translate into language understandable by hearing persons. Accordingly, we implement the WPS (Wearable Personal Station)-based embedded KSL (Korean Sign Language) recognizer that can support clear communication between hearing-impaired and hearing persons in CSCW domains, and then suggest extended CSCW architecture using our application, which recognizes sentential KSL models and then translates recognition results into a synthetic speech and visual illustration in real-time. An extended CSCW architecture is very important and essential from the view-points of a deaf person's participation in decision-making and common society. It may provide a wider range of personalized and differentiated information more effectively. In addition, for communication and decision-making of moving the hearing-impaired as a conferee on CSCW, the user need not be constrained by the limitations of a particular interaction mode at any given moment, because the portable WPS can guarantee the mobility of the embedded KSL recognizer.

2   WPS-Based Embedded KSL Recognizer

2.1   WPS (Wearable Personal Station) for the Next Generation PC

The wearable computer is a small portable computer designed to be worn on the body during use. The wearable computer differs from PDAs, which are designed for handheld use, although the distinction can sometimes be blurry. In this paper, as a wearable platform for the next-generation PC, the i.MX21 test board was selected, which is a next-generation PC platform in the Rep. of Korea, for application to our system. The i.MX21 test board consists of a ARM926EJ-S (16KB I-Cache, 16KB D-Cache) CPU, and includes ARM Jazelle technology for Java acceleration and MPEG-4 and H.263 encode/decode acceleration. The i.MX21 provides flexibility for software implementation for other video encoders, such as packet-video, real-networks and windows media. Hardware code addresses the I/O bottleneck and helps reduce power consumption, enabling greater device mobility [4].

2.2   Regulation and Components of the KSL

The KSL is a complex visual-spatial language which uses manual communication instead of sound to convey meaning, by simultaneously combining hand shapes, orientation and movement of arms or body, and facial expressions to fluidly express a speaker's thoughts. This system is used by the deaf community in the Rep. of Korea [5]. Because the KSL is very complicated, and consists of considerable numerous gestures, and motions, it is impossible to recognize all dialog components used by the hearing-impaired. Therefore, we selected 25 basic KSL gestures connected with a travel information scenario, according to the "Korean Standard Sign Language Tutor (KSSLT)" [6]. The necessary 23 hand gestures for travel information are considered - KSL gestures are classified as hand's shapes, pitch and roll degree. Consequently, we constructed 44 sentential recognition models according to associability and presentation of hand gestures and basic KSL gestures.

2.3 KSL Input Module Using Wireless Haptic Devices

A particularly useful feature is that the user may use the technology easily and routinely by using ready-to-wear articles of clothing (e.g. headsets or data glove). In addition, from the viewpoint of CSCW, VR sensors could be simply plugged into a computer system, allowing the user uninhibited control and interaction with the local computer system [7]. A traditional study on sign language recognition usually used desktop PC-based wire haptic devices or vision technology (e.g. image capture or video processing system) for the acquisition of sign language and hand signals. However, these studies and systems not only contain general restrictions such as the conditionality on space, the complexity between transmission mediums and the limitation of motion, but also problems such as the uncertainty of measurement, necessity of complex computation algorithms and sensitivity to background colors and illumination conditions.

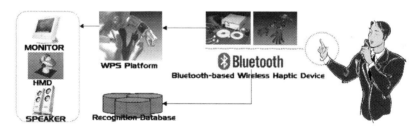

Fig. 1. The architecture and composition of the KSL input module

For this reason, as an improved KSL input module, the blue-tooth module is adopted for wire-less sensor networks. 5DT company's wireless data (sensor) gloves and fastrak® are some of the most popular input devices in the haptic application field. Wireless data gloves are basic gesture recognition equipments that can acquire and capture various haptic information (e.g. hand or finger's stooping degree, direction) using a fiber-optic flex sensor. Each flexure value has a decimal range of 0 to 255, with a low value indicating an inflexed finger, and a high value indicating a flexed finger. Also, fastrak® is an electromagnetic motion tracking system, a 3D digitizer and a quad receiver motion tracker. It provides dynamic, real-time measurements of six degrees of freedom; position (X, Y, and Z Cartesian coordinates) and orientation (azimuth, elevation, and roll) [8]. The architecture and composition of the KSL input module is shown in Figure 1.

2.4 KSL Training and Recognition Models

Statistical classification algorithms such as K-means clustering, QT (Quality Threshold) clustering, the fuzzy c-means clustering algorithm and the Self-Organizing Map (SOM), have been applied universally in traditional pattern recognition systems with unsupervised training, such as machine training, data mining, pattern recognition, image analysis and bioinformatics [9-11]. However, such classification algorithms have certain restrictions and problems such as the necessity of complicated mathematical computation, according to multidimensional features, the difficulty of applications in distributed processing systems, relativity of computation costs by pattern (data) size, and minimization of memory swapping and assignment. Accordingly, for a clustering method to achieve efficient feature extraction and construction of training/recognition models based on a distributed computing, we suggest and introduce an improved RDBMS (Relational Data-Base Management System) clustering module, to resolve such restrictions and problems.

1. Difference Between Preceding Average(preceding 3 and 1) and Current Row Value
2. Decide validity : Preceding Average - Current Value = 52-17 = 35

Average Between 3 Preceding and 1 Preceding from Current Row : 52

1. Difference between Preceding Average and Current Row Value > 5
2. 'X'(Invalidity Record) check

SerialNO	F1THUMB	F1INDEX	F1MIDDLE	F1RING	F1LITTLE	F1X-POSI	F1Y-POSI	F12-POSI	F1_Px	F1_Py	GESTURE DATA	VALIDITY
22	73	86	255	255	255	50.39	-14.53	-4.74	55.42	-5.71		X
23	51	48	255	255	255	52.05	-11.97	-2.13	53.29	-4.96		X
24	32	15	255	255	255	53.99	-9.50	0.01	50.02	-4.78		X
25	17	8	255	255	255	51.03	-10.50	-1.85	51.11	-4.83	Omission...	X
26	7	0	255	255	255	52.01	-9.85	-1.02	49.85	-5.23		
27	0	0	255	254	255	52.78	-8.77	-1.75	51.85	-6.02		
28	0	0	253	254	255	49.87	-10.18	-2.12	48.97	-5.27		
29	0	0	255	255	254	48.71	-9.43	-1.92	52.85	-4.89		
30	0	0	255	255	255	51.09	-8.75	-1.75	47.93	-4.94		

Fig. 2. The clustering rules to segment in the RDBMS classification module.

The RDBMS has the capability to recombine the data items from different files, providing powerful tools for data usage [12-13]. A clustering rule to segment valid gesture record sets and invalid record sets in the RDBMS classification module is shown in Figure 2.

- If the difference between the preceding average (preceding 3 and 1) and current row value is greater than 5, the current value is regarded as a transition sign language gesture record.
- If one of the 5th data glove system and fastrak® data values is greater than 5, the current value data is also regarded as a changing sign language gesture record.

2.5   KSL Recognition Module Based on Fuzzy Max-Min Composition

The fuzzy logic is a paradigm for an alternative design methodology, which can be applied in developing both linear and non-linear systems for embedded control, and has been found to be very suitable for embedded control applications [14]. For the design of fuzzy membership functions, many types of curves can be used, but triangular or trapezoidal shaped membership functions are the most common because they are easier to represent in embedded-controllers [15]. Therefore, we applied trapezoidal shaped membership functions for representation of fuzzy numbers-sets; this shape originates from the fact that there are several points with maximum membership. To define and describe trapezoidal shaped membership functions, we define trapezoidal fuzzy numbers-set A as A = (a, b, c, d), and the membership function of this fuzzy numbers-set will be interpreted as Equation (1) and Figure 3. The proposed the fuzzy membership functions are shown in Figure 4. In addition, suppositions and basic rules for its design and representation are as follows.

$$\mu_A(x) = \begin{bmatrix} 0 & , & x < a \\ \dfrac{x-a}{b-a} & , & a \leq x \leq b \\ 1 & , & b \leq x \leq c \\ \dfrac{d-x}{d-c} & , & c \leq x \leq d \\ 0 & , & x > d \end{bmatrix} \quad (1)$$

Fig. 3. Trapezoidal fuzzy numbers-set A as $A = (a, b, c, d)$

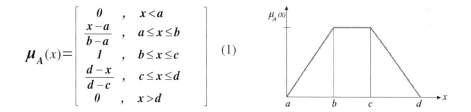

(a) Hand Gestures   (b) Basic KSSL Gestures

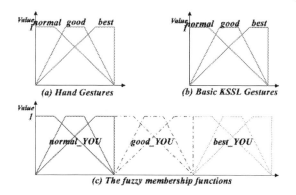

(c) The fuzzy membership functions

Fig. 4. The fuzzy membership functions for KSL recognition. Because fuzzy numbers-sets according to KSL recognition models are very various and so many, we represent membership functions partially: "YOU" in KSL).

In addition, we utilized fuzzy max-min composition to extend the crisp relation concept to relation concepts with fuzzy proposition, and reason approximate conclusions by composition arithmetic of fuzzy relations. Two fuzzy relations R and S are defined on sets *A*, *B* and *C* (we prescribed the accuracy of hand gestures and basic KSL gestures, object KSL recognition models as the sets of events that occur in KSL recognition with sets *A*, *B* and *C*). The composition $S \bullet R = SR$ of two relations *R* and *S* is expressed by the relation from *A* to *C*, and this composition is defined in Equation (2) [11].

$$For\ (x, y) \in A \times B,\ (y, z) \in B \times C,$$

$$\mu_{S \bullet R}\ (x,\ z) = \underset{y}{Max}\ [Min\ (\mu_R(x,y),\mu_S(y,z))] \tag{2}$$

$S \bullet R$ from this elaboration is a subset of $A \times C$. That is, $S \bullet R \subseteq A \times C$. If the relations *R* and *S* are represented by matrices M_R and M_S, the matrix $M_{S \bullet R}$ corresponding to $S \bullet R$ is obtained from the product of M_R and M_S; $M_{S \bullet R} = M_R \bullet M_S$. In addition, the matrix $M_{S \bullet R}$ represents max-min composition that reason and analyze the possibility of *C* when *A* occurs, this is also given in Figure 5.

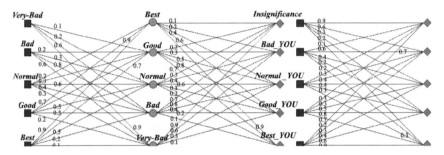

Fig. 5. Composition of fuzzy relation

3   Experiments and Performance Evaluation

The wireless data gloves transmits 14 kinds of hand gesture data (10 fingers gesture data, 4 pitch & roll data) and the motion tracker transmits 12 kinds of sign language gesture data (position X, Y, and Z Cartesian coordinates and orientation-azimuth, elevation, and roll) to the embedded WPS via a blue-tooth module. The proposed file size of the embedded KSL recognizer is 251 Kbytes, and the recognizer can process and calculate 200 samples per seconds on the WPS. The overall process of the embedded KSL recognizer using fuzzy logic consists of three major steps. In the first step, the user inputs the KSL into WPS using data gloves, and a motion tracker based on the blue-tooth module, the KSL input module captures the user's KSL. In addition, in the second step, the KSL recognition system changes the characteristics of data by fuzzy recognition module parameter. In the last step, it calculates and produces a fuzzy value of the user's dynamic KSL through a fuzzy reasoning and composition process. Ed – Please check, original meaning unclear. The recognition model by the RDBMS is used as an independent variable of fuzzy reasoning, and we decide to give a weight to each parameter. The produced fuzzy value is used as a judgment of user action and the KSL recognition system decides the user's dynamic for the KSL, according to the degree of fuzzy value. A flowchart of the embedded KSL recognition system using fuzzy logic is shown in Figure 6.

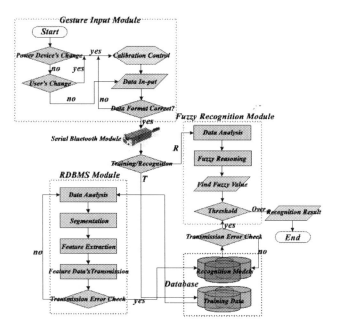

Fig. 6. The flowchart of embedded the KSL recognizer

The experimental set-up is as follows. The distance between the KSL input module and the WPS with a built-in KSL recognizer approximates radius 10M's ellipse form. In the gesture, we move the wireless data gloves and 2 receivers of the motion tracker to the prescribed position. For every 15 reagents, we repeat this action 10 times. In experimental results, we deduced an average recognition rate of 93.2% on 44 sentential the recognition models in the WPS embedded in the KSL recognizer, and recognition rates on 44 sentential recognition models are shown in Figure 7.

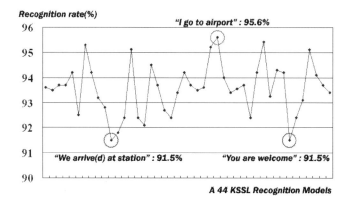

Fig. 7. Recognition rates on 44 sentential the recognition models

4 Extended CSCW Architecture Using Embedded KSL Recognizer

A virtual common workspace with a group centered interface enables participants to share a common work space, set up conferences, see other's gestures, and hear their voices in the shared space. In addition, our application enables users to remotely point into the shared document and simultaneous audio-visual communication simplifies interactions on the item of interest [16]. We describe and estimate the applicability and availability of our application with the next 3 items from the viewpoints of basic functional criteria and requirements for a CSCW system.

4.1 Interaction

A basic goal of HCI is to improve the interaction between users and computers by making computers more user-friendly and receptive to user's needs. HCI is concerned with methods for implementing interfaces, techniques for evaluating and comparing interfaces and so on. A long term goal of HCI is to design systems that minimize the barrier between the human's cognitive model of what they want to accomplish and the computer's understanding of the user's task. That is, our application computes more correctly and interprets and translates intentions of presenters or conferees required for acceptable common work and understanding in decision-making of the hearing-impaired.

4.2 Visualization

The *What-You-See-Is-What-I-See (WYSIWIS)* paradigm determines how to visualize public data used in collaboration with individual users. This application recognizes and interprets sign language by the hearing-impaired and then translates recognition results into synthetic speech and visual illustration in real-time, for presenters or conferees to satisfy visualization requirements or functions in a CSCW system.

4.3 Coordination

Coordination of interaction deals with the communication within a group of users and depends on group size and individual group members, with respect to the way they prefer to interact [16]. Especially, in a videoconference or a brainstorming session, every group member should communicate spontaneously. In contrast, a conference situation requires one person to communicate while others listen. So, our study is important for the participation and communication of the hearing-impaired.

4.4 Extended CSCW Architecture

CSCW architectures, particularly those for synchronous or interactive systems, are unique and can be difficult to design. The first step to effective design is to understand current requirements and anticipate as many future requirements as possible. After this, an early pre-design step includes forming an appropriate conceptual model of the CSCW system by leveraging well-established conceptual models or architectural pat-terns. User interfaces for CSCW systems and applications include techniques for both human-computer interaction and human-human interaction. These two modes of interaction cannot be separated strictly, for example, setting up a conference requires an action with the conference tool and first requires interaction with the conference partici-pants [16]. . In this sub-section, we examine the standard classification scheme of CSCW preferentially, and then describe and introduce the applicability and availability of the WPS-based embedded KSL recognizer in an extended classification of CSCW from the viewpoint of intersecting CSCW technologies. For example, extended CSCW architecture for application in this study in a brain-storming session, is given in Fig. 8. In other words, if the presenter is hearing-impaired, he is interpreted and represented using the application for correct communication and decision-making, and then the application translates the results into speech and visual components and delivers this in a brain-storming environment as HHI (Human-Human Inter-action). In addition, a mov-ing user can represent and communicate his own idea or intention via embedded KSL recognizer, from the viewpoint of HCI.

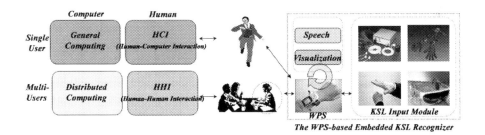

Fig. 8. Extended CSCW architecture using embedded KSL recognizer in a brainstorming

5   Conclusions

The concept of cooperation is often used in relation to the concepts of coordination and communication in CSCW. In other words, humans communicate in order to share knowledge and experience, give or receive orders, or cooperate. However, it is very difficult for the public to understand and respond to voluntary decision-making of the hearing-impaired at an internal (official) meeting or an informal talk such as brain-storming for decision-making and communication.

Consequently, in this paper, we suggested an extended CSCW architecture using the WPS-based embedded KSL recognizer, and described its applicability and avail-ability in CSCW domains. In conclusion, we clarify that this study is fundamental for participation in CSCW and decision-making of the hearing-impaired.

In the future, from the viewpoints of the decision-making and communication in the CSCW, we will focus our research with the objective for the design and imple-mentation of multi-modal CSCW architecture, integrating human's 5 sensory chan-nels such as sight, hearing, touch, smell, and taste, for efficient language processing and accurate communication of disabled persons.

Acknowledgments. This research was supported by the MIC (Ministry of Information and Communication), Korea, under the ITRC (Information Technology Research Center) support program supervised by the IITA (Institute of Information Technology Assessment) (IITA-2005- C1090-0501-0019).

References

1. Grudin, J.: Computer-supported cooperative work: Its history and participation. IEEE Computer 27(5) (1994) 19-26
2. Bannon, L. and Schmidt, K.: CSCW - four characters in search of a context. In: Bowers, J.M. and Benford, S.: Studies in Computer Supported Cooperative Work - Theory, Practice and Design. Amsterdam, North Holland (1991)
3. Dillenbourg, P., Baker, M., Blaye, A. and O'Malley, C.: The Evolution of Research on Collaborative Learning. In: Reimann, P. and Spada, H.: Learning in Humans and Machines - Towards an Interdisciplinary Learning Science. London, UK (1995)
4. I.MX21 Processor Data-sheet. URL: http://www.freescale.com/
5. Use of Signs in Hearing Communities. URL: http://en.wikipedia.org/wiki/Sign_language
6. Kim, S.-G.: Korean Standard Sign Language Tutor. 1st Edition. Osung Publishing Company, Seoul (2000)
7. Su, Y., et al.: Three-Dimensional Motion System ("Data-Gloves"): Application for Parkinson's Disease and Essential Tremor. Proceedings of IEEE International Conference on Virtual and Intelligent Measurement Systems (2001) 28-33
8. Kim, J.-H., et al.: Hand Gesture Recognition System using Fuzzy Algorithm and RDBMS for Post PC. Proceedings of FSKD2005. LNAI 3614 (2005) 170-175
9. Duda, R.O., Hart, P.E., Stork, D.G.: Pattern Classification. 2nd Edition. Wiley, New York (2001)
10. Paulus, D. and Hornegger, J.: Applied Pattern Recognition. 2nd Edition. Vieweg (1998)
11. Schuermann, J.: Pattern Classification.: A Unified View of Statistical and Neural Approaches. Wiley&Sons (1996)
12. Relational DataBase Management System. URL: http://www.auditmypc.com/acronym/RDBMS.asp
13. Oracle 10g DW Guide. URL: http://www.oracle.com
14. Chen, C.H.: Fuzzy Logic and Neural Network Handbook. 1st Edition. McGraw-Hill, New York (1992)
15. Vasantha-kandasamy, W.B.: Smaranda Fuzzy Algebra. American Research Press, Seattle (2003)
16. Reinhard, W., Schweitzer, J. and Volksen, G.: CSCW Tools: Concepts and Architectures. IEEE Computer 27(5) (1994) 28-36

Bounded Model Checking Combining Symbolic Trajectory Evaluation Abstraction with Hybrid Three-Valued SAT Solving

Shujun Deng, Weimin Wu, and Jinian Bian

Department of Computer Science and Technology,
Tsinghua University, Beijing 100084, China
dengsj04@mails.tsinghua.edu.cn,
{wuwm,bianjn}@mail.tsinghua.edu.cn

Abstract. Bounded Model Checking (BMC) based on SAT is a complementary technique to BDD-based Symbolic Model Checking, and it is useful for finding counterexamples of minimum length. However, for model checking of large real world systems, BMC is still limited by the state explosion problem, thus abstraction is essential. In this paper, BMC is implemented on a higher abstraction level -- Register Transfer Level (RTL) within an abstraction framework of symbolic trajectory evaluation and hybrid three-valued SAT solving. An efficient SAT solver for RTL circuits is presented, and it is modified into a three-valued solver for the cooperative BMC application. The experimental results comparing with the ordinary BMC without abstraction show the efficiency of our method.

1 Introduction

Functional verification of hardware designs has become one of the most expensive components of the current product development cycle. Verification methods based on SAT solvers have emerged as a promising solution. Dramatic improvements in Boolean SAT solving techniques over the past decade [1] have led to the increasing works on SAT-based verification [2].

Bounded model checking (BMC) [3-4] based on SAT is usually looked as an alternative to symbolic model checking. Given a circuit model and properties to be verified expressed in linear temporal logic (LTL) [5], the BMC problem can be efficiently reduced to a propositional satisfiability problem, and can therefore be solved by a SAT solver. A counterexample will be produced by the SAT solver if a satisfiable assignment has been found. Otherwise, the original problem is unsatisfiable in k timeframes. However, the efficiency of BMC is dependent on the bound k and the *truth/false* decisions on properties are only guaranteed for k transitions. Recently, SAT-based unbounded model checking (UMC) [6] has been proposed as a promising method to overcome the drawbacks of SAT-based BMC.

Symbolic Trajectory Evaluation (STE) [7] is an effective lattice-based model checking technique which has shown great potential in verifying large-scale hardware designs, especially those with large data paths (such as memories, FIFOs, and floating

W. Shen et al. (Eds.): CSCWD 2006, LNCS 4402, pp. 297–307, 2007.
© Springer-Verlag Berlin Heidelberg 2007

point units) [8-9]. There have been many efforts in combining STE and SAT solving. In [10], Bjesse et al. used SAT-based STE to find bugs of an Alpha microprocessor. The results presented there are as good as BMC but with negligible runtimes. In Intel, satGSTE proposed by Jin Yang et al. [11] is used for debugging and refining Generalized Symbolic Trajectory Evaluation (GSTE) [12] assertion graph. The core of satGSTE is SAT-based STE.

Recently, hybrid SAT solving for high-level circuits has gained significant improvements. Parthasarathy et al. modified the Boolean DPLL procedure [13] into an efficient finite-domain constraint solver named HDPLL [14] for RTL circuits, which integrates Boolean search and Fourier-Motzkin elimination using Finite-Domain Constraint Propagation (FDCP). Conflict-based learning is also applied in HDPLL to prune the search space. However, to our knowledge, this kind of hybrid SAT solvers was seldom used in current SAT-based STE and BMC.

In our work, a BMC framework combining STE abstraction and hybrid three-valued SAT solving was implemented. A hybrid SAT solver for RTL circuits is presented, which uses an extended DPLL procedure combining Boolean and integer decision procedures. Then we describe how a hybrid SAT solver can be changed to a SAT solver for three-valued logic. An RTL circuit is expanded into a combinational circuit with bound k which is equal to the depth of STE assertion. Properties expressed as STE assertions are translated into three-valued SAT problems with the nodes in the expanded circuits as the corresponding variables.

The remainder of this paper is organized as follows: In Section 2, some basic ideas of BMC are discussed. Section 3 describes the hybrid SAT solver used in BMC, and how it can be modified into a three-valued SAT solver. Basic concepts of STE and how to translate STE assertions into hybrid three-valued SAT problems are described in Section 4. In Section 5, the experiments and comparisons are presented. Section 6 concludes the paper.

2   Bounded Model Checking

BMC is a SAT-based model checking technique, which can be applied to verify both safety and liveness properties. The idea of BMC is to search for a counterexample in executions whose length is bounded by some integer k.

For the circuits to be verified, the properties are described in temporal logic, such as CTL (Computation Tree Logic), LTL (Linear Temporal Logic) [5]. In this paper, we focus on LTL, in which no path quantifiers (**A** or **E**) are permitted. There are four operators in LTL: the *next time* operator '**X**', the *eventuality* operator '**F**', the *globally* operator '**G**', and the *until* operator '**U**'. The meanings of these operators are illustrated in Figure 1.

Fig. 1. Illustration of LTL operators

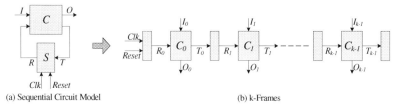

(a) Sequential Circuit Model   (b) k-Frames

Fig. 2. A sequential expansion example

Sequential circuits are expanded into combinational circuits with bound k. We call the combinational circuit *iterative logic array* (ILA). An ILA of length k is k copies of the combinational portion of the original circuit, and each copy represents a time-frame. Take the sequential circuit model in Figure 2(a) for instance, the corresponding ILA is shown in Figure 2(b). ILA can be easily translated into a hybrid SAT-problem. In BMC, the hybrid SAT-problem is to be solved by a hybrid SAT solver. If we cannot get the satisfied result (counterexample) of the expanded circuit, the value of k has to increase until a counterexample is found or k reaches the upper bound -- *completeness threshold* [4]. Given a bound that is greater than or equal to the completeness threshold, BMC is complete for finite circuit systems.

3   Hybrid SAT Solving for RTL Circuits

In our work, RTL circuits are described as net-lists (structural description extended from ISCAS'89 [15]) which is the same as HDPLL [14]. Given the structural description of an RTL circuit and a set of initial value requirements of the inputs and outputs, the hybrid SAT solving is to find the assignments to the other unassigned inputs that make these requirements satisfied.

3.1   Extended DPLL Procedure

An efficient hybrid SAT solver was developed using an extended DPLL procedure [13] as shown in Figure 3. The extended procedure is a little similar to the hybrid algorithm implemented in HDPLL [14]. However, the functions of sub-procedures shown in Figure 3 are quite different from HDPLL. The extended DPLL procedure is a branch-and-bound algorithm, which makes decisions on Boolean variables and word-level variable bits with different priorities. The main constraint propagation strategy for Boolean logic part is unit clause rule, and that for data path is based on rules corresponding to the structures of RTL circuits. Every time the value of a variable changes, variables related to it must change according to structural rules. Take operator $LT(<)$ for example, the rule for this operator is shown in Table 1. The first column denotes the old values of s and the second column denotes the current assignments, while columns 3 and 4 show the intervals for X and Y after change respectively. Column 5 shows the value of s after change. The conflict conditions are presented in the last column. Although the rule in Table 1 is complex, the operation of this rule is of linear complexity. Furthermore, one value assignment can propagate more assignments through one judgment. The reasoning rules for other RTL operators such as *multiplexers*, *ITE*, *ADD* are similar to those of *LT(<)* operator.

```
 1:  while (true)
 2:      if ( HCP() = = conflict )
 3:          blevel = hybrid_analyze();    --analyze conflict
         4:           if ( blevel = = 0 )
 5:              return UNSAT;
 6:          else
 7:              hybrid_backtrack();      --undo assignments
 8:          end if
 9:      else
10:          if ( hybrid_all_assigned() )
11:              return SAT;
12:          else
13:              hybrid_decide();
14:          end if
15:      end if
16:  end while
```

Fig. 3. The extended DPLL procedure

Table 1. Propagation rule for *LT(<)* operator

s_old	Cur Assignment	X'	Y'	s'	Conflict Conditions
Not 0	$s = 0$	$[\max(\underline{X}, \underline{Y}), \overline{X}]$	$[\underline{Y}, \min(\overline{X}, \overline{Y})]$	0	$X' < Y'$ or $X' = \phi$ or $Y' = \phi$
Not 1	$s = 1$	$[\underline{X}, \min(\overline{X}, \overline{Y}-1)]$	$[\max(\underline{X}+1, \underline{Y}), \overline{Y}]$	1	$X' \geq Y'$ or $X' = \phi$ or $Y' = \phi$
0	$X = [\underline{X'}, \overline{X'}]$	$[\underline{X'}, \overline{X'}]$	$[\underline{Y}, \min(\overline{X'}, \overline{Y})]$	-no change-	$X' < Y'$ or $Y' = \phi$
1	$X = [\underline{X'}, \overline{X'}]$	$[\underline{X'}, \overline{X'}]$	$[\max(\underline{X'}+1, \underline{Y}), \overline{Y}]$	-no change-	$X' \geq Y'$ or $Y' = \phi$
X	$X = [\underline{X'}, \overline{X'}]$	$[\underline{X'}, \overline{X'}]$	-no change-	**IF**(X'<Y') $s = 1$; **ELIF**(X'≥Y') $s = 0$	**NULL**
0	$Y = [\underline{Y'}, \overline{Y'}]$	$[\max(\underline{X}, \underline{Y'}), \overline{X}]$	$[\underline{Y'}, \overline{Y'}]$	-no change-	$X' < Y'$ or $X' = \phi$
1	$Y = [\underline{Y'}, \overline{Y'}]$	$[\underline{X}, \min(\overline{X}, \overline{Y'}-1)]$	$[\underline{Y'}, \overline{Y'}]$	-no change-	$X' \geq Y'$ or $X' = \phi$
X	$Y = [\underline{Y'}, \overline{Y'}]$	-no change-	$[\underline{Y'}, \overline{Y'}]$	**IF**(X'<Y') $s = 1$; **ELIF**(X'≥Y') $s = 0$	**NULL**

The underlying data structure of the extended DPLL procedure is an implication queue storing all implications. In Figure 3, the main function of *HCP()* is to pop the implications from the implication queue and push new implications on current level into it, until there are no more implications in the queue or some conflicts occur. Rules for RTL operators are integrated in *HCP()* to find new implications. The procedure *hybrid_decide()* is a unified process because it makes decisions on both Boolean variables and word-level variable bit-vectors. When a conflict occurs, the procedure *hybrid_backtrack()* is applied to undo the assignments and to resume the intervals and bit-vectors as before the change. If all the Boolean variables and word-level variable bits have been assigned, then the procedure *hybrid_all_assigned()* returns *true* and the original proposition is satisfied.

3.2 Hybrid Three-Valued SAT Solver

A hybrid three-valued SAT problem can be defined as a 5-tuple (V_2, V_3, W_2, W_3, C), where

V_2: the set of Boolean symbolic variables which appear in the STE assertion,
V_3: the set of Boolean three-valued variables,
W_2: the set of symbolic word-level variables,
W_3: the set of three-valued word-level variables,
C: the set of hybrid constraints.

A *three-valued assignment* is a mapping $\sigma: (V_2 \rightarrow \{0, 1\}) \times (V_3 \rightarrow \{0, 1, X\}) \times (W_2 \rightarrow \{0, 1, 2, ..., +\infty\}) \times (W_3 \rightarrow \mathbf{D})$, where "X" denotes don't care and "$\mathbf{D}$" is the set of integer intervals (integer domains). The Boolean constraints in C are expressed as conjunctive normal form (CNF). CNF is represented as a conjunction of clauses, each of which is a disjunction of literals. Each literal is a variable or its negation. A three-valued clause $c = v_1 \vee v_2 \vee ... \vee v_n$ is said to be *satisfied* by an assignment σ, written as $\sigma \models c$, if for every literal i ($1 \leq i \leq$ n), the following holds:

$$\{v_j = 0 \mid 0 \leq j \leq \text{n}, i \neq j\} \rightarrow v_i = 1$$

In other words, $\sigma \models c$, if and only if either there is at least one literal is assigned value 1 or two or more variables are assigned value X [9]. In order to propagate the information only in forward direction, CNF for basic gates are different from traditional SAT solvers. For example, CNF for an OR-gate is $(z + \overline{x} + \overline{x}) \cdot (z + \overline{y} + \overline{y})$ $\cdot (\overline{z} + x + x + y + y)$ while the traditional CNF is $(z + \overline{x}) \cdot (z + \overline{y}) \cdot (\overline{z} + x + y)$. Difference between these two CNF is that when $z = 0$, only the latter CNF can get the implications $x = 0$ and $y = 0$.

In our three-valued SAT solver, a word-level constraint is satisfied if and only if the corresponding rule holds and all the related variables are assigned with accurate values or two or more variables are assigned with integer intervals (corresponding to X for Boolean variables). A three-valued SAT problem P is satisfied by an assignment σ, written $\sigma \models P$, if and only if for every clause c in CNF $\sigma \models c$ and all the word-level constraints are satisfied at the same time.

The extended DPLL procedure presented in the former subsection can be easily changed to a hybrid three-valued SAT solver. The difference is that only the two-valued symbolic variables are selected to decide. Search trees can be generated from the decision operations and propagation steps. For a satisfiable three-valued SAT problem, the search tree contains a leaf with a weakest satisfying assignment; for an unsatisfiable problem, all the leaves are with contradictory assignments.

There are two constraint propagation rules in the hybrid three-valued SAT solver corresponding to those for the ordinary hybrid SAT solver. The first rule is unit propagation for Boolean variables which is denoted as follows:

$$\{v_i = X, v_j = 0 \mid 0 \leq j \leq \text{n}, i \neq j\} \rightarrow v_i = 1$$

The second rule is the constraint propagation based on structural rules for word-level intervals. Because we use the *forward semantics* for STE, the details of which are set out in subsection 4.1, information is only propagated in a forward fashion in the hybrid three-valued SAT solver, so the rules for RTL operators have to be changed partially. Still take the *LT* ($s \models X < Y$) operator for an instance, the first two rows in Table 1 will be changed as shown in Table 2, and other rows in the rule are the same. This means that when the output node of an RTL operator changes, the constraint won't be propagated backward.

Table 2. Part of three-valued propagation rule for *LT (<)* operator

s_old	Cur Assignment	X'	Y'	s'	Conflict Conditions
Not 0	$s = 0$	-no change-	-no change-	0	$X' < Y'$
Not 1	$s = 1$	-no change-	-no change-	1	$X' \geq Y'$

4   Symbolic Trajectory Evaluation

Symbolic Trajectory Evaluation (STE) is a model checking technique combining three-valued simulation with symbolic simulation. Three-valued abstraction improves the efficiency of STE, because if a node is not mentioned in STE assertions, the value of this node will be abstracted as the unknown value X. Thus, STE is less sensitive to the original circuit size.

4.1   Background of Symbolic Trajectory Evaluation

An *STE assertion* is denoted as an implication: $A ==> C$, where A is the *antecedent* and C is the *consequence*. A gives the stimulus and the current state, while C gives the result conditions. A *trajectory* is a sequence (path) that makes the hybrid constraints of a circuit satisfied. The assertion $A ==> C$ holds only when each trajectory satisfies both A and C. An evaluation together with a trajectory satisfies A but not C compose a counterexample of an STE assertion.

The definition of *trajectory evaluation logic (TEL)* [9] is extended as the following grammar:

$$f ::= n \text{ is } 0 \mid n \text{ is } 1 \mid w \text{ is } N \mid f_1 \text{ and } f_2 \mid P \rightarrow f \mid N f$$

where "**is**" is used to state the value of a Boolean or word-level node in the circuit.

The values of Boolean variables are logic 0, 1 and X. They can be partially ordered by their "information contents" as $X \leq 0$, $X \leq 1$, because X contains the least information. The partial orders of word-level variable values are dependent on the domain widths. In other words, $I_i \leq I_j$ iff the domain of I_j is a subset of I_i. Here, if $u \leq v$, we said that u is weaker or less specified than v.

The idea of *forward semantics* is that no more information can be propagated in a forward direction at the same time-point. We use *hybrid stable state set* to model the behavior of STE. A state ζ is in the hybrid stable state set if no more information can be derived in forward direction at the same time-point.

As defined in [9], the *stable state set F* of a circuit with a single AND-gate ($r \models p$ and q) is as follows:

$$F = \{ \zeta \mid \zeta(p) = 1 \text{ and } \zeta(q) = 1 => \zeta(r) = 1, \zeta(p) = 0 \text{ or } \zeta(q) = 0 => \zeta(r) = 0 \} = \{000,$$
$$010, 0X0, 100, 111, 1X0, 1X1, 1XX, X00, X10, X11, X1X, XX0, XX1, XXX \}$$

To construct the stable state set for a word-level operator using similar method is not easy, because word-level variables are presented as integer intervals. For the *LT* operator ($s \models X < Y$), we can only denote it as

$$F = \{\zeta \mid \zeta(X) < \zeta(Y) => \zeta(s) = 1, \zeta(X) \geq \zeta(Y) => \zeta(s) = 0\}$$

It is redundant to list all the stable states in the hybrid stable state set of *LT* operator because for a word-level variable with width n, the number of different intervals for it is

$$n + (n\text{-}1) + (n\text{-}2) + \ldots + 1 = (n^2 + n) / 2$$

The complexity of the stable state set is the product of the widths of X and Y. Thus, in our opinion, it is impossible to explicitly demonstrate the hybrid stable state set. However, it is easy to implicatively apply the hybrid stable state in hybrid three-valued SAT solver because the constraints for RTL operators are based on rules. As discussed in subsection 3.2, the rules for RTL operators need to be changed little to be consistent with the forward semantics.

4.2 Constraints for STE Assertions

In this subsection, we will explain how to translate STE assertions into constraints of a hybrid SAT problem. We use the negation of the consequent constraint to find a solution that satisfies the antecedent A but not the consequent C. Thus, the constraints for an STE assertion on circuit c, written $\mathbf{C_{STE}}(c \models A ==> C)$ can be divided into three parts:

1. Circuit constraint $\mathbf{Con}(c, k)$;
2. Antecedent constraint $\mathbf{SAT}(A)$;
3. Negation of consequent constraint $\mathbf{NSAT}(C)$.

Thus, $\mathbf{C_{STE}}(c \models A ==> C) = \mathbf{Con}(c, k) \ \& \ \mathbf{SAT}(A) \ \& \ \mathbf{NSAT}(C)$. The original STE assertion $A ==> C$ holds if and only if $\mathbf{Sol}(\mathbf{C_{STE}}(c \models A ==> C)) = \Phi$. Otherwise, $\mathbf{Sol}(\mathbf{C_{STE}}(c \models A ==> C))$ is a count-example for the original STE assertion.

Circuit Constraint: The solutions to STE assertions are corresponding to trajectories of the original circuits. Thus, the circuit constraint $\mathbf{Con}(c, k)$ can be defined as follows: $\mathbf{Con}(c, \ k) = \mathbf{Stable}(c_0) \ \& \ \mathbf{Stable}(c_1) \ \& \ \ldots \ \& \ \mathbf{Stable}(c_k) \ \& \ \mathbf{Stable_{RTL}}(c_0) \ \& \ \mathbf{Stable_{RTL}}(c_1) \ \& \ \ldots \ \& \ \mathbf{Stable_{RTL}}(c_k)$

where c_i is the partial circuit C_i in the expanded circuit shown in Figure 2(b). The stable state constraint for c_i -- $\mathbf{Stable}(c_i)$ – is built as a conjunction of the constraints for all the Boolean gates in the partial circuit C_i. $\mathbf{Stable_{RTL}}(c_i)$ means the hybrid constraints based on the RTL operator rules.

Antecedent Constraint: Given an STE assertion with the antecedent A, a node (Boolean or word-level) n, an integer value i (for Boolean variables are logic 0 and 1), and a time-point t, the *defining formula* is denoted as $\langle A \rangle(t)(n = i)$, which means that the antecedent A requires the node n to have value i at time-point t. This definition is similar to that in [8][9] except the nodes in our work are Boolean or word-level types and the values are integers instead of Boolean values.

Consequently, we define the antecedent constraint $SAT(A)$ the conjunction of all requirements that the antecedent A on any node n at any time-point t with any value i. This can be written as follows:

$$\mathbf{SAT}(A) = \prod_{0 \leq t \leq d, n \in N, i \in I} IMPLIES(\langle A \rangle(t)(n = i) \rightarrow (n_t = i))$$

Consequent Constraint: To denote the negation of the consequent constraint $\mathbf{NSAT}(C)$, we use a Boolean type array B to record whether the variables referred to in the consequent satisfy the requirements of the consequent C. If C requires the node n at time-point t to have value i and it has definite value i, then the value of the corresponding item in B is *false*. The negation of the consequent C requires one of the items in B to be *true*. This constraint can be translated into a disjunction clause $\bigvee_{0 \leq k \leq N} B[k]$. Here, the constraint for the negation of the consequent C -- $\mathbf{NSAT}(C)$ -- is given by:

$$\prod_{0 \leq t \leq d, n \in N} (IMPLIES(\langle C \rangle(t)(n = i) \text{ and } n_t = i \rightarrow B[\text{index of } n_t]) \& (\bigvee_{0 \leq k \leq N} B[k])$$

5   Experiments

We implemented the hybrid SAT solver named EHSAT in C++ programming language. The first experiment is the comparisons between EHSAT and HDPLL [14][16], a state-of-the-art hybrid constraint solver. The programs were run on a 2.4GHz/384M Pentium 4 with Linux. The test-cases were from ITC'99 benchmarks' bounded-model checking cases with initial states, which had been expanded for some time-frames with the safety properties. The results are shown in Table 3. The second column shows the number of expanded time-frames. The next two columns give the numbers of Boolean and word-level operators respectively. The CPU time for solving using EHSAT and HDPLL are presented in columns 5 and 6 respectively. The symbolic **–Abort-** indicates that the number of equalities is greater than 2056, which is defined as the maximum number in HDPLL [16]. The results show that HDPLL is competitive to the state-of-the-art hybrid SAT solver.

The second also the important experiment is about the cooperative BMC method named STE-BMC. We compared results of STE-BMC with those produced by ordinary BMC using our hybrid SAT solver. The programs were run on a 2GHz/512M Pentium-4 PC.

The test-cases were adapted from ITC'99 benchmarks. The first part of test-case names show the original benchmarks in ITC'99, and the last part present the index that we appoint to these test-cases. For example, the test-case b01_1 is the first test-case adapted from bench b01 in ITC'99. The properties we considered are: (1)

Relation between two states which are represented by values of nodes in RTL circuits; (2) Relation among values of some nodes. By translating STE assertions into LTL formulas, and with the bounds as depths of the STE assertions, BMC can verify the STE assertions on the test-cases we used. Although STE-BMC and BMC solved different problems for the same benchmark, the comparisons between STE-BMC and BMC can show how much is improved by the cooperative BMC using STE and hybrid three-valued SAT solving.

The results are shown in Table 4. The first column presents the names of the test-cases, and columns 2 and 3 show the CPU time for solving using STE-BMC and BMC respectively. The last column shows the percentages of the CPU time reduced when using STE-BMC instead of BMC.

Table 3. Runtime comparison between EHSAT and HDPLL

Test-case		Character		CPU Time (s)	
Name	Time-frames	Boolean operators	Word Operators	EHSAT	HDPLL
b01	200	7922	4556	**17.92**	25.23
	250	9922	5706	**29.19**	-Abort-
	300	11922	6856	42.34	**42.07**
	350	13922	8006	**59.45**	-Abort-
	400	15922	9156	**75.74**	91.74
	450	17922	10306	**88.65**	-Abort-
	500	19922	11456	**105.78**	132.78
b02	50	2115	2020	**1.34**	3.80
	100	4315	4120	**5.26**	14.95
	150	6515	6220	**12.23**	35.84
	200	8715	8320	**22.55**	54.16
	250	10915	10420	**34.46**	88.31
	300	13115	12520	**48.91**	140.07
	350	15315	14620	**68.36**	189.68
	400	17515	16720	**88.75**	249.51
	450	19715	18820	**120.61**	302.64
	500	21915	20920	**140.40**	376.48

Table 4. Runtime comparison between STE-BMC and BMC

Test-case	STE-BMC(s)	BMC(s)	Diff (%)
b01_1	5.79	6.15	5.85
b01_2	12.03	19.36	37.86
b01_3	30.24	41.29	26.76
b01_4	71.32	97.55	26.89
b02_1	3.43	3.53	2.83
b02_2	20.14	22.95	12.24
b02_3	51.04	65.14	21.65
b02_4	85.23	110.80	23.08
b04_1	4.29	5.26	18.44
b13_1	50.13	74.78	32.96
b13_2	67.09	89.44	25.00

As shown in Table 4, all the CPU seconds for STE-BMC are less than BMC. This means that the abstraction used in STE is beneficial when using hybrid SAT solving. Of course, the test-cases in our work are very limited and the properties verified are a little simple. In theory, BMC can outperform STE-BMC although we didn't find these cases in our work. The reason may be the limitation of our test-cases.

6 Conclusions

We presented a cooperative BMC method for RTL circuits. This method combines the expansion in BMC and the abstraction in STE. STE assertions are translated into a hybrid three-valued SAT problem. Then a three-valued SAT solver is applied to solve this problem. The experimental results are promising when compared with the ordinary BMC using hybrid SAT solver, and the reason to this improvement is due to the STE and three-valued abstraction. However, STE-BMC cannot replace the ordinary BMC. The role of the cooperative method we propose is only a complement to BMC. In the future, we will improve our approaches for practical applications.

Acknowledgments. Supported by the National Basic Research Program of China (973) under Grant No. 2005CB321605; the National Natural Science Foundation of China under Grant No(s). 60673034, 60273011, 60236020, 90607001.

References

1. Moskewicz, M.W., Madigan, C.F., Zhao, Y., Zhang, L., Malik, S.: Chaff: Engineering an efficient sat solver. Proc. of Design Automation Conference (DAC 2001). Las Vegas, NV, USA(2001) 530-535
2. Prasad, M.R., Biere, A., Gupta, A.: A survey of recent advances in sat-based formal verification. Journal on STTT 7(2) (2005) 156-173
3. Biere, A., Cimatti, A., Clarke, E.M., Fujita, M., Zhu, Y.: Symbolic model checking using sat procedures instead of bdds. Proc. of the 36th Design Automation Conference (DAC 1999). New Orleans, LA, USA (1999) 317-320
4. Biere, A., Cimatti, A., Clarke, E.M., Strichman, O., Zhu, Y.: Bounded model checking. Advances in Computers 58 (2003)
5. Clarke, E.M., Grumberg, O., Peled, D.A.: Model Checking. The MIT Press, Cambridge, Massachusetts (1999)
6. Kang, H.J., Park, I.C.: SAT-based unbounded symbolic model checking. IEEE Trans. on CAD of Integrated Circuits and Systems 24(2) (2005) 129-140
7. Seger, C.-J.H., Bryant, R.E.: Formal verification by symbolic evaluation of partially-ordered trajectories. Formal methods in System Design 6(2) (1995) 147-190
8. Roorda, J.W., Claessen, K.: A new sat-based algorithm for symbolic trajectory evaluation. Proc. Correct Hardware Design and Verification Methods (CHARME 2005). Vol. 3725 (2005) 238-253
9. Roorda, J.W.: Symbolic trajectory evaluation using a satisfiability solver. Licentiate thesis, Chalmers University of Technology (2005)
10. Bjesse, P., Leonard, T., Mokkedem, A.: Finding bugs in an alpha microprocessor using satisfiability solvers. Proc. International Conference on Computer Aided Verification (CAV) (2001) 454-464

11. Yang, J., Singerman, E.: satgste: Combining the abstraction of gste with the capacity of a sat solver. Proc. Designing Correct Circuits (DCC). Barcelona (2004)
12. Yang, J., Seger, C.J.H.: Introduction to generalized symbolic trajectory evaluation. IEEE Transactions on Very Large Scale Integration (VLSI) Systems 11(3) (2003) 345-353
13. Davis, M., Logemann, G., Loveland, D.W.: A machine program for theorem-proving. Communications of the ACM 5(7) (1962) 394-397
14. Parthasarathy, G., Iyer, M.K., Cheng, K.T., Wang, L.C.: An efficient finite-domain constraint solver for circuits. Proc. of the 41th Design Automation Conference (DAC) (2004) 212-217
15. Brglez, F., Bryan, D., Koiminski, K.: Combinational profiles of sequential benchmark circuits. Proc. International Symposium on Circuits and Systems (ISCAS) (1989) 1929-1934
16. UCSB RTL Satisfiability by Constraint Solving - HDPLL (2005). URL: http://cadlab.ece.ucsb.edu/downloads/HDPLL.html

Automatic Identification of Teams in R and D

Fabricio Enembreck[1], Edson Scalabrin[1], Cesar Tacla[2], and Bráulio Ávila[1]

[1] Pontifical Catholic University do Paraná, Rua Imaculada Conceição, 1155,
80215-901 Curitiba, PR, Brazil
{fabricio, scalabrin, avila}@ppgia.pucpr.br
[2] Federal Technolgical University do Paraná, Av. Sete de Setembro, 3165,
80-000-000, PR, Brazil
tacla@cpgei.cefetpr.br

Abstract. This paper presents a system for identifying persons who have proper skills to form a specialized team capable to execute self-managed projects of research and development. Such identification is based on techniques of textual information retrieval applied on a document base of *résumés*. The system has been evaluated with data from real projects and the results observed have shown that the system can automatically identify persons to collaborate in research projects.

1 Introduction

A common problem in organizations is to identify people or suitable competencies to form a specialized self-managed Research and Development (R&D) team in either academic or industrial environments. The concept of team formation, or join action, is central to a wide variety of disciplines including organizational design, computational organization theory, planning and learning in multi-agent systems and distributed artificial intelligence [14]. Furthermore, successful organizations generally foster the formation of teams to accomplish complicated tasks involving cooperation, collaboration, delegation, resource allocation, skill distribution and other factors are influential in an organizations' ability to leverage the collective actions of individuals [14]. Team formation is currently a wide and exciting area of research involving researchers of different communities: multi-agent systems and distributed artificial intelligence [15], CSCW [16] and recently information retrieval [12]. Information Retrieval researchers study new structures and algorithms to store, search and organize information efficiently [17]. Such structures are used to classify, group, compare documents and collections of homogeneous or multimedia documents. They can also be used to model user profiles, preferences and centers of interest. In this paper Information Retrieval is used to identify teams in R&D projects based on personal profiles extracted from the Lattes database.

In Brazil, the Lattes database is an important source of data where one can find people in a number of knowledge areas [6]. The Lattes database contains *résumés* of researchers, students, managers, professionals, and other actors of the National System of Science, Technology and Innovation. The CNPq (National Council for Scientific and Technical Development) uses such information (i) to rank candidates

W. Shen et al. (Eds.): CSCWD 2006, LNCS 4402, pp. 308–317, 2007.
© Springer-Verlag Berlin Heidelberg 2007

applying for scholarships or other kind of financial support; (ii) to select consultants, and members of committees; (iii) to assess the research and post graduation courses.

The Lattes database is representative of the Brazilian scientific population since the CNPq demands that the scholarship holders (researchers, under-graduated, master, and doctorate students), research advisors, and all the people requesting or having funds from CNPq register their *résumés* in the Lattes System. The registration is also mandatory for all researchers and students who participate of the Directory of Groups of Research in Brazil.

In this context, given an R&D project description, our objective is to extract information that allows for identifying people having the most appropriate competencies to participate in the project using the Lattes database. In order to extract such information, we apply textual retrieval techniques.

The rest of this article is organized as follows: (i) we discuss issues on forming teams; (ii) we describe the technique to extract information from the Lattes database; (iii) we present the experiments and their results; (iv) a discussion on the results and (v) finally, we offer a conclusion.

2   Forming Teams

Considering that a whole team has more resources (e.g. information, and competencies) than its members have separately, the organization, qualification, and training of teams is useful to develop tasks that are very difficult or cannot be achieved individually. The diversity of competencies in a team makes complex tasks be possible.

In general, competency managed organizations put their strategic objectives in relation with their key business processes. Applying a systematic approach to measure the individual competencies, an organization can: (i) locate and map the knowledge capital; (ii) use such information to analysis the employees and the organization in order to reduce the cost of training, to hire people with suitable competencies, to improve the performance of its workforce, to place more efficiently its human capital, and to aid its management to take strategic decisions (e.g. to launch new projects).

A team can be formed by people who work in the same or different areas. Nowadays, a modern approach is the formation of self-managed teams [1][2][7][11], with trained members to perform all or most part of the required tasks, without an immediate supervisor and taking decisions in a collective way, with support of coordinators. Each team must pursue its objectives trying to achieve a good performance level.

The formation and assessment of teams are not trivial tasks. The following measures may be considered in assessing the team: (i) the productivity, which consists of satisfying or exceeding criteria that refer to the quantity (e.g. number of products) and/or quality (e.g. quality of provided service); (ii) the personal satisfaction during the project, and finally, (iii) the engagement of the members in collaborative work.

To form a team presenting cohesion the following criteria may be considered: (i) to enroll members with diversified and complementary competencies; (ii) to enlist members with similar values and experiences; (iii) to keep the team as small as possible, but with a sufficient number of members to perform its functions and achieve the planned goals. Teams with low cohesion with a requirement of high performance generally do not succeed. In other words, the greatest possibilities of success are in multidisciplinary teams, where knowledge is transversal to the disciplines, and team members have complementary affinities and competencies, with capacity to add value to the project.

Forming teams is to select human resources. In the majority of cases, the best resources are not available. The management of the project must grant that the available resources satisfy the project requirements [8]. When the management of the project has the responsibility for composing the team, it should consider the characteristics of the available human resources. It means take into consideration previous experiences - select individuals that have worked in the same or similar projects; the personal interests - whether the individuals are interested in working in the project; the personal characteristics - whether the individuals are able to work collaboratively, and finally, the availability – whether the individuals will be available at the right moment.

Forming teams may require negotiation or previous assignments. The last case occurs when the project is the result of a proposal and the specified team was promised as part of the proposal. It may happen also in internal projects, where selected people are the ones who work in a department. In both cases, the management of the project can get external services of specific individuals or groups of individuals to carry out certain tasks of the project. So, employing external competencies is required when the organization does not have the necessary ones to satisfy the project requirements.

Members of a team work either in integral, partial, or variable time. The team starts to exist when all the members and other actors are effectively engaged in the project. Such engagement can be formal or informal, ranging from superficial to depth, depending on the project needs in relation to each person's abilities.

Forming teams involving various organizations (e.g. research laboratories, state agencies, private companies, and financial sponsors) may represent an additional difficulty in identifying and selecting members. Large projects as Genoma and Digital TV require a diversity of competencies coming from different organizations. Any tool or technique that makes easier the task of forming teams is fundamental for fast selecting the right competencies in order to answer a call for project.

3   Textual Information Retrieval

In a previous work [12], we described a textual information retrieval technique for comparing user profiles in computer supported collaborative work systems. In the present work, we use the same technique, but with a different objective: to find similarities between a description of a research project and the profiles of potential project members (candidates).

The profiles are automatically generated from knowledge items (KIs), i.e., articles, and texts written by the candidate. The KIs of a candidate are found in his/her *résumé* saved in the Lattes database. We next describe the technique used for generating the profiles and the measures for scoring the similarity between a project description and a candidate's profile.

3.1 Generating Profiles for Candidates

In order to generate a profile, we use document classification [5] and information retrieval techniques [13] on the selected KIs.

Usually, document classification is divided into two main phases: learning and classification. In the learning phase, a collection of already classified documents (the training set) is given as input for building a representation of each class. The first step consists of selecting a set of features that are important for representing the documents. A well-known approach is to consider a number of terms to represent the documents' features. Next, the classification phase puts a new document in a particular class based on the similarity between the document and each one of the classes.

In our case, the KIs coming from a *résumé* represent the training set. Hence, KIs are represented as vectors of relevant terms. A common measure of relevance for terms is the TF-IDF (Term Frequency - Inverse Document Frequency) measure [9]. TF-IDF states that the relevance of a term in a KI is in direct proportion to its frequency in the KI, and in inverse proportion to its incidence in the whole collection D of KIs. The IDF part for the ith term is given by $log(|D|/DF_i)$ where DF_i is the number of KIs containing the term i. TFi designates the frequency of the ith term in a particular KI. The TF-IDF formula is given in equation (1).

$$TFIDF(i) = TF_i \times \log\left(\frac{|D|}{DF_i}\right) \qquad (1)$$

A KI is considered to be a vector $\mathbf{d} = \{TF_1*\log (N/DF_1), TF2*\log (N/DF_2),...,TF_m*\log(N/DF_m)\}$. To learn a profile based on such KIs, machine-learning algorithms (e.g. decision trees, naïve Bayes, neural networks, and nearest-neighbor) can be applied to the data [5]. Here, we use a centroid-based approach [3] in which an average vector represents the profile of a candidate. Equation (2) gives the centroid vector c for a collection D of KIs for a candidate.

$$c = \frac{1}{|D|} \times \sum_{d \in D} d \qquad (2)$$

The greater the size of the KI collection, the more time consuming is the generation of the profile. So, in order to limit the number of KIs in the computation, we can set up the system to use only the KIs produced during a certain period or the last n KIs.

3.2 Text Classification

We use the centroid approach [3] for calculating the similarity between a project description and a candidate's profile. Classical techniques could be used such as computing the cosine or the Euclidian distance. However, we cannot use such techniques directly because the learning phase is done separately for each candidate. Their profiles have different terms and consequently different dimensions. Of course, the profiles may have common terms depending on the similarity of their KIs. For instance, candidates working on the subject probably have similar terms.

Thus, besides the similarity computation we have two additional problems: normalizing the profiles to be compared and to discover which terms best discriminate the profiles. Important terms for a candidate may not be very good for discriminating his/her profile from the other ones. For instance, the term "project" is important for most candidates, thus such a term is not a good discriminator.

In order to solve these additional problems, we propose a method for normalizing the profiles and discovering the terms that best discriminate them (Section 3.2.1). The outputs of this step are the input for the next one, i.e., scoring the similarity between a project description and a profile (Section 3.2.2).

1. Computing the Discriminating Power of Terms
In order to measure the discriminating power of the terms figuring in the profiles, we use the *Gini* index technique [10]. Let $\{c_1, c_2,..., c_m\}$ be the set of profiles computed according to Equation (2) and T_i the vector derived from the relevance of the term i in all the profiles — $T_i = \{c_{1i}, c_{2i},..., c_{mi}\}$. T'_i is the vector T_i normalized with the one-norm — $T'_i = \{c_{1i} / \| T_i \|_1, c_{2i} / \| T_i \|_1, ... c_{mi} / \| T_i \|_1 \}$ the discriminating power of i — p_i — is given by Equation (3).

$$p_i = \sum_{j=1}^{m} T'^2_{ji} \qquad (3)$$

p_i is equal to square of the length of the T'_i vector. So p_i is always in the range $[1/m, 1]$. p_i has the lower value when $T'_{1i} = T'_{2i} = ... = T'_{mi}$, whereas the higher value of p_i is given when only one profile has the term i.

The p_i measure acts as a normalizing parameter allowing profiles with different terms to be compared. We compute the p_i discriminating power for the terms of the whole collection of profiles. Such p_i measures are used in the similarity computation step described in the following sub-section.

2. Comparing a profile and a project description
In order to quantify the similarity between a project description c_1 and the profile c_2, we create a comparable vector c'_2 as follows (same size and same terms): for each term i in c_1 that exists in c_2, c'_{2i} keeps its TF_iIDF_i value. When a term i figuring in c_1 is not found in c_2 then c'_{2i} is set to zero. Next the similarity score between c_1 and c_2 is computed using the terms' discriminating power p_i according to Equation (4). It is important to stress that the score between c_1 and c_2 is not symmetric.

$$similarity(c_1, c'_2, p) = \frac{\sum_{i=1}^{|c_1|} c_{1i} \times c'_{2i} \times p_i}{|c_1|} \qquad (4)$$

In Equation 4, we compute the average quality of the terms inside the profiles, taking into account the discriminating power of each term. To increase the system performance we use only "good" discriminating terms, thus we have introduced an empirical threshold to avoid the influence of the poor ones. We consider terms having a p_i greater than or equal to 0.3, otherwise we arbitrarily set the p_i to zero.

4 Approach for Automatically Forming Teams

We use the technique presented in the previous section to develop a system able to identify people that may have the required competencies for a project. The inputs for

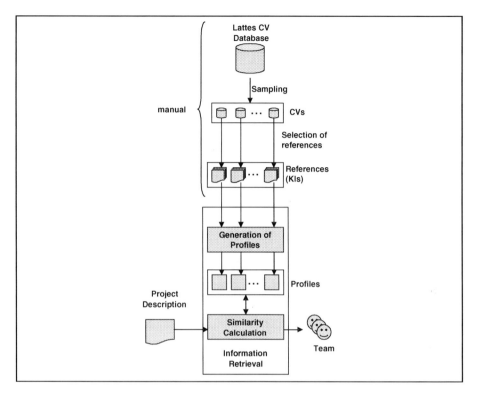

Fig. 1. System processing steps

the system are a project description and a set of *résumés* coming from the Lattes database. The output is a set of people that could form the team. Figure 1 shows the processing steps for the system.

In order to evaluate the proposed approach, we have selected *résumés* from a well-known Brazilian master course in Computer Science. For each *résumé*, we selected the 20 most important KIs according to the following priority: (i) publications in scientific journals, (ii) publications in books or book chapters, and (iii) publications in recent conferences.

A typical KI contains the following information: (i) authors, (ii) article or chapter title; (iii) journal title, book title or conference name; (iv) publishing company; (v) year of publication; (vi) keywords; (vii) knowledge areas; (viii) additional references; (ix) media. Such information follows a standard format specified by the Lattes database.

The choice of a specific master course facilitates the analysis of results because the course has three well-defined groups of research, each group with its own set of professors.

The project descriptions should be realistic and the involved teams should be known in advance in order to measure the quality of the results produced by our approach. Thus, we use the last 52 projects of master's dissertations written by the professors of the course. These projects are frequently multidisciplinary and may involve people from different groups of research. The description of each project consists of a less than 500 words text. The header of the text was not considered in order to introduce an extra difficulty to the classification task.

5 Experiments

The master program on Computer Sciences has 22 professors and 3 groups of research. For each professor 22 KIs were selected, and each KI was represented by a 500 terms vector.

The evaluation methodology compares the candidates (i.e. the potential team members) proposed by the system with the examiners of the Master's dissertation (i.e. the actual members of the project). Generally, there are three internal examiners, the advisor included, and one external. These three internal examiners give a strong indication of the professors who are interested or whose works are related with the project.

The evaluation uses two scores: FF (first-first) and AG (Advisor's Group). The FF score compares only the first candidate proposed by the system with the project manager (i.e. in our case, the advisor).

The AG score compares the team proposed by the system with the three groups of research. The AG score is higher when the system recovers people from the group of research of the advisor. Many times, people that are in the same group of research present similar profiles and even a human being would have difficulty in selecting one of them to a team. Thus, suggesting people that belong to the same group as members of a team seems a coherent alternative.

Table 1. Preliminary results

FF	AG
10/52 = 19,23%	39/52 = 75,00%

Our preliminary results (Table 1) show that the system is able to identify approximately 20% of the project managers (the advisors). The low value for the FF score is explained by the superposition of the research subjects, projects, and publications of people belonging to the different groups of research. People often work on the intersection of different themes what makes difficult to identify which of these subjects is more important for them.

On the other hand, the system has got a reasonable value for AG, demonstrating that the context of the project could be identified in the great majority of the projects. Despite the good preliminary results, we try to explain why the system fails for the 13 remaining cases.

Analyzing these cases, we remark that eight of them represent unusual situations that the system could not foresee adequately. These eight projects were qualified as innovation projects, and the advisor haven't had an important scientific production related to it. We can say that these projects represent new directions of research.

Therefore, it would be practically impossible to the system to foresee the advisor. Considering this, we revise the preliminary results of Table 1 by excluding these innovative projects. Revised results are shown in Table 2.

Table 2. Revised preliminary results

FF	AG
10/44 = 22,72%	39/44 = 88,63%

We have noticed a significant improvement in the results when the innovation projects had been excluded from the initial base of projects. Logically, a research institution has always some pioneering projects because it is essential for the research. Although this is not the objective of this work, the developed methodology allows these pioneering projects to be identified automatically, configuring itself as an important tool in the management of scientific politics in research programs.

6 Discussion

The Lattes database represents a rich source of information for the management of politics of incentive to the research. Despite this, few automatic mechanisms have been developed to explore this potential. Amongst the advantages of using the Lattes database is the standard format for describing the scientific production reducing the information noise. However, despite the effort of standardization of information in the Lattes system, many researchers have different interpretations for some inputs of the system. To make our approach more realistic and scalable, no pre-processing was done on the KIs extracted from the *résumés*.

Another possible source of noise is the use of an automatic translator from Portuguese to English used on the project abstracts. No post-processing was carried out on the text produced by the translator translator. Considering these sources of noise in the system, we believe that the results of our approach are satisfactory.

Although project management systems are capable of controlling temporal constraints, resources, scheduling and quality of tasks in projects, they fall in providing high level functionalities. Recently Artificial Intelligence has been successful exploited and tools based on Data Mining, Multi-Agent Systems and Knowledge Representation Approaches (Ontologies) are becoming common [4]. We believe that the Information Retrieval concepts discussed in this paper provide an important contribution in such a direction.

7 Conclusions

In this paper we have presented a methodology for discovering members of project teams. The discovering of the right skills in project teams is a challenge for any organization. A good choice for the work groups can reduce project risks, cost and guarantee a successful collaboration process.

In most cases, the group formation is based on the feeling of the project manager and/or organizational structure of the institution, which does not guarantee the best team. Although a successful collaboration process depends on subjective factors like confidence, friendship and other forms of interpersonal relationship, this research regards only professional aspects. This is a requirement for organizations like the CNPq where professional personnel is imperative.

The methodology has produced quite good results for the sample of *résumés* and projects used in the experiments. However many questions are open. We arbitrarily select 20 references for each researcher but why not use the entire *résumé*? Using the entire résumé could favor more experienced researchers but this could be a desired behavior! Most part of scientific articles is published in English, but the project descriptions were written in Portuguese, so English was chosen as target language. Manual translation could be more accurate but it is much more expensive too. Another important point is the size (the number of terms) of the candidate profiles. We have tested our approach varying the vector size from 200 to 5000, and the 500 terms vector has produced the best balance between the processing time and the quality of results.

References

1. Attaran, M., Nguyen, T.T.: Self-Managed Work Team. Industrial Management 41 (July/August 1999) 24
2. Elmuti, D.: Sustaining High Performance Through Self-Managed Work Teams. Industrial Management 41 (1999) 4-8
3. Enembreck, F., Barthès, J-P.: Agents for Collaborative Filtering. In: Klusch, M., Omicini, A., Ossowski, S., Laamanen, H. (eds.): Cooperative Information Agents VII. LNAI 2782 (2003) 184-191
4. Enembreck, F., Thouvenin, I., Abel, M.H., Barthès, J.P.: An Ontology-Based Multi-Agent Environment to Improve Collaborative Design. Proc. 6th International Conference on the Design of Cooperative Systems (COOP'04). Hyeres (2004) 81-89
5. Goller, C., Löning, J., Will, T., Wolf, W.: Automatic Document Classification: A thorough Evaluation of various Methods. IEEE Intelligent Systems 1(14) (2000) 75-87
6. Lattes. URL: http://lattes.cnpq.br
7. Moravic, M.: The Well-managed SMT. Management Review 87 (1998) 56-59
8. Duncan, W.R.: A Guide to the Project Management Body of Knowledge. PMI Publishing Division. North Carolina, USA (2005)
9. Salton, G.: Automatic Text Processing: The Transformations, Analysis, and Retrieval of Information by Computer. Addison-Wesley (1989)
10. Shankar, S., Karypis, G.: A Feature Weight Adjustment Algorithm for Document Categorization. Proc. SIGKDD'00 Workshop on Text Mining. Boston, MA (2000)
11. Scholtes, P.R., Joiner, B.L., Streibel B.J.: The Team Handbook. 2nd ed. Madison. Wisconsin: Oriel Incorporated (1996) 1-16
12. Tacla, C., Enembreck, F.: An Awareness Mechanism for Enhancing Cooperation in Design Teams. Proc. 9th International Conference on CSCW in Design. Coventry, UK (2005)
13. Yates, R.B., Ribeiro N.B.: Modern Information Retrieval. Addison-Wesley (1999)
14. Gaston, M., des Jardins, M.: Team formation in complex networks. Proc. 1st NAACSOS Conference (2003)

15. Gaston, M., des Jardins, M.: Agent-Organized Networks for Dynamic Team Formation, International Conference on Autonomous Agents. Proc. Fourth International Joint Conference on Autonomous Agents and Multi-Agent Systems (AAMAS) (2005) 230-237
16. Wang, W., Mogan, S.: Creating a Team Building Toolkit for Distributed Teams. Proc. 9th International Conference on CSCWD. Coventry, UK (2005) LNCS 3865 (2006) 1-10
17. Witten, I.H., Moffat, A., Bell T.C.: Managing Gigabytes: Compressing and Indexing Documents and Images. The Morgan Kaufmann Series in Multimedia and Information Systems (1997)

On Demand Consistency Control for Collaborative Graphics Editing Systems in Heterogeneous Environments

Bo Jiang[2], Jiajun Bu[1], and Chun Chen[1]

[1] College of Computer Science, Zhejiang University, Hangzhou, P.R. China
[2] College of Computer and Information Engineering,
Zhejiang Gongshang Unviersity, Hangzhou, P.R. China
{nancybjiang,bjj,chenc}@zju.edu.cn

Abstract. The wide availability of wireless devices has become one of the main challenges for designers of collaborative applications like collaborative graphics editing. Mobile devices are not as "standardized" as stationary computers but are much more diverse with respect to computing resources, connection bandwidth and display capabilities. In this paper, we present a semi-replicated architecture which supports multiple degrees of consistency maintenance for collaborative graphics editing systems in heterogeneous environments. To maintain consistency of the replicas on mobile embedded devices, either data consistency or semantic consistency is maintained based on the prediction of the regions of interest. The proposed on demand consistency maintenance scheme for mobile sites makes collaboration more efficiently. The scheme is realized in our prototype system of collaborative graphics editing system that can work well in heterogeneous environments.

1 Introduction

As one of the typical collaborative editing systems [1-3], collaborative graphics editing system (CGES) [4] enables distributed users to view and edit shared graphics documents at the same period of time. For years, CGES has been widely applied in the fields such as textile printing and weaving industry. Consistency has been widely studied in interactive groupware systems and lots of work has been done to design different types of algorithms or schemes to maintain consistency [1][5-7]. However, most of these systems are based on homogeneous computing environments, in which collaborative sites are characterized by similar computing capability, storage resources and network resources.

With the proliferation of connected devices based on platforms other than traditional desktop PCs and wireless network connections, mobile devices greatly facilitate the development of Computer-Supported Cooperative Work (CSCW) systems. With mobile networks and embedded devices people are able to participate in collaborative graphics editing sessions in ubiquitous heterogeneous environment.

Although exact replication of data is desirable to provide common grounding for collaboration in CGES, this is not feasible in heterogeneous environment, where

W. Shen et al. (Eds.): CSCWD 2006, LNCS 4402 , pp. 318–325, 2007.
© Springer-Verlag Berlin Heidelberg 2007

computing resources are limited, diverse, and variable. For example, storage capacity limits the graphics information that can be stored in the embedded sites, available network bandwidth and intermittent connection limits the amount of information that can be sent, computing power limits graphics processing and concurrency control efficiency. These constraints make it necessary to introduce a different collaborative model and consistency maintenance scheme.

In this paper, we present a semi-replicated architecture and an on demand consistency maintenance scheme for mobile devices to cooperate with desktops. We specify a scheme that can predict the regions of a shared collaborative document that mobile users may be interested in. If the operations that acted on the objects in regions of interest, they are pushed to the mobile sites. Otherwise, the operations are cradled on desktops until mobile user clicks on the region that composed of these objects. Before user pulls the detailed operations that related to the objects, the regions that are not of interest are kept semantic consistency.

The structure of this paper is as follows: Section 2 outlines the traditional replicated architecture and consistency maintenance of CGES. Also the characteristics of heterogeneous collaborative environments are analyzed. Section 3 presents the semi-replicated architecture in heterogeneous environments. Section 4 proposes Region of Interest prediction scheme that used to foresee which region will be most interested to the mobile users. Section 5 addresses the consistency maintenance scheme that designed to keep the replicas on mobile sites consistent with those on desktops. Finally, Section 6 presents conclusions of the paper.

2 Background

2.1 Traditional Replicated Architecture and Consistency Maintenance of CGES

In order to achieve high responsiveness, the replicated architecture is always adopted by former CGES. Main characteristics of the replicated architecture are as follows:

- Unconstrained editing: Multiple users are allowed to edit any part of the document concurrently and freely at any time.
- Replicated shared workspace: Users who participate in collaborative editing hold the replicas of the shared document.
- Broadcasted operations: Whenever an operation is issued by one of the collaborators, it is transmitted to all other sites. Each site maintains an operation queue that keeps all the operations that generated during a certain collaboration session.

For years, numerous researches have been done in maintaining consistency in CGES and consistency has become a broad concept with two important interpretations from the point of view of data integrity and semantic similarity [8]. Data integrity is a process-based approach for consistency, where data at collaborative sites are consistent if the operations executed on the data are up to date and executed in the same order. Semantic consistency deals with the heterogeneity that arises in the forms of naming conflicts, domain conflicts and structural conflicts. To maintain a certain degree of semantic consistency across collaborative sites requires a certain amount of system resources that might be unavailable or costly. Therefore, tradeoff between the degree of consistency with resources should be evaluated.

2.2 Characteristics of Heterogeneous Collaborative Environments

With the rapid development of mobile computing, there is a need for collaborative applications to adapt to the current new computing and communications environment. Such extension results in differences in information representations, GUI realization and collaborative behaviors when run on different platforms. The key characteristic of heterogeneous systems is that resources are heterogeneous and variable. The resources include display, communication bandwidth, CPU power, and memory of each collaborator may be quite different. Heterogeneities arise across all types of resources but it appears that network bandwidth, display and storage capabilities affect most to CEGS.

1. Display size and HCI mode: Display size on mobile devices is limited. And there are great difference in solution for human-computer interaction on desktop and palmtop computer. Mouse and keyboard designed for optimal efficiency in interacting with a computer, while styli and soft keyboards, have been used on mobile devices for their portability advantages. Therefore, the inefficiency of these input tools may make influence on collaboration behavior and somehow limit the capability of collaboration for palmtop computer holders.

2. Network connection: Abundant network resources are provided to the desktop computer by connecting to high speed networks. However, Low bandwidth wireless communication provides poor transfer speed and intermittent connection to mobile embedded collaborative sites. Network resources will sure make great influence on collaboration mode and related consistency control techniques.

Besides display size and network connection, storage is another key difference between a desktop computer and palmtop computer. Lots of mobile embedded sites have limited storage capability to cradle the whole documents.

3 Semi-replicated Architecture in Heterogeneous Environments

As CGES is characterized with variable resources that collaborative sites are in heterogeneous environments, full replicated architecture will never help to promote the efficiency of collaboration. Broadcasting each operation to other collaborators when it generated will obviously become a heavy burden for networks and intermittent connections of mobile sites may make great influence on the synchronization of shared documents. Saving the whole graphics documents with high resolution and operation queue may consume lots of storage resources. Therefore, we present a semi-replicated architecture. CGES enables both stationary sites and mobile ones to participate in the collaborative pattern design. Designers fulfill their editing job with PCs and wide width networks, whereas the main tasks for mobile embedded devices that connected to the system by wireless networks are to view the documents, add some annotations, and complete some simple editing jobs as needed.

As it is shown in Figure 1, exact replication of graphics document is cradled on a desktop computer. However, for the limited resources, mobile embedded site only holds parts of the document with high resolution which may be most interested to a certain collaborator. And also, only those operations that related to this sub-document are transmitted and stored on mobile sites. Therefore, to find the regions of interest (ROI) is a primary issue in maintaining the consistency in the semi-replicated architecture.

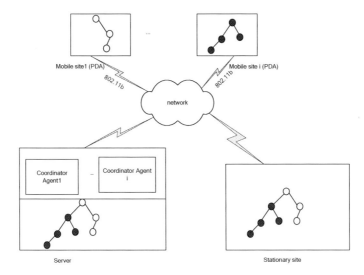

Fig. 1. Semi-replicated architecture

The graphic document can be separated into multiple drawing layers for the purpose to increase the parallelism of editing process. As the basic element of the document, drawing object can either be graphics such as rectangle, ellipse, free drawing line, image or text. When several drawing objects are bound together, drawing group is formed. Generally, operations that act on the drawing group influence all the related drawing objects.

4 Regions of Interest Prediction Scheme

While users are editing a shared document on mobile sites, the major task is to predict which region will be interested to users, and then transmit it with high resolution, but keep the others with low resolution. And also, operations that related to the drawing objects in this region are sent to mobile sites.

4.1 Key Features of Prediction

The highlighted parts are predicted based on several conditions (or attributes). As we know, time relativity and space relativity are usually referred to as important factors. In our scheme three compatible, applicable conditions are taken into account: control point location, control point history and working area. Control point is the location on the graphics document that user clicks.

Control point location attribute: User locates his control point at a position in the document, the position or those places around the position may attract the user's attention more. The attribute values are classified into {near, far}. The location attribute is set as {near} if the distance between edges of the square and the control point is less than 1/8 of diagonal of the screen; otherwise, it is set as {far}.

Control point history attribute: User clicks on the document for attention, comment or some other reasons, therefore, the clicked square is probably concerned by user. It is necessary to record the history of the clicked track. The attribute values are classified into {most recent, recent, none}. {most recent} for the square clicked most recently; {recent} for those clicked recently; {none} for no clicked record in the history list.

Working area: working area is indicated by administrator or user himself. It is an inherent duty or interest for user. Therefore, there is a close relation between user's interest and working area. The attribute values are classified into {in, edge, out}. {in} for the square within the working area; {edge} for the square that are at the edge of the working area; {out} for those out of the working area.

To find out which condition could contribute to our prediction most, we would like to evaluate the three conditions by a Rough Sets Based Prediction Scheme.

To collect supported source data for the Rough Sets Based Prediction Scheme, an experiment was carried out to get the practical return from users' activities.

Six volunteers (3 male, 3 female) from local University were invited to our lab. Four of them (2 male, 2 female) were major in computer science.

The experiment was conducted on Dell PC running simulator application, using a 17-inch monitor set to 1024x768 resolution, 256M memory and 2.4G CPU.

While volunteers were browsing a shared document, the simulator application recorded the track clicked by user's control point. We presented some questionnaires to them from time to time, asked them in which squares they were interested most for those squares would be transmitted with high resolution. Corresponding condition attributes were recorded by the simulator at the time the questionnaires were made respectively. The experiment took one hour and about 120 user's interest squares were caught for the calculation of the Rough Sets Based Prediction Scheme. By the end of the test, a number of questionnaires were collected and some random-selected data were to be analyzed.

Table 1. Condition analysis

| Fact | Condition Attributes | | | D Decision attribute |
	C1 Control point location	C2 Control point history	C3 Working area	
1	near	most recent	in	yes
2	far	none	out	no
3	far	most recent	out	yes
4	near	recent	out	no
5	far	none	out	no
6	far	none	in	no
7	far	recent	edge	yes
8	near	recent	in	no

If decision attribute is set as {yes}, it means that user is interested in the part. For the decision d = {yes, no}, Table 1 could be classified into two equivalent classes by decision attribute D: {x1, x3, x7} and {x2, x4, x5, x6, x8}. Discernibility matrix M is as follows:

$$
\begin{bmatrix}
\phi & \{c1,C2,c3\} & \phi & \{c2,c3\} & \{c1,c2,c3\} & \{c1,c2\} & \phi & \{c2\} \\
 & \phi & \{c2\} & \phi & \phi & \phi & \{c2,c3\} & \phi \\
 & & \phi & \{c1,c2\} & \{c2\} & \{c2,c3\} & \phi & \{c1,c2,c3\} \\
 & & & \phi & \phi & \phi & \{c1,c3\} & \phi \\
 & & & & \phi & \phi & \{c2,c3\} & \phi \\
 & & & & & \phi & \{c2,c3\} & \phi \\
 & & & & & & \phi & \{c1,c3\} \\
 & & & & & & & \phi
\end{bmatrix}
$$

Discernibility matrix and Core has the following relation: attribute c is the Core of condition attribute C and decision attribute D if and only if there exist i and j ($1<i<j<n$) such that $M_{ij} = \{c\}$. We can get the fact: there exist i = 4, j = 5 such that $M_{45} = \{c2\}$, therefore, the Core of Table 1 is $\{c2\}$.

In our prototype, control point history was selected as the most important factor that used to predict which part was most interested to the user.

4.2 Regions of Interest Prediction

To predict Regions of Interest (ROI), the 2D shared workspace is divided into M×N small rectangle grids, which is denoted as W[M][N]. An array is created and maintained by each collaborative session CFU[M][N]. CFU[M][N] denotes user U's clicking frequency on sub-workspace W[M][N].

For a given user U and Click Operation O that generated by U:

CFU[i][j]= CFU[i][j]+1, where i∈ [0, M-1], j∈ [0, N-1]

ROI= ∪ CF U[i][j], where i∈ [0, M-1], j∈ [0, N-1], CF U[i][j] > VU, VU is a particular value that set by the system.

5   Consistency Maintenance Scheme

In general, consistency can be classified into two categories: data integrity and semantic similarity. As for our semi-replicated architecture, data on mobile devices is synchronized by execute remote operations that generate in ROI and are pushed by the source sites or pulled by the mobile user. While semantic similarity is to keep the graphics documents' consistency at a coarse granularity level, especially regions that not in ROI.

5.1   Data Consistency Maintenance Scheme

As for object-based CGES, the operations that related to ROI are those acting on the objects of interest (OOI). ORS are the regions that objects covered and intersect with ROI. ORS donates the region that covered by the object.

ORS= ∪W[i][j], where i∈ [0, M-1], j∈ [0, N-1] and the object covers W[i][j] or intersects with W[i][j].

Consistency of mobile sites is maintained by pushing or pulling synchronized operations.

Push: when an operation related to OOI is generated, it is transmitted to the mobile sites and stores in the operation queue to refresh the view of mobile site.

Pull: when user clicks on the region that no precise information about the region is stored in the mobile sites, the request for the operations that related to this region will be broadcasted and the corresponding operations will be pulled from the original sites.

Mobile users mainly view the documents or add annotations and rarely edit the shared workspace or undo former operations. Therefore, certain kinds of operations can be incorporated to form a complex operation or be simplified.

- Do and Undo: This pair of operations can be omitted and there's no need to transmit them.
- Modify a certain attribute of an object several times: Transmit the last operation to the mobile sites.

By applying the above incorporation scheme, the operations that really need to be transmitted to mobile sites are greatly reduced.

5.2 Semantic Consistency Maintenance Scheme

As we know that the display size of mobile embedded devices is limited, those parts of patterns that are not in ROI only need semantic consistency maintenance. Semantic consistency can be maintained by displaying the major hue of that region or showing the mimic shapes of the exact objects. As it is shown in Figure 2, the ellipses in Figure 2(a) stand for flowers. When this part of region is not ROI, it is simplified as Figure 2(a) to be semantic consistent with the real pattern on PCs. Once the user clicks on them, the detailed operations that related to the ellipses can be pulled and data consistency is kept. After the detailed information is downloaded to the mobile sites, the ellipses are replaced by original flowers as shown in Figure 2(b).

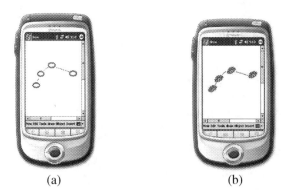

(a)   (b)

Fig. 2. Semantic consistency

6 Conclusions

Computing platforms are rapidly becoming more heterogeneous, primarily in terms of device capabilities: display characteristics, CPU speed, memory, and network connectivity. Small portable devices, such as handheld computers, smart phones and PDAs, are becoming popular means to access the Internet and participate into the collaborative graphics editing. However, the limitation of mobile embedded devices such as small screen size, low bandwidth network and intermittent connections makes it impossible for them to collaborate with desktops by former methods. To maintain the consistency of mobile sites to the stationary PCs, an on demand consistency maintenance scheme is presented. The graphics pattern is kept consistently on demand. Then the semi-replicated architecture and on demand consistency maintenance scheme has been tested in our prototype system and proved to be able to improve the cooperative capability and efficiency for mobile embedded devices.

Acknowledgments. This paper is supported by National Natural Science Foundation of China (60573176) and Zhejiang Provincial Natural Science Foundation of China under Grant No. Z603231.

References

1. Jiang, B., Chen, C., Bu, J.: CoDesign-A Collaborative Pattern Design System Based on Agent. Proceedings of the Sixth International Conference on Computer Supported Cooperative Work in Design. London, ON, CA (2001) 319-323
2. Newman-Wolfe R.E., Pelimuhandiram, H.K.: MACE: A Fine Grained Concurrent Editor. Proceedings of the ACM SIGOIS Conferecne on Organizational Computing Systems. Atlanta, Georgia (1991) 240-254
3. Ressel, M., Nitsche-Ruhland, D., Gunzenbauser, R.: An Integrating Transformation - Oriented Approach to Concurrency Control and Undo in Group Editors. Proceedings of ACM Conference on Computer Supported Cooperative Work (1996) 288-297
4. Sun, C. and Chen, D.: Consistency Maintenance in Real-Time Collaborative Graphics Editing Systems. ACM Transactions on Computer-Human Interaction 9(1) (2002) 1-41
5. Bilgin, A. and Marcellin, B.W.: JPEG2000: Highly Scalable Image Compression. In: Sayood, K. (eds): Lossless Compression Handbook. San Diego, CA: Elsevier (2003) 351–369
6. Adams, M. and Kossentini, F.: Reversible Integer-to-integer Wavelet Transforms for Images Compression: Performance Evaluation and Analysis. IEEE Trans. Image Processing 9 (2000) 1010-1024
7. Hornbaek, K. and Frokjaer, E.: Reading of Electronic Documents: The Usability of Linear, Fisheye, and Overview Detail Interfaces. Proc. ACM CHI. (2001) 293-300
8. Correa, C., Marsic, I., Sun, X.: Semantic Consistency Optimization in Heterogeneous Virtual Environment. CAIP-TR-267 (2002)

Towards an Emergence Approach to Software Systems Design

Mutaleci Miranda[1,2], Geraldo Xexeo[2,3], and Jano Moreira de Souza[2,3]

[1]Seção de Engenharia de Sistemas, Instituto Militar de Engenharia, Brazil
[2]Programa de Engenharia de Sistemas e Computação (COPPE),
Universidade Federal do Rio de Janeiro, Brazil
[3]Departamento de Ciência da Computação (IM),
Universidade Federal do Rio de Janeiro, Brazil
mmiranda@de9.ime.eb.br, xexeo@cos.ufrj.br, jano@cos.ufrj.br

Abstract. In this work, we propose a design approach which allows a large community of designers to collectively translate a set of requirement specifications into a complete design. Technically, emergence is a good way to build decentralized, fault-tolerant, scalable systems with acceptable overhead in network communication. This property makes the peer-to-peer paradigm a proper approach to build emergent systems. Hence, we have developed the COPPEER 2.0 framework, an environment for developing and running collaborative peer-to-peer applications which directly supports the main requirements elicited in our proposal.

1 Introduction

In this work, we propose an emergent system approach to allow a community to perform collective design of software systems. Emergent behavior appears when complex global behavior results, probably in an unexpected way, from the interaction of a great number of agents with different individual behaviors among themselves and with the environment. In our model, emergent design is the translation of an interrelated set of system requirements into a set of interrelated system element models performed by a great number of agents, subject to some conditions, such as no central coordination.

Technically, emergence is a good way to build decentralized, fault-tolerant, scalable systems with acceptable overhead in network communication. This property makes the peer-to-peer paradigm a proper approach to build emergent systems. Hence, we have developed the COPPEER 2.0 framework, an environment for developing and running collaborative peer-to-peer applications which directly supports the main requirements elicited in our proposal.

The remainder of this work is organized as follows. In the next section, we present some relevant emergence principles. In Section 3, we describe our emergent design model. In Section 4, we propose an illustrative example of an emergent design tool. In Section 5, we present the COPPEER framework. In Section 6, we discuss some guidelines to use COPPEER in the implementation of emergent design tools. In Section 7, we point out some related work and finally, in Section 8, we conclude and discuss some open issues.

W. Shen et al. (Eds.): CSCWD 2006, LNCS 4402 , pp. 326–334, 2007.
© Springer-Verlag Berlin Heidelberg 2007

2 Emergence

Emergent systems, also referred to as Complex Adaptive Systems (CAS), are composed of a great number of agents which can interact with one another and with an environment in such a way that system functions may be accomplished despite some degree of individual agent failures and unexpected environmental changes. A number of examples of natural CAS can be seen in [5]. The term *emergent* is an abbreviation for emergent behavior. This indicates that there are non-trivial relationships among individual element behaviors and the global system behavior.

Emergent systems are *stigmergic* and *heterarchical*. A system is said to be stigmergic if communication among its elements is mediated by an environment. Heterarchical systems are characterized by the fact that any element can influence any other element behavior according to circumstantial system needs, in contrast with hierarchical systems, in which the set of elements is partitioned in ordered levels and the behavior of each element is controlled by a fixed element from a higher level.

A peer-to-peer system can be modeled as a CAS in a very straight way: the network of peers represents the environment; programs and people that modify the state of the environment represent system agents. However, system designers must be careful with the properties of the emergent approach. First, stigmergic communication demands what we will refer to as *data bounding* principle: there must exist equilibrium among the amount of data generated by agents, the storing and propagation capacity of the environment and the processing capacity of receiving agents. Similarly, the heterarchy principle raises the need for a proper system topology. To potentially influence any other agent in the system, an agent should be able to traverse paths or propagate data to any peer in the network. An approach to efficiently achieve that is presented in Section 6.

3 Emergent Design Model

We define emergent design as the translation of an interrelated set of system requirements into a set of interrelated system element models, performed by a great number of agents with no direct communication, central coordination or global knowledge. Let R be the set of all possible requirements expressed in a given requirement language and $M \subset R$, the set of all possible model elements expressed in a given modeling language. A design is represented by a tuple $D = (S, I)$ where:

- $S \subset R$ is a set of specifications;
- I is a set of directed links of the form $(x \in S\text{-}M, y \in S)$ or $(x \in S \cap M, y \in S \cap M)$, representing that the specification x cites the specification y.

From the definition of R and M one can notice that the modeling language is a specialization of the requirement language. Hence, the first statement declares that we consider that combinations of requirements and model elements can represent a design, ranging from the initial requirement specifications to the completed design composed only of model element specifications. The second statement, in turn, claims that a requirement specification can cite an element model specification, but an element model specification can only cite another element model.

Agents must perform a sequence of operations on initial requirement specifications to derive a completed design. These operations must generate only syntactically and semantically correct designs. Syntactic correctness is assured by not creating links from model elements to requirements. Semantic correctness, in turn, is assured by the following rule: if a link from a specification *x* to a specification *y* is replaced by a link from *x* to a specification *z*, then *z* must be an *extension* of *y*, that is, the original meaning of *x* must be preserved in the operation. A detailed definition of allowed design operations in our model is provided in the following paragraphs.

Let *A* be a set of agents and $T = A^*$ the set of all subsets of *A*. The allocation of a design is a function $t:S{\rightarrow}T$ which maps each specification of a design into a team of responsible agents. If a team of agents is responsible for a specification, it is allowed to perform operations for partitioning, merging, relocating and translating the corresponding design and its allocation.

The *partitioning* operation replaces a specification *s* by a set *P* of interrelated specifications from the same type (requirement or model element) of *s*, and all links involving *s* by links involving some *P* member in the same direction. The team becomes responsible for the *P* members;

The *merging* operation replaces a set *P* of interrelated specifications from the same type by a specification *s* and all links involving some *P* member by links involving s in the same direction. The team becomes responsible for *s;*

The *relocation* operation passes the responsibility for a specification to another team of agents, changing the allocation of the design;

The *translation* operation replaces a requirement specification *r1* by a model element specification *m1* and all links involving *r1* by links involving *m1*. Furthermore, if a requirement specification *r2 is* cited by *r1*, the operation will create an element model *i(r2)* to be cited by *m1* in place of *r2*, and a citation from *r2* to *i(r2)*, which claims that its translation has to be an extension of *i(r2)*. The team becomes responsible for both *m1* and *i(r2)*. If *r2* is translated by another team into a model element *m2* in parallel to the creation of *i(r2)*, then this team must create an additional element model *a(m2)* to extend *i(r2)* and cite *m2* in place of *m1*, as depicted in Figure 1.

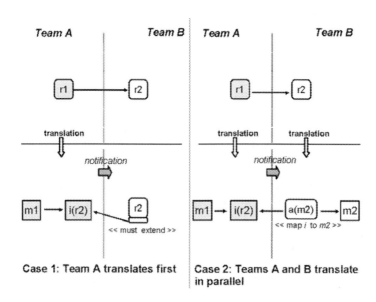

Case 1: Team A translates first
Case 2: Teams A and B translate in parallel

Fig. 1. Translation operation

As we have defined all operations in terms of teams, agents in a team need to communicate among themselves to perform these operations collectively or to elect an agent to work on behalf of the whole team. Furthermore, an operation on a specification may imply replacing or inclusion of citations in other specifications controlled by other teams. Hence, communicating among agents from different teams may be needed too. In emergent systems, both aforementioned situations involve stigmergy: information on operations has to be put in a supporting environment to be retrieved by any interested agent. In Section 6, we will explain how that can be accomplished by COPPEER.

4 Illustrative Example: UML Tool for Emergent Design

In this section, we present a simplistic example to clarify the model presented in Section 3. The requirement language is natural language and the modeling language is some textual notation equivalent to the UML class model. Hence, we can consider the modeling language as a specialization of the requirement language. Agents are human designers who use workstations connected to a common computer network. Each one joins one or more teams which, in turn, are responsible for one or more specifications.

The tool offers as support for team operations an Emergent Electronic Brainstorming System (EEBS) and a voting system. The EEBS maintains the workstation of each agent in a team connected to n neighbors on average, where n should be a small number to respect the data bounding principle. Every agent receives a specification and is asked to register in the system a proposal operation. After that, each agent reads the proposal of her neighbors, analyzes them and updates her own proposal in the system. This updating phase is repeated several times.

The expected result is the emergence of a few good proposals spread over the system in slightly different versions. Then, the voting system allows agents to browse and to vote for proposals, and applies the winning proposal to the specification. Finally, the tool notifies teams responsible for related specifications in order to allow modifications in citations.

A simplified example of requirement specification in natural language is shown in Table 1 and a possible transformation in a completed design is depicted in Figure 2. The specification corresponds to a description of a library loan log and is initially allocated to a team named *teamA*.

Table 1. Initial requirement specification

Name	*Team*	*Content*
Library loan log description	*TeamA*	"... the log registers all books each person has already loaned ... a person is described by name, address,... a book is described by title, author, ..."

After *teamA* agents agree on performing a partitioning and a relocation, the resulting design is composed of a *log description*, a *person description* and a *book description* allocated respectively to *teamA*, a second team, *teamB* and a third team, *teamC*,

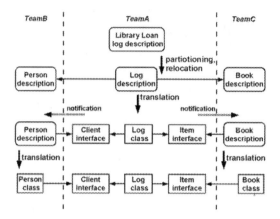

Fig. 2. Example operations

as shown in Table 2, which presents citations underlined, as do the subsequent tables. In the following step, *teamA* agents agree on performing a translation, replacing *log description* by three element models: *log class*, *client interface* and *item interface*. *TeamB* and *TeamC* are notified to add citations in person description and book description respectively. The result is shown in Table 3. Finally, *TeamB* e *TeamC* agents agree on performing translations generating the element models *person class* and *book class* respectively, shown in Table 4.

Table 2. Partitioning and relocation result

Name	*Team*	*Content*
Log description	*TeamA*	"... the log registers all <u>books</u> each <u>person</u> has already loaned."
Person description	*TeamB*	"... a person is described by name, address,..."
Book description	*TeamC*	"... a book is described by title, author, ..."

Table 3. Log description translation result

Name	*Team*	*Content*
Log class	*TeamA*	Class Log{ <u>Item</u> logItem; <u>Client</u> logClient; ... }
Client Interface	*TeamA*	Interface Client{...}
Item Interface	*TeamA*	Interface Item {...}
Person description	*TeamB*	"... a person is described by name, address, ... must extend <u>Client</u>"
Book description	*TeamC*	"... a book is described by title, author, ... must extend <u>Item</u>"

Table 4. Person and book translation result

Name	Team	Content
Person class	*TeamB*	Class Person implements Client{String name; String address ... }
Book class	*TeamC*	Class Book implements Item{String title; String author ... }

5 The COPPEER 2.0 Framework

COPPEER is a research project in progress at the Database Laboratory of the Federal University of Rio de Janeiro Graduate School and Research in Engineering (COPPE/UFRJ). The first version of COPPEER was conceived as a peer-to-peer framework to support grid computing architectures such as the Open Grid Services Architecture (OGSA) [1]. Currently, COPPEER 2.0 project goal is the implementation of a framework for developing and running collaborative peer-to-peer applications under a complex adaptive system paradigm. The global architecture of COPPEER 2.0 is composed of four layers:

- *agency layer*: performs generic P2P computations to attend needs of other layers;
- *integration layer*: encompasses application location, session management and high-level distributed computing paradigms;
- collaboration layer: handles cooperation, coordination and communication issues;
- *application layer*: is composed by user applications.

We have developed Java implementation for the agency layer as a runtime environment for complex adaptive systems named CoppeerCAS. The main entity in CoppeerCAS is the *agency*. When CoppeerCAS is started in a peer, an agency is created to manage environments, cells and agents on behalf of applications.

An *environment* is a set of interconnected cells. An agency can participate in many environments simultaneously, but can manage only one cell per environment. So, a cell is unambiguously identified by its agency and its environment.

A *cell* is a shared space based on the JavaSpace specification [3], which offers its clients an interface containing operations to write and read entries, subscribe for notification about the writing of entries containing specified data and establish or terminate connections to other known cells.

A client of a cell can be an agent or any application object. A leasing mechanism is employed to control for how much time a cell will be able to attend a client requisition. When a client wants to store an entry, it specifies an intended lease duration. Then, cells use application-specific LeaseStrategy objects to determine effective lease durations.

An *entry* is a data object which can, when stored in a cell, continuously propagate data to neighbor cells and change its own internal state. Application developers may create entries with desired rules of propagation by implementing a set of propagation cycle methods.

An *agent* is a piece of software associated with an environment which accesses cells and moves across agencies to perform distributed computations. Agents can create new agents, move from the current agency to an agency containing a neighbor cell in its environment and access the interfaces of the current cell and neighbor cells. In order to determine the behavior of agents, application developers should create a behavior object, implement methods which will be invoked when relevant events such as creating, moving or cell notification occur, and pass the object to the agency during agent creation.

An *agency* is composed of an agent manager, a cell pool and a connection manager. The agent manager is the component which effectively handles execution and mobility of agents. The cell pool manages creation of cells and controls application access to them. The connection manager handles links between cells and other objects needed to exchange data between agencies.

6 Implementing Emergent Design Tools with COPPEER

In the following paragraphs, we will explain in general terms how COPPEER features can be used to implement the emergent design model described in Section 3.

Each team can have its own COPPEER environment to handle its specifications. A specification can be stored as an entry in one cell of the environment and replicated in other cells through the propagation mechanism to decrease search time and increase system availability. In order to allow fast information dissemination in a team, a topology manager application can be employed to maintain a small-world topology in each environment.

The topology manager can be an implementation of the distributed version of the Watts-Strogatz small-network generation method [6], which we have presented in [7]. In this implementation, each cell must store an entry containing a randomly chosen position on an imaginary ring, and each node must dispatch random walker agents to discover appropriate neighbors over the network. A visiting walker agent reads the current node's position to compare to its sender position and decides if that node is near to its sender on the imaginary ring. The small-world topology is achieved by connecting many pairs of close cells and a few pairs of distant cells on the ring.

In the presence of proper topologies for team environments, mechanisms for team coordination can be implemented with basic COPPEER features. The EEBS described in Section 4, for example, can be composed of writing and reading interfaces to human agents. The writing interface stores each agent proposal as an entry in the local cell. The reading interface just reads all neighborhood proposals and presents them to the human agent when required. The voting system, in turn, can rely on the propagation mechanism to elect a proposal and an agent to perform the corresponding operation in the specification.

As an operation can imply modifications in specifications located in different environments, a global environment must encompass agents from all teams. Whenever an agent performs an operation, she must store an entry describing the operation in her cell in the global environment. Then, the global environment will propagate that entry and all agents who had subscribed to events in that specification will be notified. In order to allow for correctness of designs after operations, agents must subscribe to the global environment for events in specifications which are replicated on a local cell, cite a specification on a local cell, are cited by a specification on a local cell.

7 Related Work

Approaches for coordinating a great number of people in very complex projects are a subject in the collaborative design area. In [8] we can find a modeling similar to our emergent design modeling. However, that work focuses on negotiating to conciliate choices of agents responsible for interdependent subsystems. In its proposal, negotiations must be mediated by experienced agents and can take several iterations. In our proposal, negotiating is restricted to team members working in the same subsystem through a stigmergic brainstorming mechanism. Conciliation between interdependent subsystems is achieved through cooperation, that is, agents make efforts to build proper interfaces to subsystems designed by other agents. Information needed for cooperation is also exchanged through stigmergy.

Anthill [4] is a framework for developing P2P applications similar to CoppeerCAS. However, Anthill does not implement agent-independent data propagation. The TOTA middleware [2] offers stigmergic coordination for agents through a simple API designed from scratch. As TOTA project is mainly devoted to mobile ad-hoc networks, it doesn't explore small-world topologies.

8 Final Remarks

We have described a model for emergent design, and presented an infrastructure to build peer-to-peer collaborative applications which is well-suited for implementing the model. In the current implementation, a COPPEER environment is a set of interconnected shared memories. If an agent located in a given cell needs to be notified of an event that occurred in an unknown cell, the developer must implement an ad-hoc procedure exploring the propagation mechanism. Future implementation of the integration layer will provide general-purpose abstractions which will allow agents to treat environments as a unified shared memory. Furthermore, the implementation of the market layer will simplify management of agent teams.

Some other steps needed in our research to increase the applicability of the presented approach are the implementation of security and privacy capabilities in CoppeerCAS and the refinements in the emergent design model to comprehend physical requirements such as time constraints.

References

1. Xexeo, G., Vivacqua, A., Souza, J.M., Braga, B., D'Almeida, J.N., Almentero, B.K., et al.: COE: A collaborative ontology editor based on a peer-to-peer framework. Advanced Engineering Informatics 19(2) (2005) 113-121
2. Mamei, M. and Zambonelli, F.: Programming stigmergic coordination with the TOTA middleware. Proc. 4th International Symposium on Adaptive Agents and Multi-Agent Systems (AAMAS). Leeds, UK (2005) 415-422
3. SUN Microsystems: JavaSpaces Service Specification (2002) URL: http://www.sun.com/software/jini/specs/js1_2_1.pdf

4. Babaoglu, O., Meling, H. and Montresor, A.: Anthill: A Framework for the Development of Agent-Based Peer-to-Peer Systems. Proc. 22th International Conference on Distributed Computing Systems (2002) 15-22
5. Parunak, V.: Go to the Ant: Engineering Principles from Natural Agent Systems. Annals of Operations Research 75(1997) 69-101
6. Watts, D.J. and Strogatz, S.H.: Collective dynamics of "small-world" networks. Nature 393 (1998) 440-442
7. Miranda, M. and Xexeo, G.: A complex adaptive system approach for agent-based peer-to-peer collaborative applications. Proc. 4th Workshop de Teses e Dissertações em Bancos de Dados. Uberlândia, Brazil (2005)
8. Klein, M., Faratin, P., Sayama, H. and Bar-Yam, Y.: Protocols for Negotiating Complex Contracts. IEEE Intelligent Systems Journal 18(6) (2003) 32-38

Research of Application Modes of
Parts Library System

Yong Lu[1], Yingguang Li[2], and Wenhe Liao[2]

[1] Dept. of Mechanical Engineering, Nanjing Institute of Technology,
Nanjing 211167, P.R. China
luyong@njit.edu.cn
[2] College of Mechanical & Electrical Engineering,
Nanjing University of Aeronautics and Astronautics,
Nanjing 210016, P.R. China
{welcome.li, njwho}@nuaa.edu.cn

Abstract. Concurrent Engineering, Collaborative Design and Network Manufacturing have higher demands for parts library to share information in and among enterprises. However, various enterprises have distinctive requirements for parts library information sharing. Based on the study of the diverse parts library application status, a Parts Library Application Level Model (PL-ALM) is put forward. Firstly, the definition of PL-ALM is given. Secondly, contents of the four layers of PL-ALM are expatiated in detail, which are geometry layer, system layer, neutral layer and network layer. Thirdly, in order to upgrade parts libraries on different layers gradually, a step-up solution is provided to aiming at single geometry information, multi-view information, heterogeneous information and distributed information respectively. According to the PL-ALM, evaluation software is developed, which standardizes and advances the application level of parts library of enterprises.

1 Introduction

As common resource, web-based parts library (PLIB) is important to Concurrent Engineering, Collaborative Design and Network Manufacturing. However, different enterprises have their own particular CAD application levels and specific requirements. For example, medium and small sized enterprises emphasis on getting rid of 2D drawing boards, while virtual enterprises are engaged in collaborative design and manufacturing in distributed environment. Various application modes of PLIB systems exist, which consequently determine enterprises' individual investments and cost. According to the types of enterprises, the applications modes of parts library systems are summarized as follows:

(1) Design-oriented enterprise
  With popularization of computers, design-oriented enterprise improves development of products using advanced CAD technologies. Parts library systems of design-oriented enterprise should express parts geometric model in digital information in order to meet the requirements of products geometric modeling.

W. Shen et al. (Eds.): CSCWD 2006, LNCS 4402 , pp. 335–346, 2007.
© Springer-Verlag Berlin Heidelberg 2007

(2)   Enterprise orienting design and manufacturing

At present, many design and manufacturing oriented enterprises has turned serial product development process into current process through implementing computer integrated manufacturing system (CIMS). In order to assure one-off success of product design and manufacturing, all resources in enterprises are integrated and production starts at the moment of design process. PLIB system for these enterprises should provide part information model to ensure consistency, uniquity and share of part information so that individual application systems can access and integrate the required information from the sole part information model.

(3)   Enterprise orienting complex products design and manufacturing

Enterprise orienting complex products design and manufacturing may use different CAD systems for different product life-cycle stages (e.g. design, analysis, manufacturing). This frequently happens in practice, because a large company often buys different systems on the basis of their particular strengths in specific application areas. Catalogues of part usage are established in these enterprises, based on which a common PLIB system is provided in order to realize parts library information sharing among heterogeneous CAD systems.

(4)   Virtual enterprise

Collaborative design and manufacturing among virtual enterprises has become one of the advanced manufacturing modes in the 21st century. Virtual enterprise is a dynamic alliance, of which every single company is a key segment of the entire production chain. Taking information integration among enterprise, parts manufacturer and supplier into account adequately, PLIB systems orienting virtual enterprise should follow uniform structure and characteristic information of parts so as to realize information integration and share among the virtual enterprises and collaboration of enterprises and suppliers over Internet.

Researches about parts library have been hotspots [2][5][8][12] and International Standard Organization has issued ISO 13584 Standard [3]. Most of these studies emphasize particularly on perfect architecture and representation mechanism of PLIB systems. However, there are few studies about practical application modes and methods of upgrading application level of the existing PLIB systems of enterprises. Separation between ideal theory researches and practical application requirements and modes makes enterprises have difficulties in applying and improving parts library system effectively. Based on above discussion, Parts Library Application Level Model (PL-ALM) is put forward in order to guide enterprises evaluate their own parts library application level and solve the key problems in application. Following the stepped evolution frame in PL-ALM, enterprises can improve PLIB systems gradually, upgrade application level of PLIB and provide foundation for collaborative design and network manufacturing ultimately.

2   PL-ALM Proposal

A perfect parts library system should possess the following four capabilities: digital representation of parts geometric model, multi-view expression of parts information, exchange of parts information among heterogeneous systems and integration and share of distributed parts information, which are accordance with the application requirements of different enterprises for their own parts library systems [4][7].

(1) Digital representation of parts geometric model

Geometric model has evolved from 2-dimensional drawing, 3-dimensional wireframe model, surface model and solid model. Parts information expressed by solid model can realize parametric digital representation of part geometric model, which will consequently improve product quality, reduce product cost and shorten production cycle.

(2) Multi-view expression of parts information

Part geometric model only consists of geometric information but the engineering information required in the development process of products. Representation of part information should satisfy requirements of all processes from design to manufacturing in order to solve information incompleteness. Moreover, engineers in different fields have different viewpoints even to the same parts. For example, draftsman concerns the 2-dimensional drafts, analyst cares for stress figures and warehouseman wants to know information about stocks, as shown in Figure 1. Therefore part information should be described in an abstract method so that it can be turned into special information for some particular field according to the corresponding mapping algorithms.

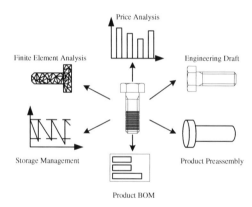

Fig. 1. Multi-view expression of parts information

(3) Exchange of parts information among heterogeneous systems

Nowadays, different CAD systems often coexist in an enterprise, which leads to the called Information Isolated Island. It is difficult to share information of parts library in enterprise. In order to solve the above problem, a general format of data file should be generated to integrate parts information represented in different CAD systems and ensure products information complete and consistent. Using the neutral mechanism and corresponding information interfaces is one of the feasible methods to represent, exchange and integrate parts information among heterogeneous systems. Shown in Figure 2, part information can be transformed into neutral files, which is then analyzed and transformed into the files identified by another CAD system by a post processor. So data exchange can be realized among different CAD systems.

(4) Integration and share of distributed parts information

Due to the advanced communication technology, the time of global manufacturing is coming. It has been a trend to share design information among different designers

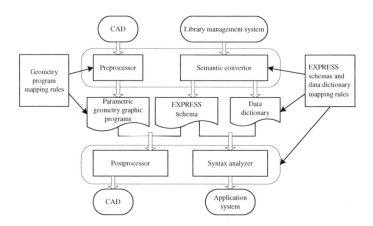

Fig. 2. Part information exchange principle among heterogeneous systems

and integrate product resources among suppliers and enterprises by Internet. Distributed technology makes it possible for users to share design results and collaborate in network environments. That is to say, appropriate person can get appropriate information at appropriate time.

Based on above requirements, the Parts Library Application Level Model (PL-ALM) is raised. PL-ALM takes capability evaluation items as the necessary conditions to achieve an application level. One capability evaluation item consists of several capability evaluation specifications. Through assessing the capability evaluation items and relevant capability evaluation specifications, parts library application level (the highest level that the company can achieve at that time) can be determined.

Definition 1. Parts Library Application Level Model (PL-ALM): PL-ALM refers to a set of modes for managing, improving and appraising parts library application level, which is put forward based on respective requirements, application status of individual company as well as knowledge and experience accumulated during the development process of the parts library system.

Definition 2. Capability evaluation item: Capability evaluation items refer to all noticeable aspects when upgrading application level of parts library system, each of which consists of a series of capability evaluation specifications.

Definition 3. Capability evaluation specification: Capability evaluation specification refers to the concrete and un-subdivided objectives constituting a capability evaluation item. Evaluation formulas in PL-ALM are expressed as following:

$$AL_p[i] = \sum_{j=1}^{N_p[i]} \{1 \,|\, G_p[i,j] = 4 \vee G_p[i,j] = 1\} \cdot \tag{1}$$

$$PAL = \max\{i \,|\, AL_p[i] \ge k \times N_p[i]\} \ . \tag{2}$$

$i = 1,2,3,4 \quad j = 1,2,3,...$

k : Level Evaluation Coefficient

G_p : Score of capability evaluation specification

N_p : Total number of capability evaluation specification

AL_p : Passed capability evaluation specification

PAL : Parts library application level

The possible values and the corresponding meanings of G_p are shown in Table 1.

Table 1. Mark criterion for capability evaluation specification

G_p	Meaning
4	Eligibility
3	Ineligibility
2	Inapplicability
1	Uncertainty

3   PL-ALM Contents

Four application levels of parts library of enterprises are established following a stepped evolution frame in PL-ALM (see Figure 3). The first level is geometry level, which regulates the basic demands for a parts library system from the points of view of geometric modeling and geometric information. The geometry level also can be considered as the static specifications that any parts library system should achieve at least. Every level in PL-ALM provides foundations for the next level above it and is distinguished from each other by continuous betterments. Skips of multi-levels are forbidden, which also embody dynamic and continuity of different levels in PL-ALM.

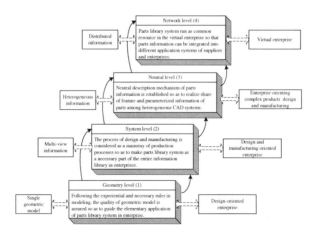

Fig. 3. Stepped configuration of PL-ALM

3.1 Geometry Level

Geometry level is at the bottom of PL-ALM, the aim of which is to satisfy basic requirements of an enterprise for the parts library system. Geometry level emphasizes on defining parts geometric information by means of geometric modeling. Nowadays 3D geometric modeling systems with powerful parametric design provide approaches for transformation and reuse of part model, which advances productive efficiency greatly and has a good effect on the wide application of PLIB systems. The two basic representation forms of parameterization are constraint-based model and history-based model [6]. Thereby parameterization of part geometric model should be verified from the above two aspects. Besides, for those medium and small sized enterprises where 2D drawings are considered as evidences in production, the drafting module in the parts library system should strictly follow relevant CAD drafting standards. Three capability evaluation items and the corresponding capability evaluation specifications are shown in Figure 4.

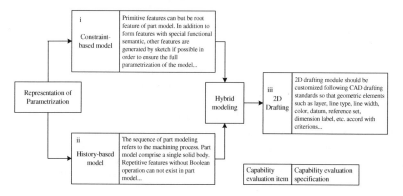

Fig. 4. Geometry level of PL-ALM (*note: capability evaluation items marked as i, ii, iii*)

3.2 System Level

From the point of view of information, parts library system comprises part geometry and topology information for product design as well as information of material and cost for the product lifecycle. The characteristics of parts library system at system level are as follows (Table 2): (1) Integrality: All part data involved constitutes logic units, and then information at various abstract hierarchies can be described and organized effectively. (2) Consistency: Part data can be represented by consistent and abstract means interiorly in favor of different application systems accessing and sharing information. (3) Multi-view: Part information can be described in many formats exteriorly in order to generate particular part views for different users.

Parts library at system level emphasizes more on configuration and structure of parts information. Based on an existing parts library system at geometry level, it is potential to advance the parts library system at geometry to that at system level by supplying the necessary parts information and organizing parts information in an effective organization mode. Parts library information at system level can be organized in diverse modes, such as objective characteristic table [1] or chained database [10].

Table 2. System level of PL-ALM

Capability evaluation item	Description of capability evaluation specification
Integrality	Geometric features, functional attributes, structural attributes, interrelation attributes, and so on, resident in PLIB system ensure that information can be used properly in the process of design, analysis, planning, manufacturing, assembly and inspection...
Consistency	Part CAD model constructed in a concept of master model can be used by other applications, such as drafting, analysis, simulation, assembly and manufacturing, which ensures inter-relationship of master model and other applications...
Multi-view	Integrated with the activities of management in enterprise, PLIB system provides part technical information for designer, real-time information for manager, inventory information for buyer...

3.3 Neutral Level

Based on a particular CAD system, information of parts library cannot be exchanged between CAD systems due to incompatibility of each other, which in turn results in poor transplant of parts library. Part information, especially information involved with the particular CAD system, should be expressed by a neutral mechanism in order to share information between heterogeneous CAD systems. Furthermore, distinguished from product, there are various kinds of parts and parts of the same kind have similar shapes with different dimensions. So the neutral representation mechanism should solve the problem of iterative storage of abundant characteristic data so as to decrease data redundancy. Information of parts library at neutral level should be organized and managed fully and abstractly from the point of methodology. Generally, capability evaluation items of a systemic parts library comprise description of part information and representation of part geometric model.

Description of part and its characteristic data of parts library at neutral level should be standardized. Parts with the same or similar characteristics forming a class, parts library information model can be created by the object-oriented method according to the hierarchical structure of parts class. The description of part information should accord with the following formal expressions:

Definition 4. Part class, marked with Π, can be represented as a binary combination (G, A), in which G represents geometric information of part class and A represents other information of part class. Then Π is referred as Part Family.

Definition 5. A collection of all instances of part family Π is referred as domain of Π, marked as $INS(\Pi)$ or $\{ins_1(\Pi), ins_2(\Pi), ...ins_n(\Pi)\}$. The relationship between any instance of part family and part family itself is defined as is-instance-of. Then the above description can be noted as $ins_i(\Pi) \overset{ins}{\in} \Pi, 1 \leq i \leq n$.

Definition 6. Hypothesizing part family Π, Π_0, Π_1 , the formula of $(\Pi_1 \subseteq \Pi_0) \wedge \forall [(\Pi \neq \Phi \wedge \Pi \subset \Pi_0) \to (\Pi \not\subset \Pi_0 - \Pi_1)]$ is certain, that is to say, Π_0 inherits Π_1 singly, which can be represented as $\Pi_0 \overset{1}{\subseteq} \Pi_1$ where Π_0 is part child family and Π_1 is part parent family.

Property 7. Hypothesizing $n > 2$ and part families $\Pi_1, ..., \Pi_n$, if the formula of $\forall i \forall j [(1 \leq i, j \leq n \wedge i \neq j) \wedge (\Pi_i \subseteq \Pi_0 \wedge \Pi_j \subseteq \Pi_0) \wedge \Pi_i \neq \Pi_j]$
$\to \Pi_i \overset{1}{\subseteq} \Pi_j \vee \Pi_j \overset{1}{\subseteq} \Pi_i$ is true, then the relationship between part child family and part parent family are impossible to be multi-inheritance.

Definition 8. Hypothesizing $n \geq 1$, part families $\Pi_0, \Pi_1, ... \Pi_n$ and the corresponding instances of every part family noted as I_k, that is $I_k \in INS(\Pi_k), k = 1, 2, ... n$, if the formula of $\forall k [(1 \leq k \leq n) \to \Pi_0 \subseteq \Pi_k] \wedge \forall i \forall j [(1 \leq i, j \leq n \wedge i \neq j)] \to (I_i \cap I_j = \Phi)$ is true, then a called is-a inheritance relationship exists between Π_0 and $\Pi_1, \Pi_2, ... \Pi_n$, which can be expressed as $\Pi_0 \overset{a}{\subseteq} \Pi_k, k = 1, 2, ... n$.

Definition 9. Hypothesizing part families $\Pi_1, \Pi_2, ... \Pi_n$, if the formula of $\forall i (1 \leq i \leq n) \to \exists \Pi = (ins_{i_1}(\Pi_1), ins_{i_2}(\Pi_2), ... ins_{i_n}(\Pi_n))$ is true, then Π is a part family and a called is-part-of relationship between Π and $\Pi_1, \Pi_2, ... \Pi_n$ exists.

Representation of part geometric model provides a parametric description mechanism of shape for different parts belonging to the same part family. The geometric representation model should meet the following formalized expressions:

Property 10. Hypothesizing part family Π , the formula of $\forall i (1 \leq i \leq n) \to R(ins_i(\Pi)) = (F, P)$ is certain, that is to say, geometric model of any part can be represented as a binary combination. In the formula, R represents the geometr[ic model of the part belonging to part family Π , F represents overall shape description of part family and P represents a set of parameters for describing the part.

Property 11. The overall shape description of a part family can be defined as a localized function $f : P \mapsto R$. That is to say, the mechanism of generating actual shape is determined by the overall description of parts family and a set of specified parameter values.

Since independence between non-geometric information and particular CAD system has been considered when establishing parts library at system level, the keys to develop parts library at neutral level are establishing neutral representation mechanisms to describe part geometric information and developing transfer interfaces of geometric information accordant with those mechanisms so that part geometric model can be exchanged by means of particular neutral programs. An in-depth discussion of developing transfer interfaces of geometric information can be found in Reference 13. All these are also key points of enhancing parts library from system level to neutral level.

3.4 Network Level

With the development of the technologies of information and network, the requirements of enterprises are continuously heightening. Developing parts library system in network to access information and resources in a wide range of environments has become the important task encountering enterprises. Parts library system in network should take place of product catalogues and integrate with supply chain management system so as to realize the share of distributed part information and network manufacturing. The key technologies of parts library system at network level include the following:

(1)   Data description norm of web-based parts library [11]: Part information should be described in a language fit for representation in network in order to realize customization of part information and information integration with different application systems.

(2)   Distributed parametric design of parts: Parts library system at network level should provide the users with the function of selecting part parameters in distributed environments and interoperating with multiform CAD systems in order to access part parameters and modify part model at real time in network.

(3)   Browse and interaction of part geometric model in network: The function of browsing part 3D geometric model independent of the particular CAD system in network ensures visualization of part information, access to part feature information and share of design intentions.

(4)   Sound mechanism for selecting parts supplier [9]: Parts library at network level should have capability of comparing performance, price, quality of parts of different suppliers and teamwork with the inventory management system in order to serve the outsourcing department of enterprise.

Although information of parts library can be shared by means of neutral files between heterogeneous CAD systems, it is difficult for distributed application systems to access information directly from them. Mapping mechanism and implementation technologies from neutral description of part information to particular representation of part information adapting to network environment are studied in Reference 14 and a practical way to enhance parts library at neutral level to that at network level is put forward.

4 Software Implementation

According to the hierarchical structure and content of PL-ALM, a software system called UG China Data Creation Standard (UCDCS) is developed using UG/Open tools, which can evaluate the application level of the parts library system and correct run-time errors of the parts library system at the geometry or system level with corresponding correction reports simultaneously (see Figure 5-7). UCDCS has been used in hundreds of enterprises, such as GM corporation. UCDCS can be used to evaluate application status of the current parts library system. On the other hand, enterprise or supplier can set the level for the parts library system in advance so as to regulate its management and usage. Only those parts passing through the examination and marked with passed notes can be stored in the parts library.

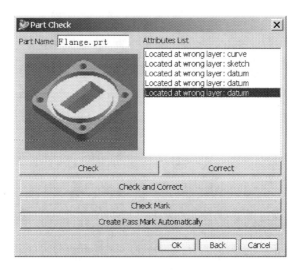

Fig. 5. Check & correction of part geometric information

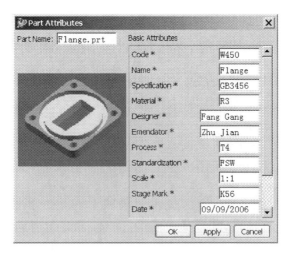

Fig. 6. Correction of non-geometric information of part

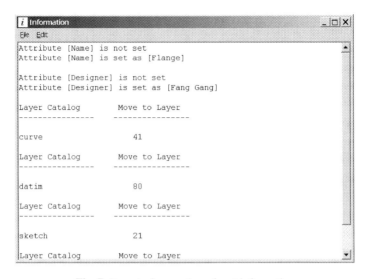

Fig. 7. Report of correction of part information

5 Conclusion

This paper proposes solutions for enterprises's part library systems based on a PL-ALM model and its four-level infrastructure. Moreover, with varying requirements, enterprises can enhance their application level gradually based on the existing parts library systems following PL-ALM. So the enterprises can not only meet the new demands quickly, but also decrease the cost of labor and waste. Future research will be focused on improving PL-ALM model considering the requirements of CAD applications in an enterprise. In addition, PL-ALM needs to collaborate with China National Institute of Standardization and International Standard Organization in order to promote wider applications of PLIB systems.

Acknowledgments. Supported by Scientific Research Fund of Nanjing Institute of Technology (Project No: KXJ06002) and China National 863 High-Tech Project (Project No: 2002AA411030).

References

1. Qin, G.: CAD Standard Components Library. Beijing: Chinese Standardization Publishing House (2000) 7-20
2. Choi, G.-H., Mun, D. and Han, S.: Exchange of CAD Part Models Based on the Macro-Parametric Approach. International Journal of CAD/CAM 2(2) (2002) 23-31
3. ISO 13584-1-1999, Industrial automation systems and integration—Parts library—Part 1: Overview and fundamental principles (1999)
4. Pierra, G., Poiter, J.C. and Sardet, E.: From digital libraries to electronic catalogues for engineering and manufacturing. International Journal of Computer Applications in Technology 18(3) (2003) 27-42

5. Wang, P. and Zhan, J.: Standard Parts Library System supporting Information Sharing in Network. World Standardization & Quality Management 10 (2001) 30-32
6. Pratt M.J.: Extension of STEP for the Representation of Parametric and Variational Models. CAD Systems Development (1995) 237-250
7. Sardet, E., Pierra, G. and Yamine, A.A.: Modelling and Exchange of Classes of Components according to Plib: A case study. Proceedings of Global Network Engineering. Antwerp (1997) 179-201
8. Sardet, E. and Pierra, G.: Simplified Representation of Parts Library: Model, Practice and Implementation. Proceedings of the 10th Product Data Technology Europe. Berkshire, UK (2001) 163-174
9. Feng, W., Chen, J., Zhao, C.: Partners Selection Process and Optimization Model for Virtual Corporations based on Genetic Algorithms. Journal of Tsinghua University (Science & Technology) 40(10) (2000) 120-124
10. Li, Y., Zhou, R., Huang, X., et al.: Research and Development of Parts Library System with Dynamic Expansion. Mechanical Science and Technology 22(3) (2003) 502-507
11. Li, Y., Lu, Y., Liao, W., et al.: Representation and share of part feature information in web-based parts library. Expert Systems With Applications 31(4) (2006) 697-704
12. Lu, Y., Liao, W. and Huang, X.: Parts Library Standard and Information Modeling Based on PLIB. Mechanical Science and Technology 22(6) (2003) 1021-1025
13. Lu, Y., Liao, W., Huang, X., et al.: Research on the Geometric Information of Parts Library Oriented to the Heterogeneous CAD Systems. Mechanical Science and Technology 23(10) (2004) 1166-1168, 1214
14. Lu, Y., Liao, W., Huang, X., et al.: Research on Data Description Norm and Building Techniques of Web-based Parts Library. Chinese Mechanical Engineering 15(11) (2004) 987-990

A Pi-calculus-Based Business Process Formal Design Method

Jing Zhang and Haiyang Wang

School of Computer and Science, Shandong University,
Shandong, Jinan 250061, China
gshzhj@public.jn.sd.cn

Abstract. The pi-calculus is a model of concurrent computation, which can express communication between correlation processes. It provides a way of constructing systems in a bottom-up manner by composing subsystems, and it also has strict formal semantics. Therefore, pi-calculus is very suitable for designing business processes which are presently becoming more and more complicated. The paper proposes a composition-oriented approach to business process design based on pi-calculus theory and gives the formal definition of business process. It also illustrates the design method by simulating an example of order processing. By this method, a complicated business process can be divided into several independent simple sub-modules, which can greatly reduce the complexity of business process design.

1 Introduction

With the development of computer and network technology, workflow technology is applied to more and more fields and the application scope is also spanning over different departments, even different enterprises. Business process represents more its complex, distributive and collaborative quality. So it is very difficult to depict all details of a whole business process in one diagram. We need to divide a business process into several parts which can be modeled independently, and then compose them to a whole process.

Pi-calculus, as a variant of process algebra, provides an approach of using concurrent operators to construct systems by composing subsystems [1]. Therefore it is very suitable to describe the business processes which are presently becoming more and more complicated. Furthermore, it has strict formal semantics. So the paper adopts pi-calculus as its formalization foundation and proposes a new design method of business process. This method supports dividing one complex business process into several independent sub-modules, and then constructs the whole process by composition. Moreover, this method supports separation of exception processing logic from main process logic, which reduces the complexity of business process design.

This paper is organized as follows: Section 1 is introduction; Section 2 discusses some related works; Section 3 introduces syntax and semantics of pi-calculus; Section 4 defines a pi-calculus-based business process model; Section 5 illustrates how to design a process by an example; Section 6 analyzes the soundness and verification of a business process; Section 7 is the conclusion.

W. Shen et al. (Eds.): CSCWD 2006, LNCS 4402 , pp. 347–356, 2007.
© Springer-Verlag Berlin Heidelberg 2007

2 Related Work

As the business process spreads different departments and even different enterprise, the research on business process design has turned to cooperative and integrated environments. Because the cooperation of many enterprises is often based on peer-to-peer interactions rather than centralized coordination, Chen [2] puts forward a peer-to-peer collaborative process model. Desai [3] describes a business process as a composition of business protocols using a dual perspective. In addition, the combination with web service technology is also a main issue of business process design, BPEL4WS [4] and DAML-S [5] are two representatives of such research. But these above business process design approaches are all descriptive and lack formalized theoretical foundation. As we know, formal analysis is essential for designing good business processes [6].

Some traditional process model methodologies are also extended to distributed and integrated environment. Inter-enterprise electronic commerce (IEEC) [7] develops inter-enterprise business processes with IDEF0. Inter-organizational workflow (IWOF) [8] employs message sequence chart (MSC) to specify the interaction between the business partners and Petri nets to design inter-organizational collaborative works. Compared with these methodologies, pi-calculus provides standards for combining sub-systems and concurrency operation to obtain bigger systems, thus a complicated business process can be designed by composing simple sub-processes.

Till now, many researches have been done on business process design based on pi-calculus theory: Förster [9] shows that pi-calculus meet essential requirements for being the foundation of a formal business process modeling language; Yang [10] gives a new approach for workflow modeling based on pi-calculus; it can characterize the dynamic behaviors of the workflow process in terms of the LTS (Labeled Transition Semantics) semantics of pi-calculus. But these works are mainly focus on those simple and centralized business processes.

Compared with these works, this paper's contribution is that we put forward a composition-oriented, pi-calculus-based business process formal design method. This method can reduce the complexity of process design by composing small process elements into entire process.

3 The Pi-calculus

The pi-calculus is a model of concurrent computation based upon the notion of naming. We assume a potentially infinite set of names N, ranged over by $a, b,..., z$, which will function as all of communication ports, variables and data values, and a set of (agent) identifiers ranged over by $A,B...$ each with a fixed nonnegative arity. The syntax of agents ranged over by P, Q is defined as following [11]:

$$P ::= 0 \mid \overline{a}\langle x \rangle.P \mid a(x).P \mid \tau.P \mid P + Q \mid P \mid Q \mid [x = y]P \mid (\vee x)P \mid A(x_1,...x_k)$$

- 0, empty agent which cannot perform any actions.
- $\overline{a}{<}x{>}.P$, name x is sent along the name a and thereafter the agent continues as P.
- $a(x).P$, a name is received along a name a, and x is a placeholder for the received name and then the agent continues as P.

- $\tau.P$, evolve to P without interaction with the environment.
- $P+Q$, agent can enact either P or Q.
- $P|Q$, combined behaviour of P and Q executing in parallel.
- $[x=y]P$, this agent will behave as P if x and y are the same name, otherwise it will do nothing.
- $(\vee x)P$, the usage of name x is constrained within P, same as new a name x in P.

Just as other process algebra, the operation semantics of pi-calculus are defined by LTS, writing as $P \overset{\alpha}{\to} Q$. In references [1] and [11], we can get detailed introductions of pi-calculus.

4   Composition-Oriented Business Process Design

Activity is the basic element describing a piece of work that forms logical steps within a process. They are divided into atomic and composite activities. An atomic activity is the smallest unit of process, which cannot be decomposed further. A composite activity is a composition of some related activities, and it provides implementation environment which we called "process context" for these sub-activities. Process context contains process relevant data and exception processing methods required by activities. The elements of our business process model are show in Figure 1.

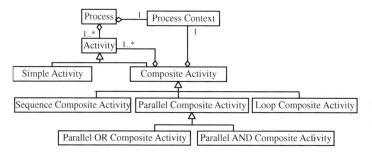

Fig. 1. Elements of business process model

4.1   Process Context

The process context is the running environment of activities. It not only provides the required data activities needed but also provides exception-processing mechanism for activities. Process context is a hierarchical structure that each sub-context inherits shared information from its parent context. Also, sub-contexts may have their own private information. When the context can't find required data or exception information, it will pass the request to its parent context.

Definition 1. Context CTX is the running environment of activities. It is divided into data context CTX_D and exception processing context CTX_E. CTX can be defined by following expression:

$$CTX(c,p_r,p_w,p_e,l_r,l_w,l_e,f,e) \stackrel{def}{=} CTX_D(c,p_r,p_w,l_r,l_w) \mid CTX_E(p_e,l_e,l_r,l_w,f) + f.\overline{e} \qquad (1)$$

$c = \{\langle r_1,d_1\rangle,....,\langle r_n,d_n\rangle\}$ are the current status of all data in the context. p_r and p_w are two ports respectively used to read and write data from its parent context. l_r and l_w are used to read and write data from this context. l_e and p_e respectively used to receive notification of exception from this context and send exception notification to parent context. f is a port receiving finish request and e is a port sending finish command.

Definition 2. Data context provides all data needed by activities and update them during activities running. It can be defined by expression (2)~(4).

$$CTX_D(c,p_r,p_w,l_r,l_w) \stackrel{def}{=} l_w(v).CTXW(v,c,p_r,p_w,l_r,l_w) + l_r(d,r).CTXR(d,r,c,p_r,p_w,l_r,l_w) \qquad (2)$$

$$CTXR(d,r,c,p_r,p_w,l_r,l_w) \stackrel{def}{=} (va)(\overline{p}_r\langle d1,a\rangle.a(v1)).\overline{r}\langle v1 \cup v2\rangle.CTX(c,p_r,p_w,l_r,l_w)$$
$$d1 = \{x \mid x \in d \wedge \neg\exists\langle x,y\rangle \in c\} \quad v2 = \{\langle x,y\rangle \mid \langle x,y\rangle \in c \wedge x \in d\} \qquad (3)$$

$$CTXW(v,c,p_r,p_w,l_r,l_w) \stackrel{def}{=} \overline{p}_w\langle va\rangle.CTX(c \cup vb,p_r,p_w,l_r,l_w)$$
$$va = \{x \mid x \in v \wedge x \notin c\} \quad vb = \{x \mid x \in v \wedge x \in c\} \qquad (4)$$

Definition 3. Context used to deal with exception circumstance during process running can be defined by following expression.

$$CTX_E(p_e,l_e,l_r,l_w,f) \stackrel{def}{=} (l_e(f_c).(\vee r)(\overline{gete}\langle f_c,r\rangle.r(s_e)).([s_e \neq o]\overline{s}_e + [s_e = o]\overline{p}_e\langle f_c\rangle)) \mid \sum_{i=1}^{k} EP_i(s_i,f,l_r,l_w,p_e) \qquad (5)$$

$EP_i(i \in \{1,...,k\})$ are exception processing sub processes. When context receives an exception, it gets the start command port s_e of exception sub-process used to deal with this exception according to the exception code. If a proper port is gotten, context will send start command along this port. If current context cannot process this exception, the gotten port will be null and context will throw this exception to its parent context.

Conditions that will result in exception must be identified in process modeling. Once such condition is matched, process must notify the context. This is performed by an exception notification activity.

Definition 4. Parameterized with start command port s, end message port e, exception notification port c_e and exception fault code f_e, exception notification activity EA is defined as:

$$EA(s,c_e,f_e) \stackrel{def}{=} s.\overline{c}_e\langle f_e\rangle \qquad (6)$$

4.2 Simple Activity

Simple activity accomplishes actual tasks with resources. After a simple activity is instanced, the following operations will be performed:

- Receive start command.
- Get initial data from context.
- Request resource to perform task.
- Receive implementation result from resource.
- Send out end message.

Definition 5. Simple Activity SA={T, R, I} performs task T by resource R with initial context I. Parameterized with start command port s, end message port e, request data port c_r and write data port c_w, SA can be formalize defined by expression (7).

$$SA(s,e,c_r,c_w) \overset{def}{=} s.(\vee x)(\overline{c_r}\langle i,x\rangle.x(v)).(\vee y)(\overline{r}\langle t,v,y\rangle.y(o)).\overline{c_w}\langle o\rangle.\overline{e} \qquad (7)$$

4.3 Composite Activity

Any activity must be executed in a context of process. It is the composite activity's responsibility to provide context for its sub-activities. The context will be created when composite activity has been instanced.

Definition 6. Sequence Composite Activity (SCA) is a composite activity that all sub-activities are executed in sequential order. SCA={A1, A2, …, An, CTX}, similarly taking port s which receives start command, port e which sends end message of activity, port c_r and c_w which request and update data respectively as parameters, SCA is defined formally as :

$$SCA(s,e,c_r,c_w) \overset{def}{=} s.(\vee l_r)(\vee l_w)(\vee a_1,...,a_n)(A1(s,a_1,l_r,l_w)\,|\,...\,|\,An(a_{n-1},a_n,l_r,l_w)\,|\,CTX(ic,c_r,c_w,o,l_r,l_w,o,a_n,e)) \qquad (8)$$

SCA will instance a local context right after it receives the start command, and then executes activities in sequence. A SCA will finally end when it receives the ending message of the last sub-activity. Since exception means deviation from normal processes and SCA has only one single branch, so there is no exception-reporting port in its context.

Definition 7. Parallel Composite Activity PCA={<A1, C1>, <A2, C2>, …, <An, Cn>, CTX}, is a composite activity composed of two or more activities that Ai will be executed only if condition Ci is satisfied. PCA is separated into ORPCA (Parallel OR Composite Activity) and ANDPCA (Parallel And Composite Activity), according to the relationship of its parallel branches.

Definition 8. ANDPCA is such a PCA that every branch meets its condition will be executed, and it will not end until all branches involved finally end. ANDPCA is formally defined as following:

$$\begin{aligned} ANDPCA(s,e,c_r,c_w) \overset{def}{=}\ & s.(((\vee l_r,l_w,l_e,f)(\vee s_1,...,s_n)(\vee e_1,...,e_n)((\vee x_1)\overline{b}\langle c_1,x_1\rangle.x_1(v_1).([v_1 = T]\\ & (\overline{s}_1\,|\,SA1(s_1,e_1,l_r,l_w)+[v_1 = F]\overline{e}_1)\,|\,...\,|\,(\vee x_n)\overline{b}\langle c_n,x_n\rangle.x_n(v_n).([v_n = T](\overline{s}_n\,|\,SAn(s_n,e_n,l_r,l_w)\\ & +[v_n = F]\overline{e}_n)\,|\,CTX(c,c_r,c_w,c_e,l_r,l_w,l_e,f,e)\,|\,(e_1\,|\,e_2\,|\,...\,|\,e_n).f) \end{aligned} \qquad (9)$$

Port b is a communication link through which PCA obtains the value of a branch's condition expression.

Definition 9. A PCA that generates only one single activity branch and ends after the single branch ends is called ORPCA, which is defined formally as:

$$
\begin{aligned}
ORPCA_E(s,e,c_r,c_w,c_e) \overset{\text{def}}{=} & s.((\forall l_r,l_w,l_e,f)(\vee s_1,...,s_n,s_{n+1},...,s_{n+k})(\vee e_1,...,e_n)((\vee x_1)\overline{b}\langle c_1,x_1\rangle.x_1(v_1) \\
& .([v_1 = T](\overline{s_1} \mid SA1(s_1,e_1,l_r,l_w)) + ... + (\vee x_n)\overline{b}\langle c_n,x_n\rangle.x_n(v_n) \\
& .([v_n = T](\overline{s_n} \mid SAn(s_n,e_n,l_r,l_w)) + (\vee x_{n+1})\overline{b}\langle c_{n+1},x_{n+1}\rangle.x_{n+1}(v_{n+1}) \\
& .([v_{n+1} = T](\overline{s}_{n+1} \mid EA_1(s_{n+1},l_e,f_1)) + ... + (\vee x_{n+k})\overline{b}\langle c_{n+k},x_{n+k}\rangle.x_{n+k}(v_{n+k}) \\
& .([v_{n+k} = T](\overline{s}_{n+1} \mid EA_k(s_{n+k},l_e,f_k)) \mid CTX(c,c_r,c_w,c_e,l_r,l_w,l_e,f,e) \mid (e_1+e_2+...+e_n).\overline{f})
\end{aligned}
\tag{10}
$$

PCA describes how to choose and execute one or several activity branches according to condition expressions and it can be used to model exception branches of a business process.

Definition 10. Loop Composition Activity LCA={A1, A2, ... An, CTX, Cl}, in which activity A1, A2, ... An compose the loop body and they are executed one by one, A1 and An are respectively the entrance and exit of the loop, C1 is the condition for exit, that is, if condition C1 is satisfied, the loop will finish, otherwise the activity A1 will be executed in a new turn. LCA can be defined by expression (11) and (12).

$$
LCA(s,e,c_r,c_w) \overset{\text{def}}{=} s.(\vee l_r,l_w)(\vee f)(CTX(ic,c_r,c_w,l_r,l_w,f,e) \mid LCAS(s,l_r,l_w,f)
\tag{11}
$$

$$
\begin{aligned}
LCAS(s,l_r,l_w,f) \overset{\text{def}}{=} & (\vee a_1,...,a_n)(A1(s,a_1,l_r,l_w) \mid ... \mid An(a_{n-1},a_n,l_r,l_w) \mid (\vee x)(a_n\overline{b}\langle c_l,x\rangle.x(v) \\
& .([v = T]\overline{f} + [v = F](\vee s_l)LCAS(s_l,l_r,l_w,f)))
\end{aligned}
\tag{12}
$$

4.4 Process

Definition 11. Composition-oriented business process COMBP={CTX, A1, A2, ... An} can be regarded as a special kind of SCA that has no parent activity, and the context what it provides is a top-layer context.

$$
COMBP(s,e,ic) \overset{\text{def}}{=} s.(\vee l_r,l_w)(\vee a_1,...,a_n)(A1(s,a_1,l_r,l_w) \mid ... \mid An(a_{n-1},a_n,l_r,l_w) \mid CTX(ic,o,o,l_r,l_w,a_n,e))
\tag{13}
$$

A COMBP will initiate the context and start the business process after receiving start message s, that is, to execute every activity in process in sequential order.

4.5 Exception Processing Process

Similar to ordinary business process modeling, an exception processing process also consists of a set of sequential activities. These activities' process context is the context where the exception processing process is defined. So exception processing process provides data-reading port l_r and data-writing port l_w for its sub-activities to read or write data in this context. It also has the exception report port c_e by which it communicates with this context.

Definition 12. Exceptional Process EP is defined formally as :

$$
EP(s,e,l_r,l_w,c_e) \overset{\text{def}}{=} s.(\vee a_1,...,a_{n-1})(A1(s,a_1,l_r,l_w,c_e) \mid ... \mid An(a_{n-1},e,l_r,l_w,c_e))
\tag{14}
$$

5   Example

We will illustrate our composition-oriented business process design method with an example of book order processing shown in Figure 2. A customer's book order is registered firstly, then stock is checked ---- if there are books out of stock, activity of

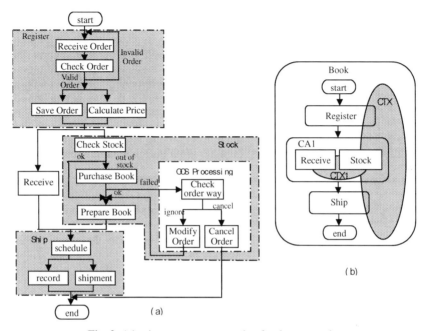

Fig. 2. A business process example of order processing

purchasing books from the supplier will be performed, receiving payment from customer is executed simultaneously, finally the books are shipped out. In the process of purchasing from the supplier, the dealer may fail in buying the needed books. In such a case, the dealer should deal with this order according to customer's demand. By the way of composition-oriented design, the complex process shown in Figure 2(a) can be described by a simple and clear process shown in Figure 2(b). Process *Book* is composed of three composite activities: *Register, CA1, Ship* and one context *CTX*, where *CA1* is a ANDPCA composed of activities *Receive* and *Stock*. Process *Book* is defined as:

$$book(s,e) \overset{\text{def}}{=} (vc_r,c_w)(va_1,a_2,a_3)(register(s,a_1,c_r,c_w) \mid CA1(a_1,a_2,c_r,c_w) \\ \mid shipp(a_2,a_3,c_r,c_w) \mid CTX(i,o,o,c_r,c_w,a_3,e)) \tag{15}$$

$$CA1(a_1,a_2,c_r,c_w) \overset{\text{def}}{=} a_1.((vl_r,l_w,f)(vs_1,s_2,e_1,e_2)(receive(s_1,e_1,c_r,c_w) \mid stock(s_2,e_2,c_r,c_w) \\ \mid CTX(o,c_r,c_w,l_r,l_r,f,a_2) \mid (e_1 \mid e_2).f) \tag{16}$$

Every sub-part of process *book* can be designed independently. For example, Figure 3 shows the design diagram of composite activity *Register*, which is modeled according to our composition-oriented method: simple activities *Receive Order* and *Check Order* constitute a sequence composite activity *register1*; *register1* and parallel AND composite activity *register2* constitute sequence composite activity *Register*. Context of *register1* and *register2* are *CTXr1* and *CTXr2* respectively, and their parent context is *CTXr*. Customer number *Cno* and order information *order* is in *CTXr*, *isValidOrder* is private data of *CTXr1*. So, if activity *Receive Order* or *Check Order* request *order* or *Cno* from *CTXr1*, *CTXr1* will request data from *CTXr*.

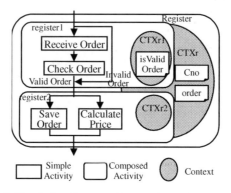

Fig. 3. The design diagram of composite activity *Register*

Activity *Register* is defined by expression (17)-(20).

$$register(s,e,c_r,c_w) \overset{\text{def}}{=} s.(\vee l_r,l_w)(\vee a_1,a_2)(register1(s,a_1,l_r,l_w) \\ \mid register2(a_1,a_2,l_r,l_w) \mid CTX(ic,c_r,c_w,l_r,l_w,a_n,e)) \tag{17}$$

$$register2(s,e,c_r,c_w) \overset{\text{def}}{=} s.(((\vee l_r,l_w,f)(\vee s_1,s_2)(\vee e_1,e_2)((\vee x_1)\overline{b}\langle c_1,\underline{x_1}\rangle.x_1(v_1) \\ .([v_1 = T](\overline{s_1} \mid saveOrder(s_1,e_1,l_r,c_w) + [v_1 = F]\overline{e_1}) \mid (\vee x_2)b\langle c_2,x_2\rangle.x_2(v_2) \\ .([v_2 = T](\overline{s_2} \mid calculate\,Price(s_2,e_2,l_r,c_w) + [v_2 = F]\overline{e_2}) \mid (CTX(ic,c_r,c_w,l_r,l_w,f,e) \mid (e_1 \mid e_2).\overline{f}) \tag{18}$$

$$register1(s,e,c_r,c_w) \overset{\text{def}}{=} s.(\vee l_r,l_w)(\vee f)(CTX(ic,c_r,c_w,l_r,l_w,f,e) \mid reg1S(s,l_r,l_w,f)) \tag{19}$$

$$reg1S(s,l_r,l_w,f) \overset{\text{def}}{=} (\vee a_1,a_2)(\underline{recOrder}(s,a_1,l_r,l_w) \mid checkOrder(a_1,a_2,l_r,l_w) \\ \mid (\vee x)(a_2.\overline{b}\langle c_1,x\rangle.x(v).([v = T]\overline{f} + [v = F](\vee s_l)register1(s_l,l_r,l_w,f))) \tag{20}$$

Other activities *Stock, Receive* and *Ship* can also be defined using the method mentioned above. In this way, a complicated business process could be divided into several simple sub-modules, and this can greatly reduce the complexity of business process modeling and analyzing.

6   Analysis of Model

If a business process is sound, then for any case, the process will terminate eventually and at the moment the process terminates all branches reach to the end of this process. Furthermore, there are no dead tasks in the process and any task can be executed according to a proper route, in other words, any activity that contains tasks can be activated.

Definition 13. A business process modeled by the way of COMBP is sound if and only if:

(1)   Any case will send end message eventually, and at that time, there is no branch that hasn't reached the end of process. Formally:

$$\forall s,e,ic \quad \exists \overset{\alpha}{\Rightarrow} = \overset{\alpha_1}{\rightarrow}\overset{\alpha_2}{\rightarrow}...\overset{\alpha_n}{\rightarrow} \quad COMBP(s,e,ic)\overset{\alpha}{\Rightarrow}\overline{e}$$

(2)   There is no activity that cannot receive a start message. Formally:

$$\forall A(s_a,e_a,c_r,c_w) \in COMBP \quad \exists \overset{\alpha}{\Rightarrow} = \overset{\alpha_1}{\rightarrow}\overset{\alpha_2}{\rightarrow}...\overset{\alpha_n}{\rightarrow}\overset{s_a}{\rightarrow},COMBP' \quad COMBP\overset{\alpha}{\Rightarrow}COMBP'$$

A business process consists of a series of composite activities. Therefore analysis on a process can be decomposed into analysis on several composite activities. A composite activity can be regarded as a sub-process whose soundness should also meet the requirement of process.

Definition 14. A composite activity is sound if and only if:

(3)   Any case will send end message eventually, and there is no branch that hasn't reached the end of activity. Formally:

$$\forall s,e,c_r,c_w \quad \exists \overset{\alpha}{\Rightarrow} = \overset{\alpha_1}{\rightarrow}\overset{\alpha_2}{\rightarrow}...\overset{\alpha_n}{\rightarrow} \quad CA(s,e,c_r,c_w)\overset{\alpha}{\Rightarrow}\overline{e}$$

(4)   There is no sub-activity that cannot receive start message. Formally:

$$\forall A(s_a,e_a,c_r,c_w) \in CA \quad \exists \overset{\alpha}{\Rightarrow} = \overset{\alpha_1}{\rightarrow}\overset{\alpha_2}{\rightarrow}...\overset{\alpha_n}{\rightarrow}\overset{s_a}{\rightarrow},CA' \quad CA\overset{\alpha}{\Rightarrow}CA'$$

Theorem 1: If every composite activity in a process is sound, then the process is sound too.

Proof: Suppose process COMBP is composed of sub-activities named as A1, A2, … An. Given that all composite activities are sound, we get that:

$$\forall CA(s,e,c_r,c_w) \in COMBP \quad \exists \overset{\alpha}{\Rightarrow} = \overset{\alpha_1}{\rightarrow}\overset{\alpha_2}{\rightarrow}...\overset{\alpha_n}{\rightarrow} \quad CA(s,e,c_r,c_w)\overset{\alpha}{\Rightarrow}\overline{e}$$

Then we get:

$$COMBP(s,e,ic) \overset{def}{=} s.(\vee l_r)(\vee l_w)(\vee a_1,...,a_n)(A1(s,a_1,l_r,l_w)|...|An(a_{n-1},a_n,l_r,l_w)|(CTX(ic,o,o,l_r,l_w,a_n,e))$$

$$\overset{\alpha_1}{\Rightarrow}(\vee l_r,l_w)(\vee a_1,...,a_n)(\overline{a_1}|...|An(a_{n-1},a_n,l_r,l_w)|(CTX(ic,o,o,l_r,l_w,a_n,e))$$

$$\overset{\alpha_2}{\Rightarrow}(\vee l_r,l_w)(\vee a_1,...,a_n)(\overline{a_2}|...|An(a_{n-1},a_n,l_r,l_w)|CTX(ic,o,o,l_r,l_w,a_n,e))$$

$$\overset{\alpha_1}{\Rightarrow}...\overset{\alpha_n}{\Rightarrow}(\vee l_r,l_w)(\vee a_1,a_2,...,a_n)(\overline{a_n}|CTX(ic,o,o,l_r,l_w,a_n,e))$$

$$\overset{\overline{a_n}}{\rightarrow}\overline{e}$$

So the process can be ended finally.

From the proof above we can obviously know that every composite activity, which directly constitutes the process, will certainly receive a start message. And every composite activity is sound, so there are no sub-activities in each composite activity that cannot receive a start message. Then there is no activity which cannot receive a start message in this process. So, the process is sound too.

7   Conclusion

Aiming at the new problems of complexity, distribution and collaboration that business processes are facing presently, we propose an approach for designing business process by composing structural process control modules. Compared with traditional business process design methods, our approach has following advantages:

- A complicated business process is decomposed into multi-layer components which can be designed independently. This makes the structure of process very simple and can be verified or analyzed easily.
- Compared with the hierarchical structure of model, we can easily generate different process views.
- The separation of exception processing logic and normal process logic makes business and technical experts focus on their own core process.
- Based on the mature formalization theory, business process can be analyzed in a strict way. This model can also be analyzed aided by pi-calculus verification tools such as Mobile Workbench (MWB) [12].

With the development of network technologies, business process technology is applied to many new areas such as B2B, web service, and EAI. In these new areas, business process design becomes more composition-oriented. The design methods proposed can exactly meet the new requirement of business process technology.

References

1. Robin, M.: Communicating and Mobile Systems: The Pi-Calculus. Cambridge University Press, New York (1999)
2. Qiming, C., Meichun, H.: Inter-Enterprise Collaborative Business Process Management. Proc. 17th International Conference on Data Engineering (2001) 253-260
3. Nirmit, D., Munindar, P.S.: Protocol-Based Business Process Modeling and Enactment. Proceedings of the IEEE International Conference on Web Services (2004) 35-42
4. Andrews, T., Curbera, F., Dholakia, H., Goland Y., Klein, J., Leymann, F., et al.: Business Process Execution Language for Web Services, Version 1.1. (2003)
5. DAML-S Coalition: Web service description for the semantic web. Proceedings of the 1st Int. Semantic Web Conference (2002) 348-363
6. Nikunj, P.D., Manjunath, K., William J.K., Eswar, S.: Toward an Integrated Framework for Modeling Enterprise Processes. Communications of the ACM 47(3)(2004) 83-87
7. Kitae, S., Choon, S.L.: A reference system for internet based inter-enterprise electronic commerce. The Journal of Systems and Software 60 (2002) 195–209
8. Wil van der, A.: Modeling and analyzing inter-organizational workflows. Proc. Int. Conf. Application of Concurrency to System Design (1998) 262-272
9. Förster M.: Theory of Business Process Modeling: The Pi-Calculus. Seminar Process-oriented Information Systems (2003) 1-17
10. Yang, D., Zhang, S.: Using pi-calculus to Formalize UML Activity Diagram. Proc. 10th IEEE Int. Conf. Engineering of Computer-Based Systems (2003) 47-54
11. Joachim, P.: An Introduction to the pi-Calculus. In: Handbook of Process Algebra. Elsevier (2001) 479-543
12. Bjorn, V., Faron, M.: The Mobile Workbench – A Tool for the pi-Calculus. Proc. Computer-Aided Verification (1994) 428-440

Achieving Better Collaboration in Global Software Design with Micro Estimation

Bin Xu[1], Hua Hu[1], Yun Ling[1], Xiaohu Yang[2], Zhijun He[2], and Albert Ma[3]

[1] College of Computer Science, Zhejiang Gongshang University,
310035 Hangzhou, China
{xubin, huhua, yling}@mail.zjgsu.edu.cn
[2] College of Computer Science & Technology, Zhejiang University,
310027 Hangzhou, China
{yangxh, hezj}@zju.edu.cn
[3] State Street Corporation, 02111 Boston MA, USA
amma@statestreet.com

Abstract. Communication delay is a main obstacle in global cooperative software design and rescheduling design tasks is essential to reduce such a impact. The duration of task and communication delay is undetermined in global software design, and the task sequence is not determined when rework is required to fix the possible defects in the progress. Therefore, it is hard to distinguish when and which task should be handled and the design task rescheduling can be difficult to accomplish. Dynamic Micro-estimation refines the estimation of effort and duration for the tasks in the next short period. Based on Multiple Component Status Transition Graph (MCSTG) and Micro-estimation, the probability of a task should be handled and the available time for this task to be finished can be easily estimated. The Micro-estimation extended MCSTG enables the project managers to reschedule the tasks according to their criticality and importance so as to facilitate the collaboration in global software design.

1 Introduction

Software outsourcing is prevalent nowadays. However, communication and coordination become the bottleneck in distributed software development. Some survey showed that the management cost actually exceeded the wages saving. Besides, some previous research [1-2] showed that distributed work items appear to take about two and one-half times longer to complete as similar items where all the work is collocated together. Such delay appears to be communication and coordination issues instead of the size or complexity of cross-sites work.

Different tactics have been suggested to reduce the cultural impact in global cooperation model [3-4] and the methodology of virtual team management in global development has also been introduced in [6][9]. Some practices to reduce the coupling of distributed work are suggested by [5][7][10], including "developing different subsystems at different sites" and "executing different process steps at different sites".

Typically, the design of a large complex system in global project bridges the requirements or specification to the development. The design activities should be finished

W. Shen et al. (Eds.): CSCWD 2006, LNCS 4402, pp. 357–366, 2007.
© Springer-Verlag Berlin Heidelberg 2007

by cooperation of different people with different skill sets. As a result, design is formidable due to frequent and large amount of communication and coordination in a global development environment.

While Communication Queue [8] may be used to minimize the impact of communication delay, task dependence including data and control dependence should be well handled so as to avoid the conflicts incurred. On the basis of analysis of task dependence between components, Multiple Component Status Transition Graph (MCSTG) is suggested so as to not only describe intra-component dependency, but also describe the inter-dependency between components [11].

Since the design activity is complex, the former design activities will be revisited if there are some defects or requirement changes. As a result, the designers are not sure which will be the following tasks when they get a certain task. Besides, the duration of each design task is not determined, so it is hard to reschedule design tasks in global cooperative environment. Therefore, duration estimation of current task and estimation of possible following task are essential for a better design tasks rescheduling.

In this paper, Micro-Estimation is proposed, which is used to handle the loop in the task network and make refined estimations so as to facilitate the cooperation in global software design.

The rest of this paper is organized as following. The problem in graph based coordination due to the contained loops is identified in Section 2, Micro-Estimation technique is proposed in Section 3. Section 4 states how to expand Fast Automatic Notification sub-system with Micro-Estimation, and Section 5 suggests a way to integrate Communication Queues sub-system with expanded Fast Automatic Notification sub-system. The summary and discussion is given in Section 6, and we also introduce the currently status of the research there.

2 Graph Based Coordination

The authors has introduced Multiple Components Status Transition Graph (MCSTG) for coordination [11], shown in Figure 1.

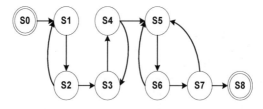

Fig. 1. Component Status Transition Graph [11]

The entry and exit criteria are studied in coordination as well as the effort pressure controlling in [12].

It will be very helpful for the project managers to master the timelines of every task, including when a task should be finished, the available time for a certain task to be started, and resource needed in the near future.

Regarding the time management, critical path arithmetic has already been introduced to calculate the timelines of a project including the ES (Early Start Time), EF (Early Finish Time), LS (Last Start Time), and LF (Last Finish Time) for each task. Giving the example in Figure 2, we may easily know that all the tasks, which in the Activity On Arrow (AOA) task network, can be finished in 71 days, and task D can be started between 7th day and 15th day with the involved formulas, ES = max(EF (Preceding tasks)) and EF = ES+ Duration.

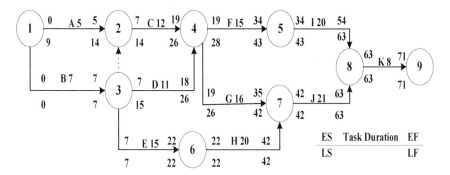

Fig. 2. Activity On Arrow (AOA) task network without LOOP

When the duration is not determined, the PERT techniques can be used to get the most possible timeline for the tasks and project. However, when considering the bug fixing, requirement change and involving development, there may be some loops in the network. The formulas above are no longer useful when there are some loops in the task network (Figure 3).

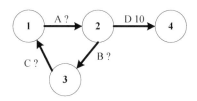

Fig. 3. A simple task network with loop

Though the network is very simple, however, the Early Start Time for Task D could not be got at the very beginning because the loops are not certain and the duration for task A, B, and C is not fixed in each loop.

3 Micro-estimation

The timeline calculation is still a problem in a real project when there are some loops in the task network before we know the possibilities of the branches, the times when the loop occurs and the duration of the tasks in the loop.

With the historical project data, the duration of the tasks can be estimated in statistics. However, it is insufficient for the decision making towards better coordination in global cooperative software design. Micro-Estimation is proposed to solve such problem. When performing Micro-Estimation, the scale of task is very small as it estimates the timeline of each piece of tasks, which can be the smallest sub-tasks in task network. Besides, the time interval is short as it only considers the current available tasks and ignores the following further steps.

3.1 Translation of MCSTG into Activity On Node (AON) Network

Giving the example in Figure 1, assume that there are some relationships between CSTG of αand β(Figure 4).

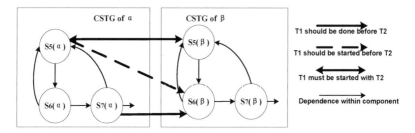

Fig. 4. Relationship between different CSTG

All these dependencies may be translated into four cases, FS (task A should be finished before the start of task B), FF (task A should be finished before the finish of task B), SF (task A should be started before the finish of task B) and SS (task A should be started before the start of task B).

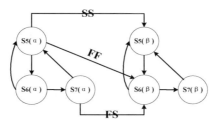

Fig. 5. Part of Activity On Node (AON) task network

MCSTG will then be translated into AON task network as in Figure 5. The dependence of FS can be ignored as it is the most possible case.

3.2 Probability Estimation for the Branches

If there is a loop in the task network, there must be at least one of the nodes with several branches behind it (Figure 6). Assume that we have generated some of the historical project data and wrapped them into (Component, Task, Duration, Time). At first, all the structured data are sorted according to the attributes of Component and Time. The probability of each branch can be calculated from the number of the tasks happened in the history. When calculating the probability of Task K happens after Task M, we need to count the number of all the task M, named Post (M), and among which how many of them are followed by Task K, named Move (Task M, Task K). The probability P(Task M, Task K) is the division of Move (Task M, Task K) of Post (Task M).

$$P(\text{Task M, Task K}) = \text{Move(Task M, Task K)} \Big/ \text{Post(Task M)} \qquad (1)$$

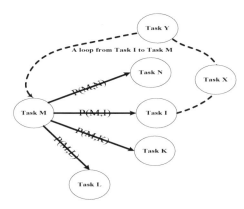

Fig. 6. Probability of branches

In practice, the probability of each branch varies from different kind of components and the complexity. However, to make it simple, the average probability of the branch may be used in the estimation. As shown in Figure 6, there shall be a loop linked by Task M, Task I, Task X and Task Y. In Micro-Estimation model, the route of Task I-X-Y-M will be ignored when estimating Task I with the attributes of Task M.

3.3 Duration Estimation

Duration estimation is based on the assumption that the duration of adjacent tasks are in the linear relationship. Regarding the example shown in Figure 6, Ratio(M,K) can be calculated from the historical data where Task K is the subsequence of Task M:

$$\text{Ratio(M,K)} = \frac{\sum (\text{Duration(Task M)})}{\sum (\text{Duration(Task K)})} \qquad (2)$$

If the duration of task M is known as Duration(Task M), the duration of task K can then be estimated as:

$$\text{Duration(Task K)} = \text{Duration(Task M)} * \text{Ratio(M,K)} \qquad (3)$$

Because the duration of each task is very important in coordination, PERT technique is used to improve the precision of estimation. Taking task M and task L in

Table 1. Ratio indicating of conjoint tasks

Task M	Task L	Ratio
10	5	0.50
6	8	1.33
7	9	1.29
12	8	0.67
...	...	...

Figure 6 as the examples, a table can be generated indicating the possible duration for task L from the historical project data (Table 1).

Regarding each pair of conjoint tasks, such as Task M and Task L in the example, the minimal, average, and maximal ratio will be calculated from Table 1, and assigned to To, Tm and Tp indicating the optimistic, most possible and pessimistic duration (Figure 7).

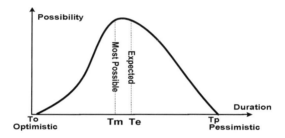

Fig. 7. Duration estimation using PERT

$$To(T,L) = \min imal(ratio(T,L)),$$
$$Tp(T,L) = \max imal(ratio(T,L)), and \tag{4}$$
$$Tm(T,L) = Ratio(T,L)$$

Typically the expected duration will be,

$$Te(T,L) = (To(T,L) + 4*Tm(T,L) + Tp(T,L))/6 \tag{5}$$

Since the design tasks are of different critical and importance, the expected duration will be large for the large scale and complex design task and the critical or important tasks will also be assigned with more time. Formula 6 shows an adjustable duration where there is three factors F1, F2 and F3.

$$Te(T,L) = (F1*To(T,L) + F2*Tm(T,L) + F3*Tp(T,L))/(F1+F2+F3) \tag{6}$$

As a result, the software engineers and architects may adjust the duration estimated according to the situation (Table 2). That is to say, if the task is of large scale, complex, critical, or important, the time will be longer so as to increase the possibility of success. On the other hand, if the task is of small scale, simple, and of low importance, the time can be lesser.

The duration of critical tasks affects the entire schedule of the design project. Therefore, the expected duration Te will be larger to ensure that there is enough buffer. In such way, if there is some estimation error, the manager can have sufficient time to handle the issue. The values of the factors in Table 2 can be adjusted case by case in a certain design project.

Table 2. Factors adjusting according to different situation

Task	F1	F2	F3
Critical	0	3	3
Complicated	1	3	2
Normal	1	4	1
Simple	2	3	1
Non-Critical	3	3	0

When the duration for current tasks are adjusted, duration of the subsequent tasks may then be estimated accordingly. The possible work can then be clarified due to the known probability of each branch and the duration for each task according to formulas 1, 2, 3, 4 and 6:

$$Effort(Task\ K) = \sum (P(M,K) * Duration(Task\ M) * Ratio(M,K) * Te(M,K)) \tag{7}$$

Each task will be specified with "required expertise", and "delay time". Therefore, the human resource usage and knowledge/expertise requirement may be generated according to the effort estimation. Besides, the possible communication delay time will be notified and other design may shift to other tasks during the period.

3.4 Critical Path Analysis

In order to shorten the entire life cycle, tasks are rescheduled according to the degree of emergency. The tasks on the critical path will be placed with a higher priority. The critical path analysis technique has been introduced in section 2 (Figure 2), and many project management tools, such as MS project, can recognize the critical path in the task network when there is no loop inside. Other tasks will be scheduled according to last finish time which will not impact the conjoint tasks. The different of time zone between distributed sites should be taken care of when calculate the available time.

When someone receives the task, the available time will be noticed so that he/she can take care of when the other will need the result and schedule the tasks efficiently.

4 Micro-estimation Expanded FAN

FAN (Fast Automatic Notification) has been used in the design phase of reengineering one module in Lattice system [11]. In Figure 8, it has been expanded with Micro-Estimation. In such way, the estimation of duration and resource message can also be generated and sent to the roles. In order to reduce the message subscription effort, the roles only need to declare their expertise and their requirement of monitoring. Message center is built to handle these requirements, filter the message and send the message to a certain group of roles.

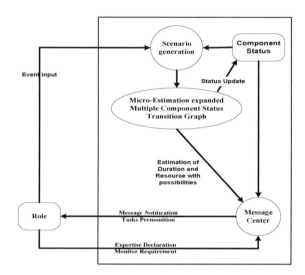

Fig. 8. Micro-Estimation expanded FAN

The software engineers or architects act as roles in the system. When they finish a task, they will record it in the system, which will be recognized as an event in the system. When an event is input, scenario will be generated, and MCSTG will be checked if the exit criterion of the node are satisfied and then find the nodes whose entry criterion are satisfied.

In the former research [11], an automatic notification mechanism was established incorporating with MCSTG, which accepted the event and response with suggestions and warning messages. Dynamic status message subscription and notification were then used to notify different roles with different messages. However, it may be boring to subscribe every small piece of task. In expanded FAN, an expertise based subscription is adopted to reduce the effort in task subscription.

With the Micro-Estimation expand mechanism, the possible tasks with estimated duration and resource will also been generated and sent to the message center. Message center will transfer the task descriptions to the roles with specified expertise or have the monitor requirement.

5 Integration of CQ and ME-FAN

Micro-Estimation expanded FAN (ME-FAN) can be used together with Communication Queue (Figure 9), the roles input events (record the finished activities) into ME-FAN, declare the expertise and require the information from ME-FAN. ME-FAN will determine if the task can be finished according to the exit condition, and generate all the Ready Tasks whose entry criteria are satisfied. Besides, the duration and resource of the possible conjoint tasks will be estimated. All these messages will be sent to Communication Queues where the tasks will be assigned to the roles according to their expertise.

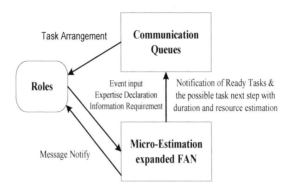

Fig. 9. Using CQ with ME-FAN

It's a future integration plan for Communication Queues sub-system and Micro-Estimation expanded FAN. However, the Communication Queue has not been expanded so as to handle the estimation data and it will just ignore such information currently. In order to exploit the Micro-Estimation technique completely, Communication Queues sub-system will be expanded and handle such estimation data so as to arrange the task efficiently and intelligently.

6 Summary and Discussion

Graph based coordination is introduced and the problem due to the loops in task network is identified. Micro-Estimation technique is proposed to estimate the conjoint tasks so as to facilitate the cooperation. Multiple Component Status Transition Graph is expanded with Micro-Estimation, and so as the FAN sub-system.

Typically, task estimation (Macro-Estimation) focuses on the macro level such as sub-system, module or component. When there are some loops in the task network or the duration of the tasks is not determined, typical critical path analysis techniques fail in finding the critical path. Micro-Estimation can be used together with critical path analysis techniques so as to find the critical tasks on demand.

Currently, ME-FAN sub-system is being tested and improved in a controlled environment. The estimation data will be pushed to the roles according to the declared expertise. The roles may view the estimation data, which will improve their decision making capabilities. Communication Queue has not been expanded due to the large effort in intelligent task allocation. As a result, the entire system could not be used in practice currently.

In future research the authors will focus on how to realize the entire computer supported cooperative design platform with Micro-Estimation. Some techniques of statistics will be used when expanding the Communication Queues sub-system.

Besides, the authors are planning to verify the Micro-Estimation method mathematically in the near future, so as to expand the research result to other domains.

Acknowledgement. This work is part of Lattice® Reengineering project which is funded by State Street Corporation, USA. The contents of this paper are the opinions and conclusions of the authors only and do not necessarily represent the position of State Street Corporation or its subsidiaries, affiliates, officers, directors or employees.

This research was also financial supported by Science and Technology Department of Zhejiang Province with No. 2005C21025 and Education Department of Zhejiang Province with No. 20061085.

References

1. Herbsleb, J.D, Mockus, A.: An Empirical Study of Speed and Communication in Globally Distributed Software Development. IEEE Trans. on Software Engi. 29(6) (2003) 481-492
2. Herbsleb, J.D., Moitra, D.: Global Software Development. IEEE Software 18(2)(2001)16-20
3. Carmel, E.: Global Software Teams: Collaborating, Across Borders and Time Zones. Prentice Hall, Upper Saddle River, N.J. (1999)
4. Carmel, E., Agarwal, R.: Tactical Approaches for Alleviating Distance in Global Software Development. IEEE Software 18(2) (2001) 22-29
5. Olson, J.S. and Teasley, S.: Groupware in the Wild: Lessons Learned from a Year of Virtual Collocation. Proc. ACM 1996 Conference on Computer Supported Cooperative work. (1996) 419-427
6. Karolak, D.W.: Global Software Development. IEEE CS Press. Los Alamitos, Calif. (1998)
7. Mockus, A. and Weiss, D.M.: Globalization by Chunking: A Quantitative Approach. IEEE Software 18(2) (2001) 30-37
8. Xu, B., Yang, X., He, Z., Ma, A.: Global Cooperative Design in Legacy System Reengineering Project. Proc. 8th CSCWD Conference. Xiamen, China (2004) 483-486
9. Allen, T.J.: Managing the Flow of Technology. MIT Press (1977)
10. Grinter, R.E., Herbsleb, J.D., Perry, D.E.: The Geography of Coordination: Dealing with Distance in R&D Work. Proc. Int' ACM SIGROUP Conf. Supporting Group Work (1999) 306-315
11. Xu, B., Yang, X., He, Z., Ma, A.: Enhancing Coordination in Global Cooperative Software Design. Proc. 9th CSCWD Conference. Coventry, UK (2005) 22-26
12. Yang, X., Xu, B.: Towards Adaptive Tasks Arrangement in Offshore Outsourcing Software Development. Proc. International Conference Machine Learning and Cybernetics (ICMLC 2005). Vol. 1. Guangzhou, China (2005) 654-657

CASDE: An Environment for Collaborative Software Development

Tao Jiang[1], Jing Ying[1,2], and Minghui Wu[1,2]

[1] College of Computer Science, Zhejiang University,
Hangzhou 310027, P.R. China
cbjtao@yahoo.com.cn
[2] Dept. of Computer, Zhejiang University City College,
Hangzhou 310015, P.R. China
{yingj, mhwu}@zucc.edu.cn

Abstract. Collaborative software development is called for to meet the requirement of the increasingly expanding software scale. A more advanced software development environment is needed to support the collaborative software development activity. The contribution of this paper is an architecture of process-centered context-aware software development environment, called CASDE, which effectively supports the collaborative development activity. We first discuss the software development activity using activity theory, and highlight its collaborative features. We then present the architecture of CASDE with a brief introduction to its key elements. The focus of the architecture lies in its support to the three levels of collaboration, i.e., co-ordinated level, co-operative level, and co-constructive level. Due to its supportive and integrated nature, the architecture can support collaboration effectively. CASDE is believed to be able to play a positive role in supporting the collaborative software development activity and improving the quality of software systems.

1 Introduction

Programming is primarily a personal activity, and a programmer could develop small software all by himself. However, as software systems became increasingly complicated, the problem of large-scale software development appeared. Complex software systems need to be built by a team, rather than a single programmer. Nowadays, software development is considered to be a kind of collaborative activity, which often involves a group of participants. Thus, collaborative development environment is particularly useful as a place where engineers may collaborate to solve problems [1].

Software process technologies are important in software development. The process-centered software development environments (PCSDEs) form one category of software engineering tools [2], which are designed to support the collaborative activities of large software teams. Ambriola et al. [13] evaluated PCSDEs. Activity theory is useful for analyzing collaborative work in general. Floyd et al. [14] discussed activity theory in the context of software development.

In this paper, based on activity theory, we analyze the nature of software development and show the key elements in the supporting environment so as to

W. Shen et al. (Eds.): CSCWD 2006, LNCS 4402, pp. 367–376, 2007.
© Springer-Verlag Berlin Heidelberg 2007

present an architecture of process-centered context-aware software development environment, CASDE. By the integration of tools and the introduction of context model, CASDE supports the development activities effectively; besides, it highlights the communication among the participants, and effectively supports the three levels of collaboration which are proposed by activity theory.

This paper is structured as follows: section 2 presents the software development activity as a kind of collaborative activity based on activity theory; Section 3 presents the architecture of process-centered context-aware software development environment, CASDE; Section 4 discusses the support of the architecture to three levels of collaboration; and Section 5, as a final conclusion, points out the demerits and gives suggestions for future explorations on the architecture.

2 Software Development Activity

Activity Theory (AT) is "a philosophy and cross-disciplinary framework for studying different forms of human practices and development processes, with both individual and social levels interlinked" [3]. Software development is a kind of design activity, which can be analyzed on the basis of AT. The entities of software development activity are shown in Figure 1.

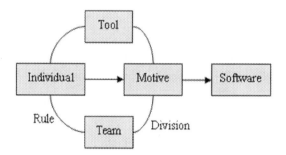

Fig. 1. The model of software development activity

Motive is an abstract concept, referring to the purpose of the development activity. Software stands for the final product. Tool is certain application that supports the operations of software development. The division of work emerges from the structure of the team, and is affected by the motive. The team-individual relationship is mediated by rules. Activity needs the mediation of tool to modify the motive iteratively. The team-individual relationship and the team-motive relationship consist of indispensable elements in successful software development. Therefore, the software development environment should support these relationships effectively to make the development activity go smoothly.

3 Key Elements and the Architecture of CASDE

Several architectures have been put forward ever since the beginning of the technology. For example, CAISE [4-5] is an extensible framework for collaborative software engineering, which supports the integration of software engineering tools. The storage and synchronous sharing of software artifacts is fully considered in CAISE. However, it does not involve the process element, thus it is not sufficient in supporting software development activity. The present condition calls for the development of an effective architecture which fully considers the key elements of software development environment.

3.1 Key Elements

CASDE has realized the relationships among the key elements which are shown in Figure 2.

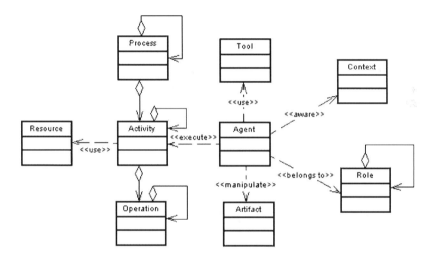

Fig. 2. The key elements of CASDE

Process is composed of activities, while activity is realized through a series of operations which possess resources. The relationship between processes, activities, and operations is not strictly one-to-one. Agents execute activities and manipulate artifacts with the help of tools. Role contains the attributes responsible for the division of work. Context is the most important element that is used to support collaborative features. Through context, agent can get proper information about the environment in which he is working.

Context is described as "any information that can be used to characterize the situation of entities (i.e. whether a person, place or object) that are considered relevant to the interaction between a user and an application, including the user and the application themselves. Context is typically the location, identity and state of people, groups and computational and physical objects." [6] This definition emphasizes objective features that can be tracked and recorded in certain ways. In software development, objective features are essential to a participant when he is working on a shared artifact. With the context element, such environment information can be captured and then processed, by the guidance of rules, to facilitate the development activity.

3.2 The Architecture of CASDE

CASDE highlights development activity which is different from the focus of the production-oriented philosophy. Communication and collaboration are emphasized in the environment. Figure 3 shows the architecture of CASDE.

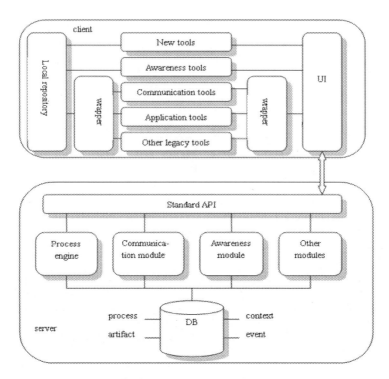

Fig. 3. The architecture of CASDE

The architecture is designed from client-server model. Client has consistent UI to interact with server, and the UI can be customized by users. Many tools are integrated to support corresponding operations. Legacy tools are wrapped by wrapper to interact with the UI and the local repository, thus other legacy tools can be easily adopted. New tools are designed to be integrated into the environment, so wrapper is not necessary for them. Local repository preserves local version of artifacts. Tools in the client may change the status of artifacts in the local repository. Awareness tools use the local repository to monitor changes made on artifacts, and with the help of such tools one developer can notice the modifications made on the shared artifact by others in time.

Server provides various services. Standard APIs are used to interact with client. In this way, the architecture can be more extensible, and new modules can be added into the environment when necessary. Process engine controls the operations of the whole project. Communication module is used to support the traditional interaction, such as email, forum, IM, and mail list. The awareness module supports collaboration in another level. Combined with the awareness tools in the client, concurrent teamwork and negotiate with project members during software development are supported.

4 Support to Collaborative Software Development

The key point of CASDE is the support to collaborative features of software development. "AT identifies a three level hierarchical structure of a collaborative activity: co-ordinated, co-operative, and co-constructive collaborative activity." [7] The software development activity has been analyzed on the basis of AT, and the supports of the architecture to the three level hierarchical structure are discussed as follows.

4.1 Co-ordinated Level

The normal and routine flows of interactions are captured in this level. Process model is an abstract representation of software development activity. A chain of work steps are enacted in the model and the work steps can guide the participants to work. Many patterns can be used to enact the process model and the model can be designed flexibly in order to obtain better performance.

Process model is represented by process modeling language. The relevant aspects of routine work are specified and enacted by the language, so it is very important in supporting the co-ordinated level. In process modeling languages, there exists a trade-off between the level of abstraction and built-in functionality provided, and the flexibility a developer has in specifying a process [2]. The use of such languages should be in accordance with specific process and seek for the balance point between flexibility and proper support level.

Division of work is an important issue in process model. If the work is divided properly, the work can be done more efficiently. In our environment, the division of work is based on roles. Role has some attributes which can be used by the process model to guide the division of work. The attributes of role are specified as domain, position, policy, and relation [8]. Domain is specified according to the work which is given by dividing the project, and it represents a management group. Position describes the status of the role within the group. Policy which can be expressed either by authorization or obligation specifies the activities related to the role. Relation gives the relationship between roles. Agents belong to roles, and they have their own personal agent BDI models [9]. By the combined use of BDI models with role's attributes, the work can be divided much more reasonably.

Participants perform their given work with the help of the environment. The environment has certain mechanisms to facilitate the participant's performance. According to the attributes of roles and the process model, work lists are generated. Thus, the participants are clear about what to do, when to do, and some other specific information. Strict sequences of operations used to be given, and this kind of operations are very suitable for applications which can do the work automatically. Sometimes, it is better to give a developer a group of choices. The developer can choose one sequence to fulfill his work, and thus his behavior becomes more flexible.

Strict control over process used to be thought good, but because of the amount of variability that is usually present in software development activity, it does not always lead to good results. The enforcement policy of process model should be flexible. Specific process should be analyzed carefully. Some parts of the process are monitored and other parts are enforced. This indicates that situated implementation of flexible sequences is more useful.

One nature of the environment is integration. Many tools are integrated into the environment to support all kinds of operations. Tool has envelope called wrapper which gives the tool a standard interface to interact with other parts of the environment. For legacy tools, the environment has not enough control over them and it simply activate them and then wait for results. New tools can be designed and implemented with the purpose of integrated into the environment, thus they can be better controlled. Awareness tools are such kind of tools that they can make full use of the local repository to support the collaborative nature of the software development.

4.2 Co-operative Level

The previous level highlights individual activities. While this level involves actors focusing on a shared problem. "By co-operative collaborative work is meant a mode of interaction in which the actors, instead of each focusing on performing their assigned actions and roles, they focus on a common object and thus share the objective of the collaborative activity."[3] Email, forum, IM, and mail list are used to facilitate communication and discussion among participants. They ensure the collaborative feature of the environment in certain degree, but they are not sufficient. Individuals do not know much about their working environment, thus the collaboration is restricted.

Synchronous communication is needed badly in the environment, but most systems miss such support. A context model is introduced to the environment in order to support synchronous communication. Context represents the environment information, such as who is working with the same artifact, what has he done, when he did that. Context information can be used in mobile collaboration in particular. Based on work contexts, Guerrero et al. [15] proposes an evaluation framework that helps developers to identify useful devices. In the context model some critical attributes [10-11] are represented.

Figure 4 shows the context model. In this model:

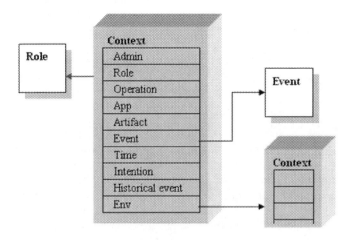

Fig. 4. The context model

- Admin sets up and manages the context.
- Context is related with role, and different roles have different kinds of contexts.
- Operation is the main action of context.
- Context is associated with various applications.
- Artifact is the object of operations. Modifications on artifact are monitored by the environment and events can be triggered accordingly.
- Event is triggered when the environment is aware of certain kind of operations on the shared artifacts.
- Time records when the context was set up.
- Intention means the motivation of the operation in the context.
- Historical event stands for a sequence of events that are associated with the same context.
- Env shows the relationship between contexts.

The context model is used by the awareness tools in the client and the awareness module in the server to support synchronous communication. The awareness tools monitor the participant's operations, and trigger events at proper times. Event can be triggered when change has been made on shared artifacts.

Participants do not always have to know the same context information with each other, and they also do not have to know all the other participants' context information. An awareness framework [10] is used in the architecture. Complete awareness and partial awareness are specified based on whether a participant has access to all possible awareness about another participant. The role, one key element of CASDE, specifies whether a participant needs complete or partial awareness of another participant. Awareness relationship characterizes the awareness information participants in one role may have about participants in another. One role can have complete, partial, or even zero awareness of another role. When two roles have access to precisely the same awareness information about each other, they have symmetrical awareness. When they do not have access to the same types of awareness information about each other, they have asymmetrical awareness.

The context information is processed as illustrated in Figure 5.

The awareness tools in client use the local repository to monitor operations. The changes to the local repository can be captured by the awareness tools, and events are triggered accordingly. Then the awareness tools send the context information to the server. The information is received and analyzed by the awareness module in the server. Based on the rules that specify the relationship between roles and contexts, the context information is processed. Then, according to the result of the analysis, the information is dispatched to related clients. The dispatched information is received by awareness tools in the destinations, and then displayed in a proper way. Thus, in a synchronous way, the participants who are working on the same shared artifact can aware each other's operations in a synchronous way. Combined with the traditional tools, the collaborative activity is supported effectively. With the context model and the context information process mechanism, the concurrent control on artifacts is properly solved. Being aware in time, consistent changes can be made, and potential conflicts can be avoided.

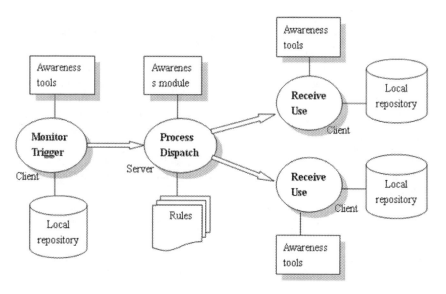

Fig. 5. The context process mechanism

4.3 Co-constructive Level

Change is always presented in the development of software, and problems in development are also discovered gradually. So, co-construction is always needed. By co-constructive collaborative activity is meant interactions in which the actors focus on re-conceptualizing their own organization and interaction in relation to their shared objects. Both the object and the script are reconceptualized, as is the interaction between the participants [12].

In CASDE, this level equates to reconceptualization of process models. Reconceptualization impacts on its associated development process, and the process evolution should be supported. Software development is a discovery process, so changes are always met. In the environment, meta-process is used to empower and constrain the participants of the process development. Special operations of process modeling language and reflective features are also used to support the changes to process. The environment can help developers to determine changes and the consequences of each change, which can be used to support co-construction.

5 Conclusion and Future Work

This paper introduces an architecture of the process-centered context-aware software development environment (CASDE). The software development, according to activity theory, is considered to be a kind of collaborative activity. CASDE effectively supports the three levels of collaboration as presented in activity theory. In particular, it fully supports the co-ordinated level, which is realized by the introduction of the context model and the context information process mechanism.

However, this architecture has demerits like other PCSDEs, such as insufficient support to the co-constructive level, and the lack of the balance between automation and flexibility. In future work, the context model will be refined to be more accurate, and the management features of such an environment should be enhanced.

As can be demonstrated above, software development environments based on CASDE support the collaborative software development activity more effectively, and it can be believed that higher quality software systems can be produced thereby. Further research on this architecture will make CASDE more powerful, providing a better environment for software development activity.

Acknowledgments. This work is partially supported by Fok Ying Tung Education Foundation (Grant No.: 94030).

References

1. Booch, G. and Brown, A.: Collaborative Development Environments. Advances in Computers 59 (2003)
2. Barthelmess, P. and Anderson K.: A View of Software Development Environments Based on Activity Theory. Computer Supported Cooperative Work 11 (1-2) (2002) 13-37
3. Kuutti, K.: Activity Theory as a Potential Framework for Human-Computer Interaction. Context and Consciousness: Activity Theory and Human Computer Interaction. MIT Press (1995) 17-44
4. Cook, C. and Churcher, N.: An Extensible Framework for Collaborative Software Engineering. Proceedings of the Tenth Asia-Pacific Software Engineering Conference. Chiang Mai, Thailand (2003) 290-299
5. Cook, C., Churcher, N. and Irwin, W.: Towards Synchronous Collaborative Software Engineering. Proceedings of the Eleventh Asia-Pacific Software Engineering Conference. Busan, Korea (2004) 230-239
6. Dey, A., Salber, D. and Abowd, G.: A Conceptual Framework and a Toolkit for Supporting the Rapid Prototyping of Context-Aware Applications. Human-Computer Interaction Journal 16 (2-4) (2001) 97-166
7. Bardram, J.: Designing for the Dynamics of Cooperative Work Activities. Proceedings of the Conference on Computer-Supported Cooperative Work. Seattle, Washington, USA (1998) 89-98
8. Lupu, E. and Sloman, M.: Towards A Role-Based Framework for Distributed Systems Management. Journal of Network and Systems Management 5(1)(1997) 5-30
9. Rao, A. and Georgeff, M.: BDI Agents: from Theory to Practice. Proceedings of the First International Conference on Multi-Agent Systems (ICMAS 95). San Francisco, USA (1995) 312-319
10. Drury, J. and Williams, M.G.: A Framework for Role-Based Specification and Evaluation of Awareness Support in Synchronous Collaborative Applications. Proceedings of the 11th International Workshops on Enabling Technologies for Collaborative Enterprises (WETICE'02). Pittsburgh, USA (2002) 12-17

11. Gross, T. and Prinz, W.: Modelling Shared Contexts in Cooperative Environments: Concept, Implementation, and Evaluation. Computer Supported Cooperative Work 13(3-4) (2004) 283-303
12. Engeström, Y., Brown, K., Christopher, L. and Gregory, J.: Coordination, Cooperation, and Communication in the Courts. In: Mind, Culture, and Activity. Cambridge University Press (1997) 369-388
13. Ambriola, V., Conradi, R. and Fuggetta, A.: Assessing Process-centered Software Engineering Environments. ACM Transactions on Software Engineering and Methodology 6(3) (1997) 283-328
14. Floyd, C., Züllighoven, H., Budde, R. and Keil-Slawik, R. (eds.).: Software Development and Reality Construction. Springer-Verlag, Berlin (1992)
15. Guerrero, L., Ochoa, S., Pino, J.A., Collazos, C.: Selecting Computing Devices to Support Mobile Collaboration. Group Decision and Negotiation 15(3) (2006) 243-271

Context Dynamics in Software Engineering Process

Flávia Maria Santoro[1], Patrick Brézillon[2], and Renata Mendes de Araujo[1]

[1] Departamento de Informática Aplicada , UNIRIO
Avenida Pasteur, 458, Rio de Janeiro, 22290-045 RJ, Brasil
`flavia.santoro@uniriotec.br, renata.araujo@uniriotec.br`
[2] LIP6 – Université Pierre et Marie Curie
8, rue du Capitaine Scott 75015 - Paris – France
`Patrick.Brezillon@lip6.fr`

Abstract. Software design processes are complex, highly collaborative and usually performed under time pressure. Knowledge is volatile due to constant turn over in software organizations and continuous advances in design technology. Software engineers usually depend on tacit knowledge shared among them in order to perform their tasks. Communicating this type of knowledge can only be facilitated by creating a shared context among actors. The aim of this paper is to present a proposal for modeling and use of shared contexts for improving software organization's knowledge management, collaboration and learning. We propose a strategy for organizing, capturing and retrieving knowledge into/from organizational memory including contextual information.

1 Introduction

Software design processes are complex, highly collaborative and usually performed under time pressure. Knowledge is volatile due to constant turn over in software organizations and continuous advances in design technology. Professionals usually depend on tacit knowledge shared among them in order to perform their tasks, share experiences and finally learn. However, software organizations' culture is still far from collaborative and productivity rush leaves few time to manage knowledge [1].

Knowledge relies on team members' background, experiences, on each software artifact, and also on the activities, facts, and situations faced during a project development. This constitutes what is usually called the Organizational Memory (OM) [1] and serves as base for organizational learning, when effectively managed. However, creating a real collaborative work environment requires more than just codifying knowledge, storing it in information systems and developing access and distribution. It is also a matter of facilitating interaction, communication and mutual understanding.

We argue that communicating knowledge can only be facilitated by creating a shared context among actors. A software designer can not use the knowledge that exists in OM if he is not able to understand its context. While performing a specific task in such a complex, social and collaborative work, software designer should be aware of overall situation, group and environment – the context – where the activity is inserted in order to effectively perform it [2-3].

The term *context* has been often used as the shared understanding and information that group participants should be *aware* of in order to perform their tasks. According

W. Shen et al. (Eds.): CSCWD 2006, LNCS 4402, pp. 377–388, 2007.
© Springer-Verlag Berlin Heidelberg 2007

to Daft and Lengel [4] total understanding of a group activity relies in the ways it is possible to reduce equivocality and uncertainty degree among members. While uncertainty refers to the absence of information, equivocality refers to ambiguity, which means, existence of conflicting interpretations about subjects or objects that groups deal with [5]. This lack of knowledge contextualization caused by equivocality and uncertainty can lead to knowledge misuse or may cause its wrong application.

Studies on how context information can be modeled and manage in collaborative applications have also started to be carried out [6-8]. However, there is still a need to detail which context information can be retained, recorded and managed in specific domains, such as software engineering activities. Furthermore, it is still an open issue how software engineering tools can provide context information in order to better support collaborative knowledge use and management.

This paper discusses the representation of context dynamics to improve collaborative software design, based on a previous characterization from Artificial Intelligence [2]. Section 2 discusses when software designers need to access the OM. Section 3 presents context concept and how knowledge is dynamically moved among its dimensions in a problem-solving situation. Section 4 shows a scenario and implications of context for collaboration in software design process. Section 5 describes our proposal to manage context dynamics and Section 6 concludes the paper.

2   Organizational Memory Approach for Software Engineering

Considering software organizations nature, some aspects such as culture and design work characteristics determine the way it must be managed:

Focus on the Process: Explicit working process serves as a reference to acquire, develop, disseminate and use organizational knowledge in a systematic way. Process becomes the infrastructure for the organization not only to perform its activities but also to learn with its execution, observe needs for change and collaborate [9].

Group support: Almost all the phases of a software project (specification, design, documentation, planning, design, programming, reviews, decision making and training) are performed collaboratively. Thus, supporting group interactions is the keystone for improving the process productivity and software quality [10].

Communities of practice: The OM can be seen as a learning environment. Solutions for collaborative and learning [11-13] are suggested to support communities of practice where a professional can find resources for performing a specific task, meet specialists, and access important aspects and organizational historical data.

In his daily activities, a software process participant has to deal with those three perspectives of using the OM somehow in a transparent manner: when following the process, a given task may be performed collaboratively and its execution may require the need of reusing and sharing experiences inside the organizational community of practice. It must be assured that each actor has access to the necessary knowledge in order to perform his activity and interpret data and information available for it.

However, when following a process using a CASE (Computer-Aided Software Engineering) tool, interacting through groupware or sharing experiences within a virtual community, the knowledge available to a participant should be more tailored, refined and precise to his needs: the specific task must be contextualized. Any actor should be aware of what is relevant or not in that specific situation in order to perform it accordingly. But, while inserted in such a complex, social and collaborative work, he should also be aware of the overall moment, situation, and environment – the *context* – where his activity is inserted in order to effectively perform it.

Organizational memory (OM) is a concept used to represent how groups should organize different kinds of information related to the activities being performed. The OM must be a "place" where group members share not only documents and products but also ideas, thoughts and discussions about the interaction. It is necessary to preserve the network of information that includes facts, restrictions, decisions and their reasons, the meaning of concepts, as well as the formal documents, in order to completely understand the interaction rationale.

3 Dynamics of Shared Context

Context is a complex description of the knowledge shared on physical, social, historical and other circumstances where actions or events happen in the real world. All this knowledge is not a part of the actions to execute or the events that occur, but influences the execution of an action or event interpretation without intervening in it explicitly. The understanding of actions and events requires contextual information on them [14]. In any domain where understanding, reasoning, problem-solving and learning are needed, the concept of context plays an important role.

We use the context model proposed by Brézillon and Pomerol [14], in which context is always related to a focus, e.g., task, problem solving or decision making. At a given step of this focus, context is the sum of all the knowledge possessed by an actor on the whole process. The authors [14] distinguish between the part of the context, which is relevant for current focus of attention, and the part, which is not relevant. The latter part is called *External Knowledge*. The former is called *Contextual Knowledge*.

Contextual Knowledge is personal to an actor and is evoked by situations and events, determined by his focus [15]. At a given focus, part of the contextual knowledge is proceduralized. *Proceduralized Context* is a part of the contextual knowledge, which is invoked, assembled, organized, structured and situated according to the focus; it is used in the task performing at this focus.

When an unpredicted event occurs, the attention of actors becomes focused on it and part of contextual knowledge is proceduralized. When the task proceeds from one step to the following one, there is a movement between the contextual knowledge and the proceduralized context because a new item enters or leaves the focus of attention. Thus, context is dynamic within the scope of a specific task accomplishment [16].

In collaborative work, only shared context is effective. It is a shared knowledge space that is explored and exploited by participants. Proceduralized context contains a sub-set of the contextual knowledge that have been assembled, structured, organized, discussed and accepted (or at least made compatible) by the agents for addressing the current focus. Consequently, the proceduralized context becomes part of the shared contextual knowledge of the actors. Making context explicit is a way of *explaining* knowledge in order to be effectively, collaboratively and correctly used [17].

As stated by Winograd [18], context emerges from the dialog among agents and the interpretation of each agent intention depends on mutually available context. So, the communication process both influences as is influenced by the underlying context. Effective communication leads, then, to an improved understanding of the problems, needs, goals, expectations, beliefs of each participant, of the overall group, and finally, of the task at hand. A shared context allows a simultaneous view of global and local information to make coherent information and corresponding action to perform. Thinking that contextual knowledge acts as a filter that defines, at a given time, what knowledge pieces must be taken into account from those that are not necessary or already shared, agents are provided with a sharper and more effective set of knowledge at each moment, turning out to increase their productivity.

Shared context also reinforces ties and trust among work team members. The more we go back-and-forth in a conversation, the more we know about each other and can tune our questions and comments to be more aligned with each others interests and needs. The shared social space provides a sense of the whole that enables members of a widely distributed group to see themselves in context [19]. Finally, turning context explicit and helping group members to visualize the ties, cohesiveness and interaction outcomes can help people to feel committed with the work, discover possibilities for improving it, and be stimulated to work collaboratively.

4   A Collaborative Software Design Scenario

We present a scenario in a software organization where different actors need to interact in order to take care of a design task. Our aim is twofold. First we illustrate different kinds of context, its dynamics, collaborative building, and relevance to effective communication and knowledge sharing among actors of a group constituted along with the problem solution building. Second, we integrate this view in the corresponding community (the group), showing how this community nature evolves along the problem solving. Thus, the scenario is discussed along three dimensions: the focus that emerge from some events, the group that is constituted and the shared context built. Each dimension evolves dynamically during the setting development.

4.1   Types of Context and Their Dynamics

Let say there is a business analyst, Daniel, who works on a software development company, Sw&Sw. He joined his manager in a meeting with the users of a system developed by Sw&Sw for a special client FunCoo. The system is an application to enable visualizing information about the projects carried out by FunCoo which is extracted from a very large integrated database. For this meeting, it is possible to distinguish the contextual knowledge related to its objective (negotiation on new requirements) from Daniel's individual external knowledge (he was not aware about some contract details and the product design). During the meeting, one of the users asks Daniel to intervene for a new maintenance. The client argues that the technology used in the implementation was not very user-friendly and they wished to migrate to a Web interface. This new focus leads Daniel to proceduralize a part of his contextual knowledge and access new external knowledge in order to address it.

Focus 1: Understanding the task

Daniel is not aware of the early development process of such system (a piece of external knowledge for him). According to his individual context, the request seemed out of project scope, since system is working well and initial specification was agreed by everybody, including the client. Daniel's conclusion is to reject the client request.

After the meeting, the manager informs Daniel that the user who asked the request is the contract leader. The enrichment of his contextual knowledge with manager's information and its consequences leads Daniel to make compatible the quite-obliged acceptance of the request but also minimize the effort on it as a new proceduralized context. There is yet a gap between the new proceduralized context and the focus, and filling this gap requires to find someone else who worked specifically on that problem to get the details about such implementation. At this point of the scenario, the group is constituted by Daniel and his Manager. They both share their individual contexts from where they jointly can build a proceduralized context.

Figure 1 summarizes context dynamics for Focus 1. We show the Knowledge Pieces and the type of context they represent to each member (Daniel and Manager) at that moment: External Knowledge (EK), Contextual Knowledge (CK) with the Interaction Context (SC) between them during the interaction, making possible to build Proceduralized Context (PC). We observe that some rules can explain and represent how PC is built from the interaction.

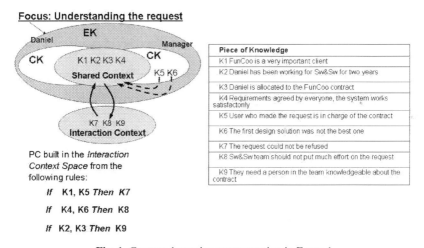

Fig. 1. Context dynamics representation in Focus 1

For filling the gap between focus and PC, the manager proposes Andrea with whom Daniel worked in previous projects (shared contextual knowledge that was proceduralized contexts at that time). They both know she is knowledgeable about this contract and could give more information to make a work plan. Thus, the group constituted now has more competence for addressing the focus and the problem solving goes to the next step.

However, Daniel needs to enrich his individual context by sharing Andrea's individual contextual information (she gets some non registered pieces of knowledge because she was there at the time the events occurred). This change of the shared context induces an evolution of the focus, which from no solution initially concerns now the selection of a solution among alternatives.

Focus 2: Deciding issues for the new design task
Based on her memory about that system, Andrea decided to reinforce the group by including Claudia because she is a specialist on such technology and thus enrich shared context. In parallel, each group member looks for enriching his/her individual context. They point out that the decision made previously was mainly for using a technology already used by FunCoo in other systems and not the best one. This solution impacted the whole product and thus it would be difficult to disassociate the interface from the rest. Thus, it is not yet possible to build an efficient proceduralized context for the current focus, and additional (external) knowledge must be added in the proceduralized context.

From Claudia's individual context, group context acquires information that there is a kind of configuration that allows capturing all the data and presents them in a Web format. They should study it because it would certainly be less expensive than rewrite the application. With this new shared context, it is possible to build a more powerful proceduralized context and thus move focus towards implementation step.

The team has now evolved in terms of its participants (Daniel, Manager, Andrea and Claudia) and shared context. Figure 2 summarizes context dynamics for Focus 2. People present new contextual information about the focus and through discussing it could reach a new proceduralized context, which turns to be the context for the design decision to be implemented.

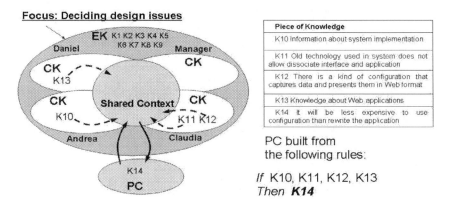

Fig. 2. Context dynamics representation in Focus 2

Focus 3: Implementing the new design solution
For addressing totally the focus, the group decides to host a new member, Alex, an interface designer. His role is to integrate the technologies and implement the solution. For that, Alex builds a prototype for the interface. Although each team member is a specialist in a specific domain, by sharing with the others, members not only enrich their individual contexts about the project, but also about their interaction with

them. This suggests that knowledge sharing is conducted through a social network that needs to be supported accordingly. In other words, to disseminate knowledge it is necessary to allow people to communicate properly creating a network where they can easily find each other and consequently the information they need to perform their tasks.

Figure 3 summarizes the context dynamics for the Focus 3. While a specialist starts implementing the design solution, the group builds the final context about the issues in the technology configuration for that system and the prototype. Part of the knowledge used in previous focus becomes external knowledge now.

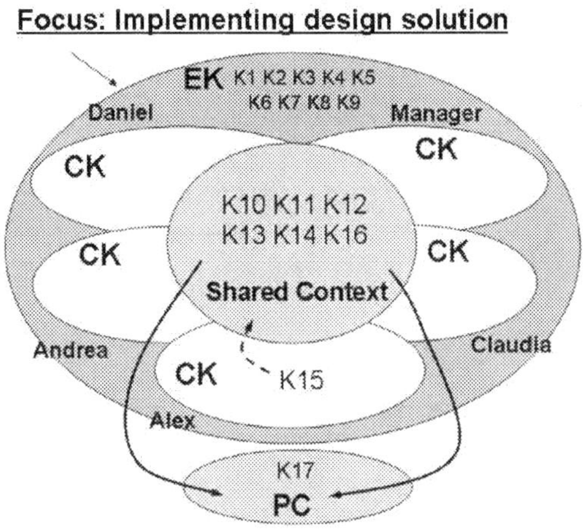

Focus: Implementing design solution

Fig. 3. Context dynamics representation in Focus 3

We may also notice that the contextual knowledge achieved different levels (in-depth view): organization, project, team, individual; and considered heterogeneous elements (in-width view): different individuals, tasks, roles and organizations. However, and most important, although they could collaborate and share information, ideas and knowledge, all the contextual information was kept informal, not registered together with the knowledge.

4.2 Building Context Through Interaction

Daniel found information for executing his task by interacting through work team. He was thus able to develop the needed contextual knowledge and then built the right proceduralized context. As a side-effect, this collaborative work enriched all the members of the team. By identifying precisely the gap between the focus and the proceduralized contexts Daniel was able to achieve (the information necessary to solve the problem and the information Daniel actually acquired), it has been possible to find the right persons with the needed contextual knowledge.

The group has evolved during the problem solving, as especially seen with the evolution of the shared context. In parallel, individual contexts also evolved either by importing directly pieces of external knowledge needed to understand parts of the problem or by integration of proceduralized contexts obtains through member interaction. The enrichment of individual contexts includes problem solving development, but also the way in which the team members worked together (e.g. need of adjustment among members).

A lesson learned from this scenario is that the most effective way for learning is by performing and sharing experiences. Learning is not just to know a procedure but to observe different alternatives put in context for performing it, identifying the gap between the focus and the proceduralized context at any moment.

This scenario points out the following other lessons learned:

- A group of actors take part at a task with specific focus, contributing with their amount of contextual knowledge, developing task contextual knowledge;
- Individual contexts act as a filter that defines what pieces of knowledge must be taken into account by the actor for the collaborative work;
- Shared context developed by a group becomes part of members contexts;
- Most of all, we can observe that the main part of shared context remained tacit, not registered, and consequently difficult to be explained, understood communicated and reused.

5   Management of Shared Context

According to the types of knowledge and contexts we found out on the scenario discussed, we propose a model that defines the main dimensions that can explain the context of a software development task: the user's *individual* context, the *team* context, the *project* context, the *software product* context, the *client* context and maybe for specific technical tasks, the context of the *software engineering domain* or the *client business domain area*. The context of a task is also explained by the context of its previous activities [20].

1. **Software Engineering Domain Area.** The software development area has many technical aspects that surrounds and are used a specific project.
2. **Individual context.** Individuals have specific experiences, expertise, motivations and interests, independently of the organization, project or roles he can assume. Each person uses a personal body of (contextual) knowledge for reasoning, interpreting, recognizing information in order to integrate the new information in this body of knowledge.
3. **Team.** The context of a team reflects the aggregation of its many participants and roles. Teams are established within a development project to perform specific tasks such as: planning, testing, specification, programming etc. Teams built with different participants will plan and perform their tasks in a different manner. The successful or unsuccessful outcomes of their tasks are new knowledge that can be stored in the organizational memory.
4. **Tasks.** The context of distinct tasks requires specific information and knowledge: testing software, for example, requires the availability of practices, tools and procedures totally different form software requirements elicitation. Additionally, the flow of activities within a project can influence each activity outcome while performed by different teams, with different skills, experiences and motivations.

5. **Project.** A specific project comprises an also specific context in respect to the product to be constructed, its goals and the process to be followed. The relationship or production of an specific individual in a project or within the organization provides new context information related to the practices performed, his performance and the need for reviewing the existing practices in order to improve them and make them tailored to the developers needs.

6. **Organization.** The context of the organization describes its business targets and its standard practices. The software development domain defines context characteristics such as new proposed practices and historical results of their application. The results obtained by organizations while providing services to their clients generate historical information of successful or unsuccessful use of practices and methodologies suggested in the market.

7. **Client.** The client has also organizational characteristics and culture that have to be taken into consideration.

8. **Client Domain Area.** Each specific client also has his business scope, domain area, priorities and business objectives.

9. **Product.** The kind of requirements, product scope that will be built, its elements and interdependence among them are a new set of relevant context information.

Based on this context model, we organized an OM by detailing each dimension into a corresponding ontology that should map context dimensions into the knowledge source objects stored into the OM (documents, databases, urls, individuals and groups). For each specific task, its corresponding contextual knowledge can be inferred from the OM based on the characteristics of the task using defined contextual rules. Each actor's individual context, not already persisted in the OM can be requested to or voluntary informed by the actor, also serving as data for determining the task context. An overview of the context capture, retrieval and persistency process is depicted in Figure 4 [21].

The result of the inference that we called the *task context set* can be presented/explained to each task participant. All other information not made available in the context set is considered as external knowledge. Anytime information is retrieved from the external knowledge, it is included in the context set as new context information. Therefore, throughout the execution of the task, the context set can change its content whenever a new external knowledge is introduced or retrieved by the actors. However, each new knowledge inserted into the context set may cause the need of new inferences to determine the new task context, e.g., the context set changes dynamically whenever the task proceeds.

The movement that allows the development of the right context in a specific individual or team focus can be expressed by "contextual rules" that transforms contextual knowledge into a proceduralized context. For a given focus, its proceduralized context is determined by the inferred contextual knowledge from the OM. To determine this contextual knowledge, we can conceive and formalize a set of rules, for example: "Depending on the actor's experience and competence in the technique needed to perform the task (information that relies into the enterprise ontology), related material such as tutorials, URL links, or experienced professionals on the technique could be retrieved from the software engineering domain ontology". This rule could be generically formalized as follows: **If actor's** experience in (technique) is low **then** retrieve software engineering domain knowledge {tutorials, URLs…}

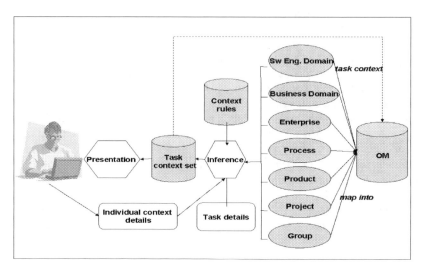

Fig. 4. Context capture, retrieval and persistency

When a task is completed, the context set that result from the interaction that occurred along the task performance is considered as its final proceduralized context. Our approach considers that the resulting proceduralized context should be stored into the OM, associated to the performed task allowing its reuse.

Considering group interactions, relationships between context management and organizational memories come to light while we explicitly formalize context dimensions along with the knowledge stored in the OM and provide services for capturing and retrieving context information from it [22-23].

6 Conclusions and Future Work

This paper discussed the use of context within knowledge management in software organizations. Our main point is that knowledge can not be managed freely. Instead, it must be managed in respect to its current context of generation and use. We described a typical software design scenario where we tried to show how the focus of attention on a specific task changes the need for knowledge and also how interaction, collaboration and the simple knowledge use in an specific context generates knew knowledge.

As long as there are different types of contexts (group context, individual contexts, focus context, shared context) evolving along the problem solving, the nature of the group that is constituted for the problem solving evolves too. Initially, there are only few persons and the group is not well structured. During the progression of the problem solving, the group becomes more organized, constituting first a community and finally a real task force with all the means for solving the problem.

We have learned from the scenario presented that the effective understanding of the collaborative situation in order to allow participants to efficiently work is proportional to the possibilities of being aware of each actor's context and of the overall group context as well. For improving the communication and coordination aspects of collaboration, participants must know their resulting shared context. In most situations, we can observe that only the focus is recorded, the shared context among actors remains unregistered. They remain implicit in each participant's knowledge. That is why sometimes it can be very difficult to explain, to communicate and, consequently to understand the underlying context.

In a shared context there are elements that are no more made explicit between participants, who refer to them implicitly (e.g., "see you tomorrow" should mean "see you tomorrow, in the lab where we work together, when you arrive because I arrive early"; the 'where' and 'when' are tacit in the first sentence). All this needs to be explained to a new participant. They also share a vocabulary in which ambiguities are removed.

We presented a proposal for assembling software organizational memory where the concept of context is used as a way for managing and sharing knowledge. In order to identify what context is in a given situation in software development, ontologies categorizes the main context dimensions available at the OM. Ontologies are being detailed allowing the formalization of rules that can be applied to discover and provide context information in its different types: external knowledge, contextual knowledge and proceduralized context.

As a next research step, we intend to use this approach for specifying and implementing an OM management system. Other research issues are concerned with the design of interface metaphors convenient for presenting and explaining context to users as well as the method for obtaining user explanations from specific context situations.

References

1. Ackerman, M.S.: Augmenting the Organizational Memory: A Field Study of Answer Garden. Proc. Conf. on Computer-Supported Cooperative Work (1994) 243-252
2. Brézillon, P.: Context in problem solving: A survey. The Knowledge Engineering Review 14(1) (1999) 1-34
3. Dey, A.K., Salber, D., Abowd, G.D.: A Conceptual Framework and a Toolkit for Supporting the Rapid Prototyping of Context-Aware Applications. Human-Computer Interaction Journal 16(2-4) (2001) 97-166
4. Daft, R.L., Lengel, R.H. and Trevino, L.K.: Message equivocality, media selection, and manager performance: Implications for information systems. MIS Quarterly 11(3) (1987) 355-366
5. Araujo, R.M., Borges, M.R.S., Dias, M.S.: A Framework for the Classification of Computer Supported Collaborative Design Approaches. Proc. III CYTED-RITOS International Workshop on Groupware. Madrid (1997)
6. Rosa, M.G.P., Borges, M.R.S., Santoro, F.M.: A conceptual framework for analyzing the use of context in groupware. Lecture Notes in Computer Science 2806 (2003) 300-313
7. Borges, M.R.S., Brézillon, P., Pino, J.A., Pomerol, J.-Ch.: Context- awareness in Group Work: three case studies. Proceedings of the IFIP Int. Conference on Decision Support Systems (DSS-2004). Prato, Italy (2004)
8. Brézillon, P., Borges, M.R.S., Pino, J., Pomerol, J-Ch.: Context-based awareness in group work. Proceedings of the 17th International FLAIRS Conference. Miami, Florida (2004)

9. Holz, H., Könnecker, A., Maurer, F.: Task-Specific Knowledge Management in a Process-Centered SEE. Proceedings of the Workshop on Learning Software Organizations (LSO'01). Kaiserslauntern, Germany (2001)
10. Araujo, R.M., Borges, M.R.S.: Extending the Software Process Culture - An approach based on groupware and workflow. Proc. 3rd Int. Conf. on Product Focused Software Process Improvement (PROFES) (2001)
11. Santoro, F.M., Borges, M.R.S., Santos, N.: Learning through collaborative projects: The architecture of an environment. International Journal of Computer Applications in Technology 16(2) (2003) 127-141
12. Schneider, K., von Hunnius, J., Basili, V.R.: Experience in Implementing a Learning Software Organization. IEEE Software 19(3) (May/June 2002) 46-49
13. Wenger, E., McDermott, R.A., Snyder, W.: Cultivating communities of practice: a guide to managing knowledge. Boston, Mass., Harvard Business School Press (2002)
14. Brézillon, P., Pomerol, J-Ch.: Contextual knowledge sharing and cooperation in intelligent assistant systems. Le Travail Humain 62(3) (1999) 223-246
15. McCarthy, J.: Notes on formalizing context. Proc. 13th IJCAI (1993) 555-560
16. Brézillon, P.: Individual and team contexts in a design process. Proc. 36th Hawaii Int.Conf. on Systems Sciences (HICSS-36) (2003)
17. Brézillon, P.: Representation of procedures and practices in contextual graphs. The Knowledge Engineering Review 18(2) (2003) 147-174
18. Winograd, T.: Architectures for Context. HCI Journal 16(2/3/4) (2001) 401-419
19. Kimball, L.; Rheingold, H.: How Online Social Networks Benefit Organizations. URL: www.rheingold.com /Associates/onlinenetworks.html (accessed on 2005)
20. Araujo, R.M., Santoro, F.M., Brézillon, P., Borges, M.R.S., Rosa, M.G.P.: Context Models for Managing Software Development Knowledge. Proc. Workshop on Modeling and Retrieval of Context. Germany (2004)
21. Araujo, R.M., Brezillon, P.: Modeling Software Organizational Knowledge through Context. Proc. Knowledge Sharing and Collaborative Engineering (2004)
22. Van Elst, L., Abecker, A.: Integrating task, role and user modeling in organizational memories. Proc. 14th International Florida Artificial Intelligence Research Society Conference. Miami, FL (2001) 295-299
23. Klemke, R.: The Notion of Context in Organisational Memories. Proc. CONTEXT 99: Modeling and Using Context. Trento, Italy (1999)

Tracking Design Dependencies to Support Conflict Management

Mohamed-Zied Ouertani, Lilia Gzara, and Gabriel Ris

CRAN – Research Centre for Automatic Control, CNRS UMR 7039
Nancy University, Faculty of Sciences and Technologies,
BP 239 Vandoeuvre-lès-Nancy 54506, France
{Mohamed-Zied.Ouertani, Lilia.Gzara}@cran.uhp-nancy.fr,
Gabriel.Ris@aipl.uhp-nancy.fr

Abstract. Due to the multi-actors interaction during collaborative design, conflicts can be revealed from disagreements between designers about proposed designs. A critical element of collaborative design would be conflict resolution. This paper proposes a methodology to support designers during the process of conflict management; focusing mainly on identifying the conflict resolution team and evaluating the selected solution impact issues. The methodology is based on product data dependencies network which is composed of the handled data and the dependency links between them. Qualification concepts are introduced to manage these dependencies. In order to identify this network, a traceability model to track the design process is proposed.

1 Introduction

Collaborative product design is involved in complicated interaction among multi-disciplinary design teams in a distributed, heterogeneous and dynamic environment, including communication, cooperation, coordination and negotiation [11]. Due to the multi-actors interaction conflicts can be revealed from disagreements between designers about proposed designs. In fact, each actor has his own point of view, concerns and objectives regarding the design project. According to Klein [6], conflicts occur when at least two incompatible design commitments are made, or when a design party has a negative critique of another design party's actions. Hence, a critical element of collaborative design would be the conflict resolution.

Insight for conflict resolution in collaborative design is available from diverse sources, which include approaches to conflict resolution in social sciences, computer-supported methods for facility design and conflict resolution in collaborative product design. The focus of these research works is on suggesting conflict detection mechanisms [16], defining conflict resolution strategies [6] and providing support to facilitate the negotiation between the different actors involved in the conflict [1][10] [15]. Indeed, all these works reveal that negotiation is a widely accepted approach for conflict resolution in collaborative design. However, none of them touches upon the problematic of identifying the actors that should be involved in the negotiation process leading to problem solving. This identification phase of the negotiation team constitutes a pre-requisite for conflict resolution. For example, the development of a business jet may involve more than 140000 data which need to be managed

W. Shen et al. (Eds.): CSCWD 2006, LNCS 4402, pp. 389–400, 2007.
© Springer-Verlag Berlin Heidelberg 2007

appropriately by the development team. In order to provide a solution to a conflict occurring on one of these data, design actors have to collaborate and negotiate forming this way the *negotiation team*. Thus, it will be difficult first to identify who are the actors involved in the design process; and second, who are the right actors (competencies, knowledge, domain, etc.) to resolve the conflict rapidly and in a proper way; i.e. to avoid the appearance of new conflicts.

The conflict management process could be perceived as the succession of five phases:

- Conflict detection: to consider means of detecting conflict occurrence depending on the method used to represent design constraints, design goals, design intents and design dependencies;
- Forming the conflict resolution team: to identify and form the team of actors (human or Software) required to participate in the resolution of the identified conflict. This phase is considered as a prerequisite to conflict resolution;
- Negotiation management: to conduct and control a collaborative negotiation session to reach a consensus;
- Solution generation: to apply actors own domain knowledge to provide the optimal solution to the considered conflict;
- Solution impact evaluation: to propagate the selected solution onto the product and the design process.

Likewise, the selected solution impact evaluation phase has not been tackled in the above reviewed works. Indeed, a selected solution may lead to modifications on the design process organisation, on a subset of the product to design or on the availability of the resources for the design.

The objective of this paper is to bring in methodological elements that allow the identification of the actors who are to be involved in the conflict resolution as well as the assessment of the propagation impact of the selected solution on the product development process. The first section of this paper describes a motivation example illustrating conflicts in a collaborative design. The second section presents the proposed methodology to support conflict management during design progress. The main concept of this methodology is the capture of the data dependencies network during design progress. This includes the proposal for a UML (Unified Modelling Language) traceability model to capture the product data dependencies. Finally, the paper concludes with a discussion of directions for future work.

2 Motivation Example

The case study concerns the design process of a Flexible Assembly System (FAS) at the training centre AIP-PRIMECA[1] Lorraine (AIPL). This system is mainly composed of an item loading station, two workstations, an item unloading station and a transportation system composed of a conveyor and a palette. We are interested in the workstation design process; which is composed of four concurrent phases:

- workstation frame design sub phase;
- workstation energy block (pneumatic and electric energy) design phase;

---

[1] http://www.aipl.uhp-nancy.fr

- Assembly Operation System (items positioning) design phase;
- Automata design phase.

A special focus is given to the design of the assembly operation system which is composed of a handler mechanism and a positionner mechanism. The handler is an arm controlled by the automata, which allows moving parts from the workstation stores to the palette. The positionner is made of three stores from which the handler picks up the parts to assemble and of a director responsible for directing the items towards a given position in order to guarantee the quality of the product.

The assembly operation system design phase is split into two parallel planned activities: the handler design process and the positionner design process. At the beginning of the assembly operation system phase, the concerned actors have to respect the following requirements:

- the palette shape and the positioning perimeter of the wholes to place the items;
- the automata's, assembly operation system's and energy block's positions;
- the jacks available for the actors to design their respective systems: three big jacks, four medium jacks, three small jacks and three rotary jacks.

The handler designer defines the mechanism by using the four medium jacks available (H_Solution1). This solution only allows four possible positions split into two positions on the workstation and two positions on the palette. Hence, the positionner designer is able to define only two alimentations composed of a vertical store with a spring each. A director is affected to each one of them (P_Solution1). The UML activity diagram Figure 1 partially describes the succession of these activities.

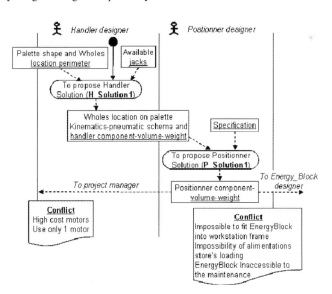

Fig. 1. Partial UML activity diagram of the operative part design process

A conflict is then detected following from an acceptability problem of the positionner planned activity solution by the Energy Block designer. He realises that it is impossible to fit the energy block subset into the workstation frame because the stores' lower parts lie within the frame dedicated to the energy block subset. Moreover, this volume problem results in the impossibility to upload the alimentations stores' as well as the inaccessibility to the maintenance of the energy subset.

Additionally, a second conflict appears: the project manager rejects the solution of a director (i.e. motor) for each alimentation because of the high cost of the motors. He requires that this subset is composed of only one engine.

Consequently, new configurations of the positionner and the handler subsystems are to be proposed taking into account the problems encountered earlier.

The FAS design process scenario has been presented to illustrate the conflicts in a collaborative design context. In the following section, a methodology support the conflict management process is presented; the design process example is used to illustrate this methodology.

3   Design Traceability Methodology to Support Conflict Management

3.1   Specifications

The design process is a succession of activities handling product data to achieve the design objective. To accomplish an activity, the actor that has been assigned to it (thanks to his know how) relies on input data to produce output data; i.e. to create new data in the case of creation activity or to transform data in the case of transformation activity. Figure 1 shows that in order to design a handler mechanism, the designer transforms the input data *wholes location perimeter* provided by the project manager into an output data *defined wholes locations on palette* and this, respecting the *available jacks* constraint. The input data of an activity correspond to:

- Data produced by a previous activity within the same design process, linked to a sequence flow [2].
- Data produced by a concurrent design process activity, linked to message flow [2].
- Constraints predefined when the design process is launched, such as standards, previous projects ...
- Constraints emerging during the design process deployment due to the actors expertise, such as trade rules.

Consequently, the data source of conflict, resulting from a transformation activity, is dependent on a whole set of input data. For instance, the data *wholes location on the palette* constitutes a conflict data for the activity *to manufacture the wholes* executed by the "mechanic machining". This data is produced by the activity *to propose handler solution* offering the solution H_Solution2 (*kinematics and pneumatic schema* and *jack type and number*). This activity has as input data the positionner configuration (*two Alimentations with vertical store each* and *one mobile director with medium jack*).

Therefore, it is necessary to resolve the conflict to go back to the input data (*positionner configuration*) of the activity (*to propose handler solution*); whereby the activity producing these data and the responsible actors are identified. Hence, identifying the actors to be involved in the conflict resolution process comes to identify the activities that produce the data on which the data source of conflict depends; since an actor is assigned to each of the design process activities.

Accordingly, the methodology proposed to identify the conflict resolution actors is based on building up the dependencies network between the handled data during the design progress. Indeed, when a conflict appears, it would be easier using the network to identify the data on which the data source of conflict depends. Once these data are extracted, it is then possible to find out the activities that produce them and consequently the actors responsible for their execution. In the following section, the data dependencies network is presented.

3.2 Data Dependencies Network

The data dependency network is an oriented graph composed of nodes, which correspond to the product data handled during the design process, and arcs, which correspond to the dependency relationships between these data. In the following, these network components are presented.

Network Nodes (Product Data). Design work returns with a succession of tasks to define a new product through the use and the generation of various product data. The handled data can be of several types: structural, functional and geometrical, etc. They correspond to the various descriptions of the product, elaborated by designers during the development process, in terms of geometrical entities, functions, bills of materials, CAD models, calculation notes, simulations, etc.

Depending on the margin left to the designer to elaborate data, on the values of data properties and on the context in which it is committed, product data can evolve through different states. Grebici et al. identify four data states: draft, exhibit, enable and deliverable [5]. These states are presented in the following.

- The draft is a piece of data that one has to apply the modalities of creation and validation of hypothesis or solutions to a project or to a design problem. It is defined by a design actor individually. For instance, in the case study presented in Section 2, the handler designer produced a handler mechanism draft composed of kinematics and pneumatic schemes.
- The exhibit is a piece of data that one applies a persuasion modality in accordance with what is represented in either for convincing about the existence of a problem or for showing a solution and allowing a common construction and the point of view exchanged. For instance, the handler designer asks the machining expert for his opinion on the possibilities to manufacture holes (support of the pieces) of a given diameter D in a manner that they are aligned on the palette. The opinion of the machining expert allows then the handler designer to define the kinematics scheme.

- The enabled traces are data the designer accepts to diffuse to others, after his consent or his agreement with a collective prescription to which he takes part. It is non-officially validated objects but sufficiently convincing to be published. For example, the handler designer publishes his design parts when he is ensured that the handler solution is validated. Indeed, the latter spreads the handler design parts in the official space to the positionner designer in order to allow him finishing his activity: to define positionner mechanism.
- The deliverable is data that transmit a strong regulation. They have been formally verified and validated (by hierarchy). They are those contractual supports to being communicated to the customer.

Network Arcs (Dependencies Links). Among the criteria that characterize links between elements (objects, tasks, design team, etc.), the dependency link criterion remains the more studied in research works and the less simple one to treat in the collaborative design modeling. Many definitions of dependency link are proposed in literature. According to Kusiak [8], a dependency between variables is the effect of change in a value of one variable on another variable, whereas for Jin [13], two components are said to have dependency relation if any of the two can not be completed without the other. These definitions reveal that two kinds of dependencies may exist between two product data: dependency at creation and dependency at modification. Two data are said "dependent at creation" if the creation of one of them depends on the creation of the second one – this corresponds to the dependency definition proposed in [13]. Two data are said "dependent at modification" if the change of one of them implies the modification of the second one – this corresponds to the dependency definition in [8]. The rest of this sub-section is devoted to characterise these dependencies. The main focus is on qualifying the dependency link through the concepts of dependency degree and dependency nature.

Dependency Degree. Depending on the dependency context (at creation or at modification), there exist different attributes that can be used to express the dependency degree between two elements in design.

Dependency at creation measure: Some research works have attempted to define attributes to express the link between data at creation, such as: the relevance, the usage and the completeness of the upstream data to the downstream data [4]. We are particularly interested in the completeness attributes which draw the actual data variation interval. The actor will express how should be the variation interval of the consumed data. Higher is the completeness attribute value, smaller would be the input data interval variation. Even if the completeness of data is defined by its user with regard to his needs to produce another data[2], it represents an absolute measure of the "at creation" dependency compared to the relevance and usage. In this paper, we are concerned with the estimation of the completeness attribute as the "at creation dependency" measure.

---

[2] A data could be considered as complete in order to be used for a given data and not for another one.

Table 1. Constructed attribute for completeness

Attribute level	Description of the attribute level
0	*Weak*: the input data could be given below a certain maximum value
1	*Not Vital*: the input data should be given within a certain value range
2	*Vital*: the input data should be given with the smallest value range
3	*Extremely Vital:* the input data should be precisely given

The completeness of data provided by an activity is arbitrarily categorized in four levels according to a discrete and subjective measurement scale using structured expert interviews. Table 1 summarises the completeness attribute values.

Dependency at change measure*:* among the attributes proposed in science management and engineering design works to define the dependency , the following are the most relevant to measure the dependency "at change": *Level Number* [12], *Importance Ratings* [9] and *Probability of Repetition* [3]. We are particularly concerned with the estimation of the last measure of dependency since it constitutes the hardest to obtain input for simulating a development process that involves iteration. The *probability of Repetition* reflects the probability of one element (activity, data) causing rework in another. Krishnan et al. define the dependency measure as the multiplication of both attributes: *Variability* and *Sensitivity* [7].

Variability is the likelihood that the output data provided by one task would change after being initially released [14]. Since the variability is associated with the *stability* of a particular element, each output element has its own variability value. The variability concerns the results of an upstream activity output that constitutes input data for the downstream activity. It is difficult, if not impossible, to come up with a universal objective measurement scale for data variability to be used in all product development situations. Therefore, a discrete, subjective measurement scale for this measure is constructed using the techniques for constructing subjective attributes. The estimated variability of data provided by a task is arbitrarily categorized in four levels, each having a numerical value, as shown in Table 2.

Table 2. Levels of data variability – adapted from [14]

Attribute level	Description of the attribute level
0	*Not variable*: the output data don't vary
1	*Low Variability:* the output data varies but few
2	*Moderate Variability*: the output data is instable
3	*High variability*: the output data is very instable

Sensitivity is the degree to which work is changed as the result of absorbing transferred data. In another words, this attribute expresses the sensitivity of output data (performed during a downstream activity) if the input data variation occurs (in the upstream activity producing this input data). Sensitivity depends on the level of dependency between two particular elements. Table 3 describes the three subjective levels of an element sensitivity developed using techniques for constructing subjective attributes.

In order to quantify the dependency link between two data, the dependency at creation and dependency at change measures are aggregated to one criterion to express the *dependency degree* between two data.

Table 3. Levels of data sensitivity – adapted from [14]

Attribute level	Description of the attribute level
0	*Not sensitive*: output data sensitivity is null to most input data changes
1	*Minor sensitivity*: output data sensitivity is low to most input data changes
2	*Moderate Sensitivity*: output data sensitivity is medium to most input data changes
3	*Major sensitivity:* output data sensitivity is high to most input data changes

Therefore, the three attributes; completeness, variability and sensitivity are aggregated to measure the dependency degree (Figure 2). As they are complementary attributes, a multiplicative utility function is utilised in the aggregation of the variability and sensitivity attributes (V*S). Furthermore, more the completeness is *high* (from *Not Vital* until *Extremely Vital*) more the required rework is long. Thus, for a given variability and sensitivity values, more the completeness is important, more the iterations are long and more the dependency degree is high. In the case when the variability value is "0" and the completeness value is different from "0", the dependency degree value must be different of "0", since that a not null completeness implies a dependency at creation. The dependency degree formula is presented in Figure 2.

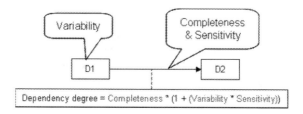

Fig. 2. Dependency degree between data D1 and D2

Accordingly, the resultant range value of the dependency degree is an integer between 0 and 30, whereas {0, 1, 2, 3 and 4} denotes a weak dependency and a low risk of rework, and {15, 20, 21 and 30} denotes a very high dependency and a high risk of rework. The values {5, 6, 7, and 8} and {9, 10, 12 and 14} describe respectively a moderate and a high dependency and risk of rework.

Dependencies Nature. For a better management of the conflict resolution process, it is interesting to distinguish the nature of the dependency link that exists between the data. This would lead to the elaboration of various network filters providing the project manager with different points of view of the handled conflict source. In this network, two various typologies can be distinguished:

• Syntactic typology: From a product model point of view, a piece of data, stated as an input or an output of a design activity, corresponds to either the creation of a new class in the model, either the addition of a new attribute to an existing, either the instantiation of an existing class or the valuation of an attribute in an existing instance. Consequently, a dependency link between two pieces of data could be between two classes, between two attributes or between a class and an attribute (already existing or newly created). Moreover, this dependency may concern the creation or the instantiation/valuation of these concepts. Figure 3 summarises these dependencies.

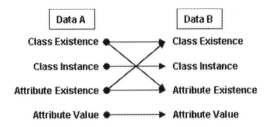

Fig. 3. Syntactic level dependencies

- Semantic typology. From a semantic point of view, various types of dependencies can be distinguished:
  - Inter-domain: dependency between data produced by actors from different domain. For example, the data "jack" and "workstation frame" are inter-domain dependent since they are produced by actors from different domain.
  - Intra-domain: dependency between data produced by two actors from the same domain. For example, the data "jack" and "wholes on palette" are intra-domain dependent since they are produced by the same actor, hence the same domain.
  - Inter-process: dependency between data produced in two different design processes. For example, the data "handler volume" and the data "energyblock volume" are inter-process dependent since they are produced within different design processes.
  - Intra-process: dependency between data produced within the same design process. For example, the data "jack" and the data "alimentation" are intra-process dependent since they are produced within the same design process (operative part design process).
  - Inter-Bill of Material (BoM): dependency between different BoMs data (Functional, Structural, etc.), of the same product or of two different products.
  - Intra-Bill of Material: dependency between the same BoM data, of the same product or of two different products.

It is then possible thanks to these two typologies to establish the dependencies network according to various levels expressing progressively the classes linked to the dependent data, the syntactic dependency between these classes and the semantic dependency between these data.

In the following section, we will present the traceability model that would allow tracking the design progress in order to extract the data dependency network.

3.3 Traceability Model to Build Up the Data Dependencies Network

To build up the dependencies network discussed in section 3.1 and 3.2, the methodology is based on a tool to trace the execution of the design process activities

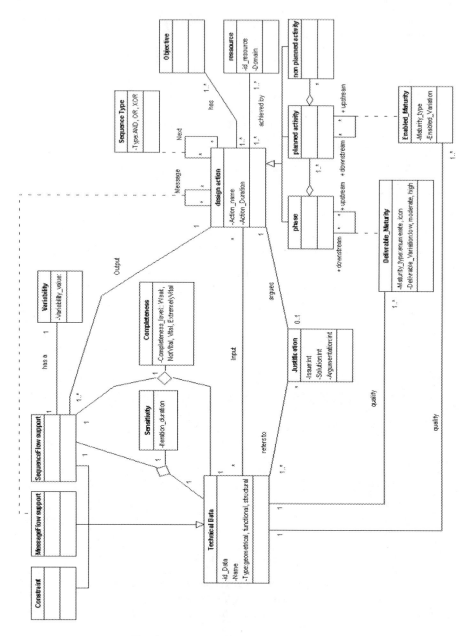

Fig. 4. The design process traceability model

taking into account the input and output data of each activity (a kind of "a posteriori" workflow). This tool relies on the proposed model (shown in Figure 4).

This model is the formalisation of the adopted concepts; i.e. *activity*, *resource*, *flow* between the *activities* (sequence flow and message flow [2]) and *data* handled by them. The "Justification" concept is added to extract the "know-how" adopted by the actor when performing their activities. The key issues for the justification herein adopted are articulated as questions, with each *issue* followed by one *solution* among several *alternatives* that responds to the issue. *Arguments* support the adopted solution and could be of Requirement-based, Rule-based, Case-based, etc.

Once the conflict is detected, the data dependencies network is built up based on the model instances, the starting point being the data source of conflict. In order to build up this network, requests on the obtained model instances are elaborated by identifying the Input/Output data of each activity and the corresponding syntactic and semantic dependencies between the handled data as discussed previously.

4   Summary and Future Work

The conflict management process is a sequence of five phases: conflict detection, formation of the conflict resolution team, negotiation management, solution generation and solution impact evaluation. In this paper, a methodology has been introduced to support conflict management; in particular the phases of negotiation team formation and of impact propagation on product data and design process organisation. The main purpose of the proposed methodology is to explicitly capture the product data dependencies during the design progress. Concepts such as the dependency degree which is based on the completeness, variability and sensitivity attributes as well as the dependency nature (i.e. syntactic and semantic) are proposed to qualify product data dependencies. Then an UML traceability model is proposed to identify these dependencies; which are represented throughout a data dependencies network. The FAS design process has been used to illustrate the whole methodology.

However, further thoughts remain to be carried out for the design process re-organisation problem. In fact, based on the data dependencies network, designers are able to identify negotiators and to propagate modifications on the already defined product data. Nevertheless, these modifications often require a re-execution of activities producing product data to be modified. In addition, the concerned actors are not often available since they can act different roles in several concurrent projects whose delivery dates are predefined. Consequently, the design process reorganisation proves to be a difficult task since it depends on availability of the actors who are able to execute these modifications.

References

1. Barker, R., Holloway, L.P., Meehan, A.: Supporting Negotiation in Concurrent Design Teams. Proc. Sixth International Conference on CSCW in Design. London, Ontario, Canada (2001)
2. Business Process Management Notation Specification. Version 1.0. (2004) URL: http://www.bpmn.org/
3. Browning, T.R., Eppinger, S.D.: Modelling Impacts of Process Architecture on Cost and Schedule Risk in Product Development. IEEE Transactions on Engineering Management 49(4) (2002) 428-442

4. Culley, S.J., Davies, S., Hicks, B.J., McMahon, C.A.: An assessment of quality measures for engineering information sources. Proc. 15th International Conference on Engineering Design. Melbourne, Australia (2005)
5. Grebici, K., Blanco, E., Rieu, D.: Toward Non Mature Information Management in Collaborative Design Processes. Proc. International Conference on Engineering Design (ICED'05). Melbourne, Australia. (2005)
6. Klein, M.: Supporting conflict resolution in cooperative design systems. IEEE Transactions on Systems, Man and Cybernetics 21(6) (1993) 1379-1390
7. Krishnan, V., Eppinger, S.D., Whitney, D.E.: A Model-Based Framework for Overlapping Product Development Activities. Management Science 43(4) (1997) 437-451
8. Kusiak, A., Wang, J.: Dependency analysis in constraint negotiation. IEEE Transactions on Systems, Man, and Cybernetics 25 (1995) 1301- 1313
9. Pimmler, T.U., Eppinger, S.D.: Integration Analysis of Product Decompositions. Proc. ASME Design Theory and Methodology Conference (DTM'94) (1994)
10. Rose, B., Gzara, L., Lombard, M.: Towards a formalization of collaboration entities to manage conflicts appearing in cooperative product design. In: Tichkiewitch, S. and Brissaud, D. (eds.): Methods and Tools for Cooperative and Integrated Design. Kluwer Academic, The Netherlands (2004)
11. Shen, W., Norrie, D.H., Barthès, J.P.: Multi-Agent Systems for Concurrent Intelligent Design and Manufacturing. Taylor and Francis, London, UK (2001)
12. Steward, D.V.: System Analysis and Management: Structure, Strategy and Design. New York: Petrocelli Books, NY, USA (1981)
13. Wang, K.L., Jin, Y.: Modelling dependencies in engineering design. Proc. ASME Design Theory and Methodology Conference. Las Vegas, Nevada (1999)
14. Yassine, A., Falkenburg, D.R., Chelst, K.: Engineering Design Management: An Information Structure Approach. International Journal of Production Research 37(13) (1999) 2957-2975
15. Zhao, G., Deng, J.: Cooperative Product Design Process Modelling. Proc. Sixth International Conference on CSCW in Design. London, Ontario, Canada (2001)
16. Zhuang, R.: Conflict Detection in Web Based Concurrent Engineering Design. Master Thesis. University of Florida (1999)

The Extended Quality Function Deployment in Product Life Cycle Design

Ming Lei, Ligang Yao, and Zuping Zhu

School of Mechanical Engineering and Automation,
Fuzhou University, Fuzhou, 350002, P.R. China
{leiming, ylgyao}@fzu.edu.cn, zhuzuping@163.com

Abstract. This paper describes the extended quality function deployment (QFD) in life cycle design (LCD) based on the traditional QFD which is often used at the requirement analysis stage. By investigating QFD in the product life cycle design, the extended QFD is proposed with the theoretical frame. The extension begins with the analysis of requirement by adding environment and cost factors, instead of only customer requirements, as the input of the 1st level house of quality (HoQ). Accordingly, multi-target values are built in. In a sequential process of the LCD, the extension carries out requirement deployment, function deployment, equipment deployment, part deployment, cost deployment and reliability deployment. Finally, this paper reveals how to apply the extended QFD in LCD and how to choose and adjust HoQ for different products.

1 Introduction

The product life cycle includes requirement analysis, conceptual design, engineering design, product manufacturing, distribution, service support, dispose and recycle. In a competitive market today, enterprises can establish their competitive advantages by means of product design taking into account the whole product life cycle. There have been many DFX methods in design, such as design for manufacture and assembly [1], design for disassembly [2], design for recycle [3], design for cost [4], design for reliability [5], design for serviceability [6] and design for environment [7]. But these methods focus on a certain stage of product life cycle and the integration is needed. Quality function deployment (QFD) proposed by Akao [8] started as a way to improve a market share by gathering as much as possible information from customers and reducing the gap between the customer's requirement and the product's performance. But the traditional QFD only focuses on the requirement analysis. In today's buyers' market, in designing their products, the enterprises should systematically consider the time (T), quality (Q), cost (C), service (S), environment (E) and so on. The extended QFD integrates various factors and becomes one of the best effective tools of products design in the LCD.

Though there is no research on the extended QFD, the improvements on the traditional QFD was carried out in a number of fields. Quality function deployment for environment (QFDE) is a tool developed by Masui et al. [9] to support designers at an

W. Shen et al. (Eds.): CSCWD 2006, LNCS 4402, pp. 401–408, 2007.
© Springer-Verlag Berlin Heidelberg 2007

early stage of designing for environment (DFE) of assembled products. It can improve products' qualities by adding environment to the "whats" of HoQ. Further, Japanese Environmental Management Association for Industry (JEMAI) issued QFDE as an effective tool of DFE activities to Japanese companies. Cristofari et al. [10] developed the green quality function deployment (GQFD) method by integrating the LCA and QFD to evaluate the products from environmental consideration. These two methods improved the environmental quality of products, but the effort for carrying them out often exceeded the limitation of the resources of product development projects. Zhang et al. [11] proposed GQFD that integrates the life cycle assessment (LCA), life cycle costing (LCC) and QFD into an efficient tool and deploys customers' environmental and cost requirements. This paper brings forward the extended QFD in the LCD. The extension includes requirement deployment, function deployment, equipment deployment, part deployment, cost deployment and reliability deployment.

2   Extended QFD in LCD

2.1   Essence of QFD

A step-by-step QFD is a method of customer-driven product design. The primary function of the QFD is to identify important issue and link priorities and target values back to the customer by a series of HoQs. Generally there are six parts in HoQ: "whats", "hows", relationship matrix, correlation matrix, competitive estimate and target as in Figure 1. There are 5 steps in the QFD approach:

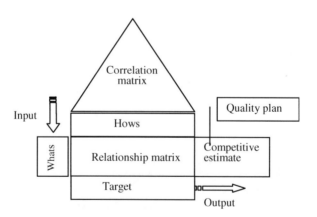

Fig. 1. HoQ

Step 1: Identifying the customer requirements as "whats" of the 1st level of HoQ.
Step 2: Mapping the subjectively demanded quality information of customers into the objectively defined technology of performances utilized to get "hows".

Step 3: Analyzing "whats" and "hows", setting up the relationship matrix and correlation matrix, finding the constraints or designing bottlenecks, and identifying and prioritizing important "hows".

Step 4: Comparing the technology with that of competitors in market, and setting up the target values.

Step 5: Defining the "hows" as the next HoQ "whats", repeating steps 1 through 4 to classify information about requirements of functions, equipments, parts, and manufacturing.

2.2 Extended QFD in LCD

Life Cycle Design is derived from Concurrent Engineering. The extended QFD is the modified model for the traditional QFD to the adapted in the LCD and composed of the requirement development (RD), function deployment (FD), equipment deployment (ED), part deployment (PD), manufacture deployment (MD), cost deployment (CD) and reliability deployment (ReD). The application of the extended QFD is similar to that of the traditional QFD by following the aforementioned five steps, repeatedly adopting the "effect-result" and linking to a series of HoQs. But the extended QFD (shown in Figure 2) has distinctive components in application as follows:

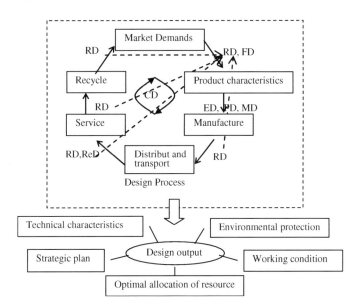

Fig. 2. Extended QFD in LCD

1. "Whats" of the 1st level of the HoQ. This illustrates the customer requirements, environmental impact and cost are integrated as the input of HoQ1. Requirements are sorted into the following decomposition. This kind of "whats" helps engineers to take into account as much as possible relevant products' information.

2. Cost deployment. In the LCD, basing on the CD of the traditional QFD, the CD penetrates other deployments, as a reverse process of calculating cost to ensure every step of design within capital constraint and realize the goal of profit.
3. Multi-target. The extended QFD establishes the quality target, environment target, and cost target.

Information about requirements is collected from all stages of the life cycle of products and put into the products with the aids of FD, ED, PD, MD, and ReD. The cost deployment goes on simultaneously with other deployments throughout design.

3   Requirement Deployment of Extended QFD in LCD

In the extended QFD, RD is beginning and fundamental. By analyzing and filtering a great deal of complex information of products, the outcome of RD is the 1st level of HoQ. The RD is developed according to the following process as shown in Figure 3.

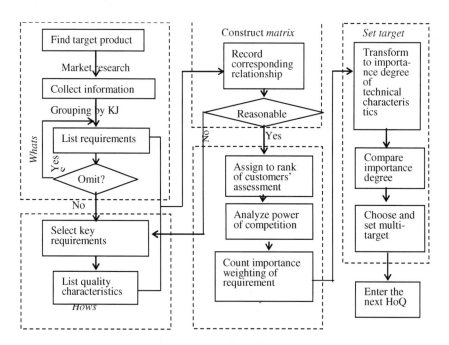

Fig. 3. The flow of requirement deployment

Specify whats. There are various kinds of products in the marketplace, enterprises should choose one or several types of products in the targeted market. By experience and marketing research, engineers find the targeted market, and pick out important requirements from collecting information as "whats" of the HoQ.

Specify hows. Within an enterprise, technical terms are used by engineers for design, so "whats" has to be translated into technical characteristics which are "hows" of HoQ.

Construct Matrix. In this step, both relationship matrix and correlation matrix are involved. The relationship matrix shows the connection between "whats" and "hows". The correlation matrix explains relation among "hows". Applying the fuzzy set theory and pair-wise trade-off value, the imprecise information is translated into the matrix.

Analyze Matrix. In the relationship matrix, engineers have to find which characteristics are more important by their importance weighting of requirement, by analyzing their power of competition. Engineers can get the rank of requirements the product offers. In the correlation matrix, perhaps some of "hows" are negative and need to be mended. So they are selected and entered into successive steps.

Set Targets. By analyzing the matrix, important characteristics and bottlenecks are defined as quality targets and environment targets. In the extended QFD, cost targets focus on the customer and enterprise and can be illustrated as cost = price – profit. Where, the cost is total spending that enterprise invested in product developing; the price is what customers afforded; and the profit is the sum which the enterprise wants to be achieved from product. The cost target will ensure the benefit in all directions.

For different products, engineers should distinguish which kind of their developing products belongs to. According to different kinds of products, the means of getting information of the requirement should be adjusted.

For same product, there are different emphases on different phases. For example, in the phases of "transportation", enterprises' requirements are focused in "after service", and the customers' requirements should be given more consideration.

4   Synthetic Deployment of Extended QFD in LCD

Synthetic deployment, involving function deployment, equipment deployment, part deployment, manufacture deployment, and cost deployment, constructs a platform to turn requirement into manufacturing (shown in Figure 4).

FD and CD. The FD inputs the attributes of the RD, generates the characteristic-function table and translates characteristics into professional terms on function. Meanwhile the important degree of function is obtained. In virtue of it, the cost target is decomposed into function cost. Key functions as the output of HoQ by the important degree of function and cost.

PD and CD. In the design of parts, engineers should consider not only the technical feasibility but also cost. Depending on enterprises, parts can be bought from suppliers or manufactured by themselves, design new one or use old one. Key parts are chosen in the same way as choosing key equipments. When the bottleneck parts can not be solved, engineers must return to ED and redesign appropriate equipments till parts meet the demands of technology and cost.

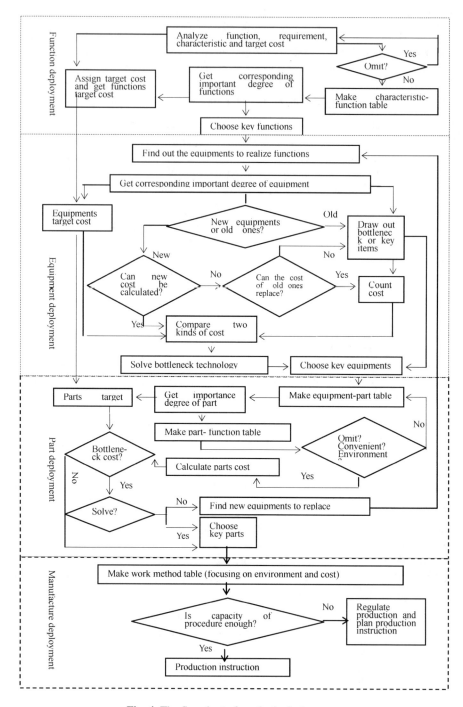

Fig. 4. The flowchart of synthetic deployment

MD and CD. Manufacturer realizes the conversion from conceptual products to material products. In the MD, the main discussion is about how to produce: the right person, by the right way, at the right time, in the right production line. In general, the result of the MD is production instruction. On the other hand, in manufacturing, pollution is hardly avoided. So engineers should put environment to the design of manufacture. Also in the MD, designers focus on cost.

Though synthetic deployment involves various deployments, it does not mean every deployment must be done. For example, when the products only need to be assembled, enterprises choose the FD, ED and MD. Anyway, engineers should apply synthetic deployment flexibly. Otherwise, the cost target is transformed into the cost of functions, equipments, and parts through the importance degree from other deployments. The CD can distribute fund rationally.

5   Reliability Deployment (ReD) of Extended QFD in LCD

Now customers pursue individuation, it makes quality more complicated and unstable. So, the goal of ReD is to keep and improve stability of products. Millions of parts of product will affect the quality. The reliability of products depends on the weakest parts. In HoQ of every step, they have been pointed out.

Reliability includes durability, maintenance and design reliability, etc. There are various types of failure with certain logic relation expressed with the tree of failure. By FKEA, potential failure can be found and analyzed. In ReD, engineers search the possible failure, trace the cause, and list the characteristic-failure table, function-failure table, equipment-failure table and part-failure table, finally choose key parts and made FMEA. The life of product will be lengthened, the maintenance will be reduced and the degree of satisfaction will be enhanced.

6   Conclusions

This paper proposed the structure of the extended QFD and introduced the extended QFD into the LCD. The extended QFD includes the environment impact and cost analysis. Based on the improved 1st level HoQ, the multi-objective extended QFD is developed. In the background of the LCD, the theoretical frame carrying out the requirement deployment, function deployment, equipment deployment, part deployment, cost deployment and reliability deployment in the extended QFD is proposed. The detailed methods on how to apply expansion QFD in the LCD is presented and how to choose and adjust HoQ according to different target product are also given.

References

1. Buttars, S., Rowland, R.: Design for Manufacture. Elektron 23 (2006) 24-26
2. Liu, T.I.: Intelligent Design for Disassembly. Int. J. Agile Manufacturing 8 (2005) 123-132

3. Wang, S., Liu, Z., Liu, G., Huang, H.: Design for Recyclability Method Based on Recycling Element. Chinese J. Mech. Eng. 41 (2005) 102-106

4. Hayek, M., Voorthuysen, E., Kelly, D. W.: Optimizing Life Cycle Cost of Complex Machinery with Rotable Modules Using Simulation. J. Quality in Maintenance Eng. 11 (2005) 333-347

5. Sadegh, P., Thompson, A., Luo, X., Park, Y., Sienel, T.: A Methodology for Predicting Service Life and Design of Reliability Experiments. IEEE Trans. on Reliability 55 (2006) 75-85

6. Barkai, J.: Design for Serviceability. Machine Design 77 (2005) 134

7. Lee, S.G., Xu, X.: Design for the Environment: Life Cycle Assessment and Sustainable Packaging Issues. Int. J. Environmental Tech. and Management 5 (2005) 14-41

8. Akao, Y.: Quality Function Development. Productivity Press, Cambridge, MA (1990)

9. Masui, K., Sakao, T., Aizawa, S., Inaba, A.: Design for Environment in Early Stage of Product Development Using Quality Function Development. Proc. Joint International Congress and Exhibition Electronics Goes Green (2000) 197-202

10. Cristofari, M., Deshmukh, A., Wang, B.: Green Quality Function Development. Proceeding of the 4th International Conference on Environmentally Conscious Design and Manufacturing. Cleveland, Ohio (1996) 297-304

11. Zhang, Y., Wang, H. P, Zhang, C.: Green QFD-II: A Life Cycle Approach for Environment Conscious Manufacturing by Integrating LCA and LCC into QFD Matrices. Int. J. Production Research 37 (2000) 1075-1091

A GA Based Task Grouping for Top-Down Collaborative Assembly Design

Youdong Yang[1,2], Shuting Zhang[1], Zhihua Li[1], and Shuming Gao[1]

[1] State Key Laboratory of CAD&CG, Zhejiang University,
Hangzhou 310027, China
[2] Zhijing College, Zhejiang University of Technology,
Hangzhou 310024, China
{yyoudong, zhangshuting, smgao}@cad.zju.edu.cn, d98lzh@263.net

Abstract. The top-down collaborative assembly design process of a product is highly concurrent and tightly coupled. Rational task planning significantly affects cycle time and efficiency of the product design. Task grouping is one of the key issues of task planning and it is discussed for top-down collaborative assembly design. An improved genetic algorithm (GA) for the task grouping is developed according to two principles: (1) the workload should be equilibrium among the design teams; (2) the tasks with high coupling relationships should be grouped into the same task group. As a case study, top-down collaborative assembly design of the shaper is demonstrated and the result illustrates the effectiveness of the proposed algorithm.

1 Introduction

The complex product design is composed of multiple design tasks and accomplished by multiple designers. Among the design tasks, there exist complex information interactions, dependencies and constraints. It is well recognized that all the design tasks should be reasonably planned in order to organize the design process effectively, that is task planning is imperative. Specifically, task planning is the process that all the design tasks are divided according to certain principles into several groups which are then assigned to appropriate design teams.

There have been several research works on task planning of complex product design. Some researchers [1-3] present task planning for concurrent design. Based on the task coupling degree, the design tasks are grouped and ordered, and the concurrency of the tasks is determined. Their approach can shorten the product design cycle to some extent. However, as there are some differences between the result of task planning and the actual design activities, the planned result needs to be adjusted according to the practice. Other researchers [4-6] discuss the resource occupation issues during the task planning process. The proposed algorithms can well schedule all resources, but can't guarantee the full resource utilization. In summary, current works aim mostly at the concurrent design, usually use only single quantitative index, and have not taken top-down collaborative assembly design into account.

By "top-down collaborative assembly design" in this study we mean that the structure design and detail design are collaboratively achieved by multiple design teams

W. Shen et al. (Eds.): CSCWD 2006, LNCS 4402, pp. 409–418, 2007.
© Springer-Verlag Berlin Heidelberg 2007

according to the concept model. As the process of top-down collaborative assembly design is highly concurrent and tightly coupled [7-8], its task grouping is more complex and difficult. To meet the task grouping requirements of top-down collaborative assembly design, two task grouping principles are proposed. One is concerned with workload equilibrium of the design teams and the other is high coupling relationship degree of the tasks in a task group. The improved genetic algorithm is utilized to search the optimal task grouping schedule to make the design cycle short and the interactions among design teams few to the fullest extent.

2 Definitions, Hypotheses and Principles

2.1 Related Definitions and Hypotheses

Definition 1: $B = (b_{ij})_{m \times n}$ is defined as the correlative information matrix, where b_{ij}, within the scope of [0,1], describes the information influence of task i on task j.

The design structure matrix is first presented by Eppinger et al.[9] to describe the relationships among all the design tasks. Here we adopt it to define the correlative information matrix. Considering that there are relationships among components correlated indirectly in actual design process, it isn't suitable to express such relationship by a Boolean value 1 or 0, so a fuzzy number with the space of [0,1] is used to represent the relationships among the tasks.

Definition 2: $R = \{r_1, r_2, \ldots, r_n\}$ is defined as the coupling matrix, where

$$r_i = \sum_{j=1, j \neq i}^{n} b_{ij} + \beta \sum_{j=1, j \neq i}^{n} b_{ji} , \quad \beta \text{ is the influencing factor whose value is less than 1 and deter-}$$

mined based on engineering experience.

Coupling matrix R is used to describe the coupling relationship degree of a task by which the influences among all the tasks can be considered comprehensively.

Definition 3: $E = \{e_1, e_2, \ldots, e_n\}$ is defined as the task evolution matrix, where $e_i > 0$ $(i=1,2,\ldots,n)$, called evolution degree is the increasing possibility of the components number of a task during top-down collaborative assembly design. It is normalized, i.e.

$$\sum_{i=1}^{n} e_i = 1 .$$

Definition 4: $C = \{c_1, c_2, \ldots, c_n\}$ is defined as the task complexity matrix, where $c_i > 0$ $(i=1,2,\ldots,n)$, indicates the structure complexity of the components in a task, it is nor-

malized, i.e. $\sum_{i=1}^{n} c_i = 1 .$

Definition 5: $T = \{t_1, t_2, \ldots, t_n\}$ is defined as the task workload matrix, where t_i is the workload of task i.

The task workload is evaluated by empirical engineers and can be measured by working day, week or other time units based on the task types.

Definition 6: $D = \{d_1, d_2, \ldots, d_n\}$ is defined as the relative coupling matrix, where $d_i = r_i / \sum_{j=1}^{n} r_j$ $(i=1,2,\ldots,n)$ and $\sum_{i=1}^{n} d_i = 1$. It is derived from the normalized coupling matrix R and used to calculate the criticality of every task.

Definition 7: $Tr = \{tr_1, tr_2, \ldots, tr_n\}$ is defined as the relative task workload matrix, where $tr_i = t_i / \sum_{j=1}^{n} t_j$ $(i=1,2,\ldots,n)$ and $\sum_{i=1}^{n} tr_i = 1$. It is derived from the normalized task workload matrix T and used to calculate the task criticality.

Definition 8: $TC = (tc_{ij})_{m \times n}$ is defined as the task grouping matrix, where n is the number of all tasks and m is the number of all design teams, $n > m$, $tc_{ij}=0$ or 1, $(i=1,2,\ldots,n$ and $j=1,2,\ldots m)$ and $\sum_{i=1}^{m} tc_{ij} = 1$.

If $tc_{ij}=1$, it indicates that task group i contains task j. A task group may have more than one task. $\sum_{j=1}^{n} (tc_{ij} \times t_j)$ is the workload of task group i. The element sum of every column is 1, namely $\sum_{i=1}^{m} tc_{ij} = 1$, because each task can only belong to a unique task group.

Hypothesis 1: Suppose each task can't be subdivided further, that is each task is an atomic task.

Hypothesis 2: Suppose each design team can only participate in a single task group.

2.2 Task Planning Principles

In this work, to effectively control the design cycle and decrease the interactions among the design teams, the following two principles are adopted for the task grouping of the top-down collaborative assembly design.

Principle 1: The workload of all design teams should be equilibrium.

Due to hypothesis 1 and 2, task grouping hardly guarantee that all the design teams have the same workload. But each design team's workload may be close to the average workload, varying within specified limits. That means the workload of all design teams can only be as equilibrium as possible.

Principle 2: The tasks with high coupling relationships should be grouped into the same task group.

The collaborative product design efficiency and consistency are affected greatly by the amount of interactions. It is necessary for the tasks with high coupling relationships to be grouped into the same task group to reduce the coupling degree among task groups and decrease the interactions among design teams.

Due to the high priority of the product design cycle, principle 1 and 2 should be firstly considered.

3 Task Categorization

Task grouping is to divide the n tasks involved in a top-down collaborative assembly design into m task groups according to principle 1 and 2. It's a multi-object and NP-complete optimization problem. In order to achieve an optimal task grouping genetic algorithm (GA) [3][6][9-12] is adopted in this work. Firstly the tasks should be categorized before presenting the algorithm. This is the predisposal of the task workload for task grouping.

Suppose the workload sum of all tasks is $T = \sum_{i=1}^{n} t_i$ (t_i indicates the workload of task i) and there are m design teams, then the average workload of each task is: $t_a = T / m$.

The tasks are classified into three categories in terms of the closeness between t_i and t_a and handled according to their categories.

Give an adjustable factor δ that can be changed flexibly according to the actual situation which is less than $0.2t_a$. The task categorization is described as follows.

(1) A task is called an 'approximately equal' task if $t_i \in (t_a - \delta, t_a + \delta)$. For this kind of tasks, each one is taken as a task group and is undertaken by one design team.

(2) A task is a 'less than' style if $t_i \leq t_a - \delta$. This task needs to be grouped with other appropriate tasks according to principle 1 and 2.

(3) A task is a 'more than' style if $t_i \leq t_a + \delta$. This kind of tasks is further divided into two cases: the first one is that its workload is in the scope of integral times of the average workload, that is $t_i - n_2 t_a \in (-k\delta, +k\delta)(n_2 = 1,2,...)$, where n_2 is an integer, and k is a factor, $k<1$. For this case, the task needn't to be grouped, and n_2 design teams will be correspondingly assigned to undertake it. The second case is that $t_a > t_i - n_3 t_a \geq k\delta, (n_3 = 1,2,...)$, where n_3 is an integer and $k<1$, For this case, the task needs to be grouped with other appropriate tasks according to principle 1 and 2, and the formed task group needs n_3+1 design teams to collaboratively undertake it.

After task categorization, task grouping for the assembly design is handled where the genetic algorithm is adopted as next section.

4 Genetic Algorithm for Task Grouping

Genetic Algorithms (GA) were originally proposed by Holland [10]. In discovering good solutions to difficult problems, these algorithms mimic the biological evolution process.

The interest of GA is that although guarantees of optimal solutions to problems cannot be given, good solutions are likely to be obtained within the time available to get one when using GA [10, 11]. So, GA can be both robust and flexible in solving hard problems like task planning.

In developing a genetic algorithm we must have in mind that its performance depends largely on the careful design and set-up of the algorithm components, mechanisms and parameters. This includes genetic encoding of solutions, initial population of solutions, evaluation of the fitness of solutions, genetic operators for the generation of new solutions and parameters such as population size, probabilities of crossover and mutation, replacement scheme and number of generations.

4.1 Chromosome Representation and Initial Population

The GA's chromosomes are represented by the task grouping matrix (definition 8), where the column denotes the scenario of each grouped task, and the row denotes the task composition of every task group. The encoding of the chromosome representation is simple and concise which facilitates the calculation of workload and coupling relationship degree of every task group.

The generation of the initial population in GA is usually done randomly. In this work, each individual of the initial population is computed by the following three steps which are repeated until all initial individuals are generated.

Suppose there are m design groups and n tasks.

Step 1: Set an adjustable factor δ, its value is less than $0.2\ t_a$ (average workload), and set integer $j=1$.

Step 2: Randomly select tasks until the workload sum of them is larger than $t_a-\delta$. If we can't select any tasks to guarantee the workload sum to be larger than $t_a -\delta$, discard this selection, and then go back to step 1. Else, let $j=j+1$, if j<m repeat step 2, else go to step 3.

Step 3: All leaving tasks are grouped into the final task group.

4.2 Fitness Function

During top-down collaborative assembly design, to ensure the workload equilibrium of every design team (principle 1), the sum of all the square differences between every task group workload and the average workload is usually used as a measurement of performance. Therefore the first part of the fitness function is determined as the sum of all the square differences, which is given by Equation (1), which can be easily calculated based on the task grouping matrix.

$$\sum_{i=1}^{m} (\sum_{j=1}^{n} (tc_{ij}t_j - t_a)^2) \tag{1}$$

At the same time, in order to reduce the interactions between task groups, the tasks with high coupling relationships should be grouped into the same task group (principle2). That means the sum of coupling relationship degrees of all the tasks in a task group should be large to the fullest extent, which is the sum of coupling relationship degrees of all the tasks in a task group in the task grouping matrix $TC_{m\times n}$, $\lambda_i(i = 1, 2,...m)$. The bigger λ_i, the higher coupling relationship degree is. Therefore the second part of the fitness function is determined as the reciprocal of λ_i—is given by **Equation (2)** .

$$\lambda_i = \sum_{j=1}^{n} tc_{ij} \left(\sum_{k=1,k \neq j}^{n} b_{jk} tc_{ik} + \sum_{k=1,k \neq j}^{n} b_{kj} tc_{ik} \right), k = 1,..., n \tag{2}$$

Combining the above two parts together (Equation (1) and (2)), eventually we use **Equation (3)** as *the final fitness function* so that the fitness function is more optimal and integrative.

$$\sum_{i=1}^{m} \left(\frac{1}{\lambda_i} \sum_{j=1}^{n} (tc_{ij} t_j - t_a)^2 \right) \tag{3}$$

4.3 Genetic Operators

The three basic operators, selection, crossover and mutation, of the genetic algorithm for task grouping are devised as follows.

The selection strategy is based on expansive sampling space where all parents and offspring have the same survival chances. Specifically the new population is determined using linear sequential selection algorithm presented by Baker [13] and the chromosomes are ranked by their fitness values from the best to the worst, thus the chromosomes with higher fitness values are selected to reproduce.

Task grouping demands chromosome codes to satisfy the constraint that each task appears in one and only one chromosome, i.e. $\sum_{i=1}^{m} tc_{ij} = 1$. If we adopt the general crossover and mutation operators, the constraint can't be satisfied, so we improve the multi-point crossover operator and the mutation operator.

Suppose there are m design groups and n tasks, i.e. the chromosome representation is $TC = (tc_{ij})_{m \times n}$. The improved operator consists of following four steps.

Step 1: Randomly select two chromosomes TC^1 and TC^2 as parents in the population, let $j=1$. Two offspring TC^{11} and TC^{22} are generated with the general multi-point crossover operator. Without the loss of generality, hereafter we just take TC^{11} as an example to demonstrate the next steps.

Step 2: Calculate the sum of each column of TC^{11} with $S_j = \sum_{i=1}^{m} tc_{ij}$, and then the further handling is divided into three cases:
1) If $S_j = 1$ and $j \neq m$, let $j = j + 1$, and repeat the step 2; else if $j = m$, go back to step 1.
2) If $S_j = 0$, which indicates that the task corresponding to this column is not put into any task group yet, go to step 3.
3) Else, which indicates that the task corresponding to this column has been put into more than one task group, go to step 4.

Step 3: Calculate the sum of every row, i.e. the workload of every task group, select the minimal workload, and then change its element of column j to 1. If $j \neq$
m, let $j = j + 1$, and go to step 2; else, go back to step1.

Step 4: Do NOR operation between the corresponding elements of the column j of
TC^{11} and the column j of TC^{1}, and update every element of column j of TC^{11}
with the corresponding element obtained, and then get the updated TC^{11}. If $j \neq$
m, let $j = j + 1$, and go to step 2; else, go back to step1.

The mutation operator is defined as the gene changes of individuals according to
small probability disturbance. The improved mutation operator is to inverse the genes
which are randomly selected in an individual. If the value of the selected gene is 0,
inverse to 1, and then inverse the gene in this column with value of 1 to 0. If the selected gene is 1, inverse to 0, which means the task that the gene denotes is not
grouped, the same way of crossover operator step 3 would be adopted to select an
approximate row and the elements of this column are changed to 1.

5 Case Study

The shaper design is taken as an example to validate the task grouping based on genetic algorithm for top-down collaborative assembly design. The structure sketch of
the shaper is shown in Figure 1 and it is supposed that the shaper is designed by five
design teams.

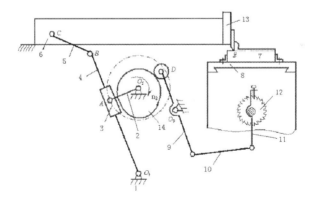

Fig. 1. Structure sketch of shaper

The shaper is a plane machining tool whose design can be divided into 10 tasks:(1)
slippery pillow 6 design, (2) tool support design, (3) lathe bed design, (4) reducing
gearing design, (5) leader structure design, (6) cam structure design, (7) four-bar
structure design, (8) ratchet wheel design, (9) helix structure design, and (10) workbench design.

Suppose the shaper design tasks are divided into five task groups, the coupling matrix B and the task workload matrix T are described as follows.

$$B = \begin{array}{c} \\ \\ \end{array} \begin{bmatrix} & 1 & 2 & 3 & 4 & 5 & 6 & 7 & 8 & 9 & 10 \\ 0 & 1 & 0.75 & 0.25 & 1 & 0.25 & 0.25 & 0.25 & 0.25 & 0.5 \\ 1 & 0 & 0.5 & 0.25 & 0.25 & 0.25 & 0.25 & 0.25 & 0.25 & 0.5 \\ 1 & 0.5 & 0 & 0.75 & 0.5 & 0.5 & 0.5 & 0.25 & 0.25 & 1 \\ 0.25 & 0.5 & 0.75 & 0 & 0.75 & 0.75 & 0.25 & 0.25 & 0.5 & 0.25 \\ 0.75 & 0.25 & 1 & 0.5 & 0 & 0.5 & 0.25 & 0.25 & 0.25 & 0.25 \\ 0.25 & 0.25 & 0.75 & 0.5 & 0.5 & 0 & 1 & 0.5 & 0.5 & 0.5 \\ 0.25 & 0.25 & 0.5 & 0.25 & 0.25 & 0.75 & 0 & 1 & 0.5 & 0.25 \\ 0.25 & 0.25 & 0.25 & 0.25 & 0.25 & 0.5 & 0.75 & 0 & 1 & 0.5 \\ 0.25 & 0.25 & 0.25 & 0.5 & 0.25 & 0.25 & 0.5 & 0.75 & 0 & 1 \\ 0.5 & 0.25 & 0.75 & 0.25 & 0.25 & 0.25 & 0.25 & 0.75 & 0.75 & 0 \end{bmatrix} \begin{array}{c} 1 \\ 2 \\ 3 \\ 4 \\ 5 \\ 6 \\ 7 \\ 8 \\ 9 \\ 10 \end{array}$$

$$T = \begin{bmatrix} 8 & 4 & 20 & 15 & 13 & 10 & 12 & 9 & 3 & 11 \end{bmatrix}$$

The parameters of the genetic algorithm for task grouping are set as follows: crossover probability (0.4), exchange mutation probability (0.1), subpopulation size (40), and the number of iteration (500).

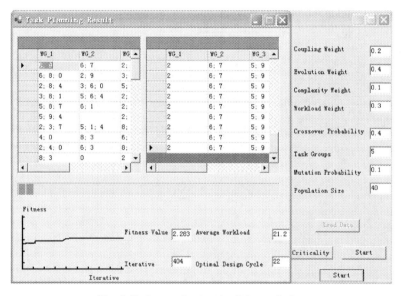

Fig. 2. Task grouping result of shaper design

Through the calculation of genetic algorithm, the task grouping result is given and shown as follows: {((1) slippery pillow, (5) leader structure), ((2) tool support, (9) helix structure, (4) reducing gearing), ((3) lathe bed), ((7) four-bar structure, (8) ratchet wheel), ((10) workbench, (6) cam structure)}; the average workload of every task group is 21.2; and the optimal design cycle of the shaper is 22 (see Figure 2). The coupling relationship degree among tasks of each task group is { (1,0.75) , {(0.25, 0.25), (0.5, 0.25), (0.5, 0.5)}, 0(single task), (1, 0.75), (0.5, 0,25)} . The result shows that there is no unrelated task in one task group, and the average of the coupling relationship degree is {0.875, 0.375, 0, 0.875, 0.375}. It can be seen that the minimal product design cycle and high coupling relationship among tasks in each task group are achieved.

The same experiment was repeated in 100 independent runs and the average was taken as the basis for evaluation. The case shows that the probability of obtaining optimal result is 76%. And the probability of obtaining optimal result is 43% while the number of iteration is less than 100. Both of the theoretical researches and experimental results show that the improved genetic algorithm has good performance on solving task grouping problem for top-down Collaborative assembly design. It can acquire high speed and improved success rate for getting optimal solution.

6 Conclusions and Future Work

The top-down collaborative assembly design process needs to be well-grouped to guarantee the given product design cycle and efficiency. This paper presents an approach to task grouping based on GA for top-down collaborative assembly design. The major contributions of the work include:

1) Two principals of task grouping for top-down collaborative assembly design are proposed.
2) A corresponding genetic algorithm for task grouping is developed, which guarantee the optimal design cycle and improve the efficiency of collaborative design.
3) The task planning for the top-down collaborative assembly design of a shaper is demonstrated. The result of the presented algorithms indicates that the requirements of task planning are well satisfied.

Since the research of task grouping is based on the abstract concept model, the granularity is rough. The future work involves the disposal of the tasks in the task group during smaller-granularity task planning and real-time task scheduling.

Acknowledgments. The authors are very grateful to the financial support from NSF of China (No.60574061) and the Trans-Century Training Programme Foundation for Talents by the Education Ministry of China.

References

1. Ren, D., Fang, Z.: Research on Task Scheduling in Concurrent Design. Computer Integrated Manufacturing Systems 1(2005) 32-38
2. Yuan, Q., Zhao, R.: The Study of Theory and Method for Design Task Scheduling in Concurrent Engineering Environment. Chinese Journal of Computers 4 (2000) 440-443
3. Zhao, J., Liu, J., Zhong, Y., et al.: New Tearing Method of Task Set Within Concurrent Design Process. Computer Integrated Manufacturing Systems 4(2001) 36-40
4. Cao, J., Zhao, H., Zhang, Y.: Research on Task Scheduling Method for Product Cooperative Design. China Mechanical Engineering 5 (1999) 500-504

5. Zhong, Q., Chen, H.: Genetic Operators in Task Matching and Scheduling. Journal of National University of Defense Technology 3(2000) 34-38
6. Sun, X., Xiao, R., Li, L.: Explore on the Workload Model and the Total Consumption Model of the Planning of Concurrent Design. China Mechanical Engineering 2(1999) 207-210
7. Gao, S., He, F.: Survey of Distributed and Collaborative Design. Journal of Computer-Aided Design & Computer Graphics 2 (2004) 149-157
8. Chen, L., Song, Z., Feng L.: Internet-Enabled Real-Time Collaborative Assembly Modeling Via an E-Assembly System: Status and Promise. Computer-Aided Design 36 (2004) 835-847
9. Eppinger, S.D., Whitney, D.E., Smith, R.P., et al: Organizing The Tasks in Complex Design Projects. ASME DE V27 (1900) 39-46
10. Holland, J.H.: Adaptation in Natural and Artificial Systems. MIT Press (1975)
11. Hartmann, S.: Project Scheduling With Multiple Modes: A Genetic Algorithm. Annals of Operations Research 102 (2001) 111–135
12. Baker, K., Scudder, G.: Sequencing with Earliness and Tardiness Penalties: A Review. Operations Research 38(1990) 22-36

An Ontology-Based Collaborative Reasoning Strategy for Multidisciplinary Design in the Semantic Grid

Li Zhang[1], Wenyu Zhang[2], Qianzhu Wang[3], and Yuzhu Wang[1]

[1] Department of Logistical Information, Logistical Engineering University
Chongqing 400013, China
Zhangli_zju@163.com
[2] School of Information, Zhejiang University of Finance and Economics
Hangzhou 310018, China
wyzhang@pmail.ntu.edu.sg
[3] 3G Academe, Chongqing University of Posts and Telecommunications
Chongqing 400065, China
Wangqz@cqupt.edu.cn

Abstract. Aiming at representing and reasoning about multidisciplinary design knowledge explicitly and exchanging it in different design environments, this paper proposes an ontology-based collaborative reasoning strategy for multidisciplinary design in the Semantic Grid. An ontology-based modeling framework is used as the basis, which adopts Web Ontology Language (OWL) to build a domain-specific multidisciplinary design repository, and allows the design agents to visit ontology repository effectively through ontology-based services. On the top of modeling framework we propose a multi-agent collaborative reasoning environment, which utilizes OWL as the content language of FIPA ACL, and supports the ontology-based collaborative reasoning for multidisciplinary design between multiple design agents. This important enhancement facilitates the implementation of Computer Supported Cooperative Work (CSCW) in multidisciplinary design for Semantic Grid applications.

1 Introduction

The distributed problem solving environments, with the high degree of heterogeneity of the design toolsets and data formats, become more and more complex, in particular for computer supported cooperative work (CSCW) in multidisciplinary design. The integration of diverse design knowledge is expected to become a key point in the multidisciplinary collaborative design. It makes an increased need for product design teams to establish and maintain a mechanism, which manages multidisciplinary design knowledge with a consistent agreement upon the heterogeneous design frameworks.

The need to create a common understanding for the multidisciplinary design knowledge becomes crucial critical for multidisciplinary collaborative design. Though diversified multidisciplinary design tools have shown their effectiveness in different design domain, the multidisciplinary collaborative design based network is still a problem, especially in representing multidisciplinary design knowledge with a uniform manner and exchanging it among product design organizations that collaborate over internet.

W. Shen et al. (Eds.): CSCWD 2006, LNCS 4402, pp. 419–427, 2007.
© Springer-Verlag Berlin Heidelberg 2007

The Semantic Grid [1] is an extension of the current Grid in which information and services are given well-defined representation through ontology-based descriptions, which maximize the potential for sharing and reuse. This has provided the driving force for research towards building open, dynamic and adaptive systems, which support flexible coordination and collaboration on a global scale. Aiming at representing and reasoning about multidisciplinary design knowledge explicitly and formally and sharing it to support CSCW in multidisciplinary design environments, this paper proposes a novel architecture, which applies Semantic Grid techniques, including an ontology-based multidisciplinary design knowledge modeling framework and an ontology-based collaborative reasoning strategy, to facilitate communication and reasoning between multiple agents for multidisciplinary collaborative design. The foundation of the proposed architecture is an ontology-based modeling framework, which has extended traditional multidisciplinary design knowledge modeling by applying ontology engineering, in particular the Web Ontology Language (OWL) [2], to support the sharing and exchange of multidisciplinary design knowledge. The top level is a collaborative virtual environment supported by the Foundation of Intelligent Physical Agent (FIPA), the standard FIPA Agent Communication Language (FIPA ACL) [3] and OWL, enabling multiple agents to exchange multidisciplinary design knowledge ontology and service ontology via an agent communication middleware, to support collaborative reasoning in multidisciplinary design.

2 Related Work

With the network rapidly proliferated all over the world, the past decade has seen a strong emphasis on the integrated product modeling to support collaboration in multidisciplinary design projects. Toye et al. [4] proposed a scalable framework and methodology for collaborative product development, including a sharable design representation and some interactive engineering tools, which links decisions and rationale with the design artifact, and supports collaborative, interactive design between different teams over the network. By integrating the sharable characteristics of other design systems in the literature, Case and Lu [5] described a discourse model to support multidisciplinary collaborative design through a three-step process. Gerhard et al. [6] suggested an open architecture, consisting of reusable available assets, anchored in the philosophy of decision-based design, to realize the platform-independent integration of distributed and heterogeneous information resources for the product realization process. Based on the architecture, a prototype platform-independent framework was described and used to design machine gears employing commonly available software assets. Bohm et al. [7] adopted an XML data format to import and export the multidisciplinary design knowledge including artifacts, functions, forms, and flows from a design repository, which supports product design knowledge archival and web-based search, display of design model and associated tool generation.

However, aiming at providing information for human understanding not for machine processing, above modeling approaches cannot rigorously and unambiguously capture the semantics of exchanged multidisciplinary design knowledge, therefore prohibiting automated reasoning in multidisciplinary collaborative design environments.

The Semantic Web [8] will enable machines to comprehend meanings of the documents. It can be employed to manage multidisciplinary collaborative design knowledge and integrate the heterogeneous design tools at the semantic level. As the pivotal part of Semantic Web, ontology technique provides a new perspective for multidisciplinary design knowledge representation. Through modeling the concepts in a knowledge domain with a high degree of granularity and formal structure, design knowledge is stored and reasoned in an ontology-based manner. An example of the use of Semantic Web in engineering design is Clockwork project [9], which combined semantic web technologies with the engineering modeling, and proposed a knowledge management methodology supported by a web-based toolkit to solve the problems of representing, sharing and reusing knowledge in a collaborative design engineering environment.

Convergence between the Semantic Web and another recent development in grid computing technologies [10] has seen grid technologies evolving towards the Semantic Grid [1]. The Semantic Grid is an extension of the current grid in which knowledge and web services are given well-defined meaning, better enabling intelligent agents to work in cooperation. Using the Semantic Grid, especially Semantic Web service techniques, Zhang et al. [11] suggested a semantic integration framework to support collaborative product design of a dynamic alliance. In this framework, all participating application systems provide their functions by means of Web services, and represent and share design knowledge through a task-oriented semantic representation model, better facilitating problem solving and cooperative work among the distributed groups on the network.

Notwithstanding the promising results reported from existing research work for multidisciplinary collaborative design, there has been little research using the ontology-based service-oriented modeling approach to support multidisciplinary collaborative design, especially, for Semantic Web or Semantic Grid enabled collaborative reasoning process.

3 An Ontology-Based Architecture for Multidisciplinary Collaborative Design in the Semantic Grid

In this section, we will present an ontology-based service-oriented modeling architecture, which combines ontology-based multidisciplinary design knowledge modeling with agent communication middleware, to facilitate multidisciplinary collaborative design on a semantic grid service platform.

3.1 Overview of the System Architecture

Product design is increasingly becoming a collaborative task among designers or design teams that are physically, geographically, and temporally distributed. Plenty of product modeling tools and engineering knowledge from various disciplines spread around different design phases, making effective capture, retrieval, reuse, sharing and exchange of these heterogeneous design knowledge a critical issue. It is difficult to implement multidisciplinary collaborative design in the multi-agent environment.

The multidisciplinary collaborative design problem can be decomposed into some sub questions. One is multidisciplinary design knowledge representation, i.e., how to

integrate the heterogeneous design knowledge with a uniform manner; the other is cooperative work, i.e., what kind of system architecture and design strategy facilitates
collaborative design in the distributed multi-agent environment. To deal with the problem of uniform design knowledge representation, we seek the ontology technology, in
particular OWL to support the explicit representation of multidisciplinary design
knowledge, and encapsulate the multidisciplinary design ontologies into FIPA ACL
message, which facilitates the semantic communication of design knowledge between
multiple design agents. On the other hand, in order to facilitate distributed work and
collaborative design on a global scale, a service-oriented infrastructure in the Semantic
Grid is proposed too. Figure 1 shows the whole suggested architecture. It evolves along
three consecutive layers, i.e., knowledge elicitation layer, ontology modeling layer, and
knowledge exchange layer, and is enabled by a Semantic Grid infrastructure.

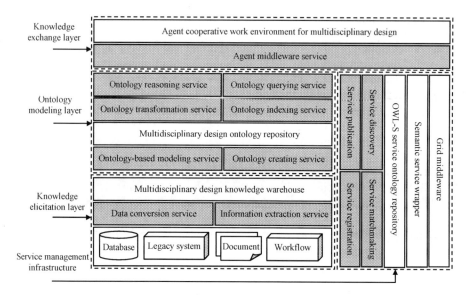

Fig. 1. An ontology-based service-oriented architecture for multi-agent collaborative design

Knowledge elicitation layer provides a service-oriented knowledge discovery
mechanism for various information sources. Through applying a set of generic knowledge acquisition services such as data conversion service, information extraction
service, knowledge engineers can elicit the multidisciplinary design knowledge which
disperse in database, legacy systems, workflow and documents, and build up multidisciplinary design knowledge warehouse as a basic part of the suggested architecture.

Ontology modeling layer is built above the knowledge elicitation layer. In this
layer, traditional multidisciplinary design knowledge modeling is extended by ontology-based approach. The key concepts in multidisciplinary design such as artifact,
function, form, flow and various discipline knowledge are represented as ontologies
with OWL, and some ontology-based knowledge services such as ontology transformation service, ontology indexing service, ontology reasoning service and ontology
querying service can be implemented effectively in this layer.

The top layer is knowledge exchange layer for the meaningful collaboration and reasoning upon the distributed multi-agent collaborative virtual environment. Java Agent Development Environment (JADE) [12] serves as a middleware to support agent representation, agent management and agent communication. The design ontologies and semantic service ontologies with OWL are used as FIPA ACL content descriptions to facilitate multidisciplinary collaborative design at the semantic level.

The backbone of the proposed architecture is a Semantic Grid platform, i.e., service management infrastructure. It is made up of Grid middleware, semantic service wrapper, service ontologies repository, supporting service publication, service registration, service matchmaking and service discovery. With an open, loosely coupled, distributed, and integrated manner, it facilitates distributed design and cooperative work effectively.

3.2 Ontology-Based Modeling to Multidisciplinary Design Knowledge

Ontology methodology is a new perspective for knowledge management. Through explicitly defining concepts, attributes and relationships, it is possible to integrate the heterogeneity of different models and tools, and supports the semantic communication. A common ontology-based modeling mechanism facilitates the semantic communication between multiple design agents in heterogeneous multidisciplinary design environment. Referring to Figure 2, this modeling framework is composed of a multidisciplinary design ontology repository and some grid services such as ontology modeling service, ontology creating service, ontology indexing service, ontology transformation service, ontology query service, ontology inference service, etc.

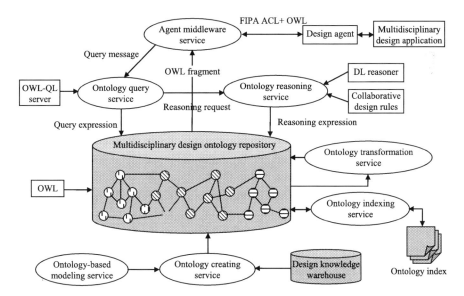

Fig. 2. An ontology-based modeling framework for multidisciplinary design knowledge

The ontology-based modeling service serves as the basis in the framework. Those fundamental design concepts such as artifact, function, form, flow, filling in various discipline knowledge, can be defined as ontologies using OWL. Through requesting for the ontology creating service by the Protégé ontology editor, the multidisciplinary design ontology repository is built.

By means of the mapping between multidisciplinary design knowledge ontology and collaborative design agent, the ontology indexing service can be used to process a quick search in the local ontology base. It helps an agent to find the required ontology or ask for the collaborative work from another agent. The ontology transformation service offers the framework capabilities to translate or map the design ontologies from one to another, and to negotiate meaning or resolve differences between different ontologies.

Based on the multidisciplinary design ontology repository, some high-level ontology-based knowledge discovery services can be processed. The typical one is ontology query service, which can deal with the question-answer ontology query message using OWL-QL [13] server. The other is ontology reasoning service through collaborative design rules, which can infer the more recent suitable design ontology with Description Logic (DL) reasoner.

4   An Ontology-Based Collaborative Reasoning Strategy in the Semantic Grid

When designer inputs a set of problem specifications into the multidisciplinary collaborative design environment, a design agent uses task decomposition service first. Overall design specifications are decomposed into simpler requirements through the task decomposition service. Figure 3 describes an ontology-based collaborative reasoning strategy by common algorithm language.

There are two important parts in Figure 3. One is a search to the local multidisciplinary design ontology repository through the ontology-based modeling method, the other is a collaborative work on the agent communication environment. To reason out design solution ontologies from design requirements, the design agent firstly searches the local multidisciplinary design ontology repository using ontology indexing service and checks whether there exist corresponding requirement ontologies. If yes, the agent will call the ontology reasoning service to perform the semantic inference, which can solve the synonym problem between different requirement ontologies. Followed by the mapping between requirement ontology and multidisciplinary product ontologies, the final product ontologies can be reasoned out. However, if the corresponding requirement ontologies are not found in the local ontology repository, the agent needs utilize the ontology indexing service to search for a collaborative remote agent, which will take over the job from the former and queries and reasons in its local ontology repository, and the remote solution ontologies will be encapsulated into FIPA packages and returned to the local

```
Design_solution Collaborative_design_reasoning (Design_agent a, Design_specification overall_specifications)
{
   Design_specification Task, Sub_tasks[ ];
   RequirementOntology Ro,Ro_remote; ProductDesignOntology Pdo[ ];
   OntologyRepository OR;
   Design_agent Remote_collaborative_agents[ ], Ra;
   FIPA_package Fp_remote, Fp_local;
   Design_solution Ds;
   Task=a.receive(overall_specifications);
   Sub_task[ ]=a.update(overall_specifications); // Update design specifications via task decomposition services
   for i=1 to Sub_task_number
   {
     Ro=a.find_match_ontology(OR, Sub_task[i]) ;// Use ontology indexing service to find the requirement ontology
     if (Ro!=NULL)  // The requirement ontology exists in the local repository
      // A search to the local multidisciplinary design ontology repository
       {
         Ro=a.reasoning(OR, Sub_task[i]); // Perform the semantic inference through ontology reasoning service
         Pdo=a.mapping(OR,Ro);// Perform the mapping between requirement ontology and product ontologies
         Ds.receive(Pdo);
       }
     else  // The requirement ontology doesn't exist in the local repository
       // A collaborative work between agents
       {
         a.sendrequest("find collaborative agent", Sub_task[i]) ;
         Ra=a.find_collaborative_agent(Remote_collaborative_agents, Sub_task[i]);
         Ro_remote=Ra.getontology(OR, Sub_task[i]);
         Ro=Ra.mapping (OR,Ro_remote);
         Fp_remote=Ro.encapsulate(); // Encapsulate the product design ontology into FIPA package
         Ra.return(Fp_remote);
         Fp_local= a.receivemessage(Ra);
         Pdo=extract(Fp_local); // Extract the FIPA package
         Ds.receive(Pdo);
       }
     }
     // Evaluate and reorganize a set of solution ontologies to choose the best solution workflow
        Ds.choose_best_solution(Ds);
   return (Ds);
}
```

Fig. 3. An ontology-based collaborative reasoning strategy for multidisciplinary design

design agent. The above process terminates after each design requirement has been visited.

When all suitable design solution ontologies are resulted, an evaluation and reorganization approach will be applied to choose the best solution workflow [14].

5   A Simple Example

As a key part of the proposed architecture, multidisciplinary design ontology knowledge is represented with OWL and encapsulated into FIPA ACL message. Figure 4 shows the representative snippets of FIPA ACL message, which includes a multidisciplinary ontology of blower design and exchanges between design agents.

```
(inform
    :sender blower_design_agent1
    :receiver blower_design_agent2
    :content ( <?xml version="1.0"?>
<rdf:RDF
    xmlns:Blower="http://cims.cqleu.edu.cn/OBMD/Blower#"
    xmlns:rdf="http://www.w3.org/1999/02/22-rdf-syntax-ns#"
    xmlns:rdfs="http://www.w3.org/2000/01/rdf-schema#"
    xml: base="http://www.owl-Ontologies.com/unnamed.owl">
    xmlns:fipaowl="http://www.fipa.org/schemas/fipaowl#">
    <fipaowl:Action rdf:ID=" blower_agent1_Action1">
    <fipaowl:actor>blower_design_agent1</rdf:actor>
    <fipaowl:act>send</rdf:act>
    <fipaowl:argument>
    </fipaowl:argument>
    </fipaowl:Action>
    <Function rdf:ID="Convert_Of_Energy">
    <Function_name
        Convert_Of_Energy
    </Function_name>
    <Function_type rdf:resource="#Convert"/>
      <Achieved_by_Flow rdf:resource="#Rotational_Motion_Sha"/>
      </Function>
      ……
</rdf:RDF>)
:language fipa-owl )
```

Fig. 4. The message snippets of multidisciplinary design ontology exchanged between agents

6 Conclusion

An ontology-based collaborative reasoning strategy is proposed to support multidisciplinary collaborative design among multiple agents. The strategy is implemented on the top of a knowledge elicitation mechanism, an ontology-based modeling framework, and a multi-agent collaborative environment, and is enabled by a service-oriented Semantic Grid platform. The ontology-based modeling framework can build the multidisciplinary design ontology repository, and ontology-based knowledge services such as ontology transformation service, ontology indexing service, ontology reasoning service and ontology querying service. At the top layer is a multi-agent collaborative environment, which utilizes OWL as the content language of FIPA ACL, and supports ontology exchange and ontology-based collaborative reasoning between multiple design agents.

The proposed enhancement in the collaborative reasoning strategy to traditional multidisciplinary design frameworks facilitates the automatic reasoning of multidisciplinary design knowledge, in an open, loosely coupled and integrated Semantic Grid service platform.

Acknowledgments. This work is supported in part by Zhejiang Natural Science Fund of China (ZJNSF) (Grant No.: Y105003), the Scientific Research Foundation of the State Human Resource Ministry for Excellent Returned Chinese Scholars (2006), and Zhejiang Provincial Education Department's Specialized Project of China (Grant No.: 20051056).

References

1. De Roure, D. and Jennings, N.: The Semantic Grid: Past, Present, and Future. Proceedings of the IEEE 93(3)(2005) 669-681
2. McGuinness, D.L. and Harmelen, F.V.: OWL Web Ontology Language Overview. URL: http://www.w3.org/TR/2004/REC-owl-features-20040210/
3. Foundation for Intelligent Physical Agents. FIPA Specifications.
   URL: http://www.fipa.org/
4. Toye, G., Cutkosky, M.R., Leifer, L., Tennenbaum, M., Glicksman,M.J.: SHARE: A Methodology and Environment for Collaborative Product Development. Proc. 2nd IEEE Workshop on Enabling Technologies: Infrastructure for Collaborative Enterprises. Morgantown, WV, USA (1993) 33-47
5. Case, M.P. and Lu, S.C.: Discourse Model for Collaborative Design. Computer-Aided Design 28(5) (1996) 333-345
6. Gerhard, J.F, Duncan, S.J., Chen, Y., Allen, J.K., Rosen, D., Mistree, F., Dugenske, A.D.: Towards a decision-based distributed product realization environment for engineering systems. Proceedings of the ASME Design Engineering Technical Conference. DETC1999/CIE-9085. Las Vegas (1999)
7. Bohm, M.R., Stone, R.B. and Szykman, S: Enhancing Virtual Product Representations for Advanced Design Repository Systems. Proceedings of the ASME Computers and Information in Engineering Conference. DETC2003/CIE-48239. Chicago, IL (2003)
8. Berners-Lee, T., Hendler, J. and Lassila, O.: The Semantic Web. Scientific American 284 (2001) 34-43
9. Zdraha, Z., Mulholland, P., Valasek, M., Sainter, P., Koss, M. and Trejtnar, L.: A Toolkit and Methodology to Support the Collaborative Development and Reuse of Engineering Models. Lecture Notes in Computer Science 2736 (2003) 856-865
10. Foster, I. and Kesselman, C.: The Grid: Blueprint for A New Computing Infrastructure. Morgan Kaufmann (1999)
11. Zhang, K.K. and Li, Q.Z.: SWSAIF: A Semantic Application Integration Framework to Support Collaborative Design. Lecture Notes in Computer Science 3865 (2005) 174-183
12. Bellifemine, F., Poggi, A. and Rimassa, G.: Developing Multi Agent Systems with a FIPA-compliant Agent Framework. Software Practice & Experience 31 (2001) 103-128
13. Fikes, R., Hayes, P. and Horrocks, I.: OWL-QL ---- A Language for Deductive Query Answering on the Semantic Web. Knowledge Systems Laboratory, Stanford University, Stanford, CA (2003)
14. Zhang, W.Y., Zhang, L., Xie, Y.: A Service-oriented Modeling Approach for Distributed Management of Multidisciplinary Design Knowledge in the Semantic Grid. Lecture Notes in Computer Science 4223 (2006) 631-640

Honey Bee Teamwork Architecture in Multi-agent Systems

Sarmad Sadik[1], Arshad Ali[1], H. Farooq Ahmad[2], and Hiroki Suguri[2]

[1] NUST Institute of Information Technology, Rawalpindi, Pakistan
sarmad@niit.edu.pk, arshad.ali@niit.edu.pk
[2] Communication Technologies, Sendai, Japan
farooq@comtec.co.jp, suguri@comtec.co.jp

Abstract. Teamwork among software agents is an emerging research area in the agent community as researchers are incorporating new architectures in multi-agent systems to facilitate coordination and collaboration among agents. We have proposed an efficient teamwork strategy for software agents which are deployed to work on distributed machines. This architecture is conceptualized from Honey Bee teamwork strategy and named after it as Honey Bee teamwork architecture. Also an abstract mapping is done between the honey bee and software agents working mechanisms. We have classified and discussed the proposed approach in context of two case studies and evaluation is made to exhibit its efficient behavior.

1 Introduction

As the application domain is becoming more complex and distributed in nature, agents have to exhibit diverse, coordinated and collaborated actions to fulfill the challenges. Since an agent cannot solely perform its operation in a better way, we need team of agents, which are specialized in some tasks and coordinate with each other to achieve desired goal. Software Agents and Teamwork jointly form a vital research area in the agent domain. The coordinating agents working jointly in a team will play a key role in information gathering and filtering as well as in task planning and execution in future [6]. An important aspect of modeling teamwork is description of goal to be achieved. The performance of teamwork depends upon goal definition, goal sharing and task distribution strategy among members. We have used two case studies, one includes Treasure Hunt application to explain the behavior of agents in teamwork, which are collaborating by using two diverse approaches. In one of the approaches, the division of plans and tasks is done based on goals and distributed to members for analyzing their performance. This is implemented using SAGE [1][8] (Scalable fault tolerant Agent Grooming Environment) multi-agent system. Also, the proposed architecture of teamwork is discussed in second case study of Earthquake Management System (EMS).

The next section provides the information about the related work. In Section 3, the system architecture is explained with highlighting the similarities between honey bee

W. Shen et al. (Eds.): CSCWD 2006, LNCS 4402, pp. 428–437, 2007.
© Springer-Verlag Berlin Heidelberg 2007

and agents teamwork. Also the teamwork analysis is shown using the case study approach. In Section 4, evaluation is made about the proposed work. In Section 5 and Section 6 conclusion and future work are presented respectively.

2   Related Work

In [4], an efficient approach has been presented on hybrid strategy of teamwork among agents and comparison of various approaches used in multi-agent systems. An agent framework is simulated [5] to model the human agent teamwork especially in space missions where mobile robots need to collaborate with human users. In [9], various properties of a design pattern are proposed for creating teams of agents but no specific architecture or framework is specified for collaboration among stationary or mobile agents. Agent architecture is proposed for teamwork [7] capabilities which enable explicit representation of team goals, plans and team's joint commitments. It supports the decision theoretic communication selectivity to address the problem of communication overhead in service of coherent teamwork. Also, it proposes the concept of team operators to monitor the team performance. In [10], a swarm based approach is presented especially for action selection problem in scenario of dynamic environment conditions. There are certain other strategies [2][3][11][12] for designing teamwork models and task allocation schemes. However, our work differs from these approaches as we have used the concept of leadership in teamwork and a hierarchical team leader approach is presented after analysis of two fundamental teamwork approaches to address the problems of clear goal definition, distribution of plan as well as monitoring the performance of member agents in team.

3   System Architecture

There are number of ways in which software agents can be used in teamwork task execution. We have designed and developed a teamwork strategy especially for use in mobile agent scenario, after perceiving idea from honey bee teamwork strategy. We have named this type of teamwork as honey bee teamwork architecture. Also, two case studies are used to explain the proposed architecture for teamwork among agents.

3.1   Honey Bee and Agents Teamwork

An abstract mapping is done of similarities between honey bee and agents teamwork strategies, which is later used in design of teamwork architecture and elaborated using prototype case studies. In case of honey bees, queen controls the nest and all other bees provides various services to queen. In agents we have developed a concept of Team Leader approach, which supervises and coordinates the operations of member agents. The team leader divides the plans to members and controls their operations by information sharing, coordination and collaboration. Honey bees move from flowers to flowers for extracting nectar which is later used to make honey. They extract it from many flowers as they move, retain it and deliver back at their nest to specified area. Mobile agents also move from machine to machine in search of their information as well as extracting out the required data. They may keep the extracted information and deliver when they come back to their parent hosts. If some queen is dead, feeding special food raises the new queen and it takes the role of next queen of nest. In agent domain, we have used the concept of agent's team leader fault tolerance measures. In this case, when team leader agent goes down, the fault is detected and based on promotion algorithm new team member agent is selected and promoted as team leader. Two types of agent promotion algorithms are specified, first is seniority and second is quantitative approach. In seniority algorithm, agent created first is made the team leader, in second approach, the system determines the performance of agents by adding points upon achievement of some predefined milestone. At the end, the agent with the highest number of points is made the team leader.

3.2   Teamwork Architecture

We have classified the general teamwork architecture as shown in Figure 1. The team is divided into two main categories. One is with the members, who are working for the same goal but no collaboration between them. The second category of teams includes those members, which are working to achieve same goal and have collaboration between them. This category is further sub-divided into two parts. One is with team leader and the other with non team leader approach. A comparison of both approaches is discussed in later part of the section.

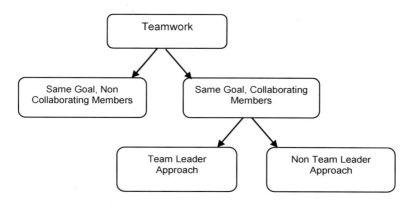

Fig. 1. Classfication of Teamwork Model

In Team Leader strategy, there is one team leader agent in team that has a job to distribute the plan or tasks to each member agent according to its domain and allotted work. In this approach, communication among agents takes place in a hierarchy fashion i.e. all communication among agents is going through their team leader. This helps in assimilation and dissimilation of information between team members. The team leader can distribute information to all members in a hierarchy fashion as shown in Figure 2. The interactions among agents or inter-agent communication can be analyzed as equal to 2n for n>1, where n is the number of agents. In our case study example of treasure hunt, the team leader divides the plan and area to each member for searching the required treasure location. If there are two agents in a team, the area to search is divided into two parts and assigned to members. If there are four, eight or sixteen members in a team then the area is divided into respective parts and each member is allotted its area of search. The team leader adds the members in beginning while creating the team and tracks their progress and current locations. When treasure is found the team leader informs all members and search is stopped.

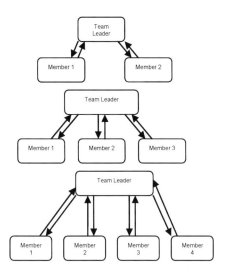

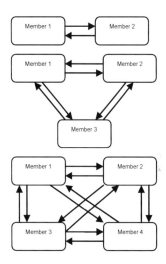

Fig. 2. Interactions among Agents in Team Leader approach

Fig. 3. Interactions among Agents in Non Team Leader

In Non Team Leader approach, there is no team leader who divides the plan or area of work for each member agent. The members have to work themselves in the designated area in direct collaboration with each other. A member has a connection with other members of the team and knows each other location and traversing path information. Considering the case study, the members are collaborating with each other while searching the area for treasure. They start searching the area from different directions and at the same time communicating with each other about their current location. If two members come face to face or in some path already traversed by other agent, they change their direction and move towards the unexplored paths. When one of the agents founds the treasure, all member agents are informed and search operation is stopped. In Non Team Leader approach every member agent has direct communication with other member agents or from implementation perspective, each member will have two streams of communication, input and output. The communication among agents in non team leader approach is much higher as compared with team leader approach as shown in Figure 3. It can be expressed in terms of formula as n(n-1) where n is the number of agents.

3.3 Teamwork in Earthquake Management System

The teamwork among agents is used in various disaster management systems. We have used a case study of earthquake management system to analyze the desired behavior of agents in monitoring and management in emergency situations using coordination and collaboration among agents. The proposed architecture of whole earthquake management system is presented as shown in Figure 4 which is divided into a number of modules. We have highlighted the coordination of mobile agents function in this domain.

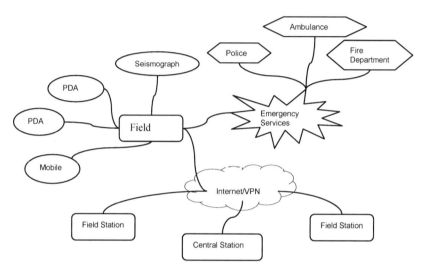

Fig. 4. EMS Proposed Architecture

We have designed the Earthquake Management System (EMS) as a distributed application using agents for monitoring and management of activities from start of earthquake to relief activities. In emergency or disaster situations, slow response of human operators cause delayed communication and suboptimal coordination. Therefore, we have shown deployment of agents in this scenario for effective performance. If the reading from seismograph goes above some benchmark value, the agent attached with it triggers the emergency services by sending the messages to other agents, which are deployed in various departments. These messages are sent using the ACL (Agent Communication Language). These agents also coordinate the activities between different departments and transfers required data from one system to other autonomously and stores in databases. In current circumstances, humans are involved in coordinating and servicing the requirements of needed data. When someone needs any information, human operators are requested to fulfill the request and after searching, they send the information manually doing all operations. Agents take the job of human operators in this regard also, and upon receiving a request to transfer or share some data, they search through database, convert it to ACL and send back the message. This is a fast mechanism for information sharing and distribution.

In a case study of EMS as shown in Figure 5, mobile agent searches information record of particular person on distributed machines. The data about injured and dead persons is deployed separately on two machines.

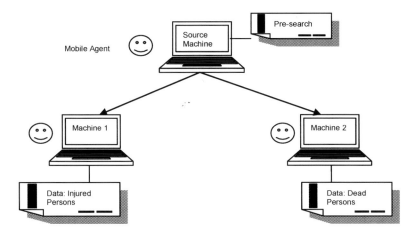

Fig. 5. Ontology based information searching and retrieval in management system

Table 1. Search operations using ontology based solutions

1. "Presearch" operation using name "Hassan" through ontology resource at source machine	2. "Opsearch" operation at destination machine
(query-ref 　　:sender(agent-identifier :name i) 　　:receiver(set (agent-identifier :name j)) 　　:content 　　　　　(action 　　　　　　　　(Search 　　　　　　　　　　:name Hassan)) 　　:language fipa-sl 　　:ontology EMS 　　:reply-with presearch-query) (inform 　　:sender(agent-identifier :name j) 　　:receiver(set (agent-identifier :name i)) 　　:content 　　　　　(result 　　　　　(action 　　　　　　(Search 　　　　　　　　:name Hassan)) 　　　　　　　　　(Status injured)) 　　:language fipa-sl 　　:ontology EMS 　　:in-reply-to presearch-query)	(query-ref 　　:sender(agent-identifier :name i) 　　:receiver(set (agent-identifier :name j)) 　　:content 　　　　　(action 　　　　　　　　(Search 　　　　　　　　　　:name Hassan)) 　　:language fipa-sl 　　:ontology EMS 　　:reply-with opsearch-query) (inform 　　:sender(agent-identifier :name j) 　　:receiver(set (agent-identifier :name i)) 　　:content 　　　　　(result 　　　　　(action 　　　　　　(Search 　　　　　　　　:name Hassan)) 　　　　　　(Parameters 　　　　　　　:ID 555-555 　　　　　　　:City Murree)) 　　:language fipa-sl 　　:ontology EMS 　　:in-reply-to opsearch-query)

In current case, mobile agent first performs a pre-search at source machine about status of a person. Then, on basis of its status injured or dead, it moves to related destination machine exhibiting a team leader approach scenario. The destination machines contains database of persons include their names, identification and related city information. Mobile agent on arrival at destination machine interacts with the local ontology resource for required information. The ontology resource is being populated by database storing the particular information. The ontology schema fields are continuously updated about the current data. Mobile agent interacts with local ontology resource at destination using ACL and receives the required information. After receiving data from mobile agents, the agent at source machine analyzes the information by extracting ACL message. It can also store or forward the data to other agents that require such information. The use of well-structured ontology based solution is more flexible for runtime information sharing and retrieval by mobile agents. The message format of "Presearch" operation at source machine as well as "Opsearch" operation at destination machine is shown in Table 1.

4   Evaluation

In first case study of treasure hunt application, teamwork approaches have been analyzed by taking measurements of their task accomplishment time. The results obtained are shown in Figure 6. In Team Leader approach, all agent members of team are executing in parallel threads, as the agents number increases and area is divided more and more, there is some overhead of parallel execution running on single machine. Non Team Leader approach has two overheads, one of parallel executions of agent members which have no area or plan division and second overhead is of the communication which they are having with each other while working for the specified goal. In light of above-mentioned performance of agents, Team Leader strategy is good choice when there is higher number of agents working in complex environments. This strategy helps in ease of implementation as well as it provides a convenient way to assimilate and dissimilate information.

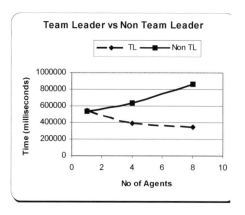

Fig. 6. TL vs Non TL approaches

The Team Leader and Non Team Leader approaches have also been tested on multiple machines as shown in Figure 7 and Figure 8. Three machines are used for this experiment. Agents are distributed on these machines and they are using multi agent systems for their execution and communication. Agents are collaborating with each other by inter-platform communication using HTTP protocol. Figure 7 shows the comparison of Team Leader approach on single and multiple machines. The single machine result shows less time consumption after start as more area division (in case study application) increases the performance of agents to achieve goal, but with the increase in number of agents and overhead of parallel execution, the performance starts degrading and more time consuming.

Fig. 7. Team Leader Approach – Single vs Multiple Machines

Fig. 8. Non Team Leader Approach – Single vs Multiple Machines

In multiple machines scenario, the time falls in the beginning but as their number starts increasing and accumulating more on one machine the time consumption starts increasing slightly. However, the performance still remains better as compared with the single machine results. The result of Non Team Leader approach is shown in Figure 8. The main difference between single machine and multiple machines results, especially in case of Non Team Leader approach, comes from the communication modes among agents. The communication is intra-machine when agents are executing on one machine. However, when they are distributed and deployed on multiple machines, the collaboration has become inter-machine communication, which increases the overhead to a great extent. As more and more agents are created and they perform their operation collaborating and coordinating with each other, the more overhead has appeared and significantly made the performance loss.

This shows more advantage of using Team Leader approach than using Non Team Leader approach in teamwork among higher number of agents especially when they are distributed and facing major overhead of collaboration due to limiting communication infrastructure or available bandwidth in networks. A hierarchy of multiple Team Leader approach may be used for more complex environments. Each team leader may have its sub-divided goal according to its hierarchy level. As the hierarchy grows, the goals or plans allotted to each individual team leader is further sub-divided (like in this treasure hunt case study sub-dividing the area of search) and shared with associated members. The goal achieved by individual members and team leaders accumulates to the main goal at the top of hierarchy.

5 Conclusion

In this paper, we have presented a teamwork approach for software agents. This approach is inferred from honey bee working strategy and named after it as the honey bee teamwork architecture. A classification is made according to goal sharing and interaction pattern among software agents. Also we have analyzed the proposed approach reflecting the hierarchical and peer-to-peer strategy using two case studies. In the first case study, treasure hunt application is described while in the second the proposed architecture of teamwork among software agents is highlighted in the domain of earthquake management system.

6 Future Work

Teamwork among software agents is emerging as a vital research area as the applications are becoming more complex and distributed. There is a need to enhance coordination and collaboration architecture among agents, which include efficient goal sharing, run-time information assimilation and dissimilation as well as making joint operation strategies. Also there is a need of joint research in teamwork as well as mobility areas for efficient task executions by a group of mobile agents.

References

1. Ali, A., Ahmad, H.F., Khan, Z.A., Mujahid, G.A. and Suguri, H.: SAGE: Next Generation Multi-Agent System. Proc. International Conference on Parallel and Distributed Processing Techniques and Applications. USA (2004)
2. Pynadath, D.V. and Tambe, M.: Team Coordination among Distributed Agents: Analyzing Key Teamwork Theories and Models. Proc. AAAI Spring Symposium on Intelligent Distributed and Embedded Systems. USA (2002)
3. Jung, H. and Tambe, M.: Performance Models for Large Scale Multiagent Systems: Using Distributed POMDP Building Blocks. Proc. Second International Joint conference on Agents and Multiagent Systems (AAMAS). Australia (2003)
4. Tambe, M., Bowring, E., Jung, H., Kaminka, G., Maheswaran, R., Marecki, J., et al.: Conflicts in teamwork: Hybrids to the rescue. Proc. Fourth International Joint Conference on Autonomous Agents and Multiagent Systems (AAMAS). Netherlands (2005)
5. Sierhuis, M., Bradshaw, J.M., Acquisti, A., van Hoof, R., Jeffers, R., Uszok, A.: Human-Agent Teamwork and Adjustable Autonomy in Practice. Proc. 7th International Symposium on Artificial Intelligence, Robotics and Automation in Space. Japan (2003)
6. Tambe, M., Shen, W., Mataric, M., Pynadath, D.V., Goldberg, D., Modi, P.J., et al.: Teamwork in Cyberspace: Using TEAMCORE to Make Agents Team-Ready. Proceedings of the AAAI. USA (1999)
7. Tambe, M.: Agent Architectures for Flexible, Practical Teamwork. Proc. National Conference on Artificial Intelligence. Rhode Island (1997)

8. Ahmad, H.F., Suguri, H., Ali, A., Mugal, M., Malik, S., Shafiq, M.O., et al.: Scalable fault tolerant Agent Grooming Environment (SAGE). Proc. Fourth International Joint Conference on Autonomous Agents and Multi agent Systems (AAMAS). Utrecht, Netherlands (2005)
9. Loke, S.W.: The A-Team Design Pattern: Useful Properties for Using Teams of Mobile Agents. Proc. International Conference on Intelligent Agents, Web Technology and Internet Commerce (IAWTIC). Vienna, Austria (2003)
10. Ferreira Jr, P.R., de Oliveira D. and Bazzan, A.L.C.: A Swarm Based Approach to Adapt the Structural Dimension of Agents' Organizations. Journal of Brazilian Computer Society - Special Issue on Agents Organizations (2005)
11. Scerri, P., Giampapa, J.A., Sycara, K.P.: Techniques and Directions for Building Very Large Agent Teams. Proc. International Conference on Integration of Knowledge Intensive Multi-Agent Systems (KIMAS '05). USA (2005)
12. Scerri, P., Farinelli, A., Okamoto S. and Tambe, M.: Allocating Tasks in Extreme Teams. Proc. Fourth International Joint Conference on Autonomous Agents and Multi agent Systems (AAMAS). Netherlands (2005)

An Agent-Mediated Service Framework Facilitating Virtual Organizations

Baohua Shan[1,2], Yanbo Han[1], and Weiqun Sun[1,2]

[1] Research Center for Grid and Service Computing,
Institute of Computing Technology, Chinese Academy of Sciences
[2] Graduate University of Chinese Academy of Sciences
{shanbaohua,sunweiqun}@software.ict.ac.cn, yhan@ict.ac.cn

Abstract. The ability to construct dynamic, flexible virtual organizations becomes one of the most desired features of a distributed application system. This paper proposes an agent-mediated service framework for constructing virtual organizations at the business level. Through dynamic matching between business services and Web services, and the negotiation between virtual organization agent and partners' agents, virtual organizations can be constructed dynamically by choosing partners on-the-fly. The framework has been implemented and tested in a real setting.

1 Introduction

Today, many business processes are so complicated that a single organization cannot accomplish efficiently and needs to collaborate with other organizations. The goal-driven dynamic assembly of organizational application tasks forms a virtual organization. However, the heterogeneous characteristic of applications in different organizations often circumscribes the inter-operation and sharing of resources between organizations. How to integrate heterogeneous applications of different organizations dynamically to form an application virtual organization is a challenging problem. The dynamically changing requirements of customers impel the organizations to provide more flexibility and adaptability in application construction so that the organization can integrate partners' applications on demand.

Grid, which targets at "the coordinated resource sharing and problem solving in dynamic, multi-institutional virtual organizations" [1], provides a feasible supporting infrastructure for virtual organizations. However, how to construct a virtual organization and how to operate it is still not well explored. In this paper, we propose an agent-mediated service framework based on VINCA [2] service grid platform we have developed. The autonomic characteristic of agents coincides with the autonomous requirements of partners in virtual organizations. An agent representing certain stakeholders can dynamically search for capable partners and negotiate with their agents to form a virtual organization on demand. Business level service composition language of VINCA service grid platform further promotes the participation of business user in the construction of virtual organizations.

W. Shen et al. (Eds.): CSCWD 2006, LNCS 4402, pp. 438–446, 2007.
© Springer-Verlag Berlin Heidelberg 2007

2 Rationale of the Framework

As is shown in Figure 1, service providers firstly publish their services into the business collective. When a virtual organization needs to be constructed, VINCA is used to define the business process which can fulfill the requirement. In the business process, tasks that should be accomplished by partners and constraints on partners are also defined using virtual organization definition tool. Virtual organization management module automatically searches in the business collective for candidates satisfying the constraints. Then for each task, virtual organization agent negotiates with candidates' agents. According to the negotiation strategy, virtual organization agent chooses one partner for each task. Finally, virtual organization management module forms a virtual organization and manages it. During negotiation, virtual organization agent also acquires detailed information about how to use partner's web services, e.g. interface definition of the service and authentication information for using the service.

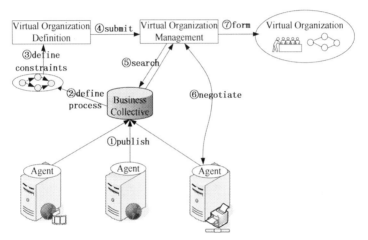

Fig. 1. Rationale of the framework

2.1 Business Collective

Business collective is a registry repository for service providers to publish their web services and other information. However, different from UDDI [3], the address published is not WSDL address of the service. It's the address of the agents located on the service providers' sides. One agent may manage several web services. In the business collective, business unit is the basic element and is defined as follows:

Definition 1: Business Unit is a three-tuple:

    Business Unit ::= <Basic Information>{<Service>} <Agent>
    Basic Information ::= <Provider Name>[<Provider Description>]
    Service ::= <Service Name>{<Service Category>}{<Service Input>}{<Service Output>}
        {<Service NFP>}[<Service Description>]
    Service Input ::= <Name><Semantic>
    Service Output ::= <Name><Semantic>

Service NFP ::= <Name><Semantic><Value>
Agent ::= <Name><Description><Address>

Each service provider corresponds to a business unit in the business collective. Virtual organization management module uses the information to search for candidates.

2.2 Virtual Organization

In the framework, a virtual organization is defined as follows:

Definition 2: A virtual organization is a set of business process, stakeholder, stakeholder tasks, outsourcing tasks, roles, users, partners, Web services, and relationships between them.

Virtual Organization ::= <Name>[<Description>]<stakeholder>
                         <business process>{<outsourcing task>}
                         {<stakeholder task>}{<partner>}
                         {<Web Services>}{<role>}{<user>}

In a virtual organization, all resources are coordinated through a business process, which is composed of business services and transitions. Tasks are divided into stakeholder tasks and outsourcing tasks. A stakeholder task is a business service that can be accomplished by virtual organization stakeholder and an outsourcing task is a task that should be accomplished by a partner. Each business service binds to a web service and can be executed by several roles. One role may be assigned to many users and one user may act as several roles.

2.3 Cooperation Mechanism

In the following sections, we will discuss the key strategies defined in our framework in detail.

2.3.1 Candidates Matching

In order to describe the virtual organizations to be constructed and constraints on partners, we've developed a language named VOML (Virtual Organization Markup Language). The schema of the language is depicted in Figure 2. It only shows the key structure of the schema.

Some basic concepts of the schema are defined below:

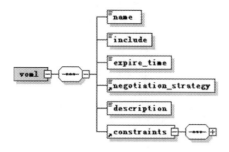

Fig. 2. Key elements of VOML

Definition 3: For each outsourcing task, constraints are satisfied only if provider restriction $pr = \{pr_1, pr_2...pr_n\}$, service restriction $sr = \{sr_1, sr_2...sr_l\}$, service provider information $pi = \{pi_1, pi_2...pi_m\}$ and service information $si = \{si_1, si_2...si_k\}$ satisfy the following rules:

- $\forall pr_i \in pr$, $\exists pi_j \in pi$ where $pr_i.semantic = pi_j.semantic$, and $pr_i.value$, $pi_j.value$ satisfy the operator.

- $\forall sr_i \in sr$, $\exists si_j \in si$ where $sr_i.semnatic = si_j.semantic$, and $sr_i.value$, $si_j.value$ satisfy the operator.

Definition 4: There are six operators '>', '<', '=', '>=', '<=', '!=' defined in our framework. $value_i$ and $value_j$ satisfy the operator only if:

- If $value_i$ and $value_j$ are both digits, then compare the value directly.

- If $value_i$ or $value_j$ is not digit, then treat $value_i$ and $value_j$ as string and compare the values of them.

Service capability is one of the most important factors in searching for candidates. Requirements of service are defined in VINCA process. The process definition is imported into VOML through 'include' element. Matching rules between requirements and service capability are defined as follows:

Definition 5: Capability required fr and service capability fp matches only if:

- $|fr.inputs| \unrhd |fp.inputs|, |fr.outpus| \unlhd |fp.outputs|$. It means that fp requires fewer inputs and produces more outputs than fr.

- $\forall fr.input \in fr.inputs$, $\exists fp.input \in fp.inputs$ where $fr.input.semantic = fp.input.semantic$

- $\forall fr.output \in fr.outputs$, $\exists fp.output \in fp.outputs$ where $fr.output.semantic = fp.output.semantic$

- $\forall fr.nfp \in fr.nfps$, $\exists fp.nfp \in fp.nfps$ where $fr.nfp.semantic = fp.nfp.semantic$ and $fr.nfp.value \subseteq fp.nfp.value$

Definition 6: A service provider is considered to be a candidate only if it satisfies definition 3 and definition 5.

If each outsourcing task has a non-empty set of candidates, then we say that a virtual organization is well defined.

Definition 7: A virtual organization is well defined only if for the outsourcing tasks set $ost = \{t_1, t_2,...,t_n\}$, $\forall t_i \in ost$, $Candidate(t_i) \neq \Phi$. $Candidate(t_i)$ represents the candidates set of t_i.

2.3.2 Negotiation Strategy

If the virtual organization is well defined, then for each task and its candidates, virtual organization agent starts negotiation with the agent of each candidate. During the negotiation phase, final partner of each outsourcing task will be chosen. In this paper, we adopt contract net protocol [4] to implement the coordination between virtual organization agent and candidates' agents. However, we provide specific contents for our framework and give more messages.

First, virtual organization agent sends task announcement message about task t_i to the agent of each candidate. The announcement message format is as follows:

```
To: Candidates' agents
From: Virtual organization agent
Type: TASK ANNOUNCEMENT
Expiration Time:
Content:
     Task abstraction:
          Name: t_i (semantic)
          Time: [t_begin, t_end] (semantic)
          Inputs:
               Input:
                    Name: i_1 (semantic)
          Outputs:
               Output:
                    Name: O_1 (semantic)
     Bid specification:
        Time: [t_1, t_2] (semantic)
```

Task announcement message contains information about the outsourcing task, e.g. inputs and outputs should be returned by candidate's services. It also contains bid information that must be provided by candidates in bidding message. Bid specification is extensible to contain other information. All information in the message must include semantic annotation. When candidate's agent receives task announcement message, it decides whether to bid for joining the virtual organization depending on the negotiation strategy defined by the service provider and services that the service provider can provide. If a candidate satisfies the requirements, then candidate's agent may send back a bid message.

```
To: Virtual Organization agent
From: Candidate's agent
Type: BID
Content:
     Task abstraction:
          Name: t_i (semantic)
     BID information:
          Time: [t_1', t_2'] (semantic)
```

Bid message contains biding information corresponding to the bid specification in the announcement message.

According to negotiation strategy, virtual organization agent chooses one bidder and sends an award message to the candidate's agent and refuse messages to other candidates.

```
To: Candidate's agent
From: Virtual Organization agent
Type: AWARD
Content:
     Task abstraction:
```

```
Name: t_i (semantic)
Time: [t_begin', t_end'] (semantic)
```

If candidate's agent receives an award message, it must reply a confirm message or a refuse message.

```
To: Virtual Organization agent
From: Candidate's agent
Type: CONFIRM
Content:
    Task abstraction:
        Name: t_i (semantic)
    WSDL:
        Address: address of wsdl file
        Operation: operation to invoke
```

In the confirm message, service providers must provide the addresses of their services and extra information for using the services, e.g. identification information for using the service. Or candidate's agent may send back a refuse message.

```
To: Virtual Organization agent
From: Candidate's agent
Type: REFUSE
Content:
    Task abstraction:
        Name: t_i (semantic)
```

When cooperating between different entities, semantics are very important. We import semantics into our framework and use ontology to describe semantics. Content of each message must have semantic annotation associated with it.

However, the negotiation process may be very complicated and sometimes may have no results. Then the framework should have some fault tolerant mechanism to guarantee robustness. It is one of our researches now.

After the negotiation process, each outsourcing task should have a partner associates with it. Or else, the virtual organization is not well constructed.

Definition 8: For outsourcing tasks set $ost = \{t_1, t_2...t_n\}$, partners set $p = \{p_1, p_2...p_l\}$ and Web services' set $ws = \{ws_1, ws_2...ws_m\}$. A virtual organization is well constructed only if $\forall t_i \in ost$ with capability requirement fr, $\exists ws_j \in ws$ with capability provided fp, where fr and fp satisfy definition 5 and $\exists p_k \in p$, $ws_j \in Service(p_k)$. $Service(p_k)$ represents the service set of p_k.

After the construction of virtual organization, the virtual organization is submitted to virtual organization management tool for running.

3 Implementation

In our framework, we choose ZEUS [5] as our agent generator. The architecture of the framework is shown is Figure 3.

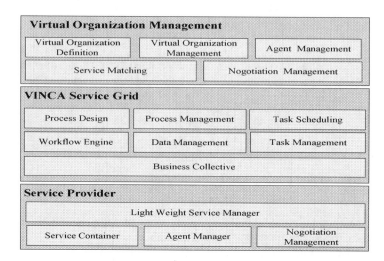

Fig. 3. Architecture of the framework

We've developed several tools to support the framework. These tools can be divided into two categories: service provider side tools and service consumer side tools. Virtual organization construction is accomplished on the service consumer side. The tools and their functionalities are introduced below.

VOD (Virtual Organization Definition tool): VOD is a service consumer side tool. Virtual organization constructor can use this tool to define constrains on partners. Output of *VOD* is a VOML file.

VOM (Virtual Organization Management tool): The tool parses voml file produced by *VOD* and search in business collective for candidates. If the virtual organization is well defined, then *VOM* provides virtual organization agent the addresses of candidates' agents and start the negotiation phase. If virtual organization is well constructed, *VOM* manages the virtual organization for running and monitors the status of virtual organization.

LSM (Lightweight Services Management tool): The tool is deployed on service provider side and manages services that service provider provided. Service provider also uses this tool to define rules of which Web services to provide depending on the contents of request message and negotiation strategy. Some other information, for example authentication information of using service is also defined in this tool.

4 Application

AmGrid [6] is a grid application platform aimed at the requirements of agile resource cooperation in network manufacturing. When there are new user requirements, the enterprise that user has submit his requirements to will evaluate its ability of accomplishing user's requirements. If the enterprise cannot accomplish the requirements by itself, then it will dynamically search for capable partners to construct a virtual organization to fulfill user's requirements.

Suppose that the enterprise needs to manufacture some notebooks, however, there are not enough CPU, hard disk and memory left. Then a new process satisfies the requirements constructed. On the left side of Figure 4, we can see that B and C can provide 30G hard disk. If the enterprise wants to buy products from B or C directly without further negotiation, then may define B or C as the hard disk provider by clicking on B or C. If the enterprise wants further negotiation to decide the final hard disk provider between B and C, by clicking "run virtual organization" button, virtual organization agent will negotiate with B and C's agents to choose the final partner. During negotiation, negotiation rules of each part will be used by the agent. The tools will automatically check whether the virtual organization is well defined or well constructed according to the definitions.

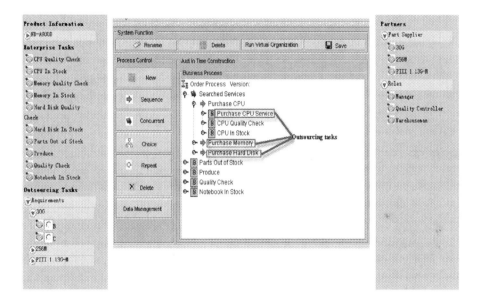

Fig. 4. Snapshot of virtual organization definition

5   Conclusions and Future Work

In paper [7], Ian Foster proposes the combination of grid and agent [8] technologies. Grid provides an infrastructure for federated resource sharing across trust domains and agent focuses on the development of concepts, methodologies, and algorithms for autonomous problem solvers that can act flexibly in uncertain and dynamic environments. So agent can be used as a means for the construction of virtual organizations underlie grid environment. CONOISE-G [9] is one of such a project. In CONOISE-G each service provider is represented as an agent. Virtual organization is constructed through the negotiation between agents. But it is not applicable to process centric virtual organizations. myGrid [10] provides a graphical interface for the modeling of workflow to link together third-party and local resources using web service protocols. Resources are statically bounded so that the workflow will fail if whichever resource the workflow used fails, although there may be some other resources available at the same time. TAEMS [11] models problem-solving activities of an intelligent agent operating in environments where responses by specific deadlines may be required. However it is difficult for non-professional users to use and at the same time it is not applicable for process-centric problem solving environment. In order to further promote the participation of non-professional users and provide much flexibility in problem solving, this paper proposes an agent-mediated service framework. Compared with other methods, this approach has the following features:

- Business user dominant: VINCA is a business user centric language, so business users can define problem solving process without the assist of computer professionals. It can further reduce the problem solving time.
- Flexibility: Each task in the process is dynamically binding to partner's service. Through the negotiation between virtual organization agent and partner's agent, the framework provides much flexibility in choose partners.

However, there are some problems needs for further research. In future, our work includes better algorithm for partner selection and further research on negotiation strategy. And of course, in reality, trust and security are two important aspects also need to be concerned.

References

1. Foster, I., Kesselman, C. and Tuecke, S.: The Anatomy of the Grid: Enabling Scalable Virtual Organizations. Int. J. Supercomputer Applications 15(3) (2001)
2. Han, Y., Geng, H., Li, H., Xiong, J., et al.: VINCA - A Visual and Personalized Business-level Composition Language for Chaining Web-based Services. Proc. International Conference on Service Oriented Computing. Trento, Italy (2003)
3. UDDI. URL: http://www.uddi.org/
4. Smith, R.G.: The Contract Net Protocol: High-Level Communication and Control in a Distributed Problem Solver. IEEE Transactions on computers 29(1980) 1104-1113
5. ZEUS. URL: http://sourceforge.net/projects/zeusagent/
6. Ying, L., Song-Lin, H., Hou-Fu, L. and Yanbo, H.: Study on the architecture and key technologies of grid application platform in network manufacture. Journal of Computer Research and Development 41(12) (2004) 2060-2065
7. Foster, I., Jennings, N.R. and Kesselman, C.: Brain Meets Brawn: Why Grid and Agents Need Each Other. Proc. International Conference on Autonomous Agents and Multi-Agent Systems (AAMAS'04). New York, USA (2004)
8. Wooldridge, M. and Jennings, N.R.: Intelligent Agents: Theory and Practice. The Knowledge Engineering Review 10(2) (1995) 115-152
9. Patel, J., Teacy, W.T.L., Jennings, N.R., Luck, M., et al.: Agent-based virtual organisations for the Grid. Int. J. Multiagent and Grid Systems 1(4) (2005)
10. myGrid. URL: http://www.mygrid.org.uk
11. TAEMS. URL: http://dis.cs.umass.edu/research/taems/

A Cooperative Game Theory Based Coalitional Agent Negotiation Model in Network Service

Zheng-Ai Bian and Jun-Zhou Luo

School of Computer Science and Engineering, Southeast University,
NanJing 210096, P.R. China
{bza,jluo}@seu.edu.cn

Abstract. The traditional non-cooperative game theory is neither Pareto optimal nor fair. It will lead to the loss of efficiency among the homogeneous network services. In this paper, a cooperative game theory based network resource negotiation model carried on by agents is presented. Compared with previous research, the current work focuses on efficiency and fairness. Its chief aim is to utilize cooperation and aggregated of the homogeneous services. The model is based on the idea of the asymmetric NBS (Nash Bargaining Solution) and coalitional game from cooperative game theory. Then a two-stage negotiation algorithm is presented. The homogeneous network services coalition reaches agreement by multi-lateral negotiation using the algorithm. Finally the comparison analysis results demonstrate the advantages of the model.

1 Introduction

The multi-agent negotiation technology is used to implement the allocation of the resource in distributed network. The competition and cooperation among agents mean that one agent can change its' policy according to any others' choices. Thus the game theory is often used in this field in recent years. And the result is that the notion of networking game arises. There are several issues that must be dealt with: 1) the efficiency of allocation solution; 2) the notion of fairness; 3) the stability of the allocation system; 4) the allocation process can be implemented in a distributed environment with minimal communication overheads.

There are two main kinds of approaches in this field. The non-cooperative game theory is given from the view point of a single agent and Nash equilibrium point and its extensions are considered [1-4]. But as [6] indicates, efficiency and fairness of allocation cannot be guaranteed by the non-cooperative game theory. Equilibrium is reached without considering the overall utility value. The second approach is the cooperative-game theory. Different agents can bargain each other and the ideal result of the bargaining is the NBS (Nash Bargaining Solution) [5] in the cooperative-game theory [11], which is a unique solution in a convex, compact strategy set. The properties of NBS prove be Pareto optimal and GPF (Generalized Proportional Fairness) [7]. The sum of utility value is maximized by bargaining.

The theory of NBS for network service was first introduced in [8-10]. But there are some fatal flaws in the NBS. The symmetric axiom leads to the loss of utility value of

W. Shen et al. (Eds.): CSCWD 2006, LNCS 4402, pp. 447–458, 2007.
© Springer-Verlag Berlin Heidelberg 2007

network service with high priority. Furthermore, the fairness only can be guaranteed when the network services are request to have the same utility section. In fact the demands for resource quantity have great discrepancy. The above studies only provided an ideal solution without considering the distributed implementation. Because the number of agent involved may be very large, the negotiation is a multilateral bargaining thread. Finally, the cooperative of different network services means the agents can form a coalition which is superadditivity. Unfortunately the NBS cannot make use of the feature.

In order to solve the above problems, an asymmetric coalitional bargaining solution (ASCBS) [11] model is proposed in this paper. It bases on this kind of idea that the homogenous network service can form a coalition and the coalitions can compete for the finite resource. The whole negotiation mechanism includes two stages. In the first stage, the coalitions finally reach an agreement point by non-cooperative alternating-offer [12] bargaining game and every coalition acts as a bargainer in the bargaining thread. The second stage is that the further allocation procedure within the coalition. In the mechanism, the agreement point in the first stage is proved to be the asymmetric NBS of the characteristic function of the coalition and the coalition for the services with high priority and more utility value section will gain more resource in the bargaining thread. In the second stage the further allocation within the coalition will give the core solution [13] of the coalition.

The rest of this paper is organized as follows: In Section 2, the basic definitions are presented, they include the normalized utility function and the negotiation zone for network service. In Section 3, we propose a new ASCBS (Asymmetric coalitional bargaining solution) model.

2   Basic Definition and Model

2.1   Normalized Utility Function of Network Service

The network service negotiation is considered as a constrained game problem. The i-th agent's utility value is constrained in an interval and the generalized utility function is presented to be a bounded continuous convex function, That is:

$$u_i(x) = f_i(x_i) - c_i(x_i) \qquad (MR_i \leq x_i \leq PR_i) \qquad (1)$$

where MR_i and PR_i are the lower bound and the upper bound of the quantity of network resource needed. Where x_i is the quantity of the resources allocated for the i-th agent. The utility function has two parts: One is the pure profit function $f_i(x_i)$, which presents the satisfaction degree of network service agent when the quantity allocated is x_i. The other is the corresponding cost function $c_i(x_i)$. It shows the cost needed in this service.

The pure profit function $f_i(x_i)$ is a continuous quadratic function. That is:

$$f_i(x_i) = c_i - a_i(x_i - b_i)^2 \qquad (2)$$

$$a_i = f_i^{'}(MR_i) \qquad (3)$$

$$b_i = \frac{1 - \beta_i}{PR_i - MR_i} \qquad (4)$$

$$c_i = \frac{f_i^{'}(MR_i)}{4} \frac{PR_i - MR_i}{1 - \beta_i} \tag{5}$$

where $1/2 \leq \beta_i \leq 1$, the smaller β_i is, the more concave is the utility curve. The limit $\beta_i = 1$ is the linear case. The cost function of the i-th agent is defined in Equation(6):

$$C_i(x_i) = \begin{cases} x_i p = x_i p^*(1 + \sum_{j \in N}(x_j - x_j^*)) & (MR_i < x_i \leq PR_i) \\ 0 & (x_i \leq MR_i) \end{cases} \tag{6}$$

where $c_i(x_i)$ is the cost which the i–th agent spends when the allocated quantity for the i-th network service is x_i. It is equal to the product of x_i and public price p. The latter denotes the current price of the network resource. It is got by multiply the initial price p^* by the variance Δx_i between initial allocated quantity x_i^* and current allocated quantity x_i. Equation (6) is interpreted as that the cost is direct proportional to the variance of the quantity of resource allocated and the initial price of the resource.

The utility function is normalized. That is:

$$M_i(x) = \frac{u_i(x_i) - u_i^{min}}{u_i^{max} - u_i^{min}} \qquad (MR_i \leq x_i \leq PR_i) \tag{7}$$

where u_i^{max} and u_i^{min} is the maximum value and minimum value of utility function of the i-th agent. The normalized utility function $0 \leq M_i(x) \leq 1$ shows the service level specification which the i-th agent attains.

2.2   Utility Value Zone and Negotiation Zone

Utility value zone U_i is the section between maximum value and minimum value of the inverse function for the utility function. That is:

$$U_i = [u_i^{-1}(u_i^{min}), u_i^{-1}(u_i^{max})] \tag{8}$$

where $u_i^{-1}(x)$ is the inverse function for the utility function. According to Equation (2) and Equation (6), it can be concluded that $u_i^{-1}(u_i^{min})$ is equal to MR_i and $u_i^{-1}(u_i^{max})$ is a variable concerning initial price p_i^* and x_i. The first derivative of $M_i(x_i)$ is shown in Equation(9):

$$\frac{\partial M_i(x_i)}{dx_i} = (\frac{df_i(x_i)}{dx_i} - p_i^* * \Delta x - xp_i^*)/(u_i^{max} - u_i^{min}) \tag{9}$$

When the i-th agent negotiates with the j-th agent, the negotiation zone T_{ij} is the intersection of the definition section of the utility function of two agents. That is:

$$T_{ij} = [\max(Z - u_i^{-1}(u_i^{max}), u_j^{-1}(u_j^{min})), \min(Z - u_j^{-1}(u_j^{max}), u_i^{-1}(u_i^{min}))] \tag{10}$$

where Z denotes the quantity of resource to be allocated between the i-th agent and the j-th agent.

3   Asymmetric Coalitional Bargaining Solution (ASCBS) Model

As section 1 describe, the homogeneous network services can form a coalition. The first stage bargaining is an inter coalition bargaining. It reaches sub-game perfect equilibrium point by alternating-offer bargaining thread among the different coalition.

The bargaining powers determinate the coalitions' concession values in the bargaining thread and the utility value when the agreement is reached. The second stage bargaining is an intra-coalition bargaining. It is the further allocation procedure within the coalition. The welfare of the members will be on proportion to the contribution to the coalition and the offer of the coalition should embody the offer of every agent. Otherwise the member will break away from the coalition.

3.1 Bargaining Coalition Model

The homogeneous agents form a coalition and they should have the same bargaining powers and the coalition will act as an active bargainer called bargaining coalition. In the bargaining stage the bargaining coalition is the delegate of the homogeneous members and it is responsible for altering offers with the opponent coalition. The utility function of the bargaining coalition is the characteristic function of the coalition. In the second stage bargaining, it forwards the opponent coalition's counter offer to every coalition member according to every member's contribution for the coalition. If every coalition member receives the counter offer unanimously, the agreement point is reached. Otherwise, the coalition member will propose a new offer for the counter offer from the opponent. The bargaining coalition can evaluate the overall offer for the coalition members' offer and the offer should make all the members satisfy the utility distribution among the members.

3.2 Negotiation Proxy Mechanism

In this paper, negotiation proxy mechanism is introduced to transform sequential bilateral-person bargaining to simultaneous multi-person bargaining. The times that bilateral bargaining cost will increase in exponential rate along with the number of bargainer involved. The cost of communication is $O(2^N)$. Moreover the bargainer should know every opponent's concession value as well as their bargaining powers. The cost is incredible. So in this paper a negotiation proxy is introduced as a "virtual bargainer" whom all agents can only bargain with. The negotiation proxy's bargaining power is standard. It means that whatever the bargaining power the bargainer has, it will meet an opponent which has the standard bargaining power. The bargainers propose the offers simultaneously. When the negotiation proxy receives all the offers from the bargainers, it will assemble all the received offers and evaluates a new counter-offer for the corresponding bargainer according to their bargaining powers. The negotiation proxy can know every bargainer's concession value and the discount rate from the offers proposed by the bargainers in a whole negotiation thread.

3.3 Inter Coalition Bargaining

According to [12], the patience of agents determines their bargaining powers in the alternating-offers game. So we have the following definition:

Definition 1: The offer λ^t_i is proposed by i-th agent at round t as well as λ^{t+1}_i is the counter offer received at round $t+1$. The bargaining power ω_i is concerned with the discount rate r_i, for any agent i,j, we have:

$$r_i / r_j = w_j / w_i \quad r_i = M_i(\lambda_i^t) - Mi(\lambda_i^{t+2}) \tag{11}$$

Equation (11) means that the bargaining power ω_i is in inverse proportion to the discount rate r_i which is the concession value of normalized utility function M_i between the offer λ_i^t and λ_i^{t+2}.

In this paper, the following rules for the service negotiation thread are defined:

Rule1: The participant should know the difference ΔM between normalized utility function value of two offers proposed by the opponent and it will propose a new count-offer to response to the variation of the opponent's offers.

Rule2: The participant is impatient and the negotiation thread should be completed as soon as possible and the time-related discount factor should be considered.

Definition 2: In the light of the negotiation decision function in [14], the negotiation decision function is:

$$\lambda_i^t = \sum W_m (\lambda_i^t)^{(m)} \tag{12}$$

The offer λ_i^t is the sum of the weighted of different discount factor $(\lambda_i^t)^{(m)}$. According to the above rules, we propose two discount factors in the negotiation thread. That is:

1) **Behavior dependent tactics** $(\lambda_i^t)^{(1)}$

$$(\lambda_i^t)^{(1)} = M_i^{-1}(M_i(\lambda_i^{t-2}) - \frac{\omega_j}{\omega_i}(M_j(\lambda_j^{t-1}) - M_j(\lambda_j^{t-3}))) \tag{13}$$

The i-th agent proportion on its discount factor to the rate between the j-th agent's bargaining power and its bargaining power.

2) **Time dependent tactics** $(\lambda_i^t)^{(2)}$

$$(\lambda)^{(2)} = \begin{cases} T^{\min} + \xi^{(t)}(T^{\max} - T^{\min}) & if(\lambda)increas \\ T^{\min} + (1 - \xi^{(t)})(T^{\max} - T^{\min}) & if(\lambda)decrea. \end{cases} \tag{14}$$

$$\xi^{(t)} = e^{(1 - \frac{\min(t, T^{\max})}{T^{\max}})^\beta \ln(\lambda^0 / T^{\max})} \qquad (\beta > 1)$$

T^{max} denotes the deadline of the bargaining thread and λ^0 is the initial offer in bargaining thread. If $\beta > 1$, the offer of the agent will reach its reserve value very quickly. This discount factor is the key element accelerating the negotiation session. The same deadline T^{max} of two participants in a negotiation session means they have the same "patience".

Two factors are considered in definition of the bargaining power w_i. The first factor is the service priority level κ_i. The agents with high priority have bigger bargaining powers. The second factor is the size of utility value section. So we have the bargaining power definition equation, that is:

$$w_i = \kappa_i * (u_i^{max} - u_i^{min}) \tag{15}$$

It can be observed from Equation(15) that the asymmetric NBS solution will be same as the NBS if the bargaining powers of the bargainers are identical.

As the above describe, the negotiation proxy mechanism is introduced to transform the sequential bilateral-person bargaining to the simultaneous multi-person bargaining. The negotiation proxy acts as a "virtual bargainer" and all the agents only can bargain with it. The bargainers propose the offers simultaneously. When negotiation proxy receives all the offers from the bargainers, it will assemble all the received offers then proposes new counter-offers to the corresponding bargainers according to their bargaining powers. The negotiation proxy knows every bargainer's concession value and the discount rate from the offers proposed by the bargainers in a whole negotiation thread.

The following algorithm procedure is used for obtaining the inter-coalition bargaining solution.

Step1: The bargaining coalitions evaluate their own coalition characteristic functions and propose a new offer to the negotiation proxies simultaneously. The offers include two elements $<\Delta M_{Gj}^{t}, \lambda_{Gj}^{t}>$. The ΔM_{Gj} is the discount rate of the coalition G_j and the λ_{Gj}^{t} is the offer value of coalition G_j at round t. The discount rate is on proportion to agents' priority level.

Step2: The negotiation proxy proposes the offers $<\Delta M_{Gj}^{t+1}, \lambda_{Gj}^{t+1}>$ in light of the bargaining power ω_{Gj} of the coalition G_j and forwards it to the j-th coalition. Where the counter-offer value is:

$$\lambda_{Gj}^{t+1} = (Z - \min(\sum_{i \in -G_j} \lambda_i^t, Z)) * (1 + \Delta M_{Gj}^{t+1}).$$

Step3: When the counter-offer value λ_{Gj}^{t+1} are accepted by the members of coalition G_j unanimously. It means that the best strategy for coalition G_j is to accept the counter-offer. Thus the coalition G_j accepts share λ_{Gj}^{t+1} and exits the bargaining thread.

Step4: The negotiation zone Z become $Z - \lambda_{Gj}^{t+1}$. If all the coalitions are satisfied with the offer values received, the bargaining thread will be ended. Otherwise the remaining coalitions will continue bargaining in the new negotiation zone Z. The process moves back to the step 1.

In order to get over the flaws of the NBS, the asymmetric NBS is introduced in this paper, that is:

Theorem 1: There is a unique asymmetric NBP (Nash bargaining point) as well as a unique asymmetric NBS $\overline{X}$ that verifies $M_i(\overline{X}) > 0$, and it is the unique solution of the problem when any normalized utility functions of every agent are convex, that is :

$$\arg \max \prod_{i \in N} (M_i(\overline{x_i}))^{w_i} \tag{16}$$

where ω_i is the bargaining power of the i-th agent.

Theorem 2: The above-mentioned inter-coalition bargaining will lead to unique SSP (stationary sub-game perfect equilibrium) and it is approximate to the asymmetric NBS $\overline{X}$ of the characteristic function of the coalition.

Proof: As the [11] says, the unique equilibrium is characterized in the n-person simultaneous alternating-offers bargaining when they have common discount factor. That is:

$$u_i(x_i)= \delta u_i(x_i+\alpha) \text{ , } i \in N \text{ ; } x(N)+\alpha=Z$$

For the i-th agent, the unique perfect equilibrium agreement point is $(x_1*+\alpha,x_{-1}*)$. Where α is the premium and δ is the discount coefficient. Variable $x_{-1}*$ is the allocated vector for all agents expect the i-th agent. According to [11], the equilibrium is approximate to the NBS of the members when the bargaining powers of the coalitions are identical. We can extend the above equations in the condition that the coalitions are not identical. It can be concluded that the equilibrium agreement is approximate to the asymmetric NBS. That is:

$$u_i(x_i)= \delta_i u_i(x_i+\alpha) \text{ , } i \in N \text{ ; } x(N)+\alpha=Z$$

As [11] describe that the alternating-offers game [2] will achieve the approximate solution of asymmetric NBS. The first advantage will disappear if the time interval between offers $\Delta \rightarrow 0$. The SPE (Sub-game perfect equilibrium) will converge to an asymmetric NBS X. □

3.4 Intra Coalition Bargaining

It's very common that the resource state is a two-state or multi-state Markov process with exponential state transition rates. For a large network system, the probability which all the services reach their peak state simultaneously is very little. Thus the homogeneous services can compensate each other with their superfluous resource. It is evident that the share model of homogeneous service will bring more resource utilization rate. Thus we have the characteristic function $V(R)$ for the coalition R, which means the best utility value for coalition R when the coalition members are in optimal collaboration states. That is:

$$V(R) = \max E(\sum_{i \in R} \tilde{u}_i(x_i ,R)) = \max E(\sum_{i \in R} \tilde{f}_i(x_i ,R) - \sum_{i \in R} \tilde{c}_i(x_i ,R)) \tag{17}$$

where $\tilde{u}_i(x_i ,R)$ is the utility value of the i-th agent when it joins the coalition R, $\tilde{f}_i(x_i,R)$, $\tilde{c}_i(x_i ,R)$ are the corresponding profit function and the cost function, It can be observed that profit function does not change for the coalition R. Thus the expected cost function is the key factor, that is :

$$E(c_i(x_i,R)) = \sum_{\substack{|m|=1 \\ m \subset neighbor(i,R)}}^{|neighbor(i,R)|} P_i(m,R)c_i(x_i - \xi(i,m)) \tag{18}$$

where $P_i(m,R)$ is the probability that the total number of collaborator for the i-th agent in collaborator set neighbor(I,R) is $|m|$. It can be observed that there are super-additivity within the coalition when the network resource is transferable. In these conditions, the coalition members can compensate each other with side payments $\xi(i,m)$. If all the services have the same transition rates, the above probaility will be a binomial distribution . Thus we have the following equations:

$$P_i(m,R) = C_{|R|}^{|m|} P_i(m,R)^{|m|} (1 - P_i(m,R))^{|R|-|m|} \tag{19}$$

Theorem 3: The homogeneous network service coalition N is a convex cooperative game coalition, that is:

For $R_3 \subset N$ and $R_1 \subset R_2 \subset N \setminus R_3$,

We have : $V(R_1 \cup R_3) - V(R_1) \leq V(R_2 \cup R_3) - V(R_2)$

Proof:

$\because V(R_1 \cup R_3) - V(R_1) - V(R_3)$

$$= \sum_{i \in R_1} \sum_{\substack{|m|=1 \\ m \subset neighbor(i,R_3)}}^{|neighbor(i,R_3)|} P_i(m, R_3) C_i(x_i - \xi(i,m)) + \sum_{i \in R_3} \sum_{\substack{|m|=1 \\ m \subset neighbor(i,R_1)}}^{|neighbor(i,R_1)|} P_i(m, R_1) C_i(x_i - \xi(i,m))$$

$V(R_2 \cup R_3) - V(R_2) - V(R_3)$

$$= \sum_{i \in R_2} \sum_{\substack{|m|=1 \\ m \subset neighbor(i,R_3)}}^{|neighbor(i,R_3)|} P_i(m, R_3) C_i(x_i - \xi(i,m)) + \sum_{i \in R_3} \sum_{\substack{|m|=1 \\ m \subset neighbor(i,R_2)}}^{|neighbor(i,R_2)|} P_i(m, R_2) C_i(x_i - \xi(i,m))$$

$$\because \sum_{\substack{m \subset R_1 \\ |m|=Num}} P_i(m, R_1) \leq \sum_{\substack{m \subset R_2 \\ |m|=Num}} P_i(m, R_2)$$

$$\Rightarrow \sum_{i \in R_1} \sum_{\substack{|m|=1 \\ m \subset neighbor(i,R_3)}}^{|neighbor(i,R_3)|} P_i(m, R_3) C_i(x_i - \zeta(i,m)) \leq \sum_{i \in R_2} \sum_{\substack{|m|=1 \\ m \subset neighbor(i,R_3)}}^{|neighbor(i,R_3)|} P_i(m, R_3) C_i(x_i - \xi(i,m))$$

$$\therefore V(R_1 \cup R_3) - V(R_1) - V(R_3) \leq V(R_2 \cup R_3) - V(R_2) - V(R_3)$$

$$\Rightarrow V(R_1 \cup R_3) - V(R_1) \leq V(R_2 \cup R_3) - V(R_2) \qquad \qquad \square$$

The convex cooperative game means that joining a bigger coalition will bring an individual agent more benefit. As [15] describes, the optimal allocation solution within a coalition is deduced from the contribution, which is called core solution. The core solution is not empty and the Shapely vector is the core solution while the coalition is convex. Thus we can extend the definition of Shapley value, that is:

$$\varphi_i(X_{Gj}) = \sum_{\substack{R \subset G_j \setminus \{i\} \\ n = |G_j|}} \frac{|R|!(n - |R| - 1)!}{n!} \left[v_{R \cup \{i\}}(X_{Gj}) - v_R(X_{Gj}) \right] \tag{20}$$

And we have the following definition:

$$V_{G_j}(X_{Gj}) = \max U_{G_j}(X_{Gj}, X - X_{Gj}) \geq \max \sum_{i \in G_j} U_i(x_i) \tag{21}$$

(Subject to $\sum_{i \in G_j} x_i = X_{Gj}$)

Variable $V_{Gj}(X_{Gj})$ is the characteristic function for coalition G_j when the overall allocated amount in the inter-coalition bargaining solution is X_{Gj}. Equation (21) shows that the characteristic function value of coalition G_j is bigger than the sum of that of the every member when they behave individually. Then we can propose a new normalized utility function for the coalition G_j. That is:

$$M_{G_j}(x_{Gj}) = \frac{V_{Gj}(X_{Gj})}{U_{G_j}^{max}} \tag{22}$$

where U_{Gj}^{max} denotes the maximum characteristic value of the coalition G_j .So we have the payoff of the member:

$$M_i(X_i) = \frac{\varphi_i(X_{Gj})}{U_i^{max}} \qquad (23)$$

where $\varphi_i(X_{Gj})$ denotes the allocated utility value for the i-th agent in the coalition G_j when the overall allocation for the coalition is X_{Gj}. If the members of coalition are all homogeneous, the core solution within the coalition doesn't change along with the change of the coalition allocation X_{Gj}.

The following steps are the further allocation procedure:

Step1: The coalition members submit their offers to the bargaining coalition simultaneously. The bargaining coalition sum the members' offer values and evaluate the characteristic function $V_{Gj}(\Sigma_i \lambda_i^t)$. For any members, if $\varphi_i(\Sigma_i \lambda_i^t) \geq u_i(\lambda_i^t)$, it means that there are no members lose their utility at this round. The coalition offer value $\Sigma_i \lambda_i^t$ is a valid offer value. Otherwise the i-th member will break away from the coalition and become an individual member.

Step2: The bargaining coalition submits the new coalition offer $<\Delta M_{Gj}^t, \lambda_{Gj}^t>$ to the negotiation proxy. The discount rate is: $\Delta M_{Gj}^t = (V_{Gj}(\Sigma_i \lambda_i^t) - V_{Gj}(\Sigma_i \lambda_i^{t-2}))/U_{Gj}^{max}$ and the offer value λ_{Gj}^t is $\Sigma_i \lambda_i^t$.

Step3: The bargaining coalition receives the new counter-offer value λ_{Gj}^{t+1} from the negotiation proxy and decomposes the counter-offer for the members. The new counter-offer value for the i-th member is $M_i^{-1}(\varphi_i(\lambda_{Gj}^{t+1})/U_i^{max})$.

Step4: The i-th member proposes a new offer and compares it with the counter-offer. The new offer value is :

$$(\lambda_i^{t+2}) = M_i^{-1}(M_i(\lambda_i^t) - \frac{(\varphi_i(\lambda_{Gj}^{t+1}) - \varphi_i(\lambda_{Gj}^{t-1}))}{u_i^{max}})$$

If counter-offer value λ_i^{t+1} is bigger than the offer value λ_i^{t+2}, it means that the best strategy for the i-th member is to accept the counter-offer.

Step5: If all the members accept their counter-offer unanimously, the bargaining coalition will accept the counter-offer λ_{Gj}^{t+1}.

For any member who belongs to the coalition G_j, the sum of the concession value when it joins the coalition should be smaller than that of the individual member in a bargaining thread. We have the following constraint:

$$\int_{\lambda_{Gj}}^{\lambda_{Gj}^{max}} \frac{\varphi_i(x_{Gj})}{u_i^{max}} dx_{Gj} < \int_{\lambda_i}^{\lambda_i^{max}} M_i(x_i) dx_i \qquad (24)$$

where λ_{Gj}^{max}, λ_i^{max} are the maximum expected offer values of the coalition G_j and the i-th coalition member, $\overline{\lambda}_{Gj}, \overline{\lambda}_i$ are the offer values of their agreement point in the bargaining thread. It's evident that the intra-coalition solution will be the Shapley value within the coalition. Where $\varphi_i(\overline{\lambda}_{Gj})$ denotes the Shapley value for the i-th coalition member when the inter-coalition bargaining points has been reached. The intra-coalition bargaining solution for the i-th coalition member is:

$$x_i = M_i^{-1}(\varphi_i(\overline{\lambda_{G_j}})/u_i^{max}) \tag{25}$$

The payoff of the i-th agent in coalition Gj is:

$$\varphi_i(\overline{\lambda_{G_j}}) = \sum_{R \subseteq G_j \backslash \{i\}} \frac{|R|!(n-|R|-1)!}{n!}\left[v_{R \cup \{i\}}(\overline{\lambda_{G_j}}) - v_R(\overline{\lambda_{G_j}})\right] \qquad n = |G_j| \tag{26}$$

4 Case Study

We can propose this scenario. There are three ASes compete for public bandwidth of Root AS. The capacity of public bandwidth is 20M. In first ASes, there are three homogeneous flows with priority 1. In second ASes, there is one aggregated flow with priority 2. In third ASes there is one aggregated flow with priority 1. The utility value sections of the flows are:$MR_1=0,PR_1=30$, $MR_2=0,PR_2=80$, $MR_3=0,MR_3=70$. In this example, the pure profit function $f_i(x)$ can be an end-to-end delay related function. Considering the equivalent bandwidth, there is extra available bandwidth for individual dataflow when three homogeneous flows are aggregated in bandwidth reservation mechanism. It means less bandwidth needed to receive the same delay performance when the individual flow joins the aggregated flow and the cost of individual flow is reduced. Thus the intra-bargaining can be looked on as a utility transferable coalitional game. The solution is Shapley value. When three flows have same traffic characteristic, Shapley value for every flow in coalition 1 is:

$$\varphi_1 = \varphi_2 = \varphi_3$$

It is assumed that the equivalent bandwidth PR_1' is approximate to $PR*0.9$. The characteristic function of coalition 1 is:

$$V_{G1} = \sum_{i \in (1,2,3)} 3f_i(x_i + 0.1x_i) - C_i(x_i)$$

The bargaining thread will hold among the coalition agents represent the aggregated flow and the bargaining solution is the coalitional asymmetric NBS of the utility value of the individual flow and the inter-bargaining solution is:

$$\arg\max \frac{V_{G1}^{3}(x_{G1})}{U_{G_j}^{max}} M_4(x_4)^{8*2} M_5(x_5)^7$$

The intra-bargaining solution for the members of coalition 1 is:

$$x_i = M_i^{-1}(\varphi_i(\overline{\lambda_{G_i}})/u_i^{max})$$

For comparison purposes we consider other optimal schemes. They are OPTIM(Global optimal), NE(Nash equilibrium),NBS(Nash bargaining solution). The normalized utility values of different schemes are listed in Table 1, that is:

Table 1. Expected solution of different schemes

	OPTIM	NE	NBS	ASCBS
Coalition1	7999	6450	7972	6709
Flow4	6815	7102	6795	7371
Flow5	5185	4021	5232	5919

Table 2. Normalized utility value of the flow

	OPTIM	NE	NBS	ASCBS
Coalition1	0.9876	0.9198	0.9870	0.9761
Flow4	0.9730	0.9874	0.9773	0.9938
Flow5	0.9328	0.8188	0.9362	0.9761

Table 1 and Table 2 show that the solution of the OPTIM is approximate to that of the NBS. The NBS can be looked on as a global optimal solution in some situations and Pareto optimal is guaranteed in this solution. The ASCBS provides the most utility value for every member. Because the superadditivity of ASCBS enables that the bargaining coalition can use the side payments of the coalition and yield more utility for the members.

Besides that, the GPF coefficient is that:

$$\sum_i (M_i - M_i^*)/M_i^*$$

where M_i^* is the reference solution. If the NBS is the reference solution, GPF coefficients of the above schemes are listed in Table 3. The result shows that the ASCBS is even more GPF than the NBS. This phenomenon attributes to the fact that the resource allocation is direct proportional to the utility function curve of coalition member.

Table 3. The GPF coefficient

	OPTIM	NE	NBS	ASCBS
Fairness coefficient	$0.879*10^{-4}$	-0.30889	0	0.0435

Table 4. The number of exchanged messages

	OPTIM	NE	NBS	ASCBS
Fairness coefficient	—	21	28	20

Besides that, it can be observed from Table 4 that the messages needed in ASCBS are less than that of traditional cooperative game model. The reason is that the altering-offer procedure only happens among the bargaining coalition and the homogeneous agents can reach agreement point more quickly in intra-coalition bargaining process. The above approaches can reduce the algorithm complexity of negotiation process considerably.

5 Conclusions and Outlook

The main purpose of the present work is to focus on several features of the homogeneous network services. The main goal is to derive a fair and optimal allocation

scheme when the differentiated service is provided. We formulate the network resource allocation problem in multi-class service systems as a cooperative bargaining
among agents. For the proposed cooperative network resource bargaining we present
the coalitional bargaining model. Based on this model we derive a new algorithm. It is
a two-stage bargaining thread including the inter-coalition bargaining and the intra-
coalition bargaining. Future work will address the development of game theoretic
models for network resource bargaining in the context of uncertainty as well as game
theory models for dynamic network resource bargaining.

Acknowledgments. This work is supported by National Natural Science Foundation
of China under Grants No.90412014 and 90604004, Jiangsu Provincial Key Laboratory of Network and Information Security under Grants No. BM2003201.

References

1. Altman, E.: Flow control using the theory of zero-sum Markov games. IEEE Transactions
   on Automatic Control 39 (1994) 814-818
2. Altman, E.: A Markov game approach for optimal routing into a queue-ing network. Annals of Dynamic Games 5 (1999) 359-376
3. Kurose, J. and Simha, R.: A microeconomic approach to optimal resource allocation in
   distibuted computer systems. IEEE Trans. On Computers 38(5) (1989) 705-717
4. La, R.J. and Anantharam, V.: Window-based congestion control with heterogeneous users.
   Proc. IEEE infocom2001. Ankorage, Alaska (2001)
5. Nash, J.: The bargaining problem. Econometrica 18 (1950) 155-162
6. Dubey, P.: Inefficiency of Nash equilibria. Math Oper Res. 11 (1986) 1-8
7. Kelly, F.P.: Charging and rate control for elastic traffic. European Trans on Telecom 8
   (1998) 33-37
8. Mazumdar, R.R., Yaiche, H. and Rosenberg, C.: A game theoretic framework for bandwidth allocation and pricing in broadband networks. IEEE/ACM Trans. on Networking
   8(5) (2000) 667-677
9. Mazumdar, R., Mason, L.G. and Douligeris, C.: Fairness in network optimal flow control:
   optimality of product forms. IEEE Trans. on Comm. 39 (1991) 775-782
10. Rextin, A.T., Irfan, Z., Uzmi, Z.A.: Games networks play a game theoretic approach to
    networks. Proc. 7th International Symposium on Parallel Architectures, Algorithms and
    Networks (2004) 451 – 456
11. Rubinstein, A.: Perfect equilibrium in a bargaining model. Econometrica 50 (1982) 97–
    109
12. Osborne, M. and Rubinstein, A.: A Course in Game Theory. MIT Press, Cambridge, Mas-
    sachusetts (1994)
13. Stefan, N.: Bilateral Bargaining: Theory and Applications. Lecture Notes in Economics
    and Mathematical Systems. Springer (2002)
14. Faratin, P., Sierra, C. and Jennings, N.R.: Negotiation Decision Functions for Autonomous
    Agents. Robotics and Autonomous Systems 24 (1998) 159-182
15. Shapley, L.: On balanced sets and cores. Naval Research Logistics Quarterly 14 (1967)
    453–460

An Agent Negotiation Approach for Establishment of Service Level Agreement

Jun Yan[1], Ryszard Kowalczyk[2], Jian Lin[2], Mohan B. Chhetri[2], Suk K. Goh[2], and Jianying Zhang[2]

[1] School of Information Systems and Technology, University of Wollongong,
Northfields Avenue, Wollongong, NSW, Australia 2522
jyan@uow.edu.au
[2] Faculty of Information and Communication Technologies,
Swinburne University of Technology,
P.O. Box 218, Hawthorn, VIC, Australia 3122
{rkowalczyk, jlin, mchhetri, sgoh, jyzhang}@ict.swin.edu.au

Abstract. Efficient management of service level agreements which govern provision of service compositions remains a big challenge in the Web services environment. This paper reports innovative research aiming at supporting autonomous establishment of a set of interrelated service level agreements for service compositions. In this paper, an agent-based framework is proposed to exploit agent interaction and negotiation capabilities for achieving agreements on service provision. Based on this framework, this paper also discusses mechanisms for agents representing service consumers and providers to negotiate quality of service constraints for constituent services in a coordinated way, with a focus on achieving end-to-end quality of service requirements.

1 Introduction

Service-Oriented Computing (SOC) is an emerging paradigm that utilises services as fundamental elements for developing distributed applications such as e-business processing [12]. In SOC, externally observable behaviours of business applications are semantically described and advertised as services so that they can be discovered and accessed by others. Moreover, oganisations are able to integrate their systems in a seamless manner by composing distributed business applications with little effort into a network of services, i.e., a service composition, to create dynamic business processes and agile applications. The most well-known integration platform for SOC is the Web Services framework which is based on a family of related XML-based standards, including WSDL, UDDI, and SOAP.

The provision of a service composition implies consumption of a set of services that are dynamically purchased from other service providers. This buy and offer relationship is commonly governed by an agreement, known as *Service Level Agreement* (SLA), which regards the guarantees of a service provision. A SLA is a contractual obligation between the service provider and the service consumer specifying mutually-agreed understandings and expectations in both functional and non-functional

W. Shen et al. (Eds.): CSCWD 2006, LNCS 4402, pp. 459–468, 2007.
© Springer-Verlag Berlin Heidelberg 2007

aspects. The functional aspects of a SLA are about interactions to be carried out to offer the service. The non-functional aspects, on the other hand, describe a set of Quality of Service (QoS) constraints, e.g., cost and response time, about how well the service should be offered.

SLA management has been the subject of intense research for several years. However, it is still at its infancy for provision of service compositions which may involve the buy and offer relationship between one service consumer and many service providers. More specifically, today's SLA management largely relies on either the customer QoS requests on individual services or manual configuration to determine the QoS constraints about individual services in a service composition. There lacks frameworks and mechanisms to manage non-functional aspects of SLAs flexibly, dynamically, and autonomously.

In view of this situation, this paper reports innovative research on SLA management for service compositions with a focus on autonomously establishing non-functional aspects of SLAs. To achieve this goal, this paper presents a framework for autonomous and coordinated SLA negotiation using intelligent agents. Based on this framework, a set of SLAs can be formed which can collectively fulfill the end-to-end QoS requirements for the service composition provision.

The rest of the paper is organised as follows. The next section briefly introduces the major related work in the area of SLA management, and the background of this research. Section 3 discusses some critical issues in the solution and proposes an overall negotiation framework. Based on this framework, Section 4 describes mechanisms for coordinated SLA negotiation, followed by a brief discussion of prototype implementation in Section 5. Finally, Section 6 concludes this document and outlines the future work.

2   Related Work and Background

Over the past a few years, active research on SLA management, mainly carried out in the context of single service offering, has covered various areas such as SLA specification and languages, SLA creation, operation, monitoring, termination, and so on. Just to name a few, Nguyen et al. [10] studied the importance of SLA management in SOC comprehensively. The Global Grid Forum (GGF) published the Web Service Agreement Specification (WS-Agreement [1]) which is an XML language for specifying an agreement between a service provider and a consumer, and a protocol for creation of an agreement using agreement templates. Keller and Ludwig presented a Web Service Level Agreement (WSLA) framework for defining and monitoring SLAs in inter-domain environments [8]. Debusmann et al. [5] presented an approach for SLA-driven management of distributed systems using common information model (CIM). Demirkan et al. [6] discussed an exploratory study to identify requirements on negotiation support for the processes associated with SLA development. In SNAP [4], a general framework is defined within which a client can reserve and acquire any resource from resources providers in a uniform fashion.

The distinct research reported in this paper is carried out in the context of the Adaptive Service Agreement and Process Management (ASAPM) project which focuses on enabling flexible, dynamic and robust management of service-oriented application provision processes that are not available in the current generation of service environments. The overall architecture of ASAPM consists of four components:

- The Negotiation Management is responsible for autonomous SLA negotiation and re-negotiation aiming at fulfilling end-to-end QoS requirements of the service composition, as explained in this paper.
- The SLA Lifecycle Management and Dynamic Service Profiling manages SLA documents over their lifetime, and maintains up-to-date service profiles which may be used for SLA negotiation and re-negotiation.
- Workflow Enactment, Monitoring and Visualisation is responsible for enactment of the service composition according to its definition, monitoring of non-functional parameters (actual QoS values), and visualisation of service composition enactment.
- Mediated Workflow Re-planning is responsible for service re-composition mediation, aiming at providing alternative plans satisfying the original user request when an unrecoverable error occurs.

Detailed information about the project, each component, and the interaction between components can be found in [13].

3 Solution Overview

The agent negotiation framework proposed in this paper supports the autonomous establishment of a set of SLAs among the service consumer and the service providers right before the enactment of services.

3.1 Requirements Analysis

As briefly indicated in Section 1, service composition provision may involve services buy and offer between one service consumer and many service providers. Generally speaking, there are two approaches to managing this multilateral relationship. One approach, as shown in Figure 1, is to have a single SLA, agreed by all the parties involved, specifying all the aspects of the service composition provision including the QoS constraints. Obviously, such an approach may result in a very complex agreement, especially when the service composition involves many services and providers. Thus, it is always difficult to manage this single SLA. In the case that the agreement needs to be modified as a response to an exception, even a very small change requires the endorsement of all the parties.

Alternatively, this research adopts a more suitable approach by managing multiple SLAs for the service composition provision. Each SLA, agreed by the service consumer and one service provider, governs the provision of a single service. Figure 2 depicts this multi-SLA approach. In such an approach, the non-functional aspects of each SLA defines the particular QoS constraints on the provision of a single service. They collectively fulfill the end-to-end QoS requirements of the whole service composition. In an exceptional scenario, the SLA modification only involves relevant SLAs and parities. Other SLAs remain unchanged as long as the overall requirements are still satisfied after modification.

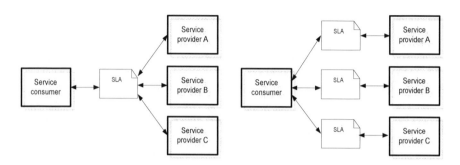

Fig. 1. Single SLA approach   **Fig. 2.** Multi-SLA approach

Although the QoS constraints of each SLA can be manually and statically designated, techniques to provide flexible, autonomous and dynamic support are highly
desirable. In more details, such techniques should satisfy the following requirements:

- The service consumer will normally give overall QoS requirements, e.g., the
  overall execution time, instead of specifying requirements on individual services, e.g., the respective execution time for services A, B, and C. It is expected
  that QoS aggregation and trade-off between services can be handled flexibly to
  collectively fulfill the overall QoS requirements.
- The agreement on QoS constraints can be achieve autonomously by the service
  consumer and the service provider through the use of software.

The agent technology which offers abilities of autonomous operations, interaction
and cooperation has been recognised as a promising technology for SLA management
in the SOC paradigm. In particular, the agent technology enables autonomous negotiation as a means of establishing service contracts. In this context, the negotiation is
normally driven by the operational policy of both the service consumer and the service provider. In addition, the agent technology offers ability of autonomous problem
solvers that can act flexibly for QoS adaptation in dynamic and exceptional environments. Therefore, the agent technology is well positioned to address the key issues in
this research.

There are two possible ways to establish SLAs for a service composition. One is
called *negotiate-all-then-enact* where SLAs are established through negotiation for all
the component services in the composition before the enactment of the first service
takes place. The other is called *step-by-step-negotiate-and-enact*, where SLA negotiation and service enactment are intertwined. In this case, the first service can be
enacted when its SLA is established. After the completion of this service, SLA negotiation is carried out for subsequent services, followed by enactment of these services.
As the preliminary goal of this research is to negotiate SLAs for the service composition to guarantee end-to-end QoS, the negotiate-all-then-enact approach is selected. In
the future, research may be carried out to investigate mechanisms for step-by-step-
negotiate-and-enact or a mixture of both methods.

3.2 Overall Negotiation Framework

SLA negotiation for a service composition involves two aspects. One aspect is the negotiation between the service consumer and one or many service providers for QoS constraints about a single service in the composition. The other aspect is the coordination of negotiation for multiple services to ensure end-to-end QoS. To address these two functional aspects, a comprehensive framework is designed, as shown in Figure 3.

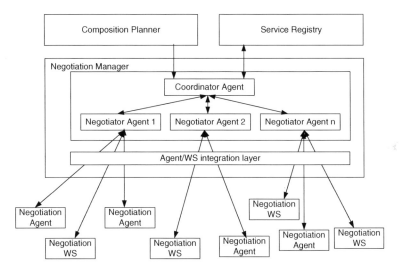

Fig. 3. SLA negotiation framework

In Figure 3, the negotiation capability of the service consumer is supported by a Multi-Agent System (MAS). This MAS consists of a *Coordinator Agent* (CA) and a set of *Negotiator Agents* (NA). The CA is responsible for the negotiation for the service composition as a whole. It interacts with the composition planner to receive the service composition definition and the overall user QoS requirements. A NA is then dynamically created to represent each service extracted from the composition. Each NA is responsible for SLA negotiation with one or many service providers for a particular service in the composition, under the guidance and control of the CA. The negotiation capabilities on the side of the service providers can be implemented in different ways, as long as they follow the same negotiation protocol and negotiation semantics. The easiest way is to have either centralised or distributed agents to act on behalf of service providers. Alternatively, for the purpose of interoperability, the negotiation capabilities on the side of the service providers can be implemented as distributed Web services called *Negotiation Web Services* (NWS) which can be registered in and retrieved from the service registry. In this case, an extra layer is needed to allow for seamless integration of agents and Web services.

4 Coordinated SLA Negotiation

Based on the framework proposed in Section 3, the agents for the service consumer autonomously negotiate with the service providers to determine local QoS constraints for individual services of the composition. This negotiation is well coordinated aiming at collectively fulfilling the given end-to-end QoS.

4.1 QoS Requirements Conversion

To enable negotiation, end-to-end QoS, i.e., the composition level requirements, need to be converted or decomposed into local QoS requirements, i.e., the service level requirements for individual services. Therefore, the negotiation objectives for each service and the coordination rules for the composition are established. In other words, the negotiation space for each service is determined.

Regarding QoS conversion, research has been done in the workflow area to calculate QoS values of a workflow process from QoS values of its constituent tasks. A well known approach called the *Stochastic Workflow Reduction (SWR) algorithm* is presented in [3]. The SWR algorithm repeatedly applies a set of reduction rules to a workflow until only one atomic task remains. Each time a reduction rule is applied, the workflow structure changes. After several iterations only one task will remain [9]. When this state is reached, the remaining task contains the QoS metrics corresponding to the workflow under analysis. In this algorithm, the set of reduction rules that can be applied to a given workflow corresponds to the set of inverse operations that can be used to construct a workflow such as sequential, parallel and conditional structures.

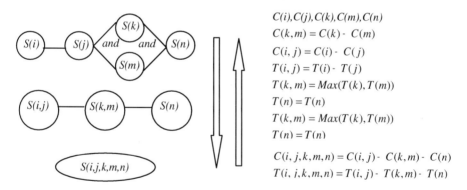

Fig. 4. Workflow reduction and QoS conversion

QoS conversion in this research is carried out by the CA in a reverse way to workflow reduction. The end-to-end QoS can be viewed as the requirements on a single composite service. While the composite service is gradually decomposed into a collection of atomic services, the overall QoS requirements are also decomposed into local requirements for these atomic services. Figure 4 depicts an example of workflow reduction and QoS conversion. For the purpose of simplicity, only two QoS parameters, i.e., cost and response time, are considered, represented as C and T in Figure 4. Using the workflow reduction algorithm, the workflow (i.e., the service composition) in Figure 4 which consists of services $S(i), S(j), S(k)$, $S(m)$ and $S(n)$ can be converted into a single service $S(i, j, k, m, n)$ which has the cost requirement $C(i, j, k, m, n)$ and response time requirement $T(i, j, k, m, n)$ (i.e., the end-to-end QoS requirements). This overall requirement can be converted into requirements on $S(i, j)$, $S(k, m)$ and $S(n)$ with specified dependencies. Finally, the requirements on individual services and the dependencies between them can be obtained. Note that the QoS requirements on a service can be specified in different formats such as the value range, e.g., cost between α and β, and the value condition, e.g., cost less than γ. During the QoS conversion, one important feature is that the profiling data of each service (type), which include historical performance such as maximum, minimum and average cost of using this service, will be retrieved from the SLA Lifecycle Management and Dynamic Profiling. These data provide estimation and expectation of the local QoS capabilities and serve as the basis for QoS conversion.

4.2 SLA Negohtiation

In the framework proposed in Section 3, SLA negotiation refers to the process by which CA, NA and one or many service providers come to mutually acceptable agreements on service QoS. In autonomous negotiation, four fundamental topics need to be taken into account. They are negotiation attributes, negotiation objectives, negotiation protocols, and decision making frameworks.

Negotiation attributes are objects to be negotiated. In this research, negotiation attributes are QoS parameters for provision of services, which may include cost of using the service, response time of the service, accessibility and reliability of the service, and so on. This research starts with two negotiation attributes, cost and response time, but can be extended to support more negotiation attributes.

The negotiation objectives are goals to be achieved through negotiation. The overall QoS requirements and the local QoS requirements obtained using QoS conversion are the objectives to be achieved.

A negotiation protocol refers to a set of rules that describe the circumstances under which the interactions between agents take place. They cover the permissible types of participants, the negotiation states, the events that cause negotiation states to be changed, and the valid actions of the agents in particular states. In this research, the Iterated Contract Net Interaction Protocol (ICNIP) [7] contributed by Foundation for Intelligent Physical Agents (FIPA) is extended to support both multi-round iterative negotiation to find a compromise for a single service, and management of concurrent negotiation for various services of the composition. The most significant extension is on negotiation triggering and negotiation confirmation. CA triggers the NA to start SLA negotiation by sending it the reserve values defining negotiation attributes and objectives. The NA then negotiates with many providers using the standard FIPA ICNIP, followed by the confirmation of negotiation or the modification of the reserve values by the CA. Following the instructions, the NA accepts an offer or restarts negotiation, respectively. After the negotiation is successfully undertaken for all services, the selected service providers commit to provide the required service with the agreed QoS.

Decision making frameworks are employed by agents to act in accordance with the negotiation protocol in order to achieve their objectives. A decision making framework includes a negotiation strategy which refers to a sequence of actions (e.g., accept and refuse) for an agent to follow. The sophistication of the framework, as well as the range of decisions that have to be made, are influenced by the negotiation protocol, the nature of the negotiation attributes, and the range of operations that can be performed on it. In this research, the decision making framework is based on the utility function which scores each point in the decision space of the negotiation object to represent the level of satisfaction [2]. In short, each service provider initially provides the NA a proposal specifying the service QoS it is willing to offer. The NA then calculates the utility value of each received proposal, selects the best proposal, and either accepts it or generates a counter proposal by making concession and/or trade-off. If a counter proposal is sent to service providers, a new negotiation iteration starts. Each service provider calculates the utility value of the counter proposal according to its own utility function, and provides the NA a new proposal by making concession and/or trade-off. This procedure is repeated until an agreement is achieved, i.e., a proposal is accepted by the NA or a counter proposal is accepted by one service provider, or the timeout.

5 Prototype Implementation

To demonstrate the key ideas presented in this paper, a prototype has been implemented for the proof-of-concept purpose. As shown in Figure 5, in this prototype, the Negotiation Manager is implemented using the FIPA compliant JADE Agent Framework which is a middleware that implements an agent platform and a development framework. The Agent/WS integration is support by a toolkit called WS2JADE [11] which enables run-time deployment and control of Web services with JADE agents and allows JADE agents to access and use Web services. The initial results are promising, demonstrating that agent negotiation can autonomously achieve interrelated SLA agreements which collectively fulfill overall QoS requirements of the service composition.

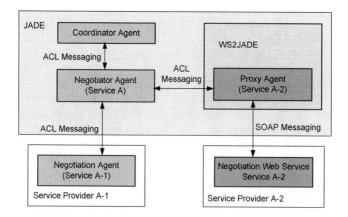

Fig. 5. Prototype Implementation

6   Conclusions and Future Work

Service level agreement management is a critical issue in the emerging paradigm of service-oriented computing. Adequate support for SLA management can guarantee both functional and non-functional aspects of the service provision. However, today's research on SLA focuses on the scenario of single service provision. SLA management in the context of the service composition which consists of a set of interrelated services has not been addressed satisfactorily. In particular, support for the management of non-functional aspects of SLA for individual services while ensuring end-to-end QoS is rather weak. There lacks mechanisms to autonomously and dynamically determine QoS values for individual services in a service composition.

This paper reports innovative research conducted in the context of the ASAPM project. In this research, SLAs for service compositions, especially those non-functional aspects of SLAs, are established and managed autonomously and dynamically. To achieve this goal, the agent technology is exploited in this research and a novel framework for coordinated SLA negotiation is presented. In this framework, autonomous negotiation can be carried out in a coordinated way to determine QoS constraints for individual services that collectively fulfill end-to-end QoS.

The framework presented in this paper builds a solid foundation for the future research work. Based on this framework, the negotiation techniques will be extended to support more QoS attributes. More complicated decision-making mechanisms will be also developed to improve the efficiency of negotiation. Quantitative results observed with the use of the architecture in real problems will be studied.

Acknowledgments. This work is supported by the Adaptive Service Agreement and Process Management (ASAPM) in Services Grid project (AU-DEST-CG060081) and the EU FP6 Integrated Project on Adaptive Services Grid (EU-IST-004617). The ASAPM project is proudly supported by the Innovation Access Program - International Science and Technology established under the Australian Government's innovation statement, Backing Australia's Ability.

References

1. Andrieux, A., Czajkowski, K., Dan, A., Keahey, K., Ludwing, H., Pruyne, J., et al.: Web Service Agreement Specification (WS-Agreement). Version 1.1 (2004) URL: http://www.gridforum.org/Meetings/GGF11/Documents/draft-ggf-graap-agreement.pdf
2. Brzostowski, J. and Kowalczyk, R.: Efficient Algorithm for Estimation of Qualitative Expected Utility in Possibilistic Case-based Reasoning. Proc. 21st Conference on Uncertainty in Artificial Intelligence (UAI 2005). Edinburgh, Scotland (2005)
3. Cardoso, J.: Stochastic Workflow Reduction Algorithm. LSDIS Lab, University of Georgia (2002) URL: http://lsdis.cs.uga.edu/proj/meteor/QoS/SWR_Algorithm.htm
4. Czajkowski, K., Foster, I., Kesselman, C., Sander V. and Trecke, S.: SNAP: A Protocol for Negotiating Service Level Agreements and Coordinated Resource Management in Distributed Systems. Proc. of the 8th Workshop on Job Scheduling Strategies for Parallel Processing. Edinburgh, Scotland (2002)

5. Debusmann, M. and Keller, A.: SLA-driven management of distributed systems using the common information model. Proc. 8th IFIP/IEEE International Symposium on Integrated Network Management (IM 2003). Colorado Springs, USA (2003)

6. Demirkan, H., Goul M. and Soper, D. S.: Service Level Agreement negotiation: A theory-based exploratory study as a starting point for identifying negotiation support system requirements. Proc. 38th Hawaii International Conference on System Sciences. Hawaii, USA (2005)

7. FIPA. Iterated Contract Net Interaction Protocol Specification (2000) URL: http://www.fipa.org/specs/fipa00030/PC00030D.pdf

8. Keller, A. and Ludwig, H.: Defining and monitoring service level agreements for dynamic e-business. Proc. of LISA 2002. Philadelphia, USA (2002)

9. Kochut, K. J., Sheth, A. P. and Miller, J.A.: Optimizing Workflow. Component Strategies 1(9) (1999) 45-57

10. Kreger, H.: Fulfilling the Web Services Promise. Communication of the ACM 46(6) (2003) 29-34

11. Nguyen, X.T., Kowalczyk, R., Chhetri, M.B. and Grant, A.: WS2JADE: A Tool for Runtime Deployment and Control of Web Services as JADE Agent Services. In: Software Agent-Based Applications, Platforms and Development Kits. Whitestein Technologies AG (2005)

12. Papazoglou, M.P. and Georgakopoulos, D.: Service-Oriented Computing. Communications of the ACM 46(10) (2003) 25-28

13. Yan, J., Zhang, J. and Lin, J.: ASAPM Requirement Analysis and Architecture. Technical Report ASAPM-TR2005.01. Swinburne University of Technology (2005)

A Web Services-Based Architecture for Wide-Area Protection System Design and Simulation

Qizhi Chen[1,2], Hamada Ghenniwa[2], and Weiming Shen[2,3]

[1] School of Electrical Engineering, Southwest Jiaotong University
Chengdu, Sichuan Province, P.R. China 610031
qzchen1625@gmail.com
[2] Department of Electrical & Computer Engineering, University of Western Ontario
London, ON Canada N6G 1H1
hghenniwa@eng.uwo.ca
[3] Integrated Manufacturing Technologies Institute, National Research Council Canada
London, ON Canada N6G 4X8
weiming.shen@nrc.gc.ca

Abstract. Wide-area protection system (WPS) is a trend of the future power system control. It monitors the contingency of a power system from the system-wide view and takes an instant action to restore the power system to its stable point. Because of the special characteristics, the WPS scheme is difficult to be simulated and tested under a conventional development environment. A Web services-based architecture for WPS design and simulation is proposed in this paper. This novel architecture wraps the legacy energy management system (EMS) functions into standard Web service interfaces, and provides standard remote computing and security evaluation services from EMS to WPS. Under this architecture, WPS scheme can be simulated and tested efficiently and the gap between simulation and running environment will be filled.

1 Introduction

The deregulation of electricity in most countries has created new control and monitoring requirements for which classical technologies may be inadequate. The first fact is that economic pressure on the electricity market and on grid operators forces them to maximize the utilization of high-voltage equipment, which very often means operation closer to the limits of the system and its components. On the other hand, reliable electricity supply is becoming more and more essential for the competing environment and any blackout is becoming more and more costly whenever it occurs.

The power system grids are extremely large and complex interconnected systems. In these grids, all generators almost rotate synchronously in dynamic equilibrium, and precisely match power generation and consumption. This balance between generation and demand must be maintained as load fluctuates and as disturbances such as equipments or transmission lines outages arise. If this balance is broken, power system will come to the insecure or emergency status. So there is a need to introduce a new protection and control methodology in power systems in order to make the power grids act as quickly as any disturbance occurs, so as to withstand the most severe credible

W. Shen et al. (Eds.): CSCWD 2006, LNCS 4402, pp. 469–478, 2007.
© Springer-Verlag Berlin Heidelberg 2007

contingency. Wide-area protection system (WPS) just appears in satisfying this critical operation requirement in power systems. It is used to save the power system from a partial or total blackout or brownout in a stable operational situation when no particular equipment is faulted or operated outside its limitations.

WPS is a new protection system proposed recently and has been an active research area during the past few years. But most of the recent research efforts focus on WPS protection algorithm design [1-2], or system architecture analysis [3]. There is no literature to discuss how to test or evaluate a WPS scheme. Because WPS is totally different from existing classical component protection, the existing testing and simulation methods for traditional protection systems are not enough for WPS testing. This paper focuses on the issue about how to test or evaluate a WPS scheme.

The paper is organized as follows. The wide-area protection for power systems and its design issues are briefly introduced in Section 2. In Section 3, a novel Web services-based WPS testing architecture that wraps legacy energy management system (EMS) functions is proposed, and the function of each wrapped Web service is discussed. Section 4 gives a WPS testing scenario and discusses its implementation details. Conclusion and future work are included in Section 5.

2   Wide-Area Protection and Its Design Issues

The classical protection in power systems is component oriented and is related to trip the circuit-breaker in order to disconnect faulty or overloaded equipment from the network, to save the electrical component, and to reestablish normal operation of the healthy part of the power system. However, this traditional protection is a local control and it only responds to the local measurement and does not have any vision about the system-wide states. But most dynamic phenomena in a power system are regional or sometimes system-wide, and the protection action needs system wide optimization and coordination.

WPS is the expansion of protection from the component level to a system level. Karlsson et al. [4] defined it as the protection to save the system from a partial or total blackout or brownout in operational situations when no particular equipment is faulted or operated outside its limitations. WPS uses system-wide information and provides a reliable security predication and optimized coordinated actions. Therefore it provides the opportunity to increase the power transmission capability and to increase the system reliability. Increasing the system reliability means that contingencies or critical events may not lead to a system wide critical situation or even to a system collapse.

In order to increase the power system reliability, the most important thing for WPS is that it must identify different contingencies as soon as possible, such as transient angle instability, small signal angle instability, frequency instability, short-term voltage instability and long-term voltage instability. Once the system instability is identified, coordinated and optimized stabilizing actions must be applied to save grid from insecure status. These actions may include: load shedding, shunt capacitors switching, transformer tap changing or even more circuit breaker tripping. So the design requirements of the WPS are [2]:

- Dynamic measurement and representation of events
- Wide-area system view

- Coordinated and optimized stabilizing actions
- Handling of cascaded outages

WPS has some characteristics that distinguish it from the classical component-based protection system. The first is that in order to determine different contingencies, WPS strongly replies on the topological information and devices parameters of target grid to determine system conditions besides system wide analog measurement. Because each power grid has its special operation mode and different devices parameters, such as impedances of transformer and transmission lines and capability curves of generators, WPS for one utility is totally different from another. That means that there is no common schema for different power grids. The second fact is that the evaluation of WPS protection actions does not depend on whether it successfully sheds loads, switches shunt capacitors or trips a circuit breaker, yet it should be evaluated by a system-wide security analysis after protection actions are taken place. If a WPS successfully trips a circuit breaker but brings system to another insecure state, this WPS scheme cannot be considered as acting correctly. So the third party security evaluation platform is necessary and important to test the validity of a WPS protection scheme.

During the design period of a WPS, the traditional component protection simulation based on power system dynamic model simulator EMTP as well as some mathematics tools such as Matlab or SIMULINK described in [5-6] can employed as the first stage for wide-area protection algorithm design. After this general algorithm simulation, an efficient security evaluation approach must be adopted for WPS validity testing.

Security assessment functions are popular and perform very well in energy management system (EMS) that locates in the control center. These EMS security functions are the best candidates to be adopted as the third party security evaluation platform for WPS. This paper proposes a Web services-based architecture for WPS design and testing. This novel architecture wraps some legacy EMS functions in the standard Web service interfaces, and provides standard remote computing and security evaluation services from EMS to WPS. Note that Dysko et al. [7] proposed a Web services-based protection simulation system, in which the power system simulator such as EMTP is wrapped as Web service so as to supply the standard simulation services to users. However, this simulation environment is for component protection and not suitable for WPS testing.

3 Web Services-Based WPS Testing Architecture

3.1 EMS

Energy management system (EMS) is the central core system for power network monitoring and control. It has been successfully employed in service for several decades. The main components in EMS are Database management system, man-machine software, data acquisition software and EMS application software. EMS application software performs various functions related to power system state estimation, security assessment, operations and so on. The main functions related with system estimation and security assessment in EMS are described in Figure 1. All these functions will be wrapped as Web services to supply parameter and security assessment services from EMS to WPS.

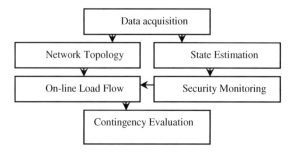

Fig. 1. Security assessment functions in EMS

3.2 Web Services

All security functions in EMS shown in Figure 1 as well as some database access functions are necessary in order to evaluate the effects of a WPS. Let us suppose the scene in which WPS can remotely access EMS functions during its design period. In this scene, WPS can get the precise system parameters of target power grid from EMS. This means that its protection schema configuration parameters will be more accurate and it will not need any modification before it is put into real use. Meanwhile, WPS can dynamically import historic disturbance data or receive real-time data from its protected target system to test its protection decisions based on a more realistic environment. Moreover, the protection action effects of WPS can be fairly evaluated by the third party's EMS security assessment functions.

Many technologies can be adopted to implement remote accesses, such as DCOM, CORBA, or RMI. But these distributed computing systems are tightly coupled and their flexibility and reusability are still limited compared to Web Services.

A Web service is a specific kind of services that is identified by a URI, whose service description and transportation utilize open Internet standards [8]. Web services provide a standard means of interoperability between different software applications running on a variety of platforms or frameworks. They are comprised of self-contained, modular applications that can be described, published, located, and invoked over the Internet. With Web services architecture, everything is a service, encapsulating behavior and providing the behavior through an interface that can be invoked for use by other services on the network.

There are three basic components in a Web services-based architecture: service provider, service consumer, and service registry. Web service providers describe their services interfaces using Web Services Definition Language (WSDL) and publish them to the service registry. Server consumers use the Universal Description, Discovery, and Integration (UDDI) APIs to find, locate, and point to a service.

Owing to the open standardization of communication protocols, extensible information representation, and pervasive Internet technology, Web service provides an appropriate approach for EMS to supply loosely-coupled, flexible remote computing services for the purpose of WPS simulation.

3.3   Web Services-Based Testing Architecture

The proposed Web services-based WPS testing architecture wraps the EMS security assessment functions and data access functions into Web services interfaces. WPS connects with EMS through Internet/Intranet and invokes these security assessment services for WPS evaluation and testing. This architecture fully utilizes the standard components of Web services, i.e., SOAP protocol for the inter-application communication between EMS and WPS, WSDL for EMS application descriptions, UDDI for EMS Web services registration and discovery. The proposed architecture is illustrated in Figure 2.

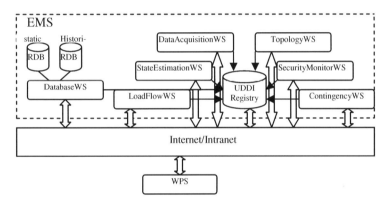

Fig. 2. Web services-based WPS testing architecture

In Figure 2, EMS is service provider and WPS is service consumer. EMS describes its services using WSDL and registers with UDDI registry. Once WPS needs invoke an EMS service, it locates the service that meets its requirement through UDDI first, obtains Web service's WSDL description, and then it establishes the link with the service provider through SOAP and communicates using XML messages.

3.4   Service Descriptions

All services supplied by EMS can be classified into two types. One serves as the purpose to supply realistic system topology and parameters to WPS. Another is used to evaluate the validity of WPS protection schemes. DatabaseWS, DataAcquisionWS and TopologyWS belong to the former, and StateEstimationWS, SecurityMonitorWS, LoadFlowWS, ContingencyWS belong to the later. The function of each Web service in EMS is described below.

DatabaseWS: It provides static or dynamic database access services to WPS. The static data are power grid network parameters, such as impedances of transformer and transmission lines, and capability curves of generators. Dynamic data are power system operation records, which include switch positions, bus voltages, currents, power values and frequencies. WPS uses static data to set up power network model and dynamic data to simulate system operation behaviors or historical disturbances.

DataAcquisitionWS: It provides real-time data acquisition service to WPS. These real-time data are acquired by SCADA in EMS control center. This service offers WPS the ability to receive the same real-time data as EMS does. Once having the same power system real-time operation parameters, the validation and correctness of WPS contingency analysis can be compared with contingency analysis results given by EMS.

TopologyWS: The network topology of a power system can be considered as a connected graph in which bus is vertex and transmission line is edge. This service supplies system topology to WPS.

StateEstimationWS: The role of state estimation is to reconstruct the most likely status of the network on the basis of real-time status taken on the network and of the topology of the network. When WPS detects a contingency, the protection scheme is taken into action. After protection scheme takes action, the system operation state is changed. Then WPS requests this service to start to evaluate the security state after this protection action. The input of StateEstimetion comes from WPS and its output will be used by SecurityMonitorWS.

SecurityMonitorWS: It receives the output of StateEstimationWS and determines whether the power system is close to, or in, the emergency state. Once SecurityMonitorWS determines that system is in the normal status, then the LoadFlowWS and ContingencyWS will be invoked to check whether there is a contingency in system.

ContingencyWS: Its role is to evaluate whether the power system is secure. It uses the output of LoadFlowWS as its input.

3.5 Security Issues

The security of this Web services-based WPS testing system should be considered from two aspects. One is EMS system security and another is Web service security.

Because of its critical importance, hardware configurations of EMS are redundant. Both database servers and application servers have their on-line hot backup servers in the control center. These redundant servers give a great opportunity to decrease the impaction when extra Web services are supplied by EMS. In order not to decrease performance of EMS and not to add extra workload to it, only backup servers are deployed to supply WPS testing services and respond services requests coming from WPS applications. Under this policy, core EMS applications will never feel any changes about environment so that the operation security will be ensured. Except this, firewall is also needed in EMS control center in order to isolate or minimize the possibility that unauthorized users access, modify or destroy any critical information.

To Web service security, WS-Security service (WSS) provides a framework within which authentication and authorization take place, so it should be applied in this Web services-based architecture. Web Services Security offers a trusted means for applying security to Web services by providing the necessary technical foundation for higher-level services. WSS builds upon existing security technologies such as XML Digital Signature, XML Encryption and X.509 Certificates to deliver an industry standard way of securing Web services message exchanges.

4   Implementation Scenario

This Web services-based WPS testing architecture can provide various services from EMS to WPS. They include power grid network configuration data retrieving, real-time data acquisition, history disturbance data retrieving and security assessment services. The following simple example of getting power grid network parameters explains how a service can be provided under this Web services-based environment.

When WPS locally finishes its protection algorithms testing and wants to apply these algorithms to its target system, it needs employs various testing Web services provided by EMS servers. The first service invoked by WPS is the one to get power grid network parameters, which is called GNPWS. GNPWS is an aggregation service, which is composed with three basic services, DatabaseWS, DataAcquisitionWS and TopologyWS. GNPWS workflow is shown in Figure 3.

Fig. 3. GNPWS workflow

The basic service DatabaseWS is a composite process that has four concurrent sub services, GetTransformerPa, GetGeneratorPa, GetLinePa and GetCapacitorPa. The composite process DatabaseWS is illustrated in Figure 4.

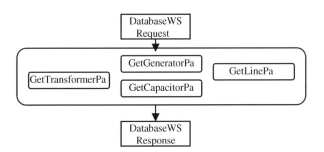

Fig. 4. Composite DatabaseWS process

All sub services in Figure 4 are orchestrated by BPEL4WS (Business Process Execution Language for Web Services) for compiling these executable processes into invoked DatabaseWS service. On receiving the database service request from WPS, DatabaseWS process initiates four sub services concurrently. WSDL for GetTransforerPa service is shown in Figure 5, and other services' WSDL documents [9] are similar to it. Observe that there are no bindings or service elements in this WSDL document, since a BPEL4WS process only reference the portTypes of the sub services involved in the process.

```
<?xml version="1.0"?>
<definitions name = "TranformerPara"
  targetNamespace= "http://ems.com/wrappedServices/DatabaseWS/Transformer/definitions"
      xmlns:tns="http://ems.com/wrappedServices/ DatabaseWS/Transformer / definitions"
      xmlns:xsd1="http://ems.com/wrappedServices/DatabaseWS/Transformer.xsd"
      xmlns:soap="http://schemas.xmlsoap.org/wsdl/soap/"
      xmlns="http://schemas.xmlsoap.org/wsdl/">

      <import namespace=" http://ems.com/wrappedServices/schemas"
          location=" http://ems.com/wrappedServices /DatabaseWS/Transformer.xsd"/>

        <message name="GetTransformerParameterInput">
          <part name="body" element="xsd1:ImpedanceRequest"/>
        </message>
        <message name="GetTransformerParameterOutput">
          <part name="body" element="xsd1: ImpedanceValue"/>
        </message>
        <portType name=" TranformerParaPortType">
          <operation name="GetTransformerParameter">
            <input message="tns: GetTransformerParameterInput "/>
            <output message="tns: GetTransformerParameterOutput "/>
          </operation>
        </portType>
</definitions>
```

Fig. 5. WSDL document for GetTransformerPa service

BPEL4WS [10] is used to definite the composition of DatabaseWS processes. Each sub service in this BPEL4WS is described as a partner link. Because they are concurrent services and have not any conversational links among them, the service composition in BPEL4WS is defined as using <flow> tag. The <flow> construct specifies activities to be performed concurrently. The BPEL4WS document for DatabaseWS process is shown in Figure 6.

5   Conclusion and Future Works

This paper proposes a Web services-based architecture for WPS schema design and simulation. This novel architecture wraps the legacy EMS functions into standard Web service interfaces, and provides the standard remote data access and security evaluation services from EMS to WPS. As a result, WPS scheme can be simulated and tested efficiently and the gap between the simulation environment and the running environment will be filled. The prototype of this architecture is under implementation.

```
<process name="DatabaseWS"
        targetNamespace="http://ems.com/wrappedServices/DatabaseWS"
        xmlns="http://schemas.xmlsoap.org/ws/2003/03/business-process/"
    xmlns:lns="http://ems.com/wrappedServices/wsdl/DatabaseWS"
    <partnerLinks>
        <partnerLink name="TransformerPara"
                <partnerLinkType="lns:TransformerParaLT"
                    myRole="GetTransformerPaService"/>
            <partnerLink name="GeneratorPara"
                <partnerLinkType="lns:GeneratorParaLT"
                myRole="GetGeneratorPaService"/>
            <partnerLink name="CapacitorPara"
                <partnerLinkType="lns:CapacitorParaLT"
                myRole="GetCapacitorPaService"/>
    <partnerLink name="LinePara"
        <partnerLinkType="lns:LineParaLT"
            myRole="GetLinePaService"/>
</partnerLinks>
<variables>
        <variable name="TransformerQuery" messageType="lns: GetTransformerParameterInput"
        <variable name="GeneratorQuery" messageType="lns: GetGeneratorParameterInput"
        <variable name="CapacitorQuery" messageType="lns: GetCapacitorParameterInput"
        <variable name="LineQuery" messageType="lns: GetLineParameterInput"
        <variablename="TransformerOut"  messageType="lns: GetTransformerParameterInput"
        <variable name="GeneratorOut" messageType="lns: GetGeneratorParameterInput"
        <variable name="CapacitorOut" messageType="lns: GetCapacitorParameterInput"
        <variable name="LineOut" messageType="lns: GetLineParameterInput"
    </variables>
    <flow>
            <invoke partnerLink="TransformerPara"
                    portType="lns:TransformerParaLT"
                    operation ="TransformerParaPortType"
                    inputVariable="TransformerQuery"
                    outputVariable="TransformerOut">
            </invoke>
            <invoke partnerLink="GeneratorPara"
                    portType="lns:GeneratorParaLT"
                    operation ="GeneratorParaPortType"
                    inputVariable="GeneratorQuery"
                    outputVariable="GeneratorOut">
            </invoke>
            <invoke partnerLink="CapacitorPara"
                    portType="lns:CapacitorParaLT"
                    operation ="CapacitorParaPortType"
                    inputVariable="CapacitorQuery"
                    outputVariable="CapacitorOut">
            </invoke>
            <invoke partnerLink="LinePara"
                    portType="lns:LineParaLT"
                    operation ="LineParaPortType"
                    inputVariable="LineQuery"
                    outputVariable="LineOut">
            </invoke>
    </flow> </process>
```

Fig. 6. BPEL4WS document for DatabaseWS process

References

1. Ingelsson, B., Lindstrom, P.-O., Karlsson, D., Runvik, G. and Sjodin, J.-O.: Wide-area protection against voltage collapse. IEEE Computer Applications in Power 10(4) (1997) 30 - 35
2. Rehtanz, C. and Bertsch, J.: Wide-area measurement and protection system for emergency voltage stability control. IEEE Power Engineering Society Winter Meeting 2(2002) 842-847
3. Crossley, P., Ilar, F. and Karlsson, D.: System protection schemes in power networks: Existing installations and ideas for future development. Proc. Seventh IEE International Conference on Developments in Power System Protection (2001) 450-453
4. Karlsson, D., Hemmingsson, M. and Lindahl, S.: Wide-area system monitoring and control: Terminology, phenomena, and solution implementation strategies. IEEE Power and Energy Magazine 2(5) (2004) 68-76
5. Wilson, R.E. and Nordstrom, J.M.: EMTP transient modeling of a distance relay and a comparison with EMTP laboratory testing. IEEE Transactions on Power Delivery 8(3) (1993) 984-992
6. Kezunovic, M. and Q. Chen: A novel approach for interactive protection system simulation. Proc. IEEE PES Transmission and Distribution Conference. Los Angeles, CA, USA (1996)
7. Dysko, A., McMorran, A., Burt, G.M., Ault, G., McDonald, J.R.: Web services-based distributed dynamic protection system simulation and testing. 2004. Proc. Eighth IEE International Conference on Developments in Power System Protection. Vol. 2. (2004) 760-763
8. Huhns, M.N. and Singh, M.P.: Service-oriented computing: Key concepts and principles. IEEE Internet Computing 9(1) (2005) 75-81
9. W3C: WSDL 1.1. URL: http://www.w3.org/TR/wsdl
10. IBM: BPWS4J. URL: http://www.alphaworks.ibm.com/tech/bpws4j

Semantic Matching of Web Services for Collaborative Business Processes

Lihui Lei, Zhunhua Duan, and Bin Yu

Institute of Computing Theory & Technology, Xidian University,
Xi'an 710071, P.R. China
{lhlei, zhhduan, yubin}@mail.xidian.edu.cn

Abstract. It is a prerequisite for automating business processes integration to dynamically discover usable web services. A formal approach to semantic matching of web services based on choreographies is presented to support it. First, an extended deterministic finite automaton (EDFA) is proposed by labeling state transitions with binary-tuples (input, output) rather than letters. EDFAs represent services more accurately: the nodes represent the states maintained by the service; the state transitions represent the communication activities of the service. Thus, the automata depicts the temporal sequences of communication activities that describe the behavior of services. Second, the semantics-based intersection of EDFAs is presented and the compatibility of services is evaluated by testing the emptiness of the languages accepted by EDFAs. Finally, component structures are introduced to describe services with two roles: invoking another service and/or being invoked by another service. The compatibility of services can be employed to discover usable services, moreover, to validate collaborative business processes.

1 Introduction

The prosperity of web services strongly depends on the ability of implementing loosely coupled e-business processes which support inter-business interaction among trading partners. There are two approaches to integrating business processes. The first one integrates different processes into a new business process executed by a centrical manager. This centrical manager coordinates the performances of the participants and routes the data flow among them. The second one is based on a common process among all participants. The execution of the common process is accomplished by a set of processes executed collaboratively with the engines of the participants. These participants synchronize their progress in the performance of the common process by an interaction protocol. Those business processes integrated by the latter approach are called *collaborative business processes* in this paper.

Automating business processes integration is a challenge, which needs dynamic and flexible binding of services. At present, most of service bindings are statically implemented, since the existing standards, e.g., WS-Inspection[1] and UDDI[2] used for searching in classification schemes or t-models, are based on string comparison and not sufficient for discovering usable services that can be safely integrated with

W. Shen et al. (Eds.): CSCWD 2006, LNCS 4402, pp. 479–488, 2007.
© Springer-Verlag Berlin Heidelberg 2007

existing components. The recent effort, semantic web services, makes the automation of business processes integration possible, because their specifications provide the semantics of services capabilities and the descriptions of services behavior. Discovering services become more precise based on semantics rather than string comparison.

To accurately and automatically discover usable services for the dynamic business processes integration, a formal approach is proposed in this paper. With this approach, the compatibility of the required service and the provided service is evaluated by the semantic matching of web services based on choreographies, i.e., the behavior of web services. In this paper, the *required service* makes requests for another service and the *provided service* provides the requested service. Moreover, with this approach, it can be determined whether collaborative business processes are performed successfully.

Firstly, an extended deterministic finite automaton (EDFA) is proposed by labeling the state transitions with binary-tuples (input, output) rather than letters. The automata can accurately describe services: the nodes represent the states maintained by the service; a state transition represents an indivisible communication activity[1] (receiving or/and returning message) of the service, which accepts 'input', produces 'output' and moves from one state to another. Thus, the automata depict the temporal sequences of communication activities which represent the behavior of services. Secondly, the semantics-based intersection of EDFAs is presented and checking the emptiness of the languages accepted by EDFAs is used to evaluate the compatibility of services. Finally, as each participant of collaborative business processes may be a required service or/and a provided service, component structures are proposed to described it.

Section 2 reviews the related work. Section 3 employs an example to illustrate the intention of matching web services based on the behavior of services. Section 4 gives the definitions of EDFAs and component structures. Section 5 illustrates the semantic matching of web services based on the behavior of services and the validating of collaborative business processes. The conclusion is drawn in the last section.

2   Related Work

Most existing approaches [3-7] focus only on certain aspects of web service descriptions such as semantics, workflow, or Quality of Service etc. Paolucci et al. [4] proposed a solution for automating web services discovery based on DAML-S [8]. The matching procedure only compares the semantics of the input and output of two services and gives the degree of similarity between two services. Although the resulting services might produce expected effects, it does not guarantee messages can be exchanged successfully between the required and the provided services. Wombacher et al. [3] proposed an approach to evaluate the compatibility of the services by comparing their behavior. This approach makes use of message sequences to describe services behavior so that messages can be exchanged successfully between the compatible services. However, the approach must be performed under the assumption that elements of two message sequences to be compared must come from the same WSDL document to guarantee that the same message-name represents the same semantics.

---

[1] All of communication activities are indivisible in this paper.

In fact, the matching of web service specifications should be done at the semantic level, because web service interfaces may be defined by various kinds of glossaries. The matching of web service specifications based on string comparison is unable to accurately discover usable web services. Although the semantic matching merely gives the degree of similarity between two concepts, it is enough for the required service to decide what to do next as long as the degree granted to the system is given. In addition, to accurately discover usable web services, the behavior of web services should be taken into account during the procedures of matching service specifications, which can guarantee that all of messages can be exchanged successfully between the provided and required services.

Our approach makes semantic matching of web service specifications based on the behavior of web services. This approach uses the sequences of the communication activities to describe the behavior of web services. Since a communication activity is indivisible, it is executed in a single step rather than in a long-running conversation. The semantics of the communication activity can be represented by the semantics of the input and output of the communication activity. This approach can guarantee exchanging messages successfully between the provided and required services and producing expected effects as much as possible. Therefore, the resulting services of our approach can be safely integrated with the existing components.

3   Motivating Example

The example is a simple procurement workflow consists of the web services: *buyer*, *book seller* and *bank*. It is depicted in Figure 1. Following italics are parameters in the messages exchanged among the services. First, the book seller accepts a message for searching *bookISBN* on *bookName* sent by the buyer and returns the message conveying the searching result to the buyer. It is a synchronous communication activity. Second, if the buyer receives *OutofStock* as the searching result, it terminates the workflow; otherwise the buyer sends *payInfo* and *delivery* respectively to the book seller, and then the book seller sends *CPayConf* and *COrder* to the buyer. Both are asynchronous communication activities performed sequentially. The communication activity between the book seller and the bank is also asynchronous. The bank receives *clientPayInfo* from the book seller, and then returns *clientPayConf* to the book seller.

Fig. 1. The interactions among the buyer, the book seller and the bank

Please note that the temporal sequences of these communication activities can be described in BPEL4WS or OWL-S [9], but cannot be described in WSDL. If the service requestor is a human user, he can decide how to interact with the service as long as he retrieves the WSDL document that describes the interface of the service. However, if the requestor is a web service, e.g., the service *buyer*, it acquires the information only by processing the description of the service.

Most of existing semantic matching approaches [7][10-11] for discovering services adopt the same idea: if the output of the provided service contain the output of the required service and the input of the required service contain the input of the provided service, the provided service matches (satisfies) the required service. However, this idea is not workable in some circumstances. For example, suppose there are three book seller services, $seller_1$, $seller_2$ and $seller_3$, shown in Figure 2. Although these services have the same input and output, $seller_1$ cannot be replaced by $seller_2$ or $seller_3$. The $seller_2$ requires *CPayInfo* and *CDelivery* to be sent by the buyer together, while the buyer of the example sends the parameters respectively. Thus, they cannot interact successfully. The service $seller_3$ requires that *CDelivery* should be received before *CPayInfo*. Suppose this is the requirement of the business logic, e.g., the business logic depicted by $seller_3$ requires that the *BPayInfo* is calculated using the *CDelivery*, the replacement of $seller_1$ by $seller_3$ will change the scenario of the business process. The buyer interacts with $seller_3$ will not produce the expected effect. Therefore, web services behavior should be taken into account for service specifications matching.

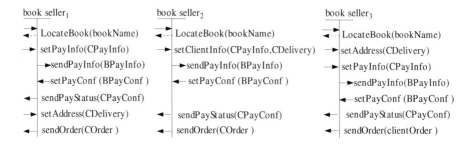

Fig. 2. Different book sellers

If the required service and the provided service satisfy the following criterions, we say they are *compatible*. First, for a pair of cooperated operations from the required service and the provided service, they are structurally and semantically compatible. Second, the required service and the provided service agree on the interaction protocol that defines all temporal sequences of the communication activities between them. That is, the required service can process all responses from the provided service and the provided service can process all requests from the required service [3].

Suppose the *buyer* wants to find a book seller to accomplish the procurement workflow. If the *buyer* finds a book seller just as the *book seller* of the example, it is necessary to find the *bank* collaborated with the *book seller* to fulfill the payment. Thus, the compatibilities of the two pairs of services should be taken into account for integrating such a collaborative business process.

4 A Formal Model for Web Services

When a web service interacts with another web service, it maintains some states [9]. Naturally, we may make use of DFAs to describe web services and regular languages to analyze web services behavior. However, the expressiveness of the standard DFAs [12] is not powerful enough to describe web services. The nodes of the standard DFAs can be used to represent the states maintained by services, whereas the state transitions of the standard DFAs are not suitable for describing the communication activities of web services. The standard DFAs accepts an input (a letter) and moves from a state to another, while a web service accepts several inputs (zero or many parameters), produces several outputs (zero or many parameters) and moves from a state to another state when it accomplishes a communication activity. Therefore, the standard DFAs need to be extended.

4.1 EDFA

The following notational conventions are used in this paper. A set is denoted by an upper case English letter; an element of the set is denoted by a lower case letter; a function or relation is denoted by a Greek letter.

Definition 1 (Extended Deterministic Finite Automata). An extended deterministic finite automata is $M = (D, I, O, Q, \delta, \lambda, q_0, F)$ where,

- D is a finite alphabet
- I and O are subsets of the power set of D, i.e., $I \subseteq 2^D$ and $O \subseteq 2^D$
- Q is a finite set of states
- q_0 is the start state with $q_0 \in Q$
- F is a set of final states with $F \subseteq Q$
- let $\Sigma \subseteq I \times O$, then the state transition function $\delta: Q \times \Sigma \to Q$, and
- the output function $\lambda: Q \times I \to 2^O$

The difference between standard DFAs and EDFAs is that the state transitions of standard DFAs are labeled by letters, while the state transitions of EDFAs are labeled by binary-tuples $(\{d_a, d_b, \cdots, d_m\}, \{d_e, d_f, \cdots, d_n\})$. Each element of the binary-tuples is a set of letters. The output function λ is proposed to represent all kinds of effects that are produced by the communication activities. In general, a communication activity might produce various kinds of outputs when it accepts an input. However, only one of them can be obtained. For example, the book seller accepts *bookName* and returns *bookISBN* or *OutofStock*; moreover, either *bookISBN* or *OutofStock* can be returned. The state transition function δ is used to describe the latter case. The output function λ is used to describe the former case. Obviously, the output function λ does not alter the automaton itself. Therefore, EDFAs is a sort of DFAs. Moreover, there exists

$$(\{d_a, d_b, \cdots, d_m\}, \{d_e, d_f, \cdots, d_n\}) = (\{d_p, d_q, \cdots, d_h\}, \{d_s, d_t, \cdots, d_k\}) \Leftrightarrow$$
$$\{d_a, d_b, \ldots, d_m\} = \{d_p, d_q, \ldots, d_h\} \text{ and } \{d_e, d_f, \ldots, d_n\} = \{d_s, d_t, \ldots, d_k\}$$

4.2 Intersection of EDFAs

A DFA generates a regular language that is the set of strings which are sequences of labels of state transitions from the start state to one of the final states. According to the closure properties of regular languages, it is known that the intersection of regular languages is a regular language. That is, the intersection of DFAs is also a DFA [12]. Furthermore, this DFA can be determined with the usual cross product construction. Since an EDFA is a variant of DFAs, the theories on DFAs are valid for EDFAs. Therefore, the intersection of EDFAs is also an EDFA which can be determined by means of the cross product construction. The intersection of EDFAs is defined as follows, which is employed to evaluate the compatibility of services in Section 5.

Definition 2 (Intersection of EDFAs). The intersection of EDFAs M_1 and M_2 is an EDFA M. If $M_1 = (D_1, Q_1, I_1, O_1, \delta_1, \lambda_1, q_{10}, F_1)$ and $M_2 = (D_2, Q_2, I_2, O_2, \delta_2, \lambda_2, q_{20}, F_2)$, then $M = M_1 \cap M_2 = (D, Q, I, O, \delta, \lambda, q_0, F)$ with

- $D = D_1 \cup D_2$ is a finite alphabet
- I and O are subsets of the power set of D, i.e., $I \subseteq 2^D$ and $O \subseteq 2^D$
- $Q = Q_1 \times Q_2$ is a finite set of states
- $F - \Gamma_1 \times \Gamma_2$ is a set of final states with $F \subseteq Q$
- $q_0 = (q_{10}, q_{20})$ is the start state with $q_0 \in Q$
- let $\Sigma \subseteq I \times O$, then $\delta((q_{1i}, q_{2j}), (i, o)) = (\delta_1(q_{1i}, (i, o)), \delta_2(q_{2j}, (i, o))$ with $(i, o) \in \Sigma$
- $\lambda((q_{1i}, q_{2j}), i) = \lambda_1(q_{1i}, i) \cap \lambda_2(q_{2j}, i)$

The output function λ of M describes the common outputs produced by M_1 and M_2 after they accept the same input. For every output $o \in \lambda((q_{1i}, q_{2j}), i)$, there exists a state $(q_{1(i+1)}, q_{2(j+1)})$ such that $(q_{1(i+1)}, q_{2(j+1)}) = \delta((q_{1i}, q_{2j}), (i, o))$, i.e., $\delta_1(q_{1i}, (i, o)) = q_{1(i+1)}$ and $\delta_2(q_{2j}, (i, o)) = q_{2(j+1)}$. Therefore, there exists an output $o \in \lambda_1(q_{1i}, i)$ and $o \in \lambda_2(q_{2j}, i)$. It is evident that λ does not alter the resulting automaton.

In order to evaluate the compatibility of the services, the common behavior of the services should be obtained. Just as the above analysis, EDFAs can be employed to depict the behavior of the services. Naturally, the common behavior of the services can be obtained according to the relations among EDFAs. Suppose there are two services S_1 and S_2 represented by EDFAs M_1 and M_2; moreover, M_1 and $M_1 \cap M_2$ are regarded as two different directed graphs: the vertexes represent the states of the ED-FAs; the arcs represent the state transitions of the EDFAs; and the labels of the state transitions of the EDFAs are neglected.

- For $M_1 \cap M_2$, if there is no path from the start state to one of the final states, then S_1 and S_2 have not the common behavior.
- For $M_1 \cap M_2$, if there are some paths from the start state to one of the final states, the set of these paths is denote by P. Similarly, for M_1, if there are some paths from the start state to one of the final states, the set of these paths is denoted by P_1. Thus if P_1 equals P, either M_1 or $M_1 \cap M_2$ can be used to depict the common behavior of S_1 and S_2, i.e., the common behavior of S_1 and S_2 is equivalent to the behavior of S_1; otherwise, only $M_1 \cap M_2$ can be used to depict the common behavior of S_1 and S_2, i.e., the common behavior of S_1 and S_2 is just a part of the behavior of S_1.

4.3 Component Structure

The implementation of the collaborative business processes is based on P2P paradigm. Therefore each service, a participant of the collaborative business process, can be invoked by some required services; moreover, it may invoke other provided services. That is to say, each web service may be a required service or/and a provided service. Component structures are introduced to represent such web services with two roles. Valid collaborative business processes are defined with the component structure.

Definition 3 (Component Structure). A component structure S = {ps, rs}, where

- ps is an EDFA. This EDFA describes this service as a provided service. If this service can not be invoked, e.g., it is a virtual service that just describes the client requirement for an expected service, ps is assigned *nil* (an unrealized service).
- rs is also an EDFA. This EDFA describes this service as a required service. If this service does not need to invoke any services, rs is assigned *empty*.

Definition 4 (Valid Collaborative Business Process). A collaborative business process is denoted by $P = (S_1,...,S_n)$ with $S_i = (ps_i, rs_i)$ ($1 \le i \le n$) representing the participants of the collaborative business processes. This collaborative business process is valid, iff for any $S_i = (ps_i, rs_i)$, if rs_i is not *empty*, there exists ps_k ($1 \le k \le n$ and $k \ne i$) that is compatible with rs_i.

5 Service Specifications Matching

Because services may use various kinds of glossaries to define their interfaces, some alterations on the intersection of EDFAs are needed to evaluate the compatibility of services. Therefore, the semantics-based intersection of EDFAs is defined as follows. The semantic matching of the communication activities is similar to the approach[2] [4].

Definition 5 (Semantics-based intersection of EDFAs). Let the required service and the provided service are represented by EDFAs $M_r = (D_r, Q_r, I_r, O_r, \delta_r, \lambda_r, q_{r0}, F_r)$ and $M_p = (D_p, Q_p, I_p, O_p, \delta_p, \lambda_p, q_{p0}, F_p)$, the semantics-based intersection of M_r and M_p is an EDFA $M = M_r \cap_{sb} M_p = (D, Q, I, O, \delta, \lambda, q_0, F)$ with

- $D = D_r \cup D_p$, $I \subseteq 2^D$ and $O \subseteq 2^D$
- $Q = Q_r \times Q_p$, $F = F_r \times F_p$ and $q_0 = (q_{r0}, q_{p0})$
- if $\delta_r(q_{ri},(i_{ri},o_{ri})) = q_{r(i+1)}$, $\delta_p(q_{pj},(i_{pj},o_{pj})) = q_{p(j+1)}$ and $Match((i_{ri},o_{ri}),(i_{pj},o_{pj})) \ge$ *threshold*, then $\delta((q_{ri},q_{pj}),(i_{ri},o_{ri})) = (\delta_r(q_{ri},(i_{ri},o_{ri})), \delta_p(q_{pj},(i_{pj},o_{pj})))$, $\{(i_{ri},o_{ri}), (i_{pj},o_{pj})\} \subseteq I \times O$
- $\lambda((q_{ri},q_{pj}),i_{ri}) = \lambda_r(q_{ri},i_{ri}) \cap_m \lambda_p(q_{pj},i_{pj})$ where, the notation '$\cap_m$' means that $\lambda((q_{ri},q_{pj}),i_{ri}) \subseteq \lambda_r(q_{ri},i_{ri})$ and for each output $o_{ri} \in \lambda((q_{ri},q_{pj}),i_{ri})$, there exists an output $o_{pj} \in \lambda_p(q_{pj},i_{pj})$, and $match(o_{ri},o_{pj}) \ge$ *threshold*.

---

[2] This approach regards a communication activity as a service which has only one operation. Let *threshold* $\in$ {*exact, plugin, subsume, fail*}, $Match((i_{ri},o_{ri}),(i_{pj},o_{pj})) \ge$ *threshold* $\Leftrightarrow |i_{ri}| = |i_{pj}|$, $|o_{ri}| = |o_{pj}|$, $match(i_{ri},i_{pj}) \ge$ *threshold* and $match(o_{ri},o_{pj}) \ge$ *threshold*. Here, $match(\phi, \phi) = exact$.

Just as the above analysis, the semantics of a communication activity can be represented with the semantics of the input and output of this communication activity. Thus, the semantics matching of the input and output of two communication activities are used to determine the degree of similarity between the communication activities. The semantic matching of the input and output of two communication activities is similar to the approach [4]. Four values, *exact*, *plugin*, *subsume* and *fail*, with priority *exact* > *plugin* > *subsume* > *fail* are employed to describe the degree of similarity.

The semantic matching of web services based on the services behavior is given as follows. The intention of this approach is to evaluate the compatibility of two services. This approach is the basis of accurately and automatically discovering usable services and validating collaborative business processes. With this approach, *incompatible*, *partial compatible* and *compatible* with priority *compatible* > *partial compatible* > *incompatible* are used to describe the compatibility of the required and the provided services. Suppose the required service and the provided service are represented by EDFAs M_r and M_p; moreover, M_r and $M_r \cap M_p$ are regarded as two directed graphs: the vertexes represent the states of the EDFAs; the arcs represent the state transitions of the EDFAs; the labels of the state transitions of the EDFAs are neglected.

- For $M_r \cap_{sb} M_p$, if there is no path from the start state to one of the final states, the required service and the provided service are *incompatible*.
- For M_r, if there are some paths from the start state to one of the final states, the set of these paths is denoted by P_r. Furthermore, for $M_r \cap_{sb} M_p$, if there are some paths (for each state (q_{ri}, q_{pj}) in these paths, $|\lambda((q_{ri}, q_{pj}), i_{pj})| < |\lambda_p(q_{pj}, i_{pj})|$ does not hold, since all of the messages returned from the provided service should be processed by the required service) from the start state to one of the final states, the set of these paths is denote by P. Therefore, if P_r equals P, the required service and the provided service are *compatible*; otherwise, the required service and the provided service are *partial compatible*.

The algorithm for checking the emptiness of the languages accepted by the DFAs is well known [12]. It is employed to evaluate the compatibility of services. With our approach, an intersection of EDFAs accepts an empty language iff there is no such path (for each state (q_{ri}, q_{pj}) in the path, $|\lambda((q_{ri}, q_{pj}), i_{pj})| < |\lambda_p(q_{pj}, i_{pj})|$ does not hold) from the start state to one of the finial states. According to the definition 5, the labels of the state transitions of $M_r \cap_{sb} M_p$ are included by that of M_r; it is easy to determine whether the path set of M_r equals that of $M_r \cap_{sb} M_p$. Further, an algorithm for validating a collaborative business processes $P = (S_1, ..., S_n)$ is given in pseudo code below.

```
CheckValidty(P){\\P =(S₁,…, Sₙ)and Sₖ =(psₖ,rsₖ)(1≤k≤n)
    for all Sₖ {
        if notempty(rsₖ)
        {   validity =false;
            for all psₘ {\\psₘ∈{ p₁,…,pₙ}
            {  if compatible(psₘ,rsₖ) and (psₖ≠ psₘ)
                validity = true;  }
            if( validity == false) return false; }
    return true;
}
```

For ease of matching, the input and output of required services are interchanged when the EDFAs representing the required services are constructed. The services of the example in Section 3, *buyer*, *book seller* and *bank*, can be represented by the component structures S_1, S_2 and S_3. Further more, $S_1 = \{nil, M_{r1}\}$, $S_2 = \{M_{p2}, M_{r2}\}$ and $S_3 = \{M_{p3}, empty\}$. M_{p2}, M_{r2}, M_{r1} and M_{p3} are shown in Figure 3. The two semantics-based intersections of EDFAs, $M_{r1} \cap_{sb} M_{p2}$ and $M_{r2} \cap_{sb} M_{p3}$, are shown in Figure 4.

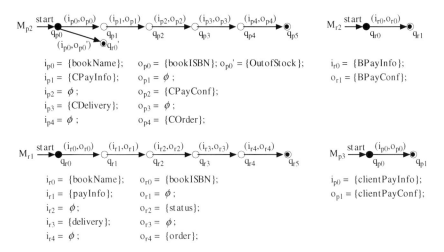

Fig. 3. Representations of the buyer, book seller and bank by component structures

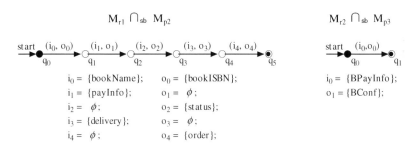

Fig. 4. Two semantics-based intersections of EDFAs: $M_{r1} \cap_{sb} M_{p2}$ and $M_{r2} \cap_{sb} M_{p3}$

As a valid collaborative business process, the services represented by M_{r1} and M_{p2} should be compatible and so should the services represented by M_{r2} and M_{p3}. In fact, the services represented by M_{r2} and M_{p3} are *compatible*, but the services represented by M_{r1} and M_{p2} are *partial compatible*: the book seller receives the *bookName* and may return *OutofStock*, while the buyer can receive *OutofStock* but does not define what to do. Thus the procurement workflow is invalid and cannot be executed successfully. On the other hand, suppose the buyer designs some interactions that are not executed by the buyer and the book seller, the book seller may receive the messages that it can not process. The procurement workflow may be broken down.

6 Conclusion and Future Work

In order to accurately and automatically discover usable services for dynamic and flexible integrating business processes, a formal approach by means of EDFAs is presented in this paper. The approach evaluates the compatibility of services based on the behavior of web services by semantic matching. It guarantees that messages can be exchanged successfully between the provided service and the required service and produces expected effects as much as possible. In contrast with those approaches presented in [3] and [4], our approach is more practicable and more accurate in an actual environment. In addition, a primary way is proposed to validate collaborative business processes based on this approach. In the future, we will validate this approach by developing a prototype system.

Acknowledgments. This research is supported by the NSFC grants 60373103 and 60433010, and the SRFDP Grant 20030701015.

References

1. Ballinger, K., Brittenham, P., Malhotra, A., Nagy, W.A. and Pharies, S.: Specification: Web services inspection language Version 1.0. (2001).
2. UDDI (2000) URL: http://www.uddi.org/
3. Wombacher, A., Fankhauser, P., Mahleko, B.: Matchmaking for Business Processes based on Choreographies. Proc. IEEE International Conference on e-Technology, e-Commerce and e-Service (2004) 359-368
4. Paolucci, M., Kawamura, T., Payne, T.R., Sycara, K.: Semantic Matching of Web Services Capabilities. Proc. ISWC 2002. LNCS 2342 (2002) 333-347
5. Zou, Z., Duan, Z., Wang, J.: A Comprehensive Framework for Dynamic Web Services Integration. Proc. 4th IEEE European Conference on Web Services (2006) 211-220
6. Bultan, T., Fu, X., Hull, R., Su, J.: Conversation Specification: A New Approach to Design and Analysis of E-Service Composition. Proc. of WWW2003 (2003) 403-410
7. Zou, Z., Duan, Z.: Building Business Process or Assembling Service Components: Reuse Services with BPEL4WS and SCA. Proc. 4th IEEE European Conference on Web Services (2006) 138-147
8. The DAML Services Coalition. DAML-S: Semantic Markup for Web Services.
9. The OWL-S Coalition: OWL-S 1.1 Draft Release. URL: http://www.daml.org/services/owl-s/1.1/
10. Xu, J., Zhu, Q., Li, J., Tang, J., Zhang, P., Wang, K.: Semantic Based Web Services Discovery. Proc. of the AWCC 2004. LNCS 3309 (2004) 388-393
11. Sycara, K.: Dynamic Discovery, Invocation and Composition. Proc. SETN 2004. LNAI 3025 (2004) 3-12
12. Hopcroft, J.E., Motwani, R. and Ullman, J.D.: Introduction to Automata Theory, Languages, and Computation. Addison Wesley (2001)

Distributed Hash Table Based Peer-to-Peer Version Control System for Collaboration

Yi Jiang, Guangtao Xue, and Jinyuan You

Dept. of Computer Science and Engineering, Shanghai Jiaotong University,
Shanghai, P.R. China
{jiangyi, xue-gt, you-jy}@cs.sjtu.edu.cn

Abstract. In this paper, we introduce a peer-to-peer system that provides versioning function on the content. The proposed system is build on top of the distributed hash tables, which provide the elementary data storing-retrieving function to the proposed system. So the data stored in our system are scattered over the network but not on a dedicated server. First, the proposed system is different from the traditional version system in that it is a peer-to-peer system rather than a client/server system that requires a central server. Second, the proposed system is different from the other peer-to-peer system in that it provides version information about the data it stored. These two features enable the reliability and robustness of the proposed system. The version management function of the system can be used in constructing team collaboration system and used as the replacement of the concurrent version managemeont system.

1 Introduction

Current version management systems, such as CVS [1], RCS [2], Subversion [3], ClearCase [4] and Visual Source Safe [5] are client-server systems, they rely on a central repository to store the version information, file content and metadata. Using those systems, it would be catastrophic when the server suffered from hardware failure or any unexpected failure. Besides, centre server based system doesn't work well in mobile environments. If mobile users cannot connect to the server, their work cannot be continued. But in this occasion, mobile users maybe still connected within a small group, because the members of the same department or modular are always together.

The peer-to-peer model is an ideal model to replace client-server computing model in many places. It is good for collaboration application because the nature of human collaboration is peer to peer. Peoples communicate with each other without a coordinator between them. It is totally self-organized and load balancing, which is lack in client-server model. Aimed at facilitate the features of the peer-to-peer technology, we try to integrate the version control with peer-to-peer system to make a distributed system with version control functionality.

W. Shen et al. (Eds.): CSCWD 2006, LNCS 4402, pp. 489–498, 2007.
© Springer-Verlag Berlin Heidelberg 2007

2 Related Works

One of the major problems of the traditional CVS system is that it uses a centre server as the repository of the version database. Using those systems, participants of the project must checkout a working copy of the shared objects before working on them. After someone has modified the object, the object was committed back into the repository. If more than one of the participants modify the same object and committed it back, the collision maybe occurred at that object. In this time, the CVS system will try to merge those modifications to form a new version. If the collision cannot be resolved, one of the committing processes will be aborted.

Brian and Jane made a distributed version control system named DRCS [6] for wide area networks. But limited to the technologies at that time, the DRCS system didn't implemented on top of a peer-to-peer platform. Instead, the DRCS system was built on top of UUCP protocol and makes use of the UUCP to synchronize the replicas of the repository. The DRCS also provides a command interface includes such commands as *co*, *ci* and *addelta* etc.

OceanStore [7] is a global storage infrastructure, automatically recovers from server and network failures, incorporates new resources, and adjusts to usage patterns. The durable data in OceanStore are read only, to overcome the deficiency, OceanStore use versioning. When a data is modified or updated, a new version created for it. We can see OceanStore is similar to our system in the aspect of the peer-to-peer storage with versioning. But the differences are oblivious. The versioning service in OceanStore is very preliminary and cannot access by the end user. It is provided as a complementary to the read only feature of data storage. The modification of the object stored in OceanStore must be stored as a revision. M-of-n data coding [8] is a useful technology used in OceanStore for fault-tolerance. A piece of data is treated as a series of m fragments that is transformed into a series of n fragments ($n > m$).

3 Design

The design of this version-enabled peer-to-peer system was inspired by the needs of developing a peer-to-peer collaboration system. When building collaboration system, the concurrent control of the shared documents and the replica management of the shared objects is a hardworking without low-level support by the infrastructure. At the same time, each participant has a copy of the documents and working on it. So peer-to-peer is what we want. In our design, the versioning function is based on a virtual file system on top of the peer-to-peer lookup protocol, such as Chord. The versioning service is built on top of virtual file system.

3.1 Design Goals

The proposed system is a distributed content distribution system with version support. On top of fully decentralized network architecture, a layer of the storage with version management function is provided. The system is designed to provide service in a peer-to-peer fashion that provides the concurrent control of version that is needed by many collaboration applications.

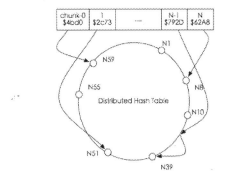

Fig. 1. Low level storage in DHT-based network, supposed that 59 = hash($4bd0) and 35=hash($62A8)

First, the system should support the concurrent editing and read-modify-write style operation on shared objects. The collision produced when the shared object been written by more than one writer should be merged automatically or manually. Second, the system must utilize the merits brought by adopting the peer-to-peer architecture to provide locality transparency and mobile user support. Third, the system provides easy to use application interface including lookup, put, get and versioning.

3.2 Peer-to-Peer Layer

This layer is the bottom layer of the architecture. Hence, it provides low level services such as peer lookup, message routing and atomic data manipulation. The main aim of this layer is to store unstructured data reliably. This layer facilitates the distributed hash table to form a pure decentralized network topology. The main reason why we choose distributed hash table based peer-to-peer routing protocol is distributed hash table can be used as a virtual memory. In such system, the value stored can be accessed through its key. The key can be randomly generated global unique number or more meaningful strings.

The overlay network of this layer is a Chord [10] overlay network, which is an outstanding peer-to-peer discovery protocol based on distributed hash table. In addition, not only Chord, but also the other structured peer-to-peer message routing protocol and distributed hash table implementation such as Pastry [9] can be used too.

3.3 Storage Layer

Currently, most of the peer-to-peer storage systems are read only. Objects been shared can not be modified. Studies in [11] present an approach to building data structures on structured peer-to-peer storage with per-participants logs. OceanStore [7] is a read only system. Every update creates a new revision of data object. Ivy [12] is a read/write file system build on top of the Chord. It uses logs to record the modifications of the objects on the peer-to-peer storage. This approach is also useful in any similar system. The version control can also use logs to track the modifications of the files with different versions. To facilitate the object manipulation in peer-to-peer system, we want to create an object system on top of peer-to-peer layer first. The basic idea is to group the objects into layers just like the directory in file system. And store the pieces of data into chunks just like the sectors in hard disk. So the storage layer is build to provide basic file system function on top of peer-to-peer layer. With the support of this layer, objects can be stored and organized in a peer-to-peer system.

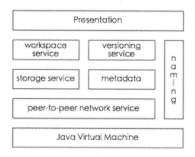

Fig. 2. Overall architecture of the system

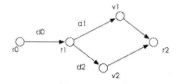

Fig. 3. Illustration of the version model

The minimal data element in the storage layer is data chunk. In the system, chunks are data that can be read or write at once. The size of chunk is limited by the Internet protocol used to transfer the data between peers. Chunk likes the block in the file system that can be read or write in one operation. Chunks are encoded with m-of-n encoding to ensure the robustness of the system. This is because the peer in the system may be offline unexpectedly; the chunks must be replicated to ensure the data consistency. The replicas are managed in the peer-to-peer layer. As shown in Figure 1, chunks stored in the peer according to its i-number, i-number is a global unique number generated when the chunk is created. The position of the chunk in the virtual cycle is computed by applying the hash function to its i-number.

Because the storage layer is on top of the peer-to-peer layer, chunks are stored in the peer-to-peer network through low level *put* and *get* operation. So each participant's local storage is used as distributed storage space of this layer.

3.4 Metadata

The metadata is stored on the head of the object. A metadata record consists of a set of attributes, or elements, necessary to describe the resource in question. We use the metadata to describe the object stored in storage layer and versioning layer. In the storage layer, the metadata mainly describes the object itself, such as length, creator, creation time, modify time, type and etc. For simplicity, the object directory that contains the object also be modeled as object. As shown in Figure 5, directory object has a metadata record also. In the versioning layer, the metadata describe the attributes related to the version, such as owner of the replica, the version, tag, branch, annotation and etc. The Dublin Core Metadata [13] is used in our system. Dublin Core is a simple yet effective element set for describing a wide range of networked resource. The Dublin Core standard includes two levels: Simple and Qualified [14]. To meet the requirements of the versioning layer, we add more elements into the metadata set. Those metadata are version, branch, tag, committer, editors and replicas.

3.5 Version Management

There are mainly two kinds of merging approach, which are state-based [15] and operation-based [16], used in developing concurrent version system. The state-based approach is widely used in source file control system such as CVS and SourceSafe. The state-based merging is based on the comparison of the original file and the new file. The data in repository are the result of *diff* of the two versions. This approach is suitable for the source file or text file control, but doesn't fit well to binary file. When applying state-based approach to binary file version control, the repository will grow faster and produce enormous space occupy, and then requires bigger bandwidth between participants, so we adopt the operation-based merging approach.

The operation-based approach is good for all kind of file under version control. The operation-based approach has the following merits over the state-based approach: First, the operation-based approach ignores the actual data structures of the object; second, the operation-based approach provides better conflict detection and it is easier to resolve the conflicts than state-based approach. Based on this, operation-based merging is used in the proposed system to cope with the variety of object types in real life.

The operation-based approach stores the operations that have been applied on the object. When committing the modified object, the changes or operations are committed and stored. If more than one participant commit to the same object, changes are to be merged. In [16], Ernst presented some algorithms of doing operation-based merge. In our prototype, we manual merge the modifications to solve the collision. When collision occurred, the collision part of the file is propagated to the user interface of the participants, and then the editor resolves the conflicts manually.

The version model can be presented as a directed acyclic graph. In the version model, A version intended to supersede its predecessor is called a revision and versions intended to coexist are called variants [17]. As shown in Figure 3, the base version is $r0$. The version $v1$ is derived from this version. The evolution from $r0$ to $r1$ is conducted by operation $d0$. In the version model, a version r1 is constructed by applying sequence of operations on the base version.

Version $r2$ in Figure 3 are constructed by merging version $v1$ and $v2$. Version $v1$ and $v2$ has the same ancestor, so the merging may result in conflicts. At this time, the versioning service notifies the participants to solve the conflicts manually.

3.6 Workspace

Many collaboration tools provide the workspace service to isolate the participants' working on the same object. In our view, the workspace is the set of the shared objects been edited or manipulated by participants locally. Because the objects in the workspace are been shared, the relation between workspaces is difficult to handle. When an object is edited in both workspaces, the modifications from different workspaces may conflict. In cooperating with other people, the workspaces need to be synchronized. We define four states for object in the workspace to easy the management of the synchronization.

The object in repository becomes an element in a workspace by *checkout* operation. This is similar to CVS, which checkout a working copy of the shared file to local working directory. When a participant editing an object in the workspace, the event of been editing is propagated to all the participants that have checked out the same object. Then the modifications were propagated to all participants. But when the modifications conflict with each other, workspace will give hints to the editor to assistant the editor to resolve them. In Figure 4, the editing state and the conflicting state are transformed by resolve and edit operation. The object in active state denotes that the object is in someone's workspace and can be edited at any time. The object can be committed only in active state. The object can enter the idle state again after the object was committed back. The offline state is activated when the participant is disconnected to the network. In this state, the editor can still edit the local replica of the object but cannot commit the changes.

In the prototype, the workspace act as a container of objects been edited, and manage the state transformation, event propagating and offering the approach to the end user to resolve the conflicts.

3.7 Architecture

The overall architecture has been shown in Figure 2. There are four layers of service on top of the Java platform in this figure. The use of the Java platform is to provide the cross-platform ability that the collaboration software needed.

The peer-to-peer service is the base of the system. In this layer, Chord is used as the underlying message routing protocol. The storage service is on top of the peer-to-peer service layer. From the view of this layer, the system is looks like other peer-to-peer storage system. The service provided by this layer is store data on the peer-to-peer network. Comparing with the centre file server, the peer-to-peer storage can be more robustness and high performance and immune from single point failure. The data stored is divided into chunks which is the minimal size of the element can be stored and retrieved. It has been proven that the bulk reading and writing is more efficient. As mentioned before, we also adopt an m-of-n encoding to ensure that any piece of data can be recovered when no more than m copies of the fragments are offline. This encoding is automatically done by the system without intervention of the user.

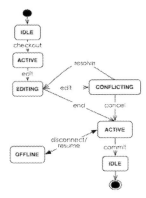

Fig. 4. The state diagram of the item in workspace

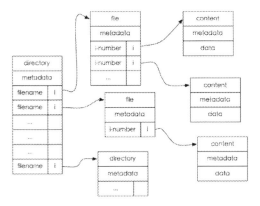

Fig. 5. Data structures of the file storage. The directory contains the mapping of the filename and the i-number of the file. The directory itself is a specify file too. The i-number is the key to address the data chunk in DHT.

Naming service is provided on top of the peer-to-peer service but can be directly used by all the other layers. The naming service provides the means one participant finding the other and finding the files can be shared. The naming service also is the rendezvous of the peers. Because distributed hash table provides a flat naming space, so it is not suitable to provide complex query. The naming service is also used to provide a hierarchical naming space to meet the habit of the user.

The workspace is the container of the object been edited and shared. The versioning service is the command interface for version management. In this layer, the version management commands are executed on top of the storage layer. Those commands are similar to those of CVS on UNIX platform.

The modification on the object will create revisions or variants of the original object. The creation of the new object as the replica is done implicitly or explicitly. When the participants check out objects into workspace, the replica of the object is created implicitly. The implicitly created object cannot be found by the versioning system, it is private to the owner. After the object was committed, the replica is deleted automatically. The explicitly created replicas are created with version management command. Those replicas will have version tag, so they can be find through the versioning system, though they cannot be edited or checked out by the other participants except the owner.

4 Implementation

The proposed system is under prototyping. In this section, we will introduce the implementation of the peer-to-peer layer, storage layer and the versioning layer.

The peer-to-peer layer has been built on top of the distributed hash tables. The naming space on this layer is flat. Values and keys are mapped through hash function. As in many DHT based peer-to-peer network, SHA-1 is used to map the value to key. In this layer, the simplest interface only contains two operations. One is *put(k,v)*, the other is *get(k)*.

As shown in Figure 5, the data structure of the storage layer is similar to the data structure in the UNIX file system. Directory is treated as special file. File is addressed by i-number, which is a random number generated when the file is created. The i-number of file is the i-number of the first block of the file. In the head of the file, metadata is stored because the metadata is frequently used. Directory file contains the mapping between the file name and the i-number. The ordinary file contains the list of the i-number of the content block that stores the data. The file storage layer builds a hierarchy structure on top of the flat naming space of the peer-to-peer layer.

The versioning system is based on file. In our system, there are some configuration and version files used to record the system configuration and the usage of the system. For example, to commit an object, the implicitly replica of the object is used as scapegoat been edited in workspace. The replica and the original file are all recorded in the configuration file. When the changes are been committed (note that the conflicts must have been resolved according to the state transformation illustrated in Figure 4), the replica is tagged as a revision of the ancestor. In the versioning service, the replica is important to the concurrency of the control. The decentralized feature makes the concurrent editing of one file difficult to control. So anyone who edits any object will edit on the replica of the object. Those replica are not synchronized during been modified. But the modification was propagated to all the replicas to determine whether the conflicts occurred. Before commit the modified object, the editor of the must resolve the conflicts, or cancel some modification. The editor can also branch the object to avoid the potential conflicts.

5 Application Scenario

Let's imaging two participants share the same file through this system. They need check out a working copy into their local workspace. After they did, replicas were created locally. When they editing the file in local workspace, the modifications made to the file are propagated to all the editors. Once there are conflicts, they are shown in the workspace. Then the editors try to communicate with each other and try to resolve the conflicts. Before the conflicts were resolved, the local copy of the object in the workspace cannot be committed. After the modifications were committed, the file modified was tagged with new version.

The mobile user can be supported in our system too. Suppose a participant disconnected from the office network. He can continue to edit the shared file locally. But he cannot commit the changes, the replica been edited is in offline state, if the user has no network connection available. If the user has wireless network connection but cannot access the office networks, he can commit the changes by mail the changes to a well-known server in the office network.

6 Conclusion

This paper illustrates a versioning-enabled peer-to-peer content distribution system based on distributed hash table. Unlike the other distributed versioning system, there is no need for a centre server in system. So the reliability should superior than those traditional systems. And due to the peer-to-peer nature of collaboration, the peer-to-peer versioning system is more suitable.

Building versioning system on top of the peer-to-peer system is a hard work. We have made our efforts in this area. In the system prototype, we only provide file storage service but not a file system view to the end user. In this way, we decrease the difficult. The versioning system is also simplified. The conflict resolving is mainly rely on the manually operation. In future, we will focus our research on the peer-to-peer merging algorithm and peer-to-peer version model.

References

1. Cederqvist, P., et al.: Version Management with CVS. Manual for CVS.
2. Ticky, W.F.: RCS – A system for version control. Software Practice and Experience 15(7) (1985) 637-654
3. Subversion. URL: http://subversion.tigris.org/
4. Leblang, D.: The CM Challenge: Configuration Management That Works. In: Tichy, W.F. (eds): Configuration Management. (1994) 1-38
5. Microsoft Visual SourceSafe. URL: http://msdn.microsoft.com/vstudio/previous/ssafe/
6. O'Donovan, B., Grimson, J.B.: A distributed version control system for wide area networks. Software Engineering Journal 5(5) (1990) 255-262
7. Rhea, S., Wells, C., Eaton, P., Geels, D., Zhao, B., Weatherspoon, H., Kubiatowicz, J.: Maintenance-free global data storage. IEEE Internet Computing 5(5) (2001) 40-49
8. Weatherspoon, H. and Kubiatowicz, J.: Erasure Coding vs. Replication: A Quantitative Comparison. Proceedings of the First International Workshop on Peer-to-Peer Systems (IPTPS 2002) (March 2002)
9. Rowstron, A. and Druschel, P.: Pastry: Scalable, distributed object location and routing for large-scale peer-to-peer systems. Proc. IFIP/ACM International Conference on Distributed Systems Platforms (Middleware). Heidelberg, Germany (2001) 329-350
10. Stoica, I., Morris, R., Karger, D., Kaashoek, M.F., and Chord, B.H.: A Scalable Peer-to-peer Lookup Service for Internet Applications. Proc. ACM SIGCOMM. San Diego, CA (2001)

11. Chen, B., Gil, T.M., Muthitacharoen, A. and Morris, R.: Building Data Structures on Untrusted Peer-to-Peer Storage with Per-participant Logs. MIT Laboratory for Computer Science TR 888. March (2003)
12. Muthitacharoen, A. Morris, R., Gil, T.M. and Chen, B.: Ivy: A Read/Write Peer-to-peer File System. Proc. Fifth Symposium on Operating Systems Design and Implementation (OSDI). Boston, MA (2002)
13. Dublin Core Metadata. URL: http://dublincore.org/
14. Using Dublin Core. URL: http://dublincore.org/documents/usageguide/
15. Mens, T.: A state-of-the-art survey on software merging. IEEE Transactions on Software Engineering 28(5) (2002) 449-462
16. Lippe, E. and van Oosterom, N.: Operation-Based Merging. ACM SIGSOFT Software Eng. Notes 17(5) (1992) 78-87
17. Conradi, R. and Westfechtel, B.: Version models for software configuration management. ACM Comput. Surv. 30(2) (1998) 232-282

Dynamic Heuristics for Time and Cost Reduction in Grid Workflows

Yingchun Yuan[1,2,3], XiaoPing Li[1,3], and Qian Wang[1,3]

[1] School of Computer Science and Engineering, Southeast University,
210096 Nanjing, P.R. China
[2] Faculty of Information Science, Agriculture University of Hebei,
071001, Baoding, Hebei. P.R. China
[3] Key Laboratory of Computer Network and Information Integration Ministry of Education,
Southeast University, Nanjing, P.R. China
nd_hd_yyc@163.com, {xpli,qwang}@seu.edu.cn

Abstract. Efficient scheduling methods are essential for time and cost reduction in grid workflow applications, depicted by directed acyclic graphs (DAG). Few of the proposed algorithms consider users' demands when allocating tasks to heterogeneous resources with different capabilities and costs. In this paper, a dynamic time and cost tradeoff heuristic is presented to optimize the cost and time of the whole workflow. The algorithm identifies the time-critical activities and cost-critical activities in each ready list generated during the workflow execution. Appropriate services are allocated to time-critical and cost-critical activities based on different QoS criteria. Experimental results show that the algorithm can achieve a better tradeoff between workflow completion time and execution cost.

1 Introduction

Open Grid Services Architecture (OGSA) introduces web services to Grid interoperability model, which makes service-oriented computing a popular application model [1-2]. In e-Business and e-Science, many important Grid applications fall into the category of workflow applications represented by directed acyclic graphs (DAG) [3]. The essential workflow scheduling becomes a challenging and complex problem. Firstly, precedence relationships among activities in workflow are very complex. Workflow scheduling must satisfy the dependencies. Secondly, for a service, it is difficult to obtain accurate predictions of its execution time, because grid resources are distributed, heterogeneous, dynamic and autonomous owned by different organizations [6]. Moreover, for each activity in a workflow, there are many service providers competent for conducting it. Different service providers implement services with different degrees of performance and execution cost. In general, the faster a service executes a task, the higher its cost is [5]. Users usually choose proper services for their tasks according to how much they want to pay and the processing time requirement. Therefore, service selection should consider users' requirements.

W. Shen et al. (Eds.): CSCWD 2006, LNCS 4402, pp. 499–508, 2007.
© Springer-Verlag Berlin Heidelberg 2007

There have been lots of recent works about resource selection and scheduling in Grids. Buyya et al proposed a computational economy framework and three independent tasks scheduling algorithms to optimize cost and time [6-7]. In contrast, the scheduling algorithm in this paper aims to schedule tasks with certain dependencies. Condor-G scheduler in literatures [9][11] considered DAG represented workflow scheduling, but it minimizes only workflows duration without consideration about the execution cost. Recently, QoS-based resource selection and mapping is a very active area of research and development. He and Sun [10] introduced a QoS-based Min-Min heuristic for independent tasks scheduling in Grids, in which those tasks with higher QoS requirements are allocated firstly. A market-based workflow management system [4] locates an optimal bid in terms of the allocated deadline of every individual activity. Indeed, it is difficult for users to give the specific QoS constraints of each activity in workflow, because most users concern about the QoS constraints of the whole workflow. Jia Yu, Buyya and Chen [5] investigated a static grid workflow scheduling algorithm to optimize cost with the whole deadline constraints. The workflow scheduling is divided into several task partition scheduling and each partition can locally optimize cost under its sub-deadline constraint. Our algorithm also adopts tasks partitions to optimize time and cost, but all tasks are grouped and allocated to services at runtime.

In this paper, a time-cost tradeoff dynamic scheduling algorithm is proposed to optimize cost while expecting to obtain the minimum duration. Different activities adaptively select services based on different QoS criteria. Moreover, services are selected and bound at runtime in accordance with the dynamic and shared characteristics in Grids. Simulated results show that this approach can achieve a better tradeoff between workflow execution cost and duration, which can effectively meet users' requirements.

This paper is organized as follows. Section 2 presents problem description. Workflow execution model and the proposed scheduling algorithm are introduced in Section 3. Section 4 shows simulated experiment results followed by conclusions in Section 5.

2 Problem Description

In grids, many important applications can be treated as workflow applications, and each workflow application consists of a collection of several interacting tasks that need to be executed in a certain partial order. These tasks have specific control or data dependencies between them. In most cases, they can be represented as a directed acyclic graph (DAG) where each node in the DAG represents a task (or activity) and the edges denote control/data dependencies.

Let $G = \{V, E\}$ denotes a directed acyclic graph, where $V = \{A_1, A_2, \cdots, A_n\}$ denotes all activities (tasks) in workflow and arcs set E represents the precedence constraint. For each arc $(i, j) \in E$, task j cannot start before i has finished. For any activity in graph G, it may be completed by only a corresponding web service (or Grid service).

In grids, multiple services may provide similar functionalities with different non-functional property values (e.g. different costs) [8]. Therefore, for each activity in a workflow, there are several execution modes corresponding to the candidate services.

Definition 1. A set of service is called *service pool* if they can perform the same task.

A service pool can be formulated as $P(A_i) = \{S_{i1}, S_{i2}, \cdots, S_{im}\}$, in which $S_{ij}(1 \le j \le m)$ denotes the *jth* service to conduct activity i, and $P(A_i)$ denotes the set of services to execute activity A_i. m is the length of the service pool, denoted as $L(A_i)$.

Definition2. Service QoS is a set of its non-functional proprieties, such as execution time, service cost, reliability, availability and so on.

According to properties stated above, Several service providers may provide similar functional services with different service QoS [12], Service execution time and service cost are considered in this paper. For a service, its execution time measures the expected delay between the moment when a request is sent and the moment when the results are received, and its cost is the amount of money that a user has to pay for executing the service. In general, service cost is closely related to its execution time. That is to say, the faster a service executes, the more a user should pay [5]. Thus, based on service QoS, each workflow activity can select the most appropriate service from its service pool. Workflow completion time is its overall execution time, and workflow execution cost is the sum of the cost of every activity.

Therefore, the paper aims to address the important problem that how to dynamically map activity $A_i \in V$ to some service $S_{ij} \in P(A_i)$ to optimize workflow execution cost with the expectation to minimum the completion time. The next section describes the approach to scheduling workflow applications.

3   Dynamic Grid scheduling Algorithm

3.1   Workflow Execution Model and Analysis

In a workflow, an activity becomes executable when its dependencies are met and may be scheduled on the selected service for execution. Figure 1 shows the major functions that a workflow engine must perform to execute a workflow.

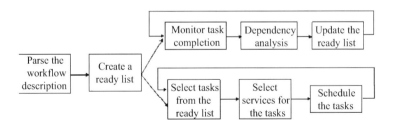

Fig. 1. Workflow execution model

From the figure, Workflow execution model is composed of DAG Manager and Scheduler. DAG Manager mainly monitors task completions, updates the ready list based on task completion events and dependencies in the workflow. Scheduler determines services for tasks in the ready list, sends control or data messages to selected service providers and drives service for execution.

The ready list is a list of executable activities. During workflow execution, all activities may be partitioned n ready lists, where the value of n and the number of activities in each ready list are determined at runtime. Activities in each ready list are mutually independent and can be executed in parallel, whereas those activities in different ready lists can be executed either in parallel or in serial (as shown in Figure 2). Let $T_i (1 \leq i \leq n)$ be all activities in a workflow, $\{RL_1, RL_2, \cdots, RL_n\}$ be n ready lists generated at runtime. In Figure 2(a), RL_i and RL_j are executed in serial because RL_j cannot begin unless RL_i completes due to the precedence constraints between them, where $\{A_1\}$ is RL_i and $\{A_2, A_3\}$ is made up of RL_j. RL_j and RL_k ($\{A_5, A_6\}$) in Figure 2(a) can execute partially in parallel if A_3 can complete earlier than A_2 in RL_j. The whole workflow completes according to constraints (serial and parallel) between ready lists (Figure 2(b)), where T_s is the start time and T_e is the completion time. It implies that the execution time of workflow is determined by two factors, ready list execution time and parallel degree between ready lists.

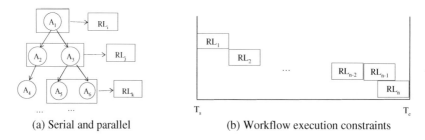

(a) Serial and parallel   (b) Workflow execution constraints

Fig. 2. Ready list execution constraints

3.2   Extended Critical Activity (ECA)

Suppose activity $A_i (1 \leq i \leq n)$ selects some service $S_{ij} (S_{ij} \in P(A_i), 1 \leq j \leq L(A_i))$. Then the completion time $c(A_i, S_{ij})$ of each activity A_i equals to the service availability time for S_{ij} plus the execution time of activity A_i on service S_{ij}, i.e., $c(A_i, S_{ij}) = A(S_{ij}) + E(S_{ij})$, where $A(S_{ij})$ is service availability time and $E(S_{ij})$ represents the service execution time. Therefore, the completion time of an activity depends on the selected service.

Definition 3. Let $\{Rl_1, Rl_2, \cdots, Rl_n\}$ be n ready lists generated during workflow execution, the number of the activities in $Rl_k (1 \leq k \leq n)$ is called the length of Rl_k, denoted as $Len(Rl_k)$. The activity that has maximum execution time in Rl_k is called *extended critical activity (ECA for short)* of Rl_k.

ECA may not be the critical activity in DAG. As well, the total number of ECA is n, namely the total number of ready lists. Because ECA of ready list Rl_k determines the minimum execution time of Rl_k, it plays an important role for the entire workflow completion time. ECA can be solved as follows.

1. Computing the minimum completion time of every activity in $Rl_k (1 \le k \le n)$, denoted as $MinTime\left(A_{k_i}\right)$ $MinTime(A_{k_i}) = Min\left\{ C\left(A_{k_i}, S_{ij}\right) | \forall A_{k_i} \in Rl_k \right\}$;

2. Finding the activity with maximum completion time from Rl_k, $A_{k_m} (1 \le m \le Len(Rl_k))$, it formulates as:

$$A_{k_m} = \{A_{k_m} \mid \underset{1 \le i \le len(RL_k)}{Max} \left\{MinTime\left(A_{k_i}\right)\right\}\}$$

Then, A_{k_m} is the extended critical activity of Rl_k. Once ECA is determined, its service can be determined.

3.3 ECA Based Dynamic Scheduling Algorithm

In general, it is NP-hard to map tasks on distributed services, especially for problems with multiple constraints (such as time and cost) [5].The dynamic workflow scheduling approach partitions the considered problem into n locally optimized subproblems, i.e. the n ready lists generated during the workflow execution. The n ready lists can be regarded as a meta-task (a set of independent tasks). All activities in each meta-task are divided into the time-critical activity and cost-critical activities. For the time-critical activity, it can be completed by the fastest resource. For the cost-critical activities, they are finished by cheaper resources whose completion time is less than or equal to that of the time-critical activity.

In section 3.2, ECA A_{k_m}, namely time-critical activity, can minimum the completion time of ready list Rl_k $(1 \le k \le n)$, so its finish time is $Deadline(k)$ of Rl_k, whereas other activities in Rl_k are cost-critical activities, they may select services whose finish time are less than or equal to $Deadline(k)$ in order to optimize workflow execution cost.

The ECA based workflow scheduling algorithm is described as follows.

1. Parse workflow graph G and k=1;
2. Repeat
3. k=k+1;
4. Rl_k ←Take ready tasks whose parent tasks have been scheduled;
5. if Rl_k is not empty
    5.1 Find ECA $A_{k_m} \in Rl_k$ and compute Deadline(k);
    5.2 For each other activity $A_{k_i} \in Rl_k$
        5.2.1 For all $S_{ij} \in P(A_{k_i})$ Compute time $C\left(A_{k_i}, S_{ij}\right)$ and cost $Cost\left(A_{k_i}, S_{ij}\right)$;
        5.2.2 Select $S_{il} \in P(A_{k_i})$ for A_{k_i}
            where $C\left(A_{k_i}, S_{il}\right) \le Deadline(k)$ and the minimum $Cost\left(A_{k_i}, S_{il}\right)$;
        5.2.3 Biding activity A_{k_i} to selected service S_{il};
    5.3 Dispatch each activity in Rl_k to selected service;
6. Wait the finished events or scheduling interval;
7. Until all tasks are completed;
8. Stop

The time complexity of service selection and assignment tasks in each ready list is $O\left(len^{2}\left(rl_{k}\right)*m\right)$, in which $len\left(rl_{k}\right)$ is the length of ready list k and m is the max length of service pool. The algorithm need to map n (the total number of ready lists) times. Therefore, The time complexity of the proposal is $O\left(len^{2}\left(rl_{k}\right)*m*n\right)$, which is similar to that of Min-min heuristic, so the proposal has little influence on the workflow completion time.

To illustrate the effectiveness and efficiency of the proposed algorithm, the proposal is compared with TMLB (Time Minimization Limited Budget) which was developed by Buyya to optimize time in Nimrod-G [7], generating solutions as quickly as possible within Budget limit. Figure 3 [8] depicts the compared workflow instance in which nodes represent tasks and arcs illustrate dependencies between nodes. Table 1 gives the service pools provided for activities in the workflow.

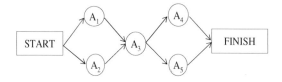

Fig. 3. A sample of workflow

Table 1. Services providers list

service	Cost	time	Service	Cost	time
$S_{1,1}$	8	8	$S_{3,1}$	5	6
$S_{1,2}$	9	10	$S_{4,1}$	15	2
$S_{1,3}$	11	6	$S_{4,2}$	10	4
$S_{2,1}$	10	5	$S_{5,1}$	20	1
$S_{2,2}$	12	4	$S_{5,2}$	10	2
			$S_{5,3}$	5	3

Table 2 shows the comparison results of service selection, execution time(s), costs ($) of the proposal against TMLB. From Table 2, it can be seen that the completion time of TMLB is as much as that of the proposed scheduling algorithm. However, the total cost spent by the proposal is 51$, which is much less than that of TMLB 63$. Therefore, the proposal can achieve a lower cost than that of TMLB with the same duration time.

Table 2. Comparison of service selection, total time and total cost using the two approaches

	A1	A2	A3	A4	A5	Total Time	Total Cost
TMLB	$S_{1,3}$	$S_{2,2}$	$S_{3,1}$	$S_{4,1}$	$S_{5,1}$	14	63
Proposal	$S_{1,3}$	$S_{2,1}$	$S_{3,1}$	$S_{4,1}$	$S_{5,2}$	14	51

4 Experiment Results

In order to evaluate performance, the proposed scheduling algorithm is compared with TMLB. Different workflow structures are tested. DAG graphs are generated randomly of which each task requires different type of service and each type of service has five different providers with different processing times and execution costs. Generally, cost is inversely proportional to processing time [5]. Five DAG graphs are randomly generated with 10, 30, 50, 80 and 100 tasks respectively, and each DAG graph has 5 different instances with different structure of tasks.

4.1 Time and Cost Comparison

First, the total cost and completion time for the two approaches are compared on the generated instances. They are performed in online mode, i.e. the next ready list is checked if it can be scheduled as soon as some task completes. The comparative results are shown in Figure 4, in which horizontal axis represents 5 instances with 10, 30, 50, 80, 100 activities respectively and vertical axis reflects completion times and costs.

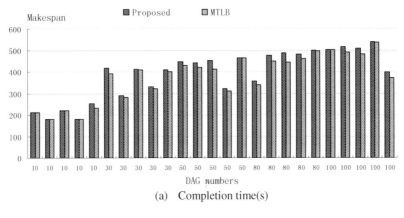

(a)   Completion time(s)

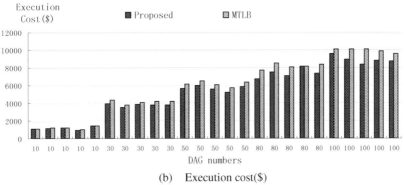

(b)   Execution cost($)

Fig. 4. Comparison of cost and completion time with different DAG instances using two approaches

It can be seen from Figure 4(a) that the proposal needs less cost than TMLB does for all cases. That is, the proposal can decrease the workflow execution cost. However, for different instances with same DAG structures, their costs are different.

Figure 4(b) implies that completion times of the two algorithms are similar in some instances with different structures under the best situations. However, the proposal may take more time than TMLB does in some instances. This is because the proposal aims to balance optimizing both cost and completion time. i.e., achieving lower cost may pay a price for more execution time. In the proposal, some tasks may select cheaper but slower services for optimizing cost and then the next ready list may be delayed. The two approaches can achieve same execution times without delay, otherwise the proposal should take a little more time than TMLB do but the gap is very narrow. Moreover, influence of the total task number of a DAG graph on both algorithms is nearly the same, i.e. the proposed algorithm can also get little executing time with the number of DAG tasks increasing.

4.2   Effect of Scheduling Intervals

The process of assigning services for tasks in ready list is called a negotiation cycle. The interval between two successive negotiation cycles is the scheduling interval [11]. During a negotiation cycle, the scheduler tries to find optimal services for all the tasks in ready list. This section tests the effect of different scheduling intervals on cost and completion time.

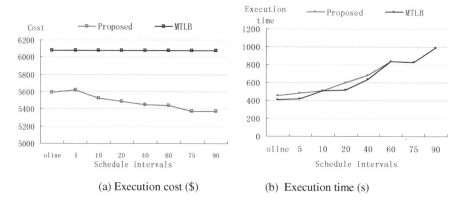

(a) Execution cost ($)   (b) Execution time (s)

Fig. 5. Execution cost and completion time in different scheduling intervals

Figure 5 shows results of effects with different scheduling intervals for a workflow instance with 50 tasks. The number of ready lists may change with different scheduling intervals in that it is generated dynamically during workflow execution. The number of ready lists may be reduced if scheduling interval increases while the total number of tasks in a ready list increases and cost is optimized. Optimal cost is obtained when scheduling interval is large enough to stop increasing the number of ready lists. However, scheduling intervals have no effect on cost in TMLB because it maps tasks onto service with minimum completion time. Figure 5(a) shows effects on cost of the two approaches. On the other hand, when scheduling interval increases, tasks in ready lists may wait and the execution time of the two approaches would increase. The two approaches can achieve the same execution time when the total number of ready lists has no change. Figure 5(b) shows workflow completion times with different scheduling intervals.

The experiment results show that both workflow execution cost and completion time are influenced by the scheduling intervals. Therefore, by setting more suitable scheduling interval, optimal workflow execution cost can be obtained, whereas workflow completion time may increase.

5 Conclusions and Future Work

Workflow scheduling is a complexity and challenging problem in economic-driven Grid resource management framework. This paper analyses Grid characteristics and workflow execution model. A dynamic workflow scheduling algorithm is proposed which emphasizes on balancing workflow execution time and cost. ECA (Extended Critical Activity) is defined for a ready list during workflow execution, which can locally minimize the execution time of the ready list, whereas other activities in the ready list may optimize their costs based on ECA. Experimental results indicate that the proposal can achieve a better tradeoff between workflow completion time and execution cost, which may effectively satisfy users' requirements in practical applications. In addition, effects of scheduling intervals on time and cost are discussed.

In the future, we will improve the proposed algorithm by considering workflow applications including hundreds of tasks or thousands of tasks. Moreover, we will further enhance our scheduling approach to adapt to different failure situations during service execution [8][12].

Acknowledgments. This work is supported by National Natural Science Foundation of China under grant numbers 60672092, 60504029 and 90412014.

References

1. Foster, I., Kesselman, C.: The Anatomy of the Grid: Enabling Scalable Virtual Organizations. International Journal of High Performance Computing Applications 15(3) (2001) 200-222
2. Foster, I., Kesselman, C. (eds.): The Grid: Blueprint for a new computing infrastructure. Morgan Kaufmannm (1998)
3. Deelman1, E., Blythe1, J., Gil, Y., Kesselman, C., Mehta, G., Vahi, K., et al.: Mapping Abstract Complex Workflows onto Grid Environments. Journal of Grid Computing 1(1) (2003) 25-39
4. Geppert, A., Kradolfer, M. and Tombros, D.: Market-based Workflow Management. International Journal of Cooperative Information Systems 7(4) (1998) 297-314
5. Yu, J., Buyya, R. and Tham, C.K.: Cost-based Scheduling of Workflow Applications on Service Grids. Proceedings of the 1st IEEE International Conference on e-Science and Grid Computing. Melbourne, Australia (2005)

6. Abramson, D., Buyya, R. and Giddy, J.: A Computational Economy for Grid Computing and its Implementation in the Nimrod-G Resource Broker. Future Generation Computer Systems (FGCS) Journal 18(8) (2002) 1061-1074
7. Buyya, R., Abramson, D., Giddy, J. and Stockinger, H.: Economic Models for Resource Management and Scheduling in Grid Computing. Concurrency and Computation: Practice and Experience Journal (Special Issue on Grid Computing Environments) 14(13-15) (2002) 1507-1542
8. Sample, N., Keyani, P. and Wiederhold, G.: Scheduling Under Uncertainty: Planning for the Ubiquitous Grid. Proceedings of the Fifth International Conference on Coordination Models and Languages (2002)
9. Frey, J., Tannenbaum, T., Livny, M., Foster, I., Tuecke, S.: Condor-G: A Computation Management Agent for Multi-Institutional Grids. Cluster Computing 5(3) (2002) 237–246
10. He, X., Sun, X., et al.: QoS Guided Min-Min Heuristic for Grid Task Scheduling. Journal of Computer Science and Technology 18(4) (2003) 442-451
11. Singh, G., Kesselman, C. and Deelman, E.: Optimizing Grid-Based workflow execution. CS Tech report. University of Southern California (2005)
12. Jin, H., Chen, H. and Chen, J., et al: Real-Time Strategy and Practice in Service Grid. Proceedings of the 28th Annual International Computer Software and Applications Conference (2004)

Measurement Model of Grid QoS and Multi-dimensional QoS Scheduling

Zhiang Wu, Junzhou Luo, and Fang Dong

School of Computer Science and Engineering, Southeast University
210096 Nanjing, P.R. China
{zawu, jluo, fdong}@seu.edu.cn

Abstract. QoS (quality of service) has become a hot topic of research in service-oriented grid environment. The key question of embedding multi-dimensional QoS into task scheduling and RMS (resource management system) evaluation is to find a scheme to integrate multiple QoS metrics. In this paper, measurement model of grid QoS is proposed to integrate multiple QoS metrics. By using this model, multi-dimensional QoS scheduling heuristics is put forward. Finally, two simulation experiments are conducted: one is to make a comparison between traditional Min-Min and multi-dimensional QoS guided Min-Min; another is to apply measurement model to evaluate the performance of grid RMS. It is indicated that the measurement model can integrate multiple QoS metrics effectively and multi-dimensional QoS scheduling can enhance the performance of grid environments remarkably.

1 Introduction

The real and specific intuition that underlies the grid computing is coordinated resource sharing and problem solving in dynamic, multi-institutional VO (virtual organization) [1-3].Varying dynamically in their purpose, scope, size, duration, structure, community, and sociology at any moment is an important feature of VO. So environment of different VO will be different, and the level of service provided by VO will also vary dynamically along with these varying attributes.

By merging with concepts and technologies from Web services, OGSA (open grid services architecture) is proposed in grid computing field, which defines a uniform exposed service semantics [4-5]. In OGSA, we focus on services: computational resources, storage resources, networks, programs, databases, and the like are all represented as services.

QoS (quality of service) is a synthetically guideline, which is used for measuring satisfaction of a service. It describes some performance characteristics of a certain service, which is expressed as a group of parameters using an understandable language to users. Limited by property of resource and policy, QoS parameters such as CPU cycle, memory, storage can not be satisfied simultaneously, and may be conflicted with each other sometimes. So, designing a kind of scheduling policy and evaluating the performance of RMS (resource management system) by considering single QoS parameter are unilateral. But the key question of considering multiple QoS

W. Shen et al. (Eds.): CSCWD 2006, LNCS 4402, pp. 509–519, 2007.
© Springer-Verlag Berlin Heidelberg 2007

parameters is to find a kind of measurement model to integrate multiple QoS parameters. And this integration should reflect utility of users profited by these multiple QoS parameters. For that, in this paper, a kind of measurement model is proposed to integrate multiple kinds of QoS parameters at VO level. And by using of this proposed measurement model, multi-dimensional QoS scheduling heuristics is proposed.

The rest of the paper is as follows. Section 2 reviews related work in grid QoS. Section 3 introduces utility model. In Section 4, the measurement model of grid QoS is put forward. In Section 5, multi-dimensional QoS scheduling is introduced based on this measurement mode. In Section 6, we conduct two experiments and discuss the experiment results. Finally, we make a conclusion and look forward to future work.

2 Related Work

Pervasive principle of network QoS is interpreted elaborately in [6]. Since QoS parameters behave dramatically different in different layers, which layer the QoS parameter is belonged to must be distinguished before research. Network QoS is viewed from application, resource and system perspectives [6]. This taxonomy is very worthy, but it fails to study QoS comprehensively and systematically. Our early work researches grid QoS from application, VO and resource device perspectives.

Since the VO layer is most important layer, the classification of VO layer has been considered further. R. Al-Ali, etc. classify the service QoS properties into five QoS domains as follows [7]: accounting QoS, service QoS, provisional QoS, service reliability and service security. Though this kind of classification has reflected some characteristics of grid QoS, but it can not totally meet the expression demands of grid QoS characteristics. For instance, the QoS of logical resource in VO have both relations and differences with physical resource. In order to describe the QoS of grid services accurately, it is necessary to distinguish them in QoS, but the classification scheme in [7] can not meet this demand. Intuitively, the problem under this classification is the classifying standard is not unified. In our early research, we classified QoS parameters into five categories in VO layer according to their properties [8]. They are system QoS, logical resource QoS, security QoS, reliability QoS and accounting QoS.

A method for representing network security is proposed in [9], which supports variant security components. A simple benefit function to measure how well a scheduler meets the goals of user preference and system priorities is also introduced. Based on this method, a flexible framework to measure the performance by a RMS using a broad range of attributes has been proposed in [10]. It quantifies various QoS attributes, such as priorities, versions, deadlines, security etc. At last it combines these QoS attributes to form flexible integrated system capability, being a critical part of a scheduler or a scheduling heuristic. This framework is very useful and can be extended for particular problem domains.

Scalable QoS metrics model is proposed in [11]. It quantifies five QoS parameters including response time, reputation, success rate, availability and price. But this model only considers how to calculate value of these five QoS parameters and fails to measure the degree of QoS parameters influencing on service performance. In this paper, recurring to the utility model, similar QoS parameters are merged into one sort and different sorts are measured by a unified value. Then we can compare the worth of different QoS parameters according to User Satisfaction.

GARA (general-purpose architecture for reservation and allocation) is proposed to support grid QoS, which provides advance reservations and end-to-end management for QoS on different types of resources [12-13]. It is a theoretic framework to support management of QoS in OGSA-based grid environment. So, more detail should be researched and embedded into it.

In scheduling research area, lots of heuristic algorithms have been proposed, such as Min-Min, Max-Min, Suffrage and XSuffrage, aiming to enhance the system throughput, utilization and makespan [14]. One-dimensional QoS guided scheduling algorithm which is improved on Min-Min has been addressed in [15]. In the current research on scheduling, user-centric approach has been proposed, concentrating on delivering maximum satisfactory to the users of the system based on their QoS requirements [16], which are usually described using QoS parameters, so the research on QoS-based scheduling will play key role on the researches of scheduling.

3   Utility Model

Users need a utility model to specify QoS requirements and constraints. To describe utility model, two definitions are proposed.

Definition 1. User Satisfaction: a real number in range [0, 1].As its value increasing, users are satisfied with the service more. When the value reaches 1, users are satisfied perfectly.

Definition 2. User Satisfaction Function: u_{ij} represents the mapping relation from the *j*-th QoS parameter of *i*-th grid service to User Satisfaction.

Three representative types of User Satisfaction Function are given in Figure 1. With CPU or network bandwidth increasing, users will be satisfied more and may not be satisfied perfectly. So the User Satisfaction Function of CPU or network bandwidth can be depicted as Figure 1(a). It is a curve infinitely closing to 1. User's demand to storage may have a minimum value. Once exceeding it, users will be satisfied perfectly, as Figure 1(b) described. User's requirement to memory may be related to the size of page in operating system. When size of memory allocated to users increases up to one page size, User Satisfaction will just increase, as Figure 1(c) depicted. The reason to choose these three types is that Figure 1(a) depicts best-effort QoS parameters, Figure 1(b) depicts discrete QoS parameters, and Figure 1(c) depicts fragment increment QoS parameters.

User Satisfaction is a subjective concept. It varies with different user's preference and grid application. User Satisfaction Function describes relation between a given QoS parameter and User Satisfaction. It is defined by user and submitted to grid resource broker with the task. It reflects how much user profits from a given level of grid service. So grid RMS can provide service to the best of its abilities according to the property of the User Satisfaction Function.

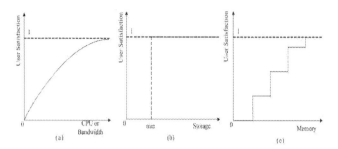

Fig. 1. Examples of User Satisfaction Function

4 The Measurement Model of Grid QoS

Since grid service performance is limited by resource ability and policy mechanism, various users' requirements cannot meet simultaneously and may be conflicted with each other. In addition, to evaluate whether a RMS is eligible, aiming at single performance objective is often unilateral. But the key problem under aiming at multiple objectives is how to integrate related various QoS requirements to form a synthetical guideline. This section tries to present such mechanism to integrate grid QoS parameters. Based on our classification of the grid QoS, we will quantify four categories excepting reliability QoS, since reliability QoS has been concerned in a multitude of literatures. Before discussing the way to measure the grid QoS, the grid application model should be proposed first.

4.1 Application Model

A grid application can be represented by a directed graph [6], where graph nodes represent Units of Work (UoW) and graph edges represent data flow between these UoWs. The data flow implicitly specifies the order in which the work must be done. The UoW is the smallest unit that resources are allocated. Each grid service usually consists of one or more UoWs, consequentially spanning lots of resources. Therefore, many grid services constitute a grid application and QoS requirements are defined for each grid service. An example of grid application is depicted in Figure 2. In this example, Service 1 and Service 3 both include one UoW, and Service 2 includes three UoWs. All these three grid services constitute one grid application. Therefore, in OGSA, we can assume simply a grid application is made up by a set of grid services.

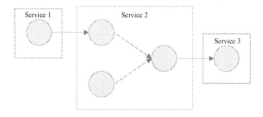

Fig. 2. Grid application model

A grid service may be realized in many different ways. Service invoker of a service negotiates the QoS of the entire service, without having to know the UoWs that make up the service. In grid application level, grid application model and utility model mentioned in section 3 both should be considered.

4.2 Measuring Logical Resource QoS, Security QoS and Accounting QoS

Logical resource QoS and security QoS may consist of many fractions, so these two categories can be quantified in the same way. Although accounting QoS is a complex issue, it can also be quantified in the same way. So, we choose representatively logical resource QoS as our QoS measurements.

Logical resource QoS is provided by producers (resource owners), which integrates global service performance of physical resource, load of local task and resource sharing strategy in VO [8]. Therefore, logical resource QoS is a kind of integrated factor reflecting service performance and may include many special parameters such as CPU time, storage and network bandwidth etc. But logical resource QoS of different grid services may include different special parameters, because different grid service emphasizes on different QoS parameters. For example, computational intensive service may not consider storage, because its storage demand can be easily satisfied.

To compare how much it influences on grid service performance, logical resource QoS including different special parameters should be represented first. Logical resource QoS can be represented by n dimensional Boolean vector L and n fractions of this vector represent all possible special parameters that can be included in logical resource QoS. A Boolean statement, for a given grid service, specifies the functional requirement for each component. So, n dimensional Boolean vector L_i can represent which kinds of special parameters are included in i-th grid service.

When QoS requirements are proposed by consumers (resource users), each specific QoS parameter has its own minimum requirement. If one of the QoS parameter's minimum requirement can not be satisfied, User Satisfaction will be 0. Only when minimum requirements of all QoS parameters included by this grid service can be satisfied, this grid service are deemed to be admitted by the grid system and User Satisfaction will not be 0. Characteristic value l_i' is used to represent whether minimum logical resource QoS requirements can be satisfied. If minimum logical resource QoS requirements are all met $l_i'=1$; else $l_i'=0$.

Next, we should calculate the user satisfaction provided by logical resource QoS. Let u_{ij} be User Satisfaction Function of j-th QoS parameter of the i-th grid service. So the measurement expression of logical resource QoS can be showed as:

$$l_i = \frac{\sum_{j=1}^{n} L_i[j] \cdot u_{ij}}{n} \tag{1}$$

The overall measurement expression of logical resource QoS is defined as: $l_i' \cdot l_i$. As soon as one of minimum logical resource QoS requirements are not all met, characteristic value l_i' will be 0 and $l_i' \cdot l_i$ will be 0 too.

Security QoS provided by producers is used to specify QoS parameters on security level and access control strategy of grid service. It is supposed to include many QoS parameters, such as level of confidentiality, integrity and user's privilege etc. Therefore, we can quantify it analogous to the logical resource QoS. Assuming $s_i{'}$ is characteristic value and s_i is the measurement expression of security QoS, measurement expression of security QoS can be defined analogously: $s_i{'} \cdot s_i$.

Accounting QoS is used to describe QoS parameters on service cost and managing approaches. The most novel approach for managing grid environments is driven by user-centric policy [16], which concentrates on delivering maximum satisfactory to the users of the system based on their QoS requirements. It introduces many of complex issues to Grid computing, especially accounting, billing and payment mechanisms. These complex mechanisms will be discussed in future work and we assume that consumers have selected a certain producer according to a kind of mechanism. So User Satisfaction produced by service cost can be derived from User Satisfaction Function. The overall measurement expression of accounting QoS can be defined as: $c_i{'} \cdot c_i$. Here, $c_i{'}$ is characteristic value and c_i is the measurement expression of accounting QoS.

4.3 System QoS

System QoS is quite different from those three categories QoS mentioned above. We propose an algorithm to determine the system QoS. System QoS specifies QoS parameters on grid system environment [8]. It is necessary to propose system QoS in multiple-VO heterogeneous grid environment. For example, if one computing node performs well in a VO and another computing node also performs well in another VO, then the comparison only using User Satisfaction would not make sense. Resources in one VO have the same sharing rules, authentication, authorization, resource access and discovery mechanisms. So the environment in one VO is assumed to be same. Since the environments are different in different VO, how well a grid service performed should be how much better it performed than the system QoS for its environment. In other words, system QoS is treated as the baseline of a VO.

To calculate the value of system QoS, the same set of tasks with same QoS requirements is deployed to different VO. The value of system QoS is the collective User Satisfaction of the given task set. If all the minimum QoS requirements of a task are met ($l_i{'} \neq 0$, $s_i{'} \neq 0$ and $c_i{'} \neq 0$), this task is said to be completed and the user satisfaction of this task can be added to the value of system QoS.

The algorithm to calculating the value of system QoS is as follows:

```
(1) all tasks in set are ordered by the same way, E=0
(2) while(task set is not null ){
(3) get the front task tᵢ in the queue
(4) if(lᵢ'≠0 && sᵢ'≠0 && cᵢ'≠0){
(5)   schedule tᵢ at soonest possible time
(6) Uᵢ=w₁·lᵢ+wₛ·sᵢ+w_c·cᵢ
(7) E=E+Uᵢ
(8) }
(9) delete task tᵢ from task set
(10)}
```

Here, E is the value of system QoS and w_l, w_s, w_c in the line 6 of the algorithm are respectively the weight of logical resource QoS, security QoS and accounting QoS. U_i is the collective user satisfaction of task t_i.

The algorithm to determine the system QoS is proposed as follows. First, the algorithm sorts the task set. For example, it can be sorted by its priorities, expected execution times, or deadlines. After the sorting, the algorithm determines whether the first task (according to the order) can be expected to achieve perfectly using the available resources. If so, it computes the User Satisfaction after the task has been completed and adds it to system QoS. The same process will continue until the task set is null.

4.4 QoS Measurement of Grid Application

Since deadline is often important limit of many tasks, especially for real time applications, to evaluate QoS of completed applications must take deadline into account. Three types of deadlines have been discussed in [10]: earliest, soft and firm. The earliest deadline is the time when the grid system is ready to execute this task. The soft deadline is the maximal time by which user is satisfied perfectly, and once exceed it the User Satisfaction will be decreased less than 1. If this task is completed after firm deadline, the User Satisfaction will be 0, because this task will be no use after that deadline. Then, we can assume t_i' represents whether i-th service is completed after firm deadline: if it does, $t_i'=0$; else $t_i'=1$. We can also assume t_i represents the User Satisfaction of deadlines. If this service is completed between earliest deadline and soft deadline, $t_i=1$; and if it exceeds soft deadline but not exceeds firm deadline, $0<t_i<1$; and once it exceeds firm deadline, $t_i=0$.

Based on the grid application model mentioned above, we assume a grid application consists of n grid services and the priority of i-th grid service is p_i according to its role played in the grid application. w_l, w_s and w_c are respectively the weight of logical resource QoS, security QoS and accounting QoS. An effective way that combines various grid QoS parameters and deadlines is introduced in this section. To allow the comparison of one VO to another VO, the QoS measurement should be normalized by the value of system QoS. The QoS measurement expression of grid application is

$$A = \frac{1}{E} \sum_{i=1}^{n} [p_i \cdot t_i' \cdot l_i' \cdot s_i' \cdot c_i' \cdot (w_t \cdot t_i + w_l \cdot l_i + w_s \cdot s_i + w_c \cdot c_i)] \qquad (2)$$

Obviously, when a service attribute is added to the measure, the worth of the service added should not lower the value of the task completed below the percentage satisfied of the least satisfied attribute. The intuition of expression 2 is that if an application is given more services and if those are satisfied perfectly, then the overall value for that application should increase.

5   Multi-dimensional QoS Scheduling

Makespan becomes the main objective function in traditional scheduling heuristic algorithms. Makespan is a standard performance metric to evaluate scheduling heuristics, which is defined as the time between the first input files is submitted to a computational server and the last output file is returned to user.

Since just computing nodes with high QoS properties can complete service request with high QoS requirements, avoiding submitting service request with low QoS requirements to computing node with high QoS properties can decreases makespan.

This intuition behaves in QoS guided Min-Min scheduling algorithm in [15] originally, but just one-dimensional QoS parameter is considered. And this one-dimensional QoS parameter is divided into high QoS and low QoS simply. By using measurement model, we can extend one-dimensional QoS to multi-dimensional QoS. Multi-dimensional QoS parameters are integrated into a synthetical metric to distinguish high or low QoS. This metric is more appropriate and the distinguishing granularity is much fine.

The smallest unit to be scheduled is UoW, and each service request may consist of one or more UoWs. Grid application can be abstracted as a set of UoWs as mentioned in section 4.1. The modified multi-dimensional QoS scheduling algorithm is as follows:

```
(1) for(each UoW i to schedule){
(2) compute Uᵢ= w₁·lᵢ+wₛ·sᵢ+w_c·cᵢ
(3) }
(4) Order UoW set in decreased order according to Uᵢ
(5) while(UoW set is not null ){
(6) get the front UoW tₖ in the queue
(7) compute minimal completion time of tₖ
(8) dispatch tₖ  to n₁ to attain minimal completion time
(9) delete tₖ from UoW set and refresh resource queue
(10)}
```

The input of this algorithm is UoW queue and resource queue, and each UoW and resource is associated with QoS parameters. The output of this algorithm is the matching queue for each UoW. It is executed as follows: first, this algorithm computes required User Satisfaction of each UoW and order UoW set according to it. Then, UoW with highest QoS requirements is in the front and will be scheduled first. In the "while" loop, for each UoW from high QoS to low QoS, this algorithm finds computing node completing UoW soonest. Then the UoW is submitted to that node. Finally, scheduled UoW will be deleted from UoW queue and resource queue will also be refreshed.

6 Simulation and Results

To illuminate the effect of measurement model, two experiments are conducted. First, traditional Min-Min algorithm and multi-dimensional QoS guided Min-Min algorithm are compared from two aspects which are makespan and resource utilization rate in three scenes. These three scenes are: (a) QoS level of 75% of the net resources is greater than average QoS demand that the net service asks, (b) 50% net QoS level of resource greater than net average QoS demand that service ask, (c)QoS level of 25% of the net resources is greater than average QoS demand that the net service asks. Grid resource becomes more and more intensely from scenes (a) to (c). 500 net resource nodes of our simulation and 2000 net service request, compare each kind of different experiment scene repeatedly with the experiment, the average result of fetching the experiment 100 times is as our experimental result. Second, the performance of grid RMS which takes either traditional Min-Min algorithm or modified Min-Min algorithm as scheduling heuristics has been compared. By assigning a set of random UoWs with deadline to one grid RMS in one VO, total User Satisfaction is calculated using formulation (2) and this User Satisfaction can be used to evaluate the quality of service of this grid RMS.

Figure 3 depicts makespan comparison between traditional Min-Min algorithm and modified Min-Min algorithm. Figure 4 depicts resource utilization rate comparison between these two kinds of algorithms. These two comparisons indicate that the performance of modified Min-Min algorithm is much better than traditional Min-Min algorithm in whatever scenes, especially in scene3.

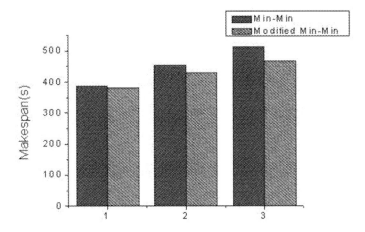

Fig. 3. The comparison chart of makespan

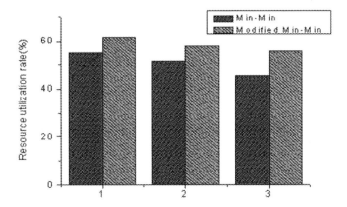

Fig. 4. The comparison chart of resource utilization rate

Another experiment has been conducted to show the measurement model which can be used to analyze and evaluate the performance of grid RMS. It is assumed that there are 500 computing nodes in one VO and exists one central RMS to schedule UoWs submitted to that VO. In our experiment, 100 grid application including 2000 grid service requests are submitted to that RMS and be scheduled according to traditional Min-Min algorithm and modified Min-Min algorithm respectively in abovementioned three scenes. User Satisfaction is calculated by formula (2). Figure 5 shows comparison of User Satisfaction gained by these two algorithms. While grid resource is very abundant such as in scene1, RMS using these two algorithms provides almost same QoS to users. But as resources becoming increasingly lacking, the difference of QoS level provided by RMS using these algorithms becomes much more obviously. For example, QoS level can be improved nearly 150% in scene3.

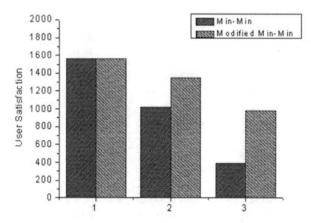

Fig. 5. Performance comparison chart of Grid RMS

7   Conclusion and Future Work

Based on the classification of the grid QoS, measurement model of grid QoS has been put forward. This measurement model is applied to task scheduling heuristics and multi-dimensional QoS scheduling is proposed. The measurement of grid QoS presented in this paper can integrate multi-dimensional QoS parameters as a critical part of a scheduling heuristic's objective function. It also can help the grid community to implement RMS and can provide a method to analyze and compare it. Multidimensional QoS scheduling heuristics can reduce makespan and improve grid resource utilization rate effectively.

In our future work, we plan to research on the grid economic issues including resource pricing schemes, negotiation protocols and accounting, billing and payment mechanisms. In addition, we also plan to apply multi-dimensional QoS scheduling to the campus grid environment. We believe it can improve makespan and resource utilization rate of campus grid in the future.

Acknowledgments. This work is supported by National Natural Science Foundation of China under Grants No. 90412014 and 90604004 and Jiangsu Provincial Key Laboratory of Network and Information Security under Grant No. BM2003201.

References

1. Foster, I., Kesselman, C: The Grid 2: Blueprint for a New Computing Infrastructure. San Fransisco: Morgan Kaufmann Publishers (2004)
2. Foster, I., Kesselman, C. and Tuecke, S.: The Anatomy of the Grid: Enabling Scalable Virtual Organizations. International Journal Supercomputer Applications (2001) 200-222
3. Foster, I., Kesselman, C., Nick, J.M. and Tuecke, S.: The Physiology of the Grid: An Open Grid Services Architecture for Distributed Systems Integration. Globus Project. (2002) URL: www.globus.org/research/papers/ogsa.pdf
4. Tuecke, S., Czajkowski, K., Foster, I., Frey, J., Graham, S., Kesselman, C., et al.: Open grid services infrastructure (OGSI). Version 1.0 (2003). URL: http://forge.gridforum.org/projects/ggf-editor/document/draft-ogsi-service-1/en/1
5. Czajkowski, K. Ferguson, D.F., Foster, I., Frey, J., Graham, S., Seduknin, I., et al.: The WS-resource framework. Version 1.0 (2004)
   URL: http://www-106.ibm.com/developerworks/library/ws-resource/ws-wsrf.pdf
6. Chatterjee, B.S.S., Sydir, M.D.J.J., Lawrence, T.F.: Taxonomy for QoS specifications. Proc. of the 3rd Int'l Workshop on Object-Oriented Real-Time Dependable Systems (WORDS'97). Newport Beach, CA, USA (1997) 100-107
7. Al-Ali, R., ShaikhAli, A., Rana, O. and Walker, D.: Supporting QoS-Based Discovery in Service-Oriented Grids. Proceedings of the International Parallel and Distributed Processing Symposium (IPDPS'03). Nice, France (2003)
8. Wu, Z, Luo, J. and Song, A.B.: QoS-Based Grid Resource Management. Journal of Software 17(11) (2006) 2264-2276
9. Irvine, C.E. and Levin, T.: Toward Quality of Security Service in a Resource Management System Benefit Function. Proc. of the 15th Annual Computer Security Application Conference. IEEE Computer Society (2000) 133-139
10. Kim, J.K., Kidd, T., Siegel H.J., Irvine, C., Levin, T., Hensgen, D.A., et al.: Collective Value of QoS: A Performance Measure Framework for Distributed Heterogeneous Networks. Proceedings of the International Parallel and Distributed Processing Symposium (IPDPS) (2001) 137-150
11. Jin, H., Chen, H., Lu, Z. and Ning, X.: QoS Optimizing Model and Solving for Composite Service in CGSP Job Manager. Chinese Journal of Computers 28(4) (2005) 578-588
12. Foster, I., Roy, A. and Sander, V.: A quality of service architecture that combines resource reservation and application adaptation. Proceedings of the International Workshop on Quality of Service (2000) 181–188
13. Roy, A.: End-To-End Quality of Service for High-End Application. PhD Thesis. The University of Chicago, August (2001)
14. Braun, T., Siegel, H.J., Beck, N., Boloni, L.L., Maheswaran, M., Reuther, A.I., et al.: A comparison study of static mapping heuristics for a class of meta-tasks on heterogeneous computing systems. Proceedings of the International Heterogeneous Computing Workshop (HCW, 99) (1999) 15-29
15. He, X., Sun, X. and von Laszewski, G.: QoS Guided Min-Min Heuristic for Grid Scheduling. Journal of Computer Science and Technology 18(4) (2003) 442-451
16. Buyya, R., Abramson, D. and Venugopal, S.: The Grid Economy. Proceedings of the IEEE 93(3) (2005) 698-714

Wrapping Legacy Applications into Grid Services: A Case Study of a Three Services Approach

Yu Xiong and Daizhong Su

Advanced Design and Manufacturing Engineering Centre
School of Architecture, Design and Built environment,
Nottingham Trent University, UK
daizhong.su@ntu.ac.uk

Abstract. In this paper, the support for legacy application, which is one of the important advantages of Grid computing, is presented. The ability to reuse existing codes/applications in combination with other Web/Internet technologies, such as Java, makes Grid computing a good choice for developers to wrap existing applications behind Intranet or the Internet. The approach developed can be used for migrating legacy applications into Grid Services, which speeds up the popularization of Grid technology. The approach is illustrated using a case study with detailed description of its implementation step by step. Globus Toolkit is utilized to develop the system.

1 Introduction

The reuse of legacy computer applications is a challenging topic in engineering research. In practice, some useful computer applications, particularly those developed long time ago, may not compatible with nowadays Internet technology. However, they may be too important to scrap or too expensive to be modified for Internet applications.

Researchers have been making efforts to resolve this problem using Web/Internet technologies to enable their distributed features. Su et al. [1] developed a method to execute large program over the Internet with Common Gateway Interface (CGI). The drawbacks of CGI are obvious, such as the slow response and difficulty of modification. Cotroneo et al. [2] presented their approach which is based on CORBA, however, CORBA is an Object-Oriented and tight-coupled technology, which means that the change of either client or server would involve the change of the other.

Xiong et al. [4] developed an approach for software sharing based on Web services. This approach solved the problems of wrapping legacy applications which are difficult other technologies and is considered to be extensible and even adaptable to any future architecture.

Based on Web services, Grid computing is considered to be the next generation network; different from traditional distributed technologies, Grid has a more global mindset; it concentrates on comparably large scale resources sharing. Therefore, Grid is

W. Shen et al. (Eds.): CSCWD 2006, LNCS 4402, pp. 520–529, 2007.
© Springer-Verlag Berlin Heidelberg 2007

a better choice for wrapping legacy applications. What's more, the situation that the large existence of legacy applications becomes obstacle of the wide-spread industrial take-up of Grid Technology because they are not accessible as Grid services [3]. It would be desirable if those stand-along resources could be wrapped into Grid services. Presented in this paper, the authors did further research and made the previous approach to support Grid Computing.

2 System Architecture

The three-services structure developed by the authors [4] is applied in this research. Figure 1 shows the architecture of the service-oriented Legacy Application Wrapping (LAW) system. There probably are multiple shared applications installed in multiple computers. Each of them is installed with the Application Proxy Factory Service (APFS). The process of activating the shared applications is represented by the Application Proxy Service (APS) created and managed by the APFS. All the APFSs are registered to the Application Manager Service (AMS) and assigned an application identifier. The AMS has an ACL table for security control.

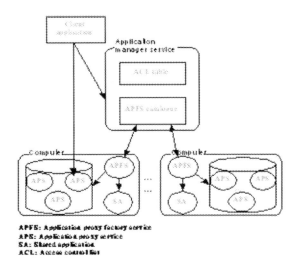

APFS: Application proxy factory service
APS: Application proxy service
SA: Shared application
ACL: Access control list

Fig. 1. Architecture of service-oriented software sharing system

When the user launches a client application, the client application issues a request to get an APS from the AMS. When the request arrives, the AMS looks up the APFS registered in the catalogue using the application identifier specified by the client application. If the APFS exists in the catalogue, the AMS then checks whether the client application has the right to use it. If the access right checking is successful, then the AMS interacts with the APFS to create an APS.

It's possible that multiple APFSs are associated with one shared application. These services may be installed in different locations. When an APFS is requested to create an

APS by AMS, the APFS determine whether a new APS is to be created or not. If the APFS cannot create a new APS, the AMS is then informed, and hence the AMS chooses another APFS instead.

After an APS is created by an APFS, the AMS returns the handle of the newly created APS to the client application. The AMS authorizes the client application with a license to access the APS so that the client application could use the handle to access the shared application. After the client application completes its task, the APS handle terminates and the corresponding resources are then released.

During the process of interaction described above, the client application cannot access the shared application without authorization. This performance issue is solved by the AMS and APFSs.

The reliability of the system is assured, such as handling the exception that one APS is down while it is being processed.

3   System Design and Overview

In this section, a legacy application for gear design optimization, GearOpt [5], is used to illustrate the Service-Oriented Architecture (SOA) based approach for LAW. Rather than using Web service, Globus Toolkit is utilized in this research to develop the system so that the system can support Grid Computing. The original GearOpt is a single user version without distributed features. As the demand of using this application for gear design is increasing, the authors decide to wrap it and enable it with network features. The Service-Oriented Architecture is employed.

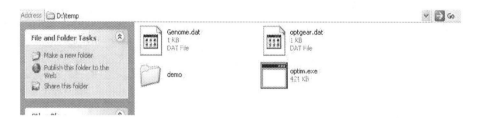

Fig. 2. The screen shot of the file folder

The original application has the functions of genetic algorithm (GA) and numerical analysis for gear strength calculation to the British Standard BS 436. As shown in Figure 2, the two data files are used to setup the optimization specifications (goals, weight factors, population size and number of tests); the .exe file, which is the GA program, conducts the optimization and the numerical analysis program is invoked by the GA program in the optimization process to calculate the tooth strength. After the calculation, the results are stored in a folder named "demo". This GA application was built long time ago; compared with nowadays applications with friendly interfaces, this application is not convenient to use for local users, lack of network invoking features.

However this program is useful and powerful; for the copyright reason, the program owner is reluctant to give it away to other unauthorized users. To solve the two problems, the authors decide to wrap it using the service-oriented approach based on Grid.

The GA and numerical analysis programs are the core of the software. So the aim is to wrap the GA program and the numerical analysis program with service and to build a GUI client application to interact with the service provider. The input parameters of GA program are stored in the .dat files and the location of the files is specified from command line arguments. In the Java language, the class Runtime has a method called exec. This method executes an executable file and specifies the command line arguments. After the GA program calculates the gear parameters, it produces the results as a file in its working directory. The Runtime.exec() method also specifies the working directory. So the input and output of the GA application can be redirected.

4 System Implementation

4.1 Implementation of Client Interface

As shown above, the Grid Portal (client application) is used by remote users to capture the input parameters. The parameters are obtained in the client side from the input of user (this process will be shown later in the experiment session). As shown in Figure 3, the main interface is pretty much friendly to the users. With the help of the Grid Portal, the user input will generate as a .dat file and this file will be transferred to the server.

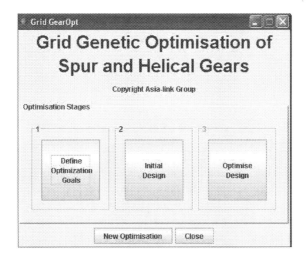

Fig. 3. The main interface of client application

4.2 Implementation of Services

The major tasks for implementation of the service-based approach for software sharing include 1) packing the application with an APS; 2) implementation of APFS; and 3) implementation of AMS.

1. Application packing

The APS represents a process of activating a shared application. When a request arrives, the APS delegates the request as local function calls to the associated process. The primary issue of this service is how to pack the GA application with an APS.

The GA application is a standalone executable file with the input from two 'dat' files and the output to specified files in a folder. This kind of application is very difficult to be packed into services. The system is written in Java language where the System.setIn() method is used to replace standard input stream with a network input stream. So aided application has been written to redirect the I/O stream of the original application, and then interface is exposed using service. APS is assigned to the GA program by executeFile=D:\\temp\\optim.exe. What's more, the original executable file 'optim.exe' is for a single user, which can only be executed once at one time in a single computer since it's developed. The authors need to change it into a multi-user enabled application, so before the APS invokes the application, APS should appoint the application run in one thread rather than in process, so that the application can simultaneously be executed many times in back office. For application in each thread, a separate folder to store its output and input is assigned.

2. The implementation of APFS

GA APFS has a function to create an APS. When a creating request arrives, the application proxy factory should check the status of the local computers to determine whether a new APS could be created or not. After a new APS is created, the APFS allocates the resource required by the APS, and then registers the APS to a proxy service catalogue. This catalogue is stored in XML format. APFS is assigned with one APS by apsURL=http://192.168.1.58:8080/ogsa/services/spb/APS. APFS should also specify the output location by outputDIR=D:\\temp.

3. The implementation of AMS

The main function of the AMS is to deal with the performance and security issues. The AMS provides a catalogue containing URIs of all registered APFSs. The application identifier identifies all the APFSs of a shared application. As mentioned in the above sections, each APFS represents a shared application in a computer. So the application identifier is used to look up all the APFSs of a shared application. In the experiments conducted by the authors, three computers are equipped as the service provider: gearopt=http://192.168.1.58:8080/ogsa/services/spb/APFS,

http://192.168.1.57:8080/ogsa/services/spb/APFS
http://192.168.1.56:8080/ogsa/services/spb/APFS

The APFS catalogue is implemented via an interface, which connects to a relational database, typically a MySQL database. Each APFS is registered as a database entry containing an application identifier and URI of the application Proxy factory service. When looking up a specific shared application, the URIs of APFSs with the same application identifier should be returned. Then the AMS interacts with the APFSs use these URIs to create an APS.

In order to achieve higher performance, a shared application could be installed in multiple computers with an APS associated with each one. Then all the APFSs are registered to the AMS. When creating an APS, the AMS polls these APSs and chooses one, which has reported that there are enough resources to create a new APS.

There is also a table used to store the Access Control List (ACL) information for a shared application in the factory service catalogue. In the current version, the AMS use PKI (Public Key Infrastructure) [6] for access control. Each entry in the ACL table contains certificate information of each application identifier with its authorized users who could use the application. When a client application requests to use a shared application, it sends its certificate information in a SOAP (Simple Object Access Protocol) header to the application manager. Then the application manager checks whether the client application could use the shared application by using the ACL table. If the client application has access right, the AMS signs a certificate to the client application. This certificate expires after the client application finishes its tasks. In the last step, the AMS uses the APFS to create an APS, and then returns the handle of the APS to the client application, which finally uses the certificate given by the application manager to interact with the created APS.

5   The Deployment of Services

After the implementation, the services need to be deployed and published. A service description file should be written for each service to be recognized by the server container—Globus Platform. A .wsdd file is used to deploy services. In this research three files are written as shown in figures 4-6. These figures represent the deployment files of APS, APFS and AMS, respectively.

```
- <service name="spb/APS" provider="Handler" style="wrapped" use="literal">
    <parameter name="operationProviders" value="org.globus.ogsa.impl.ogsi.FactoryProvider
      org.globus.ogsa.impl.ogsi.NotificationSourceProvider" />
    <parameter name="persistent" value="true" />
    <parameter name="instance-schemaPath" value="schema/GridGearOpt/APS/APSService.wsdl" />
    <parameter name="schemaPath" value="schema/ogsi/ogsi_notification_factory_service.wsdl" />
    <parameter name="baseClassName" value="org.globus.ogsa.impl.ogsi.GridServiceImpl" />
    <parameter name="handlerClass" value="org.globus.ogsa.handlers.RPCURIProvider" />
    <parameter name="className" value="org.gridforum.ogsi.NotificationFactory" />
    <parameter name="allowedMethods" value="*" />
    <parameter name="factoryCallback" value="org.globus.ogsa.impl.ogsi.DynamicFactoryCallbackImpl" />
    <parameter name="instance-baseClassName" value="edu.ntu.APS.impl.APSImpl" />
    <beanMapping qname="ns:GenomeVO" xmlns:ns="urn:APSService" languageSpecificType="java:edu.ntu.vo.GenomeVO" />
    <beanMapping qname="ns:OptGearVO" xmlns:ns="urn:APSService" languageSpecificType="java:edu.ntu.vo.OptGearVO" />
    <beanMapping qname="ns:ResultVO" xmlns:ns="urn:APSService" languageSpecificType="java:edu.ntu.vo.ResultVO" />
  </service>
```

Fig. 4. Deployment file of APS

```
- <service name="spb/AMS" provider="Handler" style="wrapped" use="literal">
    <parameter name="baseClassName" value="edu.ntu.AMS.impl.AMSImpl" />
    <parameter name="allowedMethods" value="*" />
    <parameter name="persistent" value="true" />
    <parameter name="schemaPath" value="schema/GridGearOpt/AMS/AMSService.wsdl" />
    <parameter name="authorization" value="self" />
    <parameter name="handlerClass" value="org.globus.ogsa.handlers.RPCURIProvider" />
    <parameter name="className" value="edu.ntu.AMS.AMSPortType" />
  </service>
```

Fig. 5. Deployment file of APS

```
- <service name="spb/APFS" provider="Handler" style="wrapped" use="literal">
    <parameter name="baseClassName" value="edu.ntu.APFS.impl.APFSImpl" />
    <parameter name="allowedMethods" value="*" />
    <parameter name="persistent" value="true" />
    <parameter name="schemaPath" value="schema/GridGearOpt/APFS/APFSService.wsdl" />
    <parameter name="authorization" value="self" />
    <parameter name="handlerClass" value="org.globus.ogsa.handlers.RPCURIProvider" />
    <parameter name="className" value="edu.ntu.APFS.APFSPortType" />
  </service>
```

Fig. 6. Deployment file of APS

6 Experiment

After the implementation of services and the preparation of deployment file, it is the time for doing experiment. In this experiment, AMS is deployed in the central computer, while APFS and APS are deployed in three individual computers.

Fig. 7. The login frame

Figure 7 is the login frame when the application in client is started. After login into the system, the main frame (Figure 3 in Section 4) comes out. In the main frame, the user define optimization goals in "Define Optimization Goals" panel, then input parameters in "Optimization Parameters" panel, and when ready, click on "Continue".

The list shown in Figure 8 is for the user to identify which design parameters are to be optimized. Selection of parameters will include them in the optimization process. Non selection will freeze the values to those defined in the initial design. The process is capable of optimizing the performance of both variable and fixed centre distance gear pairs.

There are five optimization goals: facewidth, contact ratio, centre distance, equal stress and equal slide/roll. The goals of the search are defined by adjusting the importance of the 5 fitness functions (shown in Figure 9).

The characteristics of the GA, i.e., population size and number of tests are set by the user with the aid of the form illustrated in Figure 10. Figure 10 is the last page of Define Optimization Goal function. After clicking "finish", the screen will changed to the entrance frame again (Figure 3 in Section 4). Now it is time to setup initial parameters of the Gear by clicking on "Initial Design".

The initial design provides the starting point of the optimization search, as shown in Figure 11 and Figure 12. For this purpose, the basic configuration of the gear must be provided, including geometry, performance and material information. These are prompted for user input or default values are provided.

After click "finish", the parameters and information will be sent for calculation and after that, the final result come out (Figure 13).

It should be noticed that the experiment is done using three computers located in three different locations, and they are providing the service in meantime.

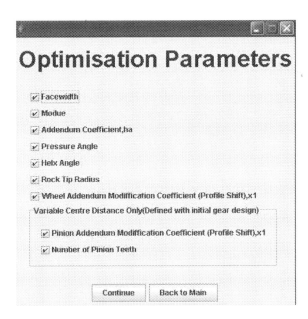

Fig. 8. The optimization parameters panel

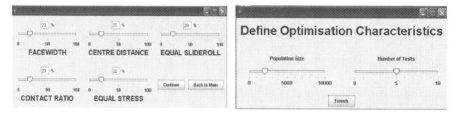

Fig. 9. Importance of the 5 fitness functions

Fig. 10. The panel to define optimization characteristics

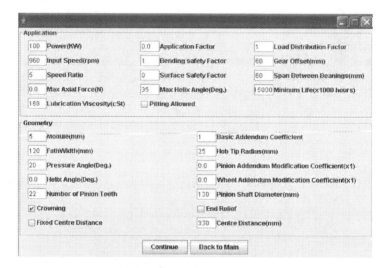

Fig. 11. The initial design parameters (part 1)

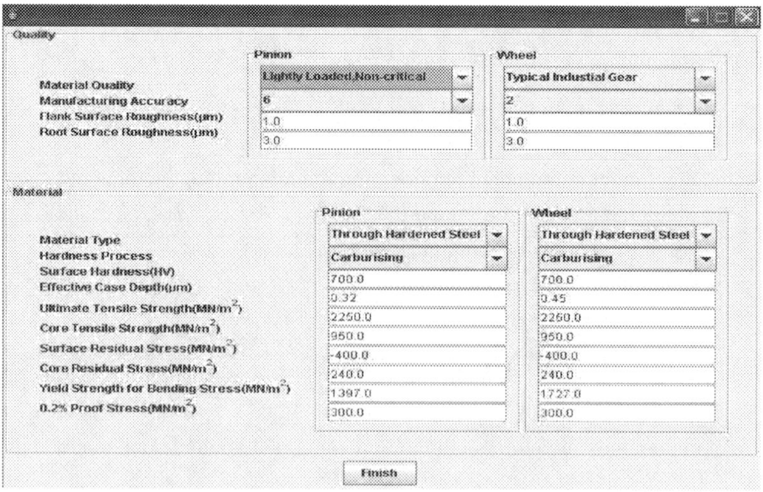

Fig. 12. The initial design parameters (part 2)

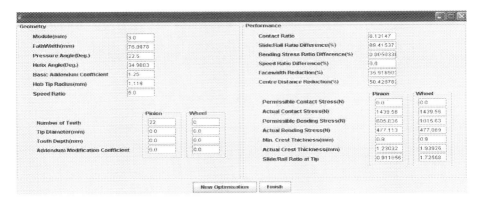

Fig. 13. The result panel

7 Conclusion

A case study for gear design optimization has conducted to illustrate the three services approach for wrapping legacy applications into Grid Services. This paper presents the details of the implementation and experiment of a service-oriented software package bank. The authors migrated a standalone and single user application into a powerful multi-user grid service with a user friendly GUI application. This approach is extremely important to solve the legacy code problem and copyright problem. Many old engineering applications can be re-used by this method.

References

1. Su, D. and Amin, N.: A CGI-based approach for remotely excusing a large program for integration of design and manufacturing over the Internet. International Journal of Computer Integrated Manufacturing 14(1) (2001) 55-65
2. Cotroneo, D., Mazzocca, N., Romano, L. and Russo, S.: Building a dependable system from a legacy application with CORBA. Journal of System and Architecture 48 (2002) 81-98
3. Kacsuk, P., Goyeneche, A., Delaitre, T., Kiss, T., Farkas, Z. and Boczko, T.: High level Grid application environment to use legacy codes as OGSA Grid Services. Proc. Fifth IEEE/ACM International Workshop on Grid Computing (2004) 428-435
4. Xiong, Y., Su, D.: A Web-Service Based Approach for Software Sharing. Lecture Notes in Computer Science 3865 (2006) 215-224
5. Su, D. and Wakelam, M.: Evolutionary optimisation within an intelligent hybrid system for design integration. Artficial Intelligence for Engineering Design, Analysis and Manufacturing Journal 5 (1999) 351-363
6. Weise, J.: Public Key Infrastructure Overview. SunPSSM Global Security Practice (2001) URL: http://www.sun.com/blueprints/0801/publickey.pdf

Service and Components Oriented Environment for Conducting Product Design Specification

Jiachen Hou and Daizhong Su

Advanced Design and Manufacturing Engineering Centre,
School of Architecture, Design and the Built Environment,
Nottingham Trent University, UK
Jiachen.hou@ntu.ac.uk, daizhong.su@ntu.ac.uk

Abstract. Product design specification (PDS) is a key step regarding the whole total design process. It is crucial for people who are involved in the product design process to efficiently share and reuse the PDS and related information. With the support of state-of-the-art technologies, in particular, Web Services and Enterprise JavaBeans (EJB), a distributed environment has been established which made future engagements in information utilizing for PDS simpler, faster and more efficient. In this paper, a brief review of the importance of PDS in the entire total design process is given first, followed by the presentation of the technologies involved in this PDS environment. This distributed environment will help manufacturers accelerate product to market and minimize potential design errors in the early product stage.

1 Introduction

Accelerating speed of product to markets is an imperative factor for manufacturers to remain a competitive position within today's turbulence environment. In the current global "climate", many factors exist and interact with each other in the process of a product development cycle in order to deliver a right product in a timely manner. Several stages are involved in the design of a new product. Eliminating errors in early stages of product development would be a greater possibility for preventing from being carried through into the high-cost end of design. Product Design Specification (PDS) is a crucial step within the total design process, which guides all the subsequent stages in the entire activities [1-3]. Many researchers have paid great attentions to the total design process from various angles, specifically, concept design and detail design [4-9]. Surprisingly, PDS stage is not particular addressed as forenamed. As an important document, a PDS is the fundamental control mechanism, which needs to be constantly referred to ensure that a product is in an appropriate track. At each review, comparisons should be made with the PDS, which itself may has changed due to additional and more up-to-date information on market shifts, or a more enhanced knowledge of the product design [1-3]. The concept of PDS refers to the whole product; however, most of products are likely broken down to the component level. As Pugh [1] suggested that to take advantages of this breakdown, it is necessary to refer to component design specification, namely, partial PDS.

W. Shen et al. (Eds.): CSCWD 2006, LNCS 4402, pp. 530–539, 2007.
© Springer-Verlag Berlin Heidelberg 2007

Partial PDS is especially important when design in teams, because it is vital that the whole team solve the same problems to meet the requirements of PDS. Sometimes, different team members will be working on slightly different problems—without knowing it. As indicated by many researchers, a common error in design is that the designers forgot to consider the impact of one or more product characteristics in their work [1][3][9]. These kinds of problems can be rather scanty but could lead to unexpected losses in efficiency and product quality. In addition, under the integrated global environment, unpredictable changes in markets and fast product development have gave pressures to design teams, and, as a result, designing a best fit product in a timely manner is evitable trend to keep a competitive position. In their survey, Hollins and Pugh discovered that the PDS was brief, incomplete and based on very poorly organized market research was a case for many companies; conversely, the most successful companies were those that had the most thorough and the complete PDS [10]. The key to a good PDS is to have the right information presented in the best possible way.

Effectively sharing and reusing partial PDS related information would reduce the time of product design, enhance reliability and finally maximize potential success and add value to the product. With Internet widely spreading, design teams can work more closely regardless of their geographical location by utilizing the Web technology; however, as reflected by the disparate and heterogeneous set of platforms and application development environments, developmental and operational inefficiencies have been driving up [11-12]. Finding an appropriate approach is vital for significantly using the PDS information. Completing an appropriate PDS involves people with different functions; asynchronous operation systems and platforms have been major barriers for efficiently accessing the information, therefore, overcoming these shortages became the top priority for more effectively using PDS information. The aim of the research is to establish a distributed environment with capabilities of exchanging and transferring partial PDS related information for people who are involved in the design process. The environment will provide the following features:

- Modular Decomposability: it can break the PDS information into smaller modules. Each module is responsible for a single function, which can be reused and extended.
- Scalability: it can support a growing number of users who use asynchrony operation systems and platform.
- Portability and Flexibility: once the code has been deployed, it can be performed by using asynchronous backend system with minimal changes

This research is concentrated on providing a distributed environment in order to effectively allocate and transfer PDS information; thus, a detailed exploration of PDS is out of the scope of the paper, and, hence, the area is not great emphasized here. In the following sections, Web-based techniques utilized for this environment are introduced first, followed by the presentation of the EJB based components and implementations that are utilized for the environment.

2 Web Technologies for the Environment Implementation

As a dynamic control document, PDS is required to span the space and time inherent in the design process and beyond [1-3]. It is vital to provide a more flexible and more efficient approach through the high degree of platform independence to capture and reuse the experience of the partial PDS in a significant way that future engagements can be made simpler and faster.

Distributed information sharing and communication are essential to support this distributed environment. The technologies, such as RPC, CORBA, Web Services, DCE, and COM exist for a few years [13]. Amongst the technologies, Web service has won exceeding popularity. Based on XML standards, Web services focus on minimizing the constraints, dependencies and manual integration effort across multiple, independent and disparate information systems. The technology was developed and widely supported by many major high--tech vendors, such as IBM, Sun Microsystems and BEA Systems. It has been considered as an excellent technology to solve distributed computing challenges for manufacturing in the Internet area. The Extensible Markup Language (XML), Simple Object Access Protocol (SOAP), Web Services Description Language (WSDL) and Universal Description, Discovery and Integration (UDDI) standards form the backbone of Web Services technology [13-15].

As a distributed environment over network, the interoperability, scalability, heterogeneity is inevitable factors when complementing the task; hence, it is crucial to apply right technology for the Web Services implementation. Java2 Enterprise Edition (J2EE) provides architecture for distributed enterprise applications. As the member of the J2EE family, Enterprise JavaBeans (EJB) is mainly utilized for the components implementation in this research. EJB has extended the functionality of applications by leveraging the penetration of browsers, which provide a solid platform for business logic and enterprise data [13][16-17]. The superior vantages of integrating the Web services and EJB technologies are to simplify the task of integrating across applications and prevent enterprise data from being locked up in an isolated application, meanwhile with the decomposability of EJB, each partial PDS could break into smaller modules, the relevant PDS documents could be reused and extended.

3 Components

Two types of EJB are employed in the Components section, in particular, session beans and entity beans. The functionality of the session beans is to implement Web services, the reasons for using session beans are because the session bean can shield the client from complexity by executing business logic inside the server, and also it can support multiple clients, which can offer better scalability for the partial PDS information that could required by large numbers of clients.

The entity beans are responsible for managing the partial PDS information in a persistent storage mechanism, such as a relational database. The entity beans can be shared by multiple clients; the beans' state exists beyond the lifetime of the application or the application server process. Two types of beans are consisted of the entity beans, namely, container managed persistence and bean managed persistence. Because of the natures of portability and flexibility, the container managed persistence is a more appropriate approach for managing PDS information than bean managed persistence. It means there is no need to modify or recompile the bean's code when applying different severs in which are performed by using various database, as EJB container handles all database access required by the entity bean.

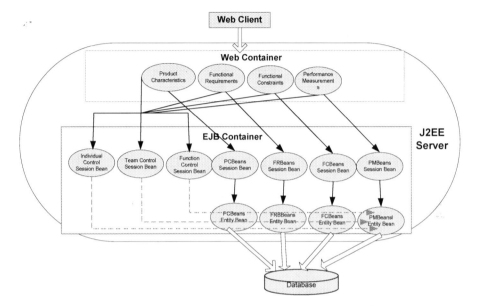

Fig. 1. EJB-oriented components

Figure 1 displays a path that session bean and entity bean can be connected together to perform the PDS information. Figure 1 indicates that the session beans and entity beans are included in the EJB container. The session beans are actually clients of the entity beans, which means the session beans are not directly access to the back end of the application; instead it works on behalf of the entity beans, because a session bean represents a single client within an Application Server which preventing the client from complexity by executing business tasks inside the server. For example, when a Web client requires the partial PDS information which relating to product's functional constraints, the request will be link to FCBeans session beans, consequently, the appropriate information will be retrieved from the backend application through PCBeans entity beans. The main advantages of using session beans and entity beans is to satisfy the demands when requestors increased, the logic can be updated easily without having to load new logic on every client's machines, meanwhile the data provided by this structure is hidden away from other components.

3.1 Functionality of Entity Beans for PDS

A partial PDS is a structured description of the purpose, functions, characteristics and other kinds of information that describes the design problem. Four kinds of information as design cores for all products, in particular, Product Characteristics, Functional

Requirements, Constrains, and Performance Metrics [1-3]. As mentioned in Introduction, the detailed exploration of PDS is out of the scope of the paper, therefore, only the brief explanation are given in the following.

PCBeans is an attribute of the product that describes the necessary characteristics of which a product must have in order for it to be succeeded in the market. The issues of affordability, usability, durability, maintainability, marketability, manufacturability, environmentally friendly, and ergonomic aesthetically pleasing are considered within the PCBeans.

FRBeans is a precise specification of the function of a product, which is focused on the operational features of the product. FRBeans define the capability and functionality of the product.

FCBeans define the performance limits of the product quantitatively. The functional constraints and the structural constraints are contained in the FCBeans.

PMBeans is a parameter that is used to measure the performance of a design with respect to relevant criterion. PMBeans are defined with respect to minimum, maximum, or optimum, which based on constraints in a design problem.

Each of the above cores has distinctive specialty to achieve certain functionality. To utilize the design cores efficiently, it is a crucial to organize them in a strategic manner.

Container managed entity bean is applied to represent the special region of PDS, which means the EJB container handles all database access requiring by the entity beans. The bean's code is not linked to a particular database, which has showed greater flexibility, scalability and portability. The reason for using entity beans to manage the PDS information is because the entity beans are considered to be long-lived, which allow shared access from multiple clients and live beyond the duration of the client's session with the server, as a result, design teams able to access PDS information synchronously without any interruptions. As mentioned earlier, generating a decent PDS requires considerable works between people from different departments; accordingly, concurrent collaboration is inevitable. In general, a product is made of different parts; each part has its unique functionality. The information for this partial PDS environment is divided into two categories. The one is the PDS information that have been completed by the design team, the reason for storing this type of information is to provide the supports for the design team, these information can be used as a reference guide for the further design; the other is the information that in their ongoing stage for design teams to complete. Due to people possess different priorities for sharing and editing the data, therefore, it is imperative to use container managed entity because the data can be transparently changed without affecting the rest of the application. In addition, entity beans are simplicity the task of accessing and manipulating, and it can be automatically reset to the state of the last committed transaction, which avoids the data loss when system crashes during the deployment.

As shown in Figure 1, the EJB container will automatically synchronize the EJB state with the database. Due to the EJB Beans run inside an EJB container, a client cannot instantiate the bean directly. Only the EJB container can instantiate an enterprise bean. Each entity bean includes an implementation of the ejbCreate() method because this enterprise bean allows callers to create new individual storage for the selected PDS information.

For convenience of manipulation, many to many relationships are established for the Entity beans: each type of information is broken up into individual table where each table represents data pertaining to the different type of PDS information. Each table has N: N relationships with its constituent individual table. The application stores the information in the database tables shown by Figure 2.

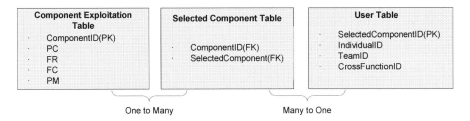

Fig. 2. Entity Bean based many-to-many relationships

Figure 2 indicates the relationship between Component Exploitation Table, Selected Component Table and User Table (The Figure 2 denotes a primary key with PK and a foreign key with FK). For example, there are four types of information for a partial PDS, and each contains several certain information, each qualified user can select related information under the components and the information can be viewed by several users concurrently. In this case, the Selected Component table can be treated as a cross-reference table. A cross-reference table containing the foreign keys can be represented a many-to-many relationship; each entity may be related to multiple occurrences of the other entity.

These tables are accessed by three EJB components, namely UserEJB, ComponentEJB, and selectionEJB. The UserEJB and ComponentEJB classes are complementary. Each class contains an ArrayList of foreign keys. The UserEJB class contains an ArrayList named ComponentIds, which identifies the Component the User is selected in. The ejbLoad method adds elements to the ComponentIds ArrayList by calling loadComponentIds, a private method. The loadComponentIds method gets the SelectedComponent identifiers from the bean. Only the selectionEJB class accesses the selection table. Therefore, the selectionEJB class manages the user-component relationship represented in the Selected Component table.

3.2 Functionality of Session Beans for PDS

As illustrated in Figure 1, seven session beans are contained in the EJB container, in particular, Individual bean, Team bean, Cross Function bean, PCBeans Control, FRBeans Controller, FCBeans Controller, and PMBeans Controller. The business methods of these session beans perform the following tasks:

- Creating and removing entity beans
- Contacting with the entity beans
- Managing the relationship between the individual, team and cross function

- Recognizing the users' identification based on priorities
- Implementing Web Services

The purpose of the session bean is to run business logic for the client. From the client's point of view, the business methods seem to run within the local machine, in fact, they actually work remotely in the session bean, which increase the security concerns and improve the performance of the process. For example, Individual bean, Team bean, and Cross Function bean guarantee that the only users who meet the security roles can access the resource. These three session beans hold the logical containers that group users who share the same information and the role membership is used to control access to specific operations exposed by the information. Unlike the Entity bean, due to the short life cycle of session beans, the bean can be removed when a client ends the session. The bean must be associated with a particular user. Each authorized user possesses individual temporary and personal storages, respectively. The statelss and stateful session beans are collaborated together to perform the task. The stateless session beans work on any temporary storage and hold no client-specific state. After a valid user requires the appropriate partial PDS information, a new storage will be created. Because a user may leave without any appropriate partial PDS information, so the storage needs to be client-specific state without persistence. Unlike the stateless session beans, the stateful session beans enable users to manipulate PDS information from their personal storage. The beans can maintain the client's state, which means they can retain information for the client. When an individual selects any particular region of the PDS, and put it into any of the four kinds of Beans, the Session bean retains a list of the selected information. Each stateful session beans holds conversational state about the user's current storage, and it allows treating the entire storage as one independent object. In this case, a visitor could theoretically stop a visiting session and later return to the system and still access to the same information. After a bean has been deployed, it can be exploited as a Web Service for service requestors to consume.

4 Implementation

The Service Oriented Architecture is applied for this distributed environment which enables people who involved in the product design process to implement PDS solutions through re-use and share EJB based components.

The environment addresses interactions and collaborations between separate parties. It blends in nicely with a service-oriented architecture which fundamentally comprises of service consumers and service providers. The interactions and collaborations are implemented using WSDL to connect EJB oriented Web Services. Figure 3 indicates that a requested Web services can also be a client of other Web services. The roles of service providers and service requestors are logical constructs and a service can exhibit characteristics of both. Those Web services have been implemented by EJB components that are assembled into module.

According to the inherency of the Web service based environment, the potential users need to receive the service from this environment first in order to carry out the process. The environment follows the "find, bind and invoke" paradigm where a user performs dynamic service location by querying the UDDI registry for the environment; UDDI Registry is the enabler for service discovery, which provides the potential user with the interface contract, and the endpoint address for the environment. The services requestors can access the Web services using either XML over HTTP or a remote procedure call API with a SOAP interface. Both techniques return structured PDS data (Product Characteristics, Functional Requirements, Constrains, and Performance Metrics). To make it possible to use the service, the service providers need to provide a WSDL file, which contains the definition of the Web Services, the messages that can be sent to the service. Services Requestors with access to this WSDL file can write a client application to visit the PDS. To efficiently implement Service-Oriented architecture, a set of EJBs are exploited as Web Services, namely, individual control service, team control service, function control service, PCBeans control service, FRBBeans control service, FCBeans control service, and PMBeans control service.

The communication is via SOAP and relies on remote procedure calls implemented with the JavaAPI for XML-based Remote Procedure Call(JAX-RPC) runtime. The PDS seeker uses JAXR to send a query searching for EJB oriented service that supports JAX-RPC to a registry server. The PDS seeker requests the specified PDS information from each of the PDS service; the remote procedure calls are made to a session Bean that represents the certain PDS information. Figure 3 shows that the PDS seeker is a client of the PDS services. For example, the PCBeans control service is a statelss session bean that implement the PCBeans method. The PCBean is the bean's web service endpoint interface that must conform to the rule of a JAX-RPC service definition interface. It hides the stateless session bean from the client.

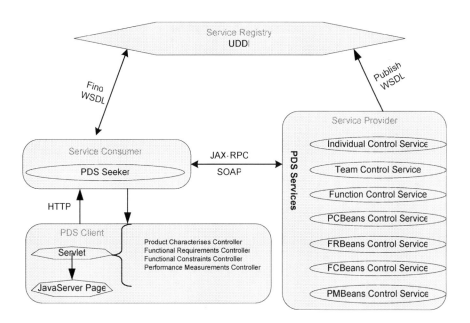

Fig. 3. Web Service oriented application flow for sharing PDS

There are several different approaches can be applied to implement the Service oriented environment, for example, a Web Service client can be based on JSP technology, or it can be a Swing-based client. As illustrates in Figure 3, the PDS Client can be a Servle-JSP based application to construct information. The Servlets is the controller. It examines the request URL, creates and initializes model EJB components, and dispatches requests to view JSP pages. For example, the Product CharacteristicsController accesses the PCBeans Control session bean through the bean's remote interfaces. PCBeans Control session beans access the PCBeans Entity Bean through their local interfaces. The Session Beans components contain the business logic for the application; they call the Web services and perform the information that returned from the services. Further illustration of these techniques is outside the scope of this paper, therefore, there is no need to present more detail implementations here.

5 Conclusions

Because PDS as a core activity that plays a vital role in total design, effectively sharing and reusing partial PDS related information for people who are engaged in the product design procedure will reduce time-to-market of the product, enhance product reliability, maximize potential success, and finally add value to the product. With the support of the-state-of-the-art technologies, a distributed environment has been developed to achieve the purposes.

The factors of interoperability, scalability, heterogeneity, decomposability and modifiability have been taken into account by utilizing Web Services and EJB technologies, which prevent data from being locked up in isolated application and increase the level of platform independence. Integrating Web Service and EJB technology within the distributed environment for sharing PDS information could improve the performance of the entire product design, separate design concerns, decrease code duplication, centralize control, and make the process more flexible. This distributed environment will help manufacturers accelerate product's time to market and minimize potential design errors in the early product stage.

Acknowledgments. The authors are grateful for the support received from the EU Asia-Link program (grant No. ASI/B7-301/98/679 -023) and Asia IT&C program (Grant No. ASI/B7-301/3152-099/71553) for carrying out the research reported in this paper.

References

1. Pugh, S.: Total Design-Integrated Methods for Successful Product Engineering. Prentice Hall (1990) 44-65
2. Booker, J.C., Raines, M., Swift, K.G.: Designing Capable and Reliable Products. Butterworth Heinemann (2001)
3. Ulrich, K.T., Eppinger, S.D.: Product Design and Development. McGraw Hill (2000)
4. Dong, Y., Tan, J.R., Xu, J.: Design reuse method for assemblies in concept design. Chinese Journal of Mechanical Engineering 18(1) (2005) 132-138

5. Yang, M.C.: Concept generation and sketching: Correlations with design outcome. Proceedings of the ASME Design Engineering Technical Conference. Vol. 3 (2003) 829-834
6. Dong, S.G.: The architectural attributes of components and the transaction patterns of detail design drawings: A case study on China's motorcycle industry. International Journal of Automotive Technology and Management 5(1) (2005) 46-70
7. De, J.H., Beukers, A., Van, T.: Two simple design problems, which illustrate the multidisciplinary concept. Applied Composite Materials 12(1) (2005) 13-19
8. Sobek, I., Durward, K.: Transitions: From conceptual ideas to detail design. Proc. ASME Annual Conference and Exposition (2005) 14539-14548
9. Farrell, R.S., Stump, G., Park, J., Simpson, T.W.: A prototype web-based custom product specification system. Proceedings of the 2003 ASME Design Engineering Technical Conference. Vol. 1B. Chicago, IL (2003) 937-945
10. Hollins, B., Pugh, S.: Successful Product Design. Butterworths (1990)
11. Hou, J., Su, D., Hull, B.: Integration of Web Service with the business models within the total product design process for supplier selection. Computer in Industry (Article in Press)
12. Su, D., Hull, B., Hou, J.: Management of networked organizations using a web-enabled collaborative environment. In: Cha, J. et al. (eds.): Advanced Design, Production and Management Systems. A.A. Balkema Publishers (2003) 259-264
13. JavaSun. Java Technology--Java Technology and Web Services.
    URL: http://java.sun.com/webservices/index.jsp
14. JavaSun. Java Technology--Java 2 Platform, Enterprise Edition (J2EE).
    URL: http://java.sun.com/j2ee/index.jsp
15. MSDN. Web Services Developer Center. URL: http://msdn.microsoft.com/webservices/
16. IBM. SOA and Web Services. URL: http://www136.ibm.com/developerworks/websevices/
17. IBM. Best Practice in EJB. URL: http://www-900.ibm.com/developerWorks/cn/java/jejbcol/index.shtml
18. IBM. Optimizing container-managed persistence EJB entity beans.
    URL: http:// www106.ibm.com/developerworks/ibm/library/i-opti

Web Service Success Factors
from Users' Behavioral Perspective

Yingwu Chen, Yan Liu, and Changfeng Zhou

College of Information System and Management,
National University of Defense Technology,
410073 Changsha Hunan Province P.R. China
{ywchen, cfzhou}@nudt.edu.cn, 6lucy@sina.com

Abstract. Web services have generated great interests both in academia and in-dustry. This study proposes an intergraded model for the empirical examination of the users' intention and behavior for using web services. An electronic ques-tionnaire is used to collect sample data. The results show that users' overall sat-isfaction, specifically explained by perceived usefulness and perceived service quality of web services, significantly affects their intention to use web services.

1 Introduction

Web services for satisfying personal needs are growing at a rate to take advantage of the basic Internet infrastructure. According to Santos [1], one of the important factors of the web is that it offers an interactive function with its customers. As the depend-ency on web services increases, so does the need to assess factors associated with web site success. From a pragmatic point of view, understanding the determinants of using web should ensure an effective deployment of information technology resources in an organization. Therefore, it is necessary to elicit the factors affecting the web service, especially from the users' behavioral perspectives.

2 Literature Review

Web-based services move services and support functions onto the Internet, away from high-cost environments where they are traditionally performed. The general definition of IS success is: the extent to which a system achieves the goals for which it was designed [2]. A Web site is a new type of information technology. It is clear that in today's highly competitive and global marketplace, a comprehensive Internet strategy is a business imperative. As many of the traditional influencers and differentiators are being removed, companies and organizations of all sizes must leverage the Internet's unique capabilities.

As businesses move key functions and processes to the Web, a strategy that utilizes the Web for competitive advantage will be a key for future success [3]. Hoffman and Novak [4], in addressing the role of marketing in a hypermedia computer-mediated environment, propose a broad structural model of consumer navigation of the Web.

W. Shen et al. (Eds.): CSCWD 2006, LNCS 4402, pp. 540–548, 2007.
© Springer-Verlag Berlin Heidelberg 2007

Atkinson and Kydd [5] also distinguished between intrinsic and extrinsic factors affecting Web use with differential usage for entertainment or research purposes. Eighmey [6] considered two questions about the benefits delivered by commercial Web sites, as well as the approach that delivers the greatest benefit. Liu and Arnett [7] concluded that four factors are critical to Web site success: information and service quality; system use; playfulness and system design quality. However, little research exists above the combination of these factors, and one important construct is not included in such research: the tasks for which the web is used. Therefore, the overall aims of this study are to develop a framework and to elicit the factors affecting the web service from the behavioral perspectives of the end users.

3   Theoretical Framework

There are three theoretical concepts that provide literature anchors at an individual level for the development of the research framework.

3.1   Technology Acceptance Model (TAM)

Technology Acceptance Model (TAM) [8] was developed to increase understanding and improve predictions of user acceptance of technology at an individual level and has been around for almost two decades [9-13]. The theory has its routes in social psychology literature, specifically, Fishbein and Ajzen's theory of reasoned action (TRA) [14], which considers norms, beliefs and attitude important in understanding behavioral intention to perform an action. The two key independent variables of perceived usefulness and perceived ease of use are said to influence the individual's attitude towards using a technology, which has a subsequent impact on behavioral intention to use and ultimately actual use of the technology.

3.2   Theory of Planned Behavior (TPB)

Theory of Planned Behavior provides comprehensive understanding of usage behaviors and intentions and serves our research as the theoretical background. A central proposition of Theory of Planned Behavior, which is closely related to Technology Acceptance Model (TAM) and has received considerable empirical support [15], in the context of information technology usage, is that the users' actual behavior (B) is determined by their behavioral intention (BI) to use the technology. That is, people tend to better adopt a new IT when they have more intention to use it. Equally important is another proposition about the so called perceived behavioral control (PBC) that the actual usage behavior is also affected by whether the users have perceived sufficient control of capability and resources necessary to adopt the IT.

3.3   Self Service Technology (SST)

Laudon and Laudon [16] emphasize that the Web and other network technologies are inspiring new approaches to customers' service and support. In addition, these changes have occurred mainly through the development of technology-based self-service formats, which enable consumers to perform services for them quickly and conveniently [17]. Some common applications of automated self-service include conducting bank transactions through automated teller machines, shipping through the Internet, making reservations and purchasing tickets through kiosks, and using self-scanning systems at supermarkets. The web-based self-service also allows customers to track orders or the status of their accounts online with our human intervention [18].

Based on such theories, our integrated model is further expanded to include the constructs and relations that might be important in web usage. We take a decomposition approach to belief structures, the user' perceived service quality (SQ) of the information provided by the web sites is determined jointly by their perceived usefulness (U) and perceived ease of use (EOU) of the web service. The users' perceived behavioral control is determined jointly by self-efficacy (SE) and Learning capability (LC). Our proposed model is summarized in Figure 1 based on the previous discuss.

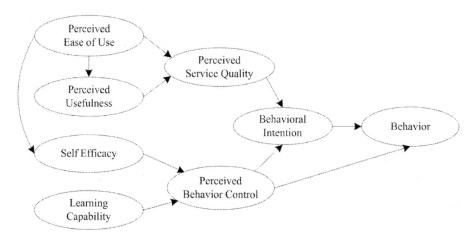

Fig. 1. The Theoretical Framework

Perceived ease of use (EOU). Ease of use is related to an easy-to-remember URL address, well-organized, well-structures, and easy to follow catalog, site navigability, and concise and understandable contents, terms and conditions. An overview of the site and appropriate navigation structures is available in [19]. According to Technology Acceptance Model mentioned previously, the users' ease of use is a direct determinant of their perceived usefulness of web. In addition to the theoretical basis, there are intuitive and practical bases to surmise that the users' perceived ease of use and their self-efficacy for adopting web is closely linked. This leads to the following hypothesis:

- H_1: Perceived ease of use affects positively Perceived usefulness.
- H_2: Perceived ease of use affects positively Self-efficacy.

Perceived usefulness (U). Perceived usefulness is defined as "the degree to which user believes that using a particular system would enhance his or her performance."

Perceived service quality (SQ). Prior studies have stressed the importance of providing high quality of service [20, 21]. In our proposed model in Figure 1, Perceived service quality is positively influenced by Perceived ease of use and Perceived usefulness. This leads to the following hypothesis:

- H_3: Perceived ease of use affects positively Perceived service quality.
- H_4: Perceived usefulness affects positively Perceived service quality.

Self-efficacy (SE). Self-efficacy reflects the users' confidence in their knowledge and ability of mastering the computing technology required by the web.

Learning capability (LC). Learning capability refers to the availability of the resources such as computers and the Internet access necessary to perform the web service. Web is an interactive function between customers and business enterprises [22]. Many studies have emphasized the importance of the two-way on-line communication between customers and firms [23,24].

Perceived behavioral control (PBC). Perceived behavioral control refers to users' confidence in having perceived sufficient control of capability and resources necessary to adopt web service. In our proposed model in Figure 1, Perceived behavioral control is positively influenced by Self-efficacy and Learning capability. This leads to the following hypothesis:

- H_5: Self-efficacy affects positively Perceived behavioral control.
- H_6: Learning capability affects positively Perceived behavioral control.

Behavioral intention (BI). Behavioral intention is modeled as a function of Perceived service quality and Perceived behavioral control. This leads to the following hypothesis:

- H_7: Perceived service quality affects positively behavioral intention.
- H_8: Perceived behavioral control affects positively behavioral intention.

End user's behavior (B). The users' actual behavior is determined by their behavioral intention (BI) to use the technology. That is, people tend to better adopt a new web service when they have more intention to use it. Equally important is another proposition about the perceived behavioral control (PBC). This leads to the following hypothesis:

- H_9: Behavioral intention affects positively End user's behavior.
- H_{10}: Perceived behavioral control affects positively End user's behavior.

4 Research Methodology

4.1 Research Sample

The research model is validated through an online survey study. Pitkow and Recker present all the advantages of the online surveying method [25]. The target population is undergraduate students who have experienced with browsing and searching for the information in Web portals.

4.2 Electronic Questionnaire Design

The electronic questionnaire is divided into two parts. The first part set out to get the general profiles of respondents in six universities. The profiles include age, gender, and level of education. The second part examines the factors that associate with the perception of service delivered through the web sites. These factors are Perceived ease of use, Perceived usefulness, Perceived service quality, Self-efficacy, Learning capability, Perceived behavioral control, Behavioral intention and End user's behavior. Twenty six questionnaire items are established to measure level of agreement or perception of users toward web service. A five point Likert scale, ranging from 1 (strongly disagree) to 5 (strongly agree), is used.

4.3 Data Analysis

The model is tested by means of the statistical analysis method of Structure Equation Model (SEM). Although the maximum likelihood (ML) approach is a frequently used estimation procedure for SEM, The proposed SEM in this article adopted the Partial Least Squares (PLS) approach. PLS is a so called component based method, which refers to the distinct estimation of LV specific measurement models and the structural model [26]. PLS is able to handle formative as well as reflective MV, potentially exclusively or jointly in one structural model. Further on, PLS estimations can handle a large model without problems and require rather only a small number of data sets. Additionally, the PLS estimation is a nonparametric calculus, i.e., none of the distribution parameters of the MV, which have to be considered with LISREL, have great influence on the results [27]. The computer program used for this analysis was the PLS Graph version 3.0 [28], and the bootstrap re-sampling method determined the significance of the paths within the structural model.

5   Results and Discussion

5.1   The Respondent Profile

A total of 160 questionnaires were distributed, eight of the returned questionnaires were incomplete and were discarded, producing a total of 152 usable questionnaires. The sample size of 152 exceeded the recommended minimum of 45 and was adequate for model testing. The demographic profile of the respondents such as age, gender, and level of education in the university are shown in Table 1.

Table 1. Characteristics of Response

	Characteristics	Number	Percentage (%)
Age	≤20	30	19.7
	21	51	33.6
	22	45	29.6
	≥23	26	17.1
Gender	Male	102	67.1
	Female	50	32.9
Level of Education	Freshman	42	27.6
	Sophomore	55	36.2
	Junior	36	23.7
	Senior	19	12.5

5.2 The Measurement Model Testing

In this paper, internal consistency and convergent validity are used to test the measurement model. Internal consistency is a measure of the homogeneity of a scale. Nunnally's recommended level of 0.7 for evaluating composite reliability can be used to assess internal consistency [29]. Convergent validity identifies whether different measurements reflect the same construct. Convergent validity is adequate when constructs have an Average Variance Extracted (AVE) of at least 0.5 [30].

Table 2. Results of Testing the Measurement Model

Construct	Mean	Std. Dev	Loading
Perceived ease of use(CR = 0.82 AVE = 0.63)			
EOU1	4.07	0.71	0.64
EOU2	3.72	0.77	0.80
EOU3	3.89	0.72	0.82
EOU4	3.90	0.75	0.88
Perceived usefulness (CR = 0.77 AVE = 0.54)			
U1	3.72	0.73	0.74
U2	3.90	0.67	0.53
U3	3.94	0.64	0.75
Perceived service quality (CR = 0.65 AVE = 0.41)			
SQ1	3.40	0.81	0.76
SQ2	3.70	0.79	0.79
SQ3	3.78	0.80	0.35
Self-efficacy (CR = 0.88 AVE = 0.79)			
SE1	4.08	0.68	0.82
SE2	4.12	0.72	0.88
SE3	3.37	0.75	0.76
Learning capability (CR = 0.76 AVE = 0.55)			
LC1	3.80	0.74	0.74
LC2	3.85	0.68	0.80
LC3	3.93	0.73	0.72
Perceived behavioral control (CR = 0.79 AVE = 0.64)			
PBC1	4.23	0.53	0.71
PBC2	3.69	0.66	0.68
PBC3	3.88	0.70	0.79
PBC4	3.83	0.69	0.66
Behavioral intention (CR =0.75 AVE =0.63)			
BI1	3.28	0.96	0.78
BI2	3.32	1.37	0.65
BI3	3.79	0.89	0.83
Behavior(CR =0.84 AVE =0.52)			
B1	3.17	0.97	0.53
B2	3.32	0.88	0.69
B3	2.74	0.76	0.52

Table 2 presents the results of the tests of measurement model. The composite reliabilities of all constructs are at least 0.70, except for the factor of Perceived service quality (0.65), thus indicating adequate internal consistency. All factor loadings are greater than 0.55 except for one item of Perceived service quality. Most of the constructs have an AVE of at least 0.5 except for Perceived service quality (0.41). The results show that convergent validity is satisfactory for the constructs.

5.3 The Structural Model Testing

Path coefficients and the R^2 values are used to test structural model. The path coefficients represent the strength and direction of the relationships among the variables. The R^2 indicates the proportion of endogenous variables that can be explained by the exogenous variables of the model. The path coefficients and R^2 values of structural model are presented in Figure 2.

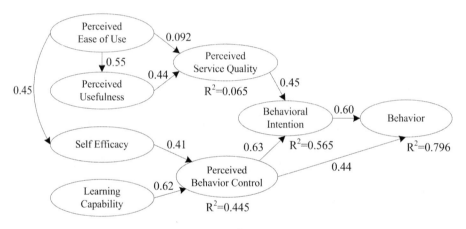

Fig. 2. Path Coefficients and R^2 Values of Structural Model

Our empirical results show that about 79.6% of variances in behavior are explained by behavioral intention and perceived behavioral control. Both hypotheses H_9 and H_{10} are verified. These factors have path coefficients of 0.60 and 0.44 respectively.

Perceived service quality and perceived behavioral control all contribute to behavioral intention, thus supporting H_7 and H_8. These factors have path coefficients of 0.45 and 0.63 respectively, with a total R^2 of 0.565.

The R^2 for perceived service quality is 0.065, suggesting that other important determinants for perceived service quality have been omitted in this model, so H_3 and H_4 are rejected.

Self-efficacy and learning capability both contribute to perceived behavioral control, supporting H_5 and H_6. These factors have path coefficients of 0.41 and 0.62 respectively, with a total R^2 of 0.445.

As hypothesized, perceived ease of use have a significant effect on self-efficacy (path =0.45), so H_2 is supported. In addition, the perceived ease of use effect perceived usefulness significantly (path =0.55), so H_1 is supported.

In sum, the results of 500 resamples indicated that, except for perceived service quality, all other paths are significant at the 0.5 level.

6 Conclusion

This study investigates success factors for web services from the end users' behavioral perspective. A theoretical framework is developed, through the integration of previous research. The model is then tested empirically through a longitudinal survey study. This exploratory work demonstrates that it is possible to develop preliminary scales for measuring user evaluation of the Web, and such scales are multidimensional. Factors identified by this research may be of interest to other researchers and providers interested in the evaluation of Web-based services.

References

1. Santos, F., e-Service quality: a model of virtual service quality dimensions. Managing Service Quality. 3 (2003) 233-246
2. Farhoomand, A.F. and Drury, D.H., Factors influencing electronic data interchange success, Data Base. 1 (1996) 45-57
3. Anton, J., Customer Service Life Cycle. Available online at: http://isds.bus.lsu.edu/cvoc/Projects/cslc/html/research.html (2000)
4. Hoffman, D.L., Novak, T.P., Marketing in hypermedia computer-mediated environments: conceptual foundations, Journal of Marketing. (1996) 50-68
5. Atkinson, M., Kydd, C., Individual characteristics associated with World Wide Web use: an empirical study of playfulness and motivation, The DATA BASE for Advances in Information Systems. 2 (1997) 53-61
6. Eighmey, J., Profiling user responses to commercial Web sites, Journal of Advertising Research. 3 (1997) 59-66
7. Liu, C., Arnett, K., Exploring the factors associated with Web site success in the context of electronic commerce, Information and Management. 1 (2000) 23-33
8. Davis, F. D., A technology acceptance model for empirically testing new end-user information systems: theory and results. Sloan School of Management, Massachusetts Institute of Technology. 1986.
9. Davis, F., Perceived Usefulness, Perceived Ease of Use, and User Acceptance of Information Technology. MIS Quarterly. 3 (1989) 319-340
10. Chau, P. Y. K., An empirical assessment of a modified technology acceptance model. Journal of Management Information Systems. 2 (1996) 185-204
11. Malhotra, Y. and Galletta, D. F., Extending the Technology Acceptance Model to Account for Social Influence: Theoretical Bases and Empirical Validation. In Thirty-Second Hawaii International Conference on System Sciences (HICSS), Maui, Hawaii. (1999)
12. Venkatesh, V. and Davis, F., A Theoretical Extension of the Technology Acceptance Model: Four Longitudinal Field Studies. Management Science. 2 (2000) 186-204
13. Brown, S. A. and Massey, A. P., Do I really have to? User acceptance of mandated technology. European Journal of Information Systems. 4 (2002) 283-295
14. Fishbein, M. and Ajzen, I., Belief, Attitude, Intentions and Behaviour: An Introduction to Theory and Research. Boston, Addison-Wesley. (1975)

15. Armitage, C. J. and Conner, M., Efficacy of the Theory of Planned Behavior: A meta-analytic review. British Journal of Social Psychology. (2001) 471–499
16. Laudon, K. C. and Laudon, J. P., Management information systems: managing the digital firm (7th ed.). NJ: Prentice Hall. (2002)
17. Bobbitt, L. M. and Dabholkar, P. A., Integrating attitudinal theories to understand and predict use of technology-based self-service: The Internet as an illustration. International Journal of Service Industry Management. 5 (2001) 423-450
18. Carlson, C., Customer service: an essential component for a successful Website. Marketing Health Services. 2 (2000) 28-30
19. Abels, E.G., Whiter, M.D. and Hahn, K., A user-based design process for Web sites. Systems and Services. 1 (1999) 35-44
20. Teas, R.K., Expectations as a comparison standard in measuring service quality: an assessment of reassess- ment, Journal of Marketing. (1994) 132-139
21. Zeuthaml, V.A., Berry, L.B. and Parasuraman, A., The behavior consequences of service quality, Journal of Marketing. (1996) 31-46
22. Bakos, J.Y., A strategic analysis of electronic marketplaces, MIS Quarterly. 3 (1991) 295-310
23. Benjamin, R.I., Electronic markets and virtual chains on the information superhighway, Sloan Management Review. 2 (1995) 62-72
24. Malone, T.W., Yates, J. and Benjamin, R.I., Electronic markets and electronic hierarchies, Communications of the ACM. 6 (1987) 484-497.
25. Pitkow, J.E. and Recker, M.M., Using the web as a survey tool: Results from the second WWW user survey. Computer Networks & ISDN Systems. 6 (1995) 809-822
26. Fornell, Claes; Bookstein, Fred L.: Two Structural Equation Models: LISREL and PLSApplied to Consumer Exit-Voice Theory, in: Journal of Marketing Research. (1982) 440-452
27. Cassel, C.; Hackl, P.; Westlund, A.H.: Robustness of Partial Least-Squares Method for Estimating Latent Variable Quality Structures, in: Journal of Applied Statistics. 4 (1999) 435-446
28. Chin W.W., PLS-Graph user' guide, version 3.0. Unpublished manuscript edition. (2001)
29. Nunnally, J., Psychometric Theory, McGraw-Hill, New York. (1978)
30. Fornell, C. and Larcker, D. F., Structural equation models with unobservable variables and measurement error. Journal of Marketing Research. 1 (1981) 39-50

Managing Knowledge in the Human Genetic Variation (HGV) Testing Context

Yulong Gu[1], James Warren[1], and Jan Stanek[2]

[1] Department of Computer Science – Tamaki, University of Auckland, New Zealand
ygu029@ec.auckland.ac.nz, jim@cs.auckland.ac.nz
[2] Advanced Computing Research Centre, University of South Australia, Australia
Jan.Stanek@unisa.edu.au

Abstract. Although human genetic variation (HGV) testing for clinical and re-search purposes produces much valuable data for health care and disease control, the knowledge management (KM) capability in this context is seldom reported or studied. We apply organizational KM theories to identify significant issues in managing HGV knowledge. We also review the essential quality of relevant KM technologies, such as database, data analysis tools, search engine, groupware, data submission tools and Workflow Management System (WfMS). Based on process analysis of key research activities in HGV testing, we propose a knowledge management system (KMS) approach to facilitate HGV knowledge flow and support cooperative HGV research work. By extending and integrating KM tools, a system architecture is designed to assist the key research procedures in HGV testing, to improve research documentation quality, to increase knowledge capture and dissemination, and to support the research cooperation and knowledge sharing in the domain.

1 Introduction

The mission statement of the Human Genome Variation Society (HGVS) identifies the aim of human genetic variation (HGV) studies as "to enhance human health through identification and characterization of changes in the genome that lead to susceptibility to illness" [1]. HGV research has centuries of history in medical science as medical practitioners observed hereditary diseases – such as Hemophilia and heart diseases. The accurate testing of HGV developed significantly since the sequencing of CFTR protein (with defects in it causing cystic fibrosis) in 1989 [2-3]. By 1991, more than 4000 genetic diseases were recognized [4]. In October 2004, the total count of human genes was estimated as 20,000 to 25,000 [5]. In the healthcare setting, genetic services test and interpret HGV of patients and/or families who are referred by a medical geneticist or a genetic counselor or a primary/specialty care provider [6-7]. Clinical HGV tests include diagnostic tests, predictive tests, carrier tests, prenatal tests, pre-implantation tests and newborn screening [8]. The test results and the information gained from family history and physical examination can be used to diagnose medical conditions, to assist in reproductive decision making, to predict future health risk and to suggest treatment in patient care [8-9]. Research-oriented HGV

W. Shen et al. (Eds.): CSCWD 2006, LNCS 4402, pp. 549–560, 2007.
© Springer-Verlag Berlin Heidelberg 2007

testing is used to better understand genetic conditions or develop clinical tests [10]. There were over 500 HGV testing laboratories in the United States at 1997 [11]. HGV testing is becoming a routine procedure in clinics and research, with at least 751 laboratories and 936 clinical chemistry/hematology centers active in the European Union alone at 2004 [12]. A 2005 international survey shows that 45% of early onset breast cancer patients discuss HGV testing with their physician and/or are referred to see a genetic counselor and 16.7% are actually tested [13].

A valid HGV testing result consists of correct variant description and interpretation. A variant interpretation may indicate the association strength between HGV and disease(s). As such, it will add knowledge on genetics and medicine, and may have some implications for health care and disease control. Despite the rapid growth of HGV knowledge, efforts to manage knowledge in the HGV testing context have seldom been reported or studied. Applying organizational knowledge management (KM) theories, we identify several significant KM issues, strategies and technologies – as presented in Section 2. We propose a system approach in Section 3 to facilitate HGV knowledge flow and to support cooperative HGV research work. The system value is discussed in Section 4 and the overall conclusion in Section 5.

2 Literature Review

Drawing on past knowledge management (KM) theories, we address a few KM issues and potential KM technologies that might be valuable for the HGV testing context.

2.1 Past KM Theories

Knowledge is a fluid mix of framed experience, values, contextual information and expert insight; it includes both explicit and tacit knowledge [14-16]. Organizational knowledge management (KM) theories suggest that KM outcomes are influenced by contextual, cultural, structural, managerial, cognitive and technological factors, e.g. the contact frequency and connection pattern between individuals, groups and organizations [17-20]. Lindsey addresses two preconditions for effective KM as the organizational "knowledge infrastructure capability" – representing social capital or the network of relationships – and "knowledge process capability" [21]. Alavi and Leidner refer the Information Systems (IS) that are applied to managing organizational knowledge as knowledge management systems (KMS) [22]. By using KMS, the workplace performance of individuals and organizations may be improved through four dimensions: (i) KMS quality; (ii) knowledge quality; (iii) perceived benefit; and (iv) system use or user satisfaction [23-25]. Accordingly, quality KMS can improve an organization's KM outcome through enhancing the KM factors – such as the relationship network, the quality of processed knowledge and user perspectives.

KM theories indicate three focuses: (i) on knowledge stocks; (ii) on knowledge flow and knowledge processing – the creation, acquisition, codification, retention, storage/retrieval, integration, coordination, transfer, sharing, distribution, application, valuation and use of knowledge; and (iii) on building core competencies, understanding the strategic advantage of know-how, and creating intellectual capital [17][20][22]. Accordingly, three KM strategies are defined as product-centric, process-centric and capability-centric approaches, but the third approach is rarely practiced. Product-centric KM captures, stores, retrieves and distributes explicitly documented knowledge by using data warehouse, searchable document repository and document management systems [20]. Process-centric KM provides pointers to the individuals who are likely to have the relevant expertise [26] and/or implements business process management [27], by using databases of experts, decision aids and expert system, workflow management systems (WfMS), groupware, and systems supporting "Community of Practice" and "hardwiring" of social networks [22][28].

Applying a product-centric strategy, HGV knowledge could be stocked in research documentations. By a process-centric approach, the KM goal should be to share knowledge among HGV researchers because of the knowledge-intensive and cooperative nature of HGV research [29]. In addition, HGV testing processes may be benchmarked and reengineered through tracking and sharing research activities. This will occur through a transition from instance decision making in interpreting each variant case to a best practice in studying the gene. The transition may eventually improve the "pattern" [30] of HGV knowledge processing and enhance HGV research methodology, since medical data analysis may discover new models to incorporate available knowledge [31]. In conclusion, the KM endeavor in the HGV testing context may take all three: product-, process- and capability-centric approaches.

2.2   Relevant KM Technologies

During HGV testing, the research done around the globe is frequently accessed, and international collaborations are performed. These activities are currently supported by Information Systems or Information Technologies (IS/IT) for: (i) data storage; (ii) data analysis; (iii) information searching; and (iv) information transferring [32-33]. In managing HGV knowledge, the functionalities of some KMS (e.g. data warehouse, WfMS and groupware [20][22][28]) and other IS/IT may be adopted. For instance, Email or messaging systems may assist communication; search engines assist information retrieval; information portals increase data and system integrity; and Web use enhances connection [34-36]. In order to facilitate HGV knowledge flow and support cooperative HGV research work, potential KM technologies may at least include database, analysis tools, search engine, groupware, data submission tools and WfMS.

2.2.1   Data Storage Tools

Enormous efforts are put into stocking the highly structured HGV data in general databases and Locus Specific Databases (LSDB) – the databases subjected in one gene normally. A few examples for international HGV databases are HGVbase [37], UMD (Universal Mutation Database) LSDB [38], OMIM (Online Mendelian Inheritance in Man) Database [39], and the proposed Central Database plus WayStation Submission tool [40-43]. These knowledge bases are the prime information resources in the genetics domain, but their data validity is questionable due to inadequate data curation [33-44].

2.2.2   Data Analysis Tools

The first HGV data analysis task is to identify a HGV by comparing the tested sequence with a reference sequence, then to name it by using a nomenclature [45-46]. In some HGV testing facilities, this sequence analysis task is assisted by sequence analysis software, such as Mutation Surveyor™ [47]. Once an HGV is identified, its clinical significance needs to be interpreted – e.g. as benign or disease-causing. Our investigation in the three South Australian HGV testing laboratories showed that interpretation for 45% of detected variants is uncertain. It mostly depends on domain knowledge on the conservation, pathological impact and significance of the variant-related DNA/RNA/Protein in humans (and, for some cases, in other organisms). Many analysis tools are developed to assist collecting relevant data, e.g. CodeLink™ Bioarray Systems [48], SNPs3D [49], STRAP [50] and the UMD central Phenotype-Genotype analysis tool [51].

2.2.3 Information Searching Tools

Evidence collection in HGV analysis is also using general and specific search engines. Two examples for HGV specific search engines are Entrez at the U.S. National Center for Biotechnology Information (NCBI) [52-53] and the UMD tools [54]. However, the searching task sometimes takes a long time because the engine users have to refine their searching keywords before getting the information they desire. Some technologies and concepts might be useful to enhance the engine effectiveness, such as metadata [55] and the Web Ontology Language (OWL) [56].

2.2.4 Information Transferring Tools

An accurate HGV interpretation should be consistent with past research results. Otherwise it has to refine the previous knowledge with convincing evidence that is acknowledged across the genetics community. International cooperation is then necessary to produce valid HGV results. At present, Internet and Email are regularly used for information exchanging and knowledge sharing, but they do not automatically facilitate collaboration or offer group decision support. Turban and Aronson state that groupware provides collaborative support to groups through a mechanism for teams to share opinions, data, information, knowledge and other resources [35]. Thus, the functionalities of groupware – such as group decision support, Community of Practice support, conferencing and messaging support – could facilitate person-to-person information transferring and knowledge sharing, and enhance the "network of relationships" by providing the opportunity of easier communication and cooperation.

Dissemination of HGV research results to international genetics knowledge bases is fundamental for global knowledge growth. At this stage, most researchers and practitioners who perform HGV testing do not often submit their test findings to databases. Consequently, a wealth of information (for example, hundreds of un-submitted variant details per HGV testing laboratory) is not accessible outside the testing facility. This might well be caused by the lack of a competent data submission tool in the domain. Most existing submission support is designed to serve particular databases, e.g. BankIt and Sequin for GenBank [57]. Hopefully, the WayStation Submission Tool – to collect HGV data into a number of databases – will provide an effective central point with consistent interface and format [40].

2.2.5 Workflow Management System (WfMS)

Workflow is the automation of a business process. WfMS software defines, creates and manages the execution of workflows [58]. WfMS has the potential to increase efficiency, reduce cost and automate research processes in science domain – as illustrated in the Taverna project [59].

3   A KMS Architecture for the HGV Testing Context

Based on a study of the research processes in HGV testing, we identify several requirements for potential KMS in the context and then design a system structure.

3.1   Process Analysis of Key Research Activities in HGV Testing

Applying an object-oriented behavior-based workflow model [60-62], as per Figure 1, provides a five-step workflow instance for producing a valid HGV report.

Step 1 Variant Naming. The procedure of comparing tested sequence with a reference sequence to find any HGV is called sequence analysis and could use sequence analysis software, such as Mutation Surveyor™ [47]. The base sequence used as reference is a cDNA (complementary DNA), or gDNA (genomic DNA), or mRNA (messenger ribonucleic acid), or protein. Base sequence databases are available to public, e.g. GenBank [63], the DNA Data Bank of Japan [64] and European Molecular Biology Laboratory (EMBL) Sequence DB [65]. Due to historical reasons, different versions of reference sequences are all in use. This causes many cases of HGV naming ambiguity, especially of locating a variant position. So the support to HGV naming activity has to apply standard nomenclature [45-46].

Step 2 Evidence Collecting. During HGV testing analysis, past relevant research results are collected from literature and (analysis) databases as evidence for a valid HGV interpretation. The gathered data needs to be incorporated into HGV report as supporting material. Therefore, a KMS has to not only support the search action itself, e.g. to enhance the searching and indexing algorithms, but also record the retrieved documents with auditing trail of the search process.

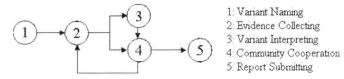

Fig. 1. Behavior-based workflow instance diagram for producing a HGV report

Step 3 Variant Interpreting. HGV interpretation decision-making is a human activity, but it can be assisted by a system-generated documentation from previous steps. This decision may be revised during community discussion in Step 4 and possibly some time later when new information becomes available. As a result, a KMS in the context has to support not only making and documenting HGV research decisions, e.g. HGV interpretation, but also the regular revision of these decisions.

Step 4 Community Cooperation. An accurate HGV interpretation should agree with previous domain knowledge and/or current community understanding. To achieve this, a discussion with research collaborators and/or domain experts could be conducted in HGV testing. During the discussion, relevant documentations will be presented and further information searching may be performed. To facilitate this co-operative work, functions of group decision support systems, Community of Practice systems, conferencing systems and messaging systems could be utilized, e.g. featuring visual argumentation support [66], video-conference support, and so forth.

Step 5 Result Submitting. The result of clinical HGV testing has to be submitted to the test requesting party - a medical geneticist or a genetic counselor or a primary or specialty care provider. And in both clinics and research cases, HGV testing result may be developed into publications for journals and databases. The submission support function of HGV KMS needs to be compatible with the dissemination targets in terms of data format and quality control methods.

3.2   Overall System Architecture

Based on above analysis, Figure 2 presents a possible KMS structure to support the five key research procedures in HGV testing. For instance, databases, search engines, and analysis tools are integrated and/or connected to assist HGV research in Step One

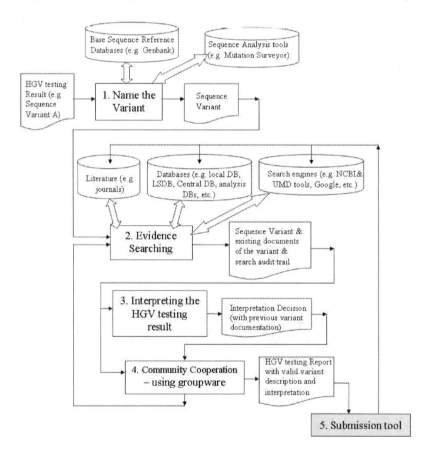

Fig. 2. Proposed system architecture (with data flow) to produce a valid HGV testing report

(Variant Naming) and Two (Evidence Collecting). The output from these tools is a full record with variant description, relevant reference and activity audit trail. This document is prepared for HGV researchers to make the interpretation decision at Step Three. The groupware features in Step Four are to support the cooperative work and knowledge sharing across the genetics community. To capture HGV knowledge in result dissemination at Step Five, a generic data submission tool will be created or an external submission tool will be connected, e.g. the WayStation. These technologies can be integrated using WfMS and Service Oriented Architecture (SOA), as a set of evocable components whose interface descriptions can be published and discovered [67]. SOA components can be integrated with Business Process Execution Language (BPEL), as an XML based programming language to produce portable business processes and enable Web Services [68].

In brief, our system approach will assist key HGV testing procedures, improve documentation quality, support the research cooperation and knowledge sharing in the domain, and eventually enhance the capture and dissemination of HGV knowledge from routine HGV testing activities to contribute to the global genetics knowledgebase. With single interface to end users, the KMS will also act as a portal system that communicates with various external toolkits or information portals, such as public or restricted (analysis) databases and search engines.

4 Discussion

Based on KM theories, we conclude that managing HGV knowledge may have to apply product-centric, process-centric and capability-centric approaches to enhancing the "network of relationship", increasing the quality of processed knowledge, and ultimately improving the KM performance of individuals and organizations. Accordingly, we design an integrated KMS architecture with features from database, analysis tools, search engine, groupware, data submission tool and WfMS.

Through extending database technologies, enhancing search engines, and integrating analysis tools, time and efforts will be saved with a single interface that connects to multiple information resources and provides powerful search and analysis support. It will deliver a HGV record with molecular and clinical data, which may be of interest to clinicians, geneticists and research biologists [54]. Groupware functionalities of the KMS will assist conducting cooperative tasks and manage all levels of information flow – i.e. connection, communication, content and process [69]. With adequate evidence and community review, the variant interpretation will be of high accuracy, validity and value, which would significantly improve HGV research documentation quality. Support to disseminate such HGV research result will start knowledge diffusion (knowledge "flow") from the testing facilities to the whole genetics community. As a result, the knowledge generated in routine HGV testing research activities will be captured and contributed to the global genetics knowledgebase. Above all, WfMS feature will monitor HGV research processes in real time, and those processes will become more easily changed [70]. In addition to facilitate process reengineering, WfMS may also help create and share tacit knowledge on HGV research methodology through tracking and sharing the research activities.

Since the major output of HGV testing is the HGV result (with variant description and interpretation), the effectiveness of knowledge dissemination task will be evaluated by the change (presumably as "increase") of HGV result submission attempts to journals and databases. The quality of our system and the quality of processed knowledge could be measured by DeLone and McLean IS Success Model [71-72], and also be evaluated by the feedback from HGV report receivers – in clinics, the medical geneticists, genetic counselors, primary or specialty care providers who request the test at the first place and receive the result eventually. Regarding the system users' perspectives, there is no evidence of consistent technology usage in the HGV context. IT adoption in the domain depends more on individual user's "technology learning ability" than on technical or other factors. Therefore, a few actions were taken to ensure the usability and acceptance of our system, such as technology readiness assessment, user information requirement study and system implementation planning (including user training plan). Our ongoing action research [73] project is to study the nature, benefits and acceptance of KM support in the HGV context. We will evaluate our KMS implementation regarding its impact on KM quality improvement at key HGV research procedures and on overall KM outcome in HGV testing facilities.

5 Conclusion

Human genetic variation (HGV) testing for clinical and research purposes routinely generate knowledge that is potentially valuable to healthcare and disease control. However, knowledge management (KM) efforts in this context are seldom studied. According to organizational KM theories, adopting quality KM technologies under appropriate strategy might significantly improve KM effectiveness through enhancing the critical KM factors. This chapter presents the design of a knowledge management system (KMS) architecture to support knowledge flow and cooperative work in HGV testing by utilizing several KM technologies, including database, analysis tools, search engine, groupware, data submission tools and Workflow Management System (WfMS). The integrated system is expected to assist key HGV testing procedures, to improve research documentation quality, to increase knowledge capture and dissemination, as well as to support research cooperation and knowledge sharing in the domain. With better KM performance in the HGV testing context, more reliable and efficient genetic services will eventually improve health care and disease control.

Acknowledgement. We would like to thank many people for their kindest assistance during this study, especially Dr. Graeme Suthers at Adelaide Women's and Children Hospital for his expertise input, his inspiring recommendations and his great effort in this project. We are also very grateful to Dr. Sui Yu and Dr. Kathryn Friend at Adelaide Women's and Children Hospital; Dr. Jacqueline Carroll, Dr. Graeme Casey and Dr. Glenice Cheetham at Adelaide Institute of Medical and Veterinary Science; Dr. Scott Grist at Flinders Medical Centre; Dr. Alexei Drummond, Ms Karen Day, Dr. Rekha Gaikwad, Prof. Andrew Shelling, Ms Carey-Ann Nel, Dr. Katie Woad and the Medical Genetics Group research students in the University of Auckland; and Mr. Tony Blomfield in Massey University for their precious information and participation.

References

1. HGVS: Society Information (2005). URL: http://www.hgvs.org/socinfo.html
2. Kerem, B., Zielenski, J., Markiewicz, D., Bozon, D., Gazit, E., Yahav, J., et al.: Identification of Mutations in Regions Corresponding to the 2 Putative Nucleotide(ATP)-Binding Folds of the Cystic Fibrosis Gene. Proceedings of the National Academy of Sciences USA 87 (1989) 8447-8451
3. Wikipedia: Genetics (2006). URL: http://en.wikipedia.org/wiki/Genetics
4. McKusick, V.A. (ed.): Mendelian Inheritance in Man. Baltimore, Md: Johns Hopkins Univ. Press (1991)
5. Genomics.energy.gov: Major Events in the U.S. Human Genome Project and Related Projects. (2005). URL: http://www.ornl.gov/hgmis
6. GeneTests: Medical Genetics Information Resource (database online). Educational Materials: Ordering Genetic Testing. Copyright. University of Washington, Seattle. 1993-2006. URL: http://www.genetests.org
7. ITPerspectives Inc.: NHS Genetic Service Information Systems Output Based Specification. (2005). URL: http://www.ngrl.org.uk/Manchester/Pages/Downloads/ITP-GEN3-OBSv05.pdf
8. GeneTests: Medical Genetics Information Resource (database online). Educational Materials: Uses of Genetic Testing. Copyright, University of Washington, Seattle. 1993-2006. URL: http://www.genetests.org
9. Genetic Tools: Using Genetic Tests. (2005). URL: http://www.genetests.org
10. GeneTests: Medical Genetics Information Resource (database online). Educational Materials: Clinical Versus Research Testing. Copyright, University of Washington, Seattle. 1993-2006. URL: http://www.genetests.org
11. Holtzman, N.A., Watson, M.S. (ed.): Promoting Safe and Effective Genetic Testing in the United States. Bethesda (MD): National Institutes of Health (1997). URL: http://www.genome.gov/10001733
12. Ibarreta, D., Elles, R., Cassiman, J.J., Rodriguez-Cerezo, E., Dequeker, E.: Towards Quality Assurance and Harmonization of Genetic Testing Services in the European Union. Nat. Biotechnol. 22 (2004) 1230-1235
13. Brown, K.L., Hutchison, R., Zinberg, R.E., McGovern, M.M.: Referral and Experience With Genetic Testing Among Women With Early Onset Breast Cancer. Genet. Test. 9 (Dec 2005) 301-305
14. Davenport, T.H., Prusak, L.: Working Knowledge: How Organizations Manage What They Know. Cambridge, MA: Harvard Business School Press (1997)
15. Nonaka, I.: A Dynamic Theory of Organizational Knowledge Creation. Organ. Sci. 5 (1994) 14-37
16. Polanyi, M.: The Tacit Dimension. Routledge & Kegan Paul, London (1966)
17. Argote, L., McEvily, B., Reagans, R.: Managing Knowledge in Organizations: An Integrative Framework and Review of Emerging Themes. Manage. Sci. 49 (2003) 571-582
18. Benbya, H., Belbaly, N.A.: Mechanisms for Knowledge Management Systems Effectiveness: An Exploratory Analysis. Knowl. Process. Manag. 12 (2005) 203-216
19. Kankanhalli, A., Tan, B.C.Y., Wei, K.K.: Contributing Knowledge to Electronic Knowledge Repositories: An Empirical Investigation. MIS Quart. 29 (2005) 59-85
20. Sambamurthy, V., Bharadwaj, A., Grover, V.: Shaping Agility Through Digital Options: Reconceptualizing the Role of Information Technology in Firms. MIS Quart. 27 (2003) 237-263

21. Lindsey, K.: Measuring Knowledge Management Effectiveness: A Task-Contingent Organizational Capabilities Perspective. Proceedings of the Eighth Americas Conference on Information Systems (2002) 2085-2090
22. Alavi, M., Leidner, D.E.: Review: Knowledge Management and Knowledge Management Systems: Conceptual Foundations and Research Issues. MIS Quart. 25 (2001) 107-136
23. Jennex, M.E., Olfman, L.: Organizational Memory/Knowledge Effects on Productivity, a Longitudinal Study. Proceedings of the 35th Hawaii International Conference on System Sciences. HICSS35. IEEE Computer Society (January 2002)
24. Jennex, M.E., Olfman, L.: A Knowledge Management Success Model: An Extension of DeLone and McLean's IS Success Model. Proceedings of the Ninth Americas Conference on Information Systems (August 2003)
25. Jennex, M.E., Olfman, L.: Assessing Knowledge Management Success/Effectiveness Models. Proceedings of the 37th Hawaii International Conference on System Sciences (2004)
26. Dennis, A.R., Vessey, I.: Three Knowledge Management Strategies: Knowledge Hierarchies, Knowledge Markets and Knowledge Communities. MIS Quart. Executive. 4 (2005)
27. Massey, A.P., Montoya-Weiss, M.M., O'Driscoll, T.M.: Knowledge Management in Pursuit of Performance: Insights from Nortel Networks. MIS Quart. 26 (2002) 269-289
28. Brown, J.S., Duguid, P.: Organizing Knowledge. Calif. Manage. Rev. 40 (1998) 90-111
29. Bossen, C., Dalsgaard, P.: Conceptualization and Appropriation: the Evolving Use of Col laborative Knowledge Management. Proceedings of the 4th Decennial Conference on Critical Computing: Between Sense and Sensibility (August 2005) 99-108
30. Firestone, J.M., McElroy, M.W.: Doing Knowledge Management. The Learning Organization 12 (2005) 189-212
31. Zupan, B., Holmes, J.H., Bellazzi, R.: Knowledge-based Data Analysis and Interpretation. Artif. Intell. Med. 37 (2006) 163-165
32. Gu, Y., Warren, J., Stanek, J., Suthers G.: A System Architecture Design for Knowledge Management (KM) in Medical Genetic Testing (MGT) Laboratories. Proceedings of the 10th International Conference on Computer Supported Cooperative Work in Design (CSCWD 2006). Nanjing, China (May 2006)
33. Gu, Y., Stanek, J., Warren, J.: Knowledge Management (KM) Technologies in Medical Genetic Testing (MGT) Laboratories: A Literature Review. Proceedings of Health Informatics Conference (HIC 2006). Sydney, Australia (August 2006)
34. Liebowitz, J.: Knowledge Management Handbook. CRC Press, Boca Raton, FL (1999)
35. Turban, E., Aronson, J.E.: Decision Support Systems and Intelligent Systems. 6th. edn. Prentice Hall, Upper Saddle River, NJ (2001)
36. Ward, J., Peppard, J.: Strategic Planning for Information Systems. John Wiley & Sons, Chichester (2002)
37. The Karolinska Institute (Sweden), The European Bioinformatics Institute (UK): Human Genome Variation Database. (2004). URL: http://hgvbase.cgb.ki.se/
38. Laboratory of Human Genetics Montpellier (France): UMD Locus Specific Databases. (2005). URL: http://www.umd.be/LSDB.html
39. NCBI: OMIM - Online Mendelian Inheritance in Man. (2005).
    URL: http://www.ncbi.nlm.nih.gov/entrez/query.fcgi?db=OMIM
40. Genomic Disorders Research Centre: Welcome to the Waystation. (2006).
    URL: http://www.centralmutations.org
41. Horaitis, O., Cotton, R.G.H.: The Challenge of Collecting Mutations Across the Genome: The Human Genome Variation Society Approach. Hum. Mutat. 23 (2004) 447-452

42. Scriver, C.R., Nowacki, P.M., Lehväslaiho, H.: Guidelines and Recommendations for Content, Structure and Deployment of Mutation Databases. Hum. Mutat. 13 (1999) 344-350
43. Scriver, C.R., Nowacki, P.M., Lehväslaiho, H.: Guidelines and Recommendations for Content, Structure and Deployment of Mutation Databases II: Journey in Progress. Hum. Mutat. 15 (2000) 13-15
44. Fredman, D., Munns, G., Rios, D., Sjöholm, F., Siegfried, M., Lenhard, B., Lehväslaiho, H., Brookes, A.J.: HGVbase: a Curated Resource Describing Human DNA Variation and Phenotype Relationships. Nucleic. Acids. Res. 32 (2004) 516-519
45. Antonarakis, S.A.: The Nomenclature Working Group: Recommendations for a Nomenclature System for Human Gene Mutations. Hum. Mutat. 11 (1998) 1-3
46. HGVS: Nomenclature for the Description of Sequence Variations. (2005). URL: http://www.genomic.unimelb.edu.au/mdi/mutnomen/
47. SoftGenetics: Mutation Surveyor™ - A Unique Research Tool. (2005). URL: http://www.softgenetics.com/ms/index.htm
48. GE Healthcare: CodeLink™ Bioarray Systems. (2005). URL: http://www4.amershambiosciences.com/aptrix/upp01077.nsf/Content/Products?OpenDocument&ParentId=568694
49. UMBI: SNPs3D. (2005). URL: http://www.snps3d.org/
50. The Medical School Charite Berlin: Multiple Sequence Alignment Interactive Program STRAPNT. (2005). URL: http://www.charite.de/bioinf/strap/
51. Laboratory of Human Genetics Montpellier (France): The UMD Central Phenotype-Genotype Analysis. (2005). URL: http://194.167.35.168:2200/CLIN.shtml
52. NCBI: Entrez, The Life Sciences Search Engine. (2006). URL: http://www.ncbi.nlm.nih.gov/gquery
53. Wheeler, D.L., Chappey, C., Lash, A.E., Leipe, D.D., Madden, T.L., Schuler, G.D., et al.: Database resources of the National Center for Biotechnology Information. Nucleic. Acids. Res. 28 (2000) 10-14
54. Laboratory of Human Genetics Montpellier (France): The UMD Central. (2005). URL: http://194.167.35.168:2200/
55. W3C: Metadata and Resource Description. (2001). URL: http://www.w3.org/Metadata/
56. W3C: Web-Ontology (WebOnt) Working Group (Closed). (2004). URL: http://www.w3.org/2001/sw/WebOnt/
57. NCBI: GenBank Overview. (2005). URL: http://www.ncbi.nlm.nih.gov/Genbank/index.html
58. Allen, R.: Workflow: An Introduction. In: Fischer, L. (eds.): Workflow Handbook 2001. WfMC (Workflow Management Coalition) (2001) 15-38
59. Taverna.sourceforge.net: Taverna 1.4. (2006). URL: http://taverna.sourceforge.net/
60. Preuner, G., Schrefl, M.: A Three-Level Schema Architecture for the Conceptual Design of Web-Based Information Systems: From Web-Data Management to Integrated Web-Data And Web-Process Management. World Wide Web Journal 3 (Mar. 2000) 125-138
61. Schmidt, M.T.: Building Workflow Business Objects, Object-Oriented Programming Systems Languages Applications. OOPSLA'98 Business Object Workshop. London (1998)
62. Schrefl, M., Stumptner, M.: Behavior-consistent Specialization of Object Life Cycles. ACM T. Softw. Eng. Meth. 11 (Jan 2002) 92-148
63. NCBI: GenBank Database. (2005). URL: http://www.psc.edu/general/software/packages/genbank/genbank.html
64. NIG: DNA Data Bank of Japan. (2005). URL: http://www.ddbj.nig.ac.jp/
65. EMBL-EBI: Nucleotide Sequence Database. (2005). URL: http://www.ebi.ac.uk/embl/

66. Wen, L., e Duh, C.: The Influential Factors in Argumentation-based Teamwork Problem Solving. Proceedings of International Conference of Internet Society Conference. Tamsui, Taiwan (2002)
67. W3C: Web Services Glossary: W3C Working Group Note 11 February 2004. (2004).URL: http://www.w3.org/TR/ws-gloss/
68. Goland, Y.Y.: The Promise of Portable Business Processes. Web Services Journal 2(2005). URL: http://ftpna2.bea.com/pub/downloads/BPEL4WS_WSJ.PDF
69. Finnie, G.: Business Intelligence and Data Warehousing. (2005). URL: http://www.it.bond.edu.au/inft323/043/Lectures/lecture%206%20023.ppt
70. Prior, C.: Workflow and Process Management. In: Fischer, L. (eds.): Workflow Handbook 2003. Future Strategies Inc., FL (2003)
71. DeLone, W.H., McLean, E.R.: Information Systems Success: the Quest for the Dependent Variable. Inform. Syst. Res. 3 (1992) 60-95
72. DeLone, W.H., McLean, E.R.: Information Systems Success Revisited. Proceedings of HICSS (2002) 238-248
73. Stringer, E.T.: Action Research: A Handbook for Practitioners. Sage Publications, Thousand Oaks, CA (1996)

A Business-Based Negotiation Process for Reaching Consensus of Meanings

Jonice Oliveira[1], Jairo de Souza[1], Melise Paula[1], and Jano Moreira de Souza[1,2]

[1] COPPE/UFRJ - Computer Science Department, Graduate School of Engineering,
Federal University of Rio de Janeiro, Brazil
[2] DCC-IM/UFRJ - Computer Science Department, Mathematics Institute,
Federal University of Rio de Janeiro, Brazil
{jonice, jairo, mel, jano}@cos.ufrj.br

Abstract. Since multi-disciplinary teams are common in business, design and manufacturing environments, it is more problematical to find a common vocabulary or an agreement over meaning. This issue especially disturbs a design project, which must be composed by people with specific and different knowledge, from diverse domains, to execute special activities. Negotiation arises from this context as a process for the construction of consensus. The goal of this work is to present a model of meaning negotiation using ontologies to obtain the consensus of meanings, based on models of business negotiation, and consequently, deal with conflicts and multiplicity of ideas, making this negotiation a way of creating value for all agents involved.

1 Introduction

In our global economic and information readiness, information overload is a fact, not a theory, and there is evidence that most people lack the skills or tools to keep up in the Knowledge Age. Nowadays, all major economic players have decentralized organizational structures, with multiple units acting in parallel and with significant autonomy [1]. Currently, computational tools and humans have to handle a variety of information sources, with data in several formats, patterns and different quality degrees. Grasping relevant information wherever it may be and exchanging information with all potential partners has become an essential challenge for enterprise survival [1]. The reason that makes semantics so important is that information now has to be sharable and disseminated in a faster way, in a distributed environment, where people or software do not necessarily share a common understanding.

Another issue which emphasizes the importance of an understanding consensus is the on growing of multi-disciplinary teams, especially in activities related on product design. There are many advantages on this kind of work, which we can cite: rapid prototyping, cost reduction and the design of a more marketable and confident product. While multi-disciplinary teams are common in design environments, it is more problematical to find a common vocabulary, a meaning agreement, which will aim in information and knowledge exchange, besides a common understanding of tasks, activities and works.

W. Shen et al. (Eds.): CSCWD 2006, LNCS 4402, pp. 561–569, 2007.
© Springer-Verlag Berlin Heidelberg 2007

Emergent semantic aims to establish semantic interoperability from a consensus, in relation to interpretations that are common in a particular context. Considering the evolving character of information, whose semantics is enriched by interpretation, handling, and use in a particular context, the interoperability is conditioned by the way as the concordance of interpretations on the meaning is established. Negotiation arises from this context as a process that is appropriate for the construction of consensus. However, as interpretations are not necessarily shared at first, semantic interoperability becomes dependent of the frequency, quality, and efficiency with which such negotiations are conducted in order to achieve agreement. In the negotiations that encompass meanings and interpretations, each participating agent can be regarded as an independent decision-maker that carries its own individual perception and judgment regarding the issues under consideration.

How in negotiation all the parties involved have to contribute for the agreement not to be reached in an unilateral fashion, it can be seen as inter-dependent decision process. Taking into account that each negotiator possesses different knowledge, experiences and focus, the conciliation of objectives or meanings contributes to the complexity of this kind of negotiation. Thus, there is the need for establishing a management of the process of consensus formation, guaranteeing the incremental and evolving aspects of these agreements.

Bearing this assertion in mind, the goal of this work is to present a model of negotiation to obtain the consensus of meanings, that is, semantic consensus, which represents a structured way to deal with the possible conflicts, and with the multiplicity of ideas, making this negotiation a productive process, and a way of creating value for all agents involved by the by the creation of an ontology. For it, some negotiation principles will be explained in Section 2 and our model will be described in Section 3. Apart from the model, we show some correlated works in this area in Section 4. Opportunities and challenges, as also conclusion and future works related to negotiation applied to consensus meaning are outlined in Section 5.

2 Negotiation

Negotiation is a process of social interaction and communication that involves distribution and redistribution of power, resources, and commitments. It involves two or more people who make decisions and engage in the exchange of information in order to determine a compromise. Many important decisions have to be negotiated because people need to share and distribute scarce resources. The interpersonal character, the participants' independence as the decision-making entities, and their interdependence in their inability to achieve goals unilaterally contribute to the complexity of the negotiation [2].

Traditionally, two types of negotiation exist: competitive and cooperative [3-5]. Competitive negotiation is classified as Win/Lose. The negotiator with a Win/Lose posture chooses the competition and the short time. Thus, the fulfillment of the wishes of one party may be directly detrimental to the fulfillment of the wishes of another party. This type of negotiation has been described as win-lose, zero-sum, pure conflict, and competitive. It is a process in which a gain for one party is a loss for the other and in which each party maximizes one's own outcome. Walton and McKersie note that distributive bargaining is often a competition over the division of resources;

who achieves more depends largely on the strategies and tactics employed [6]. Parties have a fixed-pie perception and focus on their differences, ignoring what they have in common [7].

Cooperative negotiation (also known as collaborative or integrative negotiation) is classified as Win/Win. It is a cooperative process in which involved parties find alternatives for common earnings, that is, which cater to the interests of all the parties [3][5][8].

According to Lomuscio et. al. [9], negotiation can be defined as a "Process by which a group of agents communicates with one another to try and come to a mutually-acceptable agreement on some matter". In this definition, the accent falls on words such as "agent", "communicate", and "mutually acceptable". The parties taking part in the negotiation process are not necessarily people, but can be any type of actors, such as software agents.

These actors communicate according to a negotiation protocol and act according to a strategy. The protocol determines the flow of messages between the negotiating parties and acts as the rules by which the negotiating parties must abide by if they are to interact. The protocol is public and open. The strategy, on the other hand, is the way in which a given party acts within those rules, in an effort to get the best outcome of the negotiation. The strategy of each participant is, therefore, private [10-11].

As with every process, a negotiation can be divided in phases. In Kersten and Noronha [12], the authors suggest three phases of the negotiation: pre-negotiation, conduct of negotiation and post-settlement.

In the pre-negotiation phase, the objective is the understanding of the negotiation problem. This stage involves the analysis of the situation, problem, opponent, issues, alternatives, preference, reservation levels and strategy. Moreover, in this phase, negotiators plan the agenda for the negotiations and develop their BATNA.

BATNA is the acronym for "Best Alternative To a Negotiated Agreement", created by Fisher and Ury [11]. The BATNA can be identified in any negotiation situation by the question, "What will we do if this negotiation is not successful?" In the simplest terms, if the proposed agreement is better than your BATNA, then you should accept it. If the agreement is not better than your BATNA, then you should reopen negotiations. If you cannot improve the agreement, then you should at least consider withdrawing from the negotiations and pursuing your alternative (though the costs of doing so must also be considered). One of the main reasons for entering a negotiation is to achieve better results than would be possible without negotiating [13]. More details on the BATNA can be found in [11][14-15].

The second stage in the negotiation, Conduct of negotiation, involves exchanges of messages, offers and counter-offers based on different strategies and the kinds of negotiation. The post-settlement analysis phase involves only the evaluation of the negotiation outcomes generated, and, afterwards, the negotiation activity. These outcomes include the information about the compromise and the negotiators' satisfaction.

In collaborative negotiation, an important issue we can stress, is value creation. The four key features of collaborative negotiation, which allow one to distinguish it from competitive negotiation are: value creation, focus on interests and not positions, openness, and exchange of relevant information, learning and problem restructuring [16-22]. Different authors highlight the significance of these characteristics and their impact on the parties' willingness to collaborate rather than compete, to seek new possibilities rather than defend their own positions, to work jointly on solving problems rather than demanding more resources, but value creation is what will show the benefits of cooperation. As per [23], three interpretations of value creation are possible:

1. The parties know the set of offers from the outset and select offers that dominate their previous offers.
2. The set of offers is unknown to the parties but known to someone else (e.g., analysts). The parties select dominating offers and the third party guides them in achieving an efficient compromise.
3. No one knows the set of offers; during the negotiation the parties realize the possibilities to achieve more and select offers which dominate the previous offers.

Based in these negotiation concepts, in the next section we describe our negotiation model to focus on the consensus for meaning.

3 Meaning Negotiation

Semantic interoperability is seen as an emergent phenomenon constructed incrementally, and its state at any given point in time depends on the frequency, the quality and the efficiency with which negotiations can be conducted to reach agreements on common interpretations within the context of a given task 1. As the set of mutual beliefs constitutes the "agreement" or "consensus" between the interacting agents, humans or not, we believe that the most convenient and appropriate type of negotiation, when we are envision the meaning consensus in a multidisciplinary team, is the collaborative one. The reason is the necessity of to know, to learn and to understand the special and relevant knowledge of people from different domain, knowledge which will be the base of a well done work and probably, the responsible of competitive

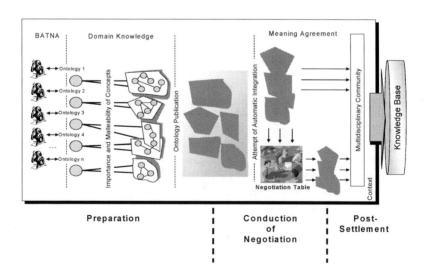

Fig. 1. Meaning negotiation process

value. Although, as per [24], meaningful exchanges can only occur on the basis of mutually accepted propositions.

So, our model is divided in 3 steps, which are: pre-negotiation, conduct of negotiation and post-settlement. This model can be seen in Figure 1.

3.1 Pre-negotiation

Pre-negotiation refers to the discussions that proceed formal negotiations. In our model for meaning negotiation, these phases are divided as follows:

1. To choose the personal or domain ontology
In this stage, the user should choose an ontology to represent the knowledge about his/her domain. Each of these ontologies (one by domain) will be the base of ontology integration process.

2. To specify the importance and malleability degrees of terms and concepts
For the ontology which was been chosen in the previous step, the user has to define the importance degree of each concept and relationship. The importance degree is an integer value, between 1 to 5 (1-the lowest value/ "it is not so important", 5-the highest value/ "it is very important") and represents the importance, the relevance, of a concept in the ontology or the importance of a relationship between two concepts in the same ontology. The definition of the importance degree is optional, and the concept and relationships which the user does not define the importance degree is automatically set as value 1.

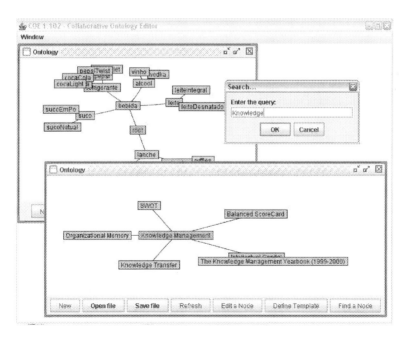

Fig. 2. An ontology edited by COE

Analogously, the user has to characterize the malleability degree. It means the range which the user accepts to modify a concept definition or a relationship between two concepts. The malleability degree is an integer value between 1 to 5 (1-the lowest value/ "it can be changed without any problem", 5-the highest value/ "it is impossible to change"). The definition of the malleability degree is optional, and the concept and relationships which the user does not define the malleability degree is automatically set as value 1. The combination of these degrees will be used in the next step, as shown in Figure 2, which means the status of concepts and its relationships in an ontology.

Having a good BATNA increases negotiating power. Therefore, it is important to improve the BATNA whenever possible. The BATNA should be fill out with all the desired possibilities to an ontology construction: all the concepts which can be negotiated, which the user waits with this negotiation process, all the alternatives, and so on.

3. To publish the personal or domain ontology

After user defines the importance and malleability degrees and constructs his/her BATNA, it is time to publish his/her ontology to a public place, where negotiators can find and access all ontologies. After the user saw other ontologies, the user can refine his/her BATNA. For the ontology definition (steps 1, 2, 3) the user uses the COE editor [25], as shown in Figure 2.

3.2 Conduct of Negotiation

The actual conduct of the negotiation during which counterparts exchange a series of messages and offers, creating a suitable atmosphere for the negotiation, presenting their side of the case, and bargaining until they reach an agreement. The parties may conduct negotiations with the assistance of one or more neutral third parties, using a person or a team as mediator. The conduct of negotiation is divided in two phases, as follows:

4. Attempt of Automatic Integration

In this stage, the environment tries to automatically integrate the ontologies, basing this action in the importance and the malleability degrees, and the syntax and semantic analysis. The syntax and semantic analysis are based on the proposal of Conceptual Schema Integration, described in [26].

The result of the automatic integration (if it was computational possible) is post to the negotiators to they evaluate the result. If all of them agree with the result, then, the next step is the 3.3 (Post-Settlement). If someone disagrees, then, all the members are invited to participate to the negotiation table.

5. Negotiation Table

Negotiations are arguments. Argumentation, not a derogatory term, is a practice of achieving a common sense through parties taking contrary positions. Here, the members can debate, espousing their positions, arguments and counter-arguments for a concept definition and its relationships in an ontology. It is not only helpful in discovering compacts, but the essence of constructive social interaction. To aim this negotiation phase, users can consult their first ontology, the BATNA, the ontologies of the other members and the ontology resulting of the step 4. This negotiation is made in a synchronous electronic environment and all the messages are categorizes using the IBIS methodology (Issue Based Information Systems). The discourse develops around single issues, in our case a concept definition or relationship between concepts, which somebody raises assuming that their treatment would be relevant for the ontology integration. The participants take different positions, defend their positions, oppose others, and weigh one aspect against another in the form of arguments.

All messages have relations. Every argument is assigned at least to one position, every position at least to one issue, every issue to at least one topic. Arguments "support" or "oppose" a position; positions "respond" to issues. Other relations can hold between all elements of IBIS. For instance, an argument can relate to another argument, also to one which belongs to another position of another issue. Or a counter-argument can relate a position of other issue, and different positions can be related (as a "derive" relation), too. The relations form a network and this network is storage after the negotiation end.

3.3 Post-Settlement

The post-settlement is the period after an agreement has already been reached, or if not, the negotiation is cancelled or a renegotiating process could be analyzed. In our case, if the meaning agreement was reached, then the next steps are done.

6. Context storage

All information which helps to represent the context - as BATNAS, previous domain ontologies, importance and malleability degrees, the attempts of ontology integration and the log negotiation table (with the messages IBIS categorization), and the final ontology - are storage.

7. Ontology dissemination

The integrated and final ontology is disseminated to the team.

4   Related Work

There are several works dealing with some related issues, such as information integration, schemas and ontology matchmaking, negotiation in agents' communication and context elicitation. An extended analysis of Emergent Semantic Systems is made in [1] and computational mechanisms can be found in this reference. In [32] we found a consensus approach for deriving semantic knowledge on the Web. The significance of information sharing and distribution of cultural knowledge has encouraged some researchers to exploit consensus, measured by inter-subject agreement, as an indicator of knowledge. The method of Consensus Analysis was first presented in several seminal papers [28-30]. In addition to introducing the formal foundation for Consensus Analysis, the initial papers cited above also provided examples of its application to modeling knowledge of general information among US college students, and the classification of illness concepts among urban Guatemalans. Other more recent applications of Consensus Analysis have focused on measuring cultural diversity within organizations [31] and different degrees of expertise in organizations and communities of practice creation [27].

Our work is different. It is an attempt to use already-known techniques of negotiation, usually employed in the business scenario, and to try and bring these concepts to ontology integration. Using this idea, our work is unique.

5 Conclusion and Future Works

The lack of any efficient semantic agreement mechanisms makes semantic integrity in heterogeneous environments very difficult for the participating parties. This problem is stressed in design project, where multidisciplinary groups have to work with and understand each other.

Initial approaches rely on some pre-defined corpus of terms serving as an initial context for defining new concepts or make use of gossiping and local translation mappings to incrementally foster interoperability in the large, but it is not enough. In this work we are based on a negotiation model to conduct a semantic agreement in a process of ontology integration. We did not find an equivalent work in literature, that is, this attempt of mapping how business negotiations are mapped into semantic agreements is exclusive.

As future work, we envision the use of data mining techniques to find patterns of: 1) meaning X domains; 2) agreement reaching x person profile; and 3) importance of terms x domains.

Acknowledgement. This work has the financial support of CAPES (The Coordination for Postgraduate Staff Improvement) and CNPq (The National Council for Scientific and Technological Development).

References

1. Aberer, K., Catarci, T., Cudre-Mauroux, P., Dillon, T.S., Grimm, S., Hacid, M.S., et al.: Emergent Semantics Systems. Proc. 1st International Conference on Semantics of a Networked World (ICSNW04) (2004) 14-43
2. Kersten, G.E.: The Science and Engineering of E-negotiation: Review of the Emerging Field. InterNeg Reports INR05/02. Montreal, Canada (2002)
3. Clarke, R.: Fundamentals of Negotiation. URL: http://www.anu.edu.au/people/Roger.Clarke/SOS/FundasNeg.html
4. Huang, P. and Mao, J.: Modeling e-Negotiation Activities with Petri Nets. Proceedings of the 35th Hawaii International Conference on System Sciences (HICSS 35). Hawaii (2002)
5. Martinelli, D.P.E and Almeida, A.P: Negociação: Como transformar confronto em cooperação. São Paulo: Atlas (1997)
6. Walton, R.E. and McKersie, R.B.: A Behavioral Theory of Labor Negotiations. New York, McGraw-Hill (1965)
7. Thompson, L.: Lose-lose Agreements in Interdependent Decision-Making. Psychological Bulletin 120(3) (1996) 396-409

8. Acuff, F.L.: How to negotiate anything with anyone anywhere around the world. New York: American Management Association (1993)
9. Lomuscio, A., Wooldridge, M. and Jennings, N.: A classification scheme for negotiation in electronic commerce. In: Agent-Mediated Electronic Commerce: A European Agent Link Perspective (2001) 19-33
10. Bartolini, C., Preist, C. and Kuno, H.: Requirements for Automated Negotiation. URL: http://www.w3.org/2001/03/ WSWS/popa/
11. Fisher, R.E, Kolpeman, E. and Schneider, A.K.: Beyond Machiavelli: Tools for Coping with Conflict. Cambridge, MA, Harvard University Press (1994)
12. Kersten, G.E. and Noronha, S.J.: Negotiations via the Word Wide Web: A Cross-cultural Study of Decision Making. Group Decision and Negotiations 8(1999) 251-279
13. Spangler, B.: Best Alternative to a Negotiated Agreement (BATNA).
    URL: http://www.beyondintractability.org/m/batna.jsp
14. Mills, H.A.: Negotiation: The art of Winning. Gower Publishing Company Limited (1991)
15. Raiffa, H: The Art and Science of Negotiation. Cambridge: Belknap Press of Harvard University Press (1982)
16. Fisher, R. and Ury, W.: Getting to Yes - Negotiating Agreement Without Giving In. New York, Penguin Books (1983)
17. Lax, D.A. and Sebenius, J.: The Manager as Negotiator. New York, The Free Press (1986)
18. Sebenius, J.K.: Negotiation Analysis: A Characterization and Review. Management Science 38(1) (1992) 18-38
19. Ury, W.: Getting Past No - Negotiating your Way from Confrontation to Cooperation. New York, Bantam Books (1993)
20. Fisher, R., Kopelman, E., et al.: Beyond Machiavelli. Tools for Coping with Conflict. Cambridge, MA, Harvard University Press (1994)
21. Raiffa, H.: Lectures on Negotiation Analysis. Cambridge, MA, PON Books (1996)
22. Bazerman, M.: Judgment in Managerial Decision Making. New York, Wiley (1998)
23. Kersten, G.: Modeling Distributive and Integrative Negotiations: Review and Revised Characterization. Group Decision and Negotiation 10(6) (2001) 493-514
24. Ouksel, A.M.: A Framework for a Scalable Agent Architecture of Cooperating Heterogeneous Knowledge Sources. Springer Verlag (1999)
25. Rezende, J., Souza, J., de Souza, J.: Peer-to-Peer Collaborative Integration of Dynamic Ontologies. Proceedings of CSCWD. Coventry, UK (2005)
26. De Souza, J.M.: Software Tools for Conceptual Schema Integration. Ph.D. Thesis. University of East Anglia (1986)
27. Rodrigues, S., Oliveira, J. and de Souza, J.: Competence Mining for Team Formation and Virtual Community Recommendation. Proceedings of CSCWD. Coventry, UK (2005)
28. Romney, A.K., Weller, S.C. and Batchelder, W.H.: Culture as consensus: A theory of culture and informant accuracy. American Anthropologist 88(2) (1986) 313-338
29. Batchelder, W.H. and Romney, A.K.: The statistical analysis of a general Condorcet model for dichotomous choice situations. In: Grofman, G. and Owen, G. (eds.): Information Pooling and Group Decision Making. Greenwich, CT: JAI Press (1986) 103-112
30. Batchelder, W.H. and Romney, A.K.: Test theory without an answer key. Psychometrika 53 (1988) 71-92
31. Caulkins, D. and Hyatt, S.: Using consensus analysis to measure cultural diversity in organizations and social movements. Field Methods 11(1) (1999) 5-26
32. Behrens, C. and Kashyap, V.: The "Emergent" Semantic Web: A Consensus Approach for Deriving Semantic Knowledge on the Web. Proc. International Semantic Web Working Symposium. Stanford, USA (2001)

Multidisciplinary Knowledge Modeling from Simulation and Specification to Support Concurrent and Collaborative Design

Jie Hu[1], Yinghong Peng[1], Dayong Li[1], Jilong Yin[1], and Guangleng Xiong[2]

[1] School of Mechanical Engineering, Shanghai Jiao Tong University,
200240 Shanghai, P.R. China
{hujie, yhpeng, dyli, yinjilong}@sjtu.edu.cn
[2] Department of Automation, Tsinghua University,
100080 Beijing, P.R. China
glxiong@cims.tsinghua.edu.cn

Abstract. This paper presents an approach of multidisciplinary knowledge modeling for concurrent and collaborative design. Firstly, a method to acquire the knowledge from simulation and specification is studied. The knowledge is used to constitute concurrent and collaborative design model. Secondly, a concurrent and collaborative design algorithm is presented to solve the model. Finally, the method is demonstrated by a design example of bogie. The results prove that multidisciplinary knowledge modeling from simulation data and specification is feasible, and the proposed method can be applied in concurrent and collaborative design process.

1 Introduction

The development process of a complex product may be involved with "time dimension" concurrence and "space dimension" collaboration. The overall performance of a complex product generally depends on a number of specifications distributed in multi-teams from different disciplines. Many researchers paid attention to concurrent and collaborative design approaches. Ahn and Kwon [1] presented an efficient reliability-based multidisciplinary design optimization (RBMDO) strategy. Rosenman et al. [2] put forward a 3D virtual world environment, which provides real-time multi-user collaboration for designers in different locations and allows for the different design disciplines to model their view of a building as different representations. Lee and Jeong [3] described the development of a decomposition based design (DBD) method using optimal sensitivity information with respect to coupled or interdisciplinary design variables. Chen and Jin [4] analyzed characteristics of multidisciplinary collaborative design (MCD) of product and proposed a new MCD-oriented product information model (MCDPM) that integrates physical structure, design semantic and collaboration management data. Kong et al. [5] developed an Internet-based collaboration system for a press-die design process for automobile manufacturers with CORBA, Java, Java3D and a relational database system. Yin et al. [6] presented an approach to component-based distributed cooperative design over the Internet where an extended multi-tier model (Browser/Server) is used to

W. Shen et al. (Eds.): CSCWD 2006, LNCS 4402, pp. 570–578, 2007.
© Springer-Verlag Berlin Heidelberg 2007

implement the web-based remote design system. Wang et al. [7] developed of a distributed multidisciplinary design optimization (MDO) environment (called WebBlow) using a number of enabling technologies including software agents, Internet/Web, and XML. Gantois and Morris [8] described a quite innovative multidisciplinary optimisation method based on robust design techniques. Giassi et al. [9] described a quite innovative multidisciplinary optimisation method based on robust design techniques: MORDACE (multidisciplinary optimisation and robust design approaches applied to concurrent engineering). Bai et al. [10] introduced the concept of the PLF (Product Layout Feature) and provided a solution to the problems of PLF modeling. As a result of the solution, collaborative design activities among multi-teams from different disciplines can be consistently carried out on PLF models in the PDM environment.

The problem with these researchers is that they focused on the coordination and optimization in concurrent and collaborative design. However, the most important problem for concurrent and collaborative design is that how to obtain the design knowledge from multidisciplinary domain.

A multidisciplinary knowledge modeling method to support concurrent and collaborative design is introduced in this paper. It collects the design knowledge from multidisciplinary simulation and specification to construct a formulated model for concurrent and collaborative design. Then, an approach of concurrent and collaborative design is presented and is illustrated by a bogie design example.

2 Knowledge Model for Concurrent and Collaborative Design

In this paper, the multidisciplinary knowledge includes the rules from multidisciplinary simulation (in Section 2.1) and the constraints from multidisciplinary specification (in Section 2.2). All knowledge is used to constitute concurrent and collaborative design model, which is presented in Section 2.3.

2.1 Knowledge from Multidisciplinary Simulation

Numerical simulation has been used more and more widely in almost all of the engineering areas. The simulation of increasingly complex phenomena leads to the

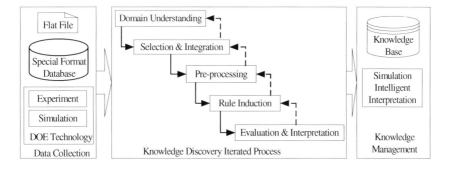

Fig. 1. Framework of knowledge discovery from simulation data

generation of vast quantities of data. Much of the output computational simulations is simply stored away on disks and is never effectively used at all. Extracting the engineering knowledge implicitly contained in simulation data is very meaningful and urgent [11-13]. It can help multidisciplinary designers understand the design parameters space more clearly and then decide which one is the optimal design. According to the characteristics of the multidisciplinary simulation data, a knowledge discovery framework is proposed as shown in Figure 1.

The detailed steps of knowledge discovery from the multidisciplinary simulation data based on fuzzy-rough sets theory are summarized as following:

Step 1. According to the domain knowledge, decide the center point for fuzzy partition. Adopt a fuzzy member function to transform the quantitative value into several linguistic term descriptions.

Step 2. Compute the decision class C_k through decision attribute subset d.

Step 3. For any condition attribute subset $B \in \rho(A)$, compute the fuzzy equivalence class $IND'(B)$.

Step 4. For each decision class C_k, compute $\underline{B}(C_k)$ and $\overline{B}(C_k)$ respectively, and insert them into certain object set and uncertain object set respectively.

Step 5. Repeat *step 3, 4* until all condition attribute subsets and all decision classes have been calculated.

Step 6. The certain rules are induced from certain object sets and the uncertain rules can be induced from uncertain object set. Calculate each rule's support degree, accuracy and efficiency measurement.

Step 7. Reduce the rule sets, and then add rules into fuzzy rule knowledge base.

After rule sets is obtained by knowledge discovery from simulation, rule sets is expressed as interval boxes such as $[x^L, x^U]$, which are adopted to describe the uncertainty of design parameters quantitatively to enhance the design robustness, and are used to construct concurrent and collaborative design model shown in Section 2.3.

2.2 Knowledge from Multidisciplinary Specification

In the process of a complex product design, we should consider multidisciplinary specifications, such as mechanics, cybernetics, dynamics and so forth. Design knowledge from specification in various disciplines can be divided into two classes: specification constraints and relation constraints. The former is design goals, including the requirements and limitations on product performance, shape size and so forth, which are determined by user requirements before starting design process. The latter is relationships between specifications and design variables, which can be obtained from design principles in each discipline. In traditional design, the information in specification constraints are not made full use, only treated as evaluated criteria.

In this paper, multidisciplinary knowledge from specification is quantitatively formulated as a set of constraints, which include equations, inequalities and ordinary differential equations (ODEs). ODEs describe the behavior of a dynamical system. All the constraints are used to construct the design model shown in Section 2.3.

2.3 Design Model Based on Multidisciplinary Knowledge

Multidisciplinary knowledge from simulation and specification are collected to construct concurrent and collaborative design model, in which interval boxes are adopted to characterize the uncertainties of design variables. The model is formulated as:

$$z(t) \in \left[z(t)^L, z(t)^U \right], x \in \left[x^L, x^U \right]$$

$$\text{s.t.} \begin{cases} g(z,x) = 0 & g = \left[g_1, g_2, \cdots, g_p \right]^T \\ h(z,x) \leq 0 & h = \left[h_1, h_2, \cdots, h_q \right]^T \\ \dfrac{dz}{dt} = f(z,x,t), f = \left[f_1, f_2, \cdots, f_n \right]^T \\ z(0) \in \left[z_0^{L0}, z_0^{U0} \right] \\ x \in \left[x^{L0}, x^{U0} \right] \end{cases} \tag{1}$$

where $z(t) \in R^n$ is a state variable vector of an n-dimensional continuous dynamical system, $x \in R^m$ is an m-dimensional design variable vector; g and h are constraint vectors of equations and inequalities respectively, and f is an nth-order ordinary differential equations (ODEs) vector describing the behavior of a dynamical system. g, h and f compose the set of constraints. $[z_0^{L0}, z_0^{U0}]$ and $[x^{L0}, x^{U0}]$ are the initial intervals, which are derived from rule sets in the knowledge discovery from simulation, $[z(t)^L, z(t)^U]$ and $[x^L, x^U]$ are consistent intervals filtered by concurrent and collaborative design algorithm which are corresponded to the given design goals. If the domain of any variable in z or x vector is empty, it means that there exists conflicts in current design project and some specifications cannot meet the requirements.

3 Concurrent and Collaborative Design

In this paper, an algorithm combined with genetic algorithm is put forward to resolve the design model. In order to use the algorithm to solve the design model, the formation of constraints must be uniformed to equalities, so the inequalities and ordinary differential equations (ODEs) should be transformed.

3.1 Model Transform

1) Transform of the inequalities

Construct a temporary vector θ for inequality constraint vector h, $\theta \in R^q$ and $\theta \geq 0$, with the help of, inequalities can be transformed into equalities.

$$h(z, X) \leq 0 \Rightarrow h(z, X) + \theta = 0 \tag{2}$$

2) Transform of ordinary differential equations

Considering the ordinary differential equations (ODE) vector f in Eqs. (1),

$$\begin{cases} \dot{z} = f(z,x,t) \quad z(t) \in R^n \quad x \in R^m \\ z(0) = z_0 \in \left[z_0^{L0}, z_0^{U0} \right] \end{cases} \tag{3}$$

If f is not dependent on time t which is coincident with engineering design requirement generally, Eqs. (3) could be rewritten as

$$\dot{z} = f(z,x) \tag{4}$$

whose solution is formulated as

$$z(x,t,z_0) = \left[z_1(x,t,z_0),...,z_m(x,t,z_0) \right]^{\mathrm{T}} \tag{5}$$

Eq. (5) shows the relationship between one of the system state variables and the its associated design variables. But in engineering design, it is difficult to obtain the analytical solution of Eq. (5), therefore some numerical methods are adopted to deal with Eq. (5) and obtain a series of values of state variables at some discrete time points:

$$z_{n+1} = z_n + f'(z_n, x, h) \tag{6}$$

where h is the iteration step size. Actually Euler method, Runge-Kutta method and so on can be used to evaluate the derivatives of f at a fixed time point t^*, then Eqs. (3) can be transformed to a group of algebra equations as result.

3.2 Concurrent and Collaborative Design Algorithm

The concurrent and collaborative design algorithm used to solve the design model is described as:

```
Procedure ModelResolve( In {C=[g,h,f],x₀,z₀}; Out {x, z})
Begin
   Transform inequality set h into equality set g₁
   Transform ODE set f into equality set g₂
   For t*=initial_time To final_time
      = Call IntervalResolve({x₀, z₀},{g,g₁,g₂})
      IF([x,z]=NULL) Then exit //conflict and exit
      EndIf
      x → x₀
      For each state_variables z_i
         z_i_max(t*)=max_GA(x, t*,z₀)
         z_i_min(t*)=min_GA(x, t*,z₀)
      EndFor
      Keep x, z_max(t*), z_min(t*) at the time point of t*
      t*= t*+h     // h is the step length of iteration
   EndFor
End
Procedure IntervalResolve(x, C(x))
Begin
   Boolean changed // a flag to judge the changes of
                      variable intervals
   While changed = TRUE Do changed← FALSE
      For j=1 TO p+q+n Do //aiming at all the constraints
         For i=1 To q+m+n Do //aiming at all the
                          variables in a constraint
            Approximate and narrow the constraints C_j(j=
            r,...,t,1≤ r≤ t≤ p+q+n) which x_i should satisfy
            approximate and narrow the interval consistent
```

```
              with the domain of (x₁,...,x_{i-1},x_{i+1},...,x_{q+m+n})
              If (the domain of xᵢ is empty)
                Then show conflict messages, Return NULL
              EndIf
              If (the interval of xᵢ is changed)
                Then changed = TRUE
                   Replace the old interval of xi with the
                   newly obtained interval
              EndIf
            EndFor
          EndFor
        EndWhile
      Return x
    End
```

The procedure of ModelResolve() is the main procedure to solve the model. The procedure of IntervalResolve() is used to solve the consistent space of design variables at every discrete time point t^*. In this algorithm, it implements two functions max_GA() and min_GA() with genetic algorithm to compute the maximum and minimum of state variables, because the arithmetic operation defined by Eqs. (14) ignores the relationships between variables which may lead divergent when solving ordinary differential equations (ODEs) (For example, when $x \in [-1,1]$, from Eqs. (14) $x - x \in [-2,2]$, not the correct answer 0). Using genetic algorithm will improve the correctness of approximation and narrowing functions with sacrificing complexity of the algorithm.

The aim of the above algorithm is to obtain the consistent space of design variables. Then, designers can use optimization method to obtain optimized solution in the consistent space.

4   Example

An example of bogie, which is shown in Figure 2, is chosen to illustrate how to design parameter based on multidisciplinary knowledge from simulation and specification. The bogie of a railway car is mainly composed of suspension, wheels and axle boxes, in which the design of dumping system including suspension spring and buffer spring is a key problem and involved with two disciplines: mechanics and dynamics.

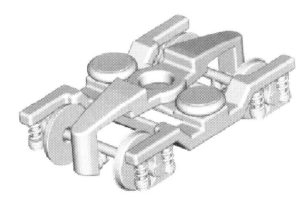

Fig. 2. An example of the railway vehicle bogie

The knowledge in bogie dumping system design is illustrated as follows.

Step 1. Multidisciplinary knowledge model
Step 1.1. Knowledge from multidisciplinary specification

1) Knowledge in mechanics

   Variables: spring ring diameter (D); spring wire diameter (d); effective round (n); compressed height of spring (H_{min}); free height of spring (H_0).
   Constants: maximal vertical load of spring (P_{max}); shear modulus (G); allowable stress ($[\tau]$).
   Constraints:

$$\tau_{max} = \frac{8P_{max}DC_m}{\pi d^3} \leq [\tau] \text{ (Stress constraint)} \tag{7}$$

$$m = D/d \text{ (Spring index)} \tag{8}$$

$$C_m = (4m-1)/(4m-4)+0.615m^{-1} \text{ (Stress correction coefficient)} \tag{9}$$

$$d = \sqrt{\frac{8P_{max}mC_m}{\pi[\tau]}} \text{ (Constraint on } d) \tag{10}$$

$$K_v = \frac{Gd}{8nm^3} = \frac{Gd^4}{8nD^3} \text{ (Stiffness contraint)} \tag{11}$$

$$H_{min} = (n+1)d = H_0 - 1.6/K_v \text{ (Compressed height constraint)} \tag{12}$$

2) Knowledge in dynamics

   Variables: bogie drift (z); time variable (t).
   Constants: wave range of the railway (a); dumping index of the dumper (C); car weight (M).
   Constraints:

$$z_t = a\sin \omega t \text{ (Equation of the railway)} \tag{13}$$

$$F = C\dot{z} \text{ (Resistance of dumper)} \tag{14}$$

$$M\dot{z} = -K_v(z-z_t) - C(\dot{z}-\dot{z}_t) \text{ (Constrained vibration equation)} \tag{15}$$

$$\beta_1 = \frac{\sqrt{1+4D_t^2 r^2}}{\sqrt{(1-r^2)^2 + 4D_t^2 r^2}} \text{ (Amplitude factor of vibration)} \tag{16}$$

$$D_t = C/2\sqrt{K_v M} \tag{17}$$

$$r = \omega \sqrt{\frac{K_v}{M}} \tag{18}$$

Step 1.2. Knowledge from multidisciplinary simulation
In this paper, the commercial finite-element program ANSYS is used for the analysis of the bogie dumping system. The simulation is carried out with different parameters. Then the concerned FEA data is collected into a decision table. According to the domain knowledge, each of the parameters is discretized into three levels. A Boolean Reasoning discretization method is carried out to discretize other condition attributes into several levels. The knowledge discovery method, which is shown in Section 2.1, is adopted to acquire explicit rules. It can deal with continuous data in simulation results and does not depend much on prior knowledge. Based on the acquired rules, the initial intervals is derived from rule sets in this example as follows:

$$D_1 \in [115,165] \, , \, d_1 \in [26,30] \, , \, n_1 \in [4,10] \, , \, D_2 \in [70,150] \, , \, d_2 \in [16,20] \, , \, n_2 \in [6,9] \, ,$$
$$D_3 \in [60,100] \, , d_3 \in [22,25] \, , n_3 \in [4,8.5] \, , C \in [220,400] \, .$$

Step 1.3. Design model based on multidisciplinary knowledge
The design model based on knowledge from multidisciplinary specification and simulation is formulated by Eqs. (1), where $x = (D_1,d_1,n_1,D_2,d_2,n_2,D_3,d_3,n_3,C)$ is design variable vector; $g=[g_1, g_2, g_3, g_4, g_5, g_6, g_7, g_8, g_9]^T$ are constraints described by Eqs. (8)-(18), $h=[h_1]^T$ is constraints described by Eq. (7), $f=[f_1, f_2]$ are described by Eqs. (14)(15), $[x^{L0},x^{U0}]$ and $[z_0^{L0},z_0^{U0}]$ are initial intervals, $[x^L, x^U]$ and $[z^L,z^U]$ are consistent intervals.

Step 2. Concurrent and collaborative design
In the design model, $[z_0^{L0},z_0^{U0}]$ and $[x^{L0},x^{U0}]$ are initial intervals, which is based on rule sets obtained by knowledge discovery from simulation; $[z(t)^L,z(t)^U]$ and $[x^L,x^U]$ are consistent intervals filtered by concurrent and collaborative design algorithm, which are corresponded to the given design goals. If the domain of any variable in z or x vector is empty, it means that there exists conflicts in current design project and some specifications cannot meet the requirements. Finally, designers can use optimization method to obtain optimized solution in the consistent intervals.

The results of initial intervals are shown as the third column in Table 1. In this table, the results of consistent interval are shown as the fourth column; and the results of optimized value are shown as the last column.

Table 1. The design results of bogie dumping components

Variable name	Denotation	Initial interval	Consistent interval	Optimized value
D_1	Outer spring ring diameter	[115, 165]	[133.3, 142.1]	140.0
d_1	Outer spring wire diameter	[26, 30]	[27.87, 30]	30.0
n_1	Outer spring effective round	[4, 10]	[4.21, 7.55]	4.3
D_2	Inner spring ring diameter	[70, 150]	[74.0, 80.6]	75.0
d_2	Inner spring wire diameter	[16, 20]	[16.95, 20.0]	20.0
n_2	Inner spring effective round	[6, 9]	[7.1, 8.89]	7.2
D_3	Dump spring ring diameter	[60, 100]	[61.1, 77.2]	65.0
d_3	Dump spring wire diameter	[22, 25]	[22.4, 24.73]	24.5
n_3	Dump spring effective round	[4, 8.5]	[4.47, 8.5]	5.0
C	Dumping index of dumper	[220, 400]	[315.3, 367.4]	330.0

5 Conclusions

In this paper, a knowledge-based concurrent and collaborative design method is presented. In the process of multidisciplinary knowledge modeling, knowledge discovery from the multidisciplinary simulation data based on fuzzy-rough sets theory is discussed. Knowledge from multidisciplinary specification is formulated as a set of constraints. Multidisciplinary knowledge model can be used to detect conflict and obtain consistent solution space for concurrent and collaborative design. A design example is given and it proves that the proposed method is efficient. The method described in this paper is used to develop knowledge driven multidisciplinary concurrent and collaborative design system, which is now running in a railway vehicle design project.

Acknowledgments. This paper is supported by the National Natural Science Foundation of China (Nos. 50575142 and 60304015) and the Shanghai Committee of Science and Technology (Nos. 055107048 and 04ZR14081).

References

1. Ahn, J., Kwon, J.H.: An efficient strategy for reliability-based multidisciplinary design optimization using BLISS. Structural and Multidisciplinary Optimization (5)(2006) 363-372
2. Rosenman, M.A., Smith, G., Maher, M.L., Ding, L., Marchant, D.: Multidisciplinary collaborative design in virtual environments. Automation in Construction (1)(2007) 37-44
3. Lee, J., Jeong, H.: A decomposition based design method coordinated by disciplinary subspace optimization. Mechanical Systems Machine Elements and Manufacturing 3 (2006) 935-941
4. Chen, L., Jin, G.: Product modeling for multidisciplinary collaborative design. International Journal of Advanced Manufacturing Technology 30(7-8) (2006) 589-600
5. Kong, S.H., Noh, S.D., Han, Y.-G., Kim, G., Lee, K.I.: Internet-based collaboration system: Press-die design process for automobile manufacturer. International Journal of Advanced Manufacturing Technology (9)(2002) 701-708
6. Yin, G., Tian, G., Taylor, D.: A web-based remote cooperative design for spatial cam mechanisms. International Journal of Advanced Manufacturing Technology (8)(2002) 557-563
7. Wang, Y., Shen, W., Ghenniwa, H.: A web/agent-based multidisciplinary design optimization environment. Computers in Industry (1)(2003) 17-28
8. Gantois, K., Morris, A.J.: The multi-disciplinary design of a large-scale civil aircraft wing taking account of manufacturing costs. Structural and Multidisciplinary Optimization (1) (2004) 31-46
9. Giassi, A., Bennis, F., Maisonneuve, J.J.: Multidisciplinary design optimisation and robust design approaches applied to concurrent design. Structural and Multidisciplinary Optimization (5)(2004) 356-371
10. Bai, Y., Chen, Z., Bin, H., Hu, J.: Collaborative design in product development based on product layout model. Robotics and Computer-Integrated Manufacturing (1)(2005) 55-65
11. Fayyad, U., Piatetsky-Shapiro, G., Smyth, P., Uthurusamy, R.: Advances in Knowledge Discovery in Databases. MIT Press, Cambridge, Mass. (1996)
12. Braha, D.: Data Mining for Design and Manufacturing: Methods and Applications. Kluwer Academic Publishers (2001)
13. Robert, L.G.: Data Mining for Scientific and Engineering Applications. Kluwer Academic Publishers (2001)

Function-Solution-Findings-Model of the Conceptual Design Based on knowledge Ontology

Dongyan Shi and Renlong Liu

College of Mechanical and Electrical Engineering, Harbin Engineering University
Harbin 150001, China
shidongyan@hrbeu.edu.cn, renlongliu@hotmail.com

Abstract. Knowledge representation is a key to the success of conceptual design where much implicit knowledge is left by different designers involved in the design. The traditional methods of knowledge representation lack explicit expressions for knowledge sharing. This paper presents a framework of functional knowledge based on ontology which can provide a good inference mechanism, in order to represent knowledge formally and explicitly in the conceptual design. The framework consists of three-level ontology constrained by semantic and syntax. In addition, a function structure meta-model (FSFM, Function-Solution-Findings-Model) is proposed for the innovative design in the conceptual design phase according to the knowledge framework. The knowledge ontology layers are defined in the meta-model and their relationship in the meta-model is discussed as well. Ontology modeling language OWL is applied to describe function ontology. Finally, an example is proposed to illustrate the process of the solving model.

1 Introduction

The conceptual design is an early stage in the design process. It consists of three parts, i.e. function, principle and structure (F-P-S). The computer support system for the conceptual design is mainly F-P-S mapping based on function expression [1]. The procedure should be an intelligent process as knowledge expression and reasoning. Pahl and Beitz [2] pointed out in *Engineer Design* that the general function of design object may be defined from the description for design task, and some proper sub-functions may be acquired through decomposing the general function; the procedure is expressed by means of the function structure tree with hierarchy relation termed the function structure diagram, which shows the relation among sub-functions. The creativity of conceptual design is from the composition of morphologism matrix after decomposing function [2]. Therefore, the composite relation of function structure is the key to research contents of conceptual design. Function has played an important role, because it not only represents function information and principle knowledge, but also provides basic information of geometry for structure design. Many scholars described function from different viewpoints [3-9], but there is no agreement on the definition of function, especially, to different designers the knowledge in the stage is usually left implicit.

W. Shen et al. (Eds.): CSCWD 2006, LNCS 4402, pp. 579–588, 2007.
© Springer-Verlag Berlin Heidelberg 2007

In addition, most of function descriptions can be used for an original or creative design. However, in the market environment, the original or creative design type only makes up of 20% in all of design types, and most of design types are the adaptable design and the mutational design that make up of 80% [1][10]. Thus, it is necessary to make a further research on these design types.

This paper presents a framework of functional knowledge based on ontology, in order to represent knowledge formally and explicitly in the conceptual design. A function-based solving model (FSFM, Function-Solution-Findings-Model) is established for the innovative design type.

2 Solving Model for Conceptual Design

Function-based solving model for conceptual design FSFM (Function--Solution--Findings--Model) is developed on the base of function-effect-principle-structure solving process and domain knowledge. Pahl&Beitz presented the framework based on Function-Effect-Principle-Structure, which provided foundation to establish design process for conventional design. F-E-P-S mapping knowledge may solve conceptual design problem on the base of the FEPS framework through using function decomposition knowledge. FEPS framework establishes a causal chain from function, through behavior, to structure, which is foundation of reasoning process for conceptual design. Based on the model, conceptual design information is abstracted in different level. Combination of information in different level provides an approach for realizing design innovation.

In the present paper, function-based conceptual design solving model FSFM is established on the basis of the model, see Figure 1.

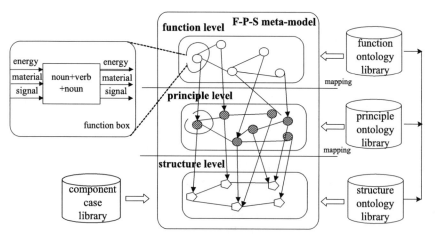

Fig. 1. Framework of function solving model

1) Effect level is removed in this model and F-P-S meta-model is constituted. This is because function definition and representation uses the method of combining functional verb, and input and output flow. Effect level may be shown in the taxonomy of input and output flow.

2) The function semantic form of "noun+verb+noun" is applied. Adding noun before verb suits representation for function. For example, the form of "verb+noun" only represents "convert energy" rather than "mechanical energy converts electrical energy" and "pressure converts force". The purpose of this kind of definition enables computer to reason better for solving process and improve solving efficiency. The function-based definition and representation leads design process to realize.

3) Ontology theory is applied and domain knowledge of conceptual design is established. Thus, domain knowledge concept consistently understood by designers may be acquired.

FSFM is an integrated design model system in which domain theory knowledge is embedded. At the same time, FSFM maintains consistency for integrated design model. FSFM model integrates conceptual ontology knowledge, model knowledge and meta-model. The description for FSFM design process is as following:

1) Establishment of initial meta-model: The initial meta-model is basic information of describing design goal. In the present paper, the initial meta-model uses function-principle-structure (FPS) system. The meta-model needs describe concepts and relation among concepts of the system, and their topological structure et al.

2) Extending meta-model: The initial meta-model doesn't contain enough information of design goal. Therefore, it needs use knowledge, such as causal knowledge (ontology knowledge) to extend information of meta-model. In this way physical principle contained in design goal can be reasoned out.

3) Synthesis and analysis on the base of design model system: Applying various design model systems evaluate design solution. The model system supports model process through input and output function semantic information of system. Design consistency is maintained in different design goal because concept consistency.

In FSFM model, stage 1 and 2 is operated in basic concept ontology level, stage 3 is operated through model and uses domain knowledge in model system to control model process, such as model management, evaluation, creation et al. Model knowledge corresponding to model system needs contain not only concepts required in creating model process, but also concepts captured as model result. Figure 2 is an abstract representing framework of FSFM model.

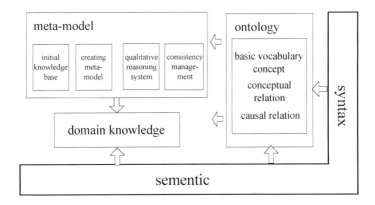

Fig. 2. Knowledge structure model of FSFM

3 The Establishment of the Knowledge Ontology Level

At present the basic idea of developing knowledge ontology may be roughly classified into two categories. One is top-down developing method. In this method, we first establish highly abstract ontology, and then establish ontology on the next layer under the constraint of the ontology. And the ontology provides constructing elements to ontology on the next layer. The other is Bottom-Up developing method, in which each system step by step expands into a general domain ontology through integration, mapping and uniting of ontology. It usually manifests itself as a large knowledge base. We apply a comprehensive plan to the knowledge expression under the framework of the FSPM model of product. First, domain experts establish domain ontology, and then ontology is automatically or semi-automatically obtained from the existing various data in domain under the instruction and constraint of the ontology.

3.1 The Function Knowledge Ontology Model

It is necessary to determine the concepts which function ontology involves and relates to function before establishing function ontology. In this way, the ontology established has enough information to provide the relatively precise and probable search to the following process.

The function ontology model established in this paper contains the core concepts as follows:

- class: function
               function flow
               flow relationship
- attributes: function object
               sub-function
               function type
               meta-function
               purpose function
               function component
               in/output flow

In which model, function representation is a function related with components; sub-function is a hierarchy among functions; function type and meta-function provide the lexicon of ontology; purpose function is connected with meta-function and function; function component and in/output flow associate function with components and flows respectively. Figure 3 shows the relation of the UML class of function. UML is an object-oriented graphical language in that is accepted by most of people and engineers. Establishing ontology also needs modeling, and so does establishing a large engineering ontology particularly. Ontology must be accepted by most of people in order to become engineering because ontology language is only a patent of a few people. Therefore, we establish UML class diagram of model and determine the relation among concepts so as to establish ontology conveniently and fast. Another method is converting the existing UML class diagram to the ontology modeling language OWL directly and automatically, that is mapping part of UML semantic to OWL. We do not pay attention to the method in the paper.

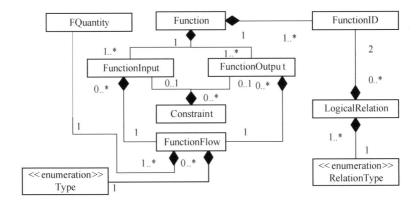

Fig. 3. UML Class diagram for FPS model

3.2 Function Ontology Semantic Tree

Function semantic tree is established in terms of Schank's Conceptual Dependency Theory. It is a kind of approach to describe semantic. Knowledge ontology of function representation uses Conceptual Dependency Theory to create function ontology library. The ontology library is represented in form of function ontology semantic tree.

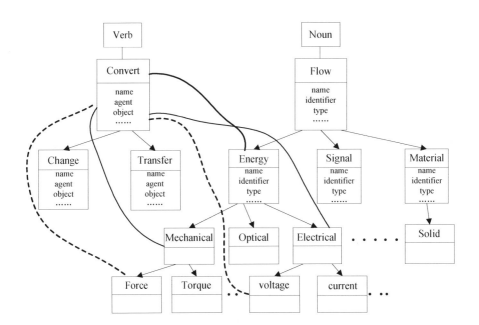

Fig. 4. Relationship of verb and noun

Function ontology semantic tree can realize connection of concept and is convenient for semantic search. Function semantic is tree structure with conceptual hierarchy. We combine existing representing method of function solving knowledge, and apply function ontology semantic tree to knowledge representation of natural semantic understanding. Tree structure is a kind of knowledge representation framework. Tree is hierarchy defined by branching relation. Tree structure widely exists in the objective world and is widely used in computer field. In addition, researchers have deeply studied all kinds of searching strategies for tree and formed lots of methods, such as deep-first search, wide-first search et al.

In function ontology semantic tree, conceptual dependency relation means that one conceptual extension contain another conceptual all extension. Root is the most abstract concept and leaf is the most concrete concept. The nodes between root and leaf are concepts on different abstract levels respectively. These nodes are connected to form tree structure through lines linking one node to the other.

Function ontology semantic tree includes verb semantic tree and noun semantic tree because function semantic representation includes verb and noun, as shown in Figure 4. Verb semantic tree and noun semantic tree are connected through definition of verb and noun concepts and attributes.

For "solid", "convert", "gas", one concept is verb and the other two is noun. But the three concepts can be connected through function ontology tree. The object of "convert" is "gas" and the subject is "solid". In the conceptual tree of "solid" and "gas", we can find both concepts are from the same nodes of the tree, i.e. through searching we can know that "solid" and "gas" belong to "material". Semantic relation among concepts can be decided through defining "convert", "solid" and "gas". Thus, although function semantic is uncertain, computer can automatically deal with non-canonical function semantic through connection among concepts.

In fact, the concept-based dependency relation can constitute conceptual network. In function ontology library, selecting conceptual dependency relation can be supplement to knowledge method.

3.3 Function Ontology Library and Its Representation

We apply object-oriented representation for function ontology library.
A definition for noun class is:

```
Noun
    name            String
    type            String
    id              String          // identifier of noun
    node            Int             // node of noun
    hasSubnodes     {[Noun]}        // children nodes of noun
    subnodeOf       [Noun]          // parent node of noun
    classifiedType  String
    resource        String
```

The attribute "resource" links other domain resources. Semantic that doesn't in the function ontology library can acquire through other resources.

A definition for verb class is:

```
Verb
    name            String
    id              String
    agent           [Noun]          // subject of verb
    object          [Noun]          // object of verb
    way             String          // realizing way
    node            Int
    hasSubnodes     {[Verb]}        // children nodes of verb
    subnodeOf       [Verb]          // parent node of verb
    resource        String
```

The attribute "object" links a noun entity. In Figure 4, "mechanical energy converts electrical energy" can be shown through the connection between noun and verb, see real line section. If input is "torque converts voltage", from connective dashed line we can acquire the information that "convert energy, mechanical energy converts electrical energy". This can provide necessary information for innovative design of product.

4 Function Representation in OWL

In ontology descriptive languages based on the artificial intelligence, we describe knowledge ontology in Web Ontology Language (OWL). OWL is the semantic descriptive framework developed by W3C organization on the basis of Resource Description Framework (RDF). OWL may clearly express the meaning of terms and the relations of them in the vocabulary list. The expression for terms and relations is termed as Ontology. OWL has more mechanisms than XML, RDF and RDF Schema to express semantic [12]. Thus, OWL exceeds XML, RDF and RDF Schema which are only able to express the documents that can be read by the computer on web. The modeling primitive in OWL include class, subclass of, property, sub-property of, domain, range and type. The words may be expanded according to our knowledge need in own domain when we use them. Then, we may use these words to make a concrete OWL data model of the related domain.

The modeling language is usually based on the descriptive logic in the development of knowledge ontology. The developing method may acquire nice reasoning supports because it is comparatively mature for the research of the reasoning mechanism describing logic.

The function is defined by "noun+verb+noun", which is the equal of natural language. It specified the relation of input and output. The exiting vocabulary resource can be applied to express the verb and noun. It is a semantic dictionary consisting of terminology and all kind of relations existing among terminologies, which may reflect semantic related concept of the domain of some subject. We may modify and expand vocabulary in terms of the feature of ontology because the existing resource may be shared. At present the majority of research is on the English standard ontology integrated vocabulary, such as the Standard Upper Ontology (SUO) created by the IEEE work group [14] and the Knowledge Systems Laboratory (KSL) created by Stanford University of USA. We classify verb. According to the English feature, we define ten general verbs at the base of five verbs presented by Roth [15]. They are Store, Change, Channel, and Guide, Connect, Transform, Produce, Provide and Measure. The principle layer followed is also classified in terms of the ten verbs. The function knowledge ontology model is expressed as shown in Figure 5.

```
</owl: Function Ontology>
<owl:Class rdf:ID="&Function; Function Verbs"/ >
<owl:Class rdf:ID="&Function; Function Input/Output">
<rdfs:subClassOf rdf:resource=" &Function; Function Verbs "/>
</owl:Class>
<owl:ObjectProperty rdf:ID="&Function; Function Type">
<rdf:type rdf:resource="&owl; Functional Property" />
</owl:ObjectProperty>
```

Fig. 5. Function representation described in OWL

5   An Instance of the Concept Design Model

Let us take mechanical hand as example to illustrate the process of conceptual design model. Function model of mechanical hand consists of function units in different levels. Its main function is "convey workpiece" and this is also the overall function of mechanical hand. For representation of overall function, verb = "convey" and noun= "workpiece". The overall function can be decomposed into "catch workpiece", "hold workpiece", "release workpiece", "return position" and "set workpiece". The sub-function "catch workpiece" can be decomposed into "convert force", "amplify force", "transmit force", and "connect force". These function verbs is directly from general function verb set or special function verb set.

The function model resulted from canonically defining product function (The system provides advices for standardization in terms of related data dictionary and connection among concepts.) reflects customers' requirement for this kind of product. This is the foundation that mechanical hand realizes physical principle of solution and simplification of structure. The decomposition according to function hierarchy ensures that the lowest function units can find physical principle and structure. The verb in function unit must be a canonical general function verb or special function verb. Figure 6 shows the function-principle-structure model of the mechanical hand.

The final solution of conceptual design is a physical scheme represented by structure diagram. The structure diagram consists of structure units. The structure unit in the example is a basic structure unit of innovative design. Note that the composition of structures is rather complexity in factual design. Structure units are not only from basic structure units of innovative design, but also from the component case library. These components are design resource.

The range of function, principle and structure is entity. This kind of definition can describe design knowledge and design constrain. Experience knowledge of designers can be convert a model saving in computer through creating the model mentioned above. This can help new designers to design.

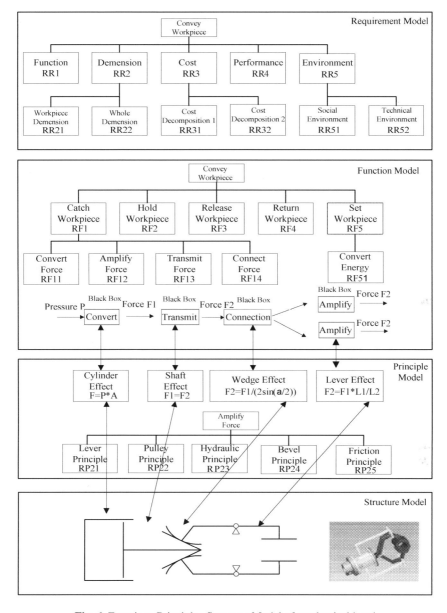

Fig. 6. Function--Principle--Structure Model of mechanical hand

6   Conclusions and Future Work

The conceptual design phase is the intelligent reasoning process based on knowledge representation. The design knowledge model is the foundation of the intelligent design. The ontology theory is applied to describe the design knowledge model, which produces an effective way to realize conceptual design intelligently and automatically. Function-based solving model FSFM (Function-Solution-Findings-Model) is presented for the conceptual design on the basis of ontology. A knowledge ontology framework is established and discussed in FSFM. The object-oriented UML class diagram is applied to map to the ontology modeling language OWL, which may establish the ontology knowledge model conveniently and efficiently. Function ontology is discussed in detail.

Our research provides the theory for the conceptual design automation.

The further research includes the realization of the reasoning process and the mapping between ontologies.

References

1. Gero, J.: Towards a Model of Designing Which Includes its Situatedness. In: Universal design Theory. Shaker Verlag, Achen (1998)
2. Pahl, G. and Beitz, W.: Engineering Design. 2nd edn. Springer-Verlag, London (1999)
3. Francis, E.H.: Product Modeling for Conceptual Design Support. Computer in Industry 48 (2002) 143-155
4. Chakrabarti, A. and Thomas, P.B.: A Scheme for Functional Reasoning in Conceptual Design. Design Studies 22 (2001) 493-517
5. Cangopadhyay, A.: Conceptual Modeling from Natural Language Functional Specifications. Artificial Intelligence in Engineering 15 (2001) 207-218
6. Sasajima, M. and Kitamura, Y.: A Representation Language for Behavior and Function: FBRL. Expert Systems With Applications 10 (1996) 471-479
7. Kitamura, Y.: A Functional Concept Ontology and its Application to Automatic Identification to Functional Structures. Advanced Engineering Informatics 16 (2002) 145-163
8. Kitamura, Y.: Ontology-based Description if Functional Design Knowledge and Its Use in a Functional Way Server. Expert Systems With Application 24 (2003) 153-166
9. Yoshioka, M.: Physical Concept Ontology for the Knowledge Intensive Engineering Framework. Advance Engineering Information 18 (2004) 95-113
10. Grabowski, H. and Huang, M.: Constraint Based Solution Finding for Multi-discipline Products. Erschienen in Photonics EAST Symposium, Boston (2000)
11. Huang, W.: The Ontology Construction and Semantic Integrated Study. East-South Universtity, Nanjing (2005)
12. Resource Description Framework(RDF). URL: http//:www.w3cchina.org
13. Cranefield, S. and Purvis, M.: UML as an Ontology Modeling Language. Proc. IJCAI-99 Workshop on Intelligent Information Integration. Stockholm, Sweden (1999) 224-228
14. Standard Upper Ontology (SUO). URL: http://suo. ieee.org
15. Roth, K.: Konstrukieren mit Konstruktionskalalogen Band II. Springer, Berlin (1994)

Towards Dynamic Cooperation of e-Services with Security Based on Trusted Right Delegation

Jingfan Tang

Institute of Software and Intelligent Technology, Hangzhou Dianzi University,
Hangzhou 310018, P.R. China
tangjf@hdu.edu.cn

Abstract. With the rapid development of e-Service market, a large number of e-Services, for example, stock trading, real-time traffic report, or travel planning, are already available on the Web. In order to achieve the complex business requirement using e-Services, there has been a growing interest in e-Services composition and cooperation. In order to make effective utilization of Internet resources, it is a trend to enable the e-Services to be dynamically deployed and executed for composition and cooperation. This paper will focus on security issues in dynamic composition and cooperation of e-Services. With the extended WSDL description and through the replication technique, the replica of an e-Service can be dynamically deployed and executed on the optimum server, which is selected from the registered servers in the enhanced UDDI center. And, a security mechanism of trusted right delegation is introduced to ensure the safely and dynamically sharing of the resources among the e-Services.

1 Introduction

In order to remain competitive in a business world, more and more enterprises utilize e-Services to encapsulate the internal business process to provide web applications to all kinds of clients. Through the interchanging of the e-Services, the business interaction of cross-enterprise application systems can be executed efficiently. Traditional service-oriented architecture is always built through the statically binding of e-Services, which is lack of the flexibility and can not cater for the dynamically changing of e-Service market. The e-Services are always bound with the specific servers after being registered into the UDDI center, and the developing and deploying of the e-Services are not fully separated. As an emerging services market, some enterprises can only provide the service servers (service execution environment) for the deploying and execution of the e-Services developed by other enterprises. In order to achieve such cooperation, some efficient mechanism should be provided to ensure the secure sharing of the cross-enterprise resources.

Replication technique has been proposed to provide scalable deployment of high-demand network services by allowing an arbitrary service to be performed by multiple service replicas [1]. Since some services need the specific resources and environment

W. Shen et al. (Eds.): CSCWD 2006, LNCS 4402, pp. 589–598, 2007.
© Springer-Verlag Berlin Heidelberg 2007

to run them, the cross-enterprise resources should be shared among the services replica, which may bring the security issue.

To address these issues, we present a novel model in this paper to support the dynamic cooperation of e-Services through the dynamic deploying of the e-Services with security. Under service-oriented architecture, the e-Service is used to encapsulate the business application to be registered into the enhanced UDDI center. The developing and deploying of the e-Services are fully separated to enable the e-Service to be dynamically deployed on the available cross-enterprise servers, which are also registered in the enhanced UDDI center. In order to ensure the safely and dynamically sharing of the cross-enterprise resources among the e-Services, a security mechanism of trusted right delegation is introduced.

2 Related Work

In the past few years, business process or workflow proposals relevant to e-Services are proliferating in the business and academic world. Most of the proposals are XML-based languages to specify e-Services interactions and compositions. For example, the Business Process Execution Language for Web Services (BPEL4WS) is a formal specification of business processes and interaction protocols [2]. And, in [3], it presented a framework to enable services that support the establishment, management and execution of business processes across enterprises boundaries. In [8], it discussed the deployment of e-services in a networked enterprise setting. A framework was introduced to support fully web-accessible legacy system services with modern business services. It also argued in favor of three faceted services combing the following constructs: a service description language, a service request language and a functional specification language. In [9], it introduced a scheme for integrating e-Services in establishing virtual enterprises. The method takes two workflow views, one representing a service request and the other a service provision (advertisement), with a mix of vital and non-vital steps and a rich set of constraints, and returns a list of possible legal combinations, if any exist.

A novel approach has been presented in [7] to address the problem of the dynamic allocation of services on the available servers for execution. XML is used to describe the services by encoding such factors as resource configuration, performance, and service-specific capabilities, which enables services to be easily developed, composed, deployed, relocated, monitored and managed in distributed environment. Based on the research in [1][6-7][10-11], we will add the capability of security in the dynamic cooperation of cross-enterprise services by introducing the mechanism of trusted right delegation to enable the safely sharing of the cross-enterprise resources among the e-Services in the emerging e-Service market.

3 Architecture Overview

Figure 1 shows the whole architecture with the interaction among the entities:

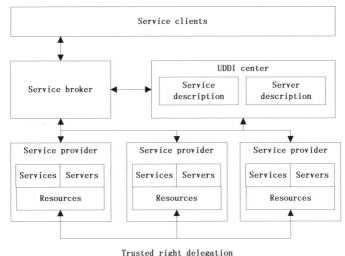

Fig. 1. Architecture overview

3.1 Extended WSDL Description

In order to support the fully separation of developing and deploying services, the WSDL document should be extended by adding the information of configuration and resources, which are described by the following items:

- *PackagesAddr*: describe the address of service replica, which can be dynamically deployed on the host server for running through dynamic replication technique.
- *ServiceShare*: describe the service share [4] which is required for running the service replica. It can also be used as search condition of selecting the available server to run the service replica.
- *Configuration*: describe the configuration information of running the service replica, which can be used by host server to initialize the running environment.
- *FaultHandlingPolicies*: describe the policies of fault tolerance [11], which can be used by host server to deal with the occurrence of fault in the service replica.
- *Resources*: describe the specific resources, which will be used during the execution process of the e-Service, such as database, etc.

3.2 Enhanced UDDI Center

An enhanced UDDI center is provided to support the registration of server descriptions by the enterprises (service providers), which provide the available servers for deploying and running the replicas of e-Services. The XML document is adopted to describe the server information including the following items:

- *ServerInterface*: describe the interface of the server, which includes the information of server name, owner, IP and open ports, etc.

- *AvailableServiceShare*: describe the available service share provided by the server to run the service replica, which can be dynamically updated at the run time.
- *PricingPolicies*: describe the pricing policies provided by the server to run the service replica, which can be used in the calculation of service evaluation function [6].
- *TrustEvaluation*: describe the trust level of the server, which will also be used in the calculation of service evaluation function.

3.3 Service Broker

As a key component in our architecture, service broker mainly implements the following functionalities:

- Receive the service request from service client.
- Query UDDI center for the service according to the service request.
- Select the optimum server according to service evaluation function with the registered service description and server description in UDDI center.
- Replicate the service and allocate the service replica on the selected server for dynamically deploying and running.

In order to support the separation of e-Services from the host server, service broker will be able to dynamically select the most available service (server) through the service evaluation function and the registration information of the service provider during the dynamic discovery of e-Service (server).

In our architecture, it also allows the separation of e-Services from required resources. The accessing of cross-enterprise resources should also be safe to assure the stable running of the service replicas. The required resources can be shared cross enterprises through the trusted right delegation to address the security, which will be introduced in Section 5.2.

As an open architecture, it supports the dynamically joining of the enterprises by registering the services or servers in UDDI center to take part in the dynamically cooperation process of the business services. During the process, the enterprises can dynamically update the registered information such as the pricing policies, etc. And, service broker will dynamically adjust its behavior to cater for such changes.

4 Dynamic Service Allocation and Execution

As shown in Figure 2, the server state collector is used to dynamically collect the state of running servers for selecting the available servers to allocate the service replica for execution. The description for each registered server is stored in server description repository, which defines the capacity of available service share, pricing policies and trust evaluation.

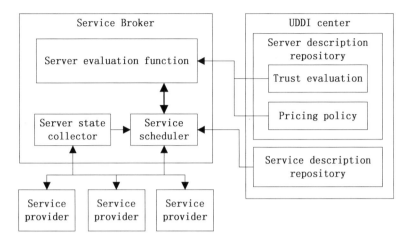

Fig. 2. Dynamic service allocation and execution

4.1 Server Evaluation Function

As introduced in [6], server evaluation function (SEF) is used to give synthetic evaluation on the available service share, pricing policy and trust evaluation. Following shows the definitions. (Let D_i denotes the service server and S_i denotes the service)

- $$Ps = \begin{cases} PS(t, p_1, p_2, ..., p_n) & (1) \\ RqC(S_i) \times CPSS(D_i) & (2) \end{cases}$$

P_s evaluates the total cost of the service S_i requested by the service server D_i for the execution of service S_i. In the case of (1), the service has been run on the service server, and the value of P_s decided by the pricing policy under the conditions of p_1, p_2, ..., p_n at the current time t. In the case of (2), the service is not running on the service server, which has the available service share to run the service. The value of P_s at this time is decided by the function of $RqC(S_i) \times CPSS(D_i)$, where $RqC(S_i)$ means the required capacity of the service share to run the service S_i and $CPSS(D_i)$ means the cost per service share proposed by the service server D_i at the current time t, which is defined in the description of server.

- $$Ts = TL(D_i) \times \Upsilon(t - t_i)$$

T_s describes the trust of the service server at current time t, where $TL(D_i)$ denotes the trust level of D_i, stored in the description of server, and $\Upsilon(t-t_i)$ denotes the decay function (where t is the current time and t_i is the time of the last update or the last transaction).

After giving the above definitions, we can define SEF using the above parameters as: $Sef=SEF(P_s, T_s)$. A simple example of SEF can be: $SEF(P_s, T_s)=P_s/T_s$.

4.2 Dynamic Allocation and Execution

According to the value of above SEF, the service can be dynamically allocated to the selected optimum server:

- If the services are already running on some service servers (provided by the service providers), the optimum service servers will be chosen for the allocation of the service due to the SEF value, which is evaluated through pricing policy.
- If the services are not running on any service servers, service scheduler should first choose the service servers with the available capacity of service share to run the service, and then, it should choose the optimum service server to allocate the service according to the SEF value, which is evaluated upon the cost per service share proposed by service server. The service can be initiated on the server for running according to the configuration information in the extended WSDL document of the service.

5 Security Mechanism

During the running process, e-Service will require some specific resources to achieve the business requirement such as database, equipment, etc. Since the e-Services are allowed to be dynamically deployed on cross-enterprise servers for running in our architecture, some efficient mechanism should be provided to support the operations on the resources with security. In this paper, we adopt the mechanism of trusted right delegation to address it. Before describing the mechanism in detail, we will introduce the definitions first.

5.1 Definitions

1. Right
"Right" means the authority owned by e-Service to do some operations on the specific resources. The deployed service replica should be authorized the right before performing the specific operation on the resources. The following shows the logical form of "right" in Prolog:

```
rightToDo(ServiceName, ResourceName, Operation, Constraint)
```

- ServiceName: the name of the e-Service, which can be used as unique ID to identify the e-Service.
- ResourceName: the name of the resource, which can be used as unique ID to identify the resource.
- Operation: the operation on the resource which the e-Service can perform.
- Constraint: the restriction on the right, i.e. Owner (ServiceName, "Serv1") means the service with the name of "Serv1" owns the right.

Using this statement, all kinds of rights can be specified with a constraint. An e-Service can do the operation only if it satisfies all the constraints.

2. Delegation

"Delegation" means the rights owned by some e-Services on the operation of the specific resources can be assigned to other e-Services. An e-Service can own some rights on the operation of some resources which is specified in the policy or has been delegated to it. It can also delegate this right to other e-Services if it has been given the right to subsequently delegate it. A delegation itself is a right which can be delegated. So, an e-Service could be given the right to perform some action but not to further delegate it or given the right to some action and the right to delegate it, or the right to delegate some action but not the right to execute it.

So, an e-Service can delegate any "delegatable" right. This leads to a chain of delegation, and if any one link is no longer valid the access is denied. We also allow for constraints on rights, delegations and ability to re-delegate.

The statement that is used to describe delegations and constraints on delegations is:

```
Delegate (IssueTime, StartTime, EndTime, From, To, canDo(X,
Rs, Operation, CDC), IDC, Redelegatable)
```

- IssueTime: when the statement was issued.
- StartTime: when the delegation becomes valid.
- EndTime: when the delegation becomes invalid.
- From: delegator service.
- To: delegatee service.
- canDo(X, Rs, Operation, Action, CDC): delegated action, X has the right to the operation on the resource Rs, only if X satisfies the condition CDC.
- IDC: condition on the delegation.
- Redelegatable: true if the To can re-delegate the operation.

There are several different types of delegations which we describe here and give simple examples.

- **Time Bound Delegation:** This is a delegation that is valid only for a certain time period.
  Delegate(IssueTime, "1105001121", "1110001120", From, X, canDo(Y, Rs, Operation, CDC), IDC, Flag): the delegation is only valid between 1105001121 and 1110001120.
- **Group Delegation:** This can be used to delegate to agents from a group who satisfy certain conditions.
  Delegate(IssueTime, StartTime, EndTime, From, X, canDo(Y, Rs, Operation, CDC), (webservice(X, fund), domain(X, "finance")), Flag): this delegates to all e-Services of fund whose domain is "finance" the ability to perform a certain operation.
- **Operation Restricted Delegation:** This is a delegation that requires the delegatee to satisfy certain conditions before the operation can be done.
  Delegate(IssueTime, StartTime, EndTime, From, X, canDo(Y, Rs, Operation, name(Y, "IBM")), (webservice(X, fund), domain(X, "finance")), Flag): only the e-Service of fund whose domain is "finance" and named "IBM" can execute this operation, even if all services of fund whose domain is "finance" have been delegated the right.

- **Redelegatable Delegation:** In this delegation, a right can be delegated along with the permission to re-delegate the right.

    Delegate(IssueTime, StartTime, EndTime, From, To, canDo(X, Rs, Operation, CDC), IDC, true): this statement allows the recipient to further delegate the right.
- **Strictly Redelegatable Delegation:** This statement allows a right to be re-delegated without giving the delegatee the right to actually do the operation.

    Delegate(IssueTime, StartTime, EndTime, From, john, canDo(Y, Rs, Operation, notname(Y, "IBM")), IDC, true): the e-Service of "IBM" is given the right to further delegate the Operation, but it cannot execute the action itself.

Through the different types of delegations, the e-Service can delegate the rights on the operations of some resources with different constraints to the e-Service replicas freely.

3. Trust

"Trust" is a complex subject relating to a firm belief in attributes such as reliability, honesty, and competence of the trusted entity [5]. Such firm belief is a dynamic value and spans over a set of values ranging from very trustworthy to very untrustworthy. The trust level is built on past experiences and given for a specific context. For example, e-Service x might trust e-Service y to provide high quality of service with fast response time. The trust level is specified within a given time because the trust level today between two entities is not necessarily the same trust level a year ago. So, the trust decays with time need to be considered when computing trust.

With the increasing scale of the internet, more and more enterprises achieve the business interaction and cooperation through internet. During the process, trust is becoming very important. An enterprise prefers to have well reputation on other enterprises to achieve more cooperation or transaction whatever as client or provider.

5.2   Trusted Right Delegation

After introducing the above definitions, we will introduce the mechanism of trusted right delegation in detail. In our framework, the right can only be delegated by an e-Service (service provider) to its trusted service (service provider). For example, the right of doing some operations on some cross-enterprise resources can be assigned to the service replica after it is dynamically deployed on some cross-enterprise server. The delegation of the right can also occur between two trusted servers. For example, some interfaces to access the internal database of one enterprise can be provided to the trusted service replica which is hosted on some server of another enterprise after the trusted right delegation.

There are different types of trusted right delegation according to the different policies. For example, there is time limitation on the accessing to some business system, which can only be accessed from 9:00AM to 12:00AM. Such trusted right delegation belongs to time bound delegation.

Figure 3 shows a whole process of dynamic cooperation of cross-enterprise services with the security mechanism of trusted right delegation.

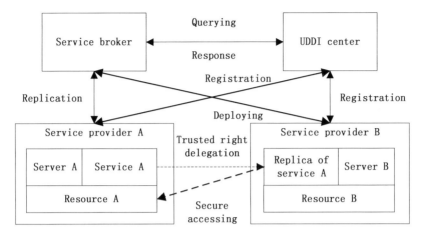

Fig. 3. A dynamic cooperation process of cross-enterprise services with security mechanism

First, service broker will query UDDI center and discover the service A, which is registered by service provider A. After synthetic evaluation on the available servers, service broker will select server B (registered by service provider B) to dynamic deploy and execute the replica of service A through the replication technique. Service A will then delegate the right of operation on resource A to the replica of service A, which will be executed on server B. After that, the replica of service A can access the resource A safely from the server B.

So, through trusted right delegation, the cross-enterprise resources can be shared safely, which also supports the dynamic cooperation of cross-enterprise services by deploying the e-Services cross-enterprise dynamically.

6   Conclusions

It is a trend to support dynamic cooperation of e-Services to achieve the complex business requirement on demand. This paper has presented a flexible model to support security in dynamic cooperation of e-Services. With the extended WSDL description, the developing and deploying of the e-Services can be fully separated. And, an enhanced UDDI center is also provided by allowing the registration of service description and server description separately. Through the replication technique, the replica of e-Service can be dynamically deployed and executed on the optimum cross-enterprise server, which is selected by service broker according to the server evaluation function. By adopting the security mechanism of trusted right delegation, the cross-enterprise resources can be safely and dynamically shared among the e-Services in the emerging e-Service market.

References

1. Tang, J., Zhou, B., He, Z.: Towards Hybrid Mechanism on Wide-Area Distributed Services. Proceedings of the International Conference on Systems, Man and Cybernetics. Hague, Netherlands (2004) 3354-3358

2. IBM Corporation: Business Process Execution Language for Web Services (BPEL4WS). Version 1.0 (2002)
3. Vaggelis, O., Volker, T.: A Framework for Virtual Enterprise Support Services. Proceedings of the 32nd Hawaii International Conference on System Sciences (1999)
4. Artur, A., Sven, G., Vadim, K., Holger, T.: Control Architecture for Service Grids in a Federation of Utility Data Centers. Hewlett Packard Laboratories. Palo Alto, USA (2002)
5. Farag, A., Muthucumaru, M.: Towards Trust-Aware Resource Management in Grid Computing Systems. Proceedings of First IEEE International Workshop on Security and Grid Computing (2002) 452-457
6. Tang, J., Zhou, B., He, Z.: Dynamic Economic- and QoS-Based Approach for Workflow-Oriented Distributed Services Allocation. Proceedings of the International Conference on Systems, Man and Cybernetics. Hague, Netherlands (2004) 3349-3353
7. Tang, J., Zhou, B., He, Z., Uros, P.: Adaptive Workflow-Oriented Services Composition and Allocation in Distributed Environment. Proceedings of the third International Conference on Machine Learning and Cybernetics. Shanghai, China (2004) 599-603
8. Yang, J., Van den Heuvel, W.J., Papazoglou, M.P.: Service Deployment for Virtual Enterprises. Proceedings of the Workshop on Information Technology for VE (2001)
9. Alan, B., Panos, C., Ioannis, T., Martha, P., Sujata, B.: A Scheme for Integrating E-Services in Establishing Virtual Enterprises. Proceedings of Research Issues in Data Engineering (RIDE) Workshop. San Jose, CA (2002)
10. Zhou, B., Tang, J., He, Z.: An adaptive model of virtual enterprise based on dynamic web service composition. Proceedings of the Fifth International Conference on Computer and Information Technology (2005) 284-289
11. Tang, J., Zhou, B., He, Z.: Policy driven and multi-agent based fault tolerance for Web services. Journal of Zhejiang University Science 6A(7) (2005) 676-682

Implementing the Coupled Objects Paradigm for Synchronizing Distributed Applications Through Firewalls

Nelson Baloian, José A. Pino, and Marc Jansen

Computer Science Department, Universidad de Chile,
Blanco Encalada 2120, Santiago, Chile
{nbaloian, jpino}@dcc.uchile.cl

Abstract. Middleware for supporting the programming of distributed systems has been proposed since the beginnings of Internet. Various approaches have been implemented to support different ways of communication, architecture, and data sharing. A schema called MatchMaker intended for developing applications requiring a replicated architecture, dynamic and partial synchronization is introduced. Two implementations of MatchMaker are presented: one based on Java RMI distributed objects for synchronizing applications running inside a local area network or networks without proxies, firewalls or NAT addresses, and the other one for applications in a restrictive environment. MatchMaker has been successfully used for developing many applications supporting collaborative distributed learning.

1 Introduction

The need for a middleware that could simplify the programming of distributed applications is clear since the development of the first ones. Sun RPC [11] schema and the CORBA [12] architecture are two of the first and most well known supporting platforms. The aim of these systems is to make distributed applications programming not too different from the programming of stand-alone applications, by encapsulating the communication protocol and offering the programmer a nice interface for executing code in another computer.

Many other platforms and architectures have been developed thereafter [1] for suiting a certain class of applications with common requirements. They differ on the distribution schemes of the shared data, communication mechanisms, and application architecture they support [2]. Rendezvous [13] and Suite [14] are groupware platforms, which use a central distribution scheme for the data of collaborative applications. GroupKit [15], DECAF [16] and MASC [17] use a replicated distribution scheme. Guerrero and Fuller [18] propose a pattern system to support the design of collaborative applications. Patterson [3], Dewan [4] and Roth [5] propose various taxonomies for groupware platforms, especially with respect to the shared data distribution schema they support. They can be grouped in the following four classes:

W. Shen et al. (Eds.): CSCWD 2006, LNCS 4402, pp. 599–608, 2007.
© Springer-Verlag Berlin Heidelberg 2007

- Centralized: A single server maintains the data for all applications. Every application has to contact this server for retrieving the state of the shared work and/or make changes. This may cause bottlenecks if the server is loaded with too much synchronizing work.
- Replicated: Every participant has a copy of all the shared data and the application is exactly replicated at every site. The application has a better performance since it has to access local data only. However, the need to keep these data coherent and synchronized at every site may lead to very complex algorithms, especially to deal with problems such as latecomers [6].
- Asymmetric: There is no pre-defined central server, but one of the participants takes that role.
- Semi-replicated: there are multiple servers in this schema. Compared to the Centralized schema, this may lead to a shorter response time and is more robust, since the crash of one of the servers does not imply the crash of the system. It has some of the problems of data coherence found in the replicated schema.

We have developed distributed applications for supporting collaborative learning in distributed environments since 1995 (http://www.collide.org). We detected we needed a support for easing development of these distributed applications. However, the synchronization requirements for our applications were quite demanding:

- Replicated architecture: It should be possible to synchronize multiple and potentially different applications already existing in a distributed environment.
- Dynamic synchronization: It should be possible to start and stop the synchronization at any point of the application lifetime. Before and after the coupling phase, applications should continue to exist independently.
- Partial synchronization: It should be possible to synchronize each component of an application interface (AI) individually with a component of another AI, thus allowing the synchronization of applications with completely different interfaces.

MatchMaker was developed on these requirements. This framework allows a programmer to easily "extend" a stand-alone application and transform it into a shared one. One of its major features is that it is based on well-known design patterns like the Model-View-Controller (MVC) architecture. MatchMaker supports collaboration by combining two architectures for collaborative systems: On the one hand, the framework has a centralized server. On the other hand, it is based on a replicated architecture. By combining them, we get the advantages of both solutions and we remove the disadvantages: e.g., a problem of a centralized server is that it is not possible for clients to continue working if this server is no longer reachable. Using a replicated architecture enables us to keep working stand-alone even if the server is not reachable. After reconnecting the server to the network it is only necessary that one client sends its data to the server and the other clients can get the data from the server again. Besides, it is easier to implement persistency if all data is saved in one central facility. Moreover, MatchMaker allows partial coupling of applications by using data structures reflecting the applications internal structures. It also has a replay function and an undo/redo framework, both based on an advanced logging mechanism.

The MatchMaker approach was first implemented over a Sun OS UNIX platform [7] and it has evolved to respond to the changing technological evolution of computers and networks. One of the last implementations [8] was based on Java and used RMI (Remote Method Invocation). However, the fact that firewalls, proxies and NAT are becoming quite frequent in the Internet moved us to implement a new solution that could also work in this new environment. The next section presents the usage of the current implementation of the MatchMaker framework. Therefore, the basic paradigm of the MatchMaker framework is described; the examples explain the needed work to extend a stand-alone application to a collaborative one.

Then, we present the implementation with SOAP to achieve the same functionality overcoming the problems created by the presence of firewalls, proxies, and NAT. Some applications developed with MatchMaker, and discussions and conclusions are presented.

2 Principles of MatchMaker and Its Usage

While building cooperative software, a developer has to decide about the mechanism he wants to use for making his application a distributed one. He basically has the choice of three major paradigms: first, he can decide to use a centralized server capable of storing the data locally and serving this locally stored data to several clients. Or second, he can decide to use a non-centralized approach in which the needed information by all clients is first sent to the server and is then multicasted to the interested clients. In these scenarios where the data does not get stored centrally, it is not possible to work with the clients any longer if the server is for some reason not accessible any more. Or third, he can choose a replicated architecture. Here, all the necessary data for the clients is replicated at the client side. The advantage of this latter approach is the clients are still operable even if they loose their network connection or the central server breaks down.

The MatchMaker framework combines the second and third paradigms for developing cooperative software. It has a centralized server, which manages to send the necessary data to the clients, but this centralized server also replicates the required internal data structure of the application. By replicating the data structure it is possible for each application to have a synchronized status compared to the other ones. Furthermore, a centralized storage of the necessary data structures also allows the handling of late-comers easily because they get an updated status of the shared data.

Within the server application, the data structure is arranged as a so-called "synchronization tree". Every application of a collaborative scenario could register itself as a listener for this synchronization tree, even for the whole tree, but also for sub trees. With the registration of an application for a part of the synchronization tree, the server ensures that the application is informed about changes in the part of the synchronization tree that the application is registered for. Usually, the synchronization tree reflects the internal data structure of the application as shown in Figure 1.

Figure 1 shows an example with two users collaboratively working in a modeling task. The application provides the possibility of using several workspaces either in private or in public mode. It can be seen the workspaces 1 and 3 are available to users A and B. Workspace 3 is only synchronized on the graph level but the handwritten annotations are not synchronized. Workspace 2 is only available for user B privately.

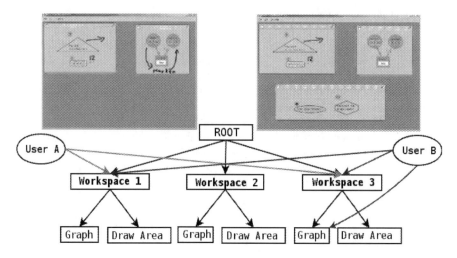

Fig. 1. An example of the MM Synchronization tree

Unlike most frameworks for synchronization, this one does not use event-based approach but a replication, according to the MVC paradigm. By doing this, it allows to interpret the models differently in different applications or scenarios. For example, a model may be fully interpreted by an application running on a PC with high performance, but on the other hand, some parts of information provided by the model may not be considered if the same model is interpreted by an application running on a PDA with limited performance especially with respect to screen facilities. The models are propagated to the clients using the Java common event architecture, whereby the events are in this case remote events since the applications run in different Java Virtual Machines. Four kinds of events can be multicasted from the server to the interested clients for changes that occur in the synchronization tree: a new node is created, a node is deleted, the model of a node has changed, or an action is executed on a certain node. Therefore, every MatchMaker client has to implement methods to handle these four operations.

We would like to stress that the class/style files and the template should not be manipulated and that the guidelines regarding font sizes and format should be adhered to. This is to ensure the end product is as homogeneous as possible.

2.1 Extended Features in MatchMaker

Besides the basic feature of synchronization of collaborative applications, the MatchMaker framework provides additional features that might be of interest while working in collaborative scenarios. Some of these features are:

Logging: It is possible to record complete MatchMaker sessions in an XML file. For example, it is recorded which client caused a certain operation, when it happened (timestamp), which sub-tree was invoked in the operation, etc. The objects themselves placed in the sub-tree might also be stored in XML format as long as the object supports it; otherwise the object will be serialized and stored as a byte array.

Replay: Having these log-files, an additional feature is the possibility of replay MatchMaker sessions, making it possible to see a MatchMaker session like a video. This might be interesting for demonstration purposes or in game scenarios in order to analyze the strategy of players but also for the analysis of collaborative groups behavior. This replay is possible either time-wise or step-wise (thus, users must decide when a certain step in the collaborative work is over and the next step starts).

Undo/Redo: Another interesting feature is an advanced Undo/Redo function. With its help, it is possible to undo/redo operations for a whole session. It is also possible to undo/redo all or some operations that happened during a certain period of time.

Persistency: Persistency is somehow related to data security. It is possible to store the status of the MatchMaker server persistently. This means the status of the server will be obtained over the server lifetime and it can be reloaded after a possible restart of the server.

2.2   Layout, Typeface, Font Sizes and Numbering

The MatchMaker framework was developed to easily extend a stand-alone application to a collaborative application. The developer has to make sure the application is capable of creating, joining and leaving MatchMaker sessions as well as updating the status of the application.

The first thing a developer has to do is to define the models for the objects he wants to synchronize. The model has to implement the java.io.Serializable interface, otherwise it will not be possible to send them over the network using RMI. The next activity is to decide which of the classes should be responsible for keeping the application synchronized. Those classes have to implement the SyncListener interface that marks the classes as a listener for the MatchMaker server. When building the interface, the developer must implement four methods, each corresponding to one of the events a MatchMaker server can multicast to interested clients:

```
public void objectChanged(SyncEvent event)
public void objectDeleted(SyncEvent event)
public void objectChanged(SyncEvent event)
public void actionExecuted (SyncActionEvent event)
```

After writing the listeners, the developer has to make sure the listeners are added to the right part of the synchronization tree. A listener will be informed about all changes that happened in a part of the synchronization tree it is registered for. It is not required all listeners be added to the root element of the synchronization tree. Most likely this will not be the case; usually the listener will only be added to a certain sub tree of the synchronization tree.

3   The SOAP-Based MatchMaker

The current version of MatchMaker works well in closed environments, such as Local Area Networks. But outside, over the Internet, there are complications. We find obstacles such as Firewalls, Proxies and Routers with Network Address Translation (NAT), which do not allow applications to act as servers. A solution for this problem is to reimplement MatchMaker using SOAP over HyperText Transfer Protocol (HTTP) as the transportation layer for communicating clients with the server, and implementing the MatchMaker server as a Web Service. HTTP is normally open to firewalls and it is easily accessible from clients behind proxies or NATs. To accomplish this task, we used Apache Axis as the platform for Web Services and consumer clients in Java. Axis is an Open Source SOAP engine written in Java.

At the sever side, Apache Axis works as a servlet, so it needs to be deployed inside a Web Servlet Container such as Jakarta Tomcat, WebLogic or the Web Application Server of J2EE. Apache Axis provides classes allowing clients to connect to a server, communicate with a remote application using the SOAP protocol and invoke Web Service methods with little effort from the developer. The new version of Match-Maker, known as SOAP MatchMaker, works the same way as the current RMI MatchMaker version. It only differs in some aspects, being the communication between clients and server the most notorious one.

The problem was how to pass Java objects through SOAP. MatchMaker passes Java Objects as arguments and it returns values between clients and server. Apache Axis BeanSerializer (AABS) utility can send a serializable Java object through SOAP if its class is written with the JavaBean pattern. But if the source code of that class is not available, we cannot assume the class was written according to the JavaBean pattern, even if it were the case. Every serializable Java object can be serialized into a byte array, and since SOAP recognizes byte arrays as a data type, we can send serializable Java objects as byte arrays through SOAP. We only need to serialize the object into a byte array at the sender side, and deserialize back into an object at the receiver side. The only restriction to deserialize a byte array back into an object is the application needs to know the class at execution time. This solution also helps to keep SOAP messages small: Java objects with too many fields could create large SOAP messages if they are serialized with ABBS.

In the RMI MatchMaker version, clients act as servers listening for events from the central server. In this new approach, the clients cannot act as servers anymore; they are forced to act in passive mode. This means clients need to contact the server to find out if new events affected the coupled objects. The basic mechanism consists of every client having an event queue at the server side. Clients are constantly requesting the server for new events, and every time a new event is available, it is sent to the client. If no new events are available, the client keeps waiting until a new event is available, but the connection with the server is kept alive.

The problem is another client to the server reports that HTTP connections have a timeout, so they cannot wait too long for a new event. A solution for this is that clients request new events once in a while, e.g., 0.5 seconds. If there are no new events available, a void event is sent back to the client. If there is at least one event available, the first event in the queue is sent back. This solution seems to work fine with simple applications with little activity, like a chat application. With large applications generating many events per second, the interaction between users is painfully slow, event queues at the server side overflow quickly and it consumes unnecessary bandwidth. A solution working much better is to have clients requesting for new events from the server and keep waiting for 10 seconds until a new event is available. If a new event is available during that period, it is sent back to the client, and the client requests the next event the same way as before. If 10 seconds have passed and there is no new events available yet, a void event is sent back to the client. This way, a client only receives void events if we get a timeout while waiting.

4 Applications Implemented with MatchMaker

MatchMaker has been successfully used to implement many applications mainly, but not only, in the Computer Supported Collaborative Work field. One of the first applications was a system for collaboratively teach/learn mathematical functions and their derivatives. In this scenario, two different versions (the teacher's version shown in the background of Figure 2 and a student version in the foreground) are used to present, discuss and practice this topic. In the scenario of a computer-integrated classroom where the teacher needs to publicly discuss a student's solution, it turned out that a full application or window synchronization is not desirable. Instead, the teacher initializes the synchronization by coupling the function input fields (i.e. the generator of the displayed curve, not the display itself). At any point in time the applications can be de-coupled, e.g. to synchronize with another student, or to synchronize with a larger group of students to distribute a special task.

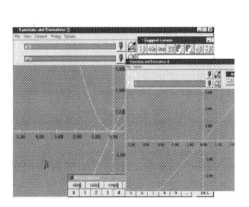
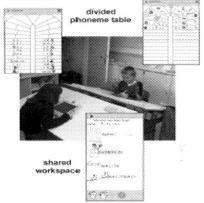

Fig. 2. A collaborative tool for discussion functions and derivatives

Fig. 3. Children collaborating with an application for early literacy

Another application is shown in Figure 3. Two children work in a collaborative mode with instances of a Java-based application for early literacy. The material (a table built up of images and letters) is distributed between the participants based on the jigsaw design principle to induce collaboration. The actual workspace is coupled by means of JMM. Two or more workspaces of this application can be coupled and decoupled by the children according to their needs and preferences. The application is in daily use at a German primary school associated to the NIMIS project [9].

Perhaps one of the most used applications has been CoolModes [10]. It is a collaborative tool framework designed to support discussions and cooperative modelling processes in various domains. Like other environments, this is achieved through a shared workspace environment with synchronized visual representations. These representations together with their underlying semantics can be externally defined, which offers the option to develop domain-dependent "plug-in" visual languages and interpretation patterns, encapsulated in so-called "palettes". The languages can differ considerably with respect to the underlying formal semantics (e.g. System dynamics simulation vs. handwriting annotation) but yet be mixed and used synchronously in the framework. From our point of view, this is a suitable approach for supporting open modelling tasks with potentially unknown means.

5 Evaluation

We assumed from the beginning that the SOAP-based MatchMaker could not outperform the RMI-based version, but we wanted to measure how worse its performance is and if it really means that the delays introduced by the serialization/deserialization process would make it useless. We first made a comparative evaluation between both implementations: we generated 100 events for an object coupled with 5 other ones with a delay of 0.5 seconds between each event. We experimented in two scenarios: the first one, for objects residing inside a local area network and the second one for objects residing all in different networks. For the delay of each event we took the maximum delay between the time of generation of the event and the time the event reached every one of the coupled objects. The results are shown in Figures 4 and Figure 5, respectively.

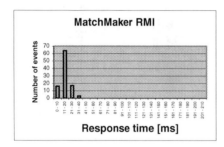
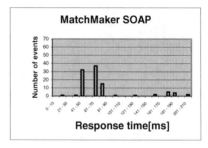

Fig. 4. The response time of the events for objects located inside a local area network

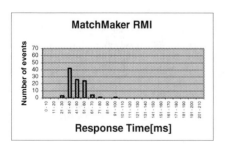
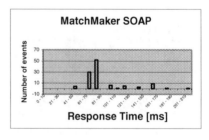

Fig. 5. The response time of the events for objects located in different networks

The obtained time performance disadvantage of the SOAP MatchMaker does not seem to be meaningful for human beings if we take the mean delay values for all events. However, the dispersion of the data is wider for the SOAP version. This means that we can expect long delays but very infrequently.

6 Conclusions

Using XML based technologies like Web Services and SOAP has drawbacks like decreased performance, basically due to the overhead in the length of sent messages and the required serialization and deserialization of XML. On the other hand, a standardized format for information exchange like SOAP allows overcoming certain drawbacks usually arising while working on collaborative systems where users are located in different physical and/or logical LANs. Often, those systems use proprietary protocols for the data exchange and thus the data exchange between applications written in different programming languages is usually considered a problem. While approaches like CORBA or RMI-IIOP try to overcome this limitation, they never are fully adopted, unlike Web Services and the corresponding XML based technologies.

Another advantage of using an XML based protocol for data exchange in Match-Maker is the sharing of data structures that were not previously known to either the server or the clients. Defining a Document Type Definition (DTD) or a Schema for the exchanged XML data allows creating the necessary data structures at runtime. Going one step further, even if no DTD or Schema is defined for the exchanged XML data descriptions, the necessary DTDs or Schemas can be calculated since it is only required to create the corresponding data structures. Afterwards, the needed data structures can be created for the respective programming language.

Nevertheless, due to the decreased performance, it becomes necessary to think about the scenario in which the new version of MatchMaker should be used, at least if the scenario is a synchronous one. Scenarios like the coupling of handwritten annotations, that usually are quite intensive in terms of the volume of exchanged data, are not good candidates for the new MatchMaker version. Whereas, in case of modelling scenarios, it is typically not very intensive with respect to the volume of exchanged data and even if a huge amount of data needs to be exchanged, a slight delay may not be considered a problem.

Acknowledgments. This work was partially supported by a research grant (No. 1040952) from Fondecyt (Chile) and a scholarship from NCIT (Japan).

References

1. Urnes, T. & Nejabi, R.: Tools for implementing groupware: Survey and evaluation. Technical Report No. CS-94-03. York University (1994)
2. Lukosch, S.: Adaptive and Transparent data Distribution Support. Lecture Notes in Computer Science 2440 (2002) 255-274
3. Patterson, J.: Taxonomy of Architectures for Synchronous Groupware Architectures. ACM SIGOIS Bulletin 15(3) (1995) 27-29

4. Dewan, P.: Multiuser Architectures. Proc. 10th ACM Symposium on Operating Systems Principles. Orcas Island, Washington, USA (1985) 63-78
5. Roth, J. & Unger, C.: An extensible classification model for distribution architectures of synchronous groupware. Proc. 4th International Conference on Design of Cooperative Systems (COOP2000). Sophia, Antipolis, France (2000)
6. Lukosh, S.: Transparent Latecomer Support for Synchronous Groupware. Lecture Notes in Computer Science 2806 (2003) 26-41
7. Zhao, J. & Hoppe, H.U.: Getting serious about flexible user interface coupling. Proc. International Workshop on the Design of Cooperative Systems. Juan-les-Pins, France (1995)
8. Jansen, M.: MatchMaker - A Framework to Support Collaborative Java Applications. Proc. 11th Conf. on Artificial Intelligence in Education. Amsterdam (2003) 535-536
9. Tewissen, F., Lingnau, A., Hoppe, U., Mannhaupt, G. & Nischk, D.: Collaborative Writing in a Computer-integrated Classroom for Early Learning. Proc. European Conf. on CSCL. Maastricht, The Netherlands (2001) 593-600
10. Bollen, L., Hoppe, H.U., Milrad, M. & Pinkwart, N.: Collaborative Modelling in Group Learning Environments. Proc. XX International Conf. of the System Dynamics Society. Palermo, Italy (2002) 53-64
11. Srinivasan, R.: RPC:Remote Procedure Call Protocol Specification Version 2. Internet RFC 1831 (1995)
12. Vogel, A. & Duddy, K.: Java Programming with CORBA. 2nd. ed. Wiley & Sons (1998)
13. Hill, R., Brinck, T., Rohall, S., Patterson, J. & Wilne, W.: The Rendezvous architecture and language for constructing multiuser applications. ACM Transactions on Computer-Human Interaction 1(2) (1994) 81-125
14. Dewan, P. & Choudhary, R.: A High-level and flexible framework for implementing multi-user interfaces. ACM Transactions on Information Systems 10(4) (1992) 345-380
15. Roseman, M. Greenberg, S.: Building real time groupware with GroupKit. ACM Transactions on Computer-Human Interaction 3(1) (1996) 66-106
16. Storm, R. Banvar, G. Miller, K., Prakash, A. & Ward, M.: Concurrency Control and vie notification algorithms for collaborative replicated objects. IEEE Transactions on Computers 47(4) (1998) 458-471
17. Aldunate, R., Ochoa, S., Pena-Mora, F. & Nussbaum, M.: Robust Mobile Ad-hoc Space for Collaboration to Support Disaster Relief Efforts Involving Critical Physical Infrastructure. ASCE Journal of Computing in Civil Engineering 20(1) (2006) 13-27
18. Guerrero, L. & Fuller, D.: A Pattern System for the Development of Collaborative Applications. Information and Software Technology 43(7) (2001) 457-467

How to Build Awareness-Supported Systems Without Sacrificing Privacy

Min-Kyung Kim and Hee-Cheol Kim

Department of Computer Science, Inje University,
Obang-dong 607, Gimhae, Gyung-Nam, South Korea
julia902@nate.com, heeki@cs.inje.ac.kr

Abstract. The success of group activities depends largely on the extent to which collaborators are aware of the characteristics and progress of a given task, the roles and activities of other members, and situational changes. This issue of awareness has become a central theme in both human–computer interaction and computer-supported cooperative work. However, to increase awareness, privacy is typically sacrificed. Emphasizing the importance of privacy, we suggest guidelines on how to deal with the issue of privacy in awareness-centered CSCW systems design, based on two interview studies and an analysis of scenarios inspired by the interviews. We discuss the results with regard to the factors of awareness of task, members, presence, schedule, and activity.

1 Introduction

Since the early 1990s, researchers have attempted to expand human–computer interaction (HCI) concepts, embracing social contexts to overcome the limits of HCI research based on cognitive science in the 1980s [1-3]. As a result, the need to understand users as social beings has been greatly emphasized. In a sense, the early 1990s gave birth to the union of HCI and computer-supported cooperative work (CSCW), or collaborative computing.

The issue of awareness is a key topic in both HCI and CSCW. Its importance stems from the realization that the more aware collaborators are of each others' activities, information, and situations, the more effective and fruitful their group activities are likely to be.

There is a substantial body of research focusing on awareness and the technologies to support it [4-9]. In addition, well-known journals have addressed awareness in special issues [6][9], and international workshops have been held to discuss the idea [4-5]. Although the notion of awareness is well supported, it does not guarantee the success of group work, mainly because there is a conflict between what information to share (awareness) and what to keep confidential (privacy).

While there have been fewer studies on privacy than on awareness in both the HCI and CSCW communities, the development of ubiquitous computing has increased interest in the concept. The issue of privacy has been addressed in the context of specific systems, such as media spaces, calendar systems, email, and file-sharing systems

W. Shen et al. (Eds.): CSCWD 2006, LNCS 4402, pp. 609–618, 2007.
© Springer-Verlag Berlin Heidelberg 2007

[10-13]. Other studies have discussed conceptual or theoretical frameworks in relation to systems design [14-15].

There is a tendency to focus research on either awareness or privacy alone. However, the creation of harmony between these two dimensions is crucial to both systems design and social reality [16]. Therefore, it is important to determine the extent to which awareness can be supported without seriously damaging privacy.

To address the balance between awareness and privacy, we propose guidelines for groupware design, and discuss how to maintain this balance based on two interview studies we have performed and an analysis of scenarios inspired by the interviews. Our aim was to shed light on the knowledge required to develop awareness systems that retain privacy.

In Section 2, we explain the objectives and methods of this research. In Section 3, we describe five types of awareness to support in groupware, as determined by interviews; they are: awareness of tasks, members, presence, schedules, and activities. Section 4 provides design guidelines that take into consideration both awareness and privacy, and Section 5 draws some brief conclusions.

2   Objectives and Methods

The ultimate goal of this paper is to provide guidelines for groupware design that offer a balance between awareness and privacy. This goal can be achieved from various points of view by which we define good groupware. In this section, we describe our objectives and our study methodology by considering the three different perspectives that we emphasize in this study.

2.1   Three Perspectives

Because groupware systems are characterized by diverse and complex factors that are both technical and social, it seems impossible to consider every single one during the development phase. Therefore, one of the important tasks at the initial stage is to determine what must be emphasized and why to do so. The choice is deeply related to system design rationales. Here, we consider three different perspectives.

First, we hope to design *usable* systems by emphasizing usability rather than technical excellence. Many studies have reported that advanced systems have not been used as much as the developers had anticipated, mainly because the gap between assumption and reality was larger than the developers had initially thought. To combat this problem, we take a more realistic approach, considering users first, based on empirical data obtained through interviews. In this sense, building usable systems can mean designing user-centered systems, which is the core endeavor of HCI research.

Second, we aim to create awareness-centered groupware. Clark and Brennan [17, 18] noted that people need "common ground" between them to coordinate and communicate their work. According to them, everything we do jointly with others is rooted in information about our surroundings, activities, perceptions, emotions, plans, and interests, but only in that part we think they share with us. This is the reason why we require the notion of common ground in order to have a dialogue or to communicate effectively. In this respect, awareness support serves to establish such common ground. Our focus on awareness is an attempt to determine how to build a crucial basis for the processes of communication and coordination.

Third, we hope to build privacy-focused systems. Privacy has not always been the primary consideration in design. However, the issue of privacy affects the usability of groupware systems, and may lead to system failure in some cases [19]. In fact, by considering awareness, we are actually considering the efficiency of group tasks. However, while it is of importance for group activities, efficiency alone does not guarantee successful cooperation. It may be critical to determine ways of supporting more subtle matters, such as privacy. Under certain circumstances, systems are rejected not because they are unusable and inefficient, but because users fear making information about themselves public. For this reason, privacy cannot be overlooked during the design phase.

2.2 Methods

We conducted two interview studies. The first was a pilot study of 20 participants with experience in group projects, such as systems development and document writing. Each interview lasted about 10–20 min, and was designed as a brainstorming session to develop a general overview on issues of awareness and privacy.

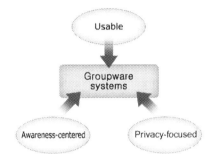

Fig. 1. Perspectives on groupware design

The topics shared with interviewees in the study were what projects they were involved in, characteristics of the group members, what kinds of information collaborators must be aware of to facilitate cooperation, when privacy matters, what difficulties they encountered when they coordinated and communicated their work, and some minor themes.

The primary concern in analyzing the data was to find out what kinds of awareness participants think are important in group activities. This was because we intended to elicit guidelines of groupware design focusing on different types of awareness. In fact, we identified five types from the interviews: awareness of task, member, presence, activity, and schedule. The first interview study was also a basis on which we planned the following interview study.

The second interview study consisted of an in-depth interview of five project participants from five different companies and organizations. We utilized the general interview approach described in Patton [20] by which both interviewers and interviewees discuss various topics and questions prepared, instead of fixed and standardized questions. Even if topics are thus determined beforehand, interviewers have the flexibility and freedom to pose more detailed questions and sequence the list of topics unless they digress from the topics selected. Each interview took 1–2 hours. Interviewees made notes on paper during and after they performed the interviews. The ten major topics discussed in the interview were as follows:

- Group coordination (e. g. coordination strategies, labor of division, group size, leadership)
- Member understanding (e. g. how to obtain information about members, official and psychological relationship, how to resolve conflicts,)

- Communication methods (e.g. what tools or systems are commonly used, why they are used, what new media are required in the future, comparison between face-to-face and other communication)
- Schedule management (e.g. who plans group meetings, how to schedule meetings and events, personal schedule management)
- Presence of members (e.g. at what place other members are currently working, what they are doing)
- Task understanding (e.g. to what extent the participants understand the group task, ways of collecting information about it)
- Document (or source code) management (e.g. what to store, how to store documents, version or change management)
- Activity understanding (e.g. how to understand work progress of other members)
- Difficult factors (e.g. what makes group work difficult, technological and social barriers)
- Crucial factors (e.g. what are important factors for the success of group activities and why)

These ten topics were developed during the process of analyzing the first interview study. The first eight themes reflected five types of awareness, and the last two involved general aspects of difficulty and the importance in performing group tasks. Even though these issues are just briefly written here together with examples of their sub-issues, more detailed topics or checkpoints were prepared while interviewers carried out each interview.

In particular, interviewers also asked the participants about whether privacy mattered, and when privacy became important concerning every issue. Therefore, while we did not categorize the issue of privacy into the ten issues, privacy was highly stressed in the interview study.

During the analysis phase of the interview, we first summarized the backgrounds of the interview cases. Then, we analyzed the data, classifying them according to five different types of awareness. At the same time, we made an attempt to maintain a balance between awareness and privacy in the analysis when dealing with the data related to privacy.

After completing the interviews and analyzing the data, we described scenarios for discussing and understanding the implications of groupware design. Such scenario-based approaches are popular in HCI research [21–23], and proved particularly useful for discussing the sensitive issue of privacy. Although we took the responses of interviewees into serious consideration, obtaining honest facts related to privacy can be problematic in an interview study or in any other retrospective studies because the interviewees may withhold sensitive and critical information, and even change real stories. Therefore, while we used the interview data in the analysis, we also wrote scenarios to address privacy from another perspective. An excerpt of one such scenario follows:

> "Chae-rin is very satisfied with the off-line login function in a messenger system. Before using the function, interventions by others could easily interfere with her work whenever she logged into the messenger system. Even when she was at home, her boss would sometimes contact her to discuss her work. However, after the function of the off-line login was permitted, she has been able to function in her own time at the computer. Recently, she has also started using two different messengers, one for her office work and the other for her private work…"

Even if the scenarios described are not real, we believe that they could be realistic, in that we have tried as much as possible to reflect the interview data, which were observations of various real situations. While we analyzed the interview data and created scenarios, we also discovered guidelines of groupware design in relation to awareness and privacy. The results are given in Section 4.

3   Five Types of Awareness

There must exist a wide variety of types of awareness. Summarizing the interview data, we identified five important types of awareness that are required for group collaboration and communication.

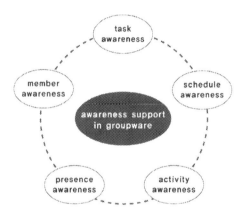

Fig. 2. Types of awareness for group work

3.1   Task Awareness

This type of awareness entails an understanding of the collaborative task itself. To perform any project, basic information about the task is required by all collaborators. Interviewees were more concerned about how to store and access information than what information was being shared. Some participants reported using a common space for groupware systems in their organization, while others utilized an ftp server if they did not have a particular groupware.

3.2   Member Awareness

Co-workers may sometimes need information about each other, such as the profile of individual members, their role in the project, and knowledge. The interviews, however, indicated that collaborators generally do not seek their colleagues' information, particularly private data. One respondent said, "I find it best to do and concentrate on my own work. Do I need to know everything about my co-worker? If I have to know something related to the task, I can ask him at a meeting." In fact, they seemed to have little curiosity concerning, or need of, collaborator information. In many cases, they believed they already knew each other sufficiently well.

3.3 Presence Awareness

Interviewees tended to agree that they need to be aware of where other members are located (e.g., at the office). However, they were not so interested in more detailed information, such as what others were doing.

Regarding messenger systems, they mainly consider the on/offline status of others, primarily because users generally do not frequently use other messenger states, such as busy, away, be right back, on the phone, and out to lunch, but also because more detailed information is related to privacy. One respondent stated, "I just use on/offline modes. There is no reason to let them know if I am having lunch or not. It is also inconvenient to change my status."

3.4 Schedule Awareness

Analysis of the interviews revealed two categories of schedule awareness: knowledge of each other's schedules, and the project manager's knowledge of each member's schedule. While the respondents indicated that collaborators share their schedules, mainly, when they have physical meetings, typically, only the project manager has each member's agenda, information the manager uses to plan meetings and assign the work tasks.

In any case, collaborators only need information that is related to the project itself. There was not a great deal of interest in knowing the detailed schedules of other group members. At the same time, collaborators did not want to expose their private schedules. For instance, some interviewees mentioned that they do not even write anything personal on their calendars on their desks to protect their privacy.

In addition, whether on paper or in a scheduling system, respondents tended to record their schedules rather sketchily, ignoring details, because plans may be easily changed, making it difficult to schedule precise times.

3.5 Activity Awareness

Based on the interviews, collaborators appeared not so concerned about knowing what other group members were doing, although this would depend on the characteristics of the project, and the position or role of members involved in that project. Even project managers tend not to attempt to know the detailed activities of other members, although they do want to understand activities overall.

Activity awareness also depends on the characteristics of the project. When a project is strongly linked to other projects, understanding the activities and schedules of other group members becomes very important. However, if a project proceeds independently, it is less important.

4   Design Recommendations

In this section, we recommend important guidelines for groupware design, based on the findings and scenario description. In particular, we focus on the balance between awareness and privacy, and discuss both concepts according to the five types of awareness.

4.1   Task Awareness

How first, what second: Interviewees were more concerned with how to store and access resources associated with tasks, than with what information was involved. Therefore, groupware designers should first consider how to best provide convenient access and storage, and place less priority on what information to provide and represent in systems.

The respondents usually stored and used the data in a common space. Specifically, they preferred a common space, such as webhard and ftp folders, in which they could easily download, upload, and access information anytime anywhere the Internet is available using drag-and-drop techniques.

4.2   Member Awareness

Same space for member awareness and presence awareness: It may be effective to use the same space to support both member and presence awareness. The interviews indicated that member awareness is less important in design than other types of awareness. However, that does not mean that member awareness should be neglected. Indeed, our scenarios revealed that, although member awareness is not supported independently of other types of awareness, it may be a part of other types of awareness.

A good solution would be to have the same space for both member and presence awareness, or other types of awareness. If an independent space for member awareness is designed, it may cause inconvenience to users, who will need to search for a space they do not visit frequently. However, if member information can be shown in the same space supporting presence awareness, which is frequently visited, member awareness would increase. For example, if member information was added to a messenger system that supports presence awareness, when a window for presence is open, users would see the list of collaborators and their status. Left-clicking the mouse on the name of a coworker would display his or her information.

4.3   Presence Awareness

Minimal expression of status: According to the interviews, when people use a messenger, they do not generally expose their detailed status to others. There are about ten different states in a messenger system. Of these, online, offline, and away are the most often used, and the respondents considered these sufficient for expressing their status. We therefore recommend that designers support these three states, and consider others according to circumstance.

Off-line login: When messenger users are on-line, other people easily request for dialogs by text chat, and so their work is likely to be interfered. This is a serious problem that most interviewees mentioned with respect to presence awareness. This matter is also related to the issue of privacy. However, messenger systems recently began to resolve it by providing the function called off-line login. Designers should consider this function in different kinds of CSCW systems for the purpose of privacy especially when they want to support presence awareness.

4.4 Schedule Awareness

Assuming support for public schedules: A tricky issue in design involves the question of how to support public and private spaces simultaneously. However, when it comes to schedulers, it may be sufficient to build a space for public schedules only. Most interviewees reported that they did not want to write their private schedules into a scheduler system, emphasizing that it should be restricted to public matters, such as training, business trips, and vacation. This indicates that users are not only concerned about official work, but actively manage their privacy, whether consciously or subconsciously.

Simple form for input: It is important not to request too much information from users. The interviewees reported that it was often difficult to input an exact time into the scheduler, especially the estimated completion time of a task. Some respondents also mentioned that they would register a starting time but skip the completion time, which is exactly what Cooper [24] reported. A form that is too detailed may impede flexibility. One way to increase flexibility is to have users input their schedules by day versus by the hour. In this case, users would select only a certain day, and would be given the option to input an exact time. Figure 3 shows an interface of a scheduler that provides a simple form for input in which users simply register their plans by the day and then add any more details they wish to share.

Fig. 3. The main window of a scheduler

4.5 Activity Awareness

Reporting important activities only: Activity awareness is concerned with understanding what members are doing and how a certain task is progressing. While it facilitates group coordination, it is also related to the sensitive issue of privacy. In fact, there is a trade-off between efficiency and privacy. A boss typically wants to be as aware as possible of an employee's activities, while employees generally want to avoid reporting their activities.

Crucially, both employers and employees are well aware that privacy is important enough that the efficiency of group work should be sacrificed to protect it, to some extent. Based on the interviews, even project leaders tended to avoid knowing every detail of each person's activities. In a sense, everyone considers and respects privacy consciously or unconsciously.

Groupware should consider privacy in terms of activity awareness. Forms that are too detailed threaten privacy. The system should request only important and necessary information from users. Even though an activity report is for activity awareness, if the system requires too many details, efficiency may decrease and users may feel that their privacy has been invaded.

5   Conclusions

Awareness is an important notion for supporting efficient group communication and coordination in groupware systems design. However, if privacy is neglected in the design process, we may fail to build usable systems. This paper investigated ways in which a balanced view between awareness and privacy may be developed, and provided design guidelines for groupware. Our results shed light on how both awareness and privacy may affect the design of groupware systems.

Acknowledgments. This work was supported by Korea Research Foundation grant (No: KRF-2004-003-D00360).

References

1. Bowers, J., Benford, S. (eds.): Studies in Computer Supported Cooperative Work: Theory, Practice, and Design. North-Holland (1991)
2. Bannon, L.: Perspectives on CSCW: from HCI and CMC to CSCW. Proc. International Conference on Human-Computer Interaction. St. Petersburg, Russia (1992) 148-158
3. Shapiro, D., Tauber, M., Traunmuller, R. (eds): The Design of Computer Supported Cooperative Work and Groupware Systems. Elsevier (1996)
4. CHI Workshop: CHI 2003 - Workshop for Elegant Peripheral Awareness. Proceedings of CHI'2003. ACM Press (2003)
5. CSCW Workshop: International Workshop on Awareness and World Wide Web. Proceedings of CSCW'2000 (2000)
6. CSCW: a special issue on Awareness on CSCW. Computer Supported Cooperative Work: The Journal of Collaborative Computing. 11(3-4)(2002) 285-530

7. Dourish, P., Bellotti, V.: Awareness and Coordination in Shared Workspaces. Proc. of CSCW'92 (1992) 107-114
8. Gutwin, C., Greenberg, S.: The Effects of Workspace Awareness Support on the Usability of Real-time Distributed Groupware. ACM Trans. on CHI 6(2) (1999) 243-281
9. HCI: A special issue on Context-aware Computing. HCI 16(2/4) (2001) 87-419
10. Dourish, P.: Culture and Control in a Media Space. Proc. of the Conference on Computer Supported Cooperative Work (ECSCW'93) (1993) 125-144
11. Palen, L.: Social, Individual, and Technological Issues for Groupware Calendar Systems. Proceedings of the CHI'99 Conference. Pittsburgh, Pennsylvania (1999) 17-24
12. Whitten, A., Tygar, J.D.: Why Johnny Can't Encrypt: a Usability Evaluation of PGP 5.0. Proceedings of the 8th USENIX Security Symposium. Washington, D.C. (1999)
13. Good, N.S., Krekelberg, A.: Usability and Privacy: A Study of Kazaa P2P File-sharing. Proceedings of the CHI'2003. Fort Lauderdale, Florida (2003) 137-144
14. Lederer, S., Hong, J.I., Dey, A.K., Landay, J.A.: Personal Privacy through Understanding and Action: Five Pitfalls for Designers. Pers. Ubiquit. Comp 8 (2004) 440-454
15. Kang, M., Kim, H-C.: A Privacy Model in Ubiquitous Environments. Proc. Int. Conf. on Multimedia, Information, Technology and its Applications. Dalian, China (2006) 273-275
16. Hudson, S.E., Smith, I.: Techniques for Addressing Fundamental Privacy and Disruption Trade-offs in Awareness Support Systems. Proc. of the Conf. on Computer Supported Cooperative Work (CSCW'96) (1996) 248-257
17. Clark, H.H.: Using Language. Cambridge University Press (1996)
18. Clark, H.H., Brennan, S.E.: Grounding in Communication. In: Resnick, L.B., Revine, R.M., Teasley, S.D. (eds.): Perspectives on Socially Shared Cognition (1991) 127-149
19. Grudin, J.: Why CSCW Applications Fail: Problems in the Design and Evaluation of Organizational Interfaces. Proc. of CSCW'88 (1988) 85-93
20. Patton, M.Q.: Qualitative Evaluation and Research Methods. 2nd ed. Sage Publications (1990)
21. Carroll, J.M.: Artifacts and Scenarios: An Engineering Approach. In: Monk, A., Gilbert, A. (eds): Perspectives on HCI: Diverse Approaches. Academic Press (1995)
22. Rosson, M.B., Carroll, J.M.: Usability Engineering: Scenario-based Development of Human-Computer Interaction. Morgan Kaufmann Publishers (2002)
23. Carroll, J.M.: Scenario-based Design: Envisioning Work and Technology in System Development. John Wiley & Sons, Inc (1995)
24. Cooper A.: The Inmates are Running the Asylum: Why High Tech Products Drive Us Crazy and How to Restore the Sanity. 2nd ed. Sams (2004)

Access Control for Workflow Environment: The RTFW Model

Hao Jiang and Shengye Lu

School of Computer Science and Engineering, Southeast University,
Nanjing, P.R. China
lvshengye_seu@hotmail.com, hjiang@seu.edu.cn

Abstract. In workflow environments, access control is an important issue of security. Especially, a suitable access control model to meet the special secure requirements is needed. In this paper, we present a formal model, called RTFW, which allows for some ubiquitous problems in workflow environments, such as separation of duty and dynamic authorization, combining the notions of role-based access control (RBAC) and task-based access control (TBAC) models. Furthermore, we describe how to design and implement its prototype system and discuss some key issues and challenges.

1 Introduction

Workflow systems can facilitate the flow of information throughout and beyond the organization [1], so it is indispensable to protect the propagated information against unauthorized access. As is known to us, idea of security models is to leave irrelevant details out and concentrate on some interesting property. There have been several access control models to address access control problems in distributed applications. Then, how to apply a suitable access control model to WFMSs is an interesting issue.

Traditional access control models are discretionary access control (DAC) and mandatory access control (MAC) models. DAC is ownership-based, flexible, and most widely used. But it does not provide high degree of security, and hence low assurance. MAC affords high level of security, based on flow control rules. But it is less flexible.

Role-based access control (RBAC) and Task-based access control (TBAC) have been proposed to address the security requirements of a wider range of applications. RBAC [2] is policy-neutral. In a RBAC model, principle of least privilege and separation of duty can be easily addressed. RBAC has easy administrative features. It is able to express policies using role hierarchy and constrains. TBAC [3] is a task-oriented authorization paradigm. In TBAC models, access permissions to objects are changing on the basis of the context of operating tasks rather than remain invariable. Unfortunately the TBAC model is at an initial stage of development.

Since workflow pays more attention to dealing with processes automatically, users who operate tasks are altering and their permissions are changing on the basis of the context of data processing. In such circumstance, DAC or MAC does not work. Adopting RBAC, however, will result in shifting roles frequently, so it is not suitable

W. Shen et al. (Eds.): CSCWD 2006, LNCS 4402, pp. 619–626, 2007.
© Springer-Verlag Berlin Heidelberg 2007

for workflow, too. But we can combine RBAC with the notion of TBAC, because the dynamic property of TBAC is highly compatible to WFMSs.

The main contribution of this paper is that it presents an access control model called RTFW, short for "Role and Task based access control model For Workflow", which incorporates the main ideas of RBAC and TBAC models, extending and adapting them to meet the need of WFMSs.

The rest of the paper includes the following parts. Section 2 introduces Core Model of RTFW with very simply security objectives. Section 3 extends Core Model to address SoD constraints. Section 4 extends it further to fulfill dynamic authorization. Section 5 goes into how to design and implement its prototype system, especially some key points and challeges. Section 6 includes conclusions.

2   Core Model of RTFW

RTFW adopts the concepts of RBAC96 [2], incorporating the notions of tasks and task instances in WFMSs. In this section we describe the simplest form of RTFW, it implements the classical RBAC model in workflow environment, without the consideration of constrains or any other administration issues.

A task can be a program, a process or a procedure that is stored in the schema of the Workflow System. A task instance is an instance of the task. The Core Model of RTFW can be described as Figure 1.

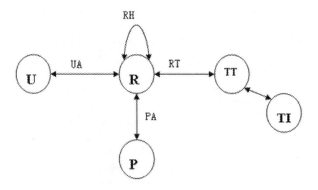

Fig. 1. Core Model of RTFW

Entities in Core Model of RTFW) are: U(set of users), R(set of roles), TT(set of tasks), TI(set of task instances), P(set of permissions), N(set of process instances).

There are some relationships among them.

UA: $UA \subseteq U \times R$, set of all user-role assignment,

$deft : TI \rightarrow TT$, a function that returns the task definition on which a task instance is based.

RT: $RT \subseteq TT \times R$, set of all task-role assignments.

trole : $TT \rightarrow R$, a function that returns the minimum roles that can perform the task. Usually, it is defined when workflow administrator defines the task.

trole' : $TT \rightarrow R$, a function that returns all the roles that can perform the task.

PA: $PA \subseteq R \times P$, set of all role-permission assignment.

RH: $RH = (R, \geq)$, Roles relate to each other through a partial order, namely Role Hierarchy. If $r1, r2 \in R$, $r1 \geq r2$, it is said that $r1$ is superior to $r2$. The following definitions describe how to compute all the roles and permissions a user could assume/be granted, using the inheritance property of Role Hierarchy.

For a user $u \in U$:

Definition 1 (Role-User assignment). If someone assumes the role r', he can also play roles junior to r' [8]. So a user may assume roles according to the function, $uroles : U \rightarrow 2^R$, where

$$uroles(u) \subseteq \bigcup_{r' \in \{ r1|(r1,u) \in UA \}} \{ r \mid r \leq r' \} \qquad (1)$$

Definition 2 (User-Permission assignment). Roles inherit the permissions of the roles that are junior to them [8]. So a user may receive permissions according to the function, $uperm : U \rightarrow 2^P$, where

$$uperm(u) \subseteq \bigcup_{r \in uroles(u)} \{ p \mid (r, p) \in PA \} \qquad (2)$$

With role hierarchy, we can specify all the roles that can perform a task. It is formulated as following,

$$trole'(tt) \subseteq \{ r_i \mid r_i \geq r \wedge r \in trole(tt) \} \qquad (3)$$

3 Separation of Duty

In this section, we describe the extended model of RTFW, which resolves one of the most famous control principles in business, Separation of Duty (SoD). Saltzer and Schroeder [4] identified SoD as a design principle for the protection of information in computer systems. We use conflicting entities to formulize the SoD problem.

3.1 Conflicting Entities

In workflow environment, conflicting entities imply the possibility of fraud if those entities are not controlled cautiously. RTFW adopts the following conflicting entities.

Conflicting Users [5]: For users $u_i, u_j \in U$, if they have the possibility to conspire, they will be considered as conflicting users (denoted as $u_i, u_j \in CU$), and they should be treated as the same one in a same process instance.

Conflicting Roles [6]: For roles $r_i, r_j \in R$, if they grant more ability than required to a single user, they will be considered as conflicting roles (denoted as $r_i, r_j \in CR$).

Conflicting Tasks [7]: For tasks $tt_i, tt_j \in TT$, if they require more ability than required of a single user to complete, they will be considered as conflicting tasks (denoted as $tt_i, tt_j \in CT$).

Conflicting roles, conflicting tasks should not be acted/performed by the same user (or the user's conflicting users).

RTFW model utilizes conflicting entities to express SoD constraints in workflow systems. Imaging there is a constraint- it says, one person cannot apply for an order and then approve the same order. Obviously, only during runtime, could workflow system know who had applied for an order and so he couldn't approve the order later. In this case, we can consider applying for an order and approving an order as conflicting tasks to each other. Since conflicting tasks cannot be performed by the same person, if one user has applied for an order, workflow system will refuse him to approve this order.

3.2   Worklist Generation Methodology

Botha [8] proposed a model, called CoSAWoE, applying SoD policy to workflow environment. His methodology is on the basis of RBAC. In this section, we modify it and make it adapted to RTFW.

To meet the SoD constraint, workflow system should know who has performed some certain tasks in the process instance, that is, the history information of a process instance. From implementing point of view, RTFW defines the history information as follows.

Definition 3 (History). The history of workflow can be described as a set, HIS. For every element, $his_i \in HIS$, it is a certain part of description information of a task instance, $ti \in TI$. $his = (n, tt, u, r)$, where,

$n \in N$, identifies the process instance to which ti belongs.

$tt \in TT$, identifies the task definition on which the task instance ti is based. It is obviously that $tt = deft(ti)$.

$u \in U$, identifies the user who performed the task instance.

$r \in R$, identities the role that the user assumed while performing the task instance

Every element is a record of a task instance which has existed in the workflow system. The worklist of every user can be easily computed after all the users of a specified task instance have been determined. Now we only focus on which users can perform a task.

Definition 4 (Worklist generation). Allowing for the SoD constraint, we can generate Worklist in two stages. Firstly, generating Worklist without the consideration of SoD; then, excluding users who violate SoD constraint [8]. The computing process goes through the following steps.

Step1: Not allowing for SoD, for a given task definition, $tt \in TT$, all the users who can work on it are returned by a function, $ul : TT \rightarrow 2^U$,

$$ul(tt) = \{u \mid trole(tt) \cap uroles(u) \neq \Phi\} \tag{4}$$

Step2: Let function, $ex_{CT} : N \times TT \rightarrow 2^U$, return the users who should be excluded because of violating conflicting tasks.

$$ex_{CT}(n, tt) =$$
$$\bigcup_{\forall tt_i \in \{tt_y | (tt,tt_y) \in CT\}} \{u \mid (n, tt_i, u_x, r) \in HIS \wedge (u = u_x \vee u \in \{u' | (u_x, u') \in CU\})\} \qquad (5)$$

Step3: Let function, $ex_{CR} : N \times R \rightarrow 2^U$, return the users who should be excluded because of violating conflicting roles.

$$ex_{CR}(n, r) =$$
$$\bigcup_{\forall r_i \in \{r_y | (r,r_y) \in CR\}} \{u \mid (n, tt, u_x, r_i) \in HIS \wedge (u = u_x \vee u \in \{u' | (u_x, u') \in CU\})\} \qquad (6)$$

Step4: Let function, $ul' : TT \rightarrow 2^U$, return all the users who can work on tt, without violating the SoD constraint. Then,

$$ul'(tt) = ul(tt) - ex_{CT}(n, tt) - ex_{CR}(n, trole(tt)) \qquad (7)$$

4 Extension for Dynamic Authorization

In this section, we extend our model further. Firstly, it classifies permissions (just 'P' in the Core Model mentioned in Section 2) into two groups. Then, it injects task-based access control notion and Object-Oriented methodology into RTFW to fulfill dynamic authorization.

4.1 Two Sorts of Permissions

We classify permissions into two groups. One represents the capability to perform an operation to a task. The other represents the capability to access and operate an object.

Definition 5 (Permission for Operation). P_{op} represents the permissions which can authorize a role to perform some operations. It is a relationship between operation and task. $P_{OP} \in PER \times TT$, where

$PER = \{execute, commit, abort, ...\}$, it is the set of all the possible operation on a task.

Definition 6 (Permission for Object). P_{ob} represents the permissions which can authorize a role to access some object or resource. It is a relationship between operation and static object. $P_{ob} \in OP \times Object$, where

$OP = \{read, write, edit, ...\}$, it is the set of all the possible access to an object.

$Object$ is the set of all the static resource in workflow environment, such as document, table, etc.

4.2 Dynamic Authorization

The P_{ob} and P_{ob} mentioned earlier can be enforced by injecting task-based access control notion and Object-Oriented methodology into RTFW.

We designed a Class, with the name *TaskControl*. Once a user selects a task from his Worklist, he begins to perform on the task instance defined by this task. At the same time, RTFW creates an instance of the *TaskControl* class. *TaskControl* instance acts as the deputy of the user, working on the task instance, activating all the roles and permissions needed for the user to fulfill the task. After the user finishes the task, *TaskControl* instance will be revoked, and all the roles and permissions will be revoked, too. One *TaskControl* instance is connected with one active task instance.

TaskControl instances have some data values for defining how task should be performed. Examples of data values include:

(1) The user who is working on the task instance.
(2) The lowest roles which a user should play when working on the task;
(3) The type of resources which a user will access during performing the task, such as document, table, etc;
(4) The allowable access permissions on such resource, such as read, write, etc;

Among these information, (1) can be set when a user selects one workitem in his Worklist and begins to work on this task. (2), (3), and (4) are determined by task definition.

So in RTFW model, while P_{op} is granted or revoked by Worklist generation methodology, the *TaskControl* instance determines the grant or revocation of P_{ob}.

5 Design and Implementation Issues

When designing and implementing RTFW prototype system, Two issues are important. One is how to implement SoD sensitive worklist generation, the other is how to authorize dynamically. To the former, we use a concrete example to illustrate the application of Worklist Generation methodology. To the latter, we look into how our prototype system uses *TaskControl* to perform dynamic authorization.

5.1 Role Hierarchy and Worklist Generation

Because Roles inherit the permissions of the roles junior to them in Role Hierarchy, the generation of worklist in Definition 4 is difficult somewhat. The influence of Role Hierarchy to worklist generation can be demonstrated as Figure 2.

In Figure 2, imagining a user, called u, is assigned a role, called f, by the Workflow administrator. Because of role inheritance, user u can also play roles h, i, j. So $uroles(u)=\{f, h, i, j\}$.

Assuming the lowest roles that a user should assume when working on the task tt is j. Then $trole(tt)=\{j\}$.

Since j appears in the set $uroles(u)$, if not allowing for SoD constraint, u can perform on the task tt. RTFW model also takes Least Privilege principle into account, so if he chooses task tt, he will assume the role j, not f, h, i, to work on it.

If the workflow administrator defines role c and role h as conflicting roles to each other, because of role inheritance, a, b, c are all conflicting roles to h.

Since conflicting roles (or conflicting tasks) can not be assumed by the same user. If user u (or his conflicting users) has assumed role a, b or c to work on some tasks, then if he assumes role h or f to perform on the task tt, he will be rejected by RTFW; but if he assumes role j to perform on tt, RTFW will grant him the permissions.

RTFW implements Worklist sub-system by means of Relational Database. The decision whether to grant POP or not involves in some relational tables, such as *HIS* table, Role-Hierarchy relation table, Conflicting entity relation table, etc.

When RTFW computes the SoD-sensitive worklist, System overhead is quite heavy. Because as long as any task instance is accomplished, *HIS* table will insert one element, and then, RTFW will compute worklist again.

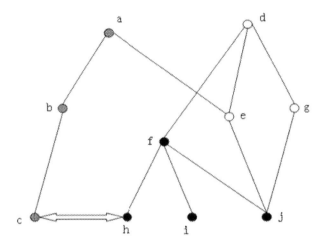

Fig. 2. Role Hierarchy

5.2 TaskControl Class

TaskControl Class defines many methods. Some of them are for setting or getting the data values mentioned earlier, invoked by systems, so that a TaskControl instance can act as the deputy of a user. Some of those methods control the lifecycle of task instance. Task instance can transfer among several states, such as start, finish, suspend, fail, etc. Only during the state of start, can the needed roles and permissions be valid. Some of those methods manage the operations on resources when user is working on a task.

6 Conclusion

In this paper, we present an access control model for WFMSs, called RTFW. It incorporates the advantages of RBAC and TBAC models, and modifies them to meet the need of WFMSs. The proposed model focuses on the issues of SoD policy and dynamic authorization. We also present some key points and challenges concerning how to design and implement its prototype system.

However, practical access control policies or constraints are very complex in workflow environments, SoD policies are only a part of them. The most difficult issue is how to model them correctly and concisely in a practical workflow application.

References

1. Fan, Y., Shi, W., Wu, C.: Fundamentals of Workflow Management Technology. Springer Verlag, Tsinghua New York (2001) 30-35
2. Sandhu, R., Coyne, E., Fenstein, H., Youman, C.: Role-based Access Control Models. IEEE Computer 29 (1996) 38-47
3. Thomas, R. and Sandhu, R.: Task-based Authorization Controls (TBAC): A Family of Models for Active and Enterprise-oriented Authorization Management. Database Security, XI: Status and Prospects-Results of the IFIP WG11.3 Workshop on Database Security. Chapman and Hall (1997) 166-181
4. Saltzer, J.H. and Schroeder, M.D.: The Protection of Information in Computer Systems. Proceedings of IEEE 63 (1975) 1278-1308
5. Ahn, G.J. and Sandhu, R.: The RSL99 Language for Rolebased Separation of duty constraints. Proceedings of the 4th ACM Workshop on Role-based Access Control (1999) 43-54
6. Nyanchama, M., Osborn, S.: The role-graph model and conflict of interest. ACM Transactions on Information and System Security 2 (1999) 3-33
7. Thomas, R., Sandhu, R.: Conceptual Foundations for a Model of Task-based Authorizations. Proceedings of the 7th IEEE Computer Security Foundations Workshop. Franconia, NH (1994) 66-79
8. Botha, R.A.: CoSAWoE: A Model for Context-sensitive Access Control in Workflow Environments. PhD Thesis. Johannesburg, South Africa (2001) 87-100

An Architecture Approach to Dynamic Policy in RBAC

Cheng Zang, Zhongdong Huang, Ke Chen, and Jinxiang Dong

College of Computer Science, Zhejiang University,
Hangzhou, P.R. China
zang623@tom.com, {hzd, chenk, djx}@cs.zju.edu.cn

Abstract. Dynamic policy enables the system to adjust the policies according to the changing circumstance, and makes the system more flexible and adaptive. We have proposed a dynamic model and the idea is to dynamically change the policy according to a pair of states rather than one state, which provides more information for the policy decision making, thus makes policy more accurate. The dynamic policy architecture based on this model is built in this paper, and we describe the components and steps of detecting a change, deciding the pair of current and previous states and picking up the policy according to the change.

1 Introduction

RBAC model [2] was proposed to improve the efficiency of access control management. It has been widely applied in various fields such as network security, database management, etc.

Meanwhile, researchers are trying to extend this model and make it more flexible. TRBAC [4] and GTRBAC [5] are developed to enhance RBAC model with a temporal user-role mapping extension which allows users to assign to different roles at different time, which extends RBAC model with dynamic and flexible features. But the way most dynamic access control systems doing is monitoring the current state of the system and apply policies according to it. If a state change is detected, the new state is focused and the previous one is abandoned. For example, in [3] and [7], they only care about what happens now, and they don't take what happened before into consideration, and the history information is dropped. And some history-based dynamic access have been proposed such as [8], but it only cares about users' behavior and does not have a full-scale view.

If history information is included into the policy decision, the policy will be more efficient and appropriate, because in this way the tendency of the system can be forecasted and the policy can then be decided. Thus we propose a state-transfer-based dynamic method in [1]. This method focuses on the state-transfer of a pair of previous and current states, taking almost all the elements of a system into consideration and changes the policy dynamically according to these state-transfers, such as the resource utilization changing, the time changing, etc. This method has some good characteristics. Firstly, it covers the states of almost all the elements in an RBAC model. Secondly, it indicates the tendency by using the former state information of the subjects in order to make policy more effective and efficient. Lastly, it doesn't need to record the former information in a log file or database as [6] does.

W. Shen et al. (Eds.): CSCWD 2006, LNCS 4402, pp. 627–634, 2007.
© Springer-Verlag Berlin Heidelberg 2007

We build the architecture in this paper using the STB dynamic policy in order to build a dynamic architecture which can make policy decision by a state-transfer but not only a current state, and make policy more appropriate for the current system and future condition.

The remainder of this paper is organized as follows: Section 2 is an overview of state-transfer-based dynamic policy and some features of the architecture. In section 3 we explain the structure of this architecture. We give a detailed example in Section 4. And we draw a conclusion in Section 5.

2 Overview of Architecture

2.1 STB Policy Idea

The STB dynamic policy [1] is a dynamic policy method. It changes policy according to the pair of previous state and current state in a state changing.

In STB dynamic method, we consider all users, roles, objects, permissions and environment as Subjects. And we call the set of values of subjects as Partial State, for example, the IP address, the time, the ON/OFF state of a switch. Based on partial state, there is a Partial-State-Based Policy (PSBpolicy), which is changed according to different current partial state. And State is composed of both partial state and PSBpolicy. When a state changes to another one, we say a State-Transfer occurs, and the policy based on this transfer is the State-Transfer-Based Policy (STBpolicy). And Policy is a set containing PSBpolicy and STBpolicy.

When a state-transfer occurs, we know both the previous state and the current state, based on which the corresponding policy can be picked up from the policy set. Consider three states: A, B and C. In most RBAC systems or extends, each state has a corresponding policy, for example state A has a policy P_A, state B has a policy P_B, state C has a policy P_C. When the state changes from A to B, the policy changes from P_A to P_B correspondingly. On the other hand, when the state changes from C to B, the policy changes from P_C to P_B too. But in STB dynamic policy, a state-transfer from A to B results a policy P_{AB}, while a state-transfer from C to B results a policy P_{CB}, which

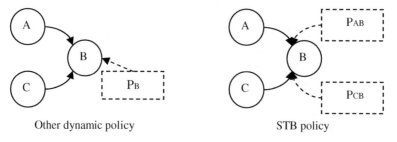

Other dynamic policy	STB policy

Fig. 1. The difference between STB dynamic policy and other dynamic policies approaches. Although these two state-transfers lead to the same state, they get different policy.

2.2 Expressions

The expressions of the rules are listed in Table 1. Here, sbj is a subject, pst is a partial state, stp and stc are states, p is policy. Statement 1 means a PSBpolicy can be decided if a partial state is decided and a PSBpolicy according to this partial state is predefined. Statement 2 implies that a state is decided by both partial state and PSBpolicy. Statement 3 shows that a state-transfer is decided when both a previous and a current state are decided. And statement 4 indicates that a policy is decided if a state-transfer and a STBpolicy according to this state-transfer is predefined.

This method shows a characteristic that it can use both previous and current information to make a more appropriate policy and also it can be compatible with the state based dynamic policy.

Table 1. Expressions

1	partial_state_decided(sbj,pst)$\land$PSBpolicy_defined(sbj,pst,p)$\rightarrow$ PSBpolicy_decided (sbj,p)
2	PSBpolicy_decided(sbj,p)$\land$partial_state_decided(sbj,pst)$\rightarrow$ current_state_decided (sbj,stc)
3	current_state_decided(sbj,stc)$\land$previous_state_ecided(sbj,stp)$\rightarrow$ state_transfer_decided(sbj, stp, stc)
4	state_transfer_decided(sbj, stp, stc)$\land$STBpoicy_defined(sbj, stp, stc, p) $\rightarrow$ policy_decided(sbj,p)

2.3 Features

The STB dynamic policy architecture mainly provides a dynamic mechanism to manage the access control policy in a network or database or workflow system. And it should provide features of dynamic, full-scale and extensible. That is, firstly, it can change policy dynamically according to different situations, especially by a state-transfer. Secondly, it can represent all changeable elements in a system, including user, resource, permission, environment variable, etc. And at last, this architecture should be open to any new element.

3   Structure of Architecture

The structure of this architecture is similar to most dynamic access control system, but some component is different so that it can qualify this architecture with a state-transfer-based feature. We draw an overall structure in Figure 2.

The arrows indicate the directions of the information transfer. For example, the arrow from "subject" to "State-transfer decision engine Dynamic policy layer I" means that the value-changing information of the subjects is transferred through the arrow. Also, the   arrow from "STBPolicy decision engine Dynamic policy layer II" to "subject" means that the policy is decided and applied for the "subject".

3.1 Subject

Subject includes users, roles, objects, permissions and environment variables. Generally speaking, every element in a system should be included into the subject set.

In a network or database or workflow system, usually there are users, resources, environment and the permissions between users and resources, and in a RBAC system, there also exists roles. Dynamic policy is a mechanism based on the change of these elements, and also there are many ways to implement this mechanism. As we have mentioned above, our method is changing the policy according to a state-transfer of subject. The method monitors these elements and detects their changes and applies the policies accordingly.

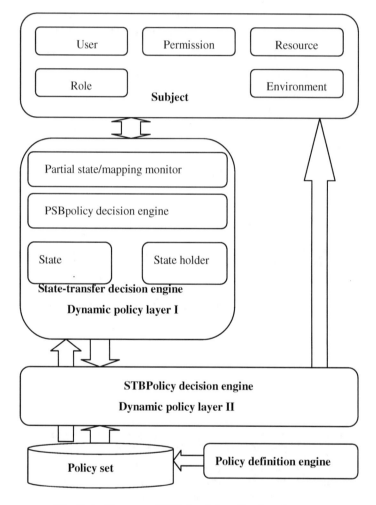

Fig. 2. Architecture of STB dynamic policy based system

3.2 State-Transfer Decision Engine

As state-transfer is the key of our dynamic access control method, the state-transfer decision engine is definitely the key of this architecture too. It decides state-transfers, on which each PSBpolicy change is based.

The task of this component is detecting the partial state change or mapping change of the system, applying the PSBpolicy and deciding the state-transfer. Partial state/mapping monitor and PSBpolicy decision engine work together to decide a new state and provide it to the state monitor. To decide a new state, firstly, partial state/mapping monitor must detect a partial state change or a mapping change, and if there is a partial state change, the PSBpolicy should be picked from the predefined policy set and applied according to the new partial state. The expression partial_state_decided(sbj,pst) $\land$ PSBpolicy_defined(sbj, pst,p)→PSBpolicy_decided (sbj,p) is implemented by this step. Now that the new partial state and the new PSBpolicy are both known, a new state can be decided. PSBpolicy_decided(sbj,p)$\land$

partial_state_decided(sbj,pst) → current_state_decided (sbj, stc) is implemented by this step. Figure 3 shows these steps.

State holder is a part of the state-transfer decision engine, and it holds the run-time states of all subjects in the system. Once any subject changes its state, the state monitor will detect the change and fetch the new state of this subject. Thus, the state-transfer decision engine gets

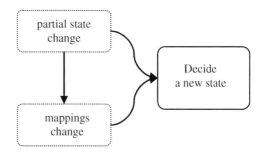

Fig. 3. Decide a state

the run-time state information from state holder as the previous state and the new state information from state monitor as the current state. If these two states are different, then a state-transfer (SBJ, Sp, Sc) is decided, and the state-transfer decision engine will inform the policy decision engine that a state-transfer occurs. At last, the run-time state held in state holder will be replaced with the new state. current_state_decided (sbj,stc) $\land$ previous_state_decided(sbj,stp)→state_transfer_ decided(sbj, stp, stc) is implemented by this step.

Specially, when a new subject appears, for example, a new computer logs on the network, there would be no run-time state held in the state holder. In this case, the decision engine gets a new state from state monitor, but it cannot get any information from state holder. So the decision engine finally decides a state-transfer from NULL to current state, expressing as (SBJ, 0, Sc).

We can consider this procedure as dynamic policy layer I, since in this procedure the PSBpolicy is changed directly according to the partial state change or mapping change.

3.3 STBPolicy Decision Engine

After the state-transfer decision engine sends the state-transfer information to policy decision engine, a policy can be decided correspondingly. Expressions state_transfer_ decided(sbj, stp, stc)$\land$STBpoicy_defined(sbj, stp, stc, p)→policy_decided(sbj,p) is implemented by this step.

Because this policy decision is based on state-transfer, we must define the policies related to state-transfers. A policy is defined as a quaternion, expressing as (SBJ, Sp, Sc, P). SBJ is the subject whose change triggers a state-transfer, and Sp, Sc is the previous and current state of the subject. P is the policy according to this state-transfer. When the state-transfer information (SBJ, Sp, Sc) is sent by state-transfer decision engine, a policy matched can be picked up from the policy set.

There are two special states in our method. State 0 means NULL and state-transfer (SBJ, 0, Sc) means an initial state, so the policy defined as (SBJ, 0, Sc, P) can be explained as the policy triggered by the initialization of SBJ at state Sc. And another state * means any state in the state set, but the policy (SBJ, *, Sc, P) does not necessarily mean the policy when SBJ is at state Sc since there may exist some conflicts. If we want policy P to be applied when SBJ is at state Sc, then (SBJ, *, Sc, P) does mean "the policy when SBJ is at state Sc" (we call it current state based policy), but if we define another policy (SBJ, Sp, Sc, P') which means a policy P' triggered by the state-transfer of SBJ from Sp to Sc, a conflict rises: when a state-transfer (SBJ, Sp, Sc) occurs, which policy should be applied?

We give them different priorities to solve this problem. We grant the low priority to the policies containing '*', so that the policies defined as (SBJ, *, Sc, P) have a lower priority than the policies defined as (SBJ, Sp, Sc, P'). If both of these two policies are defined, they mean that policy P' is applied to the system when a state-transfer of SBJ from state Sp to state Sc occurs, and a state-transfer of SBJ from any other states to state Sc results a policy P.

We can consider this procedure as dynamic policy layer II, and it is set up based on the dynamic policy layer I.

3.4 Policy Definition Engine and Policy Set

The policy definition engine is a configuration interface, and the policies are stored in the policy set. The policy is divided into two categories, one is the PSBpolicy and the other one is the STBpolicy.

Since the state is composed of partial state and PSBpolicy, we can express their relationship as $S \leftarrow \rightarrow (PS, PSBpolicy)$. And, the STBpolicy is expressed as (SBJ, Sp, Sc, P), especially, we define the current state based policy as (SBJ, *, Sc, P). We have that $(SBJ, *, Sc, P) \leftarrow \rightarrow (SBJ, *, (PSc, PSBpolicy), P)$ because we have $Sc \leftarrow \rightarrow (PSc, PSBpolicy)$. If we leave the PSBpolicy blank in the expression, we get (SBJ, *, (PSc, 0), P), which is the very formation can be used to define the partial state based policy, that is, the PSBpolicy. Thus we unify the formation of the definitions for both PSBpolicy and STBpolicy as (SBJ, Sp, (PSc, PSBpolicy), P). The benefit of the unification is that we don't need to emphasize whether it is a STBpolicy or it is a PSBpolicy when we store the policy, and the system does not need to care about when to apply PSBpolicy and when to apply STBpolicy because there is a unified policy match mechanism, if and only if the policy is matched, it is applied.

4   An Example

In this example, we assume that there is an information service in the LAN, and using this resource needs two steps: logon and access the information. The CPU load of this service is appropriate between 20%-50%, since high CPU load may cause other services jammed and low utilization may waste the capacity of CPU. Also, there are two groups of users in LAN who may use the resource. One is high_priority_user (HPU) whose IP address is 192.168.11.* and the other one is low_priority_user (LPU) whose IP address is 192.168.10.*. Each user belongs to one and only one of them. When the CPU load is over 50%, both of them can logon but only HPU can get access to the information, and when the CPU load is lower than 20%, both of them are authorized to logon and access the information. Now the problem remaining is what is the policy when CPU load is between 20% and 50%? Usually people tend to do the same thing together, for example, at daytime the office LAN is always busy but at night it is idle since employees work at the same time and rest at the same time, or when a big news is published, people all go to visit web pages, and some days later they take no interest any more. So here we consider that when the utilization of this resource is increasing, it tends to keep increasing since it may indicate that the more access is coming, on the other hand, if the utilization is decreasing, it tends to keep decreasing too. Thus we define the policy in Table 2.

Table 2. PSBpolicy and STBpolicy

service state A	partial state	CPU load < 20%
	PSBpolicy	HPU logon = true; LPU logon = true HPU access= true; LPU access= true
	STBpolicy in A	NULL
service state B	partial state	CPU load 20%-50%
	PSBpolicy	HPU logon = true; LPU logon = true HPU access= true
	STBpolicy in B	state transfers from C to B: LPU access= true
		state transfers from A to B: LPU access= false
service state C	partial state	CPU load > 50%
	PSBpolicy	HPU logon = true; LPU logon = true HPU access= true; LPU access= false
	STBpolicy in C	NULL
user state D	partial state	IP = 192.168.10.*
	PSBpolicy	role assignment = LPU
	STBpolicy	NULL
user state E	partial state	IP = 192.168.11.*
	PSBpolicy	role assignment = HPU
	STBpolicy	NULL

We have mentioned policies in state A and C before, so here we only explain the policy for service in state B. When the CPU load is between 20% and 50%, the PSBpolicy is decided as "both of them can logon, and HPU can access the information." The STBpolicy is decided by both previous and current state, describing as "LPU can access the information according to a state transfer from C to B" and "LPU cannot access the information according to a state transfer from A to B". As we assumed above, When CPU load increasing from <20% to 20%-50%, it tends to increase to >50%, so the STBpolicy "LPU can not access the information" tries to prevent the load from keeping increasing. These STBpolicies obviously maintain the CPU load in the appropriate utilization for a longer time.

Suppose there is a computer and its IP address is 192.168.10.33. When it logs on the network, the partial state/mapping monitor discovers it and finds a suitable policy (user, *, (IP=192.168.10.*, 0), role assignment =LPU) in the policy set, so this computer is assigned as LPU. At this time, the state monitor detects a new state, thus a state-transfer (user, 0, state D) is decided. But the STBpolicy is not defined, so the STBpolicy decision engine cannot match anything, thus no policy is applied according to this state-transfer.

If the CPU load of the server is 15%, there is a policy (service, *, (CPU load <20%, 0), P) where P is defined as HPU logon = true, LPU logon = true, HPU access= true, LPU access= true. At this time, the attempt of this computer to access the information is allowed. Then the CPU load increases to 35%, the partial state/ mapping monitor detects the change of CPU load, and the PSBpolicy (service, *, (CPU load >20% and < 50%, 0), P) where P is defined as HPU logon = true, LPU logon = true, HPU access= true is applied,   also a new state is decided. State-transfer decision engine then decides a state-transfer (service, (CPU load <20%, P1), (CPU load >20% and < 50%, P2)) where P1 and P2 are the STBpolicies applied according to these states. And in the policy set, there matches a policy (service, (CPU load <20%, P1), (CPU load >20% and < 50%, P2), P) where P is defined as LPU access= false. On the other hand, if the CPU load decreases from 70% to 35%, another STBpolicy (service, (CPU load >50%, P3), (CPU load >20% and < 50%, P2), P) where P is defined as LPU access= true would be matched.

5   Conclusions

We propose an access control architecture using STB dynamic policy, which can provide dynamic policies in the network of database or workflow systems. This architecture is able to forecast the system's tendency by using the information from the pair of previous and current states and make appropriate policies. We propose an overall structure and describe its components and functions, including detecting the partial state change, applying PSBpolicy, deciding state, monitoring the state-transfer, matching the policy and defining the policy. The purpose is to provide a dynamic access control system which is effective, efficient and practical.

References

1. Zang, C., Huang, Z., Chen, G., Dong, J.: A State-Transfer-Based Dynamic Policy Approach for Constraints in RBAC. LNCS 3739 (2005) 755-760
2. Sandhu, R.S., Coyne, J., Feinstein, H.L., Youman, C.: Role-based access control models. IEEE Computer 29(2) (1996) 38-47
3. Huang, Y., Yang, Z., Ping, L, Pan X.: Practical way to implement role-based access control in security administration system. Journal of Zhejiang University 38(4) (2004) 408-413
4. Bertino, E., Bonatti, P.A., Ferrari, E.: TRBAC: A temporal role based access control model. ACM Transactions on Information and System Security 4(3) (2001) 191-233
5. Joshi, J.B.D., Bertino, E., Ghafoor, A.: Temporal hierarchies and inheritance semantics for GTRBAC. Proc. 7th ACM Symp. on Access Control Model and Technologies (2002) 74-83
6. Neumann, G., Strembeck, M.: An Approach to Engineer and Enforce Context Constraints in an RBAC Environment. Proc. SACMAT'03. Villa Galllia, Italy (2003) 65-79
7. Bhide, M., Pandey, S., Gupta, A., Mohania, M.: Data Dynamic access control framework based on events: a demonstration. Proc. 19th Int. Conf. on Engi. (2003) 765-767
8. Edjlali, G., Acharya, A. and Chaudhary, V.: History-based Access Control for Mobile Code. Proc. 5th ACM Conference on Computer and Communications Security (1998)

A Fractal Watermark Solution for Product Data

Ke Chen, Gang Chen, Cheng Zang, and Jinxiang Dong

College of Computer Science, Zhejiang University,
Hangzhou, P.R. China 310027
{chenk, cg, djx}@cs.zju.edu.cn, zang623@tom.com

Abstract. Copyright and integrity protection over product data is becoming an urgent requirement, because in a Distributed Networked Manufacturing environment, enterprises have to interact with each other to share product data. In this paper, we introduce a novel watermarking solution for product data based on the idea of fractal, which classifies product data watermarks into three tiers: fractal watermark, tree-structure watermark, and tree-node watermark. It embeds watermarks not only in value-carrying nodes but also in product structures that "glue" all the nodes together by embedding multiple structure watermarks in product data. Simulation results show that the proposed technique is robust against various forms of malicious attacks of product data, and naturally immune from structure transformation attacks and subtractive (sub-tree) attacks. Moreover, the solution can protect tree-structure data whose knowledge is mainly embodied in the tree structure efficiently. It is very easy to implement and popularize.

1 Introduction

The Internet is currently the main driving force in the area of advanced manufacture applications. With the development of Distributed Networked Manufacturing, there appear more and more collaborations on complex product between different departments in a company, or even between two companies, which brings more challenges to Computer Supported Collaborative Work Design (CSCWD). Consequentially, product data security begins to be an important research topic. Traditionally, we believe there is no data security problem when two organizations, such as two departments in a company or two different companies, collaborate on the same product component or part. However, when different organizations working on different product components separately, there is a need for data security mechanism, which guarantees that users cannot access private data of other collaborators, including component structure information and part information. This mechanism can be successfully achieved with the help of access control technology. In fact, many commercial PDM softwares, such as Windchill and IMAN, have supported this mechanism.

However, with the development of Mass Customization, most enterprises must form one kind of generalized CSCW with its suppliers and even its customers. Under this situation, if an enterprise keeps its product data secret to suppliers or customers, it is impossible for suppliers to produce necessary component or part, and the enterprise

W. Shen et al. (Eds.): CSCWD 2006, LNCS 4402, pp. 635–646, 2007.
© Springer-Verlag Berlin Heidelberg 2007

would also be unable to provide better customer support. In other word, the enterprise must interact with their suppliers and customers to share product information. Consequently, copyright and integrity protection over product data is becoming an urgent requirement. Because the product information consists of two parts: product structure and part content, besides protecting the three-dimensional (3D) model of part by watermarking, we also need to protect product structure information, which describes the relations among product parts. This paper proposes a general product data watermark model, which simultaneously realizes the copyright and integrity protection of the two parts, product structure information and part content.

The rest of this paper is organized as follows: Section 2 discusses some related work, and describes limitations of existing digital watermark technologies in processing product data watermark. Section 3 sketches out the watermark model for product data. Section 4 proposes a novel watermark solution on product data and gives corresponding algorisms. Section 5 gives our simulation and discusses resilience analysis. We conclude with summary and future directions in Section 6.

2   Related Work

As an important area in information hiding [1-3], digital watermarking techniques have been extensively exploited and regarded as a potentially effective solution against illegal reproduction or theft of digital assets. Digital watermarking techniques have been successfully applied in multimedia data such as image [4-5], audio [7], video [6], etc.

At the same time, the 3D model watermark technology also made the very big progress. Ohbuchi [8] first discussed concept of watermarking 3D polygonal models, and proposed two kind of revision models geometry attribute watermark algorithms: TSQ (Triangle Similarity Quadruple) and TVR (Tetrahedral Volume Ratio). He also further presented a new robust watermarking method [9-10] that added watermark into a 3D polygonal mesh in the mesh's spectral domain. A watermark was embedded by modifying the magnitude of the spectra. The algorithm computed spectra of the mesh by using Eigen value decomposition of a Laplacian matrix derived only from connectivity of the mesh. Watermarks embedded by this method were resistant to similarity transformation, random noise added to vertex coordinates, mesh smoothing, and partial resection of the meshes. Wagner, Aspert designed and realized respective for 3D Polygonal Meshes watermark algorithm [11-12]. Based on the digital signature technology, Fornaro proposed a private Key Watermarking algorithm for authentication of CSG (Constructive Solid Geometry) [13]. While more recent research has extended to some new digital domains, such as relational data [14-15], software [16-17], natural language [18-19], categorical data [20], sensor streams [21] and so on.

Meanwhile, watermarking XML data also has received much attention. The typical work includes: Agrawal et. al. [14] presented an effective watermarking technique geared for relational data. His technique ensured that some bit positions of some of the attributes of some of the tuples contained specific values. Wilfred Ng and Ho-Lam Lau [23] extended Agrawal's techniques on XML data by defining locators in XML in their selective approach which allowed embedding non-destructive hidden information content over XML data. Sion et. al. [22] discussed the watermarking of abstract structured aggregates of multiple types of content, such as multi-type/media documents, and represented them as graphs by characterizing the values in the structure and individual nodes. He also proposed a general watermarking algorithm that made use of the encoding capacity of different types of nodes. Chen [25] proposed a novel watermark scheme for tree-structured data based on the value lying both in the tree structure and in the node content, which gives a comprehensive protection for both node content and structure of XML tree.

In this paper, based on the 3D Polygonal Meshes watermark technology, the structure/semi-structure data watermark technologies and the idea of Fractal [26], we propose a novel watermark scheme for tree-structure product data with the value lying both in product structure and in part node content, which gives a more comprehensive and resilient right protection for both part node content and product structure.

3 Preliminaries

In this section, we present some basic definitions for better discussion in the following sections.

3.1 Definitions

Definition 1 Product Data
Let product data T be a triple: $T = \{G, V, S\}$ where:

- G is the root of the product tree.
- V is a set of all nodes in the product tree, which constitute components of the product, includes 3D model set and its attached information.
- S is a set of all Parent/Child Relationships in the tree, which represents product structure.

Tree is the simplest fractal structure. Fractal, in brief, is a geometric pattern that is repeated at ever smaller scales to produce irregular shapes and surfaces that cannot be represented by classical geometry. In fractal, geometrical objects are self-similar under a change of scale, for example, magnification. We innovatively propose fractal watermark for tree-structure data based on tree's fractal feature, which is classified to fractal watermark, structure watermark and node watermark. The definitions are given in the following:

Definition 2 Fractal Watermark for Product Data
Let a fractal watermark W be a triple $M = \{T, SW, F\}$, where:

- T is the product data to be embedded with fractal watermark.
- SW is a set of all fractal watermarks embedded in product data.
- F is a set of usability constraints which need to be met before and after the fractal watermarks embedding.

Definition 3 Tree-structure Watermark for Product Data
Let a tree-structure watermark SW be a triple $SW = \{T, NW, F\}$, where:

- T is the product data to be embedded with tree-structure watermark.
- NW is a set of all tree-node watermarks embedded in product data.
- F is a set of usability constraints which need to be met before and after the tree-structure watermarks embedding.

Definition 4 Tree-node Watermark for Product Data

Let a tree-node watermark NW be a quintuple $NW = \{ t, d, s, \xi, w \}$, where:

- t is the type of the attribute of the node.
- d is the content of the node.
- S is the structural information of the node in the product tree.
- ξ, related to t closely, represent usability constraints needed before and after the node's watermark insertion.
- w is the watermark information embedded in the node.

3.2 Desirable Properties

Based on the idea of Agrawal [14], to achieve a "perfect" product data watermark, the following properties are desirable:

1. **Detectability (validity):** Detectability indicates the ability of the watermark system to detect a watermark after being embedded. It is demonstrated by two aspects: low false negative rate and low false positive rate.
2. **Imperceptibility:** The modifications caused by embedded watermark should be below a perceptible threshold, which means that the data user should not be able to recognize any visible difference in the watermarked data.
3. **Robustness:** Robust marks have the property that they can still be detected after some certain degree attacks on the tree node or tree structure.
4. **Blind System:** Watermark detection requires no knowledge of original data or watermark. This property is critical as it allows the watermark to be detected in a copy of the tree-structured data, irrespective of later updates to the original one.
5. **Following Kerckhoffs' principle:** The watermarking system should assume that the method used for inserting a watermark is public. Defense must lie only in the choice of the private key. The folly of "security by obscurity" has been shown repeatedly since the first enunciation of Kerckhoffs' principle in 1883 [27].

3.3 Malicious Attacks

The product data watermark may suffer the following attacks:

A. *Node-content attacks* are traditional attacks. i.e. adversary modifies 3D model information of the part node within usability vicinity, such as scaling, rotation or combinations of geometrical transformations.

B. *Structure transformation Attacks.* These are some special attacks for product structure watermark, mainly including:

B1. Adversary inserts some insignificant nodes to the product structure.

B2. Adversary deletes some insignificant nodes from the product structure.

B3. Adversary changes the relation among the product part nodes.

C. *Invertibility Attacks.* Adversary may launch an invertibility attack [29] to claim ownership if he can successfully discover a fictitious watermark. The claimed watermark is in fact a random occurrence.

D. *Additive Attacks.* In an additive attack, adversary inserts his own watermarks over the original product data and claims the "legal" ownership of the product data.

4   A Solution

Traditional techniques about how to embed a resilient and indelible mark in 3D model only focus on right protection for single component or part, and not for another key element, product structure information. However, for modern complicated product, design information is also embodied in product structure, which becomes the emphasis protection object of enterprise. Trivial changes of the structure may result in significant changes on product knowledge. So the watermarking technique for product data without the protection of the structural information is very fragile.

Based on this observation, this paper proposes one Fractal Watermark Solution for product, whose major characteristics include embedding watermark into each 3D part model that constitutes the product and embedding the same watermark into product structure. This feature embodies a totally different idea with former watermark solutions. In fact, good resilience protection can be achieved not only in product structure, but also in the individual nodes.

4.1   The Outline

Before the description of our solution, we enunciate one basic property of tree, which is the theory foundation of our proposed solution.

Theorem 1. All the nodes traversed from the node V tracing back to the root R of the tree determines identically the structural information of the tree node V.

Naturally, we can deduce the theorem from the definition of a tree, so the proof is omitted here.

By the theorem, each node in a tree has two parts of information, one is node content, the other is structure information of the node, which is absolutely determined by the path traversed from the node tracing back to the root R of the tree. The simple but important feature forms one of the theoretical foundations of our solution. The other theoretical foundation is the Fractal Theory. Every part is self-similar with a whole under a change of scale in fractal, and tree can be regarded as the simplest fractal. Inspired by the fractal theory, we insert corresponding watermark into each sub-tree, which constructs fractal at the watermark level. The advantage of fractal watermark is that, first, it can conceal in many sub-trees by embedding watermark into product data many times, which can be effectively used against tree-structure transformation attacks; second, it overcomes the disorder and changeability of tree-structure data and protect the whole structure as well as every sub-tree efficiently; third, it is naturally immune from sub-tree attacks at the same time.

4.2   Watermarking 3D Models

Inserting watermark to each part node in the product is a typical problem of 3D Model watermark. Our work in this paper adopts the blind watermarking algorithm for 3D Model suggested by Harte et al. [28]. Its basic idea is ensuring a minimal visibility of the distortions in the watermarked object. The 3D watermark embedding algorithm has two stages. In the first stage the algorithm identifies the vertices, whose distances to their neighborhood smaller than a threshold T and are suitable for embedding the watermark. Then, the selected vertices are ranked according to the distances from all the vertices, and form a bounding volume. A "1" bit is embedded by moving the selected vertex inside the bounding volume while a "0" bit is embedded by moving the vertex outside the bounding volume, ensuring also a minimal distortion in the resulting watermarked model.

4.3 Labeling the Part Nodes

To embed watermarks in product structure, the key challenge is to design a mapping function to calculate the corresponding labels according to tree node content (3D model). It is of paramount importance that the function must have the ability to uniquely ascertain label value and to "recognize" the labeled node after the action of watermark embedding or malicious attacking (e.g. transform 3D model or changes the relations of the nodes within the usability vicinity). So, the main idea of designing the function is that we must have the label in accordance with the most valuable part (i.e. the usability of content will degrade greatly with minor changes to the part) in the 3D model. Apparently, the mapping function is correlated closely to watermark insertion method for 3D model. In our algorithm, based on the Harte's method, the mapping function is described as following: firstly by using a key, select and order a set of vertices whose distances to their neighborhood bigger than a threshold T; then calculate the node labels based on the 3D vectors.

4.4 Watermarking Insertion

To better illustrate our idea, we represent the product tree structure using son-sibling method, and denote node content, son and sibling use *item, lson, rsibling* respectively. Furthermore, we adopt a one-way hash function $F(x) = H(K \cdot x)$, which returns an unique integer value depending on input x and a private key K known only to the owner. *Label ()* is the function that calculates the label for 3D tree node content. The array *a[ ]* demonstrates the "weight" of node content and path information respectively in the data, which are control and adjust by the user against structural attacks. The calculation of L appeared between line 6 and line 10 in Algorithm 2 illustrates that the value of L synthesizes inherent information of part node and structure information of the part node, which is represented as path traversed from the node tracing back to the root of the tree. The watermark insertion algorithms are given in the following:

Algorithm 1 The fractal watermark insertion algorithm

// The parameter r is also private to the owner. r represents the gap value of marked nodes in the product tree (the watermark ratio)

product_wm_insertion(tree_node G, secret_key K)
1: **if** (G is NULL ‖ getTreeNodeCount(G) < δ)
2:     return;

3: markStructure(G, G, K);   //insert the global watermark for tree structure

4: product_wm_insertion (G->lson, K);   //implement watermark insertion by recursion
5: product_wm_insertion (G->rsibing, K); //implement watermark insertion by recursion

---

Algorithm 2 The structure watermark insertion algorithm for tree structure

---

// *N*: the current node
// The parameter *r* is also private to the owner. *r* represents the gap value of marked nodes in the product tree (the watermark ratio)
markStructure(tree_node *G*, tree_node *N*, secret_key *K*)
1: **if** (*N* is NULL)
2:     return;

3: **if** (*N* is a candidate node for marking) {//the part node is suitable for embedding the watermark

4:     tree_node *T = N*;
5:     int *L = 0*, i = 0;
6:     **while** (*T* is not NULL){//calculate the combination value of structural and node content information
7:         *L = L + a[i]*Label(T);*
8:         *T = Parent(T);*
9:     *i = i + 1;*
10:    }// while
11:    **if** (*F(L)* mod *r* equals 0)   //mark this node
12:         markNode(*N*) ; // insert watermark to the 3D node by Harte algorithms.
13: }
14:    markStructure(*G* , *N*->lson, *K*)
15:    markStructure(*G* , *N*->rsibling, *K*)

4.5 Watermarking Detection

Product data watermark detection detects structure watermark and part node watermark respectively by traversing the whole product data tree and finding out the watermarked part nodes. In the traversing process, each watermarked node will experience the detections of two watermarks embedded in product structure and in part node.

The specific description of the detection algorithm is as follows:

Algorithm 3 The fractal watermark detection algorithm

// The parameters *α* represents the significance level of the test for detecting a fractal watermark.
product_wm_detection (product_root _node *G*, secret_key *K*)
1: *totalcount = matchcount = 0*;
2: get_structure_wm_count (*G, K, &totalcount, &matchcount*);
3: **if** (*matchCount/totalCount ≥ α*)
4:    the watermark detection is success;

Algorithm 4 The structure watermark detection algorithm

// The parameters *β* represents the significance level of the test for detecting a structure watermark.
get_structure_wm_count (tree_node *G*, secret_key *K*, **pTotalcount*, int **pMatchcount*)
1: **if** (*G* is NULL)
2:     return;   // the outlet of the recursive function
3: **if**(getTreeNodeCount(*G*) > δ)
4:    **pTotalcount = *pTotalcount + 1*;
5:    *t_count = m_count = 0* ; // *t_count* is the count of all nodes watermarked, *m_count* is the count of all
                                nodes detected in fact
6: get_node_wm_count(*G, G, K, &t_count, &m_count*);
7: **if**(*m_count* > Threshold(*t_count, β*))
8:    **pMatchcoun=*pMatchcoun+1*;
9: get_structure_wm_count (*G* ->lson, *K*, *pTotalcount, pMatchcount1*);
10: get_structure_wm_count (*G* ->rsibling, *K*, *pTotalcount, pMatchcount*);

Algorithm 5 The node watermark detection algorithm

get_node_wm_count (tree_node *G*, tree_node *N*, secret_key *K*, int **pt_count*, int **pm_count*)
1: **if** (*N* is NULL)
2:      return;   // the outlet of the recursive function
3: int *L* = *0*, *i* = *0* ;
4: **while** (*N* is not NULL){ // calculate the combination value of structural and node content information
5:          *L* = *L* + *a[i]*Label(T)*;
6:          *T* = *Parent(T)*;
7:   *i* = *i* + *1*;
8: }// while
9: **if** (*F(L)* mod *r* equals 0) {// this node was marked
10:   **pt_count* = **pt_count* + 1;
11:   **if**(detectingNodeisSuccess(N))
             *pm_count = **pm_count*+1;
12:   }
13: get_node_wm_count (G, *N* ->*lson, K* , *pt_count, pm_count*);
14: get_node_wm_count (G, *N* ->*rsibling, K, pt_count, pm_count*);

---

5 Simulation and Resilience Analysis

We now report a series of experimental results for all kinds of attacks mentioned above. For the convenience of experiments, we develop a product data Generator (PDG) which can generate product data randomly. The first step of the PDG is to produce Document Type Definitions (DTD) of XML entity with max height *H* of the tree as the input, and the second step is to random generate XML documents with node number *N* of the tree as the input. In our preliminary experiments, the nodes in the DTD are all numeric ones.

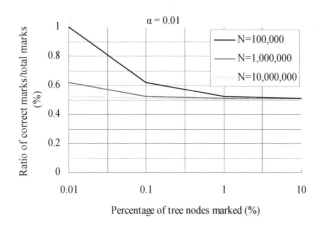

Fig. 1. Proportion of correctly marked nodes that need detection

Figure 1 shows the proportion of the correctly marked nodes required for a successful detection with 99% confidence against different watermark ratios. We notice that the required proportion of the correctly marked nodes decreases as the percentage of marked nodes and the watermark ratio $1/\gamma$ increases. we also find that the proportion is amazingly low in order to attain 99% confidence. For example, in a product data with 100,000 nodes, if 1% of the nodes are marked, only 62% of correctly detected marks are needed to provide 99% confidence. With the tree nodes and the watermark ratio increase, the percentage can drop to less than 51% and approaching 50%. Note that 50% is the lower bound to differentiate a watermark from a chance of random occurrence.

We now report a series of simple analysis for all kinds of attacks mentioned in Section 3.3:

Node-content Attacks. Node-Content Attacks are the most common ones. According to Harte [28], due to the geometrical nature of the watermarking algorithm, the watermark can be recovered after scaling, rotation or combinations of geometrical transformations. So we dwell on it here.

Tree-structure Transformation Attacks. The ability against attacks on tree structure transformation is the feature of the watermarks on the abstract tree-structured data. Immunity from attacks on tree structure transformation is the principal contribution of our algorithm.

For *attacks on addition of nodes* to the tree, for example, we randomly select a node as the father node and add one child (a relatively insignificant node). Obviously, the addition does not influence any node content, and also not alter the path info from the original node traced to the root of the tree. As a result, it does not affect the search of the watermarked nodes. Theoretically speaking, the fractal watermark algorithm can identify the watermarked nodes accurately in addition attacks.

For *attacks on deletion of nodes* to the tree, for example, we randomly select a leaf node to delete. The deletion also does not influence any node content, not alter the path info, and not affect identifying of the rest watermarked nodes. The only way to make successful attacks may be the deletion of a large number of nodes, which causes an excessive loss in the watermarked nodes. We cannot detect the watermarks correctly if the number of the deleted nodes is greater than a threshold, which is the only possible way to make successful attacks. However, in this case, deletion attack will do enormous damage to the usability of the product data. Moreover, if multiple structure watermarks have been inserted in the product data, it is an impossible mission to remove all the structure watermarks. Simulation results from Figure 2 have confirmed this.

We eliminate tree nodes randomly to calculate the probability of a success attack on the 1 million nodes with the parameter setting unchanged. Figure 2 plots the proportion of watermark detected for various γ. As expected, when γ increases (i.e. less nodes are marked), we need a lower percentage for deletion to be able to detect the watermark. For $\gamma = 100$, the watermarks are detected even if only about 0.3% sub-trees remaining. And even for $\gamma = 10,000$, the attacks for watermarks failed in need of about 20% reserved sub-trees. In other words, only above 80% nodes deleted, deletion attacks can success. So the PNW algorithm is also resistant to the attacks on tree node deletion.

For *attacks on the relations among the nodes*, it changes a node position in the tree, which actually destroys the node's structural information and results in that the algorithm cannot identify the watermarked node and extract the watermark from the node. This kind of attacks is basically equivalent to the deletion attack, so the result of experiments shown in Figure 2 is also applicable here. In fact, this kind of attacks influences the usability of the tree-structured data so greatly that it is seldom adopted by the adversaries.

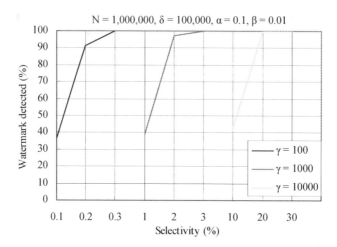

Fig. 2. Proportion of watermarks detected

Subtractive (Sub-tree) Attacks. Subtractive attacks mean the attacks that partition a tree into many independent usable trees. In order to survive these attacks, the watermarks must be preserved in every tree partition. Immunity from sub-tree attacks is another contribution of this paper. Obviously, the fractal watermark in our solution is composed of tree structure watermarks scattering in each sub-tree, which are concealed even when the tree is partitioned and the global structure watermark is damaged.

Additive Attacks. In the additive attack, adversary simply inserts his own watermark in the watermarked data and claim ownership. The original ownership claim can be resolved by locating the overlapping regions of the two watermarks in which the bit values of the marks conflict and determining which owner's marks win. The winner must have overwritten the loser's bits and hence have inserted the watermark later. Depending upon the significance level α chosen for the test, it is possible not to reach a decision if only a few marks collide. Clearly, adversaries may try to reduce the size of the overlapping region by using a low watermark ratio such as 0.1% or 0.01%. Similarly, the true owner of the data can confront the additive attacks by decreasing γ to increase the density of the watermarks.

Invertibility Attacks. In the invertibility attack, adversary may be able to find a key that generates a satisfactory watermark for some value of α. For high values of α, adversary can stumble upon such a key by repeatedly trying different key values. This attack is thwarted by using low values of α, rendering negligible the probability of accidentally finding a good key. On the premises of each sub-tree concealing structure watermark, there is little or no possibility that adversary can find an appropriate value of a key. So the solution in our paper is also very resistant to invertibility attacks.

6 Conclusion

The main contributions of this paper can be reduced to the following: (1) give formalized definitions of the fractal watermark, which achieves better resilience right protection for product data; (2) enunciate the desirable properties of a watermarking system for tree-structured product data; (3) analyze the various forms of possible malicious attacks to tree-structured product data, especially those to product structure; (4) propose a new watermark scheme for product data based on the combination of part-node content as well as path information, which gives a more comprehensive and resilient right protection for both part node content and product structure. Moreover it is particularly effective when resisting to invertibility attacks.

In the future, we would like to take more experiments for all kinds of attacks to improve our algorithms and to extend the fractal technique to also mark non-tree structure product data, such as graph, and also focus on marking various types of nodes except 3D model.

References

1. Anderson, R.J. (eds.): Information Hiding. Lecture Notes in Computer Science 1174. Springer-Verlag, Cambridge, U.K (1996)
2. Petitcolas, F.A.P., Anderson, R.J. and Kuhn, M.G.: Information Hiding -A Survey. Proceedings of the IEEE 87(7) (1999) 1062-1078
3. Bender, W., Gruhl, D., Morimoto, N. and Lu, A.: Techniques for Data Hiding. IBM Systems Journal 35(3/4) (1996) 313-336
4. Tirkel, A.Z., Rankin, G.A., van Schyndel, R.M., Ho, W.J., Mee, N.R.A., Osborne, C.F.: Electronic watermark. In: The Digital Image Computing - Techniques and Applications, Proceedings. Volume 2. Sydney, Australia (1993) 666-673
5. Ruanaidh, J.J.K.O., Dowling, W.J., Boland, F.M.: Watermarking digital images for copyright protection. IEEE Proceedings. Vision, Image and Signal Processing 143(4) (1996) 250–256
6. Hartung, F., Girod, B.: Watermarking of uncompressed and compressed video. Signal Process 66(3) (1998) 283-301
7. Bone, Y.L., Tewfik, A.H., Hamdy, K.N.: Digital watermarks for audio signals. Proc. International Conference on Multimedia Computing and Systems. Hiroshima (1996) 473-480
8. Ohbuchi, R., Masuda, H. and Aono, M.: Watermarking 3D polygonal models. Proc. Fifth ACM International Multimedia Conference (1997) 261-272
9. Ohbuchi, R., Takahasi, S. and Miyazawa, T: Watermarking 3D Polygonal Meshes in the Mesh Spectral Domain. Proc. Graphics Interface (2001) 9-17
10. Ohbuchi, R., Mukaiyama, A. and Takahashi, S.: A Frequency-Domain Approach to Watermarking 3D Shapes. Computer Graphics Forum 21(3) (2002) 1-10
11. Wagner, M.G.: Robust Watermarking of Polygonal Meshes. Proc. International Conference on Geometric Modeling & Processing. Hong Kong (2000) 201-208
12. Aspert, N., Drelie, E., Ebrahimi, T.: Steganography for three-dimensional Polygonal Meshes. Proc. SPIE 47th Annual Meeting, Application of Digital Image Processing XXV. Seattle (2002)
13. Fornaro, C., Sanna, A:. Private Key Watermarking for Authentication of CSG Models. Computer-Aided Design 32 (2000) 727–735

14. Agrawal, R., Haas, P.J., Kiernan, J.: Watermarking relational data: framework, algorithms and analysis. The VLDB Journal 12(2) (2003) 157-169
15. Sion, R., Atallah, M. and Prabhakar, S.: Rights protection for relational data. IEEE Transactions on Knowledge and Data Engineering 16(6) (2004) 1-17
16. Nagra, J. and Thomborson, C.: Threading software watermarks. Proc. Sixth International Workshop on Information Hiding. Toronto, Canada (2004) 208-223
17. Yuan, L., Pari, P.R. and Qu, G.: Soft IP protection: watermarking HDL codes. Proc. Sixth International Workshop on Information Hiding. Toronto, Canada (2004) 224-238
18. Atallah, M.J., Raskin, V., Hempelmann, C.F., et al.: Natural language watermarking and tamperproofing. Proc Fifth International Workshop on Information Hiding. Noordwijkerhout, The Netherlands (2002) 196-212
19. Chiang, Y.-L., Chang, L.-P., Hsieh, W.-T., et al.: Natural language watermarking using semantic substitution for Chinese text. Proc. Second International Workshop on Digital Watermarking. Seoul, Korea (2003) 129-140
20. Sion, R.: Proving ownership over categorical data. Proc. IEEE International Conference on Data Engineering (2004) 584-596
21. Sion, R., Atallah, M., Prabhakar, S.: Resilient rights protection for sensor streams. Proc. 30th International Conference on VLDB. Toronto, Canada (2004) 732-743
22. Sion, R., Atallah, M., Prabhakar, S.: Resilient information hiding for abstract semi-structures. Proc. Second International Workshop on Digital Watermarking. Seoul, Korea (2003) 141-153
23. Ng, W. and Lam, L.H.: Effective Approaches for Watermarking XML Data. Proc. 10th Database Systems for Advanced Applications. Beijing, China (2005) 68–80
24. Inoue, S., et al.: A Proposal on Information Hiding Methods using XML. Proc. First NLP and XML Workshop. Tokyo, Japan (2001) 55-62
25. Chen, G., Chen, K., Hu, T., Dong, J.: Watermarking Abstract Tree-Structured Data. Lecture Notes in Computer Science 3739 (2005) 221-232
26. Barnsley, M.F. and Rising, H.: Fractals Everywhere. 2nd ed. Boston, MA: Academic Press (1993)
27. Kerckhoffs, A., La cryptographie militaire. Journal des sciences militaires IX (1883) 5–83
28. Harte, T., Bors, A.G.: Watermarking Graphical Objects. Proc. IEEE International Conference on Image. Rochester, New York (2002)
29. Craver, S., Memon, N., Yeo, B.-L., Yeung, M.M.: Resolving rightful ownerships with invisible watermarking techniques: Limitations, attacks, and implications. IEEE Journal of Selected Areas in Communications 16(4) (1998) 573-586

Optimization of Workflow Resources Allocation with Cost Constraint

Zhijiao Xiao, Huiyou Chang, and Yang Yi

School of Information Science & Technology, Sun Yat-sen University,
510275 Guangzhou, China
mmousecindy@yahoo.com.cn

Abstract. A resource allocation method is proposed to determine the proper number of resources added to each resource class with cost constraint in order to optimize workflow time performance. The average throughput time of workflow instances is used to measure the workflow time performance. An approach which calculates the average throughput time of workflow instances is proposed. An improved genetic algorithm is presented to realize the allocation method. Experimental results show that the algorithm has good evolution performance and is superior to other allocation methods.

1 Introduction

Workflow is the automation of a business process, in whole or part, during which documents, information or tasks are passed from one participant to another for action, according to a set of procedural rules [1]. Nowadays, workflow technology has received much attention by its capability to support complex business processes.

Resource is an important indicator of workflow performance. In the workflow context, a resource indicates an actor or agent to carry out workflow tasks. Depending on the application domains, resources can be machines, manpower, money, software, etc. Here, we only consider durable resources, i.e. resources that are claimed and released during the execution, but not created or destroyed [2].

Resource management has been recognized as an important issue in a workflow management system (WfMS) [1]. Most of the works in the area of resource management have focused on modeling and scheduling issues [3-4]. Little attention has been devoted to the allocation of workflow resources. A proper resource allocation ensures that each activity is performed by a suitable resource. And it is a key issue in providing efficient use of workflow resources. Here, we consider the allocation on the level of resource classes, instead of individual resources. A resource class is a group of resources with similar characteristics.

Goldratt et al. [5] suppose to add resources at bottlenecks to improve the overall time performance of the workflow measured. Reijers [6] distinguishes two interpretations of the bottleneck definition as the resource queue with the maximal mean queue time and the resource with the highest mean utilization. He uses an example to show that it is not optimal resource allocation strategy to add resources at bottlenecks for

W. Shen et al. (Eds.): CSCWD 2006, LNCS 4402, pp. 647–656, 2007.
© Springer-Verlag Berlin Heidelberg 2007

both interpretations of the bottleneck. Van Hee et al. [7] propose a method of marginal allocation to add resources at the place that can bring the maximal improvement of the time performance. They have proved it is optimal for two subclasses of resource-extended stochastic workflow nets. But the method is in general not optimal if concurrency is allowed in the workflow [6]. It is because the marginal allocation strategy assigns resources one by one and cannot reallocate resources. Jin et al. propose a method to determine the processing capacities for certain activities so that most workflow instances can satisfy the deadline. But they all have not considered that different activities need different kinds of resources, and the costs of different resources are different.

This paper studies how to determine the number of resources within each resource class with cost constraint in order to optimize workflow performance. The workflow performance can be evaluated by many indicators such as time, cost, quality, etc. Time is one of the most important indicators. Many researches have been done on optimizing workflow time performance [8-9]. So we use workflow time performance as the goal of the optimization. The throughput time of a workflow is used to measure the workflow time performance. An improved genetic algorithm (GA) is proposed to solve the optimization of resources allocation problem (ORAP).

The rest of the paper is organized as follows. Section 2 describes the problem and the objective function. In Section 3, a method to calculate the throughput time of a workflow is proposed. Section 4 addresses the improved GA solving the ORAP. Experimental results are given in Section 5 to illustrate the feasibility and validity of the method proposed in this paper. Finally, a conclusion and proposals for future research directions are presented in Section 6.

2   Optimization of Workflow Resources Allocation Problem

Suppose there is a workflow wf composed with n different activities a_i (i=1, 2, ..., n) whose executions involve n different classes of resources. It is assumed that the routing structure of the considered workflow contains no temporal and logical errors. Assume that the execution of activity a_i involves resources within class i. The unit price of each resource within class i is c_i.

The goal is to minimize the throughput time of wf through adding e_i units of resources within class i with cost restricted below C. The problem can be stated as:

$$\textbf{ORAP:} \qquad \min tt = \min f(e_i). \tag{1}$$

$$\textbf{s.t.} \qquad \sum_{i=1}^{n} (e_i \cdot c_i) \leq C. \tag{2}$$

$$e_i \geq 0, e_i \text{ is an integer.} \tag{3}$$

Equation (1) is the objective function that means to minimize tt (the throughput time of wf), whose value varies with variable e_i; Equation (2) is the cost constraint on adding resources; Equation (3) guarantees the values of e_i are integers which are not less than zero.

3 Throughput Time of a Workflow

The throughput time of a workflow can be expressed in several ways. This is caused by the fact that instances that undergo the same workflow often do not share the same throughput time. A very common approach is to express the throughput time of a workflow as the average throughput time of the instances it handles [10]. So we use the average throughput time of workflow instances to measure the throughput time of a workflow. Here we assume that there are only instances of one kind of workflow in the WfMS in order to simplify the computational process.

3.1 Average Throughput Time of *wf*'s Instances

Suppose the number of executable paths of *wf* is *m*, and the probability that *wf*'s instances execute according to path A_j (*j*=1, 2, ..., *m*) is p_j, the average throughput time of A_j is t_{A_j}. Then the average throughput time of *wf* can be calculated as:

$$tt = \sum_{j=1}^{m}(p_j \cdot t_{A_j}).\tag{4}$$

3.2 Average Throughput Time of Path A_j

An executable path, called a path for short, is a possible routing path of a workflow instance. It is a series of activities from the beginning to the end of a workflow that an instance executed according to this path must execute. A workflow is decomposed into several executable paths by splitting OR structures. The relationship between any two activities in each executable path can only be the following three kinds:

Sequence
A series of activities $\{a_1, a_2, ..., a_c\}$ are executed in sequence. The average throughput time is $\sum_{i=1}^{c}t_i$, where t_i denotes the average process time of activity a_i.

Parallel
$\{[(a_1, ..., a_c), ..., (a_d, ..., a_f)]\}$ denotes a parallel relationship between $(a_1, ..., a_c)$, ..., and $(a_d, ..., a_f)$, where $a_1, ..., a_c, ...,$ and $a_d, ..., a_f$ denotes the activities in each parallel branch. Since the synchronization time of a *n*-branches parallel structure is mainly determined by the path with the longest average throughput time [8], we calculate the average throughput time as $\max(\sum_{i=1}^{c}t_i, ..., \sum_{i=d}^{f}t_i)$, where t_i denotes the average process time of activity a_i.

Iteration
Iteration structures can result in infinite executable paths. So we transform iteration structures into equivalent sequence structures using the method mentioned in [8]. Suppose there is an iteration structure as shown in Figure 1, where *p* denotes the

probability of workflow instances arriving this iteration structure, q denotes the probability of workflow instances leaving the iteration structure.

The executive probability of activities in set A is:

$$p_A = \sum_{i=0}^{\infty}[p \cdot (1-q)^i] = p/q . \tag{5}$$

The executive probability of activities in set B is:

$$p_B = \sum_{i=1}^{\infty}[p \cdot (1-q)^i] = p(1-q)/q . \tag{6}$$

Fig. 1. An iteration structure and its equivalent sequence structure

Then the iteration structure in the left of Figure 1 can be transformed into the sequence structure as shown in the right of Figure 1.

The iteration structure is expressed as $\{\frac{1}{q}a_1,...,\frac{1}{q}a_c,\frac{1-q}{q}a_{(c+1)},...,\frac{1-q}{q}a_d\}$, where $\{a_1,...,a_c\}$ is the activities in set A and $1/q$ is the executive coefficient of those activities; $\{a_{(c+1)},...,a_d\}$ is the activities in set B and $(1-q)/q$ is the executive coefficient of those activities. Then, the average throughput time is calculated as $\frac{1}{q} \cdot \sum_{i=1}^{c}t_i + \frac{1-q}{q} \cdot \sum_{i=c+1}^{d}t_i$, where t_i denotes the average process time of activity a_i.

Up till now, we can calculate the average throughput time of each executable path according to its structure.

3.3 Average Process Time of Activity a_i

Suppose the service time of activity a_i has a negative exponential distribution, characterized by μ_i. Then the average process time of activity a_i can be calculated as:

$$t_i = 1/\mu_i + w_i. \tag{7}$$

where $1/\mu_i$ is the average service time of activity a_i and w_i is the average waiting time of activity a_i.

3.4 Average Waiting Time of Activity a_i

Suppose the arrival process of wf's instances is Poisson-distributed with intensity λ. The decomposition of independent Poisson processes is known to be Poisson processes. Thus, the arrival process of each executable path is a Poisson process.

As far as the activities in an executable path are concerned, the arrival and departure processes of activities in sequence are Poisson processes. Since iteration structures can be transformed into sequence structures, the arrival and departure processes of activities in iteration structures are Poisson processes too. Though the arrival processes of activities in parallel structures are Poisson processes, the departure processes are not actually because all parallel branches must be synchronized. It can be assumed that the departure processes are Poisson processes since the synchronization time of a n-branches parallel structure is mainly determined by the path with the longest average throughput time [8].

As mentioned above, the execution of wf's instances involves n different classes of resources. It can be assumed that the execution of activity a_i involves resources within class i. Thus resources of class i can be approximated to an M/M/(r_i+e_i) queuing system, with negative exponential distributed service time with intensity μ_i, and Poisson arrival rate of $(q_i \cdot \lambda)$, where r_i is the initial number of resources within class i, e_i is the number of resources added within class i, μ_i is the intensity of the negative exponential distributed service time of activity a_i; q_i is the executive probability of activity a_i, $(q_i \cdot \lambda)$ is the arrival rate of instances of activity a_i.

Using queuing theory, the average waiting time of activity a_i can be computed as following:

$$y_i = (r_i + e_i) \cdot \mu_i - q_i \cdot \lambda. \tag{8}$$

$$w_i = \frac{(q_i \cdot \lambda)^{r_i+e_i} \cdot (r_i+e_i)}{u_i^{r_i+e_i-1} \cdot y_i^2 \cdot (r_i+e_i)! \cdot \left(\sum_{k=0}^{r_i+e_i-1} \frac{(q_i \cdot \lambda)^k}{\mu_i^k \cdot k!} + \frac{(q_i \cdot \lambda)^{r_i+e_i} \cdot (r_i+e_i)}{u_i^{r_i+e_i-1} \cdot y_i \cdot (r_i+e_i)!} \right)}. \tag{9}$$

3.5   Executive Probability of Activity a_i

The executive probability of activity a_i is the probability of an instance of activity a_i being executed when a new workflow instance arrivals. It can be calculated as:

$$q_i = \sum_{j=1}^{m} (p_j \cdot \sigma_{ij}). \tag{10}$$

where σ_{ij} is the executive coefficient of activity a_i in path A_j. If a_i is included in a sequence or a parallel structure of A_j, $\sigma_{ij} =1$; if a_i is included in an iteration structure of A_j, σ_{ij} is computed as mentioned above; if a_i is not included in A_j, $\sigma_{ij} =0$.

4   Improved GA Solving the ORAP

4.1   Unbounded Knapsack Problem

The unbounded knapsack problem (UKP) can be formulated as follows: a knapsack of capacity c is given, into which we may put n types of objects. Each object of type i has a profit, and a weight. The object is to determine the number of objects of type i, that maximize the total profit without exceeding capacity.

If we regard cost constraint as the capacity of a knapsack, the unit price of each resource within class i as the weight of each object of type i, the improvement of workflow time performance achieved by adding one resource within class i as the profit of each object of type i, then the problem can be come down to an unbounded knapsack problem which is a classic NP-hard problem in combinational optimization.

4.2 Improved GA

The genetic algorithm (GA) developed by John Holland at the University of Michigan is based on genetic processes of biological organisms [11]. Literature [12-13] reveals that GA based optimization techniques are effective to solve optimization problems. So we propose an improved GA to solve the Optimization of Resources Allocation Problem (ORAP).

Coding. A chromosome is a feasible solution to the problem and is encoded as an extended natural number string. The ith gene in a chromosome is the number of resource(s) added within class i. The creation of the initial population follows the following steps:

> Step 1: Initialize every gene of a chromosome to 0;
> Step 2: Choose a class of resources randomly within the cost constraint, and add one unit of resource within that class;
> Step 3: Repeat Step 2 until cost constraint is not satisfied;
> Step 4: Add the chromosome into the initial population S;
> Step 5: Repeat above steps until the size of S reaches the population size np.

Fitness Function. The following function is used as the fitness function:

$$F(e_i) = M - f(e_i). \tag{11}$$

where M is the maximal $f(e_i)$ of current population.

Genetic Operator
Selection: A number of chromosomes are selected according to their fitness to form the next population. The roulette wheel selection strategy combined with the elitist strategy is used here. The steps are as follows:

> Step 1: Initialize the greedy solution as the fittest chromosome (the one with the best fitness) so far;
> Step 2: Each chromosome ch_k in the current generation is allotted a roulette wheel slot sized in proportion p_k to its fitness value $F(ch_k)$. This proportion p_k can be calculated as follow:

$$p_k = F(ch_k) / \sum_{j=1}^{np} F(ch_j). \tag{12}$$

> Step 3: The roulette wheel is spun np times to choose chromosomes to form the new population;
> Step 4: Find the fittest and the least fit chromosome of current population;
> Step 5: If the fittest chromosome of current population is better than the fittest chromosome so far, then the fittest chromosome of current population becomes the fittest chromosome so far;
> Step 6: Use the fittest chromosome so far to replace the least fit chromosome of current population.

This type of selection has the advantage that the population may only become fitter. And it can be guaranteed that the solution obtained will be fitter than the greedy solution at least.

Crossover: An improved partially-mapping crossover as illustrated in Figure 2 is used as the crossover operator.

Mutation: Mutation used here is the swapping mutation which is the simple swapping of two unique genes in a chromosome.

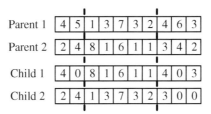

Fig. 2. Improved partially-mapping crossover. Two chromosomes are chosen at random from the population as the parents. Two crossover points are generated randomly, and the segments between the crossover points of the parents are exchanged. For those genes beyond the segments, if they won't lead to the infeasibility of the chromosome, they are preserved; otherwise they are set to 0. Thus, we get two children.

Mending Operator. It is obvious that there would not be any infeasible chromosome produced by crossover operator. But there would be infeasible chromosomes produced by mutation. Here, the infeasible chromosomes are those that violate the cost constraint.

Since infeasible chromosomes cannot be decoded and evaluated, they need to be mended. The mending process is to shrink e_i in the proportion of $C / \sum_{i=1}^{n} (e_i \cdot c_i)$, and round it towards zero.

Improving Operator. There are some chromosomes that do not make the most of the cost. There is at least one unit of resource within one class that can be added. If

$$C - \sum_{i=1}^{n} (e_i \cdot c_i) > \min(c)$$ is met, choose a class of resources randomly within the

cost constraint, and add one unit of resource within that class.

Algorithm steps. The GA follows the following steps:

Step 1: Initialize parameters: population size: np, max generation: ng, crossover rate: p_c, mutation rate: p_m;
Step 2: Create a random initial population S;
Step 3: Obtain the greedy solution;
Step 4: Stop if the number of generations reaches the value of max generation ng; otherwise go ahead;
Step 5: Evaluate each member of the current population S by calculating its fitness;
Step 6: Apply Selection;

Step 7: Apply Crossover and improving;
Step 8: Apply Mutation, mending and improving;
Step 9: Return to Step 4.

5   Experimental Results

The algorithm was implemented in Matlab 7.0 and the tests were run on a P4 2.4G/512M RAM computer.

First, we apply our algorithm to optimize a workflow whose routing structure is depicted by Petri net as shown in Figure 3.

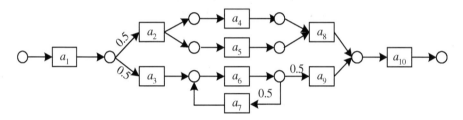

Fig. 3. A workflow and its parameters. The arrival process of the workflow's instances is Poisson with intensity $\lambda=2$. There are ten activities in the workflow. The service times of those activities have a negative exponential distribution, characterized by $\mu_i = \{1/5, 1, 1/5, 1/5, 1/6, 1/2, 1/3, 1/2, 1/2, 1/4\}$. There are two executable paths: A_1 and A_2, and $p_j=\{0.5,0.5\}$. Then $\sigma_{i2}=\{1,0,1,0,0,2,1,0,1,1\}, \sigma_{i1}=\{1,1,0,1,1,0,0,1,0,1\}$.

The executions of those activities involve ten different classes of resources. Activity a_i is executed by resources within class i. The unit price of each resource within class i is $c_i = \{2, 5, 6, 4, 6, 8, 3, 7, 5, 9\}$. The initial number of resources within class i is $r_i = \{11, 2, 6, 6, 7, 5, 4, 3, 3, 9\}$. Suppose $C=99$. The solution obtained by our algorithm is $e_i = \{4, 1, 2, 1, 3, 2, 2, 1, 1, 2\}$ and $tt=21.4803$.

Table 1 lists five groups of experimental results. It can be concluded from Table 1 that our algorithm has good evolution performance and can achieve or approach the optimal solutions.

Table 1. Experimental results. Each time the algorithm runs 150 times, and the first 50 times are for data training and learning.

				$np=50, ng=1000, p_c=0.8, p_m=0.1$			
#	best solution	worst solution	average solution	percentage of optimal solution	standard deviation	average CPU time(seconds)
1	21.4803	21.5082	21.4831	89%	0.0081	61.4994
2	21.4803	21.5082	21.4828	90%	0.0077	85.8230
3	21.4803	21.5082	21.4841	85%	0.0091	84.1810
4	21.4803	21.5082	21.4823	92%	0.0070	86.0030
5	21.4803	21.5082	21.4818	94%	0.0061	110.7100

Table 2. Comparison of the best solutions of different problems obtained by different methods. The parameters of our method are: np=50, ng=1000, p_c=0.8, p_m=0.1.

#	Adding at bottleneck			Marginal allocation	Greedy method	Our method
	maximal queue time	mean	highest mean utilization			
1	42.9573		42.4219	42.4219	42.3349	42.2518
2	23.8944		24.3472	23.4083	23.4498	23.3997
3	90.4549		89.0453	88.0502	87.6179	87.3412
4	62.4976		62.4976	65.578	65.578	61.2945
5	85.3779		85.2958	86.1434	86.1434	84.4598

Table 2 lists the comparison of the best solutions obtained by several different allocation methods to solve problems with different workflow structures and parameters.

As shown in Table 2, the method of adding at bottlenecks cannot achieve or even approach the optimal solutions. In many cases, especially when parallel structures become the bottlenecks of workflow time performance, marginal allocation method and greed method cannot achieve or approach the optimal solutions. The best solutions obtained by our method are equal or superior to those obtained by other methods, which shows that our method performs best and outperforms other allocation methods.

6 Conclusion

This paper studies how to optimize the allocation of workflow resources with cost constraint to minimize the average throughput time of a workflow. Since the problem can be concluded as an unbounded knapsack problem (UKP), an improved genetic algorithm (GA) suitable to solve the UKP is proposed to solve the problem. Examples are given to illustrate the feasibility and validity of the allocation method. It is argued that our method has good evolution performance and can achieve or approach the optimal solutions. And through comparing different solutions, we show that our allocation method is superior to other allocation strategies.

There are many other aspects, such as cost, quality, flexibility, etc., which should be considered when we allocate workflow resources. Furthermore, there are many other aspects in workflow resource allocation, such as generalization and specialization of resources, etc., which are our future research directions.

Acknowledgments. This work is supported by the Natural Science Foundation of China (Grant No. 60573159) and the Natural Science Foundation of Guangdong Province of China (Grant No. 05200302).

References

1. Workflow Management Coalition: Terminology & Glossary. WfMC-TC-1011. Workflow Management Coalition (1999)
2. Van Hee, K., Serebrenik, A., Sidorova, N., Voorhoeve, M.: Soundness of resource-constrained workflow nets. LNCS 3536 (2005) 250-267

3. Du, W.M., Shan, M.C.: Enterprise workflow resource management. Technical Report HPL-99-8. HP Software Technology Laboratory. Palo Alto (1999)
4. Lee, K.M.: Adaptive resource scheduling for workflows considering competence and preference. Proc. KES 2004. LNAI 3214 (2004) 723-730
5. Goldratt, E.M., Cox, J.: The Goal. Aldershot, Gower (1984)
6. Reijers, H.A.: Design and Control of Workflow Processes. Springer-Verlag, Berlin (2003)
7. Van Hee, K.M., Reijers, H.A., Verbeek, H.M.W. and Zerguini, L.: On the optimal allocation of resources in stochastic workflow nets. Proc. 17th UK Performance Engineering Workshop. Leeds, UK (2001) 23-34
8. Jin, H.S., Myoung, H.K.: Improving the performance of time-constrained workflow processing. The Journal of Systems and Software 58 (2001) 211-219
9. Eder, J., Panagos, E., Pozewaunig, H., Rabinovich, M.: Time management in workflow systems. Proc. International Conference on Business Information Systems (1999) 265-280
10. Van Hee, K.M., Reijers, H.A.: Using formal analysis techniques in business process redesign. LNCS 1806 (2000) 142-160
11. Goldberg, D.E: Genetic Algorithm in Search, Optimization and Machine Learning. Addison, Wesley Massachusetts (1989)
12. Lee, Z.J., Lee, C.Y.: A hybrid search algorithm with heuristics for resource allocation problem. Information Sciences 173 (2005) 155-167
13. Chang, H.Y., Yi, Y., Wang, D.W.: Soft computing for partner selection problem. Journal of System Simulation 15 (2003) 1756-1758

Implementation of Policy Based Management in Workflow Management System

Song Ouyang

School of Information Science and Engineering, Central South University,
Changsha 410083, P.R. China
ouyangsong@yahoo.com

Abstract. The foundation of a traditional workflow management system is process-based management. We have proposed to integrate policy-based management in workflow management systems to improve the flexibility and the dynamic behavior. In this paper, how to implement policy-based management in a workflow system is discussed. To construct policy model, a meta modeling method with four layer structure is introduced. The main tasks in each layer of the meta modeling architecture are described. To define where and when to apply policies in a workflow, a Control Point model is introduced. A workflow process meta model supporting policy-based management is presented. The architecture of a simple prototype system to support policy based management is also presented. The new approach has better flexibility in design time and higher adaptability at run-time.

1 Introduction

With the increase of complexity, traditional workflow management systems are facing many challenges in meeting the requirements of flexibility and adaptability and implementing resource management and security control in new applications [3-4].

To improve adaptability a Petri net formalism is presented to analyze the structural changes in workflow process modeling [5]. A new workflow modeling method is proposed to improve flexibility and adaptability of system [6]. A meta-model is proposed to support dynamic changes of workflow process [7]. Similar approach can be found in [8].

To address various software and/or hardware resources management issues, a resource management system that can handle a large number of workflow resources is proposed [9]. A generic framework for the resources representation that can be addressed by a workflow activity is presented [10]. A workflow resource pattern that captures various ways in which resources are represented and utilized in workflows is proposed [11].

The foundation of a traditional workflow management system is process-based management. The features of this management are: the execution of each step of a task is based on an instruction and its parameters; the description of the instruction is imperative and it invokes execution components directly; after one instruction completed, another pre-defined instruction is initiated based on the pre-defined rules and

W. Shen et al. (Eds.): CSCWD 2006, LNCS 4402, pp. 657–666, 2007.
© Springer-Verlag Berlin Heidelberg 2007

conditions. The controlling mechanism between steps is accurate and there are plenty of mathematic analysis tools available. In some workflow systems, better flexibility and adaptability in flow control are achieved through expanding the types of activities and adding more collaboration between activities. For the applications with comprehensive requirements in resources management and security control, however, it is difficult to improve the flexibility and adaptability by using similar methods that are used in control flow since the requirements are more complicated.

Another management paradigm that is widely used in information management systems is policy-based management. The features of this management are: the execution of each step of a task is based on the objective or behavior constraints; the description of instruction is declarative and it can not invoke execution components directly in most cases; after one step completed the subsequence step will be executed based on the analysis of active policies and the status of whole system. Now most telecom service providers have accepted that the policy-based management system is the right way to go and consider adopting it. Internet Engineering Task Force (IETF) has put forward a basic architecture for policy-based network management system [12].

Although some workflow systems used policies to manage resources and security control [14], it is not real policy-based management system. The distinct features of a policy-based management from a process-based management are: a centralized policy repository, dynamic policy transformations, dynamic looking up for policies, independent policy engine, and decision-making based on active policies.

To meet the challenges we proposed a new approach for workflow system: integrate policy-based management and process-based management in workflow system [1]. In this paper, we make deeper discussion on how to implement policy-based management in a workflow system. A meta modeling method to construct policy model and a workflow process meta-model to support policy-based management are presented. The system architecture is also presented. The new approach has better flexibility in design time and higher adaptability at run-time. It can keep the business rules consistent across the whole enterprise. It offers a standard uniform way to deal with business rules, resources management and security access control. It may provide an easier way to apply artificial intelligence in workflow system.

The remainder of the paper is organized as follows. In Section 2 meta modeling method for constructing a policy model is introduced. The Control Point model is described in Section 3. In Section 4 a process meta-model is presented. In Section 5, the system architecture is presented. Finally in Section 6 the conclusion is made.

2 Policy Model

In a policy based workflow management system, policies are used in both built time and run time. In built time polices are used to describe the business rules and the activity's goals in different abstract levels. Policies are also used to specify the constraints to the resources management and the security controls. This gives the designers more flexibility to define the task and deal with different perspectives (control flow, resource management and security control) in a uniform way. At run time, policies in a centralized policy repository are manipulated dynamically; the policy engine can make decisions for next step based on the active policies and the status of whole system; a policy and the component to execute this policy can be late bound by system, so higher adaptability can be achieved. To construct policies in a standard way, a policy model must be addressed first.

To construct a policy model meta modeling method is adopted in this paper. The framework for meta modeling is based on a four layers architecture specified in OMG's MOF specification [13]. These layers are conventionally described as follows:

- M0 layer (object layer): It contains the data that the designers wish to describe.
- M1 layer (model layer): It contains the model (meta data) that describes the data in the object layer. Meta data are informally aggregated as models.
- M2 layer (meta-model layer): It contains the descriptions (i.e., meta-meta data) that define the structure and semantics of model.
- M3 layer (meta-meta-model layer): It contains the descriptions of the structure and semantics of meta model. Objects in this layer are defined by OMG (MOF Model).

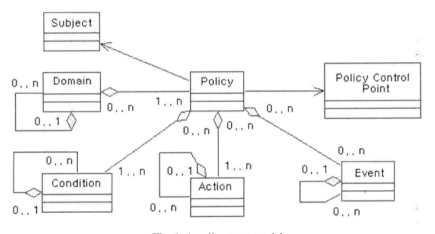

Fig. 1. A policy meta model

With meta modeling method the main tasks in three layers are described as follows:

M2 Layer: In this layer, the main task is to construct a policy meta model. This meta model provides the core elements to construct the policy in M1 layer. A simple policy meta-model is shown in Figure 1. The basic elements in the figure are described as follows:

Condition: It is represented as a Boolean expression. If the expression is TRUE, the behavior to be performed is indicated by TrueAction (not show in Figure 1) in the Action element. If the expression is FALSE, the FalseAction (not show in Figure 1) in the Action element is executed.

Action: It contains two parts: TrueAction and FalseAction. TrueAction represents the necessary actions that should be performed if the Condition evaluates to TRUE. These actions are applied to a set of managed objects. FalseAction represents the actions that should be performed if the Condition evaluates to FALSE.

Event: It is an occurrence of an important event, and can be used to trigger the evaluation of a Condition in a Policy. This element is optional.

Domain: To manage the policy efficiently, domain is used to group policies. A domain can have some sub-domains.

Subject: It represents the policy subject, i.e. the software component that will perform the specific behavior described by the policy.

Policy Control Point: The purpose of Policy Control Point is to define the proper point in a workflow to apply the policies (see ACP and BCP in Section 3).

The Subject and Policy Control Point, which are associated with Policy, are developed to support policy-based management in workflow system. The component that is specified by Subject can be bound at run-time to improve the adaptability of the system. The Policy Control Point specifies where and when to apply the policies in a workflow.

The following is a simple meta policy expressed in XPDL language:

```
<policy:Policy id="10" name="B1">
<policy:Policy Control Point type="ACP" activity="T3"/>
<policy:Subject name="ActivityManager "/>
<policy:Condition><policy:Expression>
      <policy:LessThan                      parameter="$process$/fund"
value="10000000"/>
      </policy:Expression></policy:Condition>
<policy:Action>
      <policy:TrueAction method="routeActivity">
    <policy:Parameter  name="activity"  type="ActivityInstance"
value="T4"/>
   </policy:TrueAction>
   <policy:FalseAction>
      <policy:FalseAction method="routeActivity">
    <policy:Parameter  name="activity"  type="ActivityInstance"
value="T5"/>
    </policy:FalseAction>
   </policy:Action>
  </policy:Policy>
```

This policy specifies the operation after T3 activity. The operation is to judge weather $process$/fund is greater than 100,000. If the result is true, then the method:routeActivity of component:ActivityManager is invoked with parameter T4, otherwise the method is invoked with parameter T5. Translate it into natural language: "After financial manager's review; if the money is more than $100,000, it needs chief manager's approval (T4 activity); otherwise the system informs the applicant (T5 activity)."

M1 Layer: In this layer, the main objects are policies that are constructed using the basic elements defined in M2 layer. The main task in this layer is to design different types of policies based on policies' attributes. Policies can be categorized into three types:

Action policies: An Action policy defines the action that should be taken whenever the system is in a given state. It can invoke an execution component directly.

Goal policies: A Goal policy specifies a single desired state of the system.

Function policies: A Function policy is an objective function that expresses the value of each possible state. Function policies generalize Goal policies.

Neither Goal policy nor Function policy can invoke an execution component directly. They have to be transformed into a set of Action policies.

Based on the policies' targets, policies can also be categorized into many types. For example:

Resource policies: A Resource policy specifies the behavior of the resource involved in an activity or a sub-process.

Security policies: A Security policy is used to specify the controlling of access to resources, define the roles related to positions in organizations and so on.

In addition to define various policies, the designers of workflow management system need to define the transformation rules between Goal/Function policies and Action policies.

M0 Layer: In this layer, the main objects are policy instances. The main task in this layer is to define a set of operations to manipulate the policy instances in all life cycle phases.

3   Control Point

To take the advantages of policy-based management in a workflow system, it is important to define appropriate positions in a workflow to enable the policy engine to make policy evaluations and then apply the policy. Control Point Model (CPM) enables workflow designers to define where and when to apply policies. It also provides a base to integrate policy-based management in a workflow system. CPM consists of Decision Point, Routing Control Points and policy Control Points.

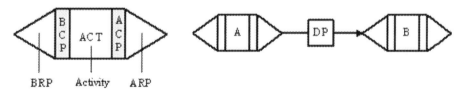

Fig. 2. Control Point Model, RCP and ECP are not shown

The main elements of CPM are described as follows:

Decision Point (DP)

A DP is a point to enforce decision-making for the workflow process. During the workflow build time DPs are inserted at some key points of a workflow process by workflow designers. At a DP the policy engine evaluates the active Goal policies, and make the decisions based on the status of whole system. A decision may include modifications of the process definition, updating of the active policies and so on. A DP is also a convenient way to enforce artificial intelligence in a workflow management system. A DP can be defined as a tuple of two elements:

```
DP = (Policy_ID_List, Constraints)
```

Policy_ID_List: IDs of active goal policies
Constraints: policy evaluation rules

After Activity Routing Point (ARP)

An ARP is a routing controller. It determines the routing of successor activities of current activity. An ARP can be defined as a tuple of three elements:

```
ARP=(Owner_ActID, Next_ActID_List, Routing_Type)
```

Owner_ActID: Owner activity of this ARP (see Figure 2)
Next_ActID_List: Successor activities of owner activity
Routing Type: Routing types of all successor activities.
                    Four choices of Routing_Type can be used:
        ONE: sequential, only one successor activity
        ALL: all successor activities are executed concurrently
        CHOICE: some successor activities are executed by selection
        DEFINED: activity specified by system dynamically

Before Activity Routing Point (BRP)

A BRP is a routing controller. It determines the routing of all predecessor activities of current activity. A BRP can be defined as a tuple of four elements:

```
BRP=(Owner_ActID, Join_Type, Branch_Arrived, State)
```

Owner_ActID: Owner activity of this BRP (see Figure 2)
Join_Type: Join types of predecessor activities of all predecessor activity. Four choices of Join_Type can be used:
        ONE: Sequential, one predecessor activity
        ALL: All predecessor activities are executed concurrency
        CHOICE: Some predecessor activities are executed by selection
        DEFINED: Activity specified by system dynamically
Branch_Arrived: The number of completed predecessors
State: The status of predecessor activities. Three choices can be used:
        Waiting: no predecessor activity completed
        Pending: part of predecessor activities is completed
        Completed: all of predecessor activities are completed

Before Activity Control Point (BCP)

A BCP is a place to define the policies to control the behavior. It takes effect before the start of execution of current activity. At this point, the policy engine evaluates the policies on the resources, security, and so on. A BCP can be defined as a tuple of three elements:

```
BCP= (Owner_ActID, Policy_ID_List, Constraints)
```

Owner_ActID: The owner activity of this BCP;
Policy_ID_List: The list of policies to control the status in the flow;
Constraints: The policy evaluation rules.

After Activity Control Point (ACP)

An ACP is a place to define the policies to control the behavior. It takes effect at the end of execution of current activity. At this point, the policy engine evaluates the policies on the system status checking, goals checking, security auditing, and so on. An ACP can be defined as a tuple of three elements:

```
ACP= (Owner_ActID, Policy_ID_List, Constraints)
```

Owner_ActID: Owner activity of this ACP
Policy_ID_List: The list of policies to control the status in the flow;
Constraints: The policy evaluation rules.

Around Activity Control Point (RCP)

An RCP is a routing controller. It takes effect at the end of execution of current activity based on the cycle checking, Multiple Instance (MI), and so on. An RCP can be defined as a tuple of five elements:

```
RCP= (Owner_ActID, MI_Type, Cycle_To, Cycle_laps, Con-
straints)
```

Owner_ActID: Owner activity of this RCP
MI_Type: The type of Multiple Instance
Cycle_To: The point to transfer to
Cycle_laps: The number of loops needed
Constraints: The rules on the termination of the cycle.

Event Control Point (ECP)

An ECP is a place to define the policies to control the behavior. It takes effect at specified events during the execution of current activity. An ECP can be defined as a tuple of three elements:

```
ECP=(Owner_ActID, Event_ID_List, Resoponse_Rules)
```

Owner_ActID: Owner activity of this ECP
Event_ID_List: The list of events to response
Resoponse_Rules: The rules for the responses;

CPM offers two advantages: (1) By combination of BRP, ARP and RCP, the system can deal with very complicated workflow patterns. (2) The ACP and BCP define accurate positions in a workflow to apply policies to support the implementation of policy-based management in workflow management systems.

4 Process Meta-model to Support Policy Based Management

For a traditional workflow management system to integrate policy based management, the workflow engine needs to be enhanced to make close collaboration with policy management component (policy engine). The enhanced engine is called in this paper as workflow control engine, or workflow engine. The policy management component is called as policy engine.

Workflow process meta-model is the base for the process definition modeling [15]. A meta-model to support policy based management is called as Policy Enabled Meta-Model (PEMM). The main objectives of designing a PEMM are: (1) to support the description of local objectives or constraints of activities by using policies in the built-time to achieve better flexibility; (2) to support a uniform policy management to different perspectives of workflow system and simplify the development of workflow management system; (3) to support the dynamic policy instances management at run-time, and the collaboration between workflow engine and policy engine. A process meta-model to support policy management is shown in Figure 3.

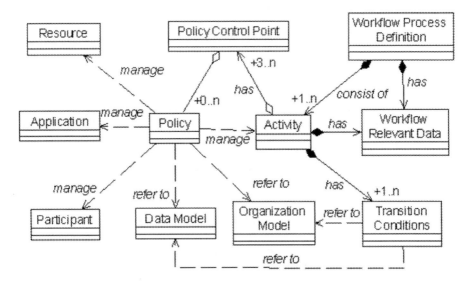

Fig. 3. A process meta-model to support policy management

The elements in the model are described as follows.

Process Activity: A logical step or description of a piece of work that contributes toward the achievement of a process.

Transition Condition: Criteria for moving, or state transitioning, from the current activity to the next activity(s) in a process instance.

Workflow Relevant Data: Data that is used by a workflow management system to determine the state transition of a process instance.

Policy: A Policy describes the constraint for resources management, security control, and the behavior of business rules.

Organization Model: The model of an enterprise's organizational structures.

Participant: A resource that performs partially, or in full, the work represented by a workflow activity instance.

Policy Control Point: See Section 3.

With the new process meta model, the workflow system has better flexibility in design time and higher adaptability at run-time. It can keep the business rules consistent across the enterprise. It offers a standard uniform method to deal with business rules, resources management and security management. It may provide an easier way to apply artificial intelligence in workflow system.

5 System Architecture

Figure 4 shows the system architecture based on the J2EE technology. The functionality of each part is described as follows:

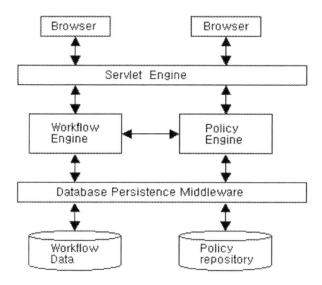

Fig. 4. System architecture

Servlet Engine: It is the user interface. It manages the interactions between users and the workflow system such as user log in, log off, register, monitoring, and querying system status;

Workflow Engine: It manages the whole system components such as process instance and process definition.

Policy Engine: It evaluates the policies and makes the decisions based on the system status. Policy Engine is the most difficult part in the implementation of the new system.

Policy Repository: It keeps and manipulates the policy instances;

6 Conclusion

To implement policy-based management in a workflow management system, some key issues must be solved. In this paper, meta modeling method and main tasks in each layer are described. CPM is introduced to specify where and when to apply policies in a workflow. The process meta-model to support policy management is presented. At last the architecture of a prototype workflow system to integrate policy management and process management is presented. The new approach has better flexibility in the design time and higher adaptability at the run-time.

References

1. Ouyang, S.: Integrate Policy based Management and Process based Management - A New Approach for Workflow Management System. Proc. CSCWD2006. Nanjing China (2006) 1196-1201
2. van der Aalst, W.M.P. and ter Hofstede, A.H.M.: Workflow Patterns: On the Expressive Power of (Petri-net-based) Workflow Languages. Proc. 4th Workshop on the Practical Use of Coloured Petri Nets and CPN Tools (CPN'02). Aarhus, Denmark (2002) 1-20
3. Bolcer, G.A. and Taylor, R.N.: Advanced workflow management technologies. Software Process Improvement and Practice 4 (1998) 125-171
4. Shi, M., Yang, G., Xiang, Y., Wu, S.: Workflow Management Systems: A Survey. Proc. IEEE Intl Conf on Communication Technology. Beijing, China (1998) 1-5
5. Ellis, C.A., Keddara, K., Rozenberg, G.: Dynamic change within workflow systems. Proc. COOCS'95. Milpitas, CA (1995)
6. Fan, Y., Wu, C.: Research on a Workflow Modeling Method to Improve System Flexibility. Journal of Software 13(4) (2002) 833-839
7. Sun, R., Shi, M.: A Process Meta-Model Supporting Dynamic Change of Workflow. Journal of Software 14 (2003)
8. Zhao, W., Hu, W., Zhang, S., Wang, L.: Study and Application of a Workflow Meta-Model. Journal of Software 13 (2003)
9. Du, W., Shan, M.-C.: Enterprise Workflow Resource Management. Proc. RIDE'99. (1999) 108-115
10. zur Muehlen, M.: Resource Modeling in Workflow Applications. Proc. 1999 Workflow Management Conference. Muenster (1999) 137-153
11. Russell, N., van der Aalst, W.M.P., ter Hofstede, A.H.M., Edmond, D.: Workflow Resource Patterns: Identification, Representation and Tool Support. Proc. CAiSE. (2005) 216-232
12. Westerinen, A., Schnizlein, J., Strassner, J., Scherling, M., Quinn, B., Herzog, S. et al.: Terminology for Policy-Based Management. Policy Framework (2001)
13. OMG: Meta Object Facility (MOF) Specification. Version 1.4 (2002) URL: http://www.omg.org/docs/formal/02-04-03.pdf
14. Huang, Y., Shan M.-C.: Policies in a resource manager of workflow systems: Modeling enforcement and management. HP Software Technology Laboratory. Technical Report HPL-98-156 (1998)
15. Workflow Management Coalition: The Workflow Reference Model. URL: http://www.wfmc.org/standards/standards.htm

Refinement of Petri Nets in Workflow Integration

Zhijun Ding [1,2], Yaying Zhang[1], Changjun Jiang[1], and Zhaohui Zhang[1]

[1] Department of Computer Science & Engineering,
Tongji University, Shanghai, P.R. China
[2] College of Information Science & Engineering,
Shandong University of Science & Technology, Qingdao, P.R. China
zhijun_ding@hotmail.com

Abstract. The current refinement of Petri nets is used mainly as a top down approach for supporting hierarchical Petri net models. In this paper, it is stepped further as a tool for modeling and verifying workflow integration. First, a series of concepts are defined for formalizing the refinement of workflow net. Then the structure, language and dynamical properties preservation of the refinement are studied. These work proves that a reliable refined workflow net preserves not only properties such as soundness, but also dynamical behavior. Moreover, the net language of the refined net can be resolved by the language of the original net and subnets, which can reduce complexity of model analysis. Finally, the results are successfully applied to design, modeling and verification of workflow integration in Shanghai Traffic Information Service Application Grid.

1 Introduction

Petri nets are frequently used to model and analyze workflow process, and a plenty of research results have been achieved in recent years [1]. However most of them are limited in single workflow modeling and analysis, such as process design methods, properties verification and performance evolution [2]. They have not considered workflow cooperation and integration. In fact, the number of business processes where multiple organizations or multi-departments are involved is increasing rapidly. van der Aalst contributes a lot in this field and introduces how to model and analyze inter-organizational workflow using Petri nets [3]. This paper focuses on using refinement technique of Petri nets as a tool for modeling and verifying integrated workflow, i.e., several participants involved in shared workflow processes. In general, refinement technique was used as a top down approach for supporting hierarchical Petri net models and complex systems' properties analysis based on properties preservation criteria [4]. Valette presents the conditions under which a subnet can be substituted for a single transition while preserving dynamical properties [5]. Suzuki and Murata generalize the results obtained by Valette, and use refinement technique for system design [6]. Huang et al. study structure properties preservation as well as dynamical properties preservation in refinement [7]. Especially for workflow management, Wachtel et al. propose a top-down Petri net-based approach for the purpose of modeling dynamic workflow [8]. van Hee K et al. studied how to preserve soundness property in the refinement of

W. Shen et al. (Eds.): CSCWD 2006, LNCS 4402, pp. 667–678, 2007.
© Springer-Verlag Berlin Heidelberg 2007

workflow nets [9]. Here in this paper we expand the application scope of refinement techniques to modeling and verifying multi-workflow integration.

The paper is structured as follows. Section 2 formulates the definitions related to refinement of workflow nets. Section 3 studies the structure, language and dynamical properties of the refined net for analysis and verification of integrated workflow model. Section 4 describes how to applying our research to design, model and verify of layered workflows and their integration in Shanghai Traffic Information Service Application Grid(STISAG) [10]. Section 5 concludes the paper.

2 Refinement of WF-Nets

The notation and terminology of Petri nets can be found in [1].

In this paper we primarily focus upon the WF-nets (workflow nets) [12]. A net $PN = (P, T; F)$ is called a WF-net iff 1) PN has two special places: ε and θ, where ε is a source place: $^{\bullet}\varepsilon = \Phi$ and θ is a sink place: $\theta^{\bullet} = \Phi$; and 2) if we add a new transition t which connects θ with ε, namely, $^{\bullet}t = \{\theta\}, t^{\bullet} = \{\varepsilon\}$, then the resulting extended net $\overline{PN}$ is strongly connected.

Moreover, a correctly modeled workflow should first transfer the token from the source place and finally transfer the token to the sink place. When there is a token at the sink place, there should be no token in any other places. Secondly, any transition in the workflow net can be triggered in a path through out the network. This property is called the soundness. Let initial marking i of PN be $i(\varepsilon) = 1 \wedge (\forall p \neq \varepsilon, i(p) = 0)$ and marking o of PN be $o(\theta) = 1 \wedge (\forall p \neq \theta, o(p) = 0)$. A WF-net PN satisfies soundness if and only if (1) For every marking M reachable from marking i, o is reachable. Formally $\forall M : i[\sigma > M$, such that $M[\tau > o$ where σ, τ are transition sequences; (2) o is the only marking reachable from marking i with at least one token in place θ. i.e., $\forall M : i[\sigma > M \wedge M \geq o$, such that $M = o$; (3) There are no dead transitions in (PN, i), that is $\forall t \in T, \exists M, M' : i[\sigma > M[t > M'$.

The refinement of Petri net is defined in [7] as follows.

Definition 1. Let $WF_1 = (P_1, T_1; F_1)$ and $WF_2 = (P_2, T_2; F_2)$ be original net and subnet respectively, where $t_r \in T_1$, $r_i^{\bullet} = \{t_r\} = {}^{\bullet}r_o$ and $|{}^{\bullet}t_r| = |t_r^{\bullet}| = 1$ as shown in Figure 1. Replacing transition t_r of WF_1 with WF_2 results in a refined net $WF = (P, T; F)$, where

(1) $P = P_1 \cup P_2 \cup \{p_i, p_o\} - \{r_i, r_o, \varepsilon_2, \theta_2\}$;

(2) $T = T_1 \cup T_2 - \{t_r\}$;

(3) $F = F_1 \cup F_2 \cup \left(\{(p_i, x) | x \in \varepsilon_2^{\bullet}\} \cup \{(x, p_o) | x \in {}^{\bullet}\theta_2\} \cup \{(x, p_i) | x \in {}^{\bullet}r_i\} \right.$

$\cup \{(p_o, x) | x \in r_o^{\bullet}\} \right) - \left(\{(r_i, t_r), (t_r, r_o)\} \cup \{(x, r_i) | x \in {}^{\bullet}r_i\} \cup \{(r_o, x) | x \in r_o^{\bullet}\} \right.$

$\left. \cup \{(\varepsilon_2, x) | x \in \varepsilon_2^{\bullet}\} \cup \{(x, \theta_2) | x \in {}^{\bullet}\theta_2\} \right)$

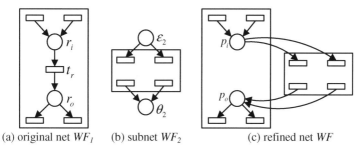

(a) original net WF_1 (b) subnet WF_2 (c) refined net WF

Fig. 1. The refinement of net

For the rest of this paper, WF_1 denotes the original net, WF_2 the subnet and WF the refined net.

Definition 2. Let WF_1 and WF_2 be WF-nets. Refined net WF is obtained by replacing transition t_r of original net WF_1 with subnet WF_2. The initial marking of WF defines as $i(\varepsilon_1) = 1 \wedge (\forall p \neq \varepsilon_1, i(p) = 0)$. The net WF is called reliable if and only if :

(1) Original net WF_1 satisfies soundness;
(2) Subnet WF_2 satisfies soundness;
(3) Place $r_i \in P_1$ is safe in the net system (WF_1, i_1).

Definition 3. $\Gamma_{\overline{T} \rightarrow \overline{T_j}} : \left(\overline{T}\right)^* \rightarrow \left(\overline{T_j}\right)^*$ $(j = 1, 2)$ is mapping of transition sequence from $\overline{WF}$ to $\overline{WF_1}$ ($\overline{WF_2}$) as defined below.

(a1) $\Gamma_{\overline{T} \rightarrow \overline{T_1}}(\lambda) = \lambda$, where λ is a null sequence;

(b1) For $\sigma \in \left(\overline{T}\right)^*$, $\Gamma_{\overline{T} \rightarrow \overline{T_1}}(\sigma \cdot t) = \begin{cases} \Gamma_{\overline{T} \rightarrow \overline{T_1}}(\sigma), & t \in T_2 - {}^\bullet p_o \\ \Gamma_{\overline{T} \rightarrow \overline{T_1}}(\sigma) \cdot t, & t \in T_1 - \{t_r\} \\ \Gamma_{\overline{T} \rightarrow \overline{T_1}}(\sigma) \cdot t_{01}, & t = t_0 \\ \Gamma_{\overline{T} \rightarrow \overline{T_1}}(\sigma) \cdot t_r, & t \in {}^\bullet p_o \end{cases}$

(a2) $\Gamma_{\overline{T} \rightarrow \overline{T_2}}(\lambda) = \lambda$, where λ is a null sequence;

(b2) For $\sigma \in \left(\overline{T}\right)^*$, $\Gamma_{\overline{T} \rightarrow \overline{T_2}}(\sigma \cdot t) = \begin{cases} \Gamma_{\overline{T} \rightarrow \overline{T_2}}(\sigma), & t \in T_1 - \{t_r\} \\ \Gamma_{\overline{T} \rightarrow \overline{T_2}}(\sigma) \cdot t \cdot t_{02}, & t \in {}^\bullet p_o \\ \Gamma_{\overline{T} \rightarrow \overline{T_2}}(\sigma) \cdot t, & t \in \overline{T_2} - \{t_{02}\} \cup {}^\bullet p_o \end{cases}$

where $\overline{WF}$, $\overline{WF_1}$ and $\overline{WF_2}$ is extended net of WF, WF_1 and WF_2 respectively (t_0, t_{01} and t_{02} is additive transition).

Definition 4. Let $PN = (N, M_0)$ be a Petri net, and $L(PN)$ be the net language of PN. $\hat{L}(PN)$ is called the termination language of PN defined as follows:

$$\hat{L}(N, M_0) = \{\sigma | \sigma \in L(N, M_0) \wedge \sigma \cdot t \notin L(N, M_0), \forall t \in T\}$$

Definition 5. Let $\alpha = \alpha_1 \cdot t \cdots \alpha_i \cdot t \cdot \gamma$ be a finite character string, where $t \in \|\alpha\|$ and $t \notin \|\alpha_i\|$, here $\|\ \|$ represents the set of all elements composing the string. Δ is a set of finite character strings. $\alpha|_{t \to \Delta} = \{\alpha_1 \cdot \beta_1 \cdots \alpha_i \cdot \beta_i \cdot \gamma | \beta_i \in \Delta\}$ is the refined language of α on Δ.

3 Property Preservation of the Refined WF-Net

In this section we will investigate what properties are preserved when a transition t_r in a WF-net WF_1 is replaced by WF-net WF_2 to obtain a refined Petri net WF.

3.1 Structure Properties

The refinement of Petri nets, which is defined above, could preserve structure properties such that place/transition invariant, repetitiveness, strong connectedness, and so on [7]. Moreover the refinement operation of workflow nets satisfies the following theorem:

Theorem 1. Let WF be a refined net obtained by replacing transition t_r of original net WF_1 with subnet WF_2. If both WF_1 and WF_2 are WF-nets, so is WF.

Note our focus in this paper is on refinement in workflow integration and its application in traffic grid information service system. Theorem proofs are not given for paper limit. The proof details can be found in [11]. Theorem 1 states that the refined net is still a workflow net as the original net and subnet are. So the refinement technique supports hierarchical modeling. It can be used as a top down approach for designing complex workflow model. At the same time it also provides different representations for model details on corresponding levels, which helps designers or users to understand or analyze the workflow. Furthermore the refinement operation gives one of efficient ways for modeling and analysis workflow integration.

As it is known that the language properties and dynamical properties preservation are more helpful for model analysis and verification than the structure properties preservation. Therefore we study the relation between dynamical behavior of refined net and of original net and subnet.

3.2 Language Properties

In the rest of this section, some good properties of a reliable refined WF-net will be described. Let $WF = (P, T; F)$ be a reliable refined WF-net. The following results can be satisfied:

Theorem 2. $\forall \sigma \in L(\overline{WF}, i)$, $M : i[\sigma > M$, we have $\Gamma_{\overline{T} - \overline{T_j}}(\sigma) \in L(\overline{WF_j}, i_j)$ $j = 1, 2$, and $i_1 \left[\Gamma_{\overline{T} \to \overline{T_1}}(\sigma) > M_1 \right.$, $i_2 \left[\Gamma_{\overline{T} \to \overline{T_2}}(\sigma) > M_2 \right.$, where $\chi = \#(\sigma, p_i) - \#(\sigma, {}^{\cdot}p_o)$

$$M_1(p) = \begin{cases} M(p_i) + \chi & p = r_i \\ M(p_o) & p = r_o \\ M(p) & p \in P_1 - \{r_i, r_o\} \end{cases} \qquad M_2(p) = \begin{cases} 1 - \chi, & p = \varepsilon_2 \\ 0, & p = \theta_2 \\ M(p), & p \in P_2 - \{\varepsilon_2, \theta_2\} \end{cases}$$

Theorem 2 denotes that any possible firing sequence in the refined WF-net is a simulation of some firing in original WF-net and subnet, using the mapping $\Gamma_{\overline{T} \to \overline{T}_j}$. At the same time theorem 2 states that for each reachable marking in the refined net, there always exist corresponding marking in the original net and subnet.

Theorem 3. $L\left(\overline{WF_j}, i_j\right) \subseteq \Gamma_{\overline{T} \to \overline{T}_j}\left(L\left(\overline{WF}, i\right)\right), \quad j = 1, 2$

Theorem 3 states that if we refined a transition of workflow net by another workflow net, any firing sequence in these two net can be simulated by some firing sequences of the refined net. Combining the above theorems, we can have a corollary as follows.

Corollary 1. $\Gamma_{\overline{T} \to \overline{T}_j}\left(L\left(\overline{WF}, i\right)\right) = L\left(\overline{WF_j}, i_j\right), \quad j = 1, 2$

Corollary 1 states that the refined WF-net is behavior equivalent with the original WF-net, that is, the mapping language from refined net to original net (subnet) is the same as original net (subnet) language.

Moreover we can have a language expression of the reliable refined WF-net.

Theorem 4. $\hat{L}(WF, i) = \hat{L}(WF_1, i_1)\Big|_{t_r \to \hat{L}(WF_2, i_2)} = \left\{ \sigma \middle| \sigma \in \alpha \Big|_{t_r \to \hat{L}(WF_2, i_2)}, \alpha \in \hat{L}(WF_1, i_1) \right\}$

According theorem 4, the termination language of a refined net can be resolved by the language of the original net and subnet. This means that the complex workflow analysis can be simplified by this way.

3.3 Dynamical Properties

As stated in Section 2, soundness is an important property of WF-net. It is proved that a WF-net is sound if and only if its extended net is bounded and live [12]. In this section we will indicate that the reliable refined WF-net satisfies soundness. Let $WF = (P, T; F)$ be a reliable refined WF-net. We have the following results.

Theorem 5. $\left(\overline{WF}, i\right)$ is bounded.

Theorem 6. $\left(\overline{WF}, i\right)$ is live.

Theorem 5 and 6 state that a reliable refined WF-net could preserve dynamical properties such as boundedness and liveness. From above results we can directly have conclusion as follows.

Theorem 7. WF satisfies soundness.

To sum up, a reliable refined WF-net satisfies not only structure properties preservation, but also behavior and dynamical properties preservation. This means that we can use original workflow analysis to verify the refined workflow. In general it is easier to verify certain properties of original system than of refined system.

When we develop Shanghai Traffic Information Service Application Grid (STISAG), we apply refinement technique and workflow net model to modeling, analyzing and verifying traffic workflows and their integration. In fact, workflow integration depicts the cooperation and interaction for multiple workflows to achieve a more overall workflow. The architecture of STISAG consists of hierarchical layers in which every layer has its own workflow. Therefore STISAG fits well with workflow integration. The refinement technique stated in this paper is helpful to modeling, analyzing and verifying complex workflow in the workflow process definition phase.

4   Modeling and Verifying Workflow Integration in STISAG

STISAG, an intelligent transportation system based on information service grid, is designed to deal with the traffic jam issues in Shanghai and provide real-time traffic information services for different kinds of transportation users. The system integrates various traffic data, service and legacy application from different traffic fields, such as Shanghai Taxi Company, Shanghai Bus Company, and Shanghai Transportation Information Center. The system also integrates computation and storage resources from Shanghai Grid nodes for real-time traffic information processing and massive traffic data storage. Figure 2 demonstrates route status query service presented in STISAG.

According to the requirement of the traffic information services, the architecture of STISAG is divided into four layers as Figure 3 shows.

Information Presentation Layer (IPL) provides users with interfaces of service on-demand and information presentation, so that users can access the information provided by STITAG using various terminals, such as mobile phone, computer, PDA and in-vehicle terminal devices.

Application Service Layer (ASL) integrates traffic application services such as Route Status Service, Optimum Travel Scheme Service and Public facility Query Service.

Grid Service Support Layer (GSSL) provides Task Scheduling, Resource Management, Data Management, and other grid services. The Task Scheduling service assigns computing tasks to corresponding grid nodes. Resource Management takes charge of monitoring and scheduling local resources. Data Management supports accessing to heterogeneous databases and transferring massive traffic data such as GPS data.

Resource Layer (RL) includes computers and storage devices and corresponding software in Shanghai Grid and SPTN (Shanghai Public Traffic Network).

4.1 Workflow Models of Each Layer

For the functions provided by STISAG, we design the work process of each layer, and construct corresponding workflow model formally using WF-net as process definition tool, shown as PN_1 in Figure 4(a), PN_2 Figure 4(b) and PN_3 Figure 4(c), respectively.

Moreover, the specific description of every transition is shown in Table 1.

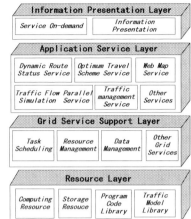

Fig. 2. Route status query service in STISAG   **Fig. 3.** The architecture of STISAG

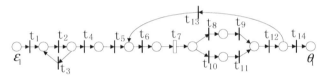

(a) WF-net PN_1 of workflow for **IPL**

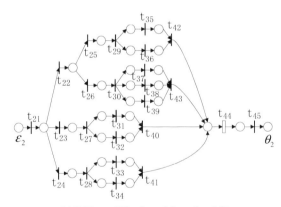

(b) WF-net PN_2 of workflow for **ASL**

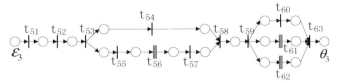

(c) WF-net PN_3 of workflow for **GSSL**

Fig. 4. Workflow model of each layer

Table 1. Description of transitions of *PN*

Transition	Description	Transition	Description
t_1	Open the Web Page	$t_{27}, t_{28}, t_{29}, t_{30}$	Data integration
t_2	Register user name and password	$t_{31}, t_{33}, t_{35}, t_{37}$	obtain the map data
t_3	Fail to login in	t_{32}, t_{39}	Requirement to the real-time traffic data
t_4	Success to login	t_{34}, t_{36}, t_{38}	Obtain the Service data
t_5	Open the map file	$t_{40}, t_{41}, t_{42}, t_{43}$	Create a RSL file
t_6	Choose function through menu	t_{44}	Service computing(Task)
t_7	Call corresponding services	t_{45}	Return the result of service computing
t_8	Fail to service response	t_{51}	Accept task
t_9	Notify user to failure	t_{52}	Waiting schedule in task buffer pool
t_{10}	Return the results of the service	t_{53}	Task scheduling
t_{11}	Presentation results to the web	t_{54}	Obtain service meta data
t_{12}	Record log	t_{55}	Resource requirement
t_{13}	Begin to new requirement again	t_{56}	Resource scheduling
t_{14}	Log out	t_{57}	Resource allocation
t_{21}	Response the service call	t_{58}	Task allocation
t_{22}	Optimum Travel Scheme Service (OTSS)	t_{59}	Startup task
t_{23}	Route Status Service	t_{60}	Execute task
t_{24}	Public facility Query Service	t_{61}	Task management
t_{25}	Static OTSS	t_{62}	Resource management
t_{26}	Dynamical OTSS	t_{63}	Finish task

There are three class of transition in our WF-nets model:

(1) The first class of transitions, presented by black thick line"❙", denotes a atomic activity. For example, t_5 means a activity of opening the map file;

(2) The second class of transitions, presented by black rectangle"❚", denotes a sub-workflow that includes some activities to realize special function, for example transition t_{56} expresses the resource schedule. In fact resource schedule is defined as a sub-workflow, which includes a series of activities such as resource query, resource choice, updating resource information table and return ID of resource etc. Based on the refinement operation in this paper, we could expand such transition into a subnet to obtain more detailed WF-net model;

(3) The third class of transitions, presented by the blank rectangle"❑", denotes an activity which needs to call the lower layer workflow to realize required operation. For example, transition t_7 describes an activity of "calling the corresponding service". It needs to transfer service parameters to the lower Application Service layer and call the workflow of ASL to perform function. We use the refinement operation to model and verify the workflow integration.

In the next section we will introduce how to construct the model, depict the system behavior and analyze the dynamical properties of the integrated workflow based on the above research results.

4.2 Integrated Workflow Model of STISAG

For ease of understanding we first consider the integration of application service layer (ASL) and grid service support layer (GSSL) in the traffic information system. As in above Figure 4(b), Figure 4(c) and Table 1, ASL needs to provide Shanghai urban traffic service such as route status service and optimum travel scheme service to its upper layer. To accomplish the service computing task, integration with its lower layer GSSL is needed to implement the traffic computing task scheduling, re-source/data management and task execution and so on. Integration of each adjacent layer is fundamental to make the application into reality.

Next, the overall integrated workflow model of STISAG is presented from the aspect of net language in that language property can furthermore depict the whole system behavior more integrally.

Accordingly we analyze the WF-net model of each layer of STISAG respectively. Based on the reachable analysis method, it is verified that each WF-net satisfies soundness, which indicates its expanded net is bounded and live. So corresponding workflow could execute the predefined process correctly and perform the functions effectively as we expect. Moreover we can obtain its termination language as follows.

$$\hat{L}(PN_1, i_1) = t_1 t_2 (t_3 t_2)^* t_4 t_5 S_1 (t_{13} S_1)^* t_{14}$$

$$\hat{L}(PN_2, i_2) = t_{21} (S_2 + S_3 + S_4) t_{44} t_{45}$$

$$\hat{L}(PN_3, i_3) = t_{51} t_{52} t_{53} (t_{54} \otimes t_{55} t_{56} t_{57}) t_{58} t_{59} (t_{60} \otimes t_{61} \otimes t_{62}) t_{63}$$

where

$$S_1 = t_6 t_7 (t_8 t_9 \otimes t_{10} t_{11}) t_{12},$$

$$S_2 = t_{22} (t_{25} t_{29} (t_{35} \otimes t_{36}) t_{42} + t_{26} t_{30} (t_{37} \otimes t_{38} \otimes t_{39}) t_{43})$$

$$S_3 = t_{23} t_{27} (t_{31} \otimes t_{32}) t_{40}$$

$$S_4 = t_{24} t_{28} (t_{33} \otimes t_{34}) t_{41}$$

Note $\otimes$ denotes shuffle operation.

The above termination language depicts all possible behavior sequences and process routing so that we can have the whole sight of system execution.

That independent workflows of each layer can run correctly is still not enough. They should also cooperate effectively with each other for realizing the service of STISAG. Therefore we design the integrated workflow based on the each layer's workflow, and modeling the workflow integration using the refined WF-nets model.

The overall integrated workflow model can be seen in Figure 5. First we replace transition t_7 of PN_1 shown in Figure 4(a) with PN_2 shown in Figure 4(b) . This results in a refined net PN', then similar operation continues, which substitutes PN_3 shown in Figure 4(c) for transition t_{44} of PN'. We will obtain final refined net PN namely the integrated workflow model of STISAG.

Based on above-mentioned refinement methods, we could analyze the integrated workflow model PN. Firstly, according to theorem 1, the model PN' is a WF-net because PN_1 and PN_2 are WF-nets. Then PN is also a WF-net since PN_3 is WF-net. Secondly, PN' can be proven to be a reliable refined WF-net because PN_1 and PN_2

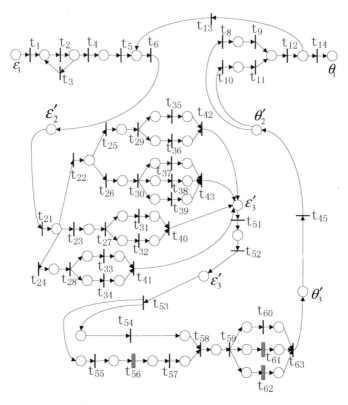

Fig. 5. WF-net *PN* of integrated workflow

satisfy soundness and safeness. So *PN′* satisfies safeness and soundness by theorem 5 and 7. Moreover, since PN_3 satisfies soundness, *PN* satisfies soundness too according to theorem 7, namely its expand net is live and bounded. Finally we can obtain a set of language properties of *PN* by corollary 1:

(1) $\Gamma_{\overline{T}\to\overline{T_1}}\left(L\left(\overline{PN},i\right)\right)=L\left(\overline{PN_1},i_1\right)$

(2) $\Gamma_{\overline{T}\to\overline{T_2}}\left(L\left(\overline{PN},i\right)\right)=L\left(\overline{PN_2},i_2\right)$

(3) $\Gamma_{\overline{T}\to\overline{T_3}}\left(L\left(\overline{PN},i\right)\right)=L\left(\overline{PN_3},i_3\right)$

The above formulas states the integrated workflow model is behavior equivalent with the layered workflow models. Moreover, the termination language of *PN* is resolved according to theorem 4.

$$\hat{L}(PN',i')=\hat{L}(PN_1,i_1)\Big|_{t_7\to\hat{L}(PN_2,i_2)}$$

$$=t_1t_2\left(t_3t_2\right)^*t_4t_5t_6t_{21}\left(S_2+S_3+S_4\right)t_{44}t_{45}\left(t_8t_9\otimes t_{10}t_{11}\right)t_{12}$$

$$\cdot \left(t_{13}t_6t_{21} \left(S_2 + S_3 + S_4 \right) t_{44}t_{45} \left(t_8t_9 \otimes t_{10}t_{11} \right) t_{12} \right)^* t_{14}$$

$$\hat{L}(PN,i) = \hat{L}(PN',i') \Big|_{t_{44} \to \hat{L}(PN_3,i_3)} = t_1t_2 \left(t_3t_2 \right)^* t_4t_5 S' \left(t_{13}S' \right)^* t_{14}, \text{ where }$$

$$S' = t_6t_{21} \left(S_2 + S_3 + S_4 \right) t_{51}t_{52}t_{53} \left(t_{54} \otimes t_{55}t_{56}t_{57} \right) t_{58}t_{59} \left(t_{60} \otimes t_{61} \otimes t_{62} \right) t_{63}t_{45} \left(t_8t_9 \otimes t_{10}t_{11} \right) t_{12}$$

For example, $\sigma = t_1t_2 \left(t_3t_2 \right)^* t_4t_5 S'' \left(t_{13}S'' \right)^* t_{14}$, where

$$S'' = t_6t_{21}S_3t_{51}t_{52}t_{53} \left(t_{54} \otimes t_{55}t_{56}t_{57} \right) t_{58}t_{59} \left(t_{60} \otimes t_{61} \otimes t_{62} \right)$$

σ describes the whole process that STISAG provides route status service to application users. Firstly user logs in the Web portal through in-vehicle terminal, mobile phones, PDAs or PCs, and selects the route status service (t_1t_2); then IPL transfers this requirement to the ASL to call correspondent service ($t_4t_5t_6t_7$). The route status service integrates the map data, GPS data and service parameter to form a RSL file ($t_{21}S_3$), and then deliver the RSL file to GSSL and call GSSL workflow to implement the task computing. Finally GSSL deploy meta data and grid resources according to RSL file ($t_{51}t_{52}t_{53} \left(t_{54} \otimes t_{55}t_{56}t_{57} \right) t_{58}$), then executes the task and at the same time applies resource and task management workflow to control resource and task ($t_{59} \left(t_{60} \otimes t_{61} \otimes t_{62} \right) t_{63}$). When the task is finished, the route status results are returned layer by layer up ($t_{45}t_8t_9$) and finally displayed via terminal devices (t_{12}).

5 Conclusion

Refinement of WF-net is provided in this paper for modeling and analyzing workflow integration. Preserving properties such as structure, language and dynamical properties are studied. This work proves that the reliable refined nets satisfy soundness. And dynamical behavior of refined Petri nets is consistent with of original nets and subnets. Therefore the property analysis and verification of refined workflow nets can be realized by properties of subnets. Thus the refinement can reduce complexity of model analysis. Moreover, how to apply refinement of Petri net is presented by designing, modeling and verifying the workflow integration in STISAG. This paper indicates that refinement operation with step-by-step refinement of transitions could realize hierarchical modeling of workflow as well as composite modeling of workflow integration.

Acknowledgments. This work is support partially by projects of National Basic Research Program of China (973 Program) (2003CB317002, 2004CB318001-03), National Natural Science Funds (90412013, 60473094, 60573018), Shanghai Science & Technology Research Plan (04XD14016) and Engineering Foundation for Young Faculty in Tongji University.

References

1. Murata, T.: Petri nets: Properties, Analysis and Applications. Proceedings of the IEEE IEEE 77(4) (1989) 541-580
2. Li, J., Fan, Y., Zhou, M.: Performance Modeling and Analysis of Workflow. IEEE Transactions on System, Man, Cybernetics. Part A. 34(2) (2004) 229-242
3. van der Aalst W.M.P.: Loosely Coupled Inter-organizational Workflows: Modeling and Analyzing Workflows Crossing Organizational Boundaries. Information and Management 37(2) (2000) 67-75
4. Zuberek, W.M.: Hierarchical Analysis of Manufacturing Systems Using Petri Nets. Proc. IEEE Int. Conf. on S.M.C. Nashville, TN, USA (2000) 3021-3026
5. Valette, R.: Analysis of Petri nets by stepwise refinements. Journal of Computer and System Science 18 (1979) 35-46
6. Suzuki, I., Murata, T.: A Method for Stepwise Refinement and Abstraction of Petri Nets. Journal of Computer and System Science 27 (1983) 51-76
7. Huang, H., Cheung, T.Y., Mak, W.M.: Structure and Behavior Preservation by Petri-net-based Refinements in System Design. Theoretical Computer Science 328(3) (2004) 245-269
8. Chrzastowski-Wachtel, P., Benatallah, B., Hamadi, R., et al.: A Top-Down Petri Net-Based Approach for Dynamic Workflow Modeling. LNCS 2678 (2003) 415-438
9. van Hee, K., Sidorova, N., Voorhoeve, M.: Soundness and separability of workflow nets in the stepwise refinement. LNCS 2679 (2003) 335-354
10. Jiang, C. et al.: Urban Traffic Information Service Application Grid. Journal of Computer Science & Technology 20(1) (2005) 134-140
11. Ding, Z., Jiang, C.: Petri Nets Modeling and Analysis Method Based on The Refinement Operation. Control and Decision 22(2) (2007) to appear (in Chinese)
12. van der Aalst W.M.P.: The Application of Petri Nets to Workflow Management. Journal of Circuits, Systems, and Computers 8(1) (1998) 21-66

Flexible Organizational Process Deployment

Andrea M. Magdaleno[1], Vanessa T. Nunes[1], Renata M. Araujo[2],
and Marcos R.S. Borges[1]

[1] *PPGI* - Graduate Program in Informatics, IM&NCE, UFRJ, Brazil,
PO Box 2324, 20001-970, Rio de Janeiro, Brazil
{andrea.magalhaes,vanunes}@gmail.com, mborges@nce.ufrj.br
[2] Department of Applied Informatics, UNIRIO, Brazil,
Av. Pasteur, 458, Urca, Rio de Janeiro, 22290-240, Brazil
renata.araujo@uniriotec.br

Abstract. Organizations are increasingly interested in modelling and automating their business processes using workflow technology. One of the difficulties in this approach is that organizations must adapt their defined processes to each different situation and that workflow systems are yet not flexible enough to allow changes for each new process instance to be enacted. This research work proposes a strategy for achieving a higher compliance with the organization's guidelines based on building up processes using pre-defined process units.

1 Introduction

Organizations have been adopting approaches for defining their business processes as a strategy for improving productivity. In those organizations where this definition already exists, each new process enactment may vary according to the participants involved, and to the context of the situation being focused. Therefore, it has been noticed that defining a standard process for the entire organization encompassing all the possible and unpredicted variations in its enactment is almost an impossible task.

Organizations often try to enclose all possible cases of work enactment into a single or set of processes. However, the complexity of understanding, use and maintenance of this process tends to increase if it is continuously updated to incorporate work variability. The ideal situation would be having a standard process defined in an adaptable and flexible infrastructure, being able to be easily, although still in a controlled manner, redefined by the organization without losing its legibility.

The main issue this work addresses is how to adapt/configure the organization standard business process into a new process to be enacted at different new situations. This motivation raised the idea of defining the concept of reusable process components – called *process beans*. Process beans are definitions of process steps/practices for any business domain implemented in a workflow management system (WFMS).

An organization can define and register a set of process beans based on its process policies, rules and strategies. Each new process enactment can be designed by combining and adapting existing organizational beans. A tool – Beans Composer – was developed in order to facilitate the management of process beans. We claim that the process beans bring more flexibility for adapting and using organization's standard process.

W. Shen et al. (Eds.): CSCWD 2006, LNCS 4402, pp. 679–688, 2007.
© Springer-Verlag Berlin Heidelberg 2007

This paper comprises six sections. The following section details the difficulties in maintaining consistency between process definition and its effective use. Section 3 presents the concept of process beans and how the process beans approach can be used in order to make process adaptation and use more flexible. Section 4 presents Beans Composer, the tool that implements the proposed solution. Section 5 discusses related work. Finally, Section 6 concludes the paper discussing how this approach helps to reduce the gap presented in Section 2.

2   The Gap Between Process Definition, Adaptation and Effective Use

In general, the process definition organizational flow occurs as depicted in Figure 1. A process definition group is assigned as responsible for organizing and registering the organization's processes strategies, goals, activities, templates etc, making this information concrete and available for the whole organization in documents, manuals, or process repositories (Figure 1-1). Usually these definitions rely on the organization's business strategies and on quality models available and demanded by the market [1-4]. The whole set of these definitions comprises what is called the organization *standard process*.

It is assumed that this material is enough to enable organization workers to perform their activities according to the defined process. The process repository, guides and manuals would be available, providing new and updated information about the process (if we agree that these definitions continuously change) and instructions about why and how to use the process in their daily work activities (Figure 1-2).

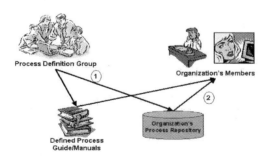

Fig. 1. Process definition flow

Considering this view, we can outline some of the gaps that may exist between process definition and its effective use. First of all, while building the organization's standard process, the process definition group is challenged with the need of defining a somehow general process which can encompass the greater part of the details and specific needs of a group or department. For instance, teams that do not have sufficient skill or training in a specific task should need more details to guide their work. However, other teams may have better qualification, so its members may feel limited with high level of control of its activities. Using the software development domain as an example, we could state that one single process could not be detailed enough if the organization desires to use different development methodologies – Object Oriented or Structured Analysis – depending on project context.

This gap may result in two different outcomes: 1) an excessively detailed process definition, making it difficult for workers to follow it and rendering process maintenance too expensive and complex; 2) an excessively general definition, adding effort for workers to interpret and to adapt it to each new situation.

Another gap is that, even if the organization members are able to understand the defined process and adapt it to their needs, it is often difficult to register how the adaptation has occurred. Therefore, possibilities for process improvement are lost.

Very often, organizations try to shorten this gap by automating the process through computational systems that implement the desired process. The automated system will make sure that the process will be followed as desired. The problem with this approach is that the process is seldom mature enough to be disciplined by a tool and costs of maintenance and adaptation are very high. Another consequence can be that the tool becomes the focus, due to the maintenance efforts, with process definition and rationale being neglected.

Workflow systems were suggested as an approach for rendering process automation more flexible. By causing process definition and its enactment to be more explicit, WFMS are a strong candidate for process automation. The main advantage of using WfMS is that costs of process maintenance are considerably reduced when compared to the maintenance of a computational system which embeds process activities.

The way processes are implemented in a WFMS still focuses on the attempt to implement the whole organization's standard process and to perform and control it as defined. However, we argue that, as a workflow system deals explicitly with the concept of process and its parts, it can be a potential platform for creating a flexible environment for process definition, adaptation and effective use.

3   Process Beans

Process beans are reusable process components. Mainly, they are definitions of business process steps/practices, implemented on a workflow management system. They can be combined or adapted for each case of enactment. They may also be connected to the defined processes of the organization to refine the existing activities or to model new processes through composition with other beans.

Process beans can be of two types: *framework beans* or *blackbox beans*. The framework beans are containers of common activities for a great number of processes. They are useful for providing a process architecture, which guides definition of new processes based on the organization rules. In the software engineering domain, an example of a framework bean would be the definition of the development lifecycle. As a high-level process, it allows each activity to be defined in a customized way, following the organization's guidelines.

Blackbox beans are smaller components with more specific use. They are designed to be used without modifications. In the software development context, an example would be the implementation of a class inside an activity of code programming.

The main difference between framework and blackbox beans is the presence of open slots in framework beans. These slots can be optionally filled with other beans of any type (framework or blackbox).

In Figure 2, we can see two possible associations of beans. First, both blackbox and framework beans can be connected in a linear sequence. This occurs when we choose not to fill in any of the open spaces in the framework bean. Moreover, it shows the ability of the framework bean to be complemented by both types of beans. It becomes clear that the combination of beans may have unlimited levels according to the desired degree of detail during the process definition step.

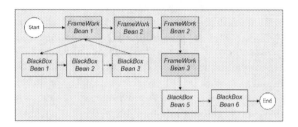

Fig. 2. Possible association of process beans

Taking as an example an organization, which adopted the waterfall model lifecycle, each activity (Requirement Analysis, Design, Code, Test or Deployment) can be considered as a process bean. The type of each bean will be determined based on the desired level of control. For instance, if the organization understands that the coding activity can only be executed in a specific way, then this bean will be classified as blackbox bean. However, other activities, like Requirements Analysis, can be framework beans (Figure 3). Therefore, for each new development project, the process to be followed can be constructed by combining related beans.

It is also important to understand that a blackbox bean (for instance, "Using Rational Rose"), might fill in more than one framework bean. This is one of the most important of the beans properties: being able to be reused in different cases of enactment, without it being necessary to repeat all its definition. Thus, we expect to reduce the time spent on process definitions in organizations and use the experience acquired in successful previous cases.

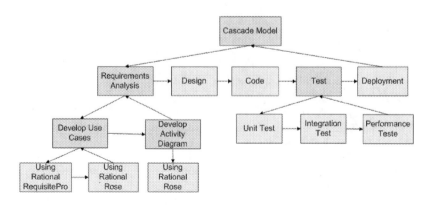

Fig. 3. Beans association in software engineering

4 Deploying Processes with Beans Composer

Process beans will be the reusable building blocks from which the organization can develop a tailored process from the defined process standards. Figure 4 presents this idea. The group responsible for defining the organization process is also responsible for translating the standard definitions into process beans implemented in the WFMS. Any member of the organization can adapt the standard process using the available process beans based on the characteristics of the situation/process they face (time, budget, available human resources etc). Other organization's members using the WFMS will further enact the specialized process.

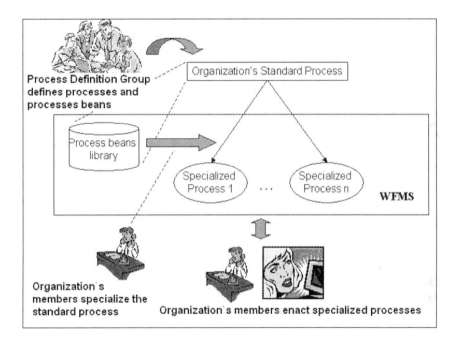

Fig. 4. Tailoring the standard process using process beans

In order to implement this approach, a tool - Beans Composer – was built, which is able to provide resources to create, manipulate, adapt and combine process beans, as also as enacting the resulting processes. Beans Composer was designed and developed over a commercial workflow system (Lotus Workflow), which provides all the functionalities for modeling and enacting processes.

Based on this scenario, there are two basic users of the Beans Composer: *Beans Administrator* and *Process Manager*. To the Beans Administrator concerns the process definition group responsible for maintaining the Beans Library by defining the desired organization's process domains (called Beans Classification), modelling and registering organization's beans. To the Process Manager concerns project/business managers who use the Beans Library to create new processes by combining different beans or creating new processes, according to the singularities of each situation.

4.1 Defining Beans

Modeling a Bean. There is no difference in modeling a framework or a blackbox bean, since they both correspond to a process. The difference will happen, later, in their use. While blackbox beans are used without any adaptation, framework beans may be completed with other beans. A bean is created in Beans Comporser by defining its underlying process in the workflow system. For instance, to construct the software engineering process proposed in Figure 3, the Beans Administrator models a first bean, called Waterfall Cycle, with five steps (Requirement Analysis, Design, Code, Test and Deployment) as shown in Figure 5. Activities performers, instructions, inputs and outputs are also defined in the workflow system.

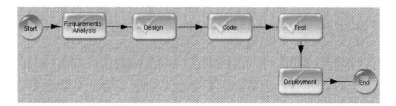

Fig. 5. Modeling a bean

Registering a Bean in the Library. All beans registered are available in the Beans Library (Figure 6). In order to include a bean in the organization library, the following information should be provided: a name; which organization standard process the bean is specializing; the bean type (framework or blackbox); its classification (domain it is able to attend); the definition of which activities will be possibly filled in (in a framework bean); its objective; the context in which it should be used; details on how to use the bean and important information about the output generated; documents, data or products necessary to start its enactment; documents, data or products that will be released; and roles committed with the execution of the bean.

Classifying Beans. As Beans Composer aims at supporting more than one application domain, the Beans Administrator must register the possible beans classifications for the whole organization. A classification must contain a name and a description which helps understand its meaning. The same bean can belong to more than one domain because the same type of problem occurs across different domains. The Beans Administrator can also create new classifications. Some examples of classifications would be: Software Engineering, Meeting, Human Resources, etc…

4.2 Creating a Project

Considering again the example of a software development organization, where a new development project will start. The software development project manager, or the software quality assurance group, will start project planning and its corresponding detailed process, based on the organization's standard process.

Imagining that the standard process is decomposed into beans and made available in the beans library, a Process Manager can start the combination of beans for defining a specific process for this project. Therefore, the project is a starting point for the

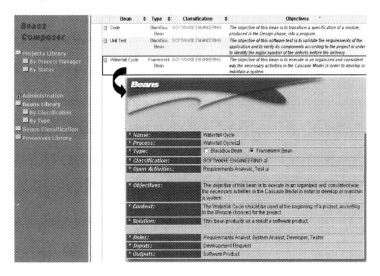

Fig. 6. R egistering a bean

combination of beans. In fact, when combining and adapting beans, the Process Manager is establishing a new process according to his needs without violating the organization's rules/standards.

In the Beans Composer, the combination of beans to define a new process is called a *project*. Each project has a unique name and can only be modified by the Process Manager who created it. A project has two possible status: "In Elaboration" or "Active". The first one represents a project still being defined by the Process Manager. The second one represents a project with all of its beans combined and ready to be executed.

The Process Manager must provide a unique name and a description, which explains the project objectives. The system records the name of the Process Manager responsible for this new project, the date of creation, the description and the initial status ("In Elaboration"). All projects are listed in the Projects Library.

A project is composed of an unlimited number of stages. Stages are steps to be executed during the project. Each stage has a bean associated to it. The Process Manager can associate any blackbox or framework bean to a stage (Figure 7).

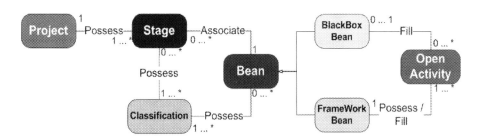

Fig. 7. Concepts of the Beans Composer

For example, in a software development project, the first stage can be composed by the Waterfall Cycle bean (Figure 8). From a framework bean, the Process Manager has two options: use the process exactly as defined, or use another bean as a subprocess of a stage. The first option is useful for teams that already have considerable knowledge of tasks involved and do not need many details or control over their execution. The second allows the adaptation of a specific task, but still guides the team toward following the organization rules.

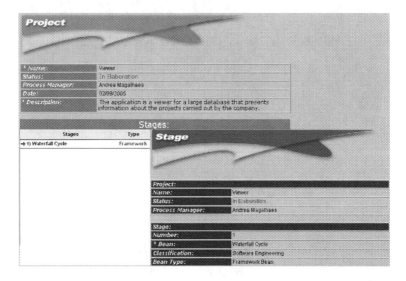

Fig. 8. Stage of the project

To offer this second option, it was created the concept of an *open activity*, available only in framework beans. An open activity represents a point where the Process Manager can fill in with another bean of any type. According to our example, the open activities will be Requirement Analysis and Test. The requirements analysis activity will be filled in with the blackbox bean "Develop Use Cases".

The Beans Composer has this drawback characterized by the fact that the Process Manager is able to fill in any bean presented in the Beans Library. Because of this, he or she must be aware of the inputs and outputs so as to maintain the integrity of documents and products that are produced and used while executing the process.

4.3 Activating a Project

A defined project comprises a set of integrated framework and blackbox beans. Therefore, a project will correspond also to a process resulting from this integration. After the Process Manager finishes the definition of the new project, it can be activated, which means, one of its instances is started to be enacted by the WFMS. Participants will enact the process by interacting with the workflow system.

5 Related Work

The process beans concept also has been studied in a variety of domains. Parrini, Campos and Borges [5] focus on using beans for documenting analysts´ queries in OLAP applications. Recently this beans concept was used to provide effective support for post-meeting activities [6-8]. The great benefit of Beans Composer is that it helps organizations to establish a process beans library in any domain of application, helping the search for appropriate processes to use and the integration of beans from different domains.

The lack of flexibility still has been an obstacle to the use of workflow systems. Thus, this topic is widely discussed in literature and there are several publications with different proposals to handle processes that deviate from the definition during the execution step.

For instance, Wainer and Bezerra [9] present an approach based on overriding constraints that aim at supporting partial workflows, which means workflows that do not have a complete definition and therefore can be dynamically planed.

Van der Aalst et al. [10] define the concept of *proclets* which are workflow process components that act as objects (as in the object-oriented programming paradigm). They encapsulate a defined process and preserves information about previous interactions.

The approaches presented above all deal with the need of defining new workflow engines that can implement the new concepts/strategies for enacting workflow. What is interesting in Beans Composer is that its approach uses existing commercial workflow tools and tries to bring flexibility by combining process definitions through process beans.

The concept of process patterns has also been explored by Ambler [11] in the software engineering context. In this work, it is argued that process patterns are an appropriate mechanism for communicating approaches to software development that have proven to be effective in practice.

White [12] used two graphical modeling notations, the BPMN Business Process Diagram from the Business Process Management Initiative (BPMI) and the UML 2.0 Activity Diagram from the Object Management Group (OMG) trying to model the patterns suggested in [13]. He concludes that both notations can adequately model most of the patterns proposed. These results help us to consider that modelling and using process patterns are a good strategy for defining organization processes.

6 Conclusion

The "divide and conquer" or "reuse" approach of managing process beans facilitates creating new process definitions for each new situation to be enacted by the workflow system. Considering that the definition of beans will be performed based on the organization's business process model, it is expected that any new project created in Beans Composer will be compliant with the organization's guidelines for enacting processes.

Each new project is recorded in Beans Composer, and their instances are recorded in the workflow engine. This is relevant information for maintaining the organization process memory, where alternatives to the organization standard process can be registered. This memory also helps in identifying process patterns among the project set that can be later defined as new organizational process beans. Finally, process beans definition, management and enactment are directly performed over a workflow system, cutting the gap between process definition and its implementation.

Studies on how the process beans concept and environments such as Beans Composer can be enhanced, to serve as knowledge management and organizational learning infrastructure for process definitions and practices are our intentions as future research work.

Acknowledgments. The work of Professor Marcos R. S. Borges was partially supported by a grant from CNPq (Brazil) No. 305900/2005-6.

References

1. Capability Maturity Model for Software (CMM). URL: http://www.sei.cmu.edu/cmm
2. Capability Maturity Model Integration (CMMI). URL: http://www.sei.cmu.edu/cmmi
3. International Organization for Standardization (ISO). URL: http://www.iso.org
4. Control Objectives for Information Technology (COBIT).
   URL: http://www.isaca.org/cobit.htm
5. Parrini, E., Campos, M.L., Borges, M.R.S.: AMPA: Knowledge Management in Analytical-based Decision Processes. Journal of Decision Systems 13 (2004) 263-286
6. Mendes, C.D.L.: Support for Post-meeting Activities using Workflow Technology. M. Sc. Dissertation. IM&NCE/UFRJ, Rio de Janeiro, Brazil (2003) (In Portuguese)
7. Araujo, R.M., Borges, M.R.S., Mendes, C.D.L.: Process Beans for Supporting Post-meeting Activities. Proc. Brazilian Workshop on Technologies for Collaboration (WCSCW). Ribeirão Preto, Brazil (2004) 165-172 (In Portuguese)
8. Borges, M.R.S., Pino, J.A., Araujo, R.M.: Bridging the Gap Between Decisions and Their Implementations. Proc. 10th International Workshop on Groupware (CRIWG). Lecture Notes in Computer Science 3198 (2004) 153-165
9. Wainer, J., Bezerra, F.L.: Constraint-based Flexible Workflows. Proc. 9th International Workshop on Groupware (CRIWG). Grenoble, France (2003) 151-158
10. Van der Aalst, W.M.P., Barthelmess, P., Ellis, C.A.: Workflow Modeling using Proclets. Technical Report CUCS-900-00. Computer Science Department, University of Colorado (2000)
11. Ambler, S.W.: Process Patterns: Building Large-Scale Systems Using Object Technology. In: SIG Books/Cambridge University Press, New York (1998)
12. White, S.A.: Process Modeling Notations and Workflow Patterns.
    URL: http://www.bpmn.org
13. Van der Aalst, W.M.P., Barros, A.P., ter Hofstede, A.H.M., Kiepuszewski, B.: Advanced Workflow Patterns. Proc. 7th International Conference Cooperative Information Systems (COOPIS). Lecture Notes in Computer Science 1901 (2000) 18-29

An Ontology Based Workflow Centric Collaboration System

Zhilin Yao[1], Shufen Liu[1], Liquan Han[1], Y.V. Ramana Reddy[2], Jinqiao Yu[3],
Ye Liu[1], Chan Zhang[1], and Zhaoqing Zheng[1]

[1] College of Computer Science and Technology, Jilin University,
Qianwei Road No.2699, Changchun 130012, China
{yaozl, liusf}@jlu.edu.cn, jlu_cscw@163.com
[2] SIPLab, Concurrent Engineering Research Center,
Lane Department of Computer Science and Electrical Engineering,
West Virginia University, 26506 Morgantown, WV, USA
ramana.reddy@mail.wvu.edu
[3] Department of Mathematics and Computer Science, Illinois Wesleyan University,
61761 Bloomington, IL, USA
jyu@iwu.edu

Abstract. This article introduces a workflow centric collaboration system based on ontology, which is context-aware and adaptive. Using ontology to represent most collaboration elements and rules of the system, we introduce an ontology repository into the framework. It gives the system the capability to represent collaboration knowledge smoothly. The system focuses on business workflow transition and business data manipulation. It can be easily extended and up-graded by modifying the ontology repository when the requirements change. Based on ontology, the system can also interact with other ontology based systems and applications.

1 Introduction

Traditional workflow systems, which can define the service management flows, lack reasonable methods to define the relevant objects, the relationships among objects and the logics of services. Without the flexibility, the flow settings may not be adapted to users' service data in this kind of system. So it is unable to meet user requirements. Most collaboration systems focus on tools to enhance communication of group, so they can not include collaboration knowledge efficiently.

The requirement of today's collaboration is more flexible then ever. Current collaboration activities are more random. Many of them do not happen in anticipated way, because they are based on an open, interactive and ever-changing computing environment, namely, the Internet. Roles of collaboration participants are inconstant. People may join a project and leave at any time. Most of current workflow systems are not flexible enough to cope with this kind of situation.

Most of workflow systems can only process the flows according to the predefined models and can not change the models dynamic when computing environment changed. Moreover, the implementation of workflow system often requires the

W. Shen et al. (Eds.): CSCWD 2006, LNCS 4402, pp. 689–698, 2007.
© Springer-Verlag Berlin Heidelberg 2007

development of special client applications, which are low-efficiency and high-cost activities. Because of the lack of interactive foundation in different workflows, this kind of patterns severely restricts the development of workflow system.

The paper is organized as follows. We first describe the design motivation of system. Then related work is reviewed. Next, we describe the system structure and the ontology repository compositions. Following this, we introduce detail ontology representation in system. After that the implementation of the system is introduced, and the method that how engine works are described. Finally, we wrap up our paper with a brief conclusion and a discussion on future work.

2 Motivation

Consider of a typical routine scene that may happen in any company. John is an employee and is participating in two projects. He would quit his job within two weeks for some reason. If the company uses some kind of workflow system, the system or the administrator of the system had to notice other *related employees* the fact, tell them to perform *relative operations*. The system or the administrator may also need to create some *relative workflow instances* to handle the quitting procedures and *relative data*. They also need to adjust the *workflows as well as corresponding models* that John participating in now.

Of course administrator can do all those tasks manually. But it is lagging in response and some mistakes may occur or some important work may be omitted due to administrator's fault. Or we can predefine detail modals and write program to enumerate all the situations that may happen in the system. When something happened, let the system handle it according to those predefined models. But the work of modeling would be enormous and very complex, and most of them may be never used at all. When business logical changes, we must do a lot of adjustment work to modify the predefined system.

The limitation of traditional collaboration systems mainly lies in the non-integrity to represent collaborative knowledge. Workflow system is a kind of collaborative system, which is an information exchange and state transition system based on domain knowledge. In this kind of system, collaborative knowledge includes domain definitions, the relationship among these definitions, states of system objects, triggering, transition and flow restriction, as well as domain restriction rules.

Traditional workflow system only defines the relationship of triggering, transition and the restriction of workflows. These definitions can not represent the elements of collaborative knowledge integrally. Other elements need to be created in an explicit or implicit way while developing the customer client system on the basis of workflow engine. Therefore, complexity is increased in order to implement the workflow system. Developers usually hand code the domain collaborative rules & regulations into the system, which makes the system hard to maintain and extend.

These problems can be resolved more effectively by introducing ontology theory.

Ontology is originally a concept in Philosophy domain. In recent years, ontology has been emphasized extensively in Information Science to generate good outcomes in many applications. Especially, the use on Web technology results in the development of Semantic Web. It plays a significant role in many domains that need the representation of knowledge.

In 1993, Gruber [1] defined ontology as "An ontology can be defined as the specification of a conceptualization". Then, Borst and Studer conducted deeper researches on the definition of ontology, and they defined ontology as "An ontology is a formal, explicit specification of a shared conceptualization" [2-3], which indicated the sharing function of ontology in information representation and information exchange. In 1998, Guarino discussed the difference between ontology theory and conceptualization further, and thus modified Gruber's definition accordingly: "An ontology is a logical theory accounting for the intended meaning of a formal vocabulary, i.e. its ontological commitment to a particular conceptualization of the world." [4].

Ontology languages allow users to write explicit, formal conceptualizations of domains models [5]. Recently, some workflow researches based on ontology have been introduced in some papers. In paper [6], the author proposed a dynamic grid service oriented ontology workflow language used in grid environment, paper [7] proposed a semantic oriented DAML based workflow model and workflow system framework, authors of paper [8] proposed mechanisms that enable dynamic flexible workflow execution by using ontologies to capture semantic relationships between workflows, resources and users. But full collaboration system solution based on ontology is not found yet.

3   System Structure

3.1   Main Structure

This article proposes a workflow centric collaboration system based on ontology. The system employs ontology to represent the various elements in workflow and thus characterize the knowledge system of workflow in a uniformed way. Based on workflow reference model [9] of WfMC-Workflow Management Coalition, we introduced the ontology repository into the system, which includes six main components: the workflow engine, ontology definition, workflow client application, administration & monitor tools, invoked applications and other workflow engines. These parts are illustrated in Figure 1.

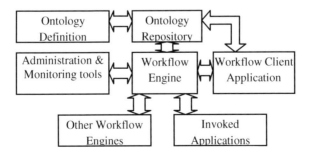

Fig. 1. System structure

3.2 Ontology Repository Compositions

The ontology repository is constructed in three levels, which are Static Abstract Level, Static Concrete Level, and Dynamic Concrete Level (as shown in Figure 2).

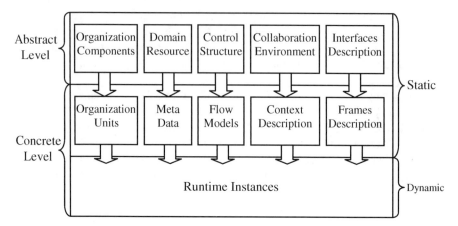

Fig. 2. Ontology repository compositions

The Static Abstract Level ontologies are mainly those that describe basic common attributes and rules of the collaboration system, as well the essential relations between them. For example, the Organization Components ontologies depict what kind of components the collaboration system must have, like Units, Roles, and Users. They should also contain the relations and rules between them. For examples, units should have some kind of structure between them, users should belong to some units and should have some roles, etc. In fact, ontologies at this level define the system framework.

The Static Concrete Level ontologies are more concrete than those at Static Abstract Level. They are usually subclasses or instances of those abstract ontologies. They depict the domain related classes and models. We may define different set of ontologies to make the system extended to different domains usage. The procedures that we build up ontologies at this level are exactly the procedures that we make system customized to special domain application. For instance, when we customize the system to special use, we should add concrete units' structure, concrete roles, and user description into the Ontology Repository. And what we added must conform to Static Abstract Level ontologies. The ontologies at this level are relatively more dynamic than Static Abstract Level ontologies, but relatively more stable than those ontologies at Dynamic Concrete Level.

The ontologies at Dynamic Concrete Level are mainly those runtime instances that the upper levels ontologies required to be included into the repository. In fact they together constitute the system runtime context.

When the system is released, the Static Abstract Level ontologies are included in the system. It represents the relationship of different parts of the system, ensures the consistency of concepts and related constrains of the collaboration procedures, and makes the knowledge shared and exchanged in domains.

The Static Concrete Level domain correlative ontologies are constructed when customize domain applications based on the system. This kind of ontology can be built by application provider or by users themselves. Users can modify and expand it later to make the system adaptive to the changes of domain.

3.3 System Usage

In the context of workflow system, there is domain collaborative knowledge in system flows and users' data. When defining the collaborative data and service flow, users embed the domain knowledge into the system. However, this knowledge is far from integration. There is a lot of domain knowledge in workflow client applications. The diversity of the knowledge determines the complexity and diversity of client application. Therefore, without a universal framework to satisfy all clients' applications, the implementations of workflow always require developing special client application aimed at special requirement.

In view of this situation, we can abstract the application framework that focuses on special kinds of applications. Although these applications may belong to different domains and have different domain knowledge, they have similar application pattern and knowledge structure.

The proposed system is intends to be used in the database-oriented applications to access data. In the system, users' service data are mostly stored in the database and users' different service flows and steps in the flows share the service data. In given context, the step will carry out the operations user defined, which are mainly the insert, delete and modify functions on the service data in database, and this will alter the state of flows. By distilling the general characters of such systems, building the system framework, the system will be customizable, because it separates the knowledge dependent on special domain with framework and uses ontology to represent knowledge uniformly.

There are not only the user data and service flow in the ontology repository, but also the support for the ontology definition of application client. With the ontology modeling tools, users can deploy the definitions into the system, including the application interface, application data, relationships between interface and data, data management logic and service flow in workflow system. With the framework system it provides, the system will present the users data according to users' customization and drive the system with flow engine that supports ontology.

4 Ontology Representation in the System

Our system is based on ontology to define system framework, which consists of five sub-models: organization ontologies, resource ontologies, process ontologies, context ontologies and interface ontologies. Each of them has three levels representation as mentioned before.

There are different kinds of ontology definitions. In this article, we adopt the definition of ontology in reference [10]. An ontology is defined as a 5-tuple $O = \{CD,$

RD, FD, ID, AD}, in which CD is a set of class definitions, RD is a set of relation definitions, FD is a set of function definitions, ID is a set of instance definitions, and AD is a set of axiom definitions.

In the following, we will briefly introduce some main parts of abstract ontologies of the system.

4.1 Organization Ontologies

The organization model is the constituent in workflow description, and also includes the settings of authority, participators, roles and organizing structures. In most cases, the structure of common organization is a tree. So we here take is for an example to demonstrate the ontology of organization model. Of course we can support other kind of structures by adding corresponding ontology definitions into the ontology repository.

A tree organization structure can be defined as ontology: $O_t = \{C_t, R_t, F_t, I_t, A_t\}$.

In Which, C_t are organization unit classes definitions. R_t is relations between units. For a tree structure organization, there are two typical relations: $R_t = R_i \cup R_b$; $R_i = \{include\}$; $R_b = \{belongsTo\}$. A_t is set of axiom and rules correlative with C_t, R_t and I_t, like follows. The two kinds of relations are both transitive properties. That means, $R_t(x, y) \wedge R_t(y, z) \rightarrow R_t(x, z)$. These two relations are inversed to each other, i.e. $R_i(x, y)$ iff $R_b(y, x)$. Further more, there should be at least one root unit in the C_t: $\exists x C_t(x) \wedge \forall y C_t(y) \rightarrow \neg R_b(x, y)$. There should also be some other axioms, Classes and relations, for the limit of paper, we don't write too much here. The ontologies stated above can be represented in OWL form, like follows:

```
<owl:Class rdf:ID="OrgnizationUnit"/>
<owl:TransitiveProperty rdf:ID="Include">
  <owl:inverseOf>
    <owl:TransitiveProperty rdf:ID="belongsTo"/>
  </owl:inverseOf>
  <rdfs:range rdf:resource="# OrgnizationUnit "/>
  <rdfs:domain rdf:resource="# OrgnizationUnit "/>
</owl:TransitiveProperty>
<owl:TransitiveProperty rdf:about="#belongsTo">
  <rdfs:range rdf:resource=" OrgnizationUnit "/>
  <rdfs:domain rdf:resource=" OrgnizationUnit "/>
  <owl:inverseOf rdf:resource="#Include"/>
</owl:TransitiveProperty>
```

Similarly, we can define role ontology: $O_r = \{C_r, R_r, F_r, I_r, A_r\}$, user ontology: $O_u = \{C_u, R_u, F_u, I_u, A_u\}$. For O_r, C_r are role definitions and privilege definitions, R_r are properties of classes in C_r and relations between classes in C_r, as well as relations between C_r, C_t and C_u, etc. Namely, the ontology classes in the repository are pervasively related. For example, user class is C_u belongs to one or several unit that defined in C_t, $R_{belongstoU\ nit} = \{R(x, y) \mid x \in C_u, y \in C_t\}$. and user could have one or several roles that defined in C_r, $R_{hasRole} = \{R(x, y) \mid x \in C_u, y \in C_r\}$. There are also relations that only between classes in C_u, like collaboration relations. This is a kind of symmetric relation, means that: $R(x, y) \rightarrow R(y, x)$. There are so many ontologies in the repository that we can't enumerate them all here. Therefore, we only list some typical ones above. In the following, we only talk about key attribute of them instead of going into every detail.

4.2 Resource Ontologies

The workflow processes need various kinds of resources, including data, service software, hardware, etc. These resources can define their operation authority according to the organization structure depicted by ontology. We also introduce meta-data of business data into this part of ontologies. That would give the system more powerful ability of manipulating business data.

4.3 Process Model

Generally, the process modeling tools lack the methods of formal definition, and thus can not define the semantic and restriction in processes or support reasoning. Nevertheless, the process models based on ontology can describe the semantics of different actions and do the restriction modeling by restriction description language.

The models define here are based on enhanced Petri-net. The control structure ontologies support most common and advanced workflow patterns. Using ontology to depict workflow models can enhance workflow system with semantic functions. When some models need to change at runtime due to some emergency events, the system engine would find alternative solutions by reasoning and searching the ontology repository.

4.4 Context Ontologies

Context ontologies almost cover all aspects of the system, because the system must be aware of the context before it can make decision according to it. In this paper, we view context from two aspects: (1) business logic context or collaboration logic context, and (2) computing environment context in collaboration. They define the essential things that the system should know.

Collaboration logic context involves business scenarios through the entire cooperative work. Computing environment context mainly describe the work load, bandwidth, computer configuration, screen size, and so on.

4.5 Interface Ontologies

The interface ontologies define how system could be invoked. That enables the system to interact with other system.

There are also ontologies of a set of client application frames in it. For a customizable system, the ability to provide mechanisms to define user system could make the system more adaptive.

5 System Implementation

The system mainly consists of two major subsystems which are specification subsystem and execution subsystem. The specification subsystem provides the function to define ontology, which includes the ontology definition of service flows, ontology definition of service data and ontology definition of interfaces. The process of defining ontology is actually a process which expresses specific domain knowledge in a workflow framework that is domain irrelevant, and thus reflects the domain knowledge with ontology, which has high complexity. In the users' viewpoint, if the costs of building ontology repository are too high, the usability of the system will decrease greatly. Therefore, the system needs a set of ontology definition tools. Based on Protégé APIs, we can create such tools to define data and flows. With these tools, users can create domain ontology in a visible way and the system will also provide the necessary information. The execution subsystem mainly consists of workflow engine, client applications and monitor tools.

Workflow engine is the core of system while the ontology repository mining is the core function of workflow engine. The flow is defined as ontology, which is expressed in OWL. Thus the engine flow should be able to parse the definitions of service flows defined in ontology repository. In our system, the service flow would be modeled according to the Time-Extended and Hierarchy-Extended Petri Net [11].

By incorporating ontology repository, the workflow engine and client are irrelevant to specific domain knowledge. The domain knowledge can be added into the ontology repository in the system dynamically with ontology definition, and the knowledge can be shared among workflow engines and other client applications.

The workflow system provides not only the application programming interface, but also a set of customizable general application systems in client system. By distilling the application model oriented for database to construct the framework and with the ontology repository, this workflow client system transfers the relationship between system framework and domain knowledge from embedment to dynamic combination. When the service data, service flows and even the requirements for the application interface change, the system can expand dynamically by altering or extending the ontology repository, which enables the system domain and dynamic extensibility.

With the definition mechanisms of client system in ontology repository, we can dynamically add following objects into the system, such as interface elements, the relationship among interface elements, the relationship between interface elements and application data and relationship between interface elements and service flow. When the system is running, by parsing the domain ontology information in ontology repository, flow ontology information and client system ontology information, the application framework can distill the service data, present according to the definition in ontology, carry out the service logics and restriction rules represented by ontology, drive the flow with the interaction between client application interface and workflow engine and alter the service data and task state by workflow engine.

6 Work Procedure of Engine

When tasks are triggered by users or some kinds of system events, the engine of the system would create the data and object for the users according to the ontology definition. When users fetch the tasks, the engine would determine how to represent the data to the users according to the client application elements in the process ontology definition, and to make any restriction valid. When users complete the tasks, the engine would check whether the condition has been satisfied according to the process ontology definition. Once the tasks have been completed, the engine would create or make any modifications to the system business data according to the resource ontology and process ontology, and decide who is the next operator according to the organization ontology or the tasks have been finished.

7   Conclusion and Future Work

By introducing the ontology definition of domain knowledge into the ontology repository, the collaboration system we proposed in this article can increase the expression ability and apply to different domains, which enables the system's domain extensibility. When collaborative requirements change, users can modify or add ontology definitions in the ontology repository, and thus the system would have the ability to dynamically upgrade and expand. With the help of a set of visible ontology definition tools, user can define the relevant objects in a convenient and effective way, which increases the usability of the system. At last, because the system is ontology repository centered, it is a good foundation for different workflow systems to interact and cooperate.

In reference [12], Professor Reddy proposes a collaboration framework, which is named as Eksarva. This framework includes essential elements in collaborative environments, such as Person, Project, Place, Situation, Signal and Smart Transcript, and can be summarized as the "PPP/SST" model. With this kind of collaborative system, users can deploy his collaborative process more efficiently, in a workflow centric manner.

The system we proposed in this paper defines the essential elements of Eksarva in the ontology repository and extends the basic workflow engine, which makes a significant progress of Eksarva collaborative system.

References

1. Gruber, C.T.R.: A Translation Approach to Portable Ontologies. Knowledge Acquisition (1993) 199-220
2. Borst, W.N.: Construction of Engineering Ontologies for Knowledge Sharing and Reuse. PhD thesis. University of Twente, Enschede (1997)
3. Studer, R., Benjamins, V.R., Fensel, D.: Knowledge Engineering, Principles and Methods. Data and Knowledge Engineering (1998) 161-197
4. Guarino, N.: Formal ontology and information systems. Proceedings of the 1st Int. Conf. on Formal Ontology in Information Systems. Trento, Italy (1998) 13-15
5. Antoniou, G., van Harmelen, F.: Web Ontology Language: OWL. Handbook on Ontologies in Information Systems. Springer-Verlag (2003) 67-92
6. Beco, S., Cantalupo, B., Giammarino, L., Matskanis, N. and Surridge, M.: OWL-WS: A Workflow Ontology for Dynamic Grid Service Composition. Proceedings of the First International Conference on e-Science and Grid Computing (2005)
7. Wu, Y., Lu, J., Yao, S., Zheng, Z.: Mechanism of Semantic Oriented Flexible Workflow. Proceedings of the Third International Conference on Information Technology and Applications (2005)

8. Vieira T.A.S.C., Casanova, M.A., Ferrao, L.G.: An Ontology-driven Architecture for Flexible Workflow Execution. Proceedings of the Web Media & LA-Web 2004 Joint Conference 10th Brazilian Symposium on Multimedia and the Web 2nd Latin American Web Congress (2004) 70-77

9. WfMC Standards. URL: http://www.wfmc.org/standards/model.htm

10. Visser, P.R.S., Jones, D.M., Bench-Capon, T.J.M. and Shave, M.J.R.: Assessing Heterogeneity by Classifying Ontology Mismatches. Proc. FOIS'98. Trento, Italy (1998) 148-162

11. Wang, B., Zhang, S., Zhu, Y.: A Workflow Model Based on Time-Extended and Hierarchy-Extended Petri Net. Proceedings of the 8th International Conference on Computer Supported Cooperative Work in Design. Volume 2. Xiamen, China (2004) 318-322

12. Yu, J., Reddy, Y.V.R., Seliah, S., Bharadwaj, V., Reddy, S. and Kankanahalli, S.: A Workflow-Centric Context-Aware Collaboration framework. Proceedings of the 9th International Conference on computer Supported Cooperative Work in Design. Volume 1. Coventry, UK (2005) 514-519

New Data Integration Workflow Design for e-Learning

Shengtian Xi[1] and Jianming Yong[2]

[1] School of Management, Tianjin University
Tianjin, 300222, China
[2] Department of Information Systems
Faculty of Business, University of Southern Queensland, Australia
yongj@usq.edu.au

Abstract. E-learning has been adopted by more and more educational institutions to implement their new learning and teaching strategy around the world. Students can study their courses which could be run by different universities which run different e-learning platforms. A universal data integrated e-learning platform is essential to transparentise the significant difference among disparate data sources which are used by different e-learning systems. This paper proposes an effective data integration mechanism for e-learning system. At the same time security concerns are discussed. The workflow-based data integration approach is shown in this paper.

1 Introduction

E-learning is becoming one of most important educational means. As more and more educational organisations are moving into e-learning, more and more useful disparate data are distributed over the Internet. How to form a universal e-learning environment for all e-learning users becomes a challenge job. Like in the United States, an academic member is called a faculty member, sometimes directly called a faculty, while in the United Kingdom and Australia, a faculty has a totally different meaning, which is an academic organisation under the university. Also sometimes one same thing can be represented by different words, like in USA, an assistant professor has the same meaning as the British word, lecturer. These differences have caused a big confusion for the users of e-learning. In order to solve this problem, an effective mechanism of data integration for e-learning systems is definitely needed. WFMS-based data integration for e-learning is suggested and analysed to meet this challenge.

The reminder of the paper is organised as follows. Section 2 discusses workflow-based environment. Section 3 addresses general traditional approaches for data integration. Section 4 shows the architecture of data integration for e-learning and WFMS-based data integration is discussed. Section 5 discusses the security concerns to data integration for e-learning. Section 6 gives the conclusion remarks.

2 Workflow Environment for e-Learning

Workflow [1] has been used in many large organisations to control their business processes and business re-engineering. According to Workflow Management Coalition

W. Shen et al. (Eds.): CSCWD 2006, LNCS 4402, pp. 699–707, 2007.
© Springer-Verlag Berlin Heidelberg 2007

(WfMC) [2] , workflow focuses on handing business processes. It is concerned with the automation of procedures where information and tasks are passed between partici- pants according to a defined set of rules to achieve, or to contribute to, an overall busi- ness goal. It is often associated with business process re-engineering, which is concerned with the assessment, modeling, definition and subsequent operational im- plementation of the core business process of an organization (or other business entity). In order to implement an effective workflow system, WfMC has published its refer- ence model of the workflow system. In April 2000, Object Management Group (OMG) [3] also published its workflow management facility specification in order to use its CORBA and relevant technologies to implement workflow systems. The workflow mechanism has been used in e-learning design [9]. In [9], the e-learning system is modeled into four sub-systems, teaching workflow system, learning workflow system, admin workflow system, and infrastructure workflow system. These four sub- workflow systems need seamlessly work together to form an efficient e-learning envi- ronment. Furthermore a new e-learning system needs good connections with "legacy systems" which are used prior to an e-learning platform. With the extension of e-learning, more and more e-learning systems need more co-operations. All these con- nections and co-operations need involving in using diverse data sources [10]. It is essential to have a mechanism of data integration for e-learning systems.

3   Traditional Data Integration Approaches

The vast diversity of data sources for e-learning systems has put forward a big challenge for data integration. In [4], semantic and syntactic interoperability is very important for data integration. Semantic interoperability is the knowledge-level inter- operability that provides cooperating businesses with the ability to bridge semantic conflicts arising from differences in implicit meanings, perspectives, and assump- tions, thus creating a semantically compatible information environment based on the agreed concepts between different business entities. Syntactic interoperability is the application-level interoperability that allows multiple software components to cooper- ate even though their implementation languages, interfaces, and execution platforms are different. Syntactic interoperability gives a technology solution, while semantic interoperability provides semiotic, linguistic, philosophical, and social solutions. For aged care information systems, the focus will be put on the semantic interoperability because the aged care organisations definitely need accurately understanding all the semantic aspect of all the data sources, aged care records.

Previous research in semantic interoperability can be categorized into three broad ar- eas: mapping-based [5], intermediary-based [6-7], and query-oriented approaches [8].

- Mapping-based approach: The mapping-based approach attempts to construct mappings between semantically related information sources. It is usually ac- complished by constructing a federated (or global) schema and by establishing mappings between the federated (or global) schema and the participating local schemas.
- Intermediary-based approach: This approach depends on the use of intermediary mechanisms (e.g., mediators, agents, ontologies, etc.) to achieve interoperability.

- Query-oriented approach: The query-oriented approach is based on interoperable languages, most of which are either declarative logic-based languages or extended SQL. They are capable of formulating queries spanning several databases.

All three approaches depend on the schemes of databases. For e-learning systems, the data sources are far broader than databases. It is not enough to focus only on the database scheme integration.

The available data sources include databases, knowledge bases, traditional files, Web page files, email messages, maps and images, videos and audios. With the growing number of information sources available, the problem of exploiting and integrating distributed and heterogeneous data sources is becoming more and more critical. Data gathering and integration is the fundamental requirement for e-learning systems. Usually different organisations have different data sources. Even some organisations possibly have the same data sources, like the same databases, the format of these data sources might be in significantly different formats. It is essential to have an effective approach of data integration for the Internet-based e-learning systems. In the following section, we will demonstrate an effective architecture of data integration for e-learning systems.

4   Architecture of Data Integration for e-Learning System

It is hard to describe the very details of data integration for e-learning systems. In order to understand the essentials of data integration for e-learning systems, the following subsections are presented to address some issues of data integration for e-learning systems.

4.1   Data Formats of e-Learning System

In order to work out an effective way to integrate the data of e-learning systems, it is important to identify the data formats of e-learning systems. Generally speaking, all data are categorised into three categories: structured data, semi-structured data, and unstructured data.

Structured Data: Many systems use structured data to manage their large data sets, like relational database systems, object-oriented database systems. Currently Oracle, Sybase, MySQL, PostgreSQL, MS Access are popular DBMS systems for large systems or individual computers. Structured data is managed by technology that allows for querying and reporting against predetermined data types and understood relationships. Many large systems use structured data to manage their large amount of data. Most e-learning systems use structured data to manage their large volume data, like student records, administration information, course information, staff record, financial data, etc. These structure data can be well managed by its operating languages, like SQL.

Semi-structured Data: Semi-structured data is that the information is usually associated with a schema and contained within the data [11], like HTML files and XML files. E-learning systems are using more and more semi-structured data, Web pages and files, to communicate between instructors/lecturers, students/learners, administration staff and technical support people [9].

Unstructured Data: Except for structured and semi-structured data, some information is totally non- structure. Usually unstructured data have two categories, map files and text files. Map files are non-language based, such as image, video or audio files. Text files are based on a written or printed language, such as Microsoft Word documents, e-mails or Microsoft Excel spreadsheets. These unstructured data are widely used in e-learning systems by all participants.

4.2 Data Integration Between New e-Learning Systems and "Legacy" Systems

E-learning systems have been developed only in recent years. Many education organisations or institutions used their old systems, usually called "legacy systems", to manage their learning, teaching, and administration for many years prior to adopting modern e-learning systems. It is vital to seamlessly integrate useful data from "legacy" systems into new e-learning systems. There are two ways to do data integration: once-all and on-call. Once-all is an approach that all previous data transfer to new formats which are the same as e-learning systems. After once-all transfer, the old data of "legacy" systems can be discarded. On-call is an approach that only requested data are presented to new systems based on a mediated data integration tool, while all other data keep intact. On-call can make new e-learning systems and "legacy" systems running independently if necessary or needed. First approach is rarely used because of too much cost. The second approach is often used by organisations. Figure 1 shows the architecture of data integration for new e-learning systems and its "legacy" systems.

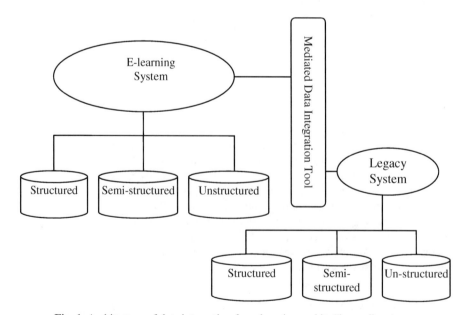

Fig. 1. Architecture of data integration for e-learning and its "legacy" systems

Mediated data integration tool (Mdtt) is a key component for data integration between e-learning and "legacy" systems. Mdtt has the capacity to process the structured data, semi-structured data and unstructured data respectively. It is a bridge across two systems to implement data integration.

4.3 Data Integration Between Different e-Learning Systems

From the learners' perspective, e-learning should be pervasive, whenever and wherever they want to access e-learning systems, they can get required and expected results in a consistent way. One of most important aspects is to achieve data integration across different e-learning systems. Currently most e-learning systems are connected by the Internet. In the networking environment, a term, architecture, can be used effectively to describe how heterogeneous systems work together while the technical details do not have to be addressed. Figure 2 shows an overall diagram of e-learning systems with a module of data integration. The data integration module is in charge of full data integration of all different data sources which belong to different e-learning systems.

The data integration module can handle all the different data sources, like database, knowledge base, semi-structure files, flat files, maps and images, videos and audios, etc. Based on different data sources, different approaches are used to implement the data integration for the e-learning systems. We do not want to discuss more technical details here. We just want to use an effective architecture to demonstrate the needs of data integration for the e-learning systems.

In order to describe the Internet as a whole for the e-learning, we do know there are countless data sources distributed over the Internet. Thus we use a logical architecture [10] to illustrate the overall data integrated systems over the Internet.

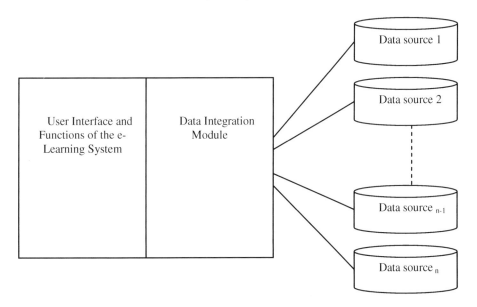

Fig. 2. Architecture of data integration for e-learning systems

4.4 WFMS-Based Data Integration Processes for e-Learning

So far data integration is still a tedious job and also involves a huge amount of labour work. In order to simplify the process of data integration for e-learning, we suggest a new approach, WFMS-based data integration for e-learning. Figure 3 shows the diagram of WFMS-based data integration for e-learning.

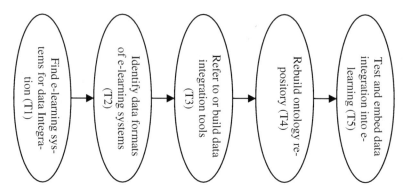

Fig. 3. Diagram of WFMS-based data integration for e-learning

Find e-learning Systems for Data Integration (Task 1): Task 1 is first step towards data integration for e-learning. At this step, the main objective is to establish a set (S) of e-learning systems for data integration. This is a dynamic process for individual systems. Prior to the start of data integration process, S is an empty set. With the more processes of task 1, more and more specific e-learning systems are added into the set, S. This process represents by the following models.

$S \leftarrow \phi$ Prior to data integration,

$S \leftarrow S1$ System S1 looking for data integration as an initiator,

$S \leftarrow S \cup Si \,\& \, Si \notin S$ More and more e-learning systems are added into the data integrated system.

Identify Data Formats of e-learning Systems (Task 2): After the completeness of Task 1, we assume an e-learning system, Si, is added for data integration, Task 2 needs staring to identify data formats (*df*) of Si. Si.*df* can have the following options.

    Si.*df*=only one of {structured, semi-structured, unstructured}, or
    Si.*df*=only two of {structured, semi-structured, unstructured}, or
    Si.*df*=all of {structured, semi-structured, unstructured}

Refer to or Build Data Integration Tools (Task 3): After the completeness of Task 2, Task 3 needs to build data integration tool for Si.*df* if data integration tool for Si.*df* does not exist yet. Otherwise if data integration tool for Si.*df* exists at data integrated e-learning system, task3 needs referring to existing tools.

Rebuild Ontology Repository (Task 4): Now the data ontology of e-learning system, Si, needs to be reflected in the central ontology repository (*OR*) for a unified e-learning system. This process can be modeled as the follows.

$$OR \leftarrow \phi$$
Prior to data integration,

$$OR \leftarrow S1.df.terms$$
System S1' terms as an initial ontology,

$$OR \leftarrow OR \cup Si.df.terms \ \& \ Si.df.terms \notin OR$$

More and more ontologies mapping are added into the central ontology repository.

For an example, there is an e-learning system in the United States, a course instructor can be an assistant professor. At another e-learning system in Australia, a course instructor usually is called a lecturer. In two systems, assistant professor and lecturer actually have the same meaning. If the mapping of these two terms has existed in *OR*, *OR* does not need to be rebuilt. Otherwise this new mapping has to be added into the central repository for data integration.

Test and Embed Data Integration into e-learning (Task 5): At this stage, the built functions of data integration for e-learning are needed testing and embedding into a universal e-learning platform. An overall e-learning architecture is shown in Figure 4.

5 Security Concern

Data integration for e-learning has brought a universal platform for the learners, instructors and administration staff. In Figure 4, any users can access e-learning system without any hurdlers. This puts e-learning in a very dangerous situation. If any individual system has a security hole, all connected e-learning system will be affected by this security hole. Through data integration, any security threats could be extended to all connected systems. This will deter the adoption of e-learning strategy. In order

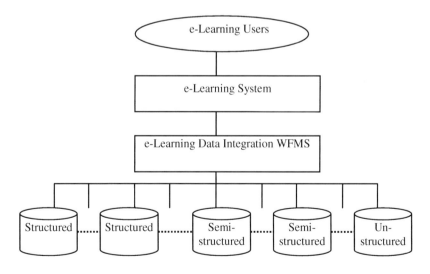

Fig. 4. Overall architecture of e-learning with the support of data integration

to overcome this security concern for data integration e-learning system, Neighbour-hood-Trust Dependency Access Control (NETDEPAL) [12] can be extended to cope this security concern. Figure 5 shows how the extended NETDEPAL works together with data integration workflow to make e-learning system more secure. Because the space limitation, there are no more details for extended NETDEPAL to be further discussed here.

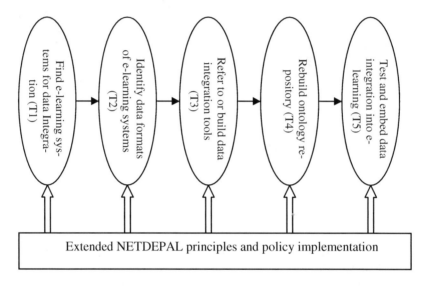

Fig. 5. Extended NETDEPAL acts on data integration workflow

6   Conclusion Remarks

This paper contributes a new modeled concept using WFMS principles to simplify data integration for e-learning. As more and more organisations are moving into e-learning and most disparate data are presented through different e-learning systems, data integration becomes a new challenge for establishing a universal e-learning environment. Through e-learning as an applicable application, data integration problem is well addressed and analysed. After security concerns are fixed by the extended NETDEPAL, data integrated e-learning system becomes more applicable. The princi-ples can be applied to other domains, like banking, health, aviation, etc. In the near future we will do some further implementations of data integration for e-learning and other application systems.

References

1. Yong, J. and Yang, Y.: Modeling and integration for Internet-based workflow systems. Proc. IASTED Int. Conf. on Internet and Multimedia Systems and Applications (IMSA2001). Hawaii, USA (2001) 345-350

2. Hollingsworth, D.: The Workflow Reference Model. WfMC-TC-1003. Version 1.1 (1995) URL: http://www.aiim.org/wfmc/standards/docs/tc003v11.pdf
3. OMG: Workflow Management Facility Specification. V1.2. (2003) URL: http://www.omg.org/docs/formal/00-05-02.pdf
4. Park, J. and Ram, S.: Information systems interoperability: What lies beneath? ACM Transactions on Information Systems 22(4) (2004) 595-632
5. Reddy, M.P., Prasad, B.E., Reddy, P.G. and Gupta, A.: A methodology for integration of heterogeneous databases. IEEE Trans. Knowledge Data Engineering 6(6) (1994) 920-933
6. Ouksel, M.and Klusch, M.: A framework for a scalable agent architecture of cooperating heterogeneous knowledge sources. In: Intelligent Information Agents: Agent-Based Information Discovery and Management on the Internet. Springer, Berlin, Germany (1999) 100-124
7. Kahng, J. and Mcleod, D.: Dynamic classificational ontologies: Mediation of information sharing in cooperative federated database systems. In: Cooperative Information Systems: Trends and Directions. Academic Press, San Diego, CA (1998) 179-203
8. Lakshmanan, L.V.S., Sadri, F. and Subramanian, I.N.: Logic and algebraic languages for interoperability in multidatabase systems. Journal of Logic Programming 33(2) (1997) 101-149
9. Yong, J.: Workflow-based e-learning platform design. Proc. 9th International Conference on Computer Supported Cooperative Design. Coventy, UK (2005) 1002-1007
10. Yong, J. and Yang, Y.: Data integration over the Internet for e-commerce. Proc. IASTED International Conference on Communications Systems and Applications (CSA'03). Banff, Alberta, Canada (2003) 253-258
11. Buneman, P.: Semistructured Data. Proc. ACM Symposium on Principles of Database Systems (PODS'97). Tucson, Arizona, USA (1997) 117-121
12. Yong, J.: Neighbourhood-Trust Dependency Access Control for WFMS. Proc. 10th International Conference on Computer Supported Cooperative Design. Nanjing, China (2006) 924-928

Design and Implementation of a Cooperative Editing System Based on Natural Language Processing

Shaoyong Yu, Shaozi Li[*], and Donglin Cao

Institute of Artificial Intelligence, Xiamen University, Xiamen, P.R. China
szlig@xmu.edu.cn

Abstract. As collaborative editing systems are becoming more and more prevalent, new requirements on collaboration are raised by users. This paper presents a novel editing system based on natural language processing, which has been used in Chinese language teaching. The proposed approach has addressed a number of problems existed in textbook editing, e.g., in order to improve the speed and accuracy of automatic phonetic notation, a method of Chinese text segmentation has been proposed; corpus retrieval is applied in the system for selection of suitable sample sentences for new words; also, in order to control the amount and recurrence rate of new words, a method of cross-text search and computing is adopted. The feedback of users has indicated that the system indeed reduces the time spent in editing collaboration.

1 Introduction

Textbook is key to teaching Chinese language as a foreign language. It dominates the effect of teaching. Thus, how to guarantee its quality has become the focus of domestic and foreign experts. Some achievements have been made, but with the development of outward Chinese language teaching, higher quality of textbooks is required. A scholar called Jianqin Wang pointed out that the modernization of textbooks, including modernization of editing concept, design pattern, means of editing and representation media is the way of innovation, then he proposed an editing pattern based on network [1]. At the same time, for most of the published textbooks, there are defects such as excessive new words, low recurrence rate of words, unsuitable example sentences and unevenly distributed language points, which affect Chinese language the teaching efficiency and effectiveness.

A number of systems have been designed to meet the requirements of collaborative editing, such as ZU-CoEditor [2] from Zhejiang University, DCA (Distributed Cooperative Editing) [3] and DMCW (Distributed Multimedia Cooperative Writing) [4] from Tsinghua University and a cooperative editing system based on J2EE Technology [5] from Shanghai University. There are also a number of foreign experts dedicated systems like AllianceWeb, COARSY (Collaborative Asynchronous Review System), WebDAV, PINS [6-7][10-11].

All these systems have done a lot of works in collaboration to improve efficiency, but all the collaborations focus on network model and work flow. The most important problem is that they do not reduce the time in inter-editor collaboration which is more

---

[*] Corresponding author.

W. Shen et al. (Eds.): CSCWD 2006, LNCS 4402, pp. 708–716, 2007.
© Springer-Verlag Berlin Heidelberg 2007

common in editing action. Editing action needs more natural language processing (NLP) collaboration between editors. This problem can not be solved only by network model and work flow. In order to make inter-editor collaboration more efficient, we investigate some inter-editor collaboration problems in Chinese collaborative editing system, and develop a collaborative multimedia editing system for Chinese language teaching material editor.

In the following sections, we will first introduce the whole system architecture and some key mechanisms that used in the system. Next we present functions used to solve the problems occur in textbook authoring and related algorithms. At the end, we give conclusions and our future work.

2   Design of System Based on Middleware

2.1   The Architecture of System

A typical collaborative editing system model is shown as Figure 1:

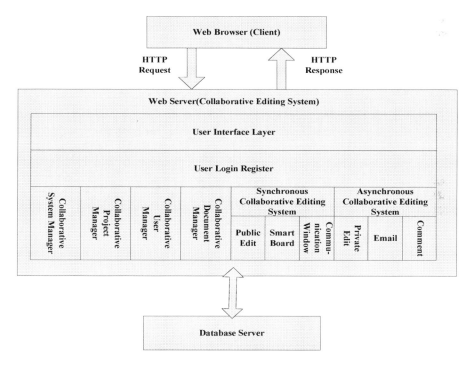

Fig. 1. A typical cooperative editing system model

The information sharing means editors would share some important materials with each other to enrich the document, the document feature computing is to check works to find out the redundancy of the document, and the Information tagging means one editor can use other editors' material to describe some concepts during editing.

In typical model, we can collaborate artificially through network communication tools such as BBS or Email, but for the document feature computing and information tagging, there are lack of the support of collaboration which is necessary. The document feature computing is very important because by statistical computing and contrast quickly between editors, editors can reduce repeated work. And through information tagging and sharing automatically, it can reduce the work of explaining some basic conceptions. These problems can not be solved essentially only by typical model and work flow, because it also relates to the natural language processing.

Considering the editing action of editors, we need to add the Shallow Nature Language Parsing to analyze the text in documents, and to realize Document Information Sharing and Computing quickly. So far, our model is shown as Figure 2.

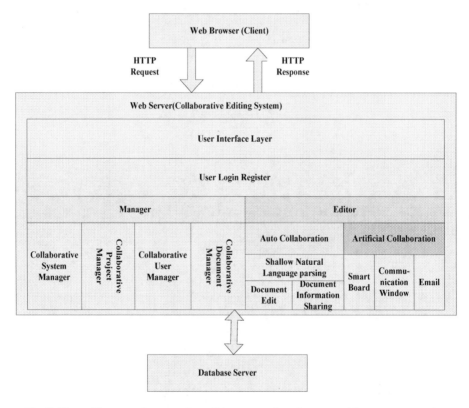

Fig. 2. The architecture of cooperative editing system based on natural language processing

We add the Role Manager in the system to detail correlative function of every role. For the role of editor, the system uses the Shallow Nature Language Parsing to realize the auto-collaboration. Through the Shallow Nature Language Parsing, we can implement the Document Information Share which is based on the document feature computing and information tagging. And make Document Edit more efficiency.

2.2 Collaborative Mechanisms in System

From the experience of co-working in daily life, we can get a conclusion that human resource management and a platform for information exchange are some of the most important facts that affect the efficiency of group work. Our collaborative mechanisms of system are designed based on the above facts.

For human resource management, we divide all the users into four groups, then different groups are given different privileges, so different users can access different parts of the system. Roles in the system are shown in Table 1.

Table 1. Roles in cooperative editing system

Roles	Privilege
Administrator	Administration of users, projects, corpus and forums
Chief Editor	Project management, task assignment, operations on chapters
Editor	Editing of assigned chapters
Commentator	Chapter review

There are two situations for information exchange, synchronous and asynchronous. To realize synchronous information exchange, we designed a sharing work area on which all the editors can work at the same time. In order to help editors to feel the existence of each other, two functions are provided: (1) Dynamic cursor, each cursor is identified by a 3-tuple "paragraph name, user ID, role", showing the role of its owner and the referred paragraph for the time being; (2) Multicolor text, it can help editors to learn what others have done. [12]

For asynchronous information exchange, the system has functions like forum, email and chatting room. By means of these functions, users can communicate with each other on line or off line.

2.3 Document Management

The process of authoring is indefinite, editors should revise their documents more than once, still the last revised version may not be the most satisfying one, so a authoring system should give supports to document version management. "file name + revised date" was used to identify different versions of the same document. Description information, which help editors to know where has been changed in document, is supported together with different version of document. [9][13] So each time, when an editor modify a document, description is compulsory to be filled.

Another function that is worth to refer to is the comparison of two documents. Documents are compared on a line basis in the same window, and the differences will be shown in highlight.

3 Key Techniques Based on NLP Applied in Editor

The authoring of textbooks for outward Chinese language teaching is different from that of common documents. In addition to supports for text, paragraph, audio and video, functions like automatic phonetic notation, generation of vocabulary, statistic on difficulty and frequency of new words, query of example sentences and generation of courseware on web are indeed necessary. A document server is created to handle the extra functions above.

When a client user want to use the services, he/she must first download an ActiveX component, then the component is responsible for the requests, it pass the request to the document server and then receive the response, at last, it hands the response to client user. The whole process is depicted in Figure3.

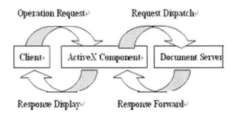

Fig. 3. The operation flow between client and server

Techniques in natural language processing, corpus, J2EE and component programming were well combined to implement all functions for Chinese language teaching. The following sections will give a detailed description.

3.1   Chinese Text Segmentation Based on HMM

In Microsoft Word, a function called "phonetic notation guide" that can help to give phonetic notations, but it has three shortages: (1) notation process is manual; (2) only 30 words are allowed each time; (3) in case of polyphone, it will make mistakes and has no chance to correct. In order to solve the above problems, a function, which can notate infinitely long text automatically with a high accuracy, is provided. The reason why a word is incorrectly notated is the word is not properly segmented. So if we want to increase the phonetic notation correctness, correctness of word segmentation should be improved first. We will now introduce how to improve the performance of phonetic notation.

As we know, basically, there are three kinds of segmentation methods for Chinese words. They are methods based on string match, understanding of the whole sentence and statistics respectively. The method based on understanding should make use of a mass of language knowledge and information. But it is difficult to transform all kinds of language information into machine-readable form for the ambiguity and complexity of Chinese language. So, this kind of method is still at an experimental stage. In our system, string match methods with statistics method are combined to implement the segmentation. The process is shown in Figure 4.

As is shown in Figure 4, a text is segmented according to the machine vocabulary in the way of reverse string match, so it will be segmented into different kinds of segmentation. We then use Part of Speech Tagging method which is the key idea of improving segmentation. Taking grammar information into consideration, this method will surely be effective.

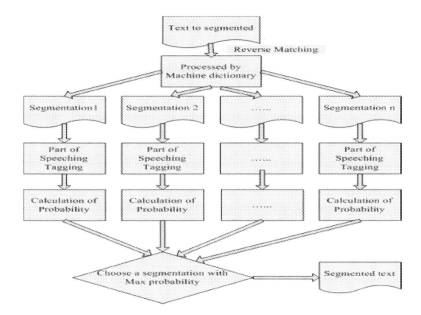

Fig. 4. The process of text segmentation

Part of Speech Tagging method is implemented based on HMM; its general idea is depicted as follows.

At first, a tagged corpus is used to get transfer probability table and emission probability table. Then we tag a sentence like this: let $w_{1,n}$ are words from the first to the nth, $t_{1,n}$ are the corresponding part of speech., $P(t_{1,n} \mid w_{1,n})$ is the probability of $w_{1,n}$ being tagged as $t_{1,n}$, $P(w_{1,n} \mid t_{1,n})$ is the probability of the sentence being constituted of $w_{1,n}$, when it is tagged as $t_{1,n}$. $P(t_{1,n})$ is the probability of a sentence being tagged as $t_{1,n}$. $P(w_{1,n})$ is the probability of a sentence being constituted of $w_{1,n}$, T represents the best part of speech tagging series.

$$T = \arg\max_{t_{1,n}} P(t_{1,n} / w_{1,n})$$

$$= \arg\max_{t_{1,n}} \frac{P(w_{1,n} \mid t_{1,n})P(t_{1,n})}{P(w_{1,n})}$$

$$= \arg\max_{t_{1,n}} P(w_{1,n} \mid t_{1,n})P(t_{1,n}) \tag{1}$$

and $P(w_{1,n} \mid t_{1,n})P(t_{1,n})$ in equation (1) equals:

$$\prod_{i=1}^{n} P(w_i \mid t_{1,n}) * P(t_n \mid t_{1,n-1}) * P(t_{n-1} \mid t_{1,n-2}) * \dots * P(t_2 \mid t_1)$$

$$= \prod_{i=1}^{n} P(w_i \mid t_i) * P(t_n \mid t_{1,n-1}) * P(t_{n-1} \mid t_{1,n-2}) * \dots * P(t_2 \mid t_1)$$

$$= \prod_{i=1}^{n} [P(w_i \mid t_i) * P(t_i \mid t_j)] \tag{2}$$

Specially, we define $P(t_1 \mid t_0) = 1.0$, and $P(w_i \mid t_i)$, $P(t_i \mid t_j)$ can be derived from transfer probability table and emission probability table which we calculate from tagged corpus.

The above algorithm can solve the problem of part of speech tagging, at the meantime, the sentence is also segmented.

3.2 Corpus Retrieval

The usage of some new words should be demonstrated by example sentence, which will help students to understand the words well. In traditional way, the author will give the example sentences just by his intuition, which will make the book unsuitable for students. But with corpus, a database of oral and written samples of language that appear naturally, the author can choose relatively difficult example sentences that suitable for students. We will now present an effective algorithm for indexing and retrieving the corpus, with which authors can derive example sentences at a satisfying degree.

We first index the tagged corpus with reverse-order file and hash file. Reverse-order file was organized as follows:

Word+The first place where the word appears in the corpus+
The place where the word appears in the sentence+
The place where the following same word appears in reverse-order file.

The hash file structure is as follows:

Word+The last place where the word appears in the reverse-order file+
The number of sentences that contain this word+
The place where the word appears in hash file.

We will get the reverse-order file by scanning the whole corpus once and then get the hash file by scanning the reverse-order file once. Indexing Corpus in this way will highly improve the performance of retrieval. All the retrieval results are returned and displayed according to the degree of similarity. A new model evolved from the model used in [8] was proposed to measure the similarity of two sentences. This model takes both the similarity of word forms and order of words into consideration, it is discussed as follows: let A represent the sentence to be inquired, B is one of the sentences in corpus, the similarity of word forms

$$FormSim(A, B) = \frac{Same(A, B)}{Len(A)} \tag{3}$$

$Same(A, B)$ in equation (3) represents the number of words both in A and B, $Len(A)$ is the number of words in sentence A..

The similarity of word order $OrderSim(A, B) =$

$$\begin{cases} 1 - \dfrac{\operatorname{Re} vOrd(A, B)}{|Once(A, B)| - 1}, while\ |Once(A, B)| > 1 \\ 1, while\ |Once(A, B)| = 1 \\ 0, while\ |Once(A, B)| = 0 \end{cases} \tag{4}$$

Here, $Once(A, B)$ is a set of words that appear only once in both A and B. Let **Vfirst(A,B)** represents the vector whose elements are the positions of words of $Once(A, B)$ in sentence A, **Vsecond(A,B)** represents the vector whose elements are the positions of words of $Once(A, B)$ in sentence B, $\operatorname{Re} vOrd(A, B)$ is the number of reverse order in **Vsecond(A,B)**.

The similarity of sentence A and B is then defined as

$Sim(A, B) = \alpha * FormSim(A, B) + \beta * OrderSim(A, B), here \alpha + \beta = 1$

Generally speaking, the similarity of word form is more important than that of word order, so we have $\alpha \gg \beta$.

3.3 Cross-Text Search and Computing

At present, few of the authors of textbooks for outward Chinese teaching can analyze language points in a way of computation and then make corresponding adjustments and controls, which will improve the quality of textbooks. Some experts realized this situation, and pointed out that excessive new words and low recurrence rate of words is the common problems that existed in published textbooks.

In order to improve the situation of low recurrence of new words, a function for counting the frequencies of words is provided, which can give detailed information about what words appear in a lesson and how frequent they are.

In some lessons, there may be some words which are not in vocabulary. If the amount of words like this is too big, it will bring down the quality of textbook. So a function is offered to calculate the proportions of all ranks of words according to HSK (Chinese language proficiency rank program), and different rank of words are highlighted in different colors. It is easy for authors to judge whether lessons are scientific or not.

In addition to the functions discussed above, this system also has some other characteristics, for example, automatic generation of vocabulary, chapters consolidation, and generation of electronic courseware.

4   Conclusion and Future Work

In this paper, we proposed a novel authoring system for teaching Chinese language as a foreign language, which provide not only collaborative mechanisms but also lots of useful functions aimed at solving the existed problems in some published textbooks. Some algorithms for improving the accuracy of words segmentation and increasing the efficiency of corpus retrieval are also discussed. The whole system is designed in a loosely coupled manner based on J2EE technology. So it can be easily extended.

One problem has not been solved in this system, i.e., an author can only learn what others have done to a chapter only when he/she is online. We expect that even if an author is off line, there should be a mechanism to help him/her to know what others have done. We are now considering a solution for off-line authors being informed of what others done through an automatic email. And this email should contain detailed information about where and what have been done by which author. Implementation of this function will greatly increase the degree of collaboration.

Acknowledgements. This project is supported by the Natural Science Fund of Fujian Province (Project Number: A0310009), the 985 Innovation Project on Information Technique of Xiamen University (2004-2007), and Academician Fund of Xiamen University, China.

References

1. Lu, W.: Design and Implementation of a Web-based Multimedia Cooperative Authoring System for Teaching Chinese as a Foreign Language. Proc. Eighth International Conference on Chinese Teaching. Beijing, China (July 2005)
2. Lu, D., Bao H. and Pan Y.: Research on Key Technology of Multimedia Cooperative Authoring. Journal on Communications 20(9) (1999) 41-46
3. Pei, Y., Shi,Y. and Xu, G.: A Cooperative Authoring System based on Distributed Computing. Journal of Tsinghua University (Science and Technology) 40(1) (2000) 76-79
4. Xie, S., Zhang, L. and An, C.: Design and Implementation of Distributed Multimedia Cooperative Authoring. Journal of Tsinghua University (Science and Technology) 37(9) (1997) 20-23
5. Wang, C., Zhao Z. and Yin, X.: A New Cooperative Authoring System Based on J2EE. Computer Engineering 29(13) (2003) 95-98
6. Decouchant, D., Favela, J., Martinez-Enriquez, A.M.: PINAS: A middleware for Web distributed cooperative authoring. Proc. 2001 Symposium on Applications and the Internet. San Diego, CA (Jan 2001) 187-194
7. Decouchant, D., Martinez, A.M.: AllianceWeb: Cooperative Authoring on the WWW. Proc. CRIWG'99, International Workshop on Groupware. Cancun, Mexico (1999)
8. Lv, X., Ren F. and Huang, Z.: Sentence Similarity Model and the Most Similar Sentence Search Algorithm. Journal of Northeastern University 24(6) (2003) 531-534
9. Moran, A.L., Favela, J., Martinez, A.M. and Decouchant, D.: Document Presence Notification Services for Collaborative Writing. Proc. CRIWG'2001, 7th International Workshop on Groupware. Darmstadt, Germany (2001) 125-133
10. Decouchant, D., Martinez, A.M.: A Cooperative, Deductive, and Self-Adaptive Web Authoring Environment. Proc. Mexican International Conference on Artificial Intelligence (MICAI'2000). Lecture Notes in Artificial Intelligence 1793 (2000) 443-457
11. Decouchant, D., Martinez, A.M. and Martinez, E.: Documents for Web Cooperative Authoring. Proc. CRIWG'99, 5th International Workshop on Groupware. Cancun, Mexico (1999) 286-295
12. Weihl, W.E.: The impact of recovery on concurrency control. Journal of Computer and System Sciences 47 (1993) 157-184
13. Wodtke, D., Weissenfels, J., Weikum, G. and Dittrich, A.K.: The MENTOR Project: Steps towards Enterprise-Wide Workflow Management. Proc. 12th International Conference on Data Engineering (1996)

"SmartContext": An Ontology Based Context Model for Cooperative Mobile Learning

Bin Hu and Philip Moore

Department of Computing, UCE Birmingham,
Birmingham, B42 2SU, UK
bin.hu@uce.ac.uk, C00625820@students.uce.ac.uk

Abstract. Context technology is a core component in cooperative mobile applications. Based on our research project "A Context Framework for Personalised Mobile Learning in Pedagogic Systems", this paper presents a semantic context model called "SmartContext", which includes a standardised context template, a context reasoning ontology and a context middleware to investigate a solution for supporting cooperative mobile learning. The integration of "SmartContext" with the current e-learning system in University of Central England is also included in this paper.

1 Introduction

With the increasing availability of mobile devices in every day life, the convergence of mobile communications and handheld computers [1] and the popularisation of wireless mobile devices [3], mobile learning (m-learning) is emerging as an important aspect of e-learning. One key benefit of m-learning is the potential for increased efficacy with learning being available "anywhere" and "anytime" [4]. Mobile devices have the power to make learning widely available and accessible, which is a natural extension to the e-learning paradigm. Imagine the power of learning that is truly "just-in-time," where access to training is available at a "precise time and place for a specific job as it is needed" [4] with learning not confined to "pre-specified times or places" [1] and is possible at the time and the place and in the order of topics that the learner wants.

A key feature in m-learning and e-learning is the emphasis on cooperative learning. "Computer Supported Cooperative learning (CSCL)" [5] is defined as groups working together for a common purpose; its aim being to investigate innovative ways of enhancing students cooperative learning based on computer supported pedagogies. Research into CSCL covers not only groupware techniques but also the "social, psychological, organisational, and learning effects" [5].

There are research projects that concentrate on mobile cooperative learning technologies. Examples are "HandLeR" [1], "KidStory" [7] and "Hunting of the Snark" [2]. "HandLeR" was aimed at enabling children aged 9–11 to capture learning events in a specific field, annotation, sharing and organisation of the learning events into learning resources and the direct communication with other learners or teachers. The "KidStory" project aimed to developing technologies that facilitated children working

W. Shen et al. (Eds.): CSCWD 2006, LNCS 4402, pp. 717–726, 2007.
© Springer-Verlag Berlin Heidelberg 2007

together to share ideas, and co-construct stories. "Hunting of the Snark" was a technology-augmented children's adventure game for pairs of children aged 7 to 8 designed to *"encourage playful learning through the developing a novel environment that engaged children in collaborative, exploratory and reflective activities"* [2]. Sharples [1] discussed and evaluated a working prototype system for children aged 9-11 to capture everyday events such as notes, images and sounds and to relate them to web-bases learning resources as an exemplar of personal mobile systems for lifelong learning.

Context plays a key role in these projects. In m-learning, context is the set of suitable environmental states and settings based on situated roles between a learner and tutor. These states and settings are relevant for context-sensitive learning systems that provide services and information adaptively based on a defined context. Nourish [6] suggests that the notion of context has a dual origin, technical and social science based. The technical "notion" relates to the relationship between human action and computational systems, the social science "notion" relating to the social setting. The observations of Nourish [6] have a corollary with computational aspects of higher education, the heterogeneous student cohort and the requirements addressed by personalised mobile learning.

This paper is based on our project, "A Context Framework for Personalised Mobile Learning in Pedagogic Systems", which investigates some key issues relevant to creating a contextual, cooperative and ambient mobile learning environment that provides cost free services to learners and tutors in 9 campuses in University of Central England (UCE) using local networks. The aim of the project is to develop an ontology based context model, called "SmartContext", to support cooperative mobile learning. The first step is to implement a standardised context template for description of user context. The following work is to develop a context reasoning ontology and a context middleware applicable in e-learning systems to match mobile user's context with those of backend services.

In this paper, Section 2 describes the "SmartContext", which covers a context template, a context reasoning ontology, and a context middleware. Section 3 discusses the integration to our e-learning system. Section 4 demonstrates a prototype and draws a comparison with some research in this field. Section 5 is a conclusion of our work.

2 "SmartContext"

The goal of the project is to develop a platform to assist in the effective implementation of context sensitive services to mobile learners/tutors. Figure 1 presents a model representing context sensitive services to learners and tutors.

2.1 Mobile Contextual Content Service

The principal motivation for this service is the provision of an intelligent, situation-dependent, customized, personalised information service to mobile learners/tutors based on heterogeneous backend resources. There are two key computer systems supporting the pedagogic systems in the School of Computing and Information at UCE, these are the School of Computing Asynchronous Network (SCAN) and "moodle".

SCAN is an on-line course management system whose facilities include module descriptions, teaching and learning resources, discussion databases and an on-line notice board. "moodle" is an open-source virtual learning environment supporting on-line, and partly on-line course delivery.

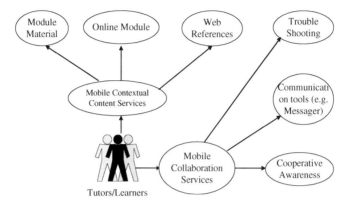

Fig. 1. Context sensitive services to learners/tutors

A contextual content service should involve the process of gathering a user's situated role (context) during the system's interaction with the user. The context is then used to select and deliver appropriate learning content services and resources tailored to the user's needs. Contextual content services are related to two key concepts, *customisation* and *personalisation*. A distinction must be drawn between customisation and personalisation.

- **Customisation:** occurs when the user can configure an interface and create a profile manually, adding and removing elements in the profile. The control of the look and / or content is explicit and is user-driven, i.e. the user is actively involved in the process and has control.
- **Personalisation:** is a condition where the user is seen as being passive, or at least somewhat less in control. It is the system that monitors, analyses and reacts to the user's situated role and behaviour. For example, content offered can be based on tracking surfing decisions.

In our project, there are the following contexts related to a mobile contextual content service:

- **Personal context:** this is part of the user context and consists of two subparts, the *physiological* and the *mental* context. The first part can contain information such as name, address, nationality, weight, height, hair colour etc with the latter part containing information such as mood, experience, interest, and habits etc. Some types of contextual information are quite static while others are fairly dynamic.
- **Task context:** this context describes users learning/teaching activities in a user context. A task context can be defined employing registered modules, specialized subjects, and goals etc.

- **Role context:** it describes a collaboration role that a learner/tutor plays in learning. The context includes his/her role (questioner, supervisor, advisor) and the areas of his/her expertise.
- **Spatio-temporal context:** this context type describes aspects of a learner/tutor's context relating to the time and spatial extent. It can contain attributes like: time, location, schedule etc.

2.2 Mobile Collaboration Service

This service is to provide a cooperative learning platform with a tool set servicing mobile learners/tutors. Learners/tutors can construct a virtual group and ask for or provide a mutual trouble shooting service. In such a service awareness plays an essential role with the ability to track the learner/tutor state and activity. Contexts related to awareness can be concluded to be as follows:

- **Activity awareness:** this relates to a learner/tutors' actions and traces in learning activities.
- **State awareness:** information on the current state of tutors/learners is very useful when a decision has to be made about when and how contact is made.
- **Social awareness:** it includes social aspects of a current learner/tutor. It contains information of his/her friends, colleagues, and other acquaintances.
- **Process awareness:** in order to follow learning/teaching procedure, a learner/tutor needs such process awareness to know the situation of learning/teaching materials and a sense of how and where his/her situation fits into the whole picture, what is the next step, and what needs to be done to move the process a step forward, etc.

2.3 The Context Template

Based on the above discussion, a context template sounds an essential requirement in this project. Additionally the context template should be standardised and domain oriented incorporating adequate flexibility to accommodate the heterogeneous requirements of learners/tutors. A context template is the means of unifying two seemingly conflicting goals, (1) the provision of a sufficiently generic context model to suit a potentially unlimited range of domains and (2) the ability to enable application developers to target contexts related to their particular application domain. Consequently the template will provide "added value" to application developers whilst improving the speed and performance of the context middleware. Having a standardised context structure within a domain such as mobile learning will also increase efficiency as an application only needs to relate to data structures that are known to it as they will be application specified being tailored to suit a specific application. Additionally a standardised context structure would make context operations less error prone.

Consider the context-matching algorithm because in the project context middleware needs to match suitable services to learner/tutor needs. If the context structure is not standardised, the matching algorithm has to accept two context structures. For example in the one structure if the "location" attribute does not exist the foundation for matching would be missing, and the algorithm would generate errors.

In our project, the context template provides a RDF (Resource Description Framework) based pattern such that all contexts that are added to a context space must be compliant to this template. Figure 2 presents a RDF class description of the context template.

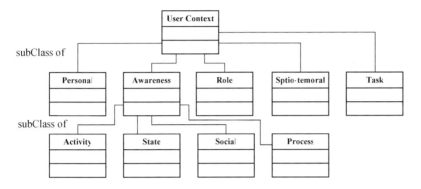

Fig. 2. An RDF description of the Context Template

Scenario: online collaboration service

- Bob has some questions about Java while he is writing the course work of A1J.
- Bob sends the help message with the question to the agent in context tag in the library.
- The agent in context tag in the library checks his context and fetches some useful contexts e.g. language preferable (English), his module name, and appreciate communication tool (Messenger) etc.
- The agent in context tag in the library sends the help message with Bob's context to other context tags located at staff office, student accommodation and other campus.
- The agent in context tag in the office matches Bob's context and his help message with his tutor -- Steven's context but is aware of his offline state.
- The agent in context tag in the office sends the message back to Bob through the agent in context tag in the library.
- The agent in context tag in the student accommodation matches Bob's context and his help message with Lisa's context and is aware of her online state.
- After negotiation, Lisa agrees to help Bob and the agent in context tag in the student accommodation sends the message to Bob.
- Bob is satisfied to consult Lisa about the question and the agent in his PDA sends a message to Lisa through the context tags in library and student accommodation.
- The agents in their PDA start Messenger and they start chatting.
- The agents in their PDA record their activities into context space using context middleware.
- The agents in context tags in the library and the student accommodation identify their context changed then update locally and execute synchronizing operation with agents in context tags in other locations.

Bobs context can be described as follows using the context template:

```xml
<xml version="1.0"?>
<rdf:RDF xmlns rdf=http://www.w3.org/1999/02/22-rdf-syntax-ns#
xmlns:uce=http://apollo.students.uce.ac.uk/mlearning/1.0/usercontext#>
<rdf:Description rdf:about="
http://apollo.students.uce.ac.uk/mlearning/1.0/usercontext/personal">
    <uce:firstname>Bob</uce:firstname>
    < uce:gender>Male< /uce:gender>
    <uce:language>English</uce:language>
    < uce:gender>Male< /uce:gender>
    <uce:language>English</uce:language>
</rdf:Description>
<rdf:Description rdf:about="
http://apollo.students.uce.ac.uk/mlearning/1.0/usercontext/task">
    <uce:module>A1J</uce:module>
    < uce:subject>JAVA</uce:subject>
</rdf:Description>
<rdf:Description rdf:about="
http://apollo.students.uce.ac.uk/mlearning/1.0/usercontext/sptio-
temporal">
    <uce:location>Library</uce:location>
</rdf:Description>
</rdf:RDF>
```

User context (like Bob's) is an instance of the context template, which means a context must be compliant to the context template. When a user registers on the system a default context instance will be created in terms of the context template. Consequently context middleware (see Section 2.5) will populate the context instance with values derived from relevant data collected from a user, this data representing his or her profile and trace record.

2.4   The Context Reasoning Ontology

The context reasoning ontology in "SmartContext" plays an extremely important role which combines context template to define the vocabularies for representing semantic links between classes and for supporting the context reasoning. A xml syntax based ontology using RDF/RDFS [8] has been developed in our project. In terms of the above scenario, a brief context reasoning ontology can be represented as Figure 3.

The properties in the ontology create the semantic links between classes. A reasoning algorithm has been implemented based on the ontology. An example is given based on the online collaboration service.

A1: Personal("Bob") IsLocatedAt Building("library")
It means Bob is in the library at the campus.
Its RDF/RDFS representation is:
```xml
<uce:Personal
rdf:about="http://apollo.students.uce.ac.uk/mlearning/1.0/usercontext/pe
rsonal/Bob">
<uce:IsLocatedAt
rdf:about="http://apollo.students.uce.ac.uk/mlearning/1.0/usercontext/Sp
tio-termoral/building/library">
</uce:Personal>
```

A2: Personal("Bob") HasAcquaintance Name("Lisa")
A3: Personal("Lisa") IsAtState State("Online")
A4: Personal("Lisa") HasActivity Activity("consulting")
A5: Activity("consulting") IsTaskAt Subject("Java")
A2+A3+A4+A5 => "Lisa is an appreciate advisor on Java and available".

The reasoning procedure is executing with a reasoning package, which is integrated with the context middleware in the implementation of Jena [9].

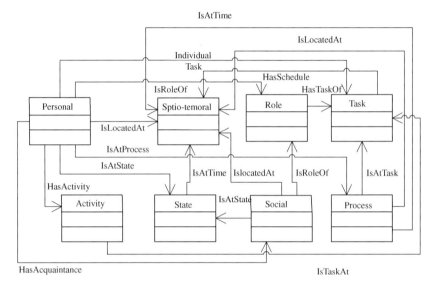

Fig. 3. A graph representation of the context reasoning ontology

2.5 The Context Middleware

The Context Middleware in "SmartContext" is responsible for efficient and appropriate storage, retrieval of any given context, and context reasoning. The component provides a common interface for interaction with context.

Before we discuss the detailed functionalities of context middleware, a notion "context space" has to be introduced. The context space means the complete set of contexts that is stored together in an electronic repository. The context space can be viewed as a database of past context, future contexts, and the current context. In context space, some contexts are more or less similar to each other. It is therefore possible to compare contexts, add contexts, delete contexts and also merge contexts within the context space.

Based on context space, the context middleware has implemented the following functionalities:

- **Context Template Function:** includes basic operations on the context template, for example, add, delete, search, get, etc.

- **Context Function:** as for Context Template Function it provides some basic operations on context but also including some advanced functionalities such as context merging, context matching, context synchronising, context reasoning etc.

One scenario of the above functionalities is context merging. Context merging is the process where two or more contexts are merged to create one new context. There may be situations where the context change process is presented with several contexts as input. This results in an activation of the context-merging component to determine the possibility of creating a new current context from the incoming contexts and the current context. The merging process uses a rule-based procedure.

3   Integration with the Current E-Learning System

The above sections have discussed the three critical parts in "SmartContext": a context template, a context reasoning ontology and a context middleware. In this section, a system architecture (Figure 4) in the project will be presented to indicate how integrate them with the current e-learning system at University of Central England.

The system is based on multi-agent architecture and agents are in charge of communication between the three roles: mobile, context tag, and E-learning server. Context middleware has been plugged into all of the three roles with the functionality of context management. E-learning server is set for the links with SCAN and Moodle as a content provider.

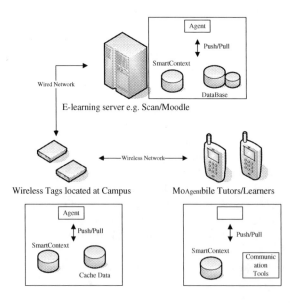

Fig. 4. The architecture of a mobile learning system

- **Context tag:** the Context Tags serve as a key component within the system architecture. Context tags are designed to be cost optimised with little system logic, simply fulfilling the task of communicating with the learner/tutor and finding her/his location. The desired flexibility of the project has a major impact on context tag architecture. The tags may differ with respect to storage capacity and transmission technology (including type, frequency and range). Moreover, some context tags may be designed to receive feedback from the learner/tutor and provide a platform for running agents.
- **Push/Pull component:** information distribution functionality is available in both push and pull mode. Push mode involves subscribing to information. Information is subsequently pushed out to a user in an asynchronous fashion. Pull mode implies synchronous requests for information.
- **Communication tools:** the tool set provides a series of software tools to support cooperative learning such as chat room, MS-Massager, white board, video talk etc.

4 Simulation and Evaluation

Figure 5 demonstrates a simulation of the Collaboration/Content Service to a learner.

Fig. 5. Demonstration of a Collaboration/Content Service scenario

There are some relevant research projects in this field, for example, Berri et al. [10] proposed an ontology-based framework for context-aware mobile learning consisting mainly of a rule-based ontology and a search agent. Another research is a design framework for mobile Computer Supported Cooperative Work [11].

Compared with the above researches in mobile learning, our work, moreover, has developed an ontology based context model in utilization of computer supported cooperative mobile learning apart of providing content oriented learning services based on user context. Supporting cooperative mobile learning is the objective of the research on an ontology based context model in our project.

5 Conclusion

Contrast to public wireless network based mobile applications, location based mobile applications appear more economic to users. For instance, a Bluetooth protocol has been utilized in the project to support communication between context tag and mobile learner/tutor without any charge. However, location based mobile applications extremely necessitate an appropriate context model to confirm successful capture of user context.

In this paper, we present an ontology based context model, "SmartContext", supporting location based contextual and cooperative mobile learning, which includes a context template, a context reasoning ontology and a context middleware. The research aim is to develop a standardised semantic context model applicable to different domains and a context middleware package with required functionality. The future work includes integration and evaluation with other current e-learning systems and investigation of ontology issues related to cooperative mobile learning with heterogeneous ontology matching.

References

1. Sharples, M., Corlett, D., Wesmancott, O.: The Design and Implementation of a Mobile Learning Resource. Personal and Ubiquitous Computing 6(3) (2002) 220-234
2. Price, S., Rogers, Y., Scaife M., Stanton, D., Neal, H.: Using "tangibles" to promote novel forms of playful learning. Interact Comp 6 (2003) 169-185
3. Meng, Z., Chu, J., Zhang, L.: Collaborative learning system based on wireless mobile equipments. Proc. CCECE. Niagara Falls (2004)
4. Kossen, J.: Mobile e-learning: When e-learning becomes m-learning.
   URL: http://www.zatz.com/authors/authorpage/jeremyskossen.html
5. Hsiao, J.W.D.L.: CSCL theories.
   URL: http://www.edb.utexas.edu/csclstudent/Dhsiao/theories.html
6. Dourish, P. What we talk about when we talk about context. Personal and Ubiquitous Computing 8 (2004) 19-30
7. Benford, S., Bederson, B.B., Åkesson, K.-P., Bayon, V., Druin, A., Hansson, P., et al.: Designing storytelling technologies to encourage collaboration between young children. Proceedings of the SIGHCI Conference in Computing Systems (CHI 2000). The Hague, Netherlands (2000) 556-563
8. W3C. RDF Concept and Abstracts Syntax. URL: http://www.w3.org/TR/2004/REC-rdf-concepts-20040210/
9. McBride, B., Boothby, D., Dollin, C.: An Introduction to RDF and the Jena RDF.
   URL: http://jena.sourceforge.net/tutorial/RDF_API/index.html
10. Berri, J., Belamri, R., Atif, Y.: Ontology-based framework for context-awareness mobile learning. Proceedings of IWCMC'06. Vancouver, British Columbia, Canada (2006)
11. Roschelle, J., Rosas, R., Nussbaum, M.: Towards a design framework for mobile computer-supported cooperative work. Proceedings of CSCL'05. Taipei, Taiwan (2006)

A Context Framework with Ontology for Personalised and Cooperative Mobile Learning

Philip Moore[1] and Bin Hu[2]

Department of Computing, UCE Birmingham, Birmingham, B42 2SU, UK
[1] ptm2me@yahoo.co.uk, [2] bin.hu@uce.ac.uk

Abstract. This paper addresses personalised cooperative mobile learning. Context, context-awareness and the application of context-awareness are considered. The development of a generic RDF context framework is presented, adaptability is considered and comparisons are drawn with related research. Context definitions are domain specific with each domain requiring specific contextual design. In this paper, the focus is the context definition for a student in the domain of higher education. A context reasoning ontology is introduced to provide support for intelligent context processing. The paper concludes that RDF/RDFS combined with OWL and Jena provides a basis for the creation of context, context reasoning with ontology enabling effective intelligent context processing.

1 Background

The increased availability of mobile devices and their convergence with hand-held/wearable computers are drivers for the popularisation of mobile wireless communications. These developments combined with the changes in the educational landscape and pedagogic systems have driven the interest in personalised mobile learning (PML) [6]. The educational and technological developments have resulted in the emergence of m-learning as an important aspect of e-learning [6]. A key benefit of m-learning is the ability to provide and access learning anytime/anywhere with learning not restricted to pre-specified times or places [15].

Pivotal to PML is the identification of users and their computational/mobile devices (in this paper collectively termed entities) to enable personalised service provision and provide support for cooperative learning. Context-aware mobile computing using an entities context provides the means to achieve these aims, mobile learning being "strongly mediated by its context" [15].

The research presented in this paper builds on the work conducted in the Department of Computing (DOC) at UCE Birmingham to develop systems to support personalised contextual and cooperative mobile learning with integration into the e-learning system in the DOC.

Section 2 addresses context, context-awareness and context processing. The context factors are presented and evaluated in section 3. Section 4 addresses the context framework, presents the RDF/RDFS class structure and considers adaptability and implementation. A context reasoning ontology is presented in section 5 with a discussion and consideration of future research provided in section 6.

W. Shen et al. (Eds.): CSCWD 2006, LNCS 4402, pp. 727–738, 2007.
© Springer-Verlag Berlin Heidelberg 2007

2 Context

The concept of context is generally agreed however an agreed common definition of the term is not [3], considerable confusion surrounding the "notion of context", its meaning and the role it plays in interactive systems [4]. In mobile computing context refers to the situated role the user of a mobile device experiences while using it [2][6]. A definition of the term context when used in PML is: "*Information consisting of properties that combine to describe and characterise an entity and its situated role in computer readable form*". An entity is defined in [3] as a *person, place* or *physical* or *computational* object

A context is created by combining property values that describe a diverse range of factors [2][4][6] including: (1) The variable tasks demanded by users (2) The mobile and computational devices (3) The service infrastructure (4) The physical situation (including location) and (5) The social setting.

Context falls into two types, *static* (termed customisation) and *dynamic* (termed personalisation) [6]:

- A *static* context occurs when a users profile is created manually, i.e. the user is actively involved in the process and has an element of control.
- A *dynamic* context relates to a condition where the user is seen as being passive, or at least somewhat less in control, the system monitoring, analysing and reacting to the user's behaviour and situated role.

The two types of context are reflected in the two principal ways context is used, these are: (1) as a retrieval clue (a static context) and (2) to tailor system behaviour to match users system usage patterns (a dynamic context).

Context is purpose and application specific requiring the identification of the function(s) and properties specific to individual domains. This requirement is exemplified in the application of context-awareness applied to learning using mobile technologies [10] where the starting point in the definition of context is to identify the purpose for the context we are interested in.

2.1 Context-Awareness

Context-awareness describes a computing paradigm in which an entities context is used to target the provision of information and resources and match users in interactive systems based on location, preferences and current need with "minimal user effort" [10]. A system can be defined as context-aware where the relevancy [2] of service provision is dependent upon a users task and situated role.

Features that identify applications as context-aware are: (1) the presentation of information and services to the user (2) automatic execution of a service and (3) tagging of context to information for later retrieval [3].

There are thee primary types of contextual information (referred to as context dimensions in [3]): (1) Spatio-Temporal (2) Identity and (3) Activity. Primary contextual information is used to derive secondary contextual information [3]. Secondary contextual information relates to property values that describe context factors such as location, device characteristics and identity information.

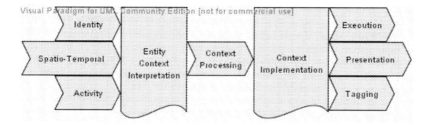

Fig. 1. Context processing

Context-aware computing relies on two principal functions: (1) context interpretation and (2) context implementation [3]. Realisation of these functions requires context processing (discussed in Section 2.2). Figure 1 models the context interpretation and implementation process.

The initial stage involves the collection of the sensor-derived input data. The data is aggregated and interpreted. Following context processing the output is a model of the individual users situated role in computer readable form represented as context property values. This enables the stored context to be implemented and context driven events (the output) activated.

2.2   A Context Process Model

A system requirement in our research is the creation, accessing and updating of stored context definitions. To meet this need a context process model has been developed. The model (presented in Figure 2) details the context processing function (see Figure 1). Notes 1 to 6 describe the process.

A context can be viewed as a *state* with *transitional states*, Figure 2 models this process commencing with a stored context (Current Context [A]) and terminating with the replacement of the initial stored context (Current Context [A]) with the (Implemented (updated) Context [D]). The process is cyclic with a back-up context always retained to address issues such as a systems failure.

- **Note 1:** the initial stored Current Context [A] is created (in the first instance default values will be used to create an initial current context [A]).
- **Note 2:** upon an event triggering the system the sensory input data is processed and the Updated Context [B] created to reflect the new situated role.
- **Note 3:** based on context processing rules if no further context processing is required the Updated Context [B] will replace the initial stored Current Context [A]. The initial Current Context [A] is stored in a back-up system.
- **Note 4:** in situations where context-processing rules dictate the Updated Context [B] will be replaced by the Updated Context [C] (following context processing) to reflect the changing situated role.
- **Note 5:** The Updated Context [C] is implemented and the Updated Context [C] becomes the Implemented Context [D].
- **Note 6:** Finally the Implemented Context [D] replaces the Current Context [A]. The initial Current Context [A] is stored in a back-up system.

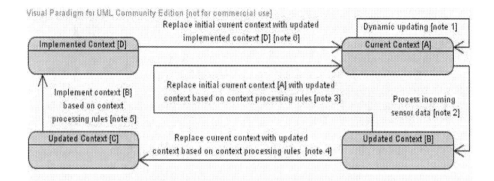

Fig. 2. Context Process Model

2.3 The Application of Context-Awareness

Context-aware solutions have been applied to many diverse domains where the provision of personalised services mapped to an entities context is a system requirement. *Cyberguide* [1] applies context-awareness to the development of a "mobile context-aware tour guide". *MOBllearn* [10] explores context-awareness using contextual information in mobile learning. *CRUMPET* [12] employs context-awareness to integrate four technology domains: (1) location-aware services (2) personalised user interaction (3) multi-media mobile communication and (4) smart component based middleware or "smartware" using multi-agent technology. Similar work has been carried out in the domain of mobile communications addressing *"Middleware for Mobile Applications Beyond 3G"* [13].

The educational and technological developments have resulted the "design and development of educational provision based on new technology enhanced paradigms that facilitate access to digital resources" [8]. There is a "natural alliance" between learning as a contextual activity and personal mobile technologies [15], context-awareness performing a crucial role in leveraging the power of mobile technologies in pedagogic systems.

3   The Context Factors

The research focus is the identification of the context factors that identify a student in the domain of HE with the development of a context framework based on the identified factors. The factors identified are listed in table 1.

The list is non-hierarchical, being analogous to a menu from which domain specific context factors can be selected to suit the domain specific nature of contextual design.

The RDF class structure (see section 4.2) uses the context factors identified, defining the RDF classes and sub-classes with their associated properties and sub-properties to provide an extensible RDF context framework generalisable to similar domains.

Table 1. The Context Factors to Describe and Define a Student Profile

Student ID / Name	Address
Student Nationality	Key Skills/First Language
Cultural Background	Social Background
Religion	Sexual Orientation
Ethnicity	Disabilities
Progression	Gender
Qualifications	Working (Y / N)
Courses Taken	Full Time/Part Time
Enrolled Course(s)	Mature Student (D of B)
Year (Enrolled Course)	Engagement
Registered Modules	Projects
Experience (Academic)	Groups
Experience (Industrial)	Interests
User Registered (Y/N)	Web Surfing Patterns
Connectivity	Screen size
Location (where contactable)	
Device Location (and therefore the user)	
Device Availability (switched on / off)	
Time Window (When contactable)	
Mode-of-Delivery (e.g. resource or message)	
Resource Formatting (documents and files)	

3.1 The Context Factor Identification

The identification of the context factors was achieved using semi-structured interviews. A potential issue identified was the relatively small population size; purposive sampling [14] addressed this issue. Purposive sampling calls for the use of populations with recognised knowledge and experience in the domain the research is designed to address thus mitigating the potential for a biased result. The selected population, drawn from the DOC, satisfied the requirements of the purposive sampling method.

Fifteen interviews were conducted, a breakdown shows that of the fifteen staff interviewed thirteen were active tutors, one was involved in student support and one was employed in technical services. The tutorial staff interviewed included computing (technical) and business oriented (soft systems) staff. A quantitative analysis shows that 66% were from a computing or technical background with 33% drawn from soft systems disciplines.

3.2 The Context Factor Evaluation

The factors were evaluated using a questionnaire, the design being based on a variation of the Likert scale. The questions were framed using the identified factors (section 3) with four levels of response to each question. The survey questions asked: *which of the following factors should be identified when defining a context*? Three pilot distributions involving tutorial staff within UCE Birmingham were conducted.

The distribution of the questionnaire involved staff and students at UCE Birmingham (UK) and Guilin University of Technology (P.R.China). Two modes of delivery were used (1) electronically using the Intranet(s) and by direct e-mail and (2) in person. 54 returns were received, a breakdown showing that 33% came from Guilin University of Technology and 66% from UCE Birmingham. The ratio of student/staff returns was 79% and 21% respectively. Response rates are difficult to quantify with any degree of accuracy due to the method of distribution.

Statistical analysis of the survey data used aggregate response values (N) (normalized to a maximum value of 1), standard deviation (SD), correlation (C) and moving averages (MA). The results obtained were analysed visually.

The questionnaire returns demonstrated a wide variation in the responses to each question, the SD with values in the range 0.33 to 1.32 and an average value of 0.81 supporting this observation. The wide range of questionnaire responses reflected the data obtained in the interview process.

To test for relationships between the interview, student and tutor data sets and to quantify the strength of any relationships, correlation coefficients were calculated. The correlation coefficients were negative ranging from weak (interview/tutor data) through moderate (interview/student data) to strong (student/tutor data). The values ranged from -0.3771 to -0.6712.

The N values were computed for each question, the N values representing a measure of the overall level of agreement respondents expressed related to the use of each factor in a student context definition. The N values fell into relatively narrow ranges for tutor and student responses with maximum values ranging from 0.97 to 0.90, minimum values being 0.59 to 0.50 and average values of 0.74 to 0.71. The interview N values show a similar maximum value of 0.93 but widely differing minimum (0.07) and average (0.31) values, the wide differences identified are explained by the relatively smaller sample used in the interviews as compared to the questionnaire sample.

The results derived from the statistical and visual analysis support the observation that there is a level of statistical significance in the data with identifiable relationships, patterns and trends. The analysis supports the conclusion that: (1) the wide variation in the identified factors noted in the interview process is reflected in the questionnaire responses and (2) the factors identified in the interviews are representative of other larger populations with greater diversity.

4 The Context Framework

Prime objectives in the development of the context framework are:

- The ability to generalise to similar domains
- The ability to accommodate a broad range of context factors
- Adaptability to diverse domains, technologies and systems.

The context framework is encoded using RDF [16]. RDF is an XML based technology providing adaptable, portable and lightweight cross platform solutions to context definition. RDF solutions can be implemented in diverse domains and systems developed using for example Java technologies, ASP and PHP [16]. This enables applications developed using RDF/RDFS to be used in diverse Internet and distributed networked applications. RDF/RDFS by representing data in computer readable form provides a basis upon which context processing using diverse back-end systems can be achieved. The creation of context definitions does not however address the issue of implementation.

To enable implementation a context reasoning ontology is introduced. Context reasoning provides a basis upon which *intelligent* context processing can be realised. RDF/RDFS alone is however incapable of supporting reasoning and to enable this RDF/RDFS will be extended using the Web Ontology Language (OWL), a component in the Semantic Web [16]. Section 5 introduces the context reasoning ontology with a typical on-line PML cooperative computing scenario to demonstrate the context reasoning process.

4.1 Personalisation Adaptability and Related Research

Significant research into personalisation and adaptability in mobile systems has been documented. Examples include: (1) *Mobile Adaptation with Multiple Representation Approach as Educational Pedagogy* [7] which addresses the issue of "web page level content adaptation" providing "guidelines for content adaptation in e-learning and mobile learning environments", (2) *Cognitive Trait Model for Persistent Student Modelling* [9] provides a "new model" to supplement performance-based modelling of students enabling the transference of relevant information to similar domains and (3) *Supporting Learning in Context: Extending Learner-Cantered Design to the Development of Handheld Educational Software* [11] in which the challenges to the development of educational software for handheld devices are considered with the design of *Pocket PiCoMap* (a learner-centered tool to support "concept mapping activities on handheld devices").

The research identified [7][9][11], while addressing issues related to portability and adaptability, fails to fully address the specific context modeling and processing requirements a context-aware PML system is designed to address.

Flanagan [5] in addressing personalisation and ontology proposes an alternative approach using unsupervised machine learning and while the "obvious advantages" of ontology are accepted it is argued that it is a "major barrier" to personalisation. A further "potential issue" identified [5] is the provision of a stored context, a system prerequisite for a context-aware PML system. The accepted advantages of ontology show that it is a viable solution, the issues relating less to the concept than the approach adopted to enable effective implementation.

A further consideration for machine learning is inductive bias. There are essentially two types of inductive bias (1) *preference bias* and (2) *restriction bias*. Examples of inductive bias include restricted relationships (e.g. conjunctions only) and for decision tree(s) the shortest tree first (based on the preference for shorter hypotheses – often called Occam's razor). Some form of inductive bias is required to enable generalisation beyond the training data, this combined with the issue of the stored context [5] makes unsupervised machine learning an unsuitable approach to for effective context processing using ontology in a context-aware PLM system.

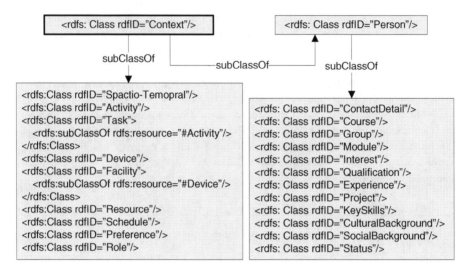

Fig. 3. The RDF Class Structure

4.2 The RDF Class Structure

To accommodate a range broad of context factors the context framework implements a class structure (Figure 3) using classes and sub-classes with associated properties and sub-properties (based on the context factors identified in section 3) to represent types and classifications of entity. The class structure provides the capability to add (and remove) classes and associated properties to tailor and refine context definitions to suit the domain specific nature of context and contextual design.

Taking an individuals role (e.g. tutor/student) as an example, properties from Class:Role (a sub-class of Class:Context) enables an individual's role to be defined. A context definition made up of a role property in combination with related properties from Class:Context and its sub-classes and Class:Person and its sub-classes enables a tutor or student context to be realised. Section 4.4 sets out example (validated) RDF/RDFS for the Class:Context with its sub-class Class:Person. Shown is the RDF description for an individuals name property with the associated datatype.

4.3 The Context Framework Evaluation

The framework evaluation involved: (1) validation of the RDF/RDFS schema vocabulary and (2) software testing.

Validation of the RDF schema was achieved using the W3c RDF validation service [16] and involved checking the schema vocabulary to verify that it is both well formed XML and compliant with the RDF/RDFS syntax and RDF data model. The successful validation represented the first step in the evaluation process.

The evaluation of the framework when implemented in software was achieved by encoding the RDF schema using the Jena RDF API (introduced in section 4.3.1). The pre-defined test data used was based on the validated RDF schema. The anticipated output was achieved.

The evaluation employed the Jena "in-memory-model" which while adequate for the testing procedure is unsuitable (when used in isolation) for full implementation, interaction with a relational database being required.

The Jena API is a Java framework for building semantic Internet and distributed networked applications. Jena provides a programming environment for RDF/RDFS and OWL and includes a rule-based inference engine. Complex context definitions can be defined using domain and application specific schema vocabularies.

Jena enables both "*in-memory*" and "*persistent storage*" with the ability to work with relational database systems including *Oracle*, *MySql*, *PosgresQL* and *Interbase*. Support is provided for multiple data storage layouts including: *Generic*, *Genericproc*, *MMGeneric*, *Hash* and *MMHash*.

4.4 The Context Properties

The RDF framework is defined in the RDF schema documents encoded in RDF/XML. This sets out the schema specific vocabularies that describe entities based on combinations of classes and properties. The RDF schema is non-hierarchical and when implemented in an application provides the ability to tailor classes and proper-ties to suit the domain and application specific nature of context.

Set out below are extracts from the validated RDF Member schema document showing the header code with qualified "namespaces" and "dataypes". Example class, sub-class, property and sub-Property definitions are shown.

```
<?xml version="1.0"?>
<!DOCTYPE rdf:RDF [<!ENTITY xsd
"http://www.w3.org/2001/XMLSchema#">]>
<rdf:RDF
    xmlns:rdf="http://www.w3.org/1999/02/22-rdf-syntax-ns#"
    xmlns:rdfs="http://www.w3.org/2000/01/rdf-schema#"
    xml:base="http://uce.mls/schemas/Member">
<rdfs:Datatype rdf:about="&xsd;string"/>

<rdfs:Class rdfID="Context"/>
<rdfs:Class rdf:ID="Person">
    <rdfs:subClassOf rdf:resource="#Context"/>
</rdfs:Class>

<rdf:Property rdf:ID="full_name">
    <rdfs:domain rdfs:resource="#Person"/>
    <rdfs:range rdf:resource="&xsd;string"/>
</rdf:Property>
<rdf:Property rdf:ID="first_name">
    <rdfs:subPropertyOf rdf:resource="#full_name"/>
    <rdfs:domain rdfs:resource="Person"/>
    <rdfs:range rdf:resource="&xsd;string"/>
</rdf:Property>
```

5 A Context Reasoning Ontology

The Class Structure and associated RDF Schema vocabulary is defined using RDF/RDFS, a component in the Semantic Web. The Semantic Web is a concept that extends the ability of XML to define customised tagging schemes and the flexible approach adopted by the RDF data model to data representation [16].

RDF is generally limited to binary ground predicates with RDFS generally restricted to subclass and property hierarchies with (and limited to) domain and range definitions for the properties. Support for context reasoning requires greater expressiveness than RDF/RDFS can provide. To enable this greater expressiveness (and reasoning support based on predicate logic) a context reasoning ontology (Figure 4) with a brief illustrative scenario is presented to demonstrate the context reasoning process.

A Bluetooth enabled PDA enables user identification and initiates event driven (in the scenario based on location change) context updating and input (task/problem) tagging. The scenario sets out a typical cooperative learning interaction with an example of context reasoning including conjunction (AND) and disjunction (OR). Context reasoning enables context processing (discussed in section 2) facilitating context matching of the questioner (the input/problem) to the advisor(s) (the output/solution).

In the scenario spatio-temporal, activity, task, preference, status, qualification, module, and role context components are identified. Context reasoning with inference using the property values enables the availability of "Lisa" and her suitability as an advisor to the questioner "Bob" to be decided with their respective roles, ("Bob"="student") and ("Lisa"= "tutor") inferred. The ontology identifies the semantic relationships for the scenario context components and the schedule, resource and device context components.

A Location Based On-Line Cooperative Computing Scenario:
A1: Spatio-Temporal<date=”2006:18:12”> [Monday]
A2: Spatio-Temporal<time=”10:50:48”> [am]
B1: Person<name=“Bob”> *IsAt* Spatio-Temporal<location=“library”>
B2: Person<name=“Bob”> *HasA* Activity<activity=“on-line”>
B3: Activity<activity=“on-line”> *HasA* Task<question<subject=“Java”>>
B4: “Bob” is on line, is located in the library and has a role of student
C1: Person<name=“Lisa”> *IsAt* Spatio-Temporal<location=“on-campus”>
C2: Person<name=“Lisa”> *HasA* Preference<availability<location=“on campus”>
                    <day = “Monday - friday”><time=“am”>>
C3: Person<name=“Lisa”> *HasAStatus* Person<available=”yes”>
C4: Person<name=“Lisa”> *HasA* Module<module=“OO Programming”>
C5: Person<name=“Lisa”> *HasA* Qualification<qualification=“Java ”>
C6: “Lisa” is available, is an appropriate advisor to “Bob” and has a role of tutor

$$((B1 \cap B2 \cap B3) \Rightarrow B4)$$
$$((A1 \cap A2) \cap (C1 \cap C2) \Rightarrow C3)$$
$$(C3 \cap (C4 \cup C5) \Rightarrow C6)$$

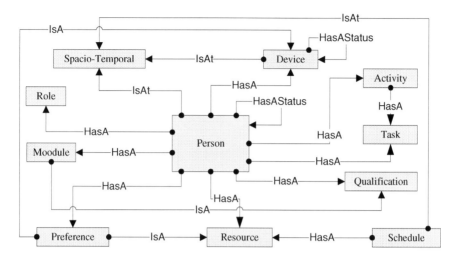

Fig. 4. Context Reasoning Ontology

Identification of individuals based on their context clearly reduces to a decision problem. The ontology in defining relationships based on the semantic links defined by context properties and their associated values (e.g. <location = "library">) enables reasoned decisions including disambiguation to be realised.

6   Conclusion

RDF/RDFS has been shown to provide the basis upon which effective context definitions can be created. Ontology using OWL provides the capability to extend RDF/RDFS and enables effective context reasoning with the aim of achieving "intelligent" context processing. Jena has the capability to enable effective implementation of the ontology in a context-aware PML system.

An aim of this research is the development of an intelligent context middleware using multi-agent technology to provide a location-based PML system to tutors and learners. The approach presented in this paper using RDF/RDFS with OWL and Jena addresses the needs of context creation and processing. The actual implementation strategy forms the basis of projected future research.

Consideration of suitable implementation strategies has identified decision trees (a type of directional graph) an interesting research direction. There is a perceived synergy between the (tree-based) RDF data model and decision trees. Assessment of implementation strategies to harness this synergy has resulted in the identification of a number of potential implementation options including:

- Knowledge-based systems with rule-based inference
- Evolutionary systems
- Hybrid approaches combining evolutionary systems with traditional search techniques

An issue to be addressed in implementing decision trees is the approach to the encoding of the problem context (tagged input) and solution context to enable effective intelligent context processing and implementation in a multi-agent context middleware. Encoding using approaches employed in ES presents an interesting potential research direction providing the potential to produce quantifiable results. However, investigation of the range of potential implementation options and approaches to encoding forms the basis of projected future research.

References

1. Abowd, G.D., Atkeson, C.G., Hong, J., Long, S., Kooper, R., Pinkerton, M.: Cyberguide: A Mobile Context-Aware Tour Guide. Wireless Networks (3) (1997) 421-433
2. Coppola, P., Della, M.A.: The Concept of Relevance in Mobile and Ubiquitous Access. LNCS 2954 (2004) 1-10
3. Dey, A.K., Abowd, G.D.: Towards a Better Understanding of Context and Context-Awareness. GVU Technical Report GIT-GVU-99-22. College of Computing, Georgia Institute of Technology (1999)
4. Dourish, P.: What we talk about when we talk about context. Personal and Ubiquitous Computing (8) (2004) 19-30
5. Flanagan, J.A.: Context Awareness in a mobile device: Ontologies versus unsupervised/ supervised learning. (2005)
   URL: http://www.cis.hut.fi/AKRR05/papers/akrr05flanagan.pdf
6. Hu, B., Moore, P.: A context Framework supporting contextual and cooperative learning. Proc. IADIS International Conference Mobile Learning. Quara, Malta (2005) 236-240
7. Kinshuk, D., Goh, T.T.: Mobile adaptation with multiple representation as educational pedagogy. In: Uhr, W., Esswein, W. and Schoop, E. (eds): Wirtschaftsinformatik 2003-Medien-Markte-Mobilitat, Physica-Verlag, Heidleberg, Germany (2003) 747-763
8. Kinshuk, D., Kommers, P. and Sampson, D.G.: Adaptivity in web and mobile learning services. Int. J. Cont. Engineering Education and Lifelong Learning 14(4/5) (2004) 313-317
9. Lin, T., Kinshuk, D., Patel, A. and Hong, H.: Cognitive trait model for persistent student modelling. (2003). Proc. World Conference on Educational Multimedia (EdMedia). Norfolk, USA (2003) 2114-2147
10. Lonsdale, P., Barber, C., Sharples, M., Arvanitis, T.N.: A context awareness architecture for facilitating mobile learning. Proceedings of MLEARN 2003. London, UK (2003)
11. Luchini, K., Curtis, M., Quintana, C., Soloway, E.: Supporting learning in context: extending learner-centered design to the development of handheld educational software. Proc. IEEE International Workshop on Wireless and Mobile Technologies in Education (2002) 107-111
12. Poslad, S., Laamanen, H., Malaka, R., Nick, A., Buckle, P., Zipf, A.: Crumpet: creation of user friendly mobile services personalised for tourism. Proc. 3G 2001. Second International Conference on 3G Mobile Communication Technologies. London, UK (2001)
13. Raatikainen, K.: Middleware for Mobile Applications Beyond 3G. Smart Networks. Proceedings of SmartNet 2002. Lapland, Finland (2002) 3-17
14. Robson, C.: Real world research second edition. Blackwell, Malden, Mass, USA (2002)
15. Sharples, M., Corlett, D., Wesmancott, O.: The Design and Implementation of a Mobile Learning Resource. Personal and Ubiquitous Computing 6(3) (2002) 220-234
16. W3C. Resource Description Framework (RDF). (2005) URL: http://www.w3.org/RDF/

A Multiagent Cooperative Learning Algorithm

Fei Liu and Guangzhou Zeng

School of Computer Science and Technology, Shandong University,
Jinan, 250061, P.R. China
lflemmon@163.com

Abstract. Some multiagent learning methods simply extend reinforcement learning to multiple agents. In these methods, large state and action spaces are the most difficult problems. Moreover, previous proposals for using learning techniques to coordinate multiple agents have mostly relied on explicit or implicit information sharing, which makes cooperation affected by communication delays and the reliability of the information received. A Multiagent Cooperative Learning Algorithm (MCLA) is presented to solve these problems. In MCLA, an evaluating strategy based on long-time reward is proposed. Thus each agent acts independently and autonomously by perceiving and estimating each other. It also considers the learning process from the holistic point of view to obtain the optimum associated action strategy in order to reduce the state and action spaces. A series of simulations are provided to demonstrate the performance of the proposed algorithm.

1 Introduction

Some research efforts are being made using reinforcement learning as an action learning method in a multiagent system [1-3]. In such reinforcement learning, some difficulties specific to multiagent systems are encountered. First, large state and action spaces problem means the enlargement of the state space due to the increase in the number of agents [1]. Since the number of combinations of the states and actions of the agent group is proportional to a power function of the number of agents, the seriousness of the problem of large state and action spaces is understandable. The complexity of reinforcement learning algorithms rely on the quantity of state and action, so simply applying these algorithms is not good for solving multiagent learning. Moreover, when improving methods focused on reduction of complexity, caused by the high number of agents and goals, some cooperative potentialities are ignored, and this subject has been studied in order to develop new approaches to the RL problem [4-6].

Second, previous proposals for using learning techniques to coordinate multiple agents have mostly relied on cooperative domains with unrestricted information sharing [7-8] has relied on explicit information sharing. Some authors [9] explore communication limits in multiagent systems, but these agents do not know how to select relevant information to share with others so that it is worth to transmit it. Adopting the "autonomous distributed system", in which each agent determines its own behavior independently, is a powerful method to solve the simultaneous learning problem.

W. Shen et al. (Eds.): CSCWD 2006, LNCS 4402, pp. 739–750, 2007.
© Springer-Verlag Berlin Heidelberg 2007

If this method were adopted, the agents other than oneself would be treated as the environment, and hence each agent would be learning independently. We show that although each agent is independently optimizing its own environmental reward, global coordination between multiple agents can emerge without explicit or implicit information sharing. These agents can therefore act independently and autonomously by perceive and estimation, without being affected by communication delays (due to other agent being busy) or failure of a key agent (who controls information exchange or who has more information) and do not have to be worry about the reliability of the information received.

The presence of multiple autonomous and self-interested agents makes multiagent cooperative learning a difficult problem. The reason is that every agent is learning, and then everyone faces a time-variant environment. Since all agents are learning, how the other learning agents will react to the strategy improvement of an individual agent will depend on how this agent improves its own strategy. To further complicate the matter, different agents may respond to the policy improvement of the same agent differently, which makes it even harder for the agents to anticipate how the environment will shift.

This paper examines a specific multiagent cooperative learning framework and presents a multiagent cooperative learning algorithm (MCLA). When some agents are learning the optimal solution of the problem directly from interaction with the environment, others can decide their action strategies by perceiving and estimating other's actions. In MCLA, an evaluating method based on long-time reward is proposed. Using it each agent acts independently and autonomously and considers the learning process from the holistic point of view to obtain the optimum associated action strategy. In addition, reinforcement learning methods have theoretical proofs of convergence; unfortunately, such convergence assumptions do not hold for some real-world applications, including many multiagent systems problems. We can learn by experiment that MCLA has good convergence and solve the large state and action spaces problems to a full extent.

The remaining of this paper is organized as follows. Section 2 introduces the related work. Section 3 describes a multiagent cooperative learning framework and MCLA algorithm in environments modeled by the framework to increase cooperation in learning and reduce complexity of cooperative learning. Section 4 discusses the effects and the role of implementing the algorithm in multiagent cooperative learning, as applied to the pursuit problem. A conclusion and some directions for future research are given in the last section.

2 Related Work

Much of the multiagent learning literature has sprung from historically somewhat separate communities-notably reinforcement learning and dynamic programming, robotics, evolutionary computation, and complex systems. Existing surveys of the work have likewise tended to define multiagent learning is ways special to these communities. Instead, we begin this survey by defining multiagent learning broadly: it is the application of machine learning to problems involving multiple agents.

One large class of learning in multiagent systems involves situations where a single agent learns while the other agents' behaviors are fixed. An example of such situations is presented in [10]. This is single-agent learning: there is only one learner, and the behaviors are plugged into only one agent, rather than distributed into multiple agents.

In team learning, there is a single learner involved: but this learner is discovering a set of behaviors for a team of agents, rather than a single agent. This lacks the game-theoretic aspect of multiple learners, but still poses challenges because as agents interact with one another, the joint behavior can be unexpected. Team learning has some disadvantages as well. A major problem with team learning is the large state space for the learning process.

The most common alternative to team learning in cooperative multiagent systems is concurrent learning, where multiple learning processes attempt to improve parts of the team. Typically each agent has its own unique learning process to modify its behavior. Bull and Fogarty [11] and Iba [12] present experiments where concurrent learning outperforms team learning, while Miconi [13] reports that team learning is preferable in certain conditions.

We propose multiagent cooperative learning that separates from both team learning and concurrent learning. First, because multiagent cooperative learning deals with problem domains involving multiple agents, the search space involved can be unusually large; and due to the interaction of those agents, small changes in learned behaviors can often result in unpredictable changes in the resulting emergent properties of the multiagent group as a whole. Second, multiagent cooperative learning involve multiple learners, each learning and adapting in the context of others; this introduces game-theoretic issues to the learning process.

In multiagent learning, explicit and implicit communication can also significantly increase the learning method's search space, both by increasing the size of the external state available to the agent, and by increasing the agent's available choices. This increase in search space can hamper learning an optimal behavior by more than communication itself may help. Thus even when communication is required for optimal performance, for many applications [14], the learning method must disregard communication, or hard-code it, in order to simplify the learning process. So we propose a cooperative learning algorithm, where global coordination between multiple agents can emerge without explicit or implicit information sharing.

In most of the reviewed researches, cooperation is unidirectional from a prespecified trainer to a preselected learner agent. In the strategy sharing method [15], each Q-learning agent learns from all of its teammates. The agents learn individually and at some special instants, each agent gathers the Q-tables of the other agents and takes the average of the tables as its own new strategy. In this system, the agents do not have the ability to find good teachers. Imitation [16-17] is one of the cooperative learning methods. In this method, the learners watch the actions of a teacher, learn them, and repeat these actions in similar situations. Genetic Programming (GP) is used for the cooperation behavior for multiple robot agents [18]. However, in the real world, cooperative learning is bidirectional and all agents learn something from each other.

To overcome the described problems, a new cooperative learning algorithm based on the observation and estimation of the other agents is proposed in the following section. We, however, concentrate on systems where agents share no problem-solving knowledge.

3   Multiagent Cooperative Learning Algorithm

3.1   Learning Agent Model

The learning agent model consists of four elementary modules, as depicted in Figure 1. These modules are Predictor, Action selector, Learning and Executing. The learning agent interacts with the environment to achieve the learning experience and constantly adjust cooperative strategy.

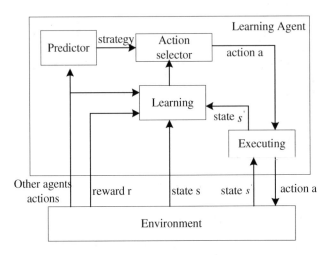

Fig. 1. Learning agent model

By observing other agents' actions execution Predictor estimates their next actions to be executed in terms of different strategies.

According to the strategy, which is provided by Predictor, Action selector selects the current best action strategy in a greater probability.

Based on state s, reward r and executed cooperative action a, Learning module adopt a learning algorithm to adjust cooperative strategy. By cooperative learning, an agent can make fast reflection on environment changes and other agents' strategy until the optimum associated strategy produces.

Executing executes the action that Action selector provides and affects the environment to transfer state s into the next state s'.

3.2   Multiagent Cooperative Learning Framework

The quality of strategies learned by a multiagent team can be significantly improved through cooperative learning. Cooperation among agents during learning is essential in directing the adjustment of strategies in the globally most beneficial direction.

Bowling [19] has made use of MDP $<n,S,A_{1..n},T,R_{1..n}>$ in multiagent environments, where n is the number of agents, A_i is the optional action set of the ith agent(Ag_i),

R_i is the immediate reward of Ag_i. We cast a multiagent cooperative system framework, which is defined as a 6-tuple $F=<M,\{A_i\}_{i\in n},S, T,R,\pi_t >$, where M is a finite set that is composed of n agents concerned with cooperative learning; $\{A_i\}_{i\in n}$ denotes that for every $Ag_i \in M$ there is a finite action set A_i and the associated action of these agents $\{a_1,a_2,...,a_n\},a_i \in A_i$ constitutes an element of the associated action space $A= \times \{A_i\}_{i\in n}$; S is state space of the model; R is a reward function, $S\times A \rightarrow \Re$, $R(s, a_1,a_2,...,a_n, s')$ is a rational representing the reward obtained from taking actions $a_1,a_2,...,a_n$ from state s and transitioning to state s', $s, s' \in S$, $a_1 \in A_1,...,a_n \in A_n$; T is a state transition function under random environment, $T:S\times A\times S\rightarrow \Pi(S)$, $\Pi(S)$ is a probability distribution over the set S and satisfies $\sum_{s'\in S}T(s,a_1,...,a_n,s')=1$. We write $T(s,a,s')$ for the probability of making a transition from state s to state s' using action a. Again s, $s' \in S$, $a_1 \in A_1,...,$ $a_n \in A_n$; π_t is a function about the strategy of multiagent learning, it denotes that at every moment agents complete a mapping between state and action.

3.3 MCLA Algorithm

In the corresponding learning framework F, agents learn the optimal solution of the problem directly from interaction with the environment. In multiagent cooperative team learning, there is not an optimum associated action that is independent from any agent. Observing other agents' past actions, an agent uses a proper method to estimate their actions and combines these with its possible action to decide to take which action to realize its object.

In MCLA, we compute the long-time reward as the multiagent learning strategy through sampling the past actions of the cooperators. The strategy for Ag_i is $\pi_t(s,a)$

$$= \sum_{\substack{A_i=a \\ A_j=\Psi(s,co-Ag_i)}} \frac{\theta_t(m,s,A_j)}{k}l(s),$$ where $\Psi(s,co\text{-}Ag_i)$ is an action set corresponding to opti-

mum solution of the cooperator co-Ag_i for Ag_i under state s, m is the memory length, k is sample length and $l(s)$ is the long-time reward of the associated action $<A_i,A_j>$. Based on this strategy, a learning agent selects an action under state s. The long-time reward estimation when taking action is the probability weighted sum of the all-possible actions under the same sate. For each action there is a queue to be maintained. In this queue there are responding actions of the cooperator as the sampling. $\frac{\theta_t(m,s,A_j)}{k}$ is the frequency of taking action A_j in k samples when the memory length is m and the number of visiting state s is $t(t\geq m\geq k)$.

The action selection strategy of a single agent usually is Boltzman formula

$$P(a)=\frac{e^{Q(s,a)/T}}{\sum_{a\in A} e^{Q(s,a)/T}}, a\in A,$$ where P(a) is the probability when selecting the action a to

take, T is the temperature parameter which reflects the searching degree and is decreased over time to decrease exploration. We propose a new action selection strategy based on π_t used for multiagent cooperative learning. The formula of this strategy is

$$Pr\,(als)=\frac{e^{\pi_t(s,a)/T}}{\sum_{y\subset\psi(s,co-Ag_i)} e^{\pi_t(s,y)/T}}.$$ The difference between P and Pr is that the latter consid-

ers the cooperators' action selection.

All the agents in the multiagent system follow this algorithm independently. Suppose a system is in state s, and action a is selected, then the system moves to state s' at the next decision-making epoch. Let R(s,a,s') be the reward generated by going from state s to state s' under action, and t(s,a,s') be the time spent during the system transition.

Step1. Let the current state be s. Initialize the reinforcement values Q_t (s,a)=0, $\forall$ s$\in$ S, and a$\in$ A. Choose the initial values of the visiting number of state s, n(s)=0, the memory length m and the sample length k. Initialize the requested number of agents n$\in$ N.

Step2. While t < lifecycle (Ag$_i$, $1\leq i\leq n$) do

   a.   When n(s)$\leq$m, choose a random action a, else observe the local associated action of the cooperator set y, the associated action<A$_i$, A$_j$>, choose an action

       according   to   Pr, $Pr(als)=\dfrac{e^{\pi_t(s,a)/T}}{\sum_{y\subset\psi(s,co-Ag_i)} e^{\pi_t(s,y)/T}}$,   where π_t (s,a)

$$=\sum_{\substack{A_i=a\\A_j=\psi(s,co-Ag)}}\frac{\theta_t(m,s,A_j)}{k}l(s)$$

   b.   Allow simulation of the system in state s, with the chosen action to continue until the next decision epoch be s', τ (s,a,s') be the transition time due to action a. Then update the longtime reward l(s) $\leftarrow$ (1-α)l(s)+α (R(s,a,s')+γ Q(s,a)), where γ is the discount factor, α is the learning rate. $Q(s,a)\leftarrow Q(s,a)+\alpha(R(s,a,s')+\gamma\max_{a'}Q(s',a')-Q(s,a))$

   c.   In case a nonrandom action was chosen in step 2.a

       • update cumulative time t $\leftarrow$ t+ τ (s,a,s')

       • update the total cost for the agent r$_{t+1}$ $\leftarrow$ r$_t$ +R(s,a,s')

Step3. Modify the queue of the cooperators under s, n(s)=n(s)+1, s ← s'.

In MCLA, the strategy is based on the associated action. Based on this strategy every agent considers the learning process from the holistic point of view to obtain the optimum associated action. Due to considering the subsequent state and action reward, MCLA uses the long-time reward of the associated action as a learning clew, in favor of searching the optimum associated action strategy.

4 Simulation Experiments

In order to achieve a task, it is often possible to accomplish through cooperation among agents what is impossible to accomplish with only one agent. Hence, the pursuit problem can ultimately be considered as one of organizing. Most analyses of the pursuit problem have been conducted with one of the two purposes: either the aim is to examine how agents organize in order to solve the problem [20], or the intention is to show the effectiveness of a proposed method [21].

4.1 Description of the Simulator

For complicating the learning problem and in order to show the differences in efficiency of the cooperative learning algorithms more clearly, a complicated version of the pursuit problem is used. In the simple case, similar to the other researches, the prey moves randomly. In the complicated case, the prey moves based on the potential field model and escapes from the hunter.

For the current research, in an environment in which there exist multiple hunters and two preys, we treated the hunters and preys as agents and made the hunters learn to capture preys.

Many hunters treated as a cooperative team can collaborate to pursuit the prey agents. The hunter agents independently search a 10 by 10 grid world to capture two prey agents, as shown by Figure 2. The hunter and prey agents determine their actions

○ Hunter Agent   △ Prey Agent

Fig. 2. Pursuit problem

simultaneously at each time step, and each agent (hunter or prey) has five possible actions to choose from: moving one cell up, down, left, right, or staying in the same cell.

Hunter agents may occupy the same square, and they capture a prey by occupying its square in sufficient numbers, rather than by surrounding the target cell. There are always a fixed number of preys on the grid. The user determines the number of preys at system initialization. In any given simulation run, all preys have an equal fixed lifetime, which is determined by the user. If, at the end of a prey's lifetime, three or more hunters occupy one of the prey squares, then that prey is deemed to have been "killed" or "captured". Alternately, if a prey square is occupied by less than three hunters, then that prey is deemed to have "expired". The instant that one prey disappears from the grid, another prey appears immediately, with each prey at a random location. Upon capturing a prey, the hunter or hunters involved receive +1 reward. Hunters receive –0.1 rewards for each move when they do not capture a prey. Such learning episodes can verify whether the learning efficiency of the system is enhanced and whether convergence time of the algorithm is as short as possible.

4.2 Experimental Results

We conduct four tests and set variable values on those parameters. Each test has 100 times learning episodes. Each episode fails at the end of all preys' lifetime. We take 10 times episodes as a team and get 10 teams of data. In the process, the following parameters are set, the reward value r=1, the temperature T=0.2, the learning rate =0.04, the discount rate γ =0.9 and the initial Q value=0.1.

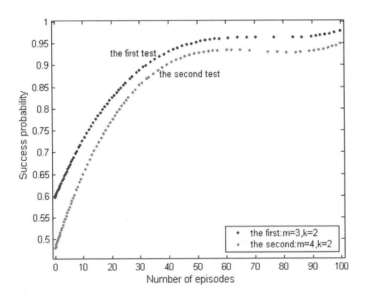

Fig. 3. The variability of success-probability of the first and the second test

Figure 3 shows the variability of success-probability of the first and the second test. In the first test, the parameters are set to m=3, k=2. In the second test, the parameters are set to m=4, k=2. From these two tests we can conclude that no matter what different parameters are set the success-probability of the algorithm can converge into the section [0.9,1] and the different set on parameters can affect the convergent rate and stable value. When k is the same and m is different, the convergence speed is basically very close, but the stable value is different. The less m is, the bigger successful probability is.

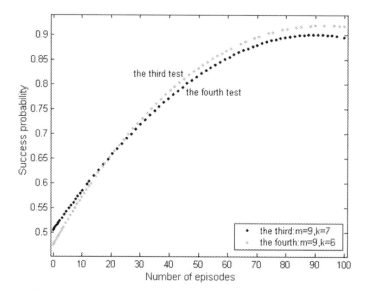

Fig. 4. The variability of success-probability of the third and the fourth test

Figure 4 presents the variability of success-probability of the third and the fourth test. In the third test, the parameters are set to m=9, k=7.In the fourth test, the parameters are set to m=9, k=6. From these two tests we can conclude that no matter what different parameters are set the success-probability of the algorithm can converge into the section [0.9,1] and the different set on parameters can affect the convergent rate and value. When k is different, the convergence rate is different. The less k is, the faster convergent rate is.

Figure 5 summarizes the performance of MCLA, with differing numbers of hunters, from 3 to 7, but exactly two preys. For each prey life and each number of hunters, 500 prey pairs were sequentially placed at random on the grid. The percentage of preys killed was then plotted. The lines join together the points for equal numbers of hunters. The right of the figure gives a legend that describes which line corresponds to a certain number of hunters.

With five or less hunters, optimal performance for the algorithm is 50%, since only one of the two preys can be killed. With six hunters, optimal performance is 80%, and with seven hunters, optimal performance is near to 90%.

The above four tests show that adopting the algorithm MCLA these agents can all learn to act cooperatively. The estimate of one another is gradually exact and the associated action is more coherent to be the optimum action. m is the factor that affects the convergent speed and k is the factor that affects the stable value. Accordingly the success-probability gradually convergence into a higher value and then the validity of this algorithm may be validated. In addition the key benefit of using the proposed algorithm for learning in multiagent systems is to speed up learning the optimal strategy. So such learning algorithm can be applied into other domains, such as the famous Taxi problem, task scheduling and robot football.

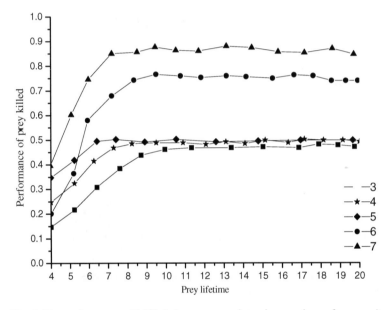

Fig. 5. The performance of MCLA (two preys and varying numbers of pursuers)

5 Conclusions and Future Work

Multiagent learning technique makes the system adapt to the uncertain environment and enhance the ability of problem explaining. Our research objective is to investigate an appropriate learning algorithm to enhance the efficiency and the whole performance of the system according to the characteristics of multiagent cooperative resolving. A multiagent cooperative learning framework is proposed. To solve some problems modeled by this framework, a new action strategy is presented according to the long-time reward estimation on the agents' actions. Using this strategy we implement a multiagent cooperative learning algorithm MCLA. This algorithm can enhance the learning rate and reduce the state space and action space of the system. This learning algorithm is tested on a pursuit problem and the results indicate that it can make cooperative agents receive the optimum action strategy. Although the simulator is a system of four agents, but the episode conclusion can be applied to more complex systems with more than four agents. In future research, we will consider the inclusion of a new state-action factor: obstacles. We expect that agents will be able to learn how to force a target toward the obstacles even though the environment space will be quite large.

The proposed long-time reward estimation method is created for the reinforcement learning algorithm, however, we believe other learning methods may reveal more problems and give a better insight into the expertness-measuring subject. Also, a substantial mathematical examination of the proposed approach is one of the subjects of our future research.

In the experiments, the impressibility factors of the agents are equal and fixed over the learning period. This parameter could be dynamically changed according to the effectiveness of the others' knowledge.

Detection of the agents with incorrect knowledge and minimizing their effects on the cooperative group learning is another direction for future research.

In the algorithm proposed in this paper, we assume that agents are able to observe the current states and current actions of each other. We believe that each agent can extend the proposed algorithm to the case when the system is not fully observable. As future work, we intend to apply the proposed algorithm to a more complex multiagent task and investigate its effectiveness in both partially observable and non-observable systems.

References

1. Mikami, S.: Reinforcement learning for multi-agent systems. J Japan Soc Artif Intell 12 (1997) 845-849
2. Arai, S.: Multiagent reinforcement learning: Uniting planning, theory, and various techniques for implementation. J Japan Soc Artif Intell 16 (2001) 476-481
3. Wolpert, D.H., Sill, J, Tumer, K.: Reinforcement learning in distributed domains: Beyond team games. Proc. 17th National Conference on Artificial Intelligence. Seattle, WA (2001) 819-824
4. Arai, S. and Sycara, K.: Credit Assignment Method for Learning Effective Stochastic Policies in Uncertain Domains. Proc. Genetic and Evolutionary Computation Conf. (2001)
5. Arai, S. and Sycara, K.: Effective Learning Approach for Planning and Scheduling in Multi-agent Domain. Proc. 6th ISAB - From Animals to Animats 6 (2000) 507-516
6. Arai, S., Sycara, K., Payne, T.: Multi-agent Reinforcement Learning for Planning and Scheduling Multiple Goals. Proc 4th Int. Conf. on MAS (2000)
7. Tan, M.: Multi-agent reinforcement learning: Independent vs. cooperative agents. Proc. Tenth Int. Conf. Machine Learning. Amherst, MA (1993) 330-337
8. Ahmadabadi, M.N. and Asadpour, M.: Expertness Based Cooperative Q-learning. IEEE Transactions on Systems, Man, and Cybernetics, Part B. 32(1) (2002) 66-76
9. Sousa, C. and Custodio, L.: Cooperative Reinforcement Learning: exploring Communication and Cooperation Problems. Proc. 2005 IEEE International Symposium on Computational Intelligence in Robotics and Automation. Espoo, Finland (2005) 445-450
10. Grefenstette, J.: Lamarckian learning in multi-agent environments. Proc. Fourth International Conference on Genetic Algorithms. San Mateo, CA (1991) 303-310
11. Bull, L. and Fogarty, T.C.: Evolving cooperative communicating classifier systems. Proc. Fourth Annual Conference on Evolutionary Programming (EP94) (1994) 308-315

12. Iba, H.: Evolutionary learning of communicating agents. Information Sciences 108 (1998)
13. Miconi, T.: When evolving populations is better than coevolving individuals: The blind mice problem. Proceedings of the Eighteenth International Joint Conference on Artificial Intelligence (IJCAI-03) (2003)
14. Berenji, H. and Vengerov, D.: Learning, cooperation, and coordination in multi-agent systems. Technical Report IIS-00-10. Intelligent Inference Systems Corp., Sunnyvale, CA (2000)
15. Eshgh, S.M., Ahmadabadi, M.N.: An Extension of Weighted Strategy Sharing in Cooperative Q-learning for Specialized Agents. Proceedings of the 9th International Conference on Neural Information Processing. Vol. 1 (2002) 106-110
16. Buchsbaum, D., Blumberg, B., Breazeal, C., Meltzoff, A.N.: A Simulation-Theory Inspired Social Learning System for Interactive Characters. Proc. 2005 IEEE International Workshop on Robots and Human Interactive Communication (2005) 85-90
17. Bryson, J.J. and Wood, M.A.: Learning discretely: Behaviour and organization in social learning. Proc. Third International Symposium on Imitation in Animals and Artifacts AISB (2005) 30-37
18. Yanai, K. and Iba, H.: Multi-agent Robot Learning by Means of Genetic Programming: Solving an Escape Problem. Lecture Notes in Computer Science 2210 (2001) 192-203
19. Bowling M.: Convergence problems of general-sum multi-agent reinforcement learning. Proceedings of the Seventeenth International Conference on Machine Learning. San Francisco, CA (2000) 89-94
20. Matsuura, K.: A study on heterogeneous agents systems learning organized behavior. Doctoral Dissertation. Department of Engineering, Hokkaido University (1996)
21. Arai, S. and Sycara, K.: Effective learning approach for planning and scheduling in multi-agent domain. Proceedings of the Sixth ISAB: From Animals to Animats. Vol. 6. (2000) 507-516

Developing a Collaborative e-Learning System Based on Users' Perceptions

Shu-Sheng Liaw[1] and Hsiu-Mei Huang[2]

[1] General Education Center, China Medical University
91, Shiuesh Rd., Taichung, 404, Taiwan, ROC
ssliaw@mail.cmu.edu.tw
[2] Department of Management Science, National Taichung Institute of Technology,
129, Sec. 3, Saming Rd., Taichung, 404, Taiwan, ROC
hmhuang@ntit.edu.tw

Abstract. The present study is to investigate learners' perceptions toward a collaborative e-learning system. First, this study provides considerations of designing a collaborative e-learning environment. After that, the implementation of a collaborative e-learning system will be discussed. Furthermore, this study investigates 68 students' perceptions toward the collaborative e-learning system. The results of factor analysis show that the five users' perception factors are: environmental characteristics, environmental satisfaction, collaboration activities, learners' characteristics, and environment acceptance. The results also indicate that these five factors should be considered at the same time when developing a collaborative e-learning system.

1 Introduction

Collaborative e-learning environments are studied in the CSCL (computer-supported collaborative learning) paradigm which has been built upon a rich history of cognitive science research about how students learn [1]. Essentially, collaborative e-learning environments can be described as a context where the computer or information technology facilitates interaction among learners for acquisition or sharing of knowledge. From previous research [2], CSCL environments, often claimed to be open, safe, and trustable, allow equal opportunities for learners to participate without the limitation on knowledge levels. In collaborative e-learning environments, students have more opportunities to be in full control of their own learning. They can also be active learners who not only absorb information, but also connect their previous knowledge to their newly-acquired information. From previous research [3], the collaborative e-learning environment enables learners to collaborate and practice critical reflection, conflict negotiation, and consensus building as in face-to-face learning environments. Besides, learners are encouraged to exchange ideas, share perspectives, and use previous knowledge or experience in order to decide on the best solution for the problem.

Indeed, collaboration may enrich individual learning experiences by motivating them to seek new insights and perspectives. The extent to which these benefits are realized depend largely on the effectiveness of group interaction, including synchronous or asynchronous. When learners do not collaborate effectively, the social and

W. Shen et al. (Eds.): CSCWD 2006, LNCS 4402, pp. 751–759, 2007.
© Springer-Verlag Berlin Heidelberg 2007

cognitive advantages of group learning are lost [4]. In other words, understanding users' perceptions toward collaborative activities is a crucial issue in enhancing learning performance.

Structuring, guiding, and mediating collaborative learning activities can increase both individual and group performance [5]. Providing these supports; however, require an understanding of individual perceptions toward CSCL environments. Based on learners' attitudes, the present study investigates how a collaborative e-learning environment assists learners in learning activities, acquiring information, exchanging ideas, and sharing knowledge. First of all, this study will explain considerations of building a collaborative e-learning environment. Then, the research will describe how to design it and also examine learners' attitudes toward the environment. And last, the study shows five critical perceptual factors for a collaborative e-learning environment.

2   Considerations of Designing Collaborative e-Learning

To develop collaborative e-learning environments, five elements should be considered [3]: environmental characteristics, environmental satisfaction, collaborative activities, learners' characteristics, and environmental acceptance. Figure 1 shows the elements of a Web-based collaborative e-learning environment.

In collaborative e-learning environments, one of the major functions is collaboration. Regarding to system functions, when a task requires a high level of collaboration, the students participate more actively in the learning process. A high-level collaborative task requires group members not only to share information, but also to determine how to retrieve useful information.

In collaborative e-learning environments, learners' experience with the use of technology might inhibit or promote their participation in the collaborative learning processes. For instance, in Web-based collaborative learning environments, a lack of computer and Internet experience might influence learners' behavioral intentions to use those environments [6]. In addition, when users feel less self-confidence toward information technology, then they also show less positive feelings toward the technology; furthermore, they even have less behavioral intention of using the technology.

In collaborative e-learning environments, collaboration refers to activities that are related to how the group is functioning in accomplishing a task. Within collaborative learning, the responsibility of learning shifts from the teachers to the learners [7]. This situation provides an opportunity for the learners to regulate their collaboration processes and goals. As a group, learners should plan the working process and ensure that it will be goal directed. In order to meet their learning objectives, learners need to support each other. Thus, learners have the responsibility to participate in collaboration processes to fulfill their learning goals.

In collaborative e-learning environments, learners' satisfaction with collaborative learning can be described as the degree to which a learner feels a positive association with his/her own collaborative learning experiences [3]. Learners' satisfaction can have repercussions on how learners work together, and whether there is a good working atmosphere among learners.

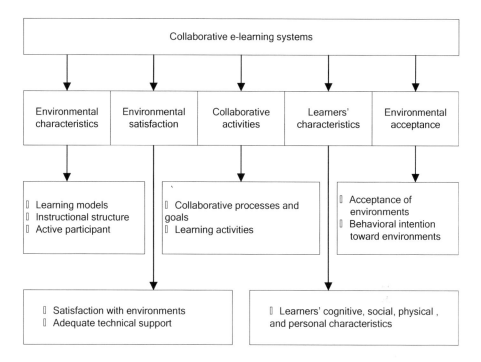

Fig. 1. Elements of designing a collaborative e-learning environment

3 Research Hypotheses

Although previous studies [3-4][8] have reported the benefits of collaborative learning, especially for online learners, there are still many issues concerning the implementation of collaborative learning in e-learning systems. Limited research has been done on learners' attitude factors during the collaboration process in asynchronous collaborative e-learning environments. Understanding users' perceptions is crucial because this might help designers to provide appropriate collaborative e-learning environments for enhancing the quality of learning process [9].

This explorative research investigates learners' feelings toward a collaborative e-learning system as well as crucial aspects concerning collaborative e-learning. Thus, this study proposes the following hypotheses:

Hypothesis 1: Five perceptual factors of the collaborative e-learning system are environmental characteristics, environmental satisfaction, collaboration activities, learners' characteristics, and environment acceptance.

Hypothesis 2: The Five perceptual factors, environmental characteristics, environmental satisfaction, collaboration activities, learners' characteristics, and environment acceptance, have high correlations with each other.

4 Proposed Solution

The issue of how to assist people work together, such as facilitating the exchange of their knowledge, enabling learning, and increasing their abilities to achieve individual and group goals, has been the target of innumerable theoretical research and practical projects. From those previous researches, it is generally recognized that communities perform better when all members adopt certain behaviors, such as sharing their knowledge or making effective use of the knowledge produced by others. Essentially, knowledge sharing is a people-to-people process, and it is the behavior of disseminating individual acquired knowledge to other members within a group. The focus of knowledge management lies in sharing knowledge to create value-added benefits to the group [10]. But sharing individual knowledge is not a simple task. People are not likely to share their knowledge unless they believe it is valuable and important for others.

The human mind is similar to a computer process which explains psychological events in terms of input, storage, and output. Based on the information processing point of view, knowledge management should include five different stages: information definition, information acquisition, information transformation, knowledge construction, and knowledge sharing [6][11].

The information definition stage is similar to the stage of knowledge objective. In this stage, the purpose of knowledge construction is to define and clarify the needed knowledge. The information acquisition stage is equal to the stage of knowledge gathering, in which an individual expresses his/her interests in finding useful information and attempts to explore and transform external stimuli by reviewing his/her own knowledge structures. The information transformation stage can be viewed as the stage of knowledge analysis whereby an individual selects appropriate information, organizes and integrates it with existing knowledge. The knowledge construction stage provides an individual constructs his/her knowledge that is not limited to the results of rote memorization, but also a kind of new knowledge that could be applied in unknown circumstances and used to solve problems. And the last stage is knowledge sharing stage. The knowledge sharing stage is to sharing and exchange individual knowledge based on collaborative activities.

5 System Implementation

The major platform of the system for end users is the Web browsers, such as Internet Explorer or Netscape, and the main system developing tools include HTML, ASP, SQL server, and ASPHTTP. Based on the system, this research creates five different functions-- the keyword function, the URL resource function, the analysis function, the construction function, and the sharing function in order to assist individuals to establish their own knowledge from Internet resources and to share their own knowledge with others.

This research builds the keyword function for the stage of knowledge objective. In the keyword function, three major sub-functions for searching desired information are: Internet medical information search, Internet general information search, and internal database search. The sub-function of Internet medical information search is to retrieve URLs from med411, medweb, and omni. The sub-function of Internet general information search is to retrieve information from general purpose search engines (such as Google, Yahoo, etc.). The sub-function of internal database search is based on historical retrieval from the database. When users request for a database search, this system does not send any request to the Internet.

The URL resource function is established for the second stage (knowledge gathering). It offers two resources that include the URL and where the resource comes from. The analysis function, the third stage, is created for the stage of knowledge analysis that includes two major sub-functions: connection and bookmark sub-functions. The connection sub-function is to connect Web pages that users are interested in and the bookmark sub-function is to mark the URLs into the database (users believe those URL addresses are all useful knowledge for them).

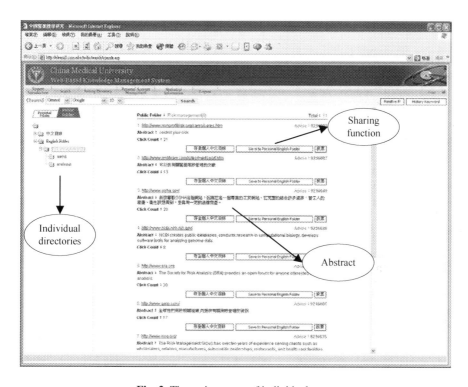

Fig. 2. The main screen of individual area

The fourth stage, construction function, is to build the explicit knowledge formats based on individual tacit knowledge. Both bookmark and abstract sub-functions assist users to create their own knowledge. As knowledge is filtered along with this knowledge construction system, individual knowledge gradually becomes increasingly classified, codified and documented, thus evolving from tacit knowledge into explicit knowledge. When knowledge is captured and processed from tacit to explicit, individuals may begin to apply it as they see appropriate [12].

The last stage, sharing function, is to offer individuals' knowledge to the group which they are involved with. The three major sub-functions are: uploading, ranking, and receiving. Individuals use the uploading sub-function to share the valuable URLs they found with others. In a group platform, users may rank every URL according to its content as well as their preferences. They can give their favorite URL a 5-point rank. Conversely, they can downgrade a useless URL to 1-point. The URLs in the group platform are all recommended by individuals. They may also incorporate communal URLs into their own. This is the major purpose of the receiving sub-function.

Figure 2 presents a screen shot including the individual area and the group area.

6 Results

Descriptive statistics (means [M] and standard deviations [SD]) of computer use were shown in Table 1. The alpha reliability of learners' attitudes toward the cooperative e-learning environment was to be highly accepted ($\alpha=0.96$) and presented in Table 2.

A principal component analysis (PCA) was conducted on factorial structure, and factor analysis requires two stages: factor extraction and factor rotation. Regarding factor extraction, the PCA yielded five components with eigenvalues greater than 1. Five eigenvalues were greater than 1. Varimax (orthogonal) rotations were used for five-factor extraction. The rotation converged in seven iterations for Varimax rotation. After Varimax rotation, the rotated eigenvalues and percentages of variance were presented in Table 3.

Using a minimum factor structure coefficient criterion of 0.61, 6 items had uniquely high saliency with component one, 6 items with component two, 4 items with component three, 4 items with component four, and 3 items with component five. The five factors (as shown in Table 2) were titled: environmental characteristics, collaborative activities, learners' characteristics, environmental acceptance, and environmental satisfaction.

The correlation analysis is needed to investigate the Hypothesis 2. The Pearson correlation coefficients among the variables are presented in Table 4. The bi-variate relationships indicated that most of the variables significantly correlated with each other.

Table 1. Descriptive statistics of computer and Internet experience (from 1 which means "no experience" to 7 which means "highly experienced")

Variables	M	S.D.
Experience using operating systems.	5.51	1.54
Experience using the Internet.	5.99	1.28
Experience using search engines (e.g. Google, Yahoo, etc.).	6.18	1.04
Experience using word processing packages.	5.56	1.47
Experience using programming languages (e.g. HTML).	3.97	1.36

Table 2. Means, standard deviations, item-total correlations and factor structure (from 1 which means "strongly disagree" to 7 which means "strongly agree")

NO	Items	M	S.D.	r*	F**
	F1: Environmental characteristics				
1.	I can use the system for collecting and managing knowledge actively.	5.19	1.30	0.68	0.79
2.	I can use the uploading function for information sharing actively.	5.13	1.42	0.68	0.86
3.	I can use the keyword function for information retrieval.	5.10	1.32	0.55	0.79
4.	I feel the system is a useful knowledge collecting tool.	5.38	1.21	0.69	0.69
5.	I can use the system for referring information to the group platform.	5.37	1.20	0.63	0.68
6.	I feel the group platform is a useful e-learning knowledge sharing system.	5.37	1.17	0.76	0.66
	F2: Collaborative activities				
7.	The system is a time-saving tool for knowledge sharing.	5.16	1.32	0.78	0.62
8.	The system is an effective tool for knowledge sharing.	5.19	1.28	0.76	0.61
9.	I am willing to use the system to share my experience with others.	4.81	1.55	0.74	0.84
10.	Other students are willing to use the system to share their experiences with me.	4.75	1.38	0.72	0.80
11.	I am willing to use the system to share my knowledge with others.	4.74	1.36	0.74	0.68
12.	Other students are willing to use the system to share their knowledge with me.	4.76	1.36	0.75	0.66
	F3: Learners' characteristics				
13.	I have confidence in using the system for collecting useful knowledge.	4.87	1.27	0.65	0.85
14.	I have confidence in using the system for knowledge sharing.	5.03	1.17	0.63	0.84
15.	I have confidence in using the system's function for information retrieval.	5.03	1.21	0.64	0.89
16.	Overall, I have confidence in using the system.	4.85	1.24	0.71	0.68
	F4: Environmental acceptance				
17.	I intend to use the system for information collection.	5.06	1.14	0.74	0.71
18.	I intend to use the system for information retrieval.	4.93	1.23	0.83	0.71
19.	I intend to use the system for knowledge construction.	4.63	1.35	0.74	0.80
20.	I intend to use the system for knowledge sharing.	4.59	1.34	0.75	0.78
	F5: Environmental satisfaction				
21.	I am satisfied with the operating methods of the system.	5.00	1.13	0.79	0.69
22.	I am satisfied with the system's speed.	4.97	1.12	0.72	0.73
23.	I am satisfied with the system's quality.	5.04	1.21	0.70	0.79

r*: Corrected item-total correlation.
F**: Factor coefficient.

Table 3. Total variance explained and percentage of variance by Varimax rotation

Component	Eigenvalue	Percentage of Variance	Cumulative Percentage
1	4.50	19.57	19.57
2	4.18	18.15	37.72
3	3.66	15.92	53.64
4	3.57	15.53	69.17
5	2.72	11.83	81.00

Table 4. Correlation analysis

NO	Variables	2	3	4	5
1	Environmental characteristics	0.59*	0.62*	0.56*	0.58*
2	Environmental satisfaction		0.69*	0.57*	0.69*
3	Collaborative activities			0.57*	0.77*
4	Learners' characteristics				0.56*
5	Environmental acceptance				

*. $p < 0.01$.

7   Discussion and Conclusion

From statistical results, learners' perceptions toward collaborative e-learning environments can be divided into five different factors (environmental characteristics, collaborative activities, learners' characteristics, environmental acceptance, and environmental satisfaction) and these five factors have high correlation with each other. In other words, these results support Hypothesis 1 and Hypothesis 2. From the items of the environmental characteristics, learners have actively collecting, retrieving, and sharing capabilities. Furthermore, learners recognize readiness of knowledge sharing and referral in the collaborative e-learning environments. From the items of collaborative activities, learners believe that the collaborative e-learning environment is a time-saving and efficient knowledge sharing system. They are also willing to share their experience and knowledge with others. Based on learners' characteristics, this study is focused on learners' perceived self-efficacy. From the result of Table 3, students demonstrate confidence to use the system for collecting and sharing knowledge. According to the items of environmental acceptance, learners have high behavioral intention to use the environment as a knowledge construction and knowledge sharing tool. As for environmental satisfaction, learners are concerned about operating methods, system speed, and system quality. The meaning of five factors having high correlation with each other is these five factors should be considered and examined at the same time when designing collaborative e-learning systems.

Learning with peers may benefit not only the overall individual performance; it may also enhance team performance by increasing the quality of team product. Students can learn to formulate ideas and opinions more effectively through group discussion. This study assesses learners' attitudes toward the collaborative e-learning environment. Vygotsky [13] explains that learning in collaboration with others is necessary for the development of personal cognitive processes. Based on social constructivism, the collaborative e-learning environment can enrich learning activities for knowledge sharing.

The rapid advance of Web technology has enabled universities and corporations to reach out and educate students across time and space barriers. Although this technology promotes collaborative learning activities, understanding learners' perceptions toward collaborative e-learning is still a critical issue. This study points out a direction of how to investigate attitude factors toward collaborative e-learning environments. By considering the formation of a collaborative e-learning and statistical results, the present article confirms the significance of understanding users' perceptions toward collaborative e-learning systems.

References

1. Koschmann, T.: (ed.) CSCL: Theory and Practice of an Emerging Paradigm. Mahwah: Lawrence Erlbaum Associates (1996)
2. Scardamalia, M. and Bereiter, C.: Computer support for knowledge-building communities. The Journal of The Learning Science 3 (1994) 265-283
3. Dewiyanti, S., Brand-Gruwel, S., Jochems, W. and Broers, N.J.: Students' experience with collaborative learning in asynchronous Computer-Supported Collaborative Learning environments. Computers in Human Behavior 23 (2007) 496-514
4. Soller, A.: Supporting social interaction in an intelligent collaborative learning system. International Journal of Artificial Intelligence in Education 12 (2001) 40-62
5. Webb, N. and Palincsar, A.: Group processes in the classroom. In: Berlmer, D. and Calfee, R. (eds): Handbook of Educa-tional Psychology. New York: Simon & Schuster Macmillan (1996) 841-873
6. Liaw, S.S.: Developing a Web assisted knowledge construction system based on the approach of constructivist knowledge analysis of tasks. Computers in Human Behavior 21 (2005) 29-44
7. Bruffee, K.A.: Sharing our toys: Cooperative learning versus collaborative learning. Change Magazine 27 (1995) 12-18
8. Guuawardena, N.C., Nola, A.C., Wilson, P.L., Lopez-Islas, J.R., Ramirez-Angel, N. and Megchun-Alpizar, R.M.: A cross-cultural study of group process and development in online conferences. Distance Education 22 (2001) 85-121
9. Liaw, S.S.: Considerations for developing constructivist Web-based learning. International Journal of Instructional Media 31 (2004) 309-321
10. Liebowitz, J.: Knowledge management and its link to artificial intelligence. Expert Systems with Applications 20 (2001) 1-6
11. Gagne, E.D., Yekovich, C.W. and Yekovich, F.R.: The Cognitive Psychology of School Learning. 2nd ed. New York: Harper Collins (1993)
12. Malone, D.: Knowledge management: A model for organizational learning. International Journal of Accounting Information Systems 3 (2002) 111-123
13. Vygotsky, L.: Mind in society: The development of higher psychological processes. Cambridge, MA: Harvard University Press (1978)

Author Index

Lecture Notes in Computer Science

For information about Vols. 1–4418

please contact your bookseller or Springer

Vol. 4479: I.F. Akyildiz, R. Sivakumar, E. Ekici, J.C.d. Oliveira, J. McNair (Eds.), NETWORKING 2007. Ad Hoc and Sensor Networks, Wireless Networks, Next Generation Internet. XXVII, 1252 pages. 2007.

Vol. 4478: J. Martí, J.M. Benedí, A.M. Mendonça, J. Serrat (Eds.), Pattern Recognition and Image Analysis, Part II. XXVII, 657 pages. 2007.

Vol. 4477: J. Martí, J.M. Benedí, A.M. Mendonça, J. Serrat (Eds.), Pattern Recognition and Image Analysis, Part I. XXVII, 625 pages. 2007.

Vol. 4476: V. Gorodetsky, C. Zhang, V.A. Skormin, L. Cao (Eds.), Autonomous Intelligent Systems: Multi-Agents and Data Mining. XIII, 323 pages. 2007. (Sublibrary LNAI).

Vol. 4475: P. Crescenzi, G. Prencipe, G. Pucci (Eds.), Fun with Algorithms. X, 273 pages. 2007.

Vol. 4472: M. Haindl, J. Kittler, F. Roli (Eds.), Multiple Classifier Systems. XI, 524 pages. 2007.

Vol. 4471: P. Cesar, K. Chorianopoulos, J.F. Jensen (Eds.), Interactive TV: a Shared Experience. XIII, 236 pages. 2007.

Vol. 4470: Q. Wang, D. Pfahl, D.M. Raffo (Eds.), Soft ware Process Dynamics and Agility. XI, 346 pages. 2007.

Vol. 4468: M.M. Bonsangue, E.B. Johnsen (Eds.), Formal Methods for Open Object-Based Distributed Systems. X, 317 pages. 2007.

Vol. 4467: A.L. Murphy, J. Vitek (Eds.), Coordination Models and Languages. X, 235 pages. 2007.

Vol. 4465: T. Chahed, B. Tuffin (Eds.), Network Control and Optimization. XIII, 305 pages. 2007.

Vol. 4464: E. Dawson, D.S. Wong (Eds.), Information Security Practice and Experience. XIII, 361 pages. 2007.

Vol. 4463: I. Măndoiu, A. Zelikovsky (Eds.), Bioinformatics Research and Applications. XV, 653 pages. 2007. (Sublibrary LNBI).

Vol. 4462: D. Sauveron, K. Markantonakis, A. Bilas, J.-J. Quisquater (Eds.), Information Security Theory and Practices. XII, 255 pages. 2007.

Vol. 4459: C. Cérin, K.-C. Li (Eds.), Advances in Grid and Pervasive Computing. XVI, 759 pages. 2007.

Vol. 4453: T. Speed, H. Huang (Eds.), Research in Computational Molecular Biology. XVI, 550 pages. 2007. (Sublibrary LNBI).

Vol. 4452: M. Fasli, O. Shehory (Eds.), Agent-Mediated Electronic Commerce. VIII, 249 pages. 2007. (Sublibrary LNAI).

Vol. 4451: T.S. Huang, A. Nijholt, M. Pantic, A. Pentland (Eds.), Artifical Intelligence for Human Computing. XVI, 359 pages. 2007. (Sublibrary LNAI).

Vol. 4450: T. Okamoto, X. Wang (Eds.), Public Key Cryptography – PKC 2007. XIII, 491 pages. 2007.

Vol. 4448: M. Giacobini et al. (Ed.), Applications of Evolutionary Computing. XXIII, 755 pages. 2007.

Vol. 4447: E. Marchiori, J.H. Moore, J.C. Rajapakse (Eds.), Evolutionary Computation,Machine Learning and Data Mining in Bioinformatics. XI, 302 pages. 2007.

Vol. 4446: C. Cotta, J. van Hemert (Eds.), Evolutionary Computation in Combinatorial Optimization. XII, 241 pages. 2007.

Vol. 4445: M. Ebner, M. O'Neill, A. Ekárt, L. Vanneschi, A.I. Esparcia-Alcázar (Eds.), Genetic Programming. XI, 382 pages. 2007.

Vol. 4444: T. Reps, M. Sagiv, J. Bauer (Eds.), Program Analysis and Compilation, Theory and Practice. X, 361 pages. 2007.

Vol. 4443: R. Kotagiri, P.R. Krishna, M. Mohania, E. Nantajeewarawat (Eds.), Advances in Databases: Concepts, Systems and Applications. XXI, 1126 pages. 2007.

Vol. 4440: B. Liblit, Cooperative Bug Isolation. XV, 101 pages. 2007.

Vol. 4439: W. Abramowicz (Ed.), Business Information Systems. XV, 654 pages. 2007.

Vol. 4438: L. Maicher, A. Sigel, L.M. Garshol (Eds.), Leveraging the Semantics of Topic Maps. X, 257 pages. 2007. (Sublibrary LNAI).

Vol. 4433: E. Şahin, W.M. Spears, A.F.T. Winfield (Eds.), Swarm Robotics. XII, 221 pages. 2007.

Vol. 4432: B. Beliczynski, A. Dzielinski, M. Iwanowski, B. Ribeiro (Eds.), Adaptive and Natural Computing Algorithms, Part II. XXVI, 761 pages. 2007.

Vol. 4431: B. Beliczynski, A. Dzielinski, M. Iwanowski, B. Ribeiro (Eds.), Adaptive and Natural Computing Algorithms, Part I. XXV, 851 pages. 2007.

Vol. 4430: C.C. Yang, D. Zeng, M. Chau, K. Chang, Q. Yang, X. Cheng, J. Wang, F.-Y. Wang, H. Chen (Eds.), Intelligence and Security Informatics. XII, 330 pages. 2007.

Vol. 4429: R. Lu, J.H. Siekmann, C. Ullrich (Eds.), Cognitive Systems. X, 161 pages. 2007. (Sublibrary LNAI).

Vol. 4427: S. Uhlig, K. Papagiannaki, O. Bonaventure (Eds.), Passive and Active Network Measurement. XI, 274 pages. 2007.

Vol. 4426: Z.-H. Zhou, H. Li, Q. Yang (Eds.), Advances in Knowledge Discovery and Data Mining. XXV, 1161 pages. 2007. (Sublibrary LNAI).

Vol. 4425: G. Amati, C. Carpineto, G. Romano (Eds.), Advances in Information Retrieval. XIX, 759 pages. 2007.

Vol. 4424: O. Grumberg, M. Huth (Eds.), Tools and Algorithms for the Construction and Analysis of Systems. XX, 738 pages. 2007.

Vol. 4423: H. Seidl (Ed.), Foundations of Software Science and Computational Structures. XVI, 379 pages. 2007.

Vol. 4422: M.B. Dwyer, A. Lopes (Eds.), Fundamental Approaches to Software Engineering. XV, 440 pages. 2007.

Vol. 4421: R. De Nicola (Ed.), Programming Languages and Systems. XVII, 538 pages. 2007.

Vol. 4420: S. Krishnamurthi, M. Odersky (Eds.), Compiler Construction. XIV, 233 pages. 2007.

Vol. 4419: P.C. Diniz, E. Marques, K. Bertels, M.M. Fernandes, J.M.P. Cardoso (Eds.), Reconfigurable Computing: Architectures, Tools and Applications. XIV, 391 pages. 2007.